The Making of American Audiences

In *The Making of American Audiences,* Richard Butsch provides a comprehensive study of American entertainment audiences from the colonial period to the present. Covering theater, minstrelsy, vaudeville, movies, radio, and television, he examines the evolution of audiences as each genre supplanted another as the primary popular entertainment. Based on original historical research, this volume exposes how audiences made themselves through their practices, and how they were made by contemporary discourses. During the nineteenth century, active audiences were represented as unruly and a threat to civic order, while in the twentieth century, audiences have been portrayed as passive and controlled by media messages. At the same time, dispersal of audiences from theaters to their homes by radio and television has made entertainment a private experience rather than a public occasion, and has severed the connection between audience practices and collective action. This timely study serves as an important contribution to communication research, as well as to American cultural history and cultural studies.

Richard Butsch is a professor of sociology at Rider University in Lawrenceville, New Jersey. A recipient of funding from the National Endowment for the Humanities and the National Science Foundation, he is the editor of *For Fun and Profit: The Transformation of Leisure into Consumption* as well as author of a variety of scholarly articles in the area of communications.

CAMBRIDGE STUDIES IN THE HISTORY OF MASS COMMUNICATION

General Editors
Kenneth Short, University of Houston
Garth Jowett, University of Houston

Cambridge Studies in the History of Mass Communication includes books that examine the communications processes and communications systems within social, cultural, and political contexts. Inclusive of empirical, effects-based research, works in this series proceed from the basis that the histories of various media are an important means to understanding their role and function in society. The history of a medium – its pattern of introduction, diffusion, acceptance, and effects – varies in each society, interacting with, and in turn, shaping its culture. Moreover, each society reacts differently to the introduction of a medium and regulatory policies are shaped by both political and cultural forces. The detailed study of various communications forms and their complex message systems is now understood to be the key to unraveling the evolution of modern society and its culture.

Other Books in the Series

THE MAKING OF AMERICAN
Audiences
From Stage to Television, 1750–1990

RICHARD BUTSCH

CAMBRIDGE
UNIVERSITY PRESS

For Ava and Noah

PUBLISHED BY THE PRESS SYNDICATE OF THE UNIVERSITY OF CAMBRIDGE
The Pitt Building, Trumpington Street, Cambridge, United Kingdom

CAMBRIDGE UNIVERSITY PRESS
The Edinburgh Building, Cambridge CB2 2RU, UK   http://www.cup.cam.ac.uk
40 West 20th Street, New York, NY 10011–4211, USA   http://www.cup.org
10 Stamford Road, Oakleigh, Melbourne 3166, Australia
Ruiz de Alarcón 13, 28014 Madrid, Spain

First published 2000

Printed in the United States of America

Typeface Caslon 224 Book 10/13 pt.   *System* QuarkXPress™   [HT]

A catalog record for this book is available from the British Library

Library of Congress Cataloging-in-Publication Data

Butsch, Richard, 1943–
    The making of American audiences : from stage to television,
1750–1990 / Richard Butsch.
        p. cm. – (Cambridge studies in the history of mass
communications)
    Includes bibliographical references and index.
    ISBN 0 521 66253 2 (hb). – ISBN 0 521 66483 7 (pb)
    1. Performing arts – Audiences – United States. 2. Radio audiences –
United States. 3. Television viewers – United States. I. Title.
II. Series.
✓ PN1590.A9B88   2000
    791′.0973 – dc21   99-36490

ISBN   0 521 66253 2   hardback
ISBN   0 521 66483 7   paperback

Contents

Figures follow page 294

Acknowledgments

About 15 years ago, I began to investigate the change from music making to music listening associated with the dispersion of phonograph and radio. I had been intrigued with historic examples of the change in western culture from production for use to production for exchange in the realm of play and leisure and the consequent division between producers/performers and consumers/audiences. After some preliminary explorations of dusty archives and old books, I concluded it would be difficult to document such private practices as the personal making and consuming of music. But in the process I stumbled across accounts of the lively theater audiences of the nineteenth century. I was struck by the comparisons to my earlier research interest in working-class consumption of television programs. I saw here a more public manifestation of what I had been looking for, the changes in audiences' participation in their own entertainment.

From the beginning I was excited about the value of this project and found it intrinsically enjoyable to do the research. It had the potential to shed light on issues of the public sphere, collective action, mass culture, and effects of television. But the work was exceedingly slow. References to audiences in the usual primary source documents were so scattered that I felt I was searching for tiny fragments of history blown across a great territory by the winds of time. Primary and secondary sources about the stage scarcely mention audiences, and typically only in passing, with little elaboration. Rarely was the term "audience" indexed in theater histories. While there is an enormous literature on audiences in mass media research from movies to television, there is very little about audiences in natural settings, and even less giving extended eyewitness descriptions. Only by persistent searching for eight years was I able to amass enough documentation to compose a series of pictures of what we have done *as* audiences and what we have said *about* audiences, so that we can imagine how we have arrived where we are.

Writing this book has been a great education. In the process I have benefited from the generosity of many scholars who shared with me their knowledge and guided me in my quests. Since I traversed such broad territory, across disciplines and eras, I seemed always the novice and in their debt as guides, now exploring colonial theater, then turn-of-the-century Italian puppets, and still later current research on the uses of VCRs. With their help, I learned the literature of each field and have arrived at the understandings of audiences that I have laid out here in this book. Equally important was their enthusiasm about my project, confirming my own sense of its value. Without this encouragement I could not have persisted.

Several colleagues stand out for special thanks for having been there with encouragement and ideas for me from the beginning through the end. Ava Baron provided insightful advice and careful, detailed criticism on every stage of this project. Bruce McConachie took me seriously while I was still a novice in theater history, and shared with me his own hard-won knowledge of theater audiences. Doug Gomery provided the same valuable service as my guide in film history; and Alison Kibler helped me learn about vaudeville. Roland Marchand shared his enthusiasm and his knowledge of the cultural history of the 1920s and 1930s. John Clarke and John Kasson each, in ways small and large, sustained my efforts.

Ava, Bruce, Kathy Fuller, Garth Jowett, and anonymous reviewers read the entire manuscript, some more than once, and were instrumental in helping me to forge the disparate chapters into a coherent book. Doug, Roland, John Clarke and John Kasson, Peter Bailey, Anne Butler, Dale Cockrell, Michael Feldberg, Paul Gilje, Sally Griffith, Alison Kibler, Kate Lacey, Kathy Peiss, Erika Rappaport, Mary Corbin Sies, Susan Smulyan, and Colin Sparks were kind enough to comment on chapter drafts over the years. Early versions of portions of the book appeared as "Bowery B'hoys and Matinee Ladies: The Re-gendering of Nineteenth Century American Theater Audiences", *American Quarterly*, 46:3 (September, 1994), 374–405; "American Theater Riots and Class Relations, 1754–1849" *Theatre Annual* 48 (1995), 41–59; and "Crystal Sets and Scarf-Pin Radios: Gender, Technology and the Construction of American Radio Listening in the 1920s" *Media Culture and Society* 20:4 (Winter, 1998), 557–72.

Many others shared ideas, their research and enthusiasm, and introduced me to yet other helpful persons. I thank Ien Ang, Gregory Bach, Pat Chmel, Lizabeth Cohen, Gary Cross, Dan Czitrom, Julie D'Acci, Richard DeCordova, Chad Dell, Faye Dudden, Lewis Freeman, Benjamin Henneke, Steve Gelber, Susan Kent, Susan Klepp, Sonia Livingstone, Elizabeth Long, Anna McCarthy, Matthew Murray, David Myers, Roy Rosenzweig, Howard Sacks, Scott Sandage, Lillian Schlissel, Phil Scranton, Lynn Spigel, Todd Swanstrom, Robert Toll, Ellen Wartella, and Robert Zecker.

My research was supported by a widespread research staff. My secretary, Marge Raynor, completed so many tasks so efficiently that I cannot name them. Mary Jo Szczekowski of Rider University's Moore Library was invaluable for delivering to my desk the resources of the nation's libraries through interlibrary loan. Perry Weston copied innumerable microfilm articles, and the rest of the library staff contributed in many ways. Alison Kibler and Alyssa Haywoode were wonderful research assistants at the University of Iowa Library Albee collection; Rosalind Taylor did the same on the Payne Fund papers at the Western Reserve Historical Society. Geraldine DuClow, at the Theatre Collection of the Philadelphia Free Library, made my work there much easier.

In addition I wish to thank the staffpersons who helped my research at the Library of Congress Manuscript Division, the National Museum of American History Archive Center, the National Archives, the National Cable Television Association, the New York Public Library at Forty-Second Street, the Annex, the Billy Rose Theater Collection, and the Picture Collection, the New York Historical Society, the City Museum of New York, the Motion Picture Association of America Library, the National Association of Broadcasters' Television Information Office, A.C. Neilsen, Inc., ASCAP, the American Federation of Musicians, the State Library of New York, the Free Library of Philadelphia, the Historical Society of Pennsylvania, the Trenton Public Library Archive, the Cincinnati Historical Society, the State Historical Society of Wisconsin, the Western Reserve Historical Society, the State Historical Society of Iowa, and the university libraries of Columbia, Harvard, Pennsylvania, Rutgers, Princeton, and Iowa, and of the Institute for Advanced Study. I also thank the remarkable generosity of numerous other collections accessed through interlibrary loan.

I received support for this research from a National Endowment for the Humanities fellowship, an American Sociological

Association/National Science Foundation grant, from research leaves, summer fellowships and grants from Rider University, and from research appointments at the Centre for Contemporary Cultural Studies of the University of Birmingham, England and the Rutgers University Center for Historical Analysis.

Finally, I wish to thank my devoted wife, companion, and colleague, Ava Baron, for her wisdom and love through all these years, and my son, Noah, for being a living reminder that there is more to life than work.

Introduction: Participative Public, Passive Private?

Perhaps, one should write theatrical history in terms of the customs of audiences.
   – George C. D. Odell, *Annals of the New York Stage* (1927), II 426.

That is why "popular culture" matters. Otherwise, to tell you the truth, I don't give a damn about it.
   – Stuart Hall, "Notes on Deconstructing 'The Popular'"
   in Raphael Samuel, ed., *People's History and Socialist Theory*
   (London: Routledge, 1981), 239.

In 1996, the American Medical Association sent out to 60,000 physicians a guide to advise their patients in children's use of television. The booklet concludes with a list of "media use suggestions for parents" that reads like the warning labels on drugs and dangerous household chemicals: use only in limited amounts, for specific purposes, and under careful guidance of adults.[1] This is just one example of the popular, professional, and scholarly discourses in the twentieth century that have been concerned with mass media's dangers to audiences. Precisely what is the danger and

1

how great it is may vary, but the issue is the foundation of almost all discussion about audiences. And the topic of audiences is pervasive, from popular magazines and books, to debates in Congress, to thousands of scientific studies of the effects of television, to scholarly debates about reception in the humanities.

It is the purpose of this book to provide a *history* of audiences, particularly one that exposes the terms of twentieth-century debate by comparing them to the terms of debate in earlier eras. Popular and scholarly discussions of audiences have long lacked a historical context. Concerns about television viewing, for example, have almost never led to consideration of earlier concerns about radio listening or moviegoing, let alone popular nineteenth-century entertainments such as melodrama, minstrelsy, and vaudeville. Yet the very issues at the heart of debates today have been played out repeatedly, sometimes in the very same terms, sometimes after inverting these terms.

How *do* nineteenth-century stage entertainments compare to twentieth-century mass media? They differ sharply in institutional form and in technology. Scholars who study one seldom are familiar with the work of those who study the other. And yet there is a continuity of concern about audiences, expressed in the public discourses of the times. Common to all these forms of entertainment is concern about the dangers of and to audiences. Audiences have been worrisome to American elites ever since the Revolution. The written record is a continual flow of worries about social disorder arising from audiences and the consequent need for social control. While the underlying issues were always power and social order, at different times the causes of the problems of audiences had different sources. In the nineteenth century, the problem lay in the degenerate or unruly people who came to the theater, and what they might do, once gathered. In the twentieth century, worries focused on the dangers of reception, how media messages, might degenerate audiences. In the nineteenth century, critics feared *active* audiences; in the twentieth, their *passivity*.

These changes in the terms of discourse highlight the importance of historicizing the concept of audience. How public discourses construct audiences, how audiences conceive themselves, and what audiences do are historically contingent. Categories like "the audience" are socially constructed, their attributes typically described in terms of dichotomies. Such dichotomies define the current ideal, what is good, deserves reward, power, privilege. The valence of dichotomies as well as the dichotomies themselves change over time. The current ideal represents the hierarchy of power within a society at a given moment of history.[2] In the nineteenth century, the active audience was bad; today it is good. One distinction ceases to be significant and another comes to the fore. In seventeenth-century England, the distinction between listening (auditing) and viewing (spectating), words and spectacle, were central to the debate about the worth of new drama. Other than a brief appearance in the 1950s of debate concerning the relative merits of radio and television, this distinction has been inconsequential. Similarly, the displacement of live performance by mass media shriveled debate about the audience-performer distinction.

Two dichotomies that persist throughout this history are the distinctions between active and passive audiences and between public and private audiences. These distinctions weave through much of the history in the ensuing chapters. Let us begin by examining these categories. I will explore the active-passive dichotomy by discussing the historical tradition of audience sovereignty, changes in the audience-performer distinction, and the concepts of attention and embeddedness from recent cultural studies of television. Then I will explore the public-private dichotomy by considering the transformation of public space from a locus of the public sphere and a ground for collective action into a marketplace of consumption. I then consider this dichotomy in its second sense as the movement of the audience from the public venue of the theater to private spaces, particularly the home.

From Active to Passive

"Passive" has been shorthand for passive reception, audiences' dependence on and unquestioning acceptance of the messages of entertainment. Critics of media-induced passivity have fretted about aesthetic degradation of the culture, social or moral disintegration of the community, or political domination of the masses.[3] The terms "passive" and "active" do not appear in nineteenth-century discourses. Instead critics talk about audience rights or rowdiness, in all cases presuming an active audience. Nineteenth-century audiences were, and were expected to be, very active. This active conception was rooted in a European tradition of audience sovereignty that recognized audiences' rights to control performances. Active audiences prevailed in London and Paris theaters and in the operas of Italy in the seventeenth and eighteenth centuries. This participative tradition was shared by the privileged as well as plebeians, to use the terms of English theater historian Ann Cook. The privileged included aristocrats and untitled but wealthy gentry who were making handsome profits from land, mercantile, and manufacturing enterprises. Plebeians included petite bourgeoisie as well as lesser classes.[4]

The privileged in early modern Europe were not barred by their own moral or aesthetic sense of superiority from engaging in the same practices as the lower classes.[5] In Elizabethan theaters, courtiers and gallants treated theater as their court where they could measure their importance by the attention they received. Fops sat on stage, interrupted performances, and even on occasion grabbed an actress. All of this annoyed the plebeian pit, who shouted, "Away with them." But pittites were hardly meek. They too ate, smoked, drank, socialized, and engaged in repartee with actors.[6] Restoration theater was more expensive and exclusive. Still, merchants and professional men, civil servants and their wives, and the critics (poets, writers, and competing playwrights) sat in the pit and squabbled, shouted, teased the women who sold oranges, baited the fops on stage, and wandered from pit to gallery and back. Nobility continued to sit on stage and in boxes, treating the theater as a place to chat, play cards, argue, and even occasionally duel.[7]

By the mid-eighteenth century, London theatergoing was popular among all classes. The privileged continued to give scant attention to the play. Some still sat on stage until David Garrick, director of the Drury Lane Theater, finally succeeded in banning them in 1762. The reputation for rowdiness shifted to the gallery where journeymen, apprentices, servants (footmen) – many of whom could afford theater because they arrived after the featured play and paid only half price – lorded over those below.[8] Instead of the individual display of courtiers of the previous era, this plebeian audience expressed collective opinions, sometimes to the point of riot.[9]

This behavior represents not only an active audience, but a discourse through which audiences insistently constructed themselves as active. Audiences asserted their rights to judge and direct performances. There were two basic traditions of such audience sovereignty which can be characterized as those of the privileged and those of the plebeians – "the people." The privileged tradition, rooted in the system of patronage, rested on the status of performers as servants to their aristocratic audience.[10] As with other servants, aristocrats ignored, attended to, or played with actors, as they desired at the moment. It would have violated social order for aristocratic audiences to defer to performers by keeping silent and paying attention. Court theaters were more formal, ritualistic examples of this. More rambunctious examples were the private theaters frequented by young gentry. Aristocratic audience sovereignty affirmed the social order.[11]

Lower classes too had an honored tradition of rights in the theater that were linked to street traditions of carnival and of crowd actions to enforce a moral economy.[12] Carnival, practiced in parades, hangings, and other public festivities, granted such prerogatives to lower classes on certain occasions when normal social order was turned upside down. The carnival tradition extended to street theater such as *commedia dell'arte* and into popular theaters, which had a rowdier tradition of audience sovereignty. Carnival, like the lesser members of the theater audience, contained lower-class rule within limits and elites to retain control of social order. But carnival also presented the threat of getting out of control.

Overactive Audiences

English immigrants and actors imported these traditions when they came to America. As we will see, American theater managers and civil authorities continued to recognize the rights of audience sovereignty until the mid-nineteenth century. They acknowledged audience prerogatives to call for tunes, chastise performers and managers, hiss, shout and throw things at intransigent performers on the stage, even riot to enforce their will. During the colonial period, gentry exercised an aristocratic sovereignty over the nascent theater. After the Revolution, common folk employed the anti-aristocratic rhetoric of the Revolution to assert their own plebeian sovereignty in the theater.

But during the Jacksonian era in the 1830s and 1840s, the upper classes grew to fear such working-class sovereignty. Too easily such collective power might be applied to larger economic and political purposes and threaten the social order. Elites labeled exercises in audience sovereignty as rowdyism. Rowdiness is a persistent phenomenon in theater history, largely associated with young men. During the Jacksonian era, rowdyism came to be considered a mark of lower-class status.[13] Elites condemned it by redefining it as poor manners rather than as an exercise of audience rights. For different reasons, reformers and entertainment entrepreneurs sought, through the nineteenth and into the twentieth century, to contain or eliminate rowdiness in audiences.

Once nineteenth-century elites and the middle class had effectively labeled the working class as rowdy and disreputable, entrepreneurs had to choose between clientele of different classes. Through the development of each major nineteenth-century stage industry profitability pushed the weight of choice against working class and rowdy and in favor of middle class and respectability. Respectability meant an audience that was quiet, polite, and passive. In drama theater, minstrelsy, variety, and even early movies, each industry grew by shifting its primary market and its image to one of middle-class respectability. Comparing different entertainments across the nineteenth and twentieth centuries, we will see how entrepreneurs who could afford the investment repeatedly have attempted to seek a middle-class audience by first attracting a female audience that signified respectability. Through this movement and with this leverage, audiences at these entertainments let slip their sovereignty and were contained if not tamed.

But, despite sustained attacks, rowdiness did not disappear. Theater entrepreneurs succeeded in segregating but not eliminating rowdy behavior. The "rowdy elements" found other, marginalized, "small time" entertainments, which still sought their patronage. Rowdies were excluded from some theaters, but there were always other, "lower-class" houses where rowdiness was tolerated, and even occasionally celebrated. Several chapters of this history will show how segmented markets serving different classes and clientele allowed rowdyism to continue in smaller theaters of all sorts where admission was cheap and young men and boys could afford to attend with some regularity. They showed up as early supporters for minstrelsy in the 1840s, as the audience for variety in the 1860s and 1870s, in small-time vaudeville and "ten-twenty-thirty" melodrama theater in the late nineteenth century, and in the new century in storefront movie shows. In the late twentieth century, rowdyism continues somewhat attenuated, at rock concerts, sporting events, and movie theaters serving particular clientele such as young urban black males or fans of cult films like *Rocky Horror Picture Show*.

Defenseless Audiences

Through the nineteenth century, public discussion focused on concerns about *active* audiences. As movies became popular in the early twentieth century, public debate shifted from a focus on audience behavior to worry about the movies' content and its effects *on* audiences, particularly on children. Attention shifted from the place to the play, from effects of dangerous people in those places to effects of dangerous media messages on people. Audiences were being redefined from active to helpless, dependent, and passive, and would remain so through the rest of the twentieth century, as we will see. Concern about what audiences were doing was superseded by what was being done to them, or more precisely what they were learning from the entertainment that they shouldn't. Some of this was evident at the turn of the century when complaints about small-time vaudeville began to focus on the lewdness of the show. With the movies, however, the attention on the show and its effects clearly became paramount over concerns about activity in the theater.

The focus of concern also shifted from women to children as the endangered group. Previously, middle-class women were the ones considered endangered and warned away from theaters and the people who frequented them. Now children were the endangered group, socialized into deviant behavior by movie content. This focus on children was part of many Progressive efforts of the times, and a new middle-class attention to childhood. From the 1880s onward children assumed a new prominence in the middle-class family, which was restructured around child rearing. Advice in child rearing grew as a profession. The helping professions from 1900 to 1930 grew by appropriating parental functions.[14]

By the 1940s these concerns were elaborated in variants of a mass culture critique, formulated as passive acceptance and control by media. These theories were formulated to explain the rise of fascism in European democracies and laid part of the blame on mass media. In the liberal version, called mass society theory, functional sociologists feared the disappearance of voluntary organizations that they saw as critical in mediating between the mass of people and the governing elites. The mass would then be susceptible to demagogues who used mass media to propagandize and manipulate the mass.[15] Left versions of mass culture critique worried that mass media "narcotized" the working class, who would become passive, develop "false consciousness," and lose the capability of acting collectively in their class interest.[16]

Audience and Performer

The shift from active to passive audiences was complemented by a change in the way in which the entertainment itself constituted the category of "the audience" in the distinction between audience and performer. In the passive construction, the performance (the message) exists independent of the audience, suggesting a boundary as well as a one-way flow across that boundary. Even recent scholarly constructions of an active resistant audience start with a preexisting "message," the preferred reading, and then rejoice in audiences' rejection or transformation of that message. But such an image is less compatible with live entertainment, particularly when audience practices include interaction with the performers, where "the message" is more obviously a collaboration between audience and performers.

The relationship between audience and performance, as well as the permeability of the boundary between the two, have varied historically. The separation between audience and performance is of modern origin. In the past the distinction between performer and audience was less clear and more open. Just as the line between work and leisure was less clear, so too the line between entertainment and other, more participative leisure. Plebeian entertainments, with the exception of a few theaters in the major cities of London and Paris, in early modern Europe were street events, part of fairs and markets. Street theater, such as *commedia dell'arte* and forms of carnival, and amateur theater blurred the lines between performer and audience. Community celebrations and parades, games and parlor theatrics were more common and participative than theatergoing.

Even in professional theater, the boundary between the two was porous. Playwrights and performers constructed an active audience through the conventions of their art. They expected and played upon audience participation, a lively dialog across the footlights. In the Elizabethan public theater, the stage was designed to advance this style, surrounded on three sides by the pit, not behind a proscenium arch. Asides and other addresses to the audience were intended to play upon and satisfy audiences' desire for involvement. Performers such as Richard Tarlton became well known for speaking out of character and taking the audience into their confidence. Such required a "knowingness" shared between audience and actor, about the topic and about theater conventions. It is equivalent to the type of humor which was essential to vaudeville three centuries later, and probably continued a practice common in street entertainments. In more exclusive Restoration theater the privileged audience also delighted in repartee. Prologues, epilogues, and asides were written to provoke reaction from the audience.[17]

As late as the Jacksonian era in America, the ability to come to the front of the stage and speak one's lines directly to the audience was considered a mark of good acting. It was only after the Civil War that this "rhetorical style" faded, though some began to criticize it in the late eighteenth century.[18] It was replaced by the "fourth wall," the front of the stage framed by the proscenium, through which the audience silently and without intervention observed the lives of the characters. Neither actors nor audience were to penetrate this invisible wall. Actors remained behind the proscenium, audiences quiet on their side.[19] As realism replaced rhetorical styles of dramatic acting in the nineteenth century, the separation of audience from performer became paramount. Realism also required silencing audiences, making them passive. The "well-behaved" audience became preferred among the middle and upper classes to audiences exercising sovereignty, which became a mark of lower class.

Changes in the relationship between live performance and audience prepared the ground for mass media. In the twentieth century, the boundary has been maintained not by policing audience behavior but by the shift from live to recorded performance, which severed audiences absolutely from performance. The possibilities of audience behavior and how it may be conceived differs from live to recorded performance. People sometimes talk back to the screen but it does not have the same effect. Live performance is a *process* to which the audience is integral, in contrast to the finished product of movie, broadcast, or recording, delivered as a fait accompli. The reintroduction of real or artificial "studio audience" reactions into television programs illustrates the significance of this process. With media this process is transformed into a *cause-effect chain,* product-response-new product. Any impact of the audience is on changing the next product, not shaping this one.

Inattention and Embedded Entertainment

Twentieth-century worries about the passive audience are contingent on the assumption that people pay attention to media messages. However, the history presented in this book shows that once people have become accustomed to new media, their behavior as audiences is notable for their *lack* of attention. Inattention has been an aspect of audience autonomy and a disproof of passivity. Moreover, inattention is not unique to mass media. Inattention weaves through the chapters of this history of American entertainment, changing in significance with different periods. Inattention to live performers in the early nine-teenth century was intimately related to matters of sovereignty and rowdiness. Long before mass media, inattention typified upper-class audiences at theater and opera. Complaints and comments about inattentive theater audiences were perennial. Theater was not a novelty for them, but a place to be seen and see others of their class. This was especially the case at European court theaters, but also among elite American audiences, such as the "Diamond Horseshoe" of New York's Metropolitan Opera, the ring of first-tier boxes reserved for founders of the house, where the new upper class of monopoly capital preserved the aristocratic tradition. Among elites inattention was a mark of their status, as masters to servile performers. Inattention at live performances then was a manner of certifying not only audience autonomy, but audience sovereignty.[20]

As we will see, working-class audiences too were inattentive, sometimes busily socializing among themselves, whether in 1830s theater or 1910 nickelodeon. The rowdy, resistant audience of the heyday of sovereignty, while often deeply engaged in the entertainment, also was wont to distract and be distracted by conversations, pranks, cards, prostitutes, and so on. As with elites, inattention was partly a matter of sociability. In the early days of movies, working-class nickelodeon audiences interspersed watching with socializing, eating, and caring for children. Conviviality, mistaken by the righteous and respectable as rowdyism, was a hallmark of almost all ethnic theaters (for drama, puppet, variety, and movie) in the years of great immigration. Immigrants brought with them old-world habits of socializing, whether from Europe or Asia.

Inattention may be an oversimplified, even misleading description. Rather than being inattentive, people might be more accurately described as exhibiting *intermittent* attention. That is, they may indeed be engaged in the story and even have an aesthetic knowledge of the genre and place aesthetic demands upon practitioners. At the same time, their attention may be divided, moving back and forth from the entertainment to conversation to other activities, and back again to the show. When radio and television were new, people listened and watched attentively.[21] Once they became commonplace, even in working-class homes, people did not sit riveted to the set but mixed viewing with other activities.

Recent communication and cultural studies researchers have emphasized that most television viewing takes place within the household or family, and that intermittent attention is a normal aspect of family communication. They focus on the *embedded* nature of viewing in the home as the fundamental characteristic of viewing that produces inattention. Radio and television became so embedded in the domestic routines in homes that they took on features of furnishings, and listening and viewing became inseparable from other household activities. This pattern applies not only to families but to many types of households. People living alone use radio and television as a kind of background, sort of pseudo-family to "people" the household. The principal reality that defines the situation in households is the relationships among its members, even when they are engaged in parallel activity rather than joint activity. Even withdrawal into lone activities presumes the preexistence of the household relationships.

We can extend the idea of embeddedness to understand nineteenth-century theater audience practices for comparison to radio and television at home. Entertainment was embedded in the larger practice of attending theater that included socializing with one's peers. While television is embedded in the family, stage entertainment was embedded in the activities of a community of peers. In the European tradition, for example, wealthy Italian families took their staff and servants with them to the opera so that they could take meals, entertain guests, send and receive messages, and conduct business in their box. In this case the family was embedded in community.

The factor of novelty applies as well. As a general rule, audiences attend to, even are absorbed by an entertainment when curious about some novelty – a star, a new technology, or an entertainment that they cannot afford regularly or that arrives infrequently. Upper-class nineteenth-century American audiences, known for talking during performances, typically fell silent in the presence of European stars. Working-class audiences often were more attentive or engaged, even when boisterous, because for them entertainments were more novel and cost more, and they could go less often.

Embeddedness contextualizes viewing and listening in the larger category of audience practices and leads us to understand that underlying the distinction between active and passive is a question of whether we should formulate the audience as a collective body or a collection of individuals. When viewing is embedded in some larger enterprise like family or community interaction, audiences are not singularly focused on the entertainment, but more on each other. The category, passive, presumes a singular focus on the entertainment.

When people define entertainment as embedded in a situation in which the paramount interaction or relationship is among audience members rather than between audience and entertainment, then we have what has been conceived as an active audience. Also, when the boundary of that interaction is communal rather than family or household, the activity is constituted as a public sphere and a foundation for collective action. Applying the idea of embeddedness to radio and television use in homes has highlighted the *dispersed* nature of these audiences. Researchers have begun to question whether it even makes sense to discuss such people as an entity called an audience. Applying the idea to nineteenth-century audiences highlights just the opposite, the degree to which these gatherings do constitute self-conscious groups that might act collectively.

To realize the aspects of a public sphere and of collective action requires going beyond inattention, more than immunity from the message, to resistance to the message, or what has come to be called reading against the grain of the preferred reading. Audience practices gain a larger significance when they are rehearsals for collective political action. Collective action theorists argue that such habits and skills, what they call a repertoire, as well as self-consciousness as a group, are necessary resources for moilizing collective action.[22] When practices are embedded in self-conscious membership in the audience and the audience as a group acts collectively, such practices foster the repertoire for collective action. Bowery b'hoys of the 1840s, rock concert fans of the 1960s, and soccer fans of the 1980s mobilized actions beyond the entertainments themselves.[23]

Public to Private

The concept of the audience as a group capable of acting to assert its will was not a theoretical exercise for nineteenth-century elites, but fed real fears of underclass rebellion. The shift in discourses documented in the following chapters, from a concern about active to passive audiences, occurred as the audience itself was tamed. Taming was achieved by reconstructing audience practices from public to private, collective to individual. The shift from public to private was a shift from community to family and ultimately to individual. It occurred in two phases.

In the first, nineteenth-century phase, public places like theater were redefined from places of community conversation and civic participation to places of private shopping and consumption; from a forum to a marketplace. The shift to consumption was simultaneously a shift from a collective/communal experience to a familial/individual experience. The person in public changed from a citizen and community member to a consumer and family member or individual. Gatherings were no longer a community with shared fate, but impersonal crowds of families or individuals with private interests. Public space was privatized. The gatherings were impersonal since people were no longer interested in engaging others outside their primary group.

The second, twentieth-century phase dismantled the gathering upon which conversations of the public sphere depended. The sense of "public" in this case is simply in contrast to privacy, though it has significance for the previous sense of "public" as a group engaged in debate about the polity. Making the gathering impersonal weakened the reasons to linger in public spaces. Radio and television broadcasting privatized entertainment and provided a reason to stay home. The home became increasingly a center of entertainment, and the family replaced the community as the group sharing the experience. This carried the process of privatization beyond privatizing public space to withdrawing to private space, raising greater barriers to community identity and participation.

Public, Participative, and Collective

The English theater tradition was public in more senses than just that theaters were open to the public by admission. They were sites of assembly, a physical gathering that was, until recently, a necessary precondition for public discussion or collective action. More particularly they were used as places of discussion, or space of discourse, as literary theorists Peter Stallybrass and Allon White phrase it, and of collective action. Theaters were public in the sense of a carnival gathering and in the sense of a public sphere. The carnivalesque, while not qualifying as and even contrasted to the bourgeois public sphere, clearly held political possibility through the potential for collective action arising from the collective celebration of "the world turned upside down" in which lower classes exercised an unaccustomed power.[24]

The tradition of participation across the footlights and within the audience, by virtue of its nature as a public conversation, was collective as well as active. It thus represented an exercise in practices of the public sphere as well as ground and rehearsal for collective action.[25] Lewd and disgusting, or politically charged, either constituted public dialog. Participants on both sides of the footlights joined in impromptu performance that the rest of the audience heartily enjoyed and to which they often gave a collective cheer. Actions for and against performers and (almost always) against managers were collective expressions. And often there were discussions among the audience and debates between factions about the performance or sometimes about entirely unrelated matters. All these represent forms of public discussion, of collective identity and even collective action.

They were abetted when audiences were composed of regular theatergoers, and performers were a resident stock company whose members and biographies were familiar to the regulars. Familiarity with the place, the performers, the plays, and the fellow audience members produced a community that was inclined to claim collective rights of audience sovereignty and to act collectively to enforce their rights, even when there may have been disagreements between factions within the audience. Members of such a community were more prone to be familiar with each other, to speak their minds, to be invested in this community, and were therefore prepared to speak up to defend or merely to participate. Neighborhood entertainments, where the sense of community persisted longer among audiences, continued to exhibit such public and collective character long after such were banished from downtown theaters or major theaters with national reputations.

From Politics to Consumption

The nineteenth-century chapters spell out how, over decades, audiences were redefined from public and collective to private and personal. The American theater audience before 1850 was conceived as a body politic and acted collectively, particularly during the early days of the republic and the Jacksonian era. In the early republic the audience in the theater was sometimes referred to as "the town" since all (politically significant) sectors of the community were present, and despite the fact that some groups were not represented or were present but had no voice.[26] Fitting the revolutionary rhetoric of egalitarianism, the audience was conceived as a body of equal citizens, all of whom held rights. These were fiercely asserted as rights of a free citizen, linking rights in theater to larger political rights. Thus the theater was defined as a public space in which the body politic deliberated. Therefore, early theater audiences, or often factions within the audience, constituted themselves as political bodies for debate or collective action, making theater an arena for public discourse and public action.

Moreover, the fact of live entertainment and the conventions of theater of the time furthered this constitution of audiences as political groups acting collectively. In live theater, meanings from text (the play) and from social interaction (performers with audience) merge, since audiences interacted with actors as both text (the characters) and as social beings (actors). In the prevailing rhetorical style of acting at the time, actors would step to the front of the stage and speak their parts directly to the audience rather than to other characters, thus denying any fourth wall between actors and audience. This style combined with the tradition of audience sovereignty to ensure a significantly active audience.[27] Thus we can speak of early theater as public sphere for both debate and for collective action.

Critical to any conception of public sphere and also to any potential for collective action is conversation, for the opportunity to assemble and discuss and come to consensus about what to do. Suppressing theater audience expression therefore eliminated the theater as a political public space. Quieting audiences privatized audience members' experiences, as each experienced the event psychologically alone, without simultaneously sharing the experience with others. During the middle of the nineteenth century managers in many theaters (and the courts) began to strip audiences of their "sovereignty" and to prohibit vocal and rowdy behavior, to bolt chairs to the floor, and in other ways restrict audiences' actions and movements. The changes culminated in the latter part of the century with darkening the theater during performances, a "benefit" of electric lighting.[28]

The combined changes quelled audience interaction. Social and physical restrictions and darkness left the audience only the stage to focus on, and here the focus was increasingly on sumptuous spectacle, a celebration of materiality and an advertisement for consumption. In theaters this translated into a further reduced identity with the rest of the audience and into consumption of entertainment as an individual experience. The establishment of middle-class decorum as the norm privatized the experience of theatergoing. The audience of late-nineteenth-century legitimate drama went as self-contained couples or groups. Interaction was inward to the group, rather than outward toward the crowd. Such small groups had aspects of a pseudo-household, perhaps with invited guests, transported to the theater, placing boundaries between each group within the theater. Moreover, they sat in a darkened room that enhanced this privacy and afterwards left the theater to discuss the experience in private. Theatergoing was redefined as a private "household" experience in distinction from its former public communal nature.

In addition to the negative prohibitions, the reformed theaters of the middle and late century offered a positive new focus, consumption. From midcentury, theaters were increasingly surrounded by and part of shopping districts, a new public space defined as domestic and feminine in contrast to the earlier public spaces that were masculine and either work related or part of the traditional public sphere. Previously, purchasing was a bourgeois male responsibility, and shops were mixed among factories, offices, and other precincts out of bounds to middle-class women. Public space was less and less considered a forum, and instead a marketplace. Even the streets, which traditionally had been important gathering places for politics, were drawn into the service of consumption through the new practice of the promenade. Political discussion retreated to private clubs, fraternal associations, union halls, and political party halls like Tammany Hall.[29]

Not all theaters and audiences, however, underwent quite the same transformation. While entertainment generally became part of this new commercial culture, some types of theaters continued to service working-class men, who continued to exercise collective authority over the stage, albeit less so than before 1850. Within these theaters they sustained an autonomous public sphere. Miriam Hansen argues that working-class immigrants constituted nickelodeon entertainment as a situation of autonomous public sphere through their convivial socializing in the movie houses. This, however, imputes too much political significance into this, unless one can demonstrate some carryover to more overt political action.

From Theater to Home

As we will see, a second historical change important to collective action was the increased delivery through the twentieth century of entertainment directly into the home, the implications of which are described in the chapters on radio and television. Recorded music technology might have brought this change earlier, but it was slow to develop and was overtaken by radio. The phonograph, marketed as early as the 1870s, spread slowly and did not become widely available in homes until the 1920s. Radio spread much more rapidly and provided more variety of uses. It therefore pioneered the new home entertainments of the twentieth century. But radio did not create a "crisis" in the public sphere. From the 1920s through the 1940s, worries about privatization were not part of the public discourse on radio. This was the era of movies, when people went *out* to the movies weekly. City centers and urban neighborhoods were vital and vibrant. The public sphere was alive and healthy, at least as a consumptive public sphere. In rural areas radio was even seen as the *solution* to isolation, linking families to the world beyond their farm.

It was not until the postwar era that commentators began to notice and decry the withdrawal of Americans into their suburban homes. Television viewing displaced moviegoing, suburban shopping centers replaced downtowns, and suburbs replaced urban neighborhoods. The 1950s and 1960s spawned doomsday theories about mass society and mass culture. Americans were retreating to their cocoons and leaving the democracy high and dry.[30]

With television the idea of audience passivity melded with the concerns over privatization. Passivity became firmly established, even an obsession, in discourses on audiences. The drug metaphor became commonplace. Viewers were addicts, "narcotized" by the "plug-in drug" television. People became thoughtless in front of the "boob tube." Such passive victims controlled by television were not capable of civic participation. The "couch potato," merely lazy or uninterested, did not leave his home to participate in the community and democracy. The imagery contrasts starkly with that of the nineteenth-century characterization of audiences.

A Note on My Choice of Entertainments

This history spans six different forms of drama and variety entertainment over two centuries. I have chosen these six because each was the dominant – or nearly dominant – commercial entertainment of its time; and because drama and variety have been the predominant genre in each, constituting a hereditary lineage traced back through the mass media of television, radio, and movies into the nineteenth-century stage entertainments of vaudeville, minstrelsy, and drama theater. These different forms have succeeded and displaced each other as the most widely available and popular forms through American history.[31] The perennial genre of drama and variety provide continuity across the forms. The combination of change and continuity makes these six forms ideal for making comparisons and tracing developments, and explains why other popular entertainments such as circus, music concerts, and spectator sports are less useful. Each form has borrowed and adapted from its predecessor. In some senses earlier forms gave birth to and nurtured the new forms that displaced them. In other senses the newer forms often succeeded by mimicking their predecessors. Minstrelsy began as *entre acte* entertainment in theater and incorporated dramatic burlesque in its developed form. Vaudeville adopted the variety form from minstrelsy and some of its performers too. High-priced or refined vaudeville too incorporated condensed one-act plays. Early talking movie comedy borrowed the vaudeville aesthetic. Radio stole stars and variety format from vaudeville and melodrama from cheap theaters. Television in turn raided radio.

Each of these forms has occupied a similar – although sometimes differentiated – niche in the array of leisure activities of their time. The similar niche is evident in their competition for audiences, with the result that each has displaced another as the most popular entertainment form. All forms of entertainment, from circus to drama to opera to novelties, were staged in the same theaters to mixed audiences before 1840s. In the 1840s, the upper classes in the largest cities began building opera houses and drama managers began in earnest to seek respectability through female audiences. Other audiences less concerned with respectability, particularly working-class men, shifted their allegiance to the new form called minstrelsy which continued to allow the rowdiness being suppressed in some theaters. Minstrelsy, however, also spawned variants, as some successful troupes drew broader audiences out of curiosity and offered respectable venues for the middle class. From the 1840s to the 1870s minstrelsy was the most widely available and popular form of stage entertainment. Minstrelsy established variety as a distinct format, with unrelated acts succeeding each other. Variants of this variety format appeared in many settings, including saloons. Once cleaned up and made respectable, variety became vaudeville. By the 1880s vaudeville had displaced minstrelsy as the predominant stage entertainment and maintained its dominance through the turn of the century.

Movies in their turn crippled cheap vaudeville and melodrama theater. In the 1910s movies began to take over darkened drama and vaudeville theaters, at first blending vaudeville with movies to broaden appeal, but soon dispensing with live entertainment as an unnecessary and expensive partner. With the arrival of sound in the late 1920s, movies had triumphed, while vaudeville and drama theater withered. The sound of radio nicely complemented silent movies in the 1920s. But the music industry as well as theater managers worried about radio stealing their audiences. During the 1930s a few feared that radio would reduce people's participation generally in community activities outside the home. After World War II television quickly supplanted both radio and movies as the principal mass medium. The attraction to television in the 1950s, combined with movies' loss of three-quarters of its audience, fed fears of privatization and theories of mass society composed of isolated families linked to the larger society through their television sets.

As popular entertainments each of these was entertainment of the "common people," but each too had its privileged constituency, and actively sought such a constituency. The story that plays out over time is therefore a recurring movement of markets and patrons and transformations of the entertainments themselves in pursuit of these markets. They cannot be solely understood as belonging to the common people or working class, except at certain moments and in certain sectors of the industries. Indeed the dynamic interplay between constituencies and the pursuit of these is necessary to understand audience practices.

Colonial Theater, Privileged Audiences

During the first third of this history, from about 1750 to the 1820s, America underwent major political, social, and cultural transformations that were reflected in theater audiences. In 1750, Colonial America, more than England itself, still was a monarchical society ruled by royal governors and gentry chartered and licensed by the king. The Revolution of course changed this and substituted a bourgeois democratic structure premised on the idea of government serving the people. Commoners challenged the authority of gentry and asserted their right to a voice in their own governance. By the 1820s early industrialization transformed class relations and the nascent working class gathered in urban neighborhoods. Throughout this time audiences were active and exercised sovereignty over performances. But who wielded this power and with what significance changed. Theater audiences continued to be important public gatherings, but the behavior and significance of the gatherings changed. Audience gender changed too, but its significance was as much about class as about gender. In the next three chapters we will detail these changes.

Professional theater arrived in the colonies in the 1750s,[1] just as the power of gentry had reached a high point and was about to enter a long process of dismantling. The colonies were a hierarchical society with a specific place for each person in a vertical structure. Relations were governed by a culture of deference, an expectation that each individual would defer to his "betters" and expect the same from his inferiors. Deference was based upon the real power of superiors to materially control the fortunes of those beneath them. A small number of elites controlled everything from government to land and commerce to religion.[2]

The most important distinction was between gentry and commoners, "lace" versus "leather aprons". Gentlemen were those of such wealth that they need not work. They proclaimed their gentility through their behavior, their demeanor, their education, their leisure. Their lifestyle provided employment for commoners.[3] Commoners were those who must work for a living, regardless of their income or skill. Gentry expected from them dutiful bows and doffed caps.

Actors were commoners and were expected to display proper deference. They were also itinerants. Even the largest cities of the colonies were only a few thousand residents, of whom only a few hundred could afford to regularly support theater.[4] Actors had to move from town to town to seek audiences. That made them vagabonds who without references could be jailed or ejected from a town, according to English laws of vagrancy.[5] Actors therefore sought powerful patrons to sponsor them when applying for license to play at a destination. The players had to submit letters of reference to the royal governor as testimony that they would cause no trouble.[6]

The culture of deference required actors to pay their respects to all the leading citizens. One manifestation of this was the custom in the 1750s for actors to call upon each of the principal inhabitants of the town to solicit their attendance at the theater for benefit performances. Announcements of benefits customarily said that, the actor "humbly begs the Gentlemen and Ladies will be so kind as to favor him with their company."[7] Public statements by managers of the 1750s express a remarkable obsequiousness, the verbal equivalent of doffing the hat and bowing. In announcing their arrival in the *New York Mercury,* Lewis Hallam, founder of one of the first acting companies in America, wrote that his company "humbly submitted to the Consideration of the Publick; whose Servants they are, and whose Protection they intreat [sic]." In part this tone was the norm even among gentry, a florid style borrowed from the Restoration court. However, it takes on significance when contrasted to the more egalitarian tone and behavior soon to replace it. A 1762 playbill for New York indicated a change in the practice of calling on patrons: "The ceremony of waiting on ladies and gentlemen at their houses with bills has been for some time left off in this company; the frequent solicitations on these occasions having been found rather an inconvenience to the person so waited on, than a compliment."[8]

An acting company's success depended to a considerable degree on these deferential relations between patrons and clients. Theater did not operate in a full market economy. While tickets were sold to the general public, a large portion of their income depended upon the willingness of wealthy gentry to purchase the lion's share and through their patronage encourage others of their class to do so too.[9] The colonial "audience," in several senses then, was the gentry.

Audiences of Gentry

Consequently, troupes frequented those southern towns that were centers of the privileged gentry life. Troupes arranged to play in Williamsburg, Virginia and other seats of royal governors to coincide with sessions of court and colonial assemblies, when markets and horseracing were also scheduled. These were sure to draw the gentry from the countryside and fill the theater. Gentry typically attended every performance when a troupe was in town.[10] Box seats where ladies and gentry families sat provided the bulk of income. The pit seated gentlemen without ladies, merchants, and others moderately well-to-do. Servants and slaves who arrived early to hold seats for their masters – there was no reserved seating – removed themselves to the gallery for the performance. Bills typically advised attendees to send servants to pick up tickets and hold seats or on where to descend from their carriages.

Managers made clear in their playbills their desire to accommodate ladies, more than they would after the Revolution. On some occasions the pit and boxes were "laid together," meaning the pit was railed off into boxes. An announcement of such intentions in 1754 stated explicitly that this was done "For the better accommodation of the Ladies" at a performance of Romeo by an actor popular with women. In April 1762 in New York City an actor postponed his benefit "as the Weather was then too bad for any Ladies to walk," indicating how important a segment of the audience were privileged women. A frequent announcement in playbills was that "Ladies will please to send their servants to keep their places."[11] Sources suggest that *young* gentlemen and ladies were an important segment of the audience. An opponent of theater in 1768 attempted to dissuade young ladies and gentlemen from attending theater, saying "I suspect that the Play-house could not long support itself from the middle-aged and grey-headed." Opponents and supporters often referred to theater's attractions for youth. It is perhaps these young ladies and gentlemen who, like their counterparts in England, featured themselves, rather than the play, as the center of attention.[12] Colonial gentry arrived late, were inattentive, and talked noisily. A playbill of 1754 for New York warned that the curtain would rise on time, despite latecomers, in order to not inconvenience those already arrived. Foppish young gentlemen took advantage of their privileged status to go backstage during the performance, pester the actresses, and even wander on stage to display their fine clothes – another English custom. In the winter of 1761–62 David Douglass, who had succeeded Hallam as the head of the acting company, had to repeatedly petition in playbills to clear the stage in New York. He complained in a public notice that "gentlemen crowd the stage and very much interrupt the performance" and announced that no one would be admitted backstage who did not have a ticket for the stage or upper boxes. Such complaints and warnings indicate managers' partially effective effort to contain unruly young gentry, probably with the support of some of the older gentry.[13]

These behaviors replicated those of English tradition in which the players were merely props in the performances of the privileged, for whom the theater was no different (in terms of these considerations) than a drawing room where they might carry on their relations with each other. Watching the play was simply one activity embedded in the more general social event of attending theater. Inattention and free trespass of the boundary between performer and audience were practices that served to affirm gentry status and the general hierarchy of colonial life.

While the upper class predominated, a few commoners appear to have attended as well. Middling artisans might afford a gallery ticket as a special occasion. The lowest ticket price was two shillings for a gallery ticket. Pit tickets were typically twice the price of the gallery. A Philadelphia laborer's wages in the mid-1750s were about ten shillings per week; a journeyman tailor, four shillings a day in 1762. For skilled workers theater was something of an expense, affordable on occasion, but most likely only in the gallery. Laborers and apprentices probably rarely attended.[14] A recurring theme raised by opponents of theater in the 1760s and 1770s was the temptation it represented to those who could not really afford it. In one example in January 1768, "Thrifty" claimed that some tradesmen who were in debt or unemployed, for whom some benefactors found work, were wasting money to "frequent the Playhouse with their families." These complaints were not the typical religious condemnations of theater and did not object to gentry attending, but expressed concern for the welfare of the town when tradesmen who could not afford such a luxury were tempted by the habits of their "betters" and by their wives and daughters to indulge themselves beyond their means. Even "middling sorts" had to be careful of their expenditures, since their fortunes could change quickly with the economy.[15]

Beginning in the 1760s there is some evidence of the rowdiness that became the trademark of the gallery in the nineteenth century. In 1762 in New York, David Douglass offered a reward to "whoever can discover the Person who was so very rude to throw Eggs from the Gallery, upon the Stage last Monday, by which the Cloaths [sic] of some Ladies and Gentlemen in the Boxes were spoiled, and the Performance in some Measure interrupted."[16] A Charleston music concert in 1765 was moved from a garden to the theater, due to some persons "so indiscreet as to attempt climbing over the fence to the annoyance of the subscribers" at the garden.[17]

Whatever the numbers of commoners in the audience, managers incorporated the English traditions of class divisions of the audience into box, pit, and gallery, reflecting the hierarchical society and its culture of deference. Each group had their proper place in the theater just as they had in society. Servants could not remain in the pit, where they held seats for their masters, but must remove themselves to the gallery. Slaves, free blacks, and other menials also would not be tolerated among gentry. Similarly the pit was no place for a lady whose status required a box where those with whom she sat were there by invitation and proper introduction. This segregation preserved proper relations of deference.

Separation was emphasized in the Williamsburg theater and the Southwark (Philadelphia) Theater, built in 1759, by installing rows of spikes separating the boxes and the stage from the pit and gallery. These spikes were not insignificant. On a night in 1752 burglars broke into the Williamsburg building and threw an actor upon a spike that penetrated his leg so deeply that he hung suspended until some passerby heard his cry for help. In the 1750s the spikes probably reflected more of the influence of English tradition of theater architecture than of an American necessity, as theater was too new in the colonies to have established the need here. But they may have gained a purpose during the 1760s as anti-aristocratic sentiment grew.[18]

Dramatic Protests

In sum, theater was an institution of the colonial aristocracy who, with their families, friends, servants, slaves, and clients, composed the audience. The actors were wholly dependent upon the aristocratic audience as their patrons. It was an active audience, but the rowdiness was of the sort based in aristocratic prerogative – young gentlemen strutting, carousing, and misbehaving themselves. Senses of an active audience engaged in collective action were absent because other classes besides servants and slaves were insubstantial in the audience. They were *outside* the theater and often opposed to theater, specifically because it was an aristocratic institution, representing from a religious point of view, decadence, and from a political view, domination.

The southern colonies were more hospitable. Williamsburg, Virginia, Annapolis, Maryland, and Charleston, South Carolina had some of the earliest active amateur theater groups and were visited by early touring professional companies, who played without opposition in the 1750s.[19] Northern colonists opposed theater on religious grounds and often succeeded in imposing bans on performances. Massachusetts banned theater in 1750 and did not repeal it until 1792; Philadelphia Quakers opposed it repeatedly in the 1750s and 1760s, whenever troupes petitioned the governor for permission to play, and Pennsylvania forbade plays in 1759. Rhode Island and New Hampshire banned theater in 1762.[20]

Opposition against Hallam's company was strong in New York and Philadelphia in the 1753–54 season. Nevertheless, supporters of theater prevailed and Hallam was granted permission in both cities. Douglass's company escaped the 1759 ban in Pennsylvania because the governor delayed its effective date long enough for them to present a five-month season of drama. Outside New England, theater had strong supporters among the most powerful and influential, including governors, and, although the opposition was not without influence, they often lost the battle.[21]

Early objections to theater were mostly to the place and people, rather than to the plays. Some even approved of reading plays while opposed to attending performances. Religious objections centered upon the theater as a depraved *place* frequented by immoral people, audience and performers alike. Opponents called the playhouse the "house of the devil," "synagogue of Satan," "school of debauchery." The actors' character more than the characters they played were at issue. In 1761 in New York City and again five years later in Philadelphia Douglass defended his actors' character from the "vilest epithets." As to the audience, one New York critic in 1761 accused all women who attended theater of lacking modesty. One critic even claimed that the problem was the people who congregated *outside* the theater, where "riots, drunkenness and obscenity are among the least of the evils nightly practised."[22]

Religious opposition, rooted in the Puritan cause of the English civil war, tended to be anti-aristocratic as well. Actors had joined the king's army against the Puritan army of Cromwell, who closed all English theaters in 1642. Upon restoration, the king reopened court theaters where plays often ridiculed Puritans. Restoration aristocracy and theater were notorious for their licentious and decadent lifestyle. Religious opponents then tended to equate theater with being both an aristocratic and decadent institution.[23]

In the 1760s circumstances began to change. A regular "assault on aristocracy," as historian Gordon Wood phrases it, arose. After the French and Indian War (1756–1763) rejection of deference intensified with a postwar depression. With the Stamp Act of 1765 resentment toward wealth and luxurious living increased further.[24] A series of incidents within and surrounding theaters indicated the beginnings of class confrontations in theater spaces that developed and continued through the Jacksonian era. Opposition to theater became openly political, and resentment of the British intertwined with class resentment. With the rising tide of anti-British feelings, theater was an obvious target. The actors were English; the plays were too. The willing patronage of the royal governors also reinforced the image of theater as a symbol of English rule. Actors, dependent upon royal governors, were reluctant to express anti-aristocratic sentiments or otherwise distance themselves from aristocracy. The American Company, renamed by Douglass in 1763 to avoid becoming a target of anti-British sentiments, still included on its advertisement in Philadelphia of April 1767 the phrase, *vivant rex et regina*. Such a public pronouncement of affiliation with the English crown on playbills, even if simple compliance with the law, must have inflamed antitheater feelings of colonists. Antitheatrical legislation expressed the anti-British feeling of northern merchants. Theater became subject to the sentiments of the boycott movement against British goods.[25]

Perceiving English rule as enforcing economic hardship, opposition to England became alloyed with opposition to aristocracy and wealth. The expense and frugality forced upon colonists by parliamentary acts produced hostility to the "extravagance" of theater. The *New York Journal* in January 1768 complained, "The money thrown away in one night at a play would purchase wood, provisions and other necessities, sufficient for a number of poor." Imported theater competed with domestic products for the scarce incomes of colonists.[26] The repeated characterization of theater as an extravagance represented a changed attitude toward wealth and toward the obligation of deference. Leisure signifiers of a gentlemen's status, such as patronizing theater, were now attacked as idleness. The gentry's association with the English justified refusing deference to them as an act of national independence. Many colonists considered English actors lackeys to aristocracy.[27]

Antitheatrical sentiments burst forth in the first major American theater riot. In New York City in 1766 the Sons of Liberty, who opposed the Stamp Act, passed a resolution to not "admit the strollers, arrived here to act, though the [British] General has given them Permission." Followers of the Sons prevented some actors, whom Douglass had sent in advance of the whole company, from performing at the Chapel Street Theater for two nights. On the third night, as a performance got underway, a "grand Rout instantly took place both Out and In the House… Lights were soon extinguished, and both Inside and Outside soon torn to Pieces and burnt by Persons unknown." Several people were injured and, according to one account, a boy killed in the attack and flight from the theater. Having cleared the audience out, rioters pulled down the theater, dragged the wood to a nearby square and built a bonfire, a typical part of street protests, all the while shouting "Liberty!" The riot revealed strong class sentiments. One newspaper said that many "thought it highly improper that such Entertainments should be exhibited at this time of public Distress, when great Numbers of poor People can scarce find the Means of subsistence."[28]

In this riot the attack was from outside, upon the theater as a British institution and symbol of the oppression of the Stamp Act. But this incident also reveals the pattern of equating the English with aristocracy and wealth, and opposing these as antidemocratic and anti-American. The pattern of equating class and nationality remained through the Jacksonian period. Artisans consistently equated the two, in the process also equating Revolutionary ideals or Americanism with the common man.

In the early 1770s a series of incidents involving artisans and laborers suggest the incipient development of class tensions *within* the theater, and the rise of an active, collectively oriented lower-class audience. After an October 28, 1772 performance by Douglass's American Company at the Southwark Theater in Philadelphia, a theater critic denounced "some Ruffians in the Gallery":

...if they call for a Song, or a Prologue, of which no Notice is given in the Bills, the Actors have an equal Demand upon them for an extraordinary Price for a Compliance with their Request – which of those vociferous gentlemen, of a Carpenter, Mason, or Taylor, will do more work than he bargains for without adequate Compensation? – Are not the Players in the same predicament? But to dismiss the Subject, the Directors of the Theatre are publicly desired to engage a Number of Constables, and dispose them in different Parts of the Gallery, who upon the smallest Disturbance, for the Future, may be authorized, by any Magistrate, and there are always enough in the House, to apprehend and carry to the Work-House, such Rioters, by which Means, Peace will be restored, and a few examples deter others from the like Outrages.[29]

This published challenge to the rights of audiences coincided with an increased presence of artisans in theaters. It was published at a time of larger strains between classes, when artisans of Philadelphia were explicitly rejecting the leadership of the merchant-lawyer elite. The calls for limitations on audience rights were directed at "carpenter, mason, or taylor" as the "ruffians" in the gallery, revealing the presence of lower classes in the audience in sufficient numbers and sufficiently active to foster the class tensions implicit in the complaint. The demands for police to enforce order indicate a desire to suppress working-class protests, a desire usually associated with the Jacksonian period.

At the same theater two months later in a small riot outside the gallery door, two people were arrested, and later that evening others broke into the theater and removed the iron spikes, the literal and symbolic class barrier that separated the gallery from the upper boxes. Douglass faced a similarly boisterous gallery when he moved to New York in the spring. There he called for the "better dispos'd People" in the audience to point out the repeated "offenders" to constables stationed in the theater or he would shut the gallery. The gallery, precinct of the lower classes, increasingly was becoming troublesome for elites.[30]

The violence, the action in the street outside the theater, and the class makeup of the crowds all indicate that theaters and theater audiences were involved in a form of lower-class political participation distinct from that after the Revolution. These incidents exemplify the operation of the moral economy of the crowd, as British historian E. P. Thompson termed it. In the early industrial settings of England and France, working-class political participation took the form of riots. Through riots, they defended what they considered their traditional rights. The term "moral economy" refers to the expectation that prices be set at what was traditionally accepted as fair, rather than by the market. This principle was applied more widely to defend political as well as economic rights.[31] Historian George Rude typified lower-class crowds as marked by direct action and violence to property more than to persons; discrimination in selecting targets; spontaneous with minimal organization and beginning with small incidents; composed of lower classes and artisans; and ideologically turned toward the past. Urban actions in particular he described as egalitarian, concerned with justice and rights of freeborn Englishmen, and class hostility to the rich.[32]

The Chapel Street riot as well as the series of incidents at Philadelphia's Southwark Theater fit these interpretations. In action and words rioters indicated that the attack was by lower classes upon wealth. Through crowd action they rectified what they considered a violation of the moral economy, that the privileged attended theater while others suffered hardship from the Stamp Act and other Acts. The crowd that removed the spikes in the Philadelphia theater was similarly taking matters into its own hands. The actions, however, differed from the moral economy in that they justified their actions not through tradition, but through new rights that would be enunciated in the Revolution and a repudiation of their traditional deference. This difference from the traditional crowd constituted the opening through which artisan political participation after the Revolution would incorporate political debate as well as riot. The use of crowd action to rectify a situation was the hallmark of the moral economy. They acted since the government, which served the king, was not expected to act in their interest. This stands in contrast to the conception of the bourgeois public sphere upon which the new polity arising from the Revolution would be premised. The public sphere was a social situation in which private persons debated public issues and let rational argument rather than power and status determine decisions. The public sphere was supposed to be a space beyond money and power. This bourgeois democracy was premised on the idea expressed in the Declaration of Independence that government served the people, and the idea expressed in the First Amendment that people would "petition the government for redress of grievance." The presumption was that people gathered together would debate and decide issues; the government as their servant would act. Public spaces would be used legitimately for debate instead of crowd actions. Thus the theater would suffice for debate, whereas the street was more suited to the action of the moral economy.

The incidents in the early 1770s, however, suggest some shifts in circumstances. Actions still indicate the exercise of a moral economy, in removing offenses by force, for example, the spikes. On the other hand, more artisans were now *inside* the theater, part of the audience, and objections to their behavior suggest both an elite unaccustomed to tolerating them inside the theater, and an increased concern about containing and controlling their behavior. Yet, the objection to the gallery's behavior also acknowledged their rights to be there and to demand the bill. The inclusion of artisans in the audience with elites seems a step toward a theater as public sphere where, in a decade or so, they would be debating each other.

This bourgeois concept of debate in public space and trust of the government to listen – and of the powerful to let argument decide – however, was never fully accepted by the artisan classes. While to some degree artisans in the theater audience accepted and participated, yet they periodically took matters into their own hands, as they did outside the theater. Street riots continued to be an important form of lower-class expression.[33] Therefore violent crowd action continued to be a part of theater disturbances through the Jacksonian era, even when at the same time participating in debate in the public space of the theater. There was a tenuous balance between debate and order on the one hand and crowd action and disorder on the other. Even the debates themselves often involved violence. Ultimately, inclusion of the lower classes created such heterogeneity that debate produced dissension rather than decision. From the elite point of view the "quality of the discourse" had degenerated. The elites eventually would withdraw from the debate and reestablish homogeneous assemblies in their own exclusive opera houses.

Drama in Early Republic Audiences

Colonial theater was barely on its feet when the Revolution halted its growth. There had been a flurry of theater construction after 1767, perhaps stimulated by the growing population.[1] But the Puritan characterization of theater as an extravagance gained wider acceptance during the hardships of the Revolution. The First Continental Congress in October 1774 passed a resolution to "discourage every species of extravagance and dissipation, especially all horse-racing, and all kinds of gaming, cock-fighting, exhibition of shews, plays, and other expensive diversions and entertainments." In October 1778, the Congress passed another resolution that states should suppress theatrical entertainments as causing "idleness, dissipation, and a general depravity of principles and manners"; and that officeholders who encouraged plays should be dismissed.[2] The language in part reflected the displacement of the culture of deference in which the leisured class was seen as creating work for commoners through their consumption, by language that condemned leisure as idleness and instead called for industriousness. Remarkably, theater was not condemned as

British – perhaps too many members of the Congress were patrons of theater to label it traitorous. Indeed some did not abide by the resolutions. Baltimore built a theater after the resolution of 1778 was passed, and there is some indication that a troupe played there and at Annapolis during the war. Plays were performed in Pennsylvania as well.[3] In general, however, theater during the war was reduced to performances by British officers in cities occupied by their troops.[4]

After the Revolution, theater became a popular amusement. The opposition, which was sufficiently strong before and during the revolution to ban theater, diminished significantly by the 1790s. An account of travels in the United States by a theater musician described the people of Annapolis as "passionately fond of theatrical entertainments," Philadelphians "very fond," and Bostonians seized by "a dramatic mania."[5]

Theater building resumed and exceeded the pace it set before the Revolution, now cropping up even in small towns. To accommodate a growing audience, new theaters were much larger and costlier buildings than the flimsy affairs of the colonial era, with lobbies, boxes, and galleries.[6] Theater troupes alone could not afford such ambitious buildings. They financed construction through stock, usually offered to leading citizens, who, according to William Dunlap, theater manager and playwright of the 1790s, "were willing to invest their money to almost any amount."[7] Stockholders received the profits, and actors who previously shared the box office were put on salary. Wealthier subscribers supported their favorite writers, performers, and accommodating managers not only with attendance but also gifts and money.[8] By this means stockholders supplanted governors as the arbiters of drama.

Greater seating capacity and a smaller proportion of boxes indicate that managers were reaching deeper into the social hierarchy for their audiences. Lower prices and higher wages made theater more affordable. A pit ticket dropped from a day's pay for an artisan before the Revolution to a third or less of that by the turn of the century; a gallery ticket was half of that. A Boston mechanic expressed appreciation in 1792 for the new theater in Broad Alley, as the only amusement to which he could afford to take his wife.[9]

A growing presence of artisans may have stimulated a change in description of theater audiences. Before the Revolution, audiences were typically referred to simply as gentry ("ladies and gentlemen" or "genteel"). Afterwards, newspaper columns on the drama began to regularly use versions of the phrase "beauty and fashion" in describing audiences. Beauty referred to upper-class ladies and fashion to the upper-class generally.[10] A theater profited to the degree it drew a "fashionable" crowd.[11]

Much commentary described their habit of watching themselves more than the stage, continuing the old aristocratic sense of the relative importance of performers and audience. Candles remained lit during performance, encouraging self-display. Attention to who was in the audience demanded that the audience be lit almost as well as the stage. There were recurring references to women in the boxes wanting sufficient light to show off their beauty, "or BEAUTY will be content no longer to blush unseen." A paper in 1804 complained about light being concentrated on the stage and insufficient light in the audience: "the Manager has not yet to learn, that all the visitors of a theatre do not attend *solely* to witness the stage exhibitions."[12]

Notwithstanding their interest in themselves, "ladies'" attendance depended as well on the play and the players. Plays with a prominent female character or plays of the sentimental school were known as "woman's plays" and the proportions of women in the audience varied greatly with the play. They did not attend Shakespeare's Falstaff plays or *Julius Ceasar*.[13]

Women seated outside the safety of the boxes did not command the title of "lady." A Frenchman in 1798 Philadelphia saw women in the pit, "but not women of distinguished appearance. Women also go in the upper gallery." Commentators of this period assumed the women in the gallery and top tier of boxes to be prostitutes. Despite the strong opposition to theater in the colonial period as licentious, there had been no accusations of prostitutes in the audience. Now their presence was noted as habitual. In 1788, a "Friend of Decency" was appalled, not at the presence of prostitutes, but that a prominent New Yorker left the ladies he had accompanied to the theater and joined "two women of notorious ill fame, in a conspicuous part of the house, with whom he continued ... caressing and feeding fruit." Prostitutes in the theater were accepted if they kept their place. A New York ad of 1795 announced, "No person of notorious ill fame will be suffered to occupy any seat in a box where places are already taken." Some did oppose their acceptance at theater. In 1794, shortly after the completion of the Federal Street Theater in Boston, some objected to the traditional separate entrance to the gallery, since "by affording a special door to that portion of the house usually the resort of the vile of both sexes, a premium on vice was offered."[14] This was a change from the past when theater was entirely condemned and banned. Now the goal was to quarantine the vice to certain sectors of the theater.

Alcohol, tobacco, and prostitution created an atmosphere unsavory for "genteel" women, but comfortable for the generally male audience. Theater had changed from an institution of the privileged classes into a masculine affair. Gentry could not exclude artisans of the republic; and association with artisans made theater less appropriate for "ladies." Cigar smoking was widespread despite the dangers of fire and the fact that smoking was not permitted in English theaters of the time. Likewise it was customary for men to send out for or bring alcohol to the theater and to return to nearby taverns at intermissions for refills. Men left their ladies in the theater while they adjourned to taverns. In 1796, New York's John Street Theater stated a new policy, that "Much confusion having arisen from the introduction of Liquor into the house, during the performance, the managers respectfully hope gentlemen will not call for any till the conclusion of the First Piece, as the Door-keepers are in the strictest manner ordered to prevent its admission."[15]

The change of theater to a more overtly masculine institution coincided with it taking on all the aspects of an institution of the classic bourgeois public sphere. The shift was less one of redefining gender roles, as historian Linda Kerber indicates that many of the ideas about women and politics predated the Revolution, than of changing theater from an exclusive institution run by and for the gentry to one where artisans and tradesmen had flooded in to claim their place. The revolutionary zeal and the flood of commoners guaranteed that theater would be a rougher place than it had been before, less suited for "ladies." But the mix of classes also guaranteed that theater, along with many other institutions of the time, such as taverns, the press, and the streets, would be a place of vigorous political debate.[16]

"No Inconsiderable Part of the Entertainment"

In this mixed-class, masculine environment audiences were very active among themselves and in relation to the stage. Unlike the colonial gentry who relied on patronage to control performers, early republic audiences intervened directly in the performances. One rowdy practice was to call for tunes, and to pelt the musicians if they did not comply satisfactorily. This tradition reached its high point in the 1790s, when Federalists and Republicans competed to demand their favorite songs.[17]

Washington Irving's humorous *Letters of Jonathan Oldstyle,* published in 1802–1803, gave a vivid and amusing sense of theater audiences of the day, encapsulating in his parody most of the antics of and complaints about audiences of the early republic, which he said "furnish no inconsiderable part of the entertainment."[18] While the ladies in the boxes busied themselves with talking and observing each other, young beaux behaved as if the theater were their personal club where they went

to lounge away an idle hour, and play off their little impertinences for the entertainment of the public. They no more regard the merits of a play, or of the actors, than my cane. They even *strive* to appear inattentive … some have even gone so far in search of amusement, as to propose a game or two of cards, in the theater, during the performance.[19]

They sat on the front of their box with their back to the stage and adjourned to the lounging room for "French brandy, Holland gin and Spanish segars."

Those in the gallery he described as making noises "similar to that which prevailed in Noah's ark [and throwing] apples, nuts and gingerbread, on the heads of the honest folk in the pit." The gallery called for tunes by "stamping, hissing, roaring, whistling." The "honest folk" in the pit were less noisy than those in the boxes or gallery. But even here the conversation was so incessant as to miss half the play, and they "stand with their dirty boots on the seats of the benches." Jonathan complained of the universal habit of eating in the theater, with tables outside heaped with apples, oranges, pies, and custards. They ate noisily, cracking nuts and crunching apples. Oldstyle's recommendations were, "To the pit – patience – clean benches and umbrellas; To the boxes – less affectation – less noise – less coxcombs; To the gallery – less grog and better constables."

Irving's parody was remarkably similar to contemporary reports. A letter by a theatergoer published in a Philadelphia newspaper in 1794 applauded plans to suppress the rowdiness when the Old American Company opened the John Street Theater in New York in 1794, arguing:

Some persons have long frequented the gallery of your Theatre, whose constant practices have been such as to render the situation of persons in other parts of the house disagreeable and irksome; & if continued must inevitably banish every person from your house except the *boys of the Gallery.* Those who frequent the Pit, have in a particular manner been the object of their ill treatment [emphasis in original].

He went on to describe how the galleryites demanded that the pittite doff his cap to them and, if he didn't, was pummeled all evening with "apples, pears, sticks and stones," "scurrility and abuse," "spitting and emptying beer bottles on him," with the result that the target as well as those around him had their clothes ruined and their bodies bruised. He later referred to the offenders as "Bucks and Bloods," that is, affluent young men.[20]

The rowdy nature of the theater contrasts sharply to the rules published for a subscription music concert in New York for 1785–86. "During the performance of the Music, no person shall either speak, rise up, move any chairs, tables or benches, walk across the room, or do any other thing to disturb or prevent the rest of the company from enjoying the Music, or by which disrespect may be shewn to the performance"; repeated violators of the rules were to be banned from the concerts.[21] Such strict regulation was due in part to the different tradition of concerts and the limitation of admissions to subscribers and their female companions. The concerts included a dance following the concert that required class exclusion in order to avoid "ladies" being forced to associate with lower classes.

Managers made efforts to contain the problem, probably to protect their property from damage as well as to appease the more sedate part of their audience, whose letters of complaint periodically appeared in newspapers. Even minor annoyances such as standing on benches, throwing refuse, and spitting required costly redecorating periodically. Managers usually put their desires in the form of requests that audiences reform their behavior. For example, the John Street Theater managers in 1795 very politely reminded their clients that "should it happen that the rules, peace or good order of the House should at any time be interrupted, they deem themselves *compelled* [emphasis in original] to point out such measures as shall if possible restore its tranquillity." The Park Theater manager in 1808 asked those in the pit to stop their habit of standing on the benches, a custom he claimed was unique to New York.[22]

Outright threats usually targeted specific individuals, typically the young or persons sitting in the gallery, who had annoyed the rest of the audience, perhaps because they could rely on the support of the rest of the house in this regard. At the opening of the Park Theater in March 1798, the manager mentioned that "for some nights past, certain ill-disposed persons have made a practice of throwing at the performers in the Orchestra and on the Stage ... offending decency and humanity." A theater in Bedlow Street, New York in 1804 referred to "young gentlemen who stile themselves BLOODS!" causing problems, and announced placement of peace officers in the house.[23]

These letters and announcements indicate that the divide between rowdies and complainants seems to have been primarily between age versus youth, more than between classes. Rowdies were often identified as young. A playbill for October 1802 complained of those who left the theater early giving their tickets to boys, presumably teenagers, who waited outside the theater for just such an opportunity. It claimed schoolboys and apprentices were "induced to leave their schools, or their master's or parent's Houses, and infest the avenues to the theatre."[24]

Federalists, Republicans, and Artisans

The post-Revolution building boom in theaters coincided with the intense conflict between Federalists and Republicans. In a climate that included the Whiskey Rebellion, Kentucky's threat of secession, the spread of Democratic-Republican Societies, and the Alien and Sedition Acts, it is understandable that public gatherings in theaters would turn political.[25] The growth of the artisan audience added a class tension to these gatherings. Fired by the powerful sentiments of equality that culminated in the Revolution and colored every aspect of society afterward, artisans joined the political debates between Federalists and Republicans.

Whereas before the Revolution confrontations were more likely between supporters and opponents of theater, afterward it was more likely a confrontation between two factions within the audience. Theater was accepted enough for it to be considered a legitimate site for debate by both sides. As before the Revolution, class sentiments were linked to national sentiments. Artisans, now in the pit and gallery instead of the street, favored the French, in the midst of their own Revolution, while the elites in boxes favored the English.[26]

Managers tried to avoid controversy. They rejected requests for reserved seats, knowing the reaction against privilege it would create.[27] They excised what they thought would be offensive lines from

English plays. The most common deletions at the Chestnut Theater in Philadelphia from its opening in 1794 to the end of the War of 1812 were passages that might inflame the anger of Republicans: references to allegiance to the English king, praise of English institutions, and the English peerage. Anything that could be interpreted as disparagement of the French was also deleted. Anything suggesting class deference was deleted.[28]

The debates were especially intense at Boston theaters. During the first two seasons of the Federal Street Theater (1794–96) the manager attempted conciliation to please both "Feds and Antis," as he needed a full house to profit. At first, the management "requested that no particular tune be called for by the audience." Then, to avoid fights, he attempted to allow Federalists and Republicans equal time to hear their favorite airs.[29] In 1796, however, the trustees of the theater encouraged Federalist plays to be performed. Some Republicans took exception to what they considered an insult to France in the play *Poor Soldier*. A quarrel between the French consul and the *Boston Gazette,* a Federalist paper, fanned the flames. The performance of the play was stopped when a riot destroyed benches, doors, and windows of the theater.[30]

Another theater manager took advantage of the conflict to build the Haymarket Theater nearby, where he offered patriotic plays like *Bunker Hill* and *West Point Preserved,* written to appeal to Republican sentiments.[31] Considerable animosity arose between the two theaters. Wealthy stockholders owned the Federal Street Theater, while artisans professing Jacobin sympathies held stock in the Haymarket. Employers gave their apprentices free tickets to the Federal if they promised to never visit the Haymarket. The Federal reduced its admission prices for pit and gallery to drive the Haymarket out of business.[32]

The tenor of feelings at the time is captured in a "Scene" published in the Federalist *Boston Gazette* in 1801, intended to satirize Republicans.[33] It was written only a few days after Republican Thomas Jefferson was elected president by the House of Representatives in very tense and uncertain circumstances. Federalists had been accusing Republicans of using the rhetoric of equality to gain the support of the lower classes against the Federalists. The column reported a fictitious conversation at a tavern. A Doctor Galen and a lawyer named Spotless are exhorting a group of artisans, called "leather breeches," from their traditional work garb, to riot at the theater, in opposition to Federalist plays and songs.

DR. GALEN: The people have within a few years been ignominiously bound and fettered by a few Ragamuffin federalists. It is time that we away and burst the Lilliputian ties... For several years the Theatre has been devoted to federal and British politics and not a republican note has been warbled within those aristocratic walls. We must begin the work of regeneration here.

LAWYER SPOTLESS: That's right! most noble doctor! the theater is an important engine in the hands of any party. It powerfully operates on public sentiment... In France it has done wonders...

DR. GALEN: ...The spirit of 1775 and 1794 is reviving. We must improve the occasion to command the performances of the Theatre. Let us rally our forces – secure the boxes, pit and gallery – hiss off *Washington's March, Adams and Liberty, Rise Columbia* [Federalist songs] and clamour for *Ça ira* and *Carmagnole* [French Jacobin songs favored by Republicans]. Let us compel the manager to bring forward Burke's *Bunker Hill...*

LAWYER: ...Tomorrow they introduce a song in which the victories of the cowardly tools of Pitt in the Aratheusa frigate, over the invincible French are sung.... My worthy friends, will you seize the opportunity to regain our wonted influence?...

LEATHER BREECHES [i.e., workmen]: I'll join you.... I'll head the [gallery] Gods...

LAWYER: And I'll rule the pit.

DOCTOR: I'll take my station in the boxes and shake the coward souls of every well-dressed federalist. (*Aside*) I am too proud to mingle with the herd I govern and direct.

LAWYER: My honest rogues! Amidst the scene of wild uproar, coats, hats and pocketbooks well filled with federalist cash will rain in showers about you.

Federalist-Republican confrontations disrupted Philadelphia theaters also. In 1798 an actor at the Chestnut Street Theater introduced at his benefit a new song, *Hail Columbia*, for Federalists to sing against the Republicans' *Ça Ira*. When he began the song the audience stood, cheered, and joined him, making that night a victory for Federalists at the theater.[34] The election of Jefferson emboldened the

Republican pit and gallery of the Chestnut Street Theater. In January 1802, each night they hissed a British actor who replaced the popular "adopted American" Thomas Cooper, to such a degree that he quit and committed suicide. Federalists in the same theater expressed their opinions just as strongly. They hissed an actor for toasting President Jefferson in 1803 and the Federalist press "fulminated" about the toast.[35] Later in the same decade the topic shifted from domestic to foreign politics. In 1808 the Chestnut Theater was the scene of patriotic displays against British impressment of American sailors at sea. The slightest remark favorable to England could lead to a disturbance. When Henry V in Shakespeare's play declared, "I thought upon one pair of English legs did march three Frenchmen," a riot ensued. Such tension was likely increased by the fact that in 1809 an English embargo was choking trade and causing distress among seamen.[36]

The struggles within the theaters of Boston and Philadelphia were part of the battle between Federalist and Republicans that flowed through the press, the streets, and all the rest of the society. The struggle had strong class overtones and these appeared in the theater disturbances as well. Theater was no longer being defined as an English or "extravagant" institution. Instead it was conceived as an arena for political expression in this intense national debate over the form of the government. Artisan Republicans, who previously would have attacked the entire institution, accepted it, adopting, as the "Scene" suggests, the French conception of theater as a valuable tool for propaganda,[37] even though they still equated the English and English actors with aristocracy and class hierarchy. Elite Federalists also accepted theater as an arena for public debate, and artisans as political opponents they could not ignore or dismiss in the theater or elsewhere. Theaters therefore became an integral part of the national confrontation between classes and their political values.

New York theaters remained relatively absent of political disputes between Federalists and Republicans. There was a demonstration of solidarity with the French at the John Street Theater in 1793 as the whole audience sang Ça ira on the anniversary of the departure of British warships from New York harbor.[38] Two incidents did occur that seem more prescient of the Jacksonian period with their more narrow focus. In March 1797, the audience at the Park theater sided with Lewis Hallam, son of the colonial company leader, in a dispute with his partner John Hogkinson, nearly creating a riot, hissing and shout-

ing at Hodgkinson. Pit and box took sides. From the pit came shouts of
"insolence" toward Hodgkinson, and someone wielded a cudgel, and
several more cried "out with the rascal." A lawyer in a side box, on the
other hand, accused those in the pit of riot and said, "You have no
right to demand any thing or person at the theater or on the stage, not
advertised expressly in the bill," echoing the 1772 attack upon audience sovereignty at the Southwark Theater in Philadelphia. Another
man in a side box then told Hodgkinson he degraded his profession by
speaking to the "rioters." Others applauded Hodgkinson. Eventually,
magistrates arrived, the rioters quelled, and the play continued. On
his next appearance, however, Hodgkinson was again hissed; he left
the stage and the play was canceled.[39]

A year later William Dunlap presented a play of his own, *Andre*, at
New York's new Park Theater. At its opening some in the audience
mistook a scene as an insult to America and hissed vociferously.
Others quieted them and the play continued. But some continued the
complaint outside the theater, and the actor, concerned for his popularity, wanted the play withdrawn. The offending scene was changed
and no further complaints occurred.[40] While neither incident was
explicitly connected to party politics, both exhibited the class antagonism that had become the mark of theater audiences, with pittites
eager to enforce their demands on the actors, and those in the boxes
equally set on thwarting the desires of the pit.[41]

In this first American era of flourishing drama, theater was as much
a place of public debate as of dramatic entertainment. It had become
the prototype of the public sphere, including a broadened range of
classes, albeit narrowed in gender. Before the Revolution, confrontation tended to be between the gentry inside and other classes at the
doors. During the early republic the other classes were represented
among the Republicans *within* the theater, in debate and competition
with Federalists.

But this public sphere did not succeed in producing rational debate
with heterogeneous participation. There was more shouting than discussing, more confrontation than consensus. The rowdiness of the
gallery and the general intensity of the competition between
Federalists and Republicans in theaters of the time indicate that managers barely contained the audience within the bounds of debate.
Audience factions sometimes became crowds taking direct action
against their targets. Unlike the traditional crowds, however, their
chosen targets were more often the actors and musicians than prop-

erty. They hissed, shouted, and threw all manner of objects at performers, mostly to force them to represent the Federalist or Republican cause. Performers, especially the musicians, were often not themselves offenders, but simply caught between the two factions.

Theaters thus were a peculiar blend of bourgeois public space and site of semitraditional crowd actions. The public space of theater was a rich soup of intense political participation by gentry, merchants, and artisans, all patrons of the same public houses. The debate would soon change, however, from a dispute between two political parties, as the Federalists faded from the political scene. It would take on a more distinct hue of class antagonism stripped of party alliance.[42]

The B'Hoys in
Jacksonian Theaters

During the colonial period theater was a place for gentry, during the early republic a place for political debate and contest between classes, but in the Jacksonian era, roughly 1825 to 1850, theater belonged to the common man. The rowdy nineteenth-century audiences so often recounted in colorful tales were the young working men of this era. Now the working class constituted a large enough market to sustain their own theaters, and the young men were the most avid theatergoers among them. These young men exercised sovereignty not through patronage, as gentry had, but through vocal expression of their will and enforcement through physical assault. This was the ultimate "active" audience. They participated in collective action more than public debate. They brought the street into the theater, rather than shaping the theater into an arena of the public sphere. Elites would be increasingly concerned about containing them.

The privileged were disinclined to engage these ruffians and instead increasingly sought refuge in more exclusive gatherings. Gustave de Beaumont, travel companion of Tocqueville, claimed that, in

Philadelphia in 1831–32, "Persons more distinguished in fortune and position do not make theatergoing a habit; only something out of the ordinary will attract them there – for example, the presence of a celebrated guest actor."[1] While this may have overstated their absence, clearly they had reduced their past support of theater. Classes were increasingly at odds with each other in theaters and increasingly the upper classes sought their own theaters, segmenting entertainment by class.

B'Hoys: A Market, a Youth Culture, an Icon

By the Jacksonian era drama had become a regular entertainment for a wide assortment of people in cities and towns, east and west, qualifying it as popular entertainment. Workmen's wages had risen significantly since the War of 1812. Theater ticket prices were reduced in 1823 and by the 1830s were half what they had been a couple of decades earlier. As a result, theater was an affordable and attractive diversion and young working men with spare time and money attended frequently.[2] Englishman Henry Fearon, touring the United States in 1817, remarked on the relative standard of living of English and American workingmen:

...men that, if in London could hardly buy a pint of porter – and should they ever think of seeing a play must take up their abode among the gods in the upper gallery: yet, in America, they can pay three-quarters of a dollar – free from care, and without feeling, on the following morning, that they must compensate, by deprivation or extraordinary labour, for their extravagance.[3]

Some theaters were known for their working-class patronage, and some managers made a concerted effort to attract a working-class clientele. In New York City, the Chatham Garden Theater attracted workmen from the late 1820s until it closed in 1832, when the Bowery Theater displaced it as the favorite haunt of workers. In Philadelphia in 1831, the Arch Street Theater lowered prices and offered American stars in American plays to attract a loyal working-class audience. Not long after, in 1834, Francis Wemyss refurbished the Walnut Street Theater in patriotic colors and formed an alliance with the Bowery in New York to produce the same shows with the same costumes and scenery, to suit working-class tastes. In Boston, the Tremont Theater became a working-class haunt in the 1830s, followed by Pelby's

National Theater.[4] The Jacksonian triumvirate of western theater pioneers Sol Smith, Noah Ludlow, and James Caldwell all paid homage to workers in their audiences. They courted riverboatmen and other workmen in New Orleans, Mobile, and St. Louis. In 1852, when a manager in St. Louis snubbed workers, he no longer could turn a profit.[5]

New York's Bowery Theater was the longest-lived and came to be emblematic of the working-class theater. The Bowery was built in 1826, and its first manager sought a fashionable upper-class audience in competition with the Park Theater. But the affluent remained at the Park Theater in their own neighborhood. Thomas Hamblin took over management of the Bowery in 1830 and instead sought a working-class audience.[6] Hamblin renamed it the American Theater, and draped it in patriotic melodramas. As Whitman described it, "the heavy tragedy business prevail'd more decidedly at the Bowery Theater, where Junius Booth and Edwin Forrest were frequently to be heard." Booth and Forrest were practitioners of a very physical "robustious" style of acting that appealed to working-class men but was becoming unfashionable among "polite society" in New York and Boston. Since most workers still could not afford theater every night, Hamblin began the practice of longer runs of the same play, instead of a new play each night, as was the custom at the Park and other upper-class theaters.[7]

Walt Whitman reminisced about the Bowery Theater audience of the 1830s as "packed from ceiling to pit with its audience mainly of alert, well dressed, full-blooded young and middle aged men, the best average of American-born mechanics."[8] But Whitman's admiration was not shared by all. Less tolerant contemporary observers wrote of a rougher crowd. The *New-York Mirror* in 1833 described "a great want of order and respectability in the conduct of the pit audience... A dirty-looking fellow a few nights since, taking it into his head that the pit was hardly comfortable enough for him, coolly stepped into the dress-circle, and there seated himself very much to the discomfort of some well-dressed females in the same box ... while his comrades in the pit, seeing that he was not to be moved, gave him three cheers." Even Whitman declared that the Bowery after 1840 "completely changed [with] vulgar programmes [and] pandemonium in the pit."[9] By midcentury, "Light and Shadow" writer George Foster colorfully described the Bowery pit, "which heaves continually in wild and sullen tumult, like a red flannel sea agitated by some lurid storm ...

the roaring crush and clamor of tobacco chewing, great coat wearing second tier – the yells and screams, the shuddering oaths and obscene songs, tumbling down from the third tier."[10]

These were the Bowery b'hoys, who became the topic of travelogues, dime novels, police gazettes, and plays.[11] They became noticeable in the 1840s when a large percentage of the New York working-class population was unmarried males living in working-class wards around the Bowery. Single men who had migrated to cities for work and journeymen tramping from city to city often lived in boarding houses, where they had a room to sleep but little more.[12] The young boarder, having no home of his own, spent much of his free time at the saloon or theater with his peers. Living and working together, these young men developed a community and culture among themselves. They were journeymen or apprentices who had limited prospects of becoming self-employed master craftsmen like their grandfathers' generation, as factories replaced shops. As their prospects shrank in their craft they turned to a youth culture constructed around leisure and consumption for the core of their identity and self esteem.[13]

These young men valued independent self-help, fairness, generosity and loyalty, vigor and strength. Egalitarianism ranked high; they opposed any form of pretensions. They showed little interest in religion or unions, but formed what may have been the first working-class youth culture, built around consumption of alcohol, clothes, and theater. Their rowdiness was a rejection of the respectability that the middle class were forging at the same time to distinguish themselves from the working class. Their flamboyant dress contrasted starkly with the somber wear of the respectable. The stereotypical "dressed-up" b'hoy wore felt top hat with "soap-locked" hair underneath, red flannel shirt, and high black boots.[14]

The geography of their distinctly masculine culture was composed of the boardinghouse, saloon, theater, and fire company. Physicality was central to their idea of a good time. The typical b'hoy ran with a volunteer fire company, which by the 1830s had become clubs of young workmen. They took considerable pride in their company, even leaving work to fight a fire. Companies raced to be first at a fire; the competition easily led to fights. Some of the companies were as notorious for brawls as the gangs that prowled the streets of New York and Philadelphia's working-class districts.[15]

The b'hoys of New York were more numerous and perhaps more distinctive than in other cities, but they were not unique. In

Philadelphia the "boys of pleasure" ran with the fire companies, made the saloon their home, and filled the pit of the Arch or Walnut Street Theaters. Young working men and boys in other cities large and small left a record of physical fun that included rowdiness and regular theatergoing. A young printer in Albany in 1828 reported attending theater several evenings a week. Englishman Henry Fearon found fourteen-year-old boys who were regulars at the theater in Pittsburgh. Descriptions of frontier theater audiences similarly depict rowdy young men.[16]

By the late 1840s the b'hoys had become the subject of much popular discourse that turned them into a cultural icon.[17] Three discourses on b'hoys are identifiable: a moralistic discourse that emphasized the dangers of poor districts and their subculture, and two commercial variants, numerous plays depicting the b'hoys and "Light and Shadow" books that pictured this subculture for outsiders.

Plays appeared through the 1830s and 1840s featuring city life of the volunteer fireman or Bowery b'hoy. But when the impudent, conceited, and exuberant character of Mose appeared in 1848 on the stage of the Olympic Theater, before a mix of workers and clerks, he was instantly recognized as the "real thing." Mose quickly became a stock characterization of the young urban worker. Within the next two years over a dozen other Mose plays were staged, presenting Mose in the working-class subculture of several different cities. Frank Chanfrau, the actor who originally created Mose, made a career of it.[18] For a rare moment, the working-class youth saw themselves presented to the world in drama. The Mose plays seem to have been written to appeal to the b'hoys themselves, and most opened at theaters in New York and Philadelphia with substantial working-class clientele.

The moralistic discourse elaborated the dangers of the Bowery subculture. Advocates of respectability used the b'hoys as a measure of what *not* to do. Newspaper drama columns contrasted the audiences at the Bowery Theater to those at respectable theaters. Guidebooks offered more hysterical versions, advising young middle-class women to constrain their appearance on the street and not to venture into certain places. Theater figured prominently in these stories as one of the principal dangerous places. The discourse made no distinctions between violence and the rowdiness of working youth. There were indeed dangerous groups and neighborhoods, but in the middle-class discourse these became grounds to suspect working-class youth generally and to divide the city into respectable or disreputable locations.

These fears spread well beyond New York and Philadelphia. A New England reformer expressed concern about the anti-authoritarian culture of what he called "Boweriness." A Charlestonian claimed that people had worried that such "Boweryisms" would spread to their fair city.[19]

Newspapers, magazines, and book publishers offered a commercial twist on this discourse, using the guise of moral warnings to offer titillating glimpses of the underworld to the middle classes. "Light and Shadow" books, travelogues of lower-class worlds, traded upon the popularity of the b'hoys as well as on middle-class fears of their subculture. Newspapers and magazines provided the middle class with a mix of lurid and fear-inspiring stories of sex and violence among the lower classes, and of higher-class young men and women becoming victims to it.[20]

B'hoys became a representation around which could be wrapped all sorts of images of what was good and bad and even what it meant to be American. The b'hoys claimed their rough style was distinctly American. Higher classes used the image to indicate why Americans needed civilizing. In this respect the b'hoy was like several other stock characters. George Foster claimed that "an unpracticed hand could not distinguish [the b'hoys from] the trapper of the Rocky Mountains and the gold hunter of California." Others compared b'hoys to the Mississippi boatmen. These characters all shared a roughness and rejection of the pretense of respectability, and were promoted as "true Americans."[21]

Cut off from the traditional avenues of rising status rooted in their craft, b'hoys found a new source of identity among their fellows in new urban working-class neighborhoods. Images of their lack of propriety in contemporary discourses furthered their identity with the group. Their rowdiness was a means of affirming their membership in the group, as well as vying for status within the group. Their behavior in theaters needs to be understood as expressions of collective identity and action. B'hoys with little other influence in the society must have taken pleasure in their collective power to control a theater.

B'Hoys at the Theater

It is not surprising that young men who shared such a rough-and-tumble culture were rowdy at the theater too. Minstrel pioneer Dan Emmet described the b'hoys at the Bowery Theater: "when their mouths were not filled with tobacco and peanuts, they were shouting to each other at the top of their voices... Their chief pastime between the acts, when not fighting, was to catch up a stranger or countryman, and toss him from hand to hand over their heads until forced from fatigue to desist."[22] On a crowded night in 1832 three hundred of the audience shared the stage of the Bowery with the actors for *Richard III.* According to the *New York Mirror* they made themselves quite at home.

...the boys [on-stage] frequently ran between King Richard and Lady Anne to snatch a stray copper. In the tent scene, so solemn and impressive, several curious amateurs went up to the table, took up the crown, poised the heavy sword, and examined all the regalia with great care... When Mr. Rice came on the stage to sing his celebrated song of Jim Crow, they not only made him repeat it some twenty times, but hemmed him in so that he actually had no room to perform the little dancing or turning about appertaining to the song; and in the afterpiece, where a supper-table is spread, some among the most hungry very leisurely helped themselves to the viands."[23]

Such behavior was not unique to the Bowery Theater. Englishwoman Frances Trollope condemned the b'hoys of both cities when she described the manners of the audience at the old Washington Theater in D.C. as uncivilized as those of Cincinnati.[24]

Rowdiness was probably encouraged by drinking, which was prevalent in theaters. Alcohol consumption reached its historic peak among Americans during this period, and theaters were no exception. Bars in theaters provided a ready supply of alcohol to add to the conviviality and measurably to the profits, making the theater much like a tavern with entertainment, distinguished only by its architecture. A visiting German aristocrat in the 1830s observed, "[Americans] looked upon the theatre with little more deference than upon a public-house." The French aristocrat Alexis de Tocqueville said they "paid not the slightest attention to the stage, but walked about, drank together, and argued as if nothing else were going on."[25]

The b'hoys reveled in the traditions of audience sovereignty by which they laid claim to the rights to call for tunes and for encores and to call performers and managers before the curtain for an accounting of their actions to the audience. The *New York Mirror* remarked in 1833, "A few evenings since they were performing an overture, which did not exactly suit the cultivated taste of some wor-

thies in the pit, 'Yankee Doodle' being more in unison with their patriotic ideas of propriety, was loudly called for, and its melting tones
forthwith breathed forth in mellifluous harmony. The pit was gratified
and evinced their satisfaction by a gentle roar." One Boston theatergoer boasted in 1846,

> We made Blangy dance her best dance twice; we made Mrs. Sequin
> repeat "Marble Halls" ... and tonight we are going to encore Mrs. Kean's
> "I Don't Believe It" in *The Gamester*.... Perhaps we'll flatter Mr. Kean by
> Making him take poison twice...[26]

Managers sometimes had to come before the curtain, pleading mercy
for exhausted performers who had already performed several encores.
B'hoys called performers, even stars, before the curtain too. The
American favorite, Edwin Forrest, was made to apologize in 1833 in
New Orleans for missing a curtain call. At his next performance he
was greeted with hisses, whistles, and cries of "apology." He immediately stepped to the footlights and explained the circumstances, for
which he was not only forgiven but even cheered. This sudden change
from jeers to cheers, which often occurred, indicates that the pit was
more concerned with recognition of their rights as an audience than
with the particular incident or actor. When the popular Junius Booth
was unrehearsed and ill for his role in Boston in 1829 and announced
that another would read his part, the entire house hissed loudly and
the play was canceled. Renowned English actor William Charles
Macready was shelled with rotten eggs, vegetables, and chairs, and, in
Cincinnati, half a carcass of a sheep.[27]

The skills of a manager and his familiarity and relationship with his
audience was crucial in preventing escalations that might evaporate
his profits. Amid the depression in 1839, when other theaters were
doing poorly, William Mitchell, manager of the Olympic Theater of
New York, quieted them, "Gentlemen of the pit, this noise must not go
on; when I say must, I mean if it *goes on* we must go off ... you now
pay one shilling for admittance [a low price at the time]; if this noise
be not stopped, I shall raise the price to three shillings." They quieted
down, although he was not always so successful.[28] An incident in the
1830s related by Sol Smith reveals the presumption of control by
audiences and efforts of managers to deflect these without offending
the presumptors. Smith had just taken management of the theater in
Mobile. A group used to "managing the former manager" hoped to do
the same with Smith. An anonymous letter was sent to him threaten-

ing to stop the night's performance before it began unless an acceptable reason was given for not casting their favorite actress. Smith felt compelled to go before the audience to explain, his answer was accepted, and the performance proceeded. On another night he was hissed for the expression "in the family way" on the grounds it was not the words of the author. He was advised to stop the play and again explain himself. He obtained a copy of the playbook, and showed the passage to the offended parties, who then withdrew their complaint. In both cases most of the audience supported Smith from the outset.[29]

Audiences were neither homogeneous nor unanimous, but often divided along class lines. Rowdiness was typically attributed by newspapers and other accounts to working-class males in the pit and gallery. Middle- and upper-class audience members in boxes were frequently exonerated of such unseemly demonstrations or cast as actively opposed to them. The middle and upper classes demanded more restraint, and young workers seemed intent on refusing to cooperate. The "respectable" classes refused to engage Bowery b'hoys in debate, as Federalist elites had done with artisan Republicans. Instead they dismissed the new proletarian standard bearers as simply illegitimate. Bourgeois discourses on rowdiness and rioting were redefining these behaviors as inappropriate and unacceptable. Middle-class writers labeled rowdies "Goths" in newspaper accounts, and demanded more forcible responses to disorders. Philip Hone, mayor of New York and a leading member of the New York elite, called them "rabble" while referring to their opponents as "gentlemen."[30]

Riots

Rowdiness easily turned to violence when actors or managers continued to resist the audience's demands or refused to recognize their traditional prerogatives. Working-class crowds typically cast themselves as defenders against some insult or attack, as working class versus upper class, locals versus outsiders, whites versus black or Irish, or Americans versus British. Invariably the working classes donned a patriotic, nativist cloak as defenders of national pride, defining the nation in terms of the common man and in contrast to any sort of pretensions, which included "respectability."

Most theater riots of this period involved insistence on the subordination of British actors to the will of the common man in the audience.[31] British actors still bore the mantle of aristocratic privilege in the minds of the American working class. Riots often arose from some anti-American remark by British actors alleged in newspapers or by handbills, but the issue often also involved some overtone of class conflict. While the working-class pit demanded redress of some "insult" to America by an English actor, the boxes defended the actor from the "unwarranted" attacks from the pit and beyond. Most evident in these riots is the working-class sections' insistence on its sovereignty over "arrogant" performers and managers, including their behavior off-stage.

There are many instances of protests against English actors, some of which erupted in riots: Joseph George Holman in Charleston and Charles Incledon in New York City, both in 1817; Joshua Anderson in New York, Boston, and Baltimore in 1831–33; Fanny Kemble in Philadelphia in 1833; Tyrone Power in 1834 and Joseph Burke in 1836, both in Albany; George Farren in 1834 and Henry Wood in 1836, both in New York City.[32] Two, however, well illustrate the issues and coincidentally also bracket this era, one at its beginning, the other at its close: the Edmund Kean protests in the 1820s and the Astor Place riot in 1849.

The great British star, Edmund Kean, was so admired that he redefined the practice of the curtain call into an acclaim for the actor. When he first appeared in Boston in 1821 demand was so great that tickets were sold at auction. But when he returned in the off-season, audiences were meager and he refused to perform. Bostonians were outraged. When he returned to the United States four years later, the "affront" to Americans remained fresh in the minds of some. An all-male audience – a sign trouble was expected – crowded New York's Park Theater. The first-tier boxes and many in the pit – reputedly three-fourths of the audience – supported Kean, but not the second tier nor "An immense assemblage of the populace [who] were at the doors and threatened to take the theatre by storm." They hissed and shouted. The play went on in pantomime, the noise too loud to hear the players. Kean was struck by oranges, apples, and a sand bag. The play ended with a shower of rotten apples upon him. The next day he published an "abject apology."

A month later he appeared in Boston, again to a packed all-male house and a large crowd outside. Again the gallery opposed Kean, while the boxes supported him. He was driven from the stage by "nuts, pieces of cake, a bottle of offensive drugs, and other missiles." The crowd broke chandeliers, railings, seats, and doors; they invaded the stage and searched for him. Not finding him they then proceeded to his hotel to capture him, but again he escaped. He continued to be harassed in other cities through his tour.[33]

The Kean riots typified the many protests against British actors in the era: the audience divided along class lines, the boxes supporting the actors, the pits and galleries opposed. As in the earlier periods, the riots conform to historian George Rude's identification of the core issue of urban crowd actions as asserting the equality and rights of lower classes against upper classes. The disturbances were the means by which working classes enforced their sovereignty in the theater.

But elites were becoming increasingly leery of such exercises of power on the part of this new emerging working class, and especially the notorious b'hoys. Less tolerant of demonstrations, they called for firmer responses to working-class demonstrations in and out of theater. This would lead to the formation of professional police forces in the 1850s.[34]

The growing intolerance came to a head in the infamous Astor Place Opera House riot of 1849 in New York City, which was the last riot of the period and the only one violently suppressed. Superficially it was a battle grown out of a dispute between the American actor Edwin Forrest and the British actor William Charles Macready, who had competed throughout the Jacksonian period upon American stages.[35] But the clash expressed underlying class antagonisms. Forrest was a favorite of the Bowery b'hoys. Macready, a favorite of the upper classes, had expressed disdain for the American working class's lack of taste.

The Opera House itself was a symbol of aristocratic pride and an affront to the egalitarian notions so dear to Jacksonian working classes. In April 1849, Macready began his engagement at the Astor Place while Forrest performed at the Broadway Theater. Newspapers played up the competition. Competitions were not unusual and were often used to increase attendance. But this was a competition between classes. Supporters of Forrest crowded the Astor gallery on Macready's opening night. Shortly into the play he was greeted with incessant howling, rotten eggs, and potatoes. His mocking responses only enraged the gallery. The play continued in "dumb show." Wooden shingles and chairs were thrown at the stage. Police reported that about 500 people were involved in the disturbance but made no effort to stop it. They halted the performance in the third act and Macready left the theater.

The next day Macready withdrew from the stage and booked passage to return to England. But a letter of support published in the daily newspapers by forty-seven of the most influential merchants, lawyers, and intellectual figures in the city persuaded him to return to the stage. This constituted a direct challenge by the elite to the working-class followers of Forrest. Two days later, May 10, Macready returned to the stage. Two hundred police were stationed in the theater, with an additional hundred and twenty-five outside. Military troops waited on alert. Such force was new, part of the recent civic determination to control the population through professional police forces. Police arrested ticketholders who created a disturbance. Outside a crowd of some five thousand heard of the arrests. Police tried to control the crowd by hosing them with water. They in turn threw stones at the police and through the windows into the theater. The militia was called and were pelted with rocks. Soldiers were given the order to fire over the rioters' heads. Infuriated, the crowd threw more rocks and attempted to disarm the soldiers, accusing the soldiers of defending a British actor against American citizens. The militia fired into the crowd, killing twenty-two people.[36]

Such deadly force had never been used against theater rioters in or outside a theater. It marked a turning point in audience rights. Thereafter managers, supported by court decisions, expanded their control over audience behavior until the 1870s, when some bemoaned the passivity of audiences and the absence of even mild hissing. After this, theater riots were rare and those rare occasions usually involved immigrants who shared much of the preindustrial culture and practices of the Jacksonian rioters.[37] Rowdy audiences continued in minstrel shows, variety halls, and cheap theaters, but "legitimate" theater would be reserved for the "respectable."

Increasingly through the Jacksonian period there arose a depoliticized form of class dispute. The working class continued their espousal of Republican ideals and their attacks on privilege as represented by English actors. Elites, however, disputed not the working class politics but their manners. They condemned working-class rowdiness and rioting as uncivil and unacceptable. They defined themselves as respectable and the working class as disreputable, as if it were a matter of morality rather than class interest. Respectability was demonstrated by decorous manners. Disreputable behavior – disturbances, riots – were grounds for suppression. The new culture of respectability imposed a new class hierarchy, justified in seemingly apolitical terms, sidestepping the egalitarian values of the Revolution that the working class continued to advocate.[38] The working class continued to assert its voice. But it gradually gave way in the face of increasing managerial efforts, backed by civil forces and justified by the distinction between respectable and disreputable, to suppress that voice.

4

Knowledge and the Decline of Audience Sovereignty

Nineteenth-century magazines and theatrical memoirs often recounted tales of greenhorns, or "green'uns," who reacted to events in the play as if they were real. In a story of Edwin Forrest's early career in an 1825 Albany performance of *The Merchant of Venice,* a canal boatman was so immersed in the characterization of Iago that he shouted "you damned lying scoundrel, I would like to get hold of you after the show and wring your infernal neck." In another story set in 1841 Baltimore, a sailor jumped on stage to help a dying heroine, saying, "I'll be damned if a woman should starve and die," giving her all the money in his pocket. After the scene was explained to him and he was led back to his seat, the audience gave him three cheers and ladies waved their white handkerchiefs to salute his generosity.[1] Typically, the green'un was an unsophisticated figure, a backwoodsman, boatman or sailor, whom the rest of the audience treated with a benign condescension. Green'uns were exemplars of the common man – generous, possessing a strong sense of fairness, uncorrupted by civilization, but naive and unsophisticated in city ways.

Green'un stories offered readers an opportunity to feel knowledgeable by contrast, and thus highlighted the value placed on knowledge
of the theater. The other members of the audience described in these
stories also express a bemused superiority. A green'un story is a kind
of insider joke shared by readers and the audience within the story,
both at the expense of the greenhorn. The core of all insider jokes is to
demonstrate membership within the group through understanding the
joke, through insider knowledge. Green'un stories, then, represented
a measure of the importance to audiences of their knowledge of theater and drama. Knowledge of theater represented cultural capital
exchangeable in different specie depending on the in-group, within
the b'hoys' subculture or the dominant culture.[2] Ironically, in both
cases this valued knowledge became the fulcrum for the demise of
their sovereignty as the audience.

Street Wisdom, Incorporation, and the Demise of Sovereignty

Contemporaries described the working-class audiences as devoted fans
of the stage, demonstrating more interest and commitment than the
fashionable crowd who came more to be seen than to see. B'hoys were
regulars who attended once a week or more and were familiar with the
actors of the resident stock company, with whom they formed a community. They were familiar also with a second kind of knowledge. They
knew Shakespeare and had seen many plays often enough to challenge
actors whose interpretations did not conform to their own reading.
Actor William Northall described the b'hoys at the Olympic Theater as

occasionally prompting some unfortunate actor in his part, and this we
have known them frequently to do, but always with good nature, and a
sort of pride they took that everything should go off well on account of
the strangers that might be present. Sometimes, too, they would join in
some popular chorus, a bit of volunteer aid which, so far from giving
offence to actors or audience was always highly relished by both parties.
These boys were always very knowing about anything which was going
on in front and behind the curtain, and any one of them who chanced to
be acquainted, in ever so remote a degree, with any one of the performers, male or female, was considerably envied for his good fortune.[3]

The b'hoys' familiarity with theater legitimated their "ownership"
of the theater as *their* place, and their right to exercise sovereignty

over its performances. Eventually performers would come to orchestrate this participation and the interaction between performers and audience. But at first such shared outlook between stage and pit did not entail a shift of control. Performers and managers attempted to gain acceptance among the b'hoys by expressing a shared viewpoint, a commercialized class solidarity. It was implicit in the popularity of Edwin Forrest, who bonded with the b'hoys through his physical style of acting and his behavior off stage.

Managers at working-class theaters expressed their solidarity through house rules and the playbill. William Mitchell, at the Olympic in the 1840s, printed farcical announcements on his playbills that parodied those found on bills of fashionable houses, indicating a shared disdain for such pompousness. These were, in the words of historian Peter Bailey, a popular discourse "to destabilize the various official knowledges that sought to order life through their languages of improvement and respectability."[4] Managers and performers conspired with the b'hoys both against the world above and in the co-production of the b'hoys themselves as streetwise "salt of the earth."

Most striking in this respect are the many Mose plays, discussed earlier. Mose was an exaggeration of the streetwise but goodhearted b'hoy. The Mose plays crystallized an image that the b'hoys themselves co-produced through their reception and reenactments. Their lively cheers and other vocal responses collectively underlined moments and imprinted their own reading of the performance on the evening.

The Mose plays appeared when a new working class was adjusting to urban life and constructing their own new identity and culture. The plays' popularity was based on their representation of the young urban workmen's shared experience. Mose was both a mirror and an "etiquette book" for the b'hoys, showing them how they looked and how to behave. The image was multiplied and distributed to a much broader audience through numerous lithographs for the thousands who hadn't seen the plays. The impact of this image was indicated by children imitating Mose in their street play.[5]

The representations by actors Frank Chanfrau and Edwin Forrest of "working-class heroes" tied the b'hoys to these figures and made their familiarity with theater all the more important to them. In few other places did they have as much control in shaping their own public image. But granting importance to such performers was the first step toward a shift in the balance of power between performers and working-class audiences. Performers were in a position to certify the b'hoys' knowledge and thus become the "bankers" of their subcultural capital. As we will see, performers would go beyond representation. They would incorporate into their acts planned dialogs with audiences. This "conversation across the footlights" was an old tradition with roots in Elizabethan drama. It was no doubt common during the farces that were the customary end of the nights' bill and were written specifically to refer to familiar local persons and events. The style became a trait of minstrelsy in the 1850s and was even more common in vaudeville late in the century. Audiences speaking up in this practice differed from calling tunes and encores; their participation was prompted and managed by performers. The balance of power shifted to the performer.

Allowing performers to lead these "conversations" presumed a new audience respect for performers that grew with the star system and was embryonic in the Mose plays and the figure of Edwin Forrest. B'hoys developed strong attachments to actors in the companies of their preferred theaters. Among the b'hoys in the pit at the Olympic in the 1840s, "Miss Taylor filled the only place in his heart unoccupied with the fire engine with which he ran. When she was on the stage he never spoke, but kept his eyes fixed upon her... At her exit he woke up." Performers used this loyalty to their advantage. William Northall described Mary Taylor, who played Mose's g'hal, Lize, at the Olympic, as "one of the finest managers of these kinds of worshippers in the world. She knew exactly how to encourage their attentions, and when to stop ... [she] was sure of a glorious reception every night."[6] In the star system every performance enacted the persona of the star, rather than the character, and furthered the audience attachment to the star.

Stars like Chanfrau, Forrest, and Mary Taylor, who embodied the b'hoys and their g'hals, became important to the identity of the group, placing them in a position to better manage the audience. The onstage affirmation of the b'hoys' identity still gave the impression that the audience was in control. As we will see, in vaudeville the adept performer would be one who could manage the crowd by letting them feel in control. This technique eventually became a means to channel the vibrant energy of working-class audiences into avenues safe and profitable to the management.

The demise of sovereignty for the b'hoys illustrates the fluid manner in which cultural resistance may transform into incorporation. The b'hoys' dominance in their Jacksonian theaters is a preeminent example of an oppositional culture, repudiating the dominant culture's valued respectability, taste, and fashion. It arose in response to significant changes in the structural circumstances of their class, including proletarianization and urbanization. Erosion of their audience sovereignty through "conversation across the lights" was an incipient form of incorporation, co-opting the b'hoys' culture and turning it into commercial profit.[7]

"Taste": Knowledge as Cultural Capital

By the 1840s, theatrical knowledge also began to be important in the dominant culture among middle- and upper-class audiences who distinguished appreciation of art (taste) from enjoyment of entertainment. American historian Lawrence Levine described the sacralization of culture after the Civil War, when a hierarchy was established between high brow and low brow. The campaign to impose such standards and manners on the audience began before the war, even though they would not predominate until the latter part of the century. Like the plebeian form of knowledge, it also was based on a heightened status for the performers on stage, redefined as gifted artists.

Cultivation was one of three middle- and upper-class discourses that distinguished these groups from the lower classes. The other two concerned respectability and fashion. People were not classifiable in terms of one criterion alone such as more fashionable, or cultivated, or respectable. They were likely to have been influenced to a degree by all three. The three bourgeois discourses appeared in the same newspapers and magazines, even in the same column, read by the middle and upper classes. Respectability implied a moral superiority; cultivation, an aesthetic/intellectual one. Fashion was more indeterminate. While ostensibly fashion was about an aesthetic judgment, it was actually more about inclusion or exclusion and about who was accepted in wealthy social circles. It was distinguished by association with persons, places, and things so labeled.[8] All three discourses shared aversion to the b'hoys. The working class constituted the essential inferior "other," about which there was no question of exclusion. Small towns and even frontier towns were as much a part of these discourses as were major cities. Civic boosters in every town, no matter how small or remote, were concerned to demonstrate their respectability, cultivation, and fashion.[9]

We will explore the discourse on respectability in detail in the next chapter; here we will concentrate on cultivation and fashion.[10] Cultivation presumes the knowledge to appreciate distinctions in aesthetic quality, knowing what is good and what is bad art. That requires quiet in order to pay attention. Complaints about those who were interfering with the listening of others became more common. The City Council of New Orleans posted in the St. Charles theater in the 1840s the city policy to maintain "the quiet and attention which should always be ascendant in a public assembly." As was usually the case in the West, the concern was directed against rowdiness, but it supported the same norms of behavior advocated by the cultivated, to sit still and pay attention.[11] Those advocating cultivation defined the performance as sacred, to be quietly appreciated, while the fashionable and the disreputable defined it as entertainment to be used to suit their needs. The latter continued to exercise their respective forms of audience sovereignty, while the cultivated granted sovereignty to the artists/performers. While the cultivated could escape the disreputable b'hoys by moving to different theaters, the fashionable wealthy were the ones who often paid for these very theaters and therefore could not be avoided or quieted. The cultivated have complained about the disinterested fashionable ever since, arriving late, leaving early, talking in-between, and generally creating distractions.

The b'hoys' knowledge did not qualify them as cultivated. Their knowledge was of their own world, which the cultivated often contrasted to "taste." The "robustious" acting style of Forrest was compared unfavorably to the intellectual style of Macready in the 1840s. Theater manager Joseph Cowell contrasted the two as "art over impulse." The New York newspaper, the *Knickerbocker,* called the Forrest style the "affected, ranting school." *Harper's Weekly* referred to a vest named for Forrest as appropriately "loud and splashy." *Harper's* in 1863 described the young women in a Forrest audience as "not refined, nor intellectual" who cried "good hearty tears," while the audience of the sophisticated young Edwin Booth was a "more cultivated and intellectual audience," who gave "refined attention" to the performance. They were "appreciative and expectant of fine points, but not irresistibly swept away."[12] The disparagement of the b'hoys cast the cultivated as intellectually superior in their understanding of drama. One safe way to demonstrate this was to prefer recognized "artists" like Macready or Booth, giving these stars considerable leverage over their "sophisticated" audiences. The star was in a position to warrant an audience's good taste, and thus could command their silent attention to his "genius." At the same time the audience had forsaken its right to chastise the star.

The fashionable, on the other hand, were portrayed as indifferent to art and narrowly interested only in fashion. Joseph Cowell – not the stereotypic snob, having managed a circus and acted on the frontier – in 1844 bewailed the economic dependence of theater on the ignorant fashionable: "what an abominable affliction have these ephemeral four syllables proved to the young and otherwise unfettered country ... introduction of fashionable atrocities to make the thoughtless laugh, the thinking grieve."[13]

The authority of stars was enhanced by the cultivated's lack of self-confidence in their own judgment. Middling and upper-class Americans were fearful of their aesthetic limitations, especially relative to Europeans. Newspaper statements rejecting this snobbery reveal the widespread nature of this concern. The *Spirit of the Times* in 1847 reassured gentlemen readers they had nothing to be ashamed of: "Fear not the few who affect to commiserate your ignorant raptures and talk learnedly of Paris and London.... [They] are neither more nor less – it is a fact – than snobs. Don't mind a word they say." An 1839 review in *Spirit of the Times* noted that pantomimist Madame Celeste was so good that "she has been able to play just where she has pleased, without fear of losing caste by appearing in a house notoriously vulgar," but that patrons of the Park Theater, hearing of her long run at the Bowery Theater, began to believe she was overrated, and therefore stayed away from her performances at the Park.[14] Patrons of the Park Theater apparently were not sufficiently sure of their own judgment of quality to attend the Bowery Theater to see her.

"Fashion" at the Opera

In their aversion to the b'hoys, the better classes began in the 1840s to stay away from theaters. "Light and Shadow" writer George Foster claimed, "The respectable and virtuous will not visit [theater] unless impelled thither in fashionable crowds by some extraordinary genius." Walt Whitman described the Park Theater in 1847 as otherwise deserted.[15]

Eventually elites sought somewhere more exclusive that they could control, providing an appropriate place for public social occasions for elite display. Through ownership they could ensure fashion, cultivation, and respectability in the *place* they frequented, rather than in the *star* they revered. Elite allegiance shifted from theater to the more fashionable opera. Opera was considered especially appropriate for ladies. At opera performances they were permitted to sit in the pit, upon the expectation that disreputable and disruptive elements would not be there.[16] Much was made in the Jacksonian era of this "aristocracy" of opera as opposed to more "democratic" theater. Opera performances offered at unfashionable houses, such as the Bowery and Richmond Hill Theaters in New York, were failures.[17]

Wealthy elites banded together to build their own opera houses. As stockholders they controlled the company and its repertoire, and determine policies. The Italian Opera House was built in New York in 1833, by wealthy stockholders exclusively for opera. Reflecting its elitist purpose it had a greater proportion of boxes to pit and gallery seats, as did colonial theaters. Moreover, the pit was priced the same as the first tier of boxes and fitted for elite use, including ladies. But there were not a sufficient number of wealthy patrons and the Opera House closed after two seasons.[18]

By the 1840s, there were enough wealthy patrons. Elites in New York, Philadelphia, and Boston began planning grand opera houses. In 1847, one hundred and fifty wealthy New Yorkers paid to build the Astor Place Opera House. Along with their newly acquired "taste" for opera, the wealthy adopted an elaborate ritual of proper behavior and an attitude of high-culture exclusiveness. It was "the resort of our exclusively aristocratic Upper Ten Thousand … filled out with the lovely forms and faces of five or six hundred of the most beautiful women in the world, dressed *a meraviglia,* and as many distinguished looking men."[19] Unlike the Park Theater, to which workers sometimes turned when the Bowery closed, the Astor Place Opera House kept such people out through a dress code of "freshly shaven faces, evening dress, fresh waistcoats, and kid gloves for gentlemen." The introduction of reserved seating also made the exclusion of undesirables more manageable.[20]

The gentleman's magazine, *Spirit of the Times,* in 1847 described the audiences of the Astor Place Opera House.[21] Among the "ermined ranks of fashion" in the opera audience, "an atmosphere of elegance and refinement makes itself palpable to the sense. There is a feeling of repose, of security from rude and impertinent interruption, a languor of voluptuous enjoyment." A "gentle buzz" of conversation was carried on around the writer.

The "gentle buzz" and "ermine rank" would continue to characterize the audiences of major opera houses. Decades later, the first circle of boxes, nicknamed the "Diamond Horseshoe," of the Metropolitan Opera House, epitomized the fashionable wealthy who demonstrated sovereignty by their inattention to the stage, reproducing the aristocratic privilege of colonial theater where performers were mere servants.[22]

5

Matinee Ladies: Re-gendering Theater Audiences

n the colonial era, when theater was an aristocratic institution, women were a prominent part of the privileged audiences. With democratization in the early republic, theater
became increasingly a male institution. During midcentury,
as theaters began to constrain audiences, women's presence
increased again. Re-gendering of theater was part of fundamental
cultural shifts, first to a middle-class culture founded on respectability, and then to a culture of consumption conceived around the
female shopper.

Respectability was instrumental in establishing antebellum class
status. It rested upon a code of manners that placed great emphasis on
restraint, self-control, and impression management. At its core it was
a gendered concept. Middle-class women, particularly wives and
mothers, were its primary carriers. The demands of etiquette fell far
more heavily on women than on men, and many of the requirements
upon men referred to their treatment of women.[1] Women could therefore signify the respectability of those with them and the places they
frequented.

The antebellum middle class delineated public spaces as respectable or disreputable, depending on whether they endangered the reputation of a middle-class woman. By mapping much of the geography of cities as dangerous, women's access was severely circumscribed. To the degree women were involved publicly – in religion, the temperance movement, charity and missionary work – it was justified as extensions of their domestic roles. When women transgressed this domestic "cover," their presence in inappropriate places or circumstances might label them as "public women," that is, prostitutes. Antebellum theaters were such places, frequented by dangerous and disreputable women – prostitutes, actresses, and working-class women.[2]

Women's acceptance in theater after midcentury resulted not from a women's movement but from entrepreneurs seeking new markets. Entrepreneurs transformed respectability from a barrier into an opportunity for women's access by redefining the theater as a place safe for mothers and children. Their acceptance in theater was justified on domestic grounds, just as the legitimation of extended domestic duty allowed middle-class women reformers more political incursions into public spaces. In both cases the boundaries between public and private were made more elastic. Once begun, however, the gender transformation of theater had less to do with respectability than with a growing consumer culture. Theaters were the first of a constellation of commercial spaces, including department stores and ice cream parlors, created for women amid the dangerous cityscape.[3]

Respectability, grounded in restraint, was ultimately incompatible with commercialization and the growth of consumption. With consumer culture, status and identity were defined through consumption. Restraint was replaced by self-indulgence. The new middle-class standard of public status would become "fashion." "Fashionable" was no longer exclusively a synonym for the upper class, but began to refer to whoever could afford the approved clothes and furnishings. A successful play in 1845, entitled *Fashion; or, Life in New York,* superimposed the new usage upon the old when it satirized the socially ambitious noveau-riche wife trying to gain acceptance through purchases of clothes and furniture.[4] *Godey's Ladies Book* promoted this middle-class interest in fashion through fashion plates, that is, dress illustrations, to inform its readers of the latest from Paris. Gradually the plates became the centerpiece of each issue. By 1863, each issue contained two hand-colored plates, fourteen black-and-white, and nine more with descriptive text.[5]

Fashion was a standard well suited to consumption. Its very essence was change, to be "in fashion," not "old-fashioned," to continually shop for the "latest" fashion. Fashion in this sense was also a much more flexible and therefore playful standard. Ever-changing fashion is built on illusion, constantly making oneself over. Founded on appearance rather than substance, fashion allowed people to "play at" being various things. It made daily life more theatrical, as one could change roles by changing costumes. At the same time, actresses' costumes became ads for new fashions. Ladies might go to theater to imitate the star's dress instead of her character.

Fashion, shopping, and female theatergoing reinforced each other. Theaters were already attracting significant female audiences to matinee performances when shopping first became a woman's job in the 1850s and before Alexander Stewart opened the first great department store. Theaters began to locate in these new shopping districts and attendance quickly became a part of the shopping day. Theater and shopping offered, as historian Kathy Peiss phrased it, "desire, emotion, sensuality and fantasy as legitimate and motivating aspects of identity."[6] Each of these aspects is well suited to the pleasures of female spectatorship in the darkened theater of the 1870s, when all of this coalesced into the culture of consumption.

Re-gendering theater was a model of the broader transformation of public space and the dismantling of the separation of the public from private space. It involved three closely related processes. Domestication, the symbolic and social reconstruction of theater into a family entertainment, was the first phase. De-masculinization entailed the gradual elimination of those aspects that were specifically masculine in their appeal and the drift of men away from drama entertainment. Feminization, which began at midcentury with the introduction of regular matinees, meant that women *as women* were recruited as the primary audience.

For Male Amusement

Antebellum theater was not exclusively male, but it was clearly a "masculine space." Drama columns appeared in the six-cent newspapers gentlemen read, rather than in the ladies' magazines that were beginning to blossom in the 1830s. Theater managers selected plays to please men. "Manly" virtues were preferred over romance, robust heroes and villains over matinee idols. *Richard III* was the most-performed play in Philadelphia from 1835 to 1855. *Macbeth* was performed at two theaters simultaneously in Baltimore (with Macready and Forrest competing) in 1848, and at three theaters in New York in 1849. Other popular plays also featured "manly" heroes, such as Spartacus the revolutionary slave, Metamora the noble savage, and Mose the Bowery b'hoy.[7]

The most popular actors were Edwin Forrest, known for his "muscular school" of acting, and Edmund Kean, whose agitated style of acting made him popular in the roles of Richard III, Othello, Shylock, Hamlet, and Lear. Junius Booth, founder of the famous acting lineage, was known for his "sustained vigor of voice, and look, and action." Thomas Cooper, who set the acting style from the turn of the nineteenth century until he was eclipsed by Kean in the 1820s, was admired for off-stage dueling, racing, and gambling.[8]

Managers attempted to attract a male audience by giving prostitutes free entry to the gallery. Prostitution was important to the profitability of theaters, and some theaters that prohibited it soon retracted. Brothels were situated close to theaters to accommodate the business. Lower-class prostitutes arrived en masse before the rest of the house opened and were confined to the gallery or third tier of boxes where they met clients. Higher-class prostitutes entered the theater escorted by their clients and might sit with them anywhere in the house.[9]

Given this masculine atmosphere, almost any theater was thought to pose a risk to respectability. Frances Trollope noted, "ladies are rarely seen" at the theater in Cincinnati in 1828. Actors noted the absence of women in their memoirs.[10]

There were sporadic efforts to attract respectable women. In the 1800s, two theaters, in Philadelphia and New York, installed coffee rooms for women. Samuel Drake renovated his Lexington, Kentucky theater in 1816 to encourage ladies to attend. Noah Ludlow built a ladies' retiring room in his St. Louis theater in 1837, but it was closed for lack of use.[11]

Managers hoped to leaven rather than displace the male audience. While respectable women were still a small minority in male space, they were considered an antidote to male rowdiness. A Bostonian in 1809 remarked, "if honest tradesmen were permitted by custom, for no regulation of the theatre is against it, to bring their wives and daughters with them, they would themselves be more cautious in their conduct, and more inclined to insist upon a like cautiousness in others." The *New York Mirror* argued in 1826 that women in the audience are "the best guarantee for the gentlemanly deportment of the other sex."[12]

"Respectable" women did attend, but not regularly and not in great numbers. They attended as men's guests and avoided the gallery, precinct of prostitutes, and the pit, full of ruffians. The boxes were reasonably safe; women could show off their finery and observe who else was there. The first night of a new play was considered experimental and not for women; they waited until reports indicated the script was safe for their reputations. Whenever a disturbance was expected – often planned in advance and warning given – women stayed away. When trouble came unexpectedly, women swiftly departed.[13]

Anna Quincy, daughter of the President of Harvard University, revealed in her diary some of the complications of theatergoing for young women in 1833 Boston. Anna and her sisters were "wild" to see the English actress Fanny Kemble, but had to wait for a man to obtain box tickets and escort them. She described a good deal of coming and going by men during the play, while the girls stayed in their box. She mentioned not going to the theater once because *Venice Preserved,* a Restoration play, was considered not quite proper, even though Kemble starred. On the last night of Kemble's engagement she mentioned a "horde of fierce barbarians ... half sort of gentlemen" occupying the box next to hers one night. Despite her several visits to see Kemble she ended her entries on the theater by observing that "it is certainly, even at the best, no fit place for '*an elegant* female.'"[14]

Respectable public entertainments did exist. Niblo's Garden in the 1830s was a place of family entertainment, patronized by New Yorkers where "whole families would go at a moment's warning to hear this or that singer, but most of all, year after year, to see the Ravels [pantomime and acrobatic troupe]." Such entertainments, however, were the exception rather than the rule. The "virtuous public" did not regularly attend even the best houses, except when "impelled thither in fashionable crowds by some extraordinary genius like Miss Cushman" or other stars. On such nights the bars in the theater typically were closed, and the audience changed accordingly. Actor Tyrone Power noted that behavior differed as well: "extreme decorum and exclusive appearance are assured by the places [in the parquet] being all secured by families."[15]

While respectability was a powerful force in middle-class culture, middle-class women's responses were not one-dimensional. Fanny

Kemble observed that even middle-class American women were brash, showy in their street dress, and unusually free to walk in the streets unescorted during the day, compared to England. At the same time, these women avoided the theater and insisted upon being called "ladies," as "woman" indicated "lower or less refined classes." The picture of women corseted in respectability and excluded from public space is oversimplified.[16]

Nevertheless, middle-class women symbolically stood for respectability. Their very constrictions made them signifiers of respectability, an important marker used to distinguish class identity. This would be the basis for their first being courted as an audience by museum theaters.

Dramas for the Family: Domestication

Theaters disguised as "lecture rooms" attached to museums were the first to systematically seek women, particularly mothers, as an audience.[17] Although proprietary museums had been in existence for some years, it was not until the 1840s that they began to present moral reform melodramas in their "museum theaters," to appeal to a new market of religious middle class who heretofore would not set foot in the "immoral" halls of theater.[18]

Moses Kimball opened the Boston Museum in 1841 by purchasing the collection of the New England Museum. Upstairs was a 1200-seat auditorium where he presented lectures, concerts, and other exhibits. In 1843, he created a resident dramatic company and presented a drama, *The Drunkard: or the Fallen Saved,* appealing to the temperance spirit of the time. It ran for more than one hundred performances at a time when theaters typically changed their bill every night. In 1848, at the American Museum in New York, P. T. Barnum imitated Kimball's success, using the same play. He expanded his theater to 3000 seats in 1850.[19]

Kimball introduced marketing strategies to achieve respectability that have been credited to B. F. Keith in his creation of "refined vaudeville" forty years later. Kimball maintained an image of morality by censoring plays to please even "the most fastidious," excluding prostitutes and prohibiting sale of alcohol. He advertised exhibits as educational and morally uplifting and distributed a pamphlet for children describing the wonders of his museum.[20] He cleverly redefined his museum theater as a way in which women could fulfill their maternal duties.

Soon museum theaters appeared in Philadelphia, Boston, Brooklyn, and even in the smaller cities of Albany, Baltimore, Providence, and Troy. They helped to create a new market for drama theater, to establish its respectability, and to lay the foundation for new norms of decorum for audiences that would become the mode of "legitimate" theaters. The Boston Museum itself came to be regarded as the principal theater of Boston and one of the best in America.[21] The success of the moral reform melodrama proved theaters could attract the respectable. Uncle Tom's Cabin was the most influential in this regard. Nineteenth century theater historian Charles Durang wrote that theaters were greatly assisted by "Uncle Tom" throughout the North and East. At the respected Chestnut Street Theater, it played for twenty-five successive nights to crowded houses and then returned after a short respite to play another month, an unheard-of run at a legitimate house in the 1850s. According to the New York Atlas in 1853, it transformed the National Theater in New York: "Among the audience we recognized many people who have been taught to look on the stage and all that belongs to it with horror and contempt."[22]

Taming the Audience: De-masculinization

The subdued qualities that ruled middle-class behavior in the 1830s and 1840s insisted on a separation from coarseness, rowdiness, and other forms of emotional outlet that characterized the lower classes. This "feminization" of middle-class culture required men to suppress the roughness that had been the mark of American masculinity, and continued to be so for the working class, and to adopt the restraint and self-control that was becoming the defining character for the middle class at midcentury.[23]

Theater managers began demanding proper decorum consistent with the new manners and excluding the lower classes, antitheses of this new respectability. The effort to exclude women identified as prostitutes from the theater began in the 1830s. Noah Ludlow excluded those he considered prostitutes from his Mobile and St. Louis theaters as early as 1837. In the 1840s, Philadelphia's Arch Street Theater announced it would exclude "improper characters" from the third tier and stop selling alcohol in the theater. Also in the 1840s, Niblo's Garden would admit only women accompanied by a man, to exclude prostitutes from plying their trade. Other theaters adopted this strategy in the 1850s. (This may have discouraged prostitutes, but it also forestalled theater becoming a "woman's place.") Prostitutes were gone from legitimate theaters by 1870.[24]

Theaters serving the upper and middle classes in the late 1840s began to rein in audience rowdiness and repudiate the extralegal prerogatives of audience sovereignty. Dramatist William Northall, in 1851, argued in favor of the rights of managers to control audiences when they disrupt the performance:

If the public has rights, so has the manager. He is not to be so much the slave of public caprice as to submit to its dictation in the conduct of his own interests, when his management does not contravene good morals, or interfere with the legitimate enjoyments of his audience in witnessing that which they paid to see.[25]

This had been said before, but it was now being enforced by theater managers.

By 1849, a very different standard of behavior was being established in middle-class theaters. A playbill for Burton's Theater in New York warned not of throwing things at the stage, a typical warning of years past, but that "fidgety individuals" not stand and put on coats early as "it is most distressing to the ladies and gentlemen on the stage" and "to respect the feelings of those who wish to see the whole of the play in quiet."[26] An 1861 parody of American theatergoers in *Spirit of the Times* cited lack of manners as the problem, such as stepping on toes, dropping a cane, standing to look around, coughing, sneezing, belching, and leaving early.[27]

To increase seating for the middle and upper classes, theaters began in the 1840s to rename the male, working-class pit the "parquet." They reconstructed it physically, with armchairs bolted to the floor replacing benches, and symbolically as a respectable place to be seated, where the upper class could display themselves almost as well as in boxes. Parquet seats were priced the same as side boxes, which redefined them as equal in status.[28] The taming of the audience would continue after the Civil War but the demise of audience sovereignty was at hand. What would be called "legitimate" theater was no longer the arena of manliness.

Historian Richard Stott claims this de-masculinzation made middle-class men marginal to their own culture and attracted them to the more masculine working-class culture of the antebellum period. Middle-class wives had to struggle to domesticate their husbands and to discourage their drinking and attendance at prizefights and working-class theaters.[29] Such tensions between class and gender codes of behavior created ambivalence among middle-class men toward the new code of civility. At a time when this class's status was uncertain, establishing one's respectability and distancing oneself from the disreputable working class were important reasons for the emphasis on self-control in middle-class manners. Yet a concept of intellectualized masculinity was still new and the emphasis on physicality, even in its self-controlled forms of athleticism, and enhanced by images of physical heroism of the Civil War, was still strong. No doubt the self-confident working-class rejection of middle- and upper-class manners during the Jacksonian period, and the expression of its own counterculture in places such as the Bowery, enticed middle-class males to throw off their middle-class constraint. At the same time that they may have supported the reform of theater manners, they also were bored by its result. Reform made theater less a male stronghold and probably eased the acceptance of women as the primary audience, beginning with the matinee.

The Matinee: Women as an Audience that Mattered

The pursuit in earnest of women as an audience in their own right began with the matinee. Holiday matinees were not uncommon in the 1830s and 1840s, but weekly matinees were rare until the 1850s. The earliest regular matinees were billed as educational experiences to which mothers could bring their children.[30]

Soon, however, theaters began to court women *as women*. A Boston matinee in 1855 by the famous touring French actress Rachel was publicized with her numerous fashionable costumes. An actor in her troupe explained:

At that hour and especially on a Saturday, all the male Americans are riveted to their office desks. So what happened? We played to an audience exclusively composed of women... Prodigious takings for a Saturday.[31]

The "prodigious takings" suggest the profitable size of the female market at the time. New York opera matinees had become a regular thing by 1858, and were better attended than evening performances – an early indicator that men's attendance was flagging. Laura Keene inaugurated Wednesday and Saturday matinees at her fashionable New York theater sometime during the 1858–59 season.[32] A gentleman's

magazine in 1858 testified to the feminine nature of New York matinees: "The ladies, unattended, can and do come in troops; and a
degree of merriment and elegant ease that characterize these assemblies make them most charming and attractive."[33]

Others were not so blasé about what they saw as neglect of women's
domestic role. The *New York Times* in 1860 predicted the matinee
would not take root in America, saying,

> We have not amongst us sufficient idle wealth to justify the surrender of
> whole days by any large part of the community to mere purposes of
> amusement. Even our very wealthiest ladies, unless they wish openly to
> repudiate all suspicion of paying any heed to domestic duties, will not
> often allow themselves to be seen attending such an entertainment.

It claimed at a matinee at Niblo's Garden the demimonde predominated.[34]

Rebutting the *Times's* editorial, a woman who signed as "Mother"
wrote:

> It is an invasion against the rights of the female portion of society in our
> city, to wish to deprive them of these legitimate and high toned amuse-
> ments, by endeavoring to throw slurs on the character of those who
> patronize them [and to] force our society to take the same tone as in
> Europe, where no woman is safe from insult, even in the street, without
> a gentleman accompanies her. It has always been the boast of American
> women that their independence and self-respect was all sufficient to
> protect them from impertinence, at least during the day time. Is the
> order of things to be changed, so that it will not be thought respectable
> to walk in the streets without a brother, father, or husband accompanies
> his lady relatives? It is simply absurd to think of such a proposition in a
> City where the whole community of men spend their time in commer-
> cial interests…[35]

Labeling the *Times's* expectations as "absurd," this "mother" highlighted how society had changed: men were not available during the
day to chaperone; women were self-sufficient and prided themselves
on their freedom. This letter constituted a manifesto for middle-class
women to claim public space as their own, justifying it on the same
patriotic grounds used by men. Attending matinees, for this woman,
suggested far more than entertainment. It represented the right to
public space and public participation. It was a revival of turn-of-the-
century Republican values and of theater as a political space – a manifesto to demand a return of women to public space.

The battle was not long in winning. As male escorts were becoming less necessary during the day,[36] matinees could tap this new market. Declining theater profits in the 1860s probably encouraged the introduction of regular matinees at more theaters. In 1865, the *New York Clipper* noted:

Matinees are on the increase. On Saturday last, *matinees* were given at the Olympic Theatre, Niblo's Garden, Broadway, New Bowery, Hippotheatron, Wood's Minstrels, Barnum's Museum, Niblo's Saloon-Gottaschalk, Varieties, Heller's Salle Diabolique, and American Theatre. The ladies are the chief patrons of these day entertainments, and no doubt attract full as many of the robustuous sex as the play attracts. Its [*sic*] worth a walk to look in at one of our *matinees,* if only to gaze at the gay plumage of the female birds.[37]

By 1869, Booth's and Wallack's Theaters and their respected stock companies began Saturday matinees whose receipts were very near as good as nighttime performances. In 1871, Boston reformer Dio Lewis recommended matinees as offering "the most decent representations."[38]

The matinee soon afforded middle-class Victorian women a public place of their own, where they could go without escort and "stop on the way home for ice punch and cream-cakes."[39] The indulgent nature of matinee and cream-cakes distinguished it from the museum theater. Drama theaters were offering entertainment for women rather than moralizing education for them and their children, an escape and a refuge for women from paternal oversight and domestic duties. Women seem to have responded quickly to this new entertainment. Moreover, men were out of place there, marking it all the more a woman's place. But this new public women's world of consumption was restricted to afternoons; evening performances still required a male escort.

Changing Gender Roles

The acceptance of matinees for women entailed some adjustments in gender expectation. To accept their growing predominance at evening performance required even more adjustment. In the 1850s and 1860s, a new kind of woman emerged. The frail, pale, willowy ideal became a buxom, hearty beauty, and fashionable women began using cosmetics and peroxiding their hair. Middle-class women began to emulate the dress of actresses. When the French actress Rachel was hailed in the mid- 1850s for her stage gowns, the appeal of fashion was limited by the constraints of home production and the considerable labor involved. By the 1880s, however, middle-class women could go to see the leading lady's gowns and then go buy them – or something like them – in the department store. Publicity for actresses and their plays increasingly emphasized their dress on- and off-stage. Even the costumes of Olive Logan, who crusaded against the degradation of drama by "leg shows," were advertised in a playbill of Philadelphia's fashionable Walnut Street Theater.[40]

In 1868, middle-class women, described by contemporaries as "comfortable middle-aged" and notable for "homely respectability," attended burlesque performances by Lydia Thompson's troupe of British Blondes, representing not only a new voluptuous model of beauty but also a new assertive femininity. As if to demonstrate this, Thompson and one of her troupe, with the aid of her publicist, horsewhipped the editor of the *Chicago Times* who had written a series of personal attacks upon Thompson.[41]

Sensation melodramas, popular during the 1860s and 1870s, offered a similar assertive model of femininity and seemed well suited to a female audience. In striking contrast to the virile male heroes favored in the 1830s, sensation melodrama often featured vigorous heroines opposite passive and conflicted male leads. The heroine of Augustin Daly's great success of 1867, *Under the Gaslight,* saves a man strapped to railroad tracks by the villain. Its success continued through the 1870s.[42]

Men, however, were finding drama theater increasingly stultifying and began patronizing alternative pastimes. The physical aspects of manliness, constrained by the new rules of etiquette, found an outlet in exercise and games, the gymnasium and sporting clubs.[43] News of horseracing and boxing and adventure stories based on sports crowded out theater news in gentlemen's magazines such as *Spirit of the Times.*[44] "Leg shows" prospered after the Civil War. At first these appeared in the guise of dramas, attracting men back to drama theaters, but by the 1870s they had developed into a separate branch of the stage – burlesque. In 1861, Adha Menken created a sensation in *Mazeppa* by riding a horse on-stage in tights. In 1866, *The Black Crook* combined ballet – considered a surreptitious "leg show" in its own right – and spectacle, drawing audiences to gawk at the unprecedented profusion of female forms. In 1872, a New Orleans newspaper

complained, "Men of good, sound sense, go night after night [to bur-
lesque] to hear repeated inanities ... which, if said ... by anyone else
than a woman in tights, they would turn from in disgust."[45]
The remarkable proliferation of male entertainments gave theater
managers even more reason to seek women as a market. Bars within
theaters were eliminated to enable managers to refuse admission to
the unruly. By 1870, beer had disappeared from the pit of American
theaters.[46] After the Civil War, managers increasingly prohibited the
stamping of feet, calls for encores, and other rowdiness. Courts upheld
the right of managers to refuse to admit or to remove those who were
drunk, boisterous, or lewd.[47] Theater, now de-masculinized, had even
less appeal to men.

Managers tamed the audiences so much that warnings in playbills
were reduced to concerns over nuisances. *Every Saturday* reported
that a man who hissed mildly in 1871 was ejected from the theater. It
bemoaned, "What mild creatures we are when sitting at a play! how
shy we are of showing our delight when delighted and with what pitiful
patience we submit to the long-drawn-out stupidity of thin melodramas." The gentlemen's magazine, *Spirit of the Times,* in 1866 referred
to "the bore of attending dull or even good performances for the sole
purpose of escorting their Mary Janes."[48]

Women at Evening Performances

The transformation of evening performances into a feminine market
was not accompanied by a specific innovation such as the matinee;
several factors played a part. Theaters remade the pit for feminine
use. In the words of *Spirit of the Times,*

Even the New Bowery, strange as it may seem, is going to surrender to
the demand for change ... the shirt-sleeved and peanut pocketed
Democracy are to be removed to the upper tiers... Respectability wants
room – wants to take its wife and daughter to the play – and Shilling
Democracy must give way.

Women occupied the parquet by the end of the Civil War. Shortly
after, the gallery in some theaters was renamed the family circle and
seats replaced benches, making it more attractive to women, although
boys remained predominant there until the twentieth century.[49]
Managers now selected plays to appeal to women. Laura Keene,
upon first opening her New York theater in 1855, presented plays

directed at middle-class women and on the last night of that season thanked the women in the audience for their support. The newly popular sensation melodramas offered heroines with whom women could identify. *Harper's* expressed the change from the past: "Where the noisy crowd of men were massed, upon hard, backless benches, there is the luminous cloud of lovely toilets mingled with the darker dress of the *jeunesse doree*." In the 1870s, one theater in New Orleans was briefly dubbed the Ladies Theater.[50]

The female audience at evening performances was growing in significance. Women probably became a more important market during the depression of 1873–78 when managers were desperate to fill empty theaters. In 1876–77, Brooklyn theaters introduced ladies' nights, when women were admitted free if accompanied by a man. By 1878, at Wallack's Theater, one of the last and finest stock companies in New York, on first nights "more than one-half of the people present are ladies, full one-third are young ladies." By 1889, the *New York Mirror* observed that older sisters "sally forth to a first night performance under the careful chaperonage of mamma," while the younger matinee girl "is forced to feed the dramatic cravings of her young soul with afternoon doses."[51]

By the 1890s, legitimate theater was a women's entertainment. A newspaper writer noted "the dramatic season of 1897–98 has been remarkable for the number of entertainments that appeal distinctly to women rather than to men ... there is plenty of amusement on our boards of the sort that New York women love."[52] In 1910, drama critic Walter Prichard Eaton claimed that women constituted three-fourths of the American theater audience. The men, he believed, "come because their wives or sweethearts want to." A survey of Shubert theaters in Manhattan on a Saturday night found galleries full, with two-thirds filled by women. Columbia University professor Clayton Hamilton, in 1911, said,

every student of the contemporary theater knows that the destiny of our drama has lain for a long time in the hands of women. Shakespeare wrote for an audience made up mainly of men and boys... Ibsen and Pinero have written for an audience made up mainly of women... Our matinee audiences are composed almost entirely of women; and our evening audiences are composed of women also, and the men that they brought with them ... in fact the theater is to-day the one great public institution in which "votes for women" is the rule, and men are overwhelmingly outvoted.[53]

Gender Shift, Status Reversal

By the time women had become an important sector of the theater audience, audience sovereignty was dead and rights of managers to regulate behavior well established. The fact of being free to go to theater constituted progress for women, as did the new femininity associated with it. But in the theater itself the authority of the female audience was minimal compared to that of the male audience a half-century earlier. Much as women repeatedly gained access to an occupation just as its wages, autonomy, and status declined, in theater their entry coincided with loss of audience autonomy, a kind of proletarianization of pleasure.[54] The statuses of audience and performer had reversed. With the growth of importance of stars over stock companies, curtain calls became a ritual of homage by the audience to the star. Floral tributes and even expensive jewelry cast upon the stage to leading ladies increased in the 1850s. It declined during the war but revived again in the 1870s. Admirers threw so many expensive bouquets on the stage, even during the performances, that managers prohibited it.[55]

The changed circumstance is revealed by the words of Joseph Jefferson, a popular actor of the second half of the century, who described the audience as "imprisoned" in a "helpless condition" during the performance, for "He cannot withdraw without making himself conspicuous."[56] No one would have characterized the audience of the early nineteenth century as "imprisoned" or "helpless." It is similarly illustrated by audience reaction to the insults of British actor Henry Miller. During a performance in New Haven in 1898, he was annoyed at a ripple of inappropriate laughter from the audience that briefly interrupted his performance. At the end of the third act he came before the curtain and received hearty applause. But, one witness said, "Without even a thanks Mr. Miller started in upon a tirade of abuse ... compared [the audience's] conduct to what might be expected in the slums of London ... [and said] there were so many hyenas in the audience." The response of the audience consisted of no more than hisses and the incident had no effect on his reception in other cities, in stark contrast to the riots against British actors in the 1830s.[57]

6

Blackface, Whiteface

The 1850s witnessed a remarkable growth in three new urban stage entertainments that competed with traditional theater: museum theater, minstrelsy, and variety. By far the most influential on nineteenth-century American culture was minstrelsy. Northern white Americans at midcentury were fascinated with stage portrayals of blacks, as slavery grew to be the issue that overshadowed all else in the nation. Minstrelsy blended politics and popular culture and its music permeated daily life. One could go nowhere outside the South without hearing "Negro melodies." *Putnam's Monthly* described *Jim Crow's* immediate and widespread popularity, "The school-boy whistled the melody... The ploughman checked his oxen in mid furrow, as he reached its chorus... Merchants and staid professional men ... unbend their dignity to that weird and wonderful posture ... it is sung in the parlor, hummed in the kitchen, and whistled in the stable."[1]

Whiteness and Blacks

The incredible popularity of whites performing as stereotyped black characters on stage confirmed the overwhelming whiteness of American theater before the Civil War. Blacks were barely a presence on-stage or in the audience. There was only a handful of black entertainers who played to white audiences, almost always as between-act diversions. Aside from the African Grove, a summer garden theater in New York City in the early 1820s, there is no record of any black theaters in the antebellum period.[2]

While not numerous, blacks attended theaters frequently enough for whites to require a policy of segregated seating. Exclusion from the theater entirely was extremely rare. Playbills frequently stated "colored" prices, restricted to the gallery. These applied to free blacks and slaves, north, south, and on the frontier. In 1834 at Fort Crawford on the upper Mississippi, soldiers mounted an amateur performance at which the audience was separated into sections for officers with their families, for the soldiers, and for Indians and Negroes.[3]

Many observers mentioned blacks sitting in galleries. Gustave De Beaumont, companion to Alexis de Tocqueville during his travels in America in the 1830s, said of a Philadelphia audience, "I was surprised at the care with which spectators of white skin were distinguished from the black faces. In the first gallery were the whites, in the second the mulattoes; in the third, the Negroes." de Tocqueville noted the same arrangement in New Orleans. Some came as servants in company of their masters; but free blacks and even slaves also attended on their own. Pete Williams, a successful black saloon owner in New York in the 1840s went regularly to the theater. William Johnson, a free Negro of Natchez, went regularly to the theater as a young man in the 1830s, including a performance of "Jim Crow." He often escorted a mulatto girl; the girl and her mother also attended without him. Johnson even signed passes for slaves to attend.[4]

There was rarely mention of behavior, and even more rarely of misbehavior of black attendees. Sol Smith referred to St. Louis blacks "as honest and virtuous a set of auditors, male and female, as can be found in any community." Any disruptive behavior by blacks almost certainly would have been subject of comment, so it is likely that the few blacks in theater audiences did not draw attention to themselves. William Johnson curtailed his attendance after an incident of fighting at the theater, even though he had no part in it.

Presumably he considered caution the wiser choice, for fear of being identified as a troublemaker.[5]

Minstrelsy: Class, Race, and Gender

Theater's whiteness is evident in the entertainments offered. While museum theaters of the 1840s can be understood in terms of the intersecting categories of class and gender, minstrelsy, born in the same decade, involved the intersection of class and race. Museum theaters tapped the righteous middle class; early minstrels appealed to the rambunctious working class. Museum theaters used the feminine as a symbol; minstrels played upon the sentiments of race.

White men wore blackface on stage even before the Revolution, and blackface was long a part of street carnival. But it was only after the War of 1812 that actors began to use blackface specifically to portray American Negroes. By the late 1820s, several performers in circuses or between acts in theaters claimed to portray southern slaves authentically. The first to experience great success was Thomas Dartmouth Rice, who created the character of Jim Crow, the happy dancing and singing slave, which he often performed on the same bill as plays.[6]

In 1843, four out-of-work musicians in New York City formed a quartet, named themselves the Virginia Minstrels, and mounted an entire evening's bill around blackface entertainment.[7] Others soon imitated them. The response by the 1850s to this new entertainment was phenomenal. Demand was so great in northern cities that troupes could hire any theater in town with confidence of filling it. They often played three shows a day, anticipating the schedule of vaudeville.[8]

Halls devoted exclusively to minstrelsy prospered in most large northern cities. During the 1850s ten major houses devoted exclusively to minstrelsy thrived in New York, five in one block of Broadway. Famous troupes played in their own halls for years. E. P. Christy's Minstrels played continuously at Mechanics Hall in New York from 1847 to 1856, and Wood's Minstrels ran for fifteen years nearby. Ordway's Aeolians in Boston, Hooley's in Brooklyn, and Sanford's in Philadelphia had similar runs of a decade. Other cities that had no resident troupe had minstrel halls continuously occupied by touring troupes. By 1857, four of the most prominent houses in San Francisco were almost exclusively devoted to minstrelsy, crowding out other entertainments. When the famous Bryant's Minstrel troupe arrived, people formed a line several hundred yards long to get tickets. Touring troupes cropped up everywhere, following rivers and railroads and even reaching the frontier. Beginning in the 1850s, G. R. Spalding's showboat, the Banjo, plied the Mississippi and its tributaries. Others followed. The boats, traveling about twenty miles a day, spread the popular new music and humor to each small town along the banks, which eagerly awaited the arrival of such "big city" entertainment.[9]

Minstrel troupes represented a reliable new source of income to theater managers struggling to survive in the depression of the early 1840s, when many theaters – including New York's Bowery, Chatham, and Park – closed or turned to circus. Philip Hone said the Ethiopian Serenaders at Palmo's Opera House in 1844 were "very popular and fills the theater in which so lately the scientific strains of Italian music floated over empty benches." Again, during the panic of 1857, when other entertainments suffered, minstrelsy grew.[10]

Supporters of drama grew alarmed at the success of and competition from minstrelsy. William B. Wood, the famous theater manager, lamented that in the 1840s many drama houses were "delivered over to jugglers, Negro singers, and the managers of such objects of low interest," as a result of the depression in the early 1840s. A German orchestra leader whose tour of America failed, complained in 1852, "the so-called minstrels have the best business here [and earn] enormous sums of money." George Holland, an actor with Wallack's stock company, defected in 1857 to Christy and Wood's Minstrels, publishing a "card" saying regular theater could not pay him a living wage and so he would perform the same roles in blackface. The *New York Clipper* remarked in 1858 that managers "were at a loss for novelties to buck against that improving institution, Negro minstrelsy," and again in 1860, "While the drama is fast losing caste, the minstrelsy business, on the other hand, is improving ... crowding the houses nightly, the weather, whether good or bad, making no difference."[11]

Tears and Laughter

What was the attraction of minstrelsy? It was primarily a musical entertainment, songs and dancing interspersed with low-brow comedy and expressed through caricatured plantation slaves and northern black dandies. By the mid-1850s, when it had settled into its own distinctive format, the typical evening's entertainment consisted of several acts, grouped into three parts, all performed by members of the troupe. A first part, sometimes presented in whiteface (without makeup), was a musical set with the performers arranged in a semicircle. The master of ceremonies, called the "interlocutor," sat in the center; and the endmen, playing tambourine ("Tambo") and bones ("Brudder Bones"), acted as comedians. Repartee between interlocutor and endmen was the source of humor. The interlocutor was portrayed as somewhat pompous, longwinded, and fond of multisyllabic terms; he played the straightman for the endmen's buffoonery. A dual message of racism and anti-intellectualism was encapsulated in the interchanges.[12]

Much of the music was sentimental ballads of love thwarted by tragedy or of men pining for home. Such sentimentalism appealed strongly to geographically displaced young men in city boardinghouses or gone West. The *New York Tribune* wrote in 1855, "Who has not often observed the tears of sensibility moistening the cheek of youth, while listening to the primitive strains of *Uncle Ned*?" Similar teary-eyed, homesick forty-niners filled western saloons as well.[13]

The second part, called the "olio," presented a variety of songs, dances, and standup routines. Here would typically be a "stump speech," a parody of a current politician or lecturer, in blackface, poking fun at intellectualism and reformers, including temperance crusaders, abolitionists, and feminists. The stump speech given by a blackface comedian was a *tour de force* in malapropism and depicted black men as fools. At the same time, however, it also parodied the lyceum lecture, an educational entertainment of the 1850s popular among the respectable middle class.

The third part, or afterpiece, typically was a one-act sketch. Originally this was allegedly a realistic scene of plantation life. Later it became a burlesque of an opera, play, or current event, in the tradition of the afterpiece in theaters of the time, but in blackface. Burlesques of opera parodied the fashionable. *Uncle Tom's Cabin* was turned into a proslavery farce for the third part of the bill. Several versions of a happy Uncle Tom were created.[14]

Historian Peter Zanger describes minstrelsy as "a systematic irreverence and antagonism toward the most prominent aspects of American Victorian high culture, toward its pomposity, its artificiality, its sanctimoniousness, as well as toward its learning, its humanitarianism, and its cultivation."[15] Recent scholars have characterized this irreverence as a form of working-class cultural resistance. However, it also was holding on to white male privilege, resisting reforms from temperance to abolition to women's rights. It unified white males in opposition to blacks and women.[16] Minstrelsy was for many whites their first vivid depiction of black life and slavery. Blacks were only 2 percent of the population in the North in 1850, and northern whites sometimes mistook whites in blackface as blacks. Taking advantage of this confusion, P. T. Barnum hired a black boy to dance but, hesitating to present a black performer, dressed the boy in blackface and woolly wig to pass as a blackface performer. To avoid being mistook as black, minstrel performers made special efforts to demonstrate their whiteness: on-stage they alluded to their whiteness; in posters and sheet music covers, they posed without blackface and dressed respectably in suits.[17] Despite such efforts, confusion still existed. Edward Dicey, a correspondent for the London *Spectator* traveling the United States, recounted a minstrel troupe in St. Louis, Missouri, then a slave state. He said "It is possible the Negro minstrels, in spite of their color, were artificially black." Northern whites were astonished at the diversity of Negro skin color when they took the stage after the Civil War.[18]

Several changes occurred in minstrelsy in the mid-1850s, perhaps in response to the growing crisis in the union over the question of slavery, perhaps to tone down lines offensive to middle-class patrons. The free, urban black dandy was added in contrast to the "contented slave." Sentimental ballads proliferated in the first part. The olio became more a variety show, with unrelated acts following each other. During the War, minstrel shows became uniformly unionist, but they continued to sentimentalize slavery.[19]

Free of Moral Criticism

Minstrels ridiculed so many groups – blacks, women, reformers, educators, cultural elites, the rich, and politicians – that it is remarkable that they themselves seldom became the target of criticism. Even the antislavery newspaper, *The Liberator,* did not print criticisms of minstrelsy.[20] Minstrelsy was spared the tag of immorality that hung on theater. The term "minstrel" was adopted from respectable family singing groups of the time. They referred to their performances as "concerts" and the venues as "halls," associating them with more respectable music concerts rather than drama theaters.[21] Female minstrels were rare in the antebellum period, and there were no waitresses – who were the center of controversy for concert saloons – to be accused of prostitution. Minstrels also benefited from a reputation for drawing men *out* of the saloons. And they sanctified the family in many sentimental songs. Occasional lewd jokes were generally overlooked by the morals patrol, perhaps because the audience was primarily male, and, like vaudeville later, the jokes were cleaned up for a more mixed or family audience.

Minstrelsy did offend those intent on creating a cultural hierarchy in music.[22] Literary magazines did not condemn minstrelsy outright, but contrasted some "golden age" of blackface to the present. There were frequent complaints in the late 1850s of minstrelsy having declined in its authenticity. *Putnam's Monthly*, for example, placed the "golden age" of Negro songs before the days of ministrelsy. According to *Putnam's*, minstrel shows were "vile parodies, sentimental love songs, dirges for dead wenches," "crude burlesque on a popular opera." In 1853, George Root, composer of many "dirges for dead wenches," complained of such criticism.[23]

Other critics cast Stephen Foster as the aesthetic savior of minstrelsy. *Atlantic Monthly* described the 1840s before Foster as in "bungling hands" who distorted Negro delineation into "slang phrases and crude jests, all odds and ends of vulgar sentiments, without regard to the idiosyncrasies of the Negro." Then Foster wrote his first "Negro song" in the mid-1840s and became the minstrel par excellence for the 1850s, and was championed by high-brow music heroes such as Ole Bull.[24]

Minstrel Audiences

Despite the fact that minstrelsy was the most popular entertainment of its time and the source of much popular music that reached even those who had never seen a minstrel show, there are very few references to actual behavior of minstrel audiences.[25] Minstrels published few memoirs. Instead they published much more profitable joke books and song books. Sheet music sales represented a large share of minstrel income.[26] Since minstrelsy was neither controversial nor highbrow, it generated little newspaper or magazine commentary by reformers or cultural elites.

Newspapers and magazines published few reviews and little artistic criticism of minstrelsy compared to drama. *Poole's Index* cites only a handful of articles under the heading of minstrelsy for the whole of the nineteenth century. From the opening of Christy's Minstrels at Mechanic's Hall in 1847 until its demise in 1861, *The Spirit of the Times* included in its "Theatrical" column a simple one-sentence reminder that "The minstrels are crowded as ever," seldom elaborating on particular halls or performances. The same column went on for a half page with detailed reviews of plays at theaters around the nation. The paper included other articles about theater that also ignored minstrelsy. At the same time the paper never uttered a negative word about minstrelsy, not even a condescending adjective, and even recommended its gentlemen readers try out this popular amusement at the most well-known halls in New York. Other magazines covering theatricals and entertainments similarly printed only minimal reviews of minstrelsy. Minstrelsy was treated as uncontroversial light entertainment, good for a hearty laugh.[27]

The workingman's paper, the *New York Herald,* printed little more. Minstrelsy was grouped with concerts under "Musical" rather than in the "Theatrical" column, but little more was said than how entertaining they were and what large crowds they drew: "hundreds are frequently obliged to return home, not being able to gain admission [to Christy's Minstrels]." The paper's police reporting in 1851 and 1855 also revealed no incidents at minstrel halls.[28]

When it began publication after the War, the trade paper, the *New York Clipper,* did carry a separate column entitled "Negro Minstrelsy." Over ten years, to 1875, while minstrelsy was still dominant, the *Clipper* reported only six disturbances at minstrel performances around the country.[29] Three were minor scuffles involving disruptive individuals. The other three were general audience protests or riots when halls failed to provide what was advertised in the bill.

The only way to decipher apparently contradictory evidence about *who* were minstrelsy's audiences is to distinguish between different decades, between big and small time, between big city and small town. Some were respectable, some not. Some was family entertainment, some for men. The *Literary World* in 1849 described the audience as "the b'hoys and their seamstress sweethearts." But minstrels also played at Barnum's Museum, where a more "respectable" crowd congregated.

The audience was undoubtedly overwhelmingly white. Minstrel songs often began with the address to the audience, "Now, white folks..." There were no mentions of "colored gallery" in minstrel playbills, as there often were for theaters. And there is no mention by contemporaries of seeing blacks in the audience. Indeed one would think this would have been felt a most threatening place for black persons to find themselves – unless they were prepared to confirm, by their own behavior, the Sambo routines enacted on-stage.

Several scholars have inferred from the entertainment itself that the audiences were men. But shows directed specifically to men were likely confined to the lesser halls in major cities. In small towns, the entire populace, including children, were likely to attend minstrelsy, or any other entertainment that came their way. Playbills often indicated children's half-price admission. Reports of actual attendance referred to boys and not to girls. Mark Twain remembered a minstrel show from his boyhood in the 1840s: "in our village of Hannibal we had not heard of it before, and it burst upon us as a glad and stunning surprise." Michael Leavitt, the creator of the burlesque business, was delighted as a boy by minstrel shows in Bangor, Maine around 1850. Minstrel Ben Cotton said upon first seeing a minstrel show in his town in the 1840s he "thought of nothing else for weeks."[30]

The presence of girls is not so evident. Minstrel Ralph Keeler referred to the many girls whom he wooed as a young performer age eleven to thirteen, in small towns in the 1850s. He apparently met them at dances offered at the end of evening performances at which, for an extra admission, townsfolk could dance, with the troupe in their best "citizens' dress" providing the music. Presumably the teenage girls Keeler met had also attended the earlier program. He notes three respectable young women of "a large Western city" whom he escorted to "theater and concerts," "ice-cream saloons [and] places of amusement," but does not specifically mention minstrel shows.[31]

Pursuing Respectability

Minstrelsy was the masculine entertainment that theater had been. Its humor was raucous and sometimes risqué; it elicited loud guffaws rather than polite smiles. This "theater of misrule" conflicted with the bodily and emotional constraint that was the mark of respectability and middle-class status. Its inappropriateness for "ladies" was expressed in 1855 by a Memphis newspaper editor:

We would suggest that for the benefit of those in our city who have some objections to attending an Ethiopian Concert, that [the Campbell Minstrels] give a *white* entertainment, and thus extend to everyone an opportunity to hear them. Great musical talent, such as this troupe has the reputation, can "draw a house" if they appear like *men*. The charm of a black surface and foolish flummery of Negro slang is not, or at least ought not, to have such additional attraction over those that appear in a more pleasing and rational a light.

It soon became common practice in Memphis to offer part of the show in "citizens' dress and white face." Buffoonery in blackface was not polite entertainment.[32]

While not confronted with the same antagonism that faced drama theater, minstrels attempted to overcome objections and to enhance their image as family entertainment. Samuel Sanford distributed free toys and presented a pantomime performance to children on Christmas morning in 1855 to promote his Twelfth Street Opera House.[33] Playbills often touted shows as family entertainment. The most successful troupes, who played permanently at major halls, toned down their populist performances for a more polite audience. An 1850 bill for Charley White's Melodeon in New York went on at length about the propriety of the place:

...all business of the stage is concluded at a reasonable hour. ... Every representation in this Saloon is chaste, moral and free from vulgarity and all objectionable allusions. No improper person (male or female) admitted. No bar allowed on the premises. FRONT SEATS RESERVED FOR LADIES... Gentlemen are most respectfully requested not to beat time with their feet.[34]

Similarly, playbills for minstrel houses in San Francisco in 1862 and 1863 announced Saturday matinees for "Ladies and Families" and "Families and Children." Some bills advertised door prizes for women.[35]

As previously mentioned, troupes made a point of referring to their program as a "concert," which had the ring of propriety. Music was one of the few acceptable Sunday entertainments, and the term "sacred concert" referred to Sunday music programs. If the serenaders were to present simply a musical concert it could be attended by "ladies" with scruples. The popularity of Stephen Foster's minstrel ballads for young women playing parlor pianos also helped to establish the respectability of minstrelsy.[36]

The lavish decorations of Christy and Wood's Minstrels' new hall in New York in 1857 was itself an advertisement to attract a female audience. The *Spirit of the Times* described its marble façade and floors, pianos and brocade sofas in the foyer, magnificent chandeliers, and other luxuries comparable to those in the best theaters. The *Spirit* concluded, "the ladies will be enraptured with the new house, and indeed they appeared so on last night."[37]

Advertising proclaiming respectability was common to all forms of stage entertainment at the time. Museum theaters, legitimate theaters, and even variety halls were advertising that their bill was "safe" and offered special accommodations and/or prices for ladies, with male escorts, and children. Certainly the widespread efforts to appeal to the new respectable middle class suggest it must have seemed an especially lucrative market to entertainment entrepreneurs of the 1850s. At least some of this advertising succeeded in drawing women to minstrel halls. Sanford's Minstrels, visiting Baltimore in 1851, drew a significant number of women. Women attended minstrel troupes playing at the Union and American Theaters of San Francisco in 1857. In 1858 a Memphis paper described the audience for the famous touring Buckley Minstrels as "a highly respectable one, including many fashionably attired ladies, who manifested the highest delight with the performance."[38] Each of these, however, constituted a special occasion, rather than a regular nightly amusement.

Working-Class Fun?

Working men probably constituted a large portion of the audience.[39] Tickets were affordable. The standard admission for minstrels in the antebellum period was 25 cents general admission, comparable to the price of gallery seats at theater, but allowing the holder to sit anywhere. This was about a quarter of an unskilled worker's daily wage in New York during the antebellum period. An English actor, H. P. Gratton, described a Buffalo, New York minstrel audience as "Erie steam boatmen," towpath teamsters, and "their ladies" sitting at tables enjoying their drinks.[40]

The entertainment suited working-class tastes and sentiments. Jokes about pompous intellectuals and self-righteous reformers struck a chord with young workers. Minstrels quickly incorporated the b'hoys' favorite character Mose into their shows. During the war, minstrels attacked the wealthy who avoided the draft. Its form too, "immediate, unpretentious, direct," fit the tastes of young working men. It had no set script, character development, plot, or musical score, allowing more of their participation. While it developed a more formalized structure by 1860, it remained strongly oriented to the audience.[41]

Minstrelsy, however, was not exclusively working class, but attracted "gentlemen" as well. Two papers in Cleveland in 1851, commenting on a minstrel show, disagreed as to whether the audience were gentlemen or rowdies.[42] The *Spirit of the Times* advised its gentlemen readers to attend performances in New York, "really scientific artiste in their line," that "the number of ladies that attend [the Campbell Minstrels] is a guarantee of the excellence of the performance," and [re Pierce Minstrels at the Olympic] "If you have not, go at the earliest opportunity."[43] The *Journal of Music* observed that "Fashion sent her cohorts to mingle with the unwashed million at the shrine of Gumbo." Drama critic H. A. Clapp claimed that the better classes of Boston had attended minstrelsy before the war, when it had concentrated on "authentic delineations." A Boston troupe performed for President Polk at the White House; and minstrel shows were Lincoln's favorite entertainment in the 1850s.[44]

White working-class men and boys may have constituted some, perhaps most of the minstrel audience in the 1840s and 1850s. But by the 1850s there were "ladies" and "gentlemen" at least in some halls sometimes.[45] They may not have attended the same performances: humor that may have played well to the "rough" would have been offensive to the "respectable"; and that which pleased the "respectable" may have bored the "rough." Lyrics and jokes cited as proof of working-class audiences were likely toned down for more "respectable" audiences. Such flexible response to audiences was integral to minstrel success. Advance agents would scout the local news and gossip in the town for the next night's stand so minstrels could incorporate it into the night's show. As one commented on the Rentz Female Minstrels, they could be whatever the audience wanted.[46]

The most famous troupes in the biggest houses in the largest cities were most likely drawing large numbers among the middle and upper classes. The distinction made between run-of-the-mill minstrels and the famous troupes was expressed by a Minneapolis newspaper in 1858: "Minstrels too often (and too justly) associated with noise, vulgarity and low aims... This troupe [Dan Emmett's] is just the opposite."[47] Less well known troupes in smaller urban halls probably depended more heavily on working-class male audiences. Smaller towns were unlikely to attract the big name troupes. Their halls likely filled with lower-middle and working class, and some middle class shyly attending. The changes in minstrelsy, from delineation to spectacle, from ribaldry to "chaste" and "monotonous," can be understood as efforts to incorporate different classes and both genders as its market. It was in the interest of minstrel managers to placate and interest the "respectable" and "fashionable" even while trying also to satisfy working-class men and boys. This is the continuing dilemma of a mass entertainment. The improvisational and variety form was well suited to this purpose, providing something for everyone.

Postwar Minstrelsy

In 1872, "Light and Shadow" author James McCabe referred to Bryant's minstrel house on Twenty-third and Sixth in New York as "filled with an audience of city people of the better class," and claimed Dan Bryant had raised

minstrelsy to the dignity of a fashionable amusement and has banished from it all that is coarse and offensive. Men worn out from business cares go there to laugh... Families come by the score to laugh at the vagaries of the sable minstrels, and the mirth of the little folks is one of the heartiest and healthiest sounds."[48]

Minstrelsy changed after the Civil War. It had to compete on the one hand with spectacles in drama theaters for the respectable patrons and on the other hand with concert saloons and variety for rough clientele.[49] Minstrelsy responded with spectacles of its own. By the late 1870s Haverly's troupe was advertised for it size: "Forty – 40 – Count 'Em – 40 – Forty – Haverly's United Mastodon Minstrels." They even changed the music. The *New York Clipper* in 1868 described minstrel shows as "snatches of opera, songs abounding in high-flown sentiment and considerable orchestral crash." Minstrels seemed like a "pack of signor Maccaronis in disguise." The transformation of minstrelsy into family entertainment that was "clean, bright amusement" was complete. The *Clipper* said, "now, and very properly too, our fair ones turn out in numbers second to none" for minstrel shows that in the past they would have looked upon with "holy horror."[50] Minstrels were met halfway by a general loosening of constraints of respectability for women in public places. A few entrepreneurs chose another strategy. To hold onto the rowdy male audience and keep it from defecting to variety, sex appeal was added in the form of female minstrel troupes. Other troupes incorporated this in the form of coquettish female impersonators.[51]

To compete, minstrelsy had moved away from portraying blacks, abandoning what made it distinctive. In the end it would lose both audiences. Respectability had given big-time minstrel troupes an advantage over variety and saloon entertainment. But in the 1870s minstrel troupes had to compete with a cleaned-up version of variety that would become vaudeville. By the 1880s, many smaller minstrel troupes could not survive the competition, and minstrelsy became dominated by a few large and lavish national traveling companies.[52]

By the 1870s, minstrelsy was a "tired businessman's show" in decline. The *New York Clipper* in 1871 stated, "Has the taste for Negro minstrelsy diminished, or is the apparent public apathy in that style of amusement to be attributed to a lack of novelty and freshness in the entertainments presented?" The *Brooklyn Eagle* in 1877 published a similar column on the decline. Minstrelsy survived a little longer in some places such as San Francisco, where it lingered throughout the eighties. Brander Matthews in 1915 explained minstrelsy's decline as due to the drift away from "its own peculiar field – the humorous reproduction of the sayings and doings of the colored man in the United States." However, whites had tired of "reproductions of the sayings and doings of the colored man" left over from antebellum debates about slavery and abolition.

Other causes of decline Matthews cited were more to the point. The lack of sex appeal and the "limited and monotonous" program could not compete with variety and musical comedy in offering "broad fun commingled with song and dance."[53] Separate performance halls and a taste for variety entertainment eventually paved the way for its replacement by vaudeville. Variety had dented the minstrel audience, and profits of New York in the late 1850s when variety halls (concert saloons) suddenly multiplied. In the 1870s and 1880s minstrelsy lost more audiences and profits to vaudeville.

Variety, Liquor, and Lust

A s theaters began to sanitize and feminize, a new entertainment appeared and began to flourish. Concert
saloons combined stage entertainment in a variety format with alcohol served from a bar by waitresses. Liquor
was the primary commodity for sale and sexuality the
lure. Variety, a bill of entertainment composed of a series of unrelated
acts or bits of entertainment, has a long history. Early American theater bills resembled variety, offering miscellaneous entertainments
between acts of a full-length play and a comic skit after the play. The
bill included whatever might divert the audience: dancing, singing,
juggling, acrobatics, demonstrations of scientific discoveries. But variety was less a descendant of drama than, like minstrelsy, of popular
musical entertainments.[1] In the 1840s, when minstrelsy swept the
country, saloons offering musical entertainment also began to appear.
By the 1850s there were numerous places variously called free-and-
easies, music halls, and concert saloons. Boundaries between the
terms were not clearly demarcated. A "Light and Shadow" book
described one such place in 1882: "It is not a bar-room, not a concert

saloon, not a pretty waiter-girl establishment, and not a free-and-easy. None of these terms describe it, for it is all those things."[2] The term used depended more on the writer's evaluation of the saloon than on any taxonomic validity. These places blended minstrelsy, burlesque, music, dance, and sexual play in a confusion of combinations. They also ranged in class and clientele. Well-to-do sporting men frequented concert saloons with lavish interiors and entertainments. At the other extreme were dance hall dives frequented by "roughs," and in between were places catering to working men of modest income.

The principle discourse on concert saloons revolved around the morality of the places and their clients.[3] Concert saloons were part of the dangerous geography bourgeois women were warned against. Some reformers considered that the most disturbing consequence was the contamination of the bourgeois home by the husbands who patronized these same saloons, attracted to their aggressive, virile, masculine mix of liquor, cigars, and commercial sex. With free time, money, and prerogative affluent men could float from working-class dives to fancy Broadway saloons as it pleased them. They could slum in this world and return home to their respectability. It may well be the polluting nature of these transgressions, as well as resentment of such amoral elite privilege, that fueled reactions specifically to the Broadway saloons that were most likely to serve the affluent. Such elite "sporting men" had the tacit cooperation of some city officials reluctant to suppress this culture. The concert saloons thus had their powerful advocates as well as adversaries.[4]

But as with theater, variety would undergo a transformation through the 1860s and 1870s from disreputable to respectable. The pattern of change and the strategies used were much the same in variety as in theater: to sanitize the environment by removing prostitution and liquor and ensuring "chaste" performance, and to invite women and children by offering matinees and reduced admissions.

Early Variety: The 1860s Concert Saloon

The panic of 1857 stimulated growth of this cheapest form of entertainment, as interest in more expensive and respectable minstrel shows temporarily slackened. In 1861 the *New York Times* counted 23 concert saloons along five blocks of Broadway between Canal and Third Streets. An 1858 statute stopped the growth of concert saloons in Massachusetts. But almost everywhere else they thrived, spreading rapidly throughout the country by the early 1860s. Some "toned down" saloons even operated in smaller towns. Michael Leavitt, the originator of burlesque, included among the "better class" of variety houses in 1862 several each in Philadelphia, Baltimore, Cincinnati, Chicago, St. Louis, Omaha, and San Francisco.[5]

Admission in the late 1850s was free or at most 12 $\frac{1}{2}$ cents, half that of minstrelsy. Liquor sales produced the profits. *Harper's Weekly* in 1859 characterized concert saloon audiences generally as men and boys of loose deportment who jeered performers. *The Night Side of New York* described the audience at one Broadway saloon as a gallery of young bootblacks and rowdies, a parquet of young men-about-town, sailors, soldiers, and old men, and an orchestra of dry goods dealers, lawyers, clerks, officers, and gentlemen with large quantities of money. The author claimed to see among the clientele of a fashionable saloon those "well known on the [stock exchange], in the gold room, and in private banking offices; faces of city officers, alderman and councilmen ... newspaper men." Like theaters of the 1830s, concert saloons served men of all classes.[6]

But regardless of class, clearly the appeal of concert saloons was sexual. Although the entertainments included "ballads, pantomime, recitations, Negro delineations, dancing," the saloons featured women performers and waitresses. Ads emphasized, often in bold and large type, the pretty and agreeable waitresses in attendance.[7]

The "depravity" of lower-class saloons in the Bowery was taken for granted. But ads of enticing waitresses at fashionable Broadway saloons, situated amid respected theaters and other middle-class entertainments, spurred controversy in the 1860s.[8] At first comments were not unfavorable. An 1859 *Harper's Weekly* article on the Sunday "sacred concerts" of a small concert saloon on the "undignified side of Broadway" described the girls as engaging in "innocent familiarities with congenial spirits among the audience." Notably absent were suggestions that the girls were prostitutes or strong language condemning the saloon as immoral.[9] *Wilkes' Spirit of the Times* reported approvingly on the Broadway saloons as late as August 1861, at the very beginning of the Civil War. The correspondent for "Music and Drama" wrote what sound like "puff pieces," describing acts at the Canterbury, American Concert Hall, and Broadway Music Hall as "delightful," "exquisitely graceful," "astonishing," "amusing and side-splitting novelties." Audiences were "well satisfied" and "Saturday matinees for ladies have proved a highly successful feature."[10]

However, in September 1861 a new columnist, signing his editorials "Bayard," jettisoned this friendly language and condemned the concert saloons as "A Great Social Evil ... The open shamelessness in some of these saloons would astound the keeper of a Water Street dance cellar."[11] Others also began to turn a more jaundiced eye on concert saloons. A New York City Grand Jury in December 1861 concluded that concert saloons were "a great source of crime" and ordered an investigation by the Superintendent of Police of New York City, who then urged legislation.[12] The following week, the *New York Evening Post* published an extended description of several saloons along Broadway, describing them as the homes of "avowed Bacchus and Phallus worship." The *Post* allowed that there were shades of difference and that some of the entertainments were good. It identified the problem as the waitresses, who it considered no more than prostitutes. It described a conversation in which one girl suggested that a dissipated-looking young fellow rent a private box "to have some fun." The column referred to the girls as having an "utter absence of womanly grace, repose or modesty and ... the indefinable but unmistakable stoop belonging to their class." It claimed these girls were met at the end of their shift at midnight by men "to conduct them to the 'Ladies Supper Rooms' of the locality, to their own equivocal boarding houses – to any unmentionable localities you please."[13]

Following the police superintendent's advice, in April 1862 the New York State legislators passed an Act to regulate places of public amusement. It required licensing, and prohibited waitresses from selling and serving liquor. Some halls complied by closing their bar or allowing no females to enter. Others claimed they could not exclude females as guests, so long as they did not wait on men. Several went out of business. The Gaieties offered free admission, changing itself thereby into a restaurant, and not an amusement hall, avoiding the new legislation.[14] The American Concert Hall defiantly protested in the *New York Herald*, calling itself "the music hall of the masses,"

since the unconstitutional efforts to crush it, the People have rallied around it, and now every evening, hundreds are turned away, unable to gain admission ... despite all efforts of Bigotry and Fanaticism ... attempts to deprive it of its rights and privileges by puritanical members from the rural districts, aided by the *New York Daily Times* and other scurrilous journals.[15]

Concert saloons prospered despite reformers and legislators. *Spirit of the Times* declared the efforts to suppress them an utter failure, claiming they were "flourishing luxuriantly all over [New York City]" and catering to "the throng of soldiers and officers in the city [and] strangers from all quarters." The mention of soldiers suggests the War helped their success. The *Spirit* added danger to previous charges of immorality, claiming "Crime of all sorts is rife in these saloons. Within a few months three or four regular murders have been done, while robberies are not only of frequent occurrence but are a part of their dependence for income ... loafers and thieves who live by sharing the earnings and stealings of the 'pretty waiter girls.'" They blamed the saloons for "decoying" young girls from "honorable pursuits to become waiters and consequently prostitutes." Editor George Wilkes criticized "'respectable' dailies [who] publish from day to day right among the announcements of the theaters, the filthy appeals of 'pretty waiter girls' and their pimps for custom," and chastised officials who would not put an end to these places.[16]

Nevertheless, reformers may have encouraged some of the Broadway saloons to improve their image. From the beginning they had an advantage over the Bowery's reputation for lower-class enter-tainments for an equally lower-class, rough audience. James McCabe called the saloons there "mere brothels, in which no man's life is safe."[17] The saloons on Broadway were in a fashionable neighborhood near the best legitimate theaters. The Broadway Music Hall of the 1860s was located in the former Wallack's Theater. The Gaieties was next door to Laura Keene's Theater, one of the first theaters with a large female patronage.[18]

The large and prosperous Broadway establishments redefined themselves in the language of fashion and respectability to counter the condemnations by some newspapers. They avoided the terms "saloon" or "concert saloon," which by the early 1860s had become pejorative. Instead they billed themselves as variety or music halls, and had full stages and balconies. Ads attested to their respectability and no longer mentioned liquor, cigars, or waitresses. In 1860 the Olympic advertised in the *New York Herald,* "the merchant, artisan, and tradesman can repair with his family and enjoy a few hours of amusement that will be found original, pungent and devoid of any-thing vulgar." The old National Theater was converted into a music hall in 1860, its motto, "to please without giving offence." Ads empha-sized the quality of entertainers rather than pretty waitresses.[19]

Variety halls adopted strategies of legitimate theaters to attract a family clientele and to seek a new market, women. The Palace Garden in 1858 excluded liquor and offered free gifts to "ladies" attending. Many halls introduced matinees that were dubbed "ladies hour," during which drinking and smoking were forbidden. Concert saloons customarily had been closed during the day, so matinees represented extended hours and a previously untapped source of profit. Frank River's Melodeon in Philadelphia offered its first matinee in 1860 "for families and children." The Broadway Music Hall followed suit in 1861, and so did others. The spread of the practice suggests its success. This set the precedent for marketing variety to women, which Tony Pastor and others developed further in the 1870s.[20]

Ads also stated policies toward containing rowdy audiences. In Philadelphia, The Eleventh Street Opera House even went so far in 1867 as to advertise itself as "The Family Resort" and announced house rules to control the audience, prohibiting loud talking, moving about during a song, standing in aisles, whistling or beating time with the feet. Frank River's Melodeon pursued respectable working-class families, providing a dress circle for ladies and children "within the capacity of the most limited purse."[21]

While most concert saloons had to advertise their respectability, German beer halls that also offered entertainment had this done for them through the unsolicited testimony of reformers and newspaper correspondents. The tone of such testimony is typically that of admiration and praise, depicting them as the epitome of working-class respectability. Despite the German habit of staging Sunday concerts, they were free of charges of religious violations, sexual immorality, or violence. Contemporaries typically contrasted the German beer halls to concert saloons, the former intrinsically a family place, the latter off limits to any decent woman. This was observed not only in New York, but in many cities with large German neighborhoods, such as Cincinnati, Milwaukee, and San Francisco.[22] Edward Dicey, correspondent for the English magazine, the *Spectator,* in his tour of America in 1862, commented that at German beer gardens, "whole families, fathers, mothers and children come and sit for hours to drink beer and listen to the music." He found the audience "as well-behaved, though not so quiet, as it would have been in Germany."[23]

The *New York Herald* confirmed Dicey's description in a front-page article, "Teutonic Sunday Amusements," in 1859. It emphasized that the German halls were "conducted peaceably and quietly." The correspondent saw "men, women, children and infants, of every rank and condition in society" seated around tables drinking beer and always in family groups. Between acts or songs "they became vivacious and loquacious in the extreme ... but as soon as [the music] struck up, all other sounds ceased, as by magic."[24]

Beer halls proliferated in the German districts of Cincinnati, Milwaukee, and St. Louis with the arrival of large numbers of immigrants in the 1840s and early 1850s. They served beer and sometimes wine and did not tolerate drunkenness or disorder. They always had music, and sometimes variety acts. The summer version was the beer garden, which added picnicking, sports, and games. Milwaukee Gardens, in the 1850s, spread over three acres on the outskirts of Milwaukee, accommodated ten thousand and offered concerts, dancing, sports, theater, and a restaurant. It had a menagerie, a midway, souvenir stalls – a predecessor of turn-of-the-century amusement parks.[25]

But aside from German halls, sex and liquor were the basis for success of concert saloons across the country. Memphis saloons were described as dangerous as well as immoral. Free-and-easies of Memphis had "wine rooms" attached where for an additional fee patrons could fraternize with the dancing girls. There were brawls, shootings, knifings, and attacks on waiter girls. But even the roughest houses of Memphis included patrons of "nearly all classes of men ... married and single, youth and old age, reputable and disreputable, the gentleman and the rough." Here too reformers attempted to stop the saloons. By 1866 local newspapers began a campaign against free-and-easies. One manager in 1866 made the mistake of publicly stating to the newspaper that many alderman attended his saloon. Shortly thereafter he was arrested several times.[26]

The familiar western saloon was part of this growth too.[27] Kansas City audiences apparently were better behaved than those in Memphis, since no reports of disturbances were made in the local press, except of drunks who were promptly removed. Managers advertised policies of "preservation of strictest order," which suggest a need to enforce order. During the Civil War the local commandant stationed a guard in one house, to control the behavior of soldiers frequenting the place. A variety hall was closed and fined in December 1869 for a performance of the can-can, which violated an ordinance requiring that female performers' legs "must be covered to below the knee." The town council, however, remitted the fine.[28]

Concert saloons continued as a low-end entertainment into the twentieth century, when they were transmogrified into cabarets. Progressive reformers echoed some of the concerns of the 1860s. A 1901 report for the elite Boston Committee of Fifty claimed, "These music halls ... are worse than ordinary saloons, since they combine the vice of prostitution with that of intemperance. Admission is free. The women, after performing, frequently circulate through the hall in order to persuade the men to 'set them up' to drinks. The same may be said of the saloon vaudeville shows."[29]

Absent from these descriptions are any accounts of audiences acting collectively to assert their will on the performers or saloon managers. The brawls and knifings mentioned in some rougher houses were generally individual affairs, not equivalent to the collective hissing or calls for tunes from performers. Given the reformers' desires to close these places, it seems likely they would have seized upon any rowdiness or disturbances as further evidence for their cause. Yet they report little. Other reporters too have little to say. This contrasts with the frequent and elaborated comment on rowdy and boisterous audiences both before this time, in the Jacksonian theaters, and after, in turn-of-the-century immigrant theaters.

We are left to conclude that both the minstrel and variety audiences of the 1850s and 1860s were not riotous and did not enforce their desires on the stage as had Jacksonians. Minstrel audiences were noisy but not riotous; concert saloon audiences may have been less focused on the stage because male attentions were affixed on sexual matters, that is, the girls in their laps. In any case the loss of sovereignty taking place in drama theaters of the time was also occurring in these other places of amusement. The growing legal rights of theater managers extended to minstrel and variety halls that charged admission. Certainly the concert saloon manager had an interest in containing audiences in order to not bring further police attention. The police were not eager to shut them down for immoral reasons, but may have been more willing to close a "disorderly" house.

Descriptions of camaraderie among audience members in variety halls also is absent from contemporary accounts. Earlier drama theater audience members tended to be familiar with each other. They attended the same theater regularly, sat in the same section – many often came from the same professions or crafts. The socializing featured in accounts of the Bowery b'hoys and forty-niners is missing in commentaries on concert saloons. Group identification among audience members appears to have been absent in the variety saloon. This absence reduced the probability of collective action and thus of audience sovereignty. It also meant that the concert saloon was not a locus of political action that might have had significance beyond its boundaries, as was the case with theater riots from the colonial times to the Jacksonian period. Going to a concert saloon was more an act of private consumption than of communal celebration, more economic and individual, less political and cultural than even attending the minstrel show of the 1840s and certainly the drama theater of the 1790s.

Variety to Vaudeville

By the early 1870s, accusations of prostitution in variety halls abated, but they still were not quite reputable. Sympathetic as well as critical observers characterized variety halls as places of working men's amusement where alcohol was consumed. The Metropolitan on Broadway in 1874 had an audience of "bootblacks and errand boys [in the gallery], parquet of clerks, shopmen and gamblers ... a class who served immigrants in their business, patronized immigrant businesses and competed with them for jobs," but not a fashionable crowd. A variety house in Kansas City in the early 1870s advertised that it desired "patronage from only the male sex" and touted its "wines, liquors and cigars."[30]

The editor of the *Southern Magazine* in 1871 described the audience in a working-class variety hall as "rough-looking, unkempt, unwashed and horribly dressed, not because they are vicious, but because they are poor and ignorant and unrefined; because their labor is degrading in character, meager in pay, and uncertain in duration." He defended the entertainment as "not quite so bad, and the jokes, though a little coarser perhaps, certainly not more impure in meaning than are enacted on the stages of prominent theaters before fashionable audiences." He saw the variety hall as providing necessary recreation for these men and as keeping them from getting drunk in a saloon, the same benefit later reformers would attribute to nickelodeons. He blamed the slumming upper-class young men and gray-haired businessmen who came here for engaging in "coarse debauchery" behind the closed curtains of the boxes.[31]

Accusations of debauchery at variety halls were becoming infrequent. Newspapers cooperated in reconstructing variety and its history, disassociating it from saloons. The panic of 1873 that closed many drama theaters was instrumental in establishing variety in its own home. Variety was a much cheaper form of entertainment than drama to produce and an obvious way to fill empty drama theaters. The *New York Times* noted, "when all other theatres except the Union Square were doing little or no business, the Comique and Metropolitan turned people away every night... The popular bias in favor of this style of evening amusement became so palpable that [the renowned legitimate theater director] Mr. Daly devoted the Olympic and Grand Opera House to it."[32]

An 1874 article in the *New York Times* on the origin and history of variety shows in New York marks a turning point in attitudes toward variety. The subtitle declared, "Morality a Striking Feature" of variety halls. It gave positive descriptions of concert saloons which only two years before it had condemned. It never mentioned waiter girls and called the long prejudice against variety "ridiculous." It credited the *Black Crook,* which played at Niblo's Garden for a year in 1866–67, with offering variety in the guise of drama and with breaking down this prejudice. Confirming the respectability of variety, the article concluded, "It is an established rule in each of these theatres that the performer who uses an immoral or objectionable phrase or gesture on the stage shall be dismissed... Can as much be said for modern society plays!"[33]

Another article in 1879 in the trade paper, the *New York Mirror,* confirmed that variety was established as a distinct entertainment more profitable than "legitimate" drama. The article's title, "The Variety Theatres," redefined them distinct from "saloons" and even "halls" and as belonging to the newly respectable and fashionable category, "theatres", with the French spelling. Instead of discussing morality it focused on the profitability of variety houses in Cincinnati, San Francisco, Chicago, St. Louis, Louisville, as well as New York City.[34]

As variety gained respectability aesthetics replaced morals as the primary criticism. Theater closings worried those in drama, and they reacted with a cry to protect "Art" from popular culture. A newspaper in Des Moines in 1871 feared, "It is really too bad that the legitimate drama cannot be better supported in this city. When every nigger show, sleight-of-hand performance, or dead-beat 'mystery man' can draw crowded houses, here we have an excellent dramatic company which comprises some star actors and actresses of more than average talent, with a good stock company to assist them, and they play night after night to empty benches."[35]

Acceptance of variety, however, hinged on its respectability more than aesthetics. Tony Pastor is usually credited with achieving this. He was in actuality only one of several entrepreneurs advancing the respectability of variety, among them Charley White and R. W. Butler, who had opened and managed several concert saloons, minstrel, and variety houses.[36] Pastor was born into the business and almost certainly was familiar with the efforts of other entrepreneurs for which he was later credited.[37]

Pastor's contribution was to pursue this new market with systematic effort beyond that of other entrepreneurs, and this perhaps earned him the title of pioneer. He opened his Opera House in the Bowery in 1865 to a clientele of East Side working-class Irish and German families. He was not yet reaching for the middle class but still seeking respectability through "family" entertainment. The *New York Herald* claimed he excluded "rowdyish and troublesome elements". It noted "good order observed and the absence of peanut feasts and boisterous applause" and that "ladies and children now form a large proportion of its audience." In 1866 he added matinees with half-price admission for children. In 1871 he removed the bar to an adjoining "refreshment saloon." In 1872 he admitted ladies free on Friday evenings when accompanied by a man. The trade paper, *New York Clipper,* confirmed the success of "ladies night," noting the audience was "about equally composed of ladies and gentlemen."

After the panic of October 1873, Pastor sought to retain his respectable working-class clientele with music lyrics that praised the virtues of workers and questioned those of the wealthy. He reduced his admission prices and gave door prizes of hams, turkeys, and dress patterns, and in February a valentine for every woman in the house. He also gave barrels of flour, tons of coal, clocks, and most popular of all, silk dresses. Prizes of domestic provisions, low admissions, and songs sympathetic to workers ensured a gender-mixed, working-class family audience.[38]

Pastor's pursuit of the middle class began with his move from the Bowery to Broadway in 1875, situating his theater among hotels and streetcar lines, businessmen, shoppers, and sightseers. He sought to become the "society Vaudeville Theatre" and apparently succeeded. The *Mirror* moved his ads to the regular theater section.[39] Pastor cemented his reputation for clean variety when he moved his theater again to Fourteenth Street near Union Square in 1881, which was New York City's new center of entertainment. The *Clipper* described an evening at Pastor's in 1884: "decidedly a 'family' audience, a large number of ladies, many of them coming in twos and threes, without escort, showing that it is politic to manage an establishment of this description in such a manner that no gentlemen need fear to bring his wife, sister, or mother to 'see the show' or even allow them to go by themselves."[40]

Pastor's efforts employed a marketing strategy used by museum theater before him, and again by B. F. Keith and movie theaters after him. The strategy involved a two-step process; first attracting women and children and, having achieved that, seeking the middle class as the target market. Women with children established the entertainment as family entertainment and thus safe for the middle class to attend without soiling their reputations. In the cases of variety and nickelodeons, proprietors sought a shift from predominantly working-class clientele to a middle-class clientele. The class transition in drama theater was more indirect. Museum theaters sought a market that included respectable working-class patrons as well as the middle class. "Legitimate" theaters that had formerly been of mixed class sought to attract middle-class women. Middle-class men were already attending without their families. Tony Pastor and other variety managers were the first to try the pure strategy of using gender to define the class of an entertainment.[41]

By 1879, variety was quite profitable, more so than "legitimate" theater. But this did not mean that all variety had followed the same path as Tony Pastor. Concert saloons in disreputable entertainment districts, such as the Bowery and the "Over the Rhine" of Cincinnati, continued to use sex to attract and liquor to sell to patrons. But in contrast to the 1860s, commentators expressed more concern about loss of money than of morals. Popular theater writer John Jennings gave an extended description of how these places fleeced gullible males. The patrons of the variety "dives" were a mixture of "young men, clerks, salesmen, and sometimes the trusted employee of a bank or broker's office," farmers and elderly country bumpkins in town on business, with "a well-dressed young man" next to "a crowd of hoodlums in jeans pants and braided coats."[42]

Bouncers maintained order while the girls manipulated the customers in planned frolics destined to take their money. The "dives" had private boxes for fifty cents which stage girls frequented to encourage purchases of drinks. For those with deeper pockets, in wine rooms for private dinner parties, the girls ordered large quantities of champagne to "shampoo" the men.[43]

Jennings included etchings of each scene to add vividness – and to picture pretty young women in half-dress for his own readers. He claimed men "with more money than brains," both young and old, sent mash notes to the girls backstage who took them for all they are worth. The weight and tone of Jennings' tales blamed the girls and cast the men as foolish victims.[44] But he stopped short of accusing the girls of prostitution as typically done by commentators of the 1850s. In the 1880s, theft was worse than immorality. The stories of the 1850s were part of the painting of public spaces as morally dangerous. The 1880s stories tend toward dangers to one's pocketbook, a plight consistent with the new culture of consumption.

The shift in stories represents a shift in control from the audience to the management. Earlier stories depicted customers as active participants in the debauchery. The 1880s stories shifted emphasis to the girls and their accomplices and employers who took advantage of their customers' foolishness. These images transformed audiences from active to passive.

8

Vaudeville, Incorporated

By the 1880s much of variety had transformed from concert saloon to vaudeville. Variety moved into regular theaters with balconies, galleries, and so on, and was independent of saloons. The entertainment was changing from something akin to minstrel turns to something more like drama. Comic sketches – abbreviated forerunners of television situation comedies – displaced standup routines.[1] But the more significant change was the nationalization and centralization of the industry wrought by Benjamin Franklin Keith, Edward F. Albee, and Frederick Freeman Proctor. These men and their partners built vaudeville theater chains and then combined them into an even more powerful nationwide booking agency that forced many independent theater owners and performers to become dependent clients of a national business. Tony Pastor had opened variety to a new audience of women and children. Keith and Albee and Proctor turned this newly respectable entertainment into big business. The United Booking Office had the power to offer or withhold employment from performers in theaters across the country, moving from house to house every week. To theater managers they offered a package of weekly changing bills of acts of predictable quality. The new generation of vaudeville entrepreneurs created what would be called big-time vaudeville in large, plush, downtown theaters, and combined these with small-time houses in outlying or less desirable locations that continued the earlier variety traditions. The booking agency made small-time circuits as a sort of minor league to big-time circuits.[2]

Accompanying the structural changes was a shift in control of the theater from audiences to managers. Management made concerted efforts to define vaudeville and resocialize audiences. But audiences did not become uniformly peaceable. Lively audiences were intrinsic to the success of many vaudeville acts, especially comedy. Performers had to delicately balance audience involvement with control of the audience in order for their act to succeed both with the immediate audience and with the longer-term goals of managers to control the theater space. Thus the history of vaudeville is one of a movement toward greater control of audiences, yet that movement was resisted by audiences and, to a degree, by performers. Managerial control was more complete at the center, the pinnacle of big-time, while audiences held control to a greater degree at the periphery, in the numerous small-time venues.

Contemporaries made much of the small-time, big-time distinction. All circuits, it was joked, called themselves big-time, no matter how small, but everyone acknowledged a difference. Big-time billed itself as "high-class vaudeville" or "family vaudeville" or "dollar" vaudeville, not variety. Keith referred to his theaters as "refined vaudeville." Vaudeville booking agent-turned-writer Robert Grau said, "There were not over fifteen high-class vaudeville theaters in the early 90's," but they quickly multiplied, "until no city with a population of 50,000 or more was without at least one establishment where 'refined' vaudeville was the attraction."[3]

Proctor contrasted "first-class" or "big-time" vaudeville, which required a constant infusion of new acts, to small-time, which he considered the "refuge" of old worn-out acts. In other words, small-time meant second rate or worse; big-time meant the best performers with fresh acts. Terms like "small-time," "cheap," "pop" (short for popularly priced) referred to vaudeville houses with lower-cost acts and lower admission prices. These included theaters not only in urban neighborhoods but also in smaller towns all over the country. Vaudevillian Eddie Shayne, reminiscing about the 1880s, equated the East with big-time vaudeville and the West with old-time concert saloons. The western house had waitresses working the all-male audiences for drinks. Shayne considered the West a training ground where the player had to learn to be flexible and versatile, where she or he honed an act until it was perfected. The eastern version was played in theaters, with curtain, restrooms, lounges, and upholstered seats. It recruited women to the audience.[4]

Whatever the terms used, the consistent point made by contemporaries was that small-time was the training ground for big-time and continued the earlier traditions of variety. Small-time was cheaper, local, and less formal. It thus had an audience that was more working class, more male, and more participative and noisy.

The creator of big-time, Benjamin Franklin Keith, began his career in Boston, not in variety, but with dime museums which had a history of respectability. With these roots he effectively severed any connection between his brand of variety from the concert saloon's unsavory reputation, very much in the same way that Moses Kimball and P. T. Barnum had separated theater in their museums from the disreputable associations of drinking and prostitution in the 1840s. Keith's strategies therefore differed from those of Tony Pastor.

Keith adopted many of the same marketing strategies proven by Kimball.[5] In 1883, to improve weak business, he opened a theater upstairs from his new dime museum and offered a variety program. Sometime between 1883 and 1885 he began his association with Edward F. Albee. His first innovation was that of continuous vaudeville in 1885. Previously several shows were offered each day, each a series of eight to ten acts. However, at the end of each the curtain was dropped and the theater cleared. Keith noticed this created a dreary atmosphere that made people more reluctant to come in for the next show. His solution was simply not to drop the curtain but to begin again with the first act immediately after the last act. The result was a continuous flow of people through the day, allowing people to come and go at their own schedule. Being in the midst of the shopping district made it attractive to women who were shopping. Its success allowed him to buy other theaters and establish a circuit. His next theater in Providence, Rhode Island was also in the center of the shopping area. In the words of a Keith publication, "It is a well-known fact that many vaudeville patrons are busy men and women who run in to see a few acts when they have a few minutes to spare – waiting for a train, filling in time before an appointment, or just to see a special act in which they are interested."[6]

Keith instituted strict regulations about clean acts, not allowing even such phrases as "slob" or "son of a gun." He proclaimed that "words unfit for the ears of ladies and children" were prohibited on his stage. His insistence on squeaky-clean acts was emphasized by the reputed source of a loan to build his first vaudeville "palace" in Boston in 1894 – the Catholic Archdiocese of Boston. His circuit was nicknamed the "Sunday school circuit." According to the *Dramatic Mirror,* men predominated in "the regular houses" where Bonnie Thornton songs caused a great deal of hilarity. But at Keith's she had to restrict herself to songs suited to the "refined audience who are characteristic of Keith's."[7]

Keith imposed constraints on the audience as well as performers. He prohibited smoking, spitting, whistling, stamping feet, crunching peanuts, and wearing hats. At the opening of his first Philadelphia house in the late 1880s, he stood in the gallery at intermission and lectured the audience on its behavior. Bouncers were stationed in the gallery. When in 1902 the *Philadelphia Inquirer* urged theaters to "suppress" the gallery gods, Edward F. Albee claimed, "We have absolutely no trouble with the gallery... There is no spitting on the floor, no stamping of feet, no whistling or noisy demonstration" at Keith's. He claimed that Keith's policy of treating everyone as ladies and gentlemen and expecting the same in return had eliminated "annoyances and bad behavior" of galleryites when the theater opened in the late 1880s.[8]

The Providence Theater published a weekly paper, the *Keith News,* beginning in 1904, which included a regular column titled "The Girl Behind the Pen." The column talked to and about the audience, and was designed to socialize patrons into proper behavior at Keith's theaters. It boasted of how great Keith's was, what it did for audience comfort, such as providing a lost-and-found, hatpins in the ladies' room, and umbrellas for a deposit on rainy days. The "Girl" explained the necessity of the rules and repeatedly requested patrons to abide by them. She described how well appointed and well behaved the second balcony (no longer called the gallery) was, while also boasting of the discipline there. Little vignettes parodied the bothersome habits of some patrons.[9]

Keith was obsessed with attracting a higher-class clientele. In 1894 he and Albee opened in Boston the most luxurious theater of its time, named simply "B. F. Keith's New Theatre." This theater was the forerunner of the movie palaces of the 1920s and included several of the innovations that film historian Douglas Gomery notes as central to their success. The theater was lavishly decorated with marbled, mirrored, and wainscoted walls, mosaic tile floors, and furnishings appointed in gold, silver, and ivory. Bathrooms included large anterooms, maids, and the most modern fixtures. A large fan in the basement pumped cool air throughout the theater in the summer, a precursor to air conditioning. Five thousand electric lights illuminated the building. One hundred and fifteen uniformed employees were carefully trained and strictly supervised to cater to patrons as though they were servants. Such luxury appealed even to the upper crust; every class was now willing to attend vaudeville. It was America's mass entertainment at the turn of the century, like movies in the 1930s and television in the 1960s.[10]

While Keith introduced refined vaudeville in Boston, Frederick Freeman Proctor was building the first vaudeville circuit. Like Keith, he built his reputation on a family show. A judge who attended Proctor's with his family remarked, "I'm recommending your theatre for all of my future domestic trouble cases. Men don't go sneaking off alone to corrupt places of entertainment now that you have provided in your Twenty-Third Street Theatre a source of real inspiration and joy." This theater was in the shopping district, ideal for continuous vaudeville, which he introduced with the motto, "After breakfast go to Proctor's, after Proctor's go to bed." The attitude expressed in the motto, of a life built upon consumption, was new in American culture, with which vaudeville grew up. According to the *New York Journal,* the Twenty-Third Street Theater at the turn of the century was "filled with abdominal shoppers and youthful gentlemen of leisure." Proctor gave souvenirs to ladies attending matinees and, like Keith, he provided uniformed ushers, and matrons in ladies' rooms, and demanded strict politeness from them. His Newark theater, which opened in 1898, was crowded with ladies.[11]

Proctor was quicker and more systematic than Keith in acquiring theaters. His first theater in Albany opened in 1880. By 1886 he had a circuit of eleven theaters when Keith still had only one, and had twenty-five by 1889. Circuits were well-suited to continuous vaudeville, which required meticulous planning to acquire enough acts and to place them in an order which would be most effective both for stage changes and for attracting the biggest audiences. This expense could be distributed across several theaters in a circuit. By the late 1880s continuous vaudeville had spread to many other houses.[12]

Keith's top manager, Edward F. Albee, is credited with much of Keith's success. Albee was different from previous managers and owners. Keith, Proctor, Pastor, and almost all the theater managers for variety and minstrelsy before him had begun as performers, in a tradition not far removed from the craft tradition. Albee was never a performer, but a modern manager trained in business. It was this business mentality that shaped vaudeville and created a centralized industry under the control of the United Booking Office.[13]

By the 1890s there were several regional vaudeville circuits throughout the country. Sylvester Poli in New England, Sullivan-Considine in the Far West, Pantages on the West Coast, Martin Beck from Chicago west, and several others. The owners of these circuits joined to form the United Booking Office, in 1900, with Albee at the head. It controlled bookings in most vaudeville houses throughout the nation, both small-time and big-time. Each year it booked about 600 acts for 20- to 40-week tours of all its theaters. Keith and Albee were compared to the robber barons for creating such a monopoly.[14]

According to theater historian Frederick Snyder, centralization increased standardization and suppressed spontaneity in the entertainment. Each performer had to fit his act to a predetermined schedule and not vary from strict time limits. Such constraints forced interaction between performer and audience into a predetermined formula in which the performer had to carefully orchestrate audience response.[15]

One way to get immediate reaction was racier material. Around 1910 there appeared a number of criticisms of vaudeville for racy and low-brow acts. While Keith's continued to tout the squeaky-clean nature of their entertainment, *American Magazine* in 1910 claimed that a husband or father could not send his wife or daughter to vaudeville confident of its clean entertainment. They claimed, "in the days before vaudeville had developed its present money-making capacities [it] was both wholesome and cheap. Those days are passed. Nowadays it is anything to get a laugh or a shock." A 1910 issue of the *Dramatic Mirror* appealed to Keith to banish vulgarity and smut from vaudeville acts appearing in motion picture houses. In 1912 another article confirmed the vaudeville shows "where the impropriety and obscenity were no whit less offensive than they are at a so-called burlesque show."[16]

Others criticized the low intellectual level of vaudeville acts. Reformer Michael Davis in 1910 said vaudeville's "most striking characteristic is simple stupidity ... the teeming vaudeville audiences often appeared bored." He concluded they went because it was one of few amusements they could afford, thus suggesting the audience was mostly lower class but avoiding condemning their intelligence. *American Magazine* condemned its effects on tastes as well as morals; "Vaudeville in the last five or six years, has done more to corrupt, vitiate and degrade public taste in matters relating to the stage than all other influences put together." An article in *The Drama* considered the illness "vaudevillitis" as ruining the ability to appreciate drama, noting that "the best people" in a city of the central states attend vaudeville regularly, to the detriment of theater. *The Moving Picture World* in 1911 claimed that movies were far superior and sustained vaudeville where it could not have otherwise survived.[17]

The vaudeville audience was also criticized for being very limited intellectually. *American Magazine* claimed the "sporting" audience at Koster and Bial's in the 1890s were able to understand the poignant performance of a French singer to which the 1909 audience at an uptown family vaudeville theater could respond only with titters. Caroline Caffin caricatured two young ladies in the vaudeville audience as having so little understanding of drama that they took an actor's turning his back on the audience during a scene as poor acting.[18]

Audience Demographics

From 1905 to 1908 was a period of rapid expansion in vaudeville. Vaudeville grew with the growing class of American white-collar workers, especially women and children. Non-English-speaking immigrants could not understand the humor and seldom attended. Segregation policies excluded blacks, except for a small number of black theaters, just as in other entertainments.[19] But there was some kind of vaudeville house for almost everyone else. Even the upper class came on special occasions. Tickets ranged from five cents to one dollar, a price for everyone's purse.[20]

At the turn of the century some sources mention changes that would have appealed to a female audience: sketches written for women and children, acts that were less rollicking, quieter, more dainty, and cute. A new emphasis was placed on the dress of the performers, to interest the female audience. Journalist and editor Hartley Davis called women and children the "backbone of the success of vaudeville."[21] Yet actor Edwin Royle remarked that, despite the appeal of Keith's to women and children, many or most of the audience were men. Theater critic Caroline Caffin wrote that men were being attracted because they could smoke in parts of the house. She claimed New York vaudeville audiences were more than half men, the tired businessman who does not want to think. She also noted that "There must be something for everyone and though the fastidious may be a little shocked ... they must not be offended, while the seekers of thrill must on no account be bored by too much mildness." Elbert Hubbard, an orator on the vaudeville stage briefly in the 1910s before becoming an advertising pioneer, similarly noted the evening audience was composed of "a goodly number of businessmen ... the lassies with their laddies" and boys in the balcony. The complaints in the 1910s about racy and vulgar acts include references to a large male clientele, including boys, presumably teenagers.[22]

These mixed observations about who predominated in the vaudeville audience again suggest a diverse audience and that an entertainer needed to perform in a way that could reach each group within the same house. An audience within a given theater represented a broad spectrum. Elbert Hubbard said, "Things must not be keyed too high, nor too low." Keith emphasized the diversity of the audience in their big-time theaters.[23] These theaters offered mass entertainment. But also to a degree it was a segmented market, with different audiences in each house. In either case no simple answer can describe the diverse audiences.

Manipulating the Audience

The appeal of vaudeville was that performers played to the audience. Vaudeville was built upon interaction between performer and audience that contrasted to drama theater of the time and appeared similar to that of minstrelsy and early theater audiences. The liveliness of the vaudeville audience was often contrasted to audience behavior in drama theater of the same period. Theatrical realism had promoted the fourth wall. The play was to proceed without any disturbance, even applause, from the audience that would break the spell of realism being created on stage. Actors ignored the audience to concentrate on the characters of the play. Vaudeville was considered inferior by theater critics due to its direct appeal across the footlights.

Vaudeville managers sometimes preferred *not* to encourage audience participation. They said it offended the more refined patrons in the orchestra, who might be more accustomed to drama theater. A Philadelphia manager objected to an act that threw a dummy at the audience and drew it back. Even in the small town of Woonsocket, Rhode Island, a manager in 1914 complained that the tactic of performers running through the audience "has long since served its usefulness ... it might appeal to some, but it grates harshly upon the finer sensibilities."[24]

And yet managers relied upon the outspoken audience for vocal approval of good acts. Historian Alison Kibler notes how vaudeville slang suggests the institutionalized expectation of a strong audience response. "Riot" described a successful act; an audience "killed" an act, or it "died," getting no reaction from the audience; an act "drew blood," meaning enthusiastic applause.[25]

Vaudeville performers considered audience responses vital to their performance. They often worked at the edge of the stage to maximize this. Vaudevillian Nora Bayes described the relationship as "an intimate chat with one or two close friends." The best seats were "down front," closer than desired in drama theater, where one could best participate in this interaction. Performers, however, had to maintain control if they were to elicit the right responses at the right time. They prided themselves on their ability to read the audience and considered themselves "mechanics of emotion." In the words of Robert Lytell of the *New Republic* in 1925, "They seize you and do pretty nearly anything they want with you and while it is going on, you sit with your mouth open and laugh and laugh again."[26]

Performers manufactured an artificial intimacy and spontaneity. Some musical acts encouraged audiences to sing along, magicians sought volunteers, and others threw things into the audience in order to enhance this illusion of audience involvement. The ultimate effort at control was to "plant" a confederate in the audience to insure that the response would be as planned. Comedy team Olsen and Johnson planted confederates who acted as hecklers. Another act began seated in the audience, with the manager announcing a cancellation of a performance. The couple stood up and criticized the manager, then rushed the stage to do their own routine.[27]

Another story about using a plant in the audience illustrates the extremes to which managers and performers would go to manipulate the audience. A little dancer of six finishes her act on stage when a man rushes forward to the stage. "Nellie ... don't you know me?" The little girl cries, "Papa! Take me home." Two ushers seize him and the little girl's manager comes forward to claim that the mother gave the child to him. The father appeals to the audience. They scream and threaten the girl's manager. The theater manager calms the audiences and says "This theatre don't want to part father and daughter. Give the child to the man! and get out of here!" The audience cheers and leaves the theater elated. It worked well for one-night stands.[28]

The participative nature of vaudeville was very different from that of early theater. In early theater the power rested in the audience, while in vaudeville it rested with the manager and performer. However much the vaudeville performers depended upon the audience, they depended on control of it even more. The enforcement of house rules of audience behavior was consistent with the need of performers to channel audience responses within narrow limits, even when those responses were much more vocal than what was acceptable in legitimate theater.

In vaudeville, performers' need for connection to their audience pushed them to transgress the boundaries of control and propriety established by managers, in order for their act to "go over." Performers were caught between managers' desires for control and audience's desires for participation/inclusion. They had to balance both to succeed. In antebellum theater there was no such delicate balance, since the audience held greater control and managers were less concerned with respectability. In vaudeville, transgressions of managerial policy, with complicity between performers and audiences, were often of the nature of sexual innuendoes. The shift in control and content produced a version of "knowingness" between them and a means to maintain the balance performers depended upon.[29]

Control of audience responses was also evident in the managers' use of audiences to evaluate acts. The one power of the vaudeville audience was to "kill the act." One that didn't get laughs or enthusiastic applause was promptly removed from the bill. The audiences of the Colonial Theater, a big-time theater in Manhattan, responded to bad acts with a cadenced applause known as the "Colonial Clap." Many performers remarked that if you did not give them something to laugh at they would laugh at you.[30]

On amateur night in small-time houses this role of the audience was enhanced further, but within the channels prescribed by the needs of the theater management. Managers encouraged audience misbehavior when they instituted amateur night.[31] Amateur night was a tool effectively used by managers to search for new talent while also allowing the audience some of the free reign they did not customarily allow. Baiting the performer was an integral part of the amateur night show. It was encouraged by managers using "the hook," signs saying "Beat It," squirts from a seltzer bottle, chasing them off with an inflated bladder, and closing the curtain. Vaudevillian Fred Allen said these audiences were "primarily in the theater to deride and laugh."[32]

The key to successful management in all these cases was to induce audience reaction while containing it. Sometimes they failed to contain it. Keith required managers of each theater to submit weekly reports in the 1900s to the head office. These reports, themselves a corporate policy of control, often cited incidents, usually from the gallery. A common complaint was the inability to prevent the "boys in the gallery" from "guying" performers. Particularly worrisome to the managers was the "guying" of high-brow acts that they believed appealed to a better class of patron they imagined to be in the orchestra.[33]

One group that perturbed managers was outspoken women in the audience. Keith's managers expected women to set a tone of refinement. Yet they sometimes reported women who were quite responsive to "unladylike" acts. Women applauded an actress who had just won a divorce suit, and got "into the spirit of things by yelling and cheering" a reenacted boxing match; many went to see a strong man in revealing tights.[34]

Small-Time Audiences

Lively audiences and rowdiness seem more prevalent in small-time compared to big-time vaudeville. In urban areas, small-time theaters were located in commercial streets fringing working-class neighborhoods. Reformers described these audiences in disapproving terms. A 1913 report on Cleveland movie theaters lumped cheap vaudeville with burlesque and stated "one sees hundreds of young men and boys at these performances and sees the frenzied manner in which they indicate their approval of the vulgar." It described an audience at cheap vaudeville responding to a dancer: "the ladies in the audience hid their faces ... older men turned their heads while the young men and boys stamped their feet, clapped their hands, many of them rising out of their seats, waving their hats, at the same time shouting vulgar suggestions to the performer." But the reference to "ladies in the audience" suggests a bill with appeal to more than rowdy young men.[35]

In small towns vaudeville shows had a wider range of patrons, but still many stories verify their liveliness. Small-time was the training ground for vaudeville performers. This was more so the case in small-town circuits in the Midwest, South, and West. Some small towns had reputations for their audiences. When vaudevillians had a difficult audience they would call it another Youngstown, Ohio, where the audience of immigrant steelworkers knew little English and did not understand the comedy. In Grand Rapids, people in the boxes put their feet up on the rail, in the front row on the orchestra rail, "and always laughed in the wrong places." In the South, audiences threw "sticks, bricks, spitballs, cigar butts, peach pits and chewed out stalks of sugar cane." Sometimes western audiences would retaliate against performers outside the theater. A cowboy threatened to kill Groucho Marx for having pointed his finger at the cowboy's sister.[36]

In 1893 a singing act, the Cherry Sisters, was so bad that the Cedar Rapids, Iowa audience turned their performance into a laughingstock, without the naive girls realizing it. People in the audience began blowing horns left over in the gallery from a political rally. Others hooted, whistled, and stomped their feet. When the girls, thinking it was an ovation, began their act again, the audience quieted to see what would happen. This led to another outburst of noise, and another as the audience toyed with and made fun of the performers. Nevertheless they toured Iowa's small towns. The bill announcing them in Marshalltown read "Bad Eggs, Black Powder, and Ten-gauge Guns Barred."[37]

Male college students had a reputation for rowdiness. Harvard students would arrive in hundreds and really "whoop it up." When Mae West performed in New Haven, Yale students purchased a block of seats down front but left them empty until her turn. Then they marched in, singing "Boola Boola." When she was canceled due to the boisterousness, the students wrecked the theater. Student crowds from the University of Michigan, Purdue, Notre Dame, Indiana, and Ohio State, in small-town Midwestern theaters often threw things at performers they disliked and harassed the female troupers as they left the theater. In one case the Ann Arbor fire department used hoses to disperse several hundred students from the stage door. Even in minor ways their antics disrupted performances. They brought alarms clocks set to go off during a performance.[38] The behavior of these privileged young men belied the image of rowdiness as a working-class trait.

The active audience, then, never entirely disappeared. It remained always a possibility if not a realization, even a necessity of the entertainer's success and the entrepreneur's profit. Rowdiness always survived on the margins. This is perhaps part of a generalization: that hegemony is in some ways always strongest in the center, in the spotlight, but never complete and always weakest at the margins and in the shadows. This difference again emphasizes the need to avoid blanket statements about entertainment forms and to differentiate times, places, and audiences even for the same entertainment.

"Legitimate" and "Illegitimate" Theater around the Turn of the Century

While decorum was well established as the norm in legitimate theaters by the last quarter of the century, complaints about audience behavior indicate that it was not always honored. The nature of the complaints had changed, however. Drama theater had subdivided along class lines, and criticism was directed mostly at the affluent audiences of legitimate theater for their inattention and lack of taste. At the same time, working-class audiences at popular and ethnic theaters were rambunctious and voluble, though not violent as before. Writers no longer disapproved of these audiences, but rather described them largely in sympathetic terms. This chapter will explore the peculiar inversions of cultural and class hierarchies in the discourse on legitimate theater audiences, and examine the continuing participative traditions among working-class audiences of popular theaters.

Around the turn of the century, aesthetic guardians replaced moral guardians as the critics of theater. Sacrilege against "Art," not against God, was the sin. Dramatic criticisms typically advocated high culture against the commercialism of theater. They described American drama theater at the turn of the century as commercially successful but artistically bankrupt: plays were second rate, acting was histrionic, and independent producers devoted to art had been driven out by the Theater Syndicate.[1]

These criticisms formed the core of the "New Theater" movement, the goals of which were to rescue drama from commercialism and to foster in its audiences an appreciation for high art. The Drama League was founded in 1910 to educate middle-class American audiences about good drama, by helping them to select plays. Dramatic Arts became a legitimate subject of college curriculum. The community theater movement established stock companies all over the country, including The Provincetown Players, who produced Eugene O'Neill's first plays, and the Washington Square Players, who provided a home for many great playwrights, actors, and directors.[2]

The term "legitimate" was recruited into the discourse on the relationship of theater to art and to mass culture. Some used it merely to distinguish drama from other stage entertainments. Critics of commercialism reserved the term for plays of artistic merit. Actor Norman Hapgood said in 1899 that classic drama was called legitimate in theatrical circles "to distinguish it from contemporary plays" that were considered of little artistic merit. Actor Joseph Jefferson in 1889 offered a similar definition, "a term used to distinguish theaters offering tragedy and comedy from those trafficking in spectacle, opera, pantomime, etc." Implicit in all usages of "legitimate" was a distinction of higher-class theater from popular theater and entertainments.[3]

The "legitimate" audience was divided between the affluent and fashionable on the one hand and the cultured and educated on the other, or what sociologist Pierre Bourdieu distinguished as those with high economic capital and those with high cultural capital. The cultivated took to their pens to criticize the shallowness of the fashionable audience and by contrast to praise the sincerity of the lower-income gallery desirous of cultivation.

The Fashionable Female Audience

Advocates of drama as art had an image problem. Drama theater by this time was considered commercial entertainment by cultural elites, and feminine entertainment at that. The growth of the numbers of women in the audience coincided with the decline of stock companies and the rise of sensation melodrama offered by combination companies under the control of the Theater Syndicate. Those who wanted to claim drama as an art had to reform theater, to educate the audience, and to dissociate it from the "flighty female" audience. The discourse had two streams, one that focused specifically on women, and one that criticized the vacuity of the fashionable orchestra audience generally, including the "men dragged there by their wives."

The criticism of female audiences was strikingly misogynist. In 1910, drama critic Walter Prichard Eaton complained, in *Woman's Home Companion,* of the "bad influence of American women on the drama," as managers sought to satisfy a woman's taste for romantic melodrama, which the woman "judges and enjoys according as it tells a pretty story with sufficient 'love interest' and preferably a happy ending." Women looked on drama as "something to be taken passively, a cross between massage and a cup of tea."[4] Eaton went on with example after example of inanities women had been heard to say in theaters.

Drama critic Clayton Hamilton found women wanting as supporters of dramatic art. In "The Psychology of Theatre Audiences," he applied Gustave Le Bon's theory of mob psychology to analyze the theater audience, claiming that, driven by passion rather than intellect, "women in the boxes and orchestra ... go less to see than be seen." He argued that, "since women are by nature inattentive, the femininity of the modern theatre audience forces the dramatist to employ the elementary technical tricks of repetition and parallelism, in order to keep his play clear."[5]

Middle-class women in galleries of legitimate drama were described very unfavorably in contrast to vaudeville and melodrama galleries of office boys. The boys were "trained and hardened critics," and the first to detect "the catchy lilt in a popular air ... the good points in a one-act sketch, the limberness in a comedian's legs." The women were "the last to apprehend a good point," laugh and applaud at the wrong places, "almost pathetic" to watch at high-brow drama such as Ibsen, they are "so mystified, so puzzled."[6]

Worst of all was, according to many, the matinee girl, for whom the "love interest" was not the character of the play but the star, the matinee idol. The matinee idol was the result of the combination of melodrama, star system, and the matinee itself. Such idols were promoted with great success by impresario Charles Frohman from 1885 to 1914, using publicity in the same way that Hollywood would in the 1930s. They wrote articles such as "Why I Like Women Who Wear Hats" for the consumption of their following.[7] Promoters stocked stores surrounding the theaters with pictures of the stars, and "hero books" bound in leather for fans to record their thoughts about the leading man.[8] Numerous articles, fiction stories, even plays and songs were written about the matinee girl.[9] These teenagers were the predecessors of movie and rock 'n' roll fans, pioneers in a privileged youth market of the new consumer culture of the late nineteenth century. Magazines characterized these girls as affluent teenagers from the suburbs who attended matinee every Saturday in noisy pairs or threes. Despite their "experience" with theater, they had little understanding of or interest in drama. Their only criterion was that a play has a "love interest." After the play, giggling girls waited at the stage door or at receptions to meet the leading man.[10]

Family magazines argued that these adolescent girls harmed themselves as well as the theater. In 1899 the *Ladies' Home Journal* ran a series of articles on theater to enlighten young girls and protect them from their own fascination.[11] Again four years later, the magazine's editor, Edward Bok, lectured parents about allowing their daughters of twelve to sixteen to attend risqué matinees weekly where they "drink in remarks and conversations to which no young girl in her teens should listen."[12] *Munsey's* accused some matinee idols of taking advantage of these girls by responding to fan mail with love letters "written by the dozen."[13] A Milwaukee doctor went so far as to claim that romantic matinees may cause "nervous prostration" in young women.[14]

Blaming women for theater's shortcomings was part of a larger discourse equating mass culture with the feminine and art with the masculine. Women were widely associated with consumption of mass culture. Affluent women were particularly to blame; they had the opportunity of receiving education, yet exhibited middle-brow tastes. According to these criticisms, they read pulp novels and supported the less expensive magazines that had displaced *Harper's, Atlantic* and the like. Mass culture was described in pejorative feminine terms.[15] Art critics at the turn of the century argued that women made inferior artists. They spoke of women as a threat to "Art," claiming their consumer demand supported mass culture. Middle-class women who had once been identified as a civilizing influence amid rowdy male audiences were now characterized as undermining that civilization.

Other criticism complained about the fashionable audience generally, including the men, as a class, and blamed them for the state of drama. The inattentive and impolite upper class, the jaded first-nighter, the tired businessman were contrasted to the devoted gallery. One theme was the ignorance of the audience in identifying good acting. Repeating a criticism made in earlier decades, theater critics complained that the affluent audiences who provided the bulk of legitimate theater income with their regular purchases of orchestra seats never bothered themselves to learn anything about drama or acting, and applauded anything. They were called dunces, indiscriminate, and a mindless mob. In 1903, *Current Literature* commented on wild applause at a performance of Eleanor Duse, saying that it was "hardly probable that over one-half of one percent of the audience at the Victoria had the mental grasp that would justify them in going into paroxysms of joy... How many of these same enthusiasts would have talked about Duse's genius if she had come to some minor theater unheralded?"[16]

The affluent Broadway theatergoers in the orchestra were often upbraided for their impoliteness both to the actors and others in the audience. The joke of the period was, "When's a gentlemen not a gentlemen? When he is at the theatre." *Theatre Magazine* wrote, "a similar statement may be made as to the conduct of supposedly well-bred women when attending theatrical performance and perhaps with more far-reaching truth." The article cited several incidents where actors, even "the charming and irreproachable" actress Margaret Anglin and the highly regarded Richard Mansfield, interrupted performances because talking in the house so distracted them.[17]

Many criticisms were rooted in the fact that the fashionable went as a Saturday night ritual that had little to do with good drama. The same couples whose teenage daughters went to the matinee, themselves had a standing date with their friends at the theater every week. The central character in this orchestra audience was the "tired businessman" who wanted a play that would make him laugh, nothing too heavy or thoughtful. A 1910 *Munsey's* article said audiences "want above all to forget the strain of the busy day ... to be entertained rather than edified." They were criticized for seeking relaxing entertainment instead of supporting dramatic arts. Their manners were upsetting as a reflection of the lightness with which they consumed plays. Their standing Saturday night date meant they were not selective about the plays they attended and knew little about them even after they went, since they gave it little attention while there. Many writers expressed irritation at the inconsiderate women of these couples who talked loudly and blocked the view of the stage with their large hats, fashionable at the time.[18] Even playwright Rachel Crothers, while defending theater against the criticism that commercialism had ruined it, considered "the largest and the most powerful and important class" in the audience to be those who went for amusement and went regularly, for whom "it is the easiest way of getting through an evening without responsibility: and the theater is always there – waiting for them." Her words have the same sarcastic ring of other critics toward this affluent urban orchestra crowd, who could go to the theater whenever they pleased.[19]

By the late 1910s, a lighter vein of commentary on audiences began to appear. Caricaturist Harriet Fish published several cartoons in *Vanity Fair* from 1914 to 1920 that parodied upper-class theatergoers. The caption of one described the fashionable people "who came an act late, left an act early, slept during the second act, and talked in between times."[20] A *Theater Magazine* article parodied "The shop girl," "the flapper," "Miss Get-rich-quick," "the housewife," "the tired business man," "the high brow." Other articles joked about people going to the theater to clear their throats, and those who talked incessantly yet complained of others who did the same. *Theater Magazine* published several cartoons in 1924–25 that caricatured the orchestra and boxes doing many things, but not attending to the play.[21]

The attacks on women and the complaints about the orchestra audience have in common their focus on class. Affluent men as well as women were criticized for their lack of cultural appreciation. Writers especially targeted women as the embodiment of the lack of cultivation they disliked among the wealthy. On the other hand, they often had kind words and praise for the less affluent women in the gallery, and nostalgia for the lower-class boys of bygone galleries. The praise extended beyond the gallery to working-class theaters as well. Uneducated working-class men and women were evaluated not in terms of their aesthetics or support of high culture, but for their "natural," sincere responses to performances.

Good Gallery Gods

In contrast to the derisive attitude toward those in the orchestra and to past complaints about nineteenth-century gallery behavior, the early twentieth-century gallery of legitimate theater was hailed as the savior of drama. The gallery had changed. In the second half of the nineteenth century, teen-age boys had replaced the prostitutes, laborers, and blacks of the Jacksonian gallery. But the boys soon left increasingly "legitimate" theaters for cheaper admissions to vaudeville and then movie theaters. By 1910 the boys were replaced by gallery goddesses and earnest devotees of drama unable to afford orchestra seats.[22] The new galleryites were middle-class and mostly women.[23] They were canonized as the true lovers of drama, and in the process the history of the earlier gallery also took on a rosier hue.

Theaters had long tried to restrain annoying gallery boys. In one of the last such efforts, the *Philadelphia Inquirer* mounted a successful campaign in 1902 to get theater managers of the city to suppress gallery antics. The newspaper cited the gallery for whistling, howling, yelling, stamping feet, jeering actors, and insulting the "well-dressed people in the boxes and orchestra circle." The article claimed galleryites made coarse remarks at ladies in low-cut gowns and hooted "old geezer" at gentlemen. Stage kisses were made ridiculous by smacking of lips, and tragic moments by mock crying. The *Inquirer* asserted that "the higher-priced places of amusement are ones which suffer most from the gallery god nuisance... Managers of the more reasonable theaters claim that the other playhouses have only themselves to blame ... the gallery is encouraged to whistle all the popular airs, and that the leaders of the orchestras and the prima donnas themselves aid and abet the crowd." The *Inquirer* was delighted to report their article had stimulated each house to station police in their galleries and to quickly apprehend anyone who persisted after a warning.[24]

But rarely was the *new* middle-class gallery criticized for disturbing the performance. Among the supporters of the gallery was Mrs. Richard Mansfield, wife of the famous actor and theater reformer at the turn of the century. In 1904 she characterized the gallery as "the true appreciative audience – the girls' club, the school teachers, the men and women who love the drama ... where the real applause comes from ... the gallery stand and applaud and applaud, while the people in the orchestra were hunting for their wraps and hurrying out for carriages."[25] Theater critic Arthur Pollock complimented the devoted galleryites for their "mental curiosity," for being "responsive, sincere, and discerning." The galleryite chose the play carefully, arrived on time, and "does not treat the theatre as a place to entertain his friends." This description was juxtaposed against that of the orchestra audience, the "stage-door Johnny, the bald-headed row, the tired business man, who don't know the name of the play or even who wrote Hamlet," and who were jaded, bored, and blasé.[26]

In response to managers' concerns about empty gallery seats (abandoned for the movies) and to plans to eliminate the gallery in constructing new theaters, articles in *Theater Magazine* in 1919 and 1920 credited the gallery's enthusiasm for a play's success. Written in the first person, the 1919 article proclaimed,

It is we who applaud when the show is good and hiss when it ought to be taken off the boards. The box-office man knows us and so do the actors. Our fifty-cent pieces are the real money. Only on rare occasion is there "paper" in the gallery. The leading lady knows where her salary is coming from – that's why she always looks up when she sings. And besides – aren't we the chaps who whistle the "hit" after the show? Many a person downstairs would like to join us, but that's not dignified, you know.

He concluded that the elimination of the gallery from new theaters "is a mistake." The 1920 article argued that "The balcony's infectious enthusiasm is vital to a musical show" and that a full balcony ensured profits.[27] Theater manager Sargent Aborn called the gallery "the backbone of the theater" and proposed reductions in prices of gallery tickets to bring them back from the movies. Two letters by galleryites to the drama editor of the *New York Times* asserted their superior dramatic appreciation and confirmed the impact of rising ticket prices.[28]

About the same time, the gallery boys were memorialized, while their annoying behavior was forgotten or excused. A *Herald Tribune* article entitled "Bringing Back the Gods to the Top Gallery" was prompted by a Broadway theater's experiment in reducing gallery prices to fifty cents. Drama critic Howard Barnes reminisced about the "small boys, street cleaners, rag-pickers, plug-uglies and ragamuffins" of the gallery, which Broadway producers and actors of the turn of the century considered essential to the success of a play. Barnes considered them benign, there to be amused rather than to cause trouble, cheering the heroine and hissing the villain.[29] By the late 1920s, the nostalgia was sufficiently widespread that some enterprising entrepreneurs opened two theaters in Hoboken to recreate the past. They revived plays such as *Black Crook* and *After Dark*. Audiences were encouraged to engage in the old-fashioned hissing of villains and the cheering of heroes and heroines. According to the *New York World,* "even highbrows, sickened by their own doctrines are to be found in hordes in Hoboken." The *New York Evening Post* said, "audiences may be turning away from the over-sophistication of the Broadway stage ... the unconscious attitude of the Hoboken audience is not one of scorn, but of wistfulness and regret for old memories."[30]

Progressive reformers also singled out working-class audiences for praise.[31] They described working-class people as appreciative, again in contrast to the bored sophisticates in the orchestras of legitimate theaters. About the same time that critics were chastising flighty matinee girls, social reformer Elizabeth McCracken, in the *Atlantic,* praised the working-class girls "from the city tenements" who went to plays as often as they could afford a gallery ticket. She claimed they were less prone to idol worship and went to the theater "for the play." Jane Addams, the settlement house pioneer, and Mrs. Mansfield, wife of the famous actor, both remarked on the enthusiasm of working-class children for Shakespeare and Moliere plays put on for their benefit. Addams wrote, "every settlement in which dramatics have been systematically fostered can also testify to a surprisingly quick response to this form of art on the part of young people ... children whose tastes have supposedly been debased by constant vaudeville, are pathetically eager to come again and again."[32]

Others credited working-class adults as well. The *New York Times* contrasted the rudeness of ladies and gentlemen who talked during the performance to the audiences at popularly priced theaters, whom they described as "seldom ill-behaved." Women's advocate Annie MacLean found theater a popular pastime for native-born and Jewish immigrant working women in New York and New Jersey. Founded on the same sentiments, the People's Institute of New York began a program in cooperation with theater managers of providing half-price tickets on weeknights to plays selected by the Institute for their superior quality. The tickets were distributed through settlement houses, YMCAs, unions, schools, and libraries. The program was based on the same premise that working people were capable and desirous of appreciating "the best dramatic, musical and art events."[33] While Progressive reformers hoped to help the lower classes and aesthetic critics hoped to elevate drama to art, both praised the lower-class audiences' interest in and appreciation of drama theater.

"Mellowdrammer" Audiences

Among the favorite subjects of writers who wrote sympathetically about the working class were ethnic theaters supported by non-

English-speaking immigrants. Reformers who worked among the immigrants and writers who told picaresque stories about the "other half" crafted images that mixed empathy with condescension.

Immigrants brought to America their traditions of lively, participative audience practices reminiscent of Jacksonian audiences, but without such violence. The Lower East Side of New York had been the home of working-class theater since the 1830s, when the Bowery Theater first began to cater to this market. From that time the Bowery was known for its rough, working-class entertainment, including melodrama, minstrelsy, concert saloons, and variety. First Germans and Irish and later Italians and Jews shared these theaters. Common to all was an earthy, peasant/working-class amusement culture. One contemporary observer described the steamy and crowded Bowery Theater in the 1870s, filled with ragged newsboys, men in their shirt-sleeves, mothers with suckling infants, sailors and their "black-eyed Susans," milliners and their "jealous-eyed lovers," "roughs, 'prentice boys and pale German tailors," "emaciated German and Italian barbers."[34]

The audience had not much changed in 1911 when playwright and critic Channing Pollock described the melodrama houses scattered across the ethnic neighborhoods of Manhattan. Pollock did not distinguish the ethnicity of the audiences, describing one as much like the other. The audiences at the Bowery Theater, now renamed the Thalia, were composed principally of peddlers, longshoremen, sweatshop girls, and small boys, with a predominance of Jews.

Reserve is not characteristic of these gatherings. They hiss steamily at what they are pleased to consider evil and applaud with equal heartiness that which seems good to them ... favoring the unfortunate under any circumstances and finding vent in bitter hatred of the prosperous. They are the natural enemies of the police, and by the same token, friends to the cracksman or the convict who expresses a particle of decency.[35]

Around the turn of the century many ethnic groups established their own native-language theaters in low-income immigrant ghettoes of the largest cities. The two most well-known are the Yiddish theater and the Italian theater, which arose in a few cities with large immigrant populations. Many other ethnic groups also established theaters, but these were seldom commercial and were very few in number.[36] Across the multitude of European ethnic theaters can be found

similarities of audience behavior that suggest common roots in peasant traditions and their transition to urban, working-class life.[37] The
Yiddish and Italian cases illustrate some of the similarities.

Italian Theater

Italian theater arrived in New York in the 1880s, peaked in the
1930s, and rapidly disappeared in the late 1940s. There were drama,
variety, and marionette theaters. Drama critic John Corbin described
the audience of the Teatro Italiano of the Lower East Side of New York
City as "for the most part men ... bootblacks and banana venders,
East-Side barbers and ex-members of Colonel Waring's Street
Cleaning Brigade ... yet there was always a sprinkling of women and
no audience I ever saw was without a baby or two... They would speak
to you on the slightest pretext, or none, and would relate all that was
happening on stage." They carried on a dialog with the play, discussed
the actions among themselves, and made a row in the more exciting
moments.[38]

One night, anticipating an especially bad performance at the Maiori
Theater in the Bowery, the audience hissed as the curtain rose to
warn the actors to perform better. Between acts the playwright came
before the curtain and disavowed any association with the poor performance. The head of the troupe came out to defend his troupe. The
audience threw insults, popcorn, hats, apple cores, and bottles at the
actor. By the second act half the audience, especially the women and
babies, were asleep, despite the clamor.[39]

A favorite performer in Italian variety theater was the mimic
Eduardo Migliaccio. Whole families, from grandmother to baby,
attended variety. They greeted Migliaccio with wild applause, hushed
as he impersonated familiar Italian characters, and again applauded
wildly when he was done. "Farfariello" was their favorite Migliaccio
impersonation, representing in humorous but sympathetic ways the
plight of the immigrant trying to become American. Migliaccio also
created several characters reminding immigrants of their home villages. The impersonations expressed the double ties of the Italian
immigrant to the past and present, to Italy and America.[40]

The Italian theater bill of the 1880s was reminiscent of the early
American theater, including a prologue, play or opera, *entre-acte* performances, and afterpiece. The evening concluded with a community
dance, much as it did in smaller towns after a minstrel show in the
1870s. Opera and drama were presented in Tuscan dialect, which

most Italians understood, but the audience was composed of those from many regions. It was a family audience, including husband, wife, and children, attending on Sundays.[41]

The loyalty of Sicilian working-class men was to marionette theater, a tradition with roots in the middle ages, when Normans ruled Sicily. The first such theater opened in Boston about 1888; two opened in Brooklyn in 1889 and 1900. These were small theaters, seating about one hundred and charging five cents admission.[42] The puppets were two to four feet tall. The stories were epic tales with plenty of action and fighting, appealing to men and boys, and presented in nightly installments that went on for months. Italian Renaissance epic poet Torquato Tasso's *Jerusalem Delivered* ran for six months, seven nights a week, to which its working-class/peasant audience came loyally night after night. *Orlando Furioso,* another epic about the fight against the Saracens in the age of Charlemagne, could last for two to five years. One puppeteer in 1908 claimed his audience would listen to nothing else.[43]

Curtain time was when sufficient numbers of spectators had arrived. The audiences were always vocal and excited, especially during the battle scenes. They followed the story closely, coming to the theater every night religiously. They knew the story well and did not hesitate to correct a performance. When a Brooklyn marionette company skipped a few pages the audience was instantly in an uproar. But by 1908 Italians were beginning to abandon the marionettes for the nickelodeon just down the block. By the 1930s only one theater on Mulberry Street remained having a few loyal followers who attended the epics every night.[44]

Yiddish Theater

Yiddish theater in the United States flourished about the same time as Italian theater, part of the same wave of immigration from eastern and southern Europe from the 1880s to 1910s. The first Yiddish theater opened in New York in 1882 and it reached its peak around the turn of the century. But the strict immigration laws of the 1920s stopped the flow of unassimilated Yiddish speakers upon which the theater was dependent. Yiddish theater was an important part of New York's Lower East Side, where some 300,000 Yiddish Jews were crowded into tenements purchased some two million tickets annually at the turn of the century. There were Yiddish theaters in some other cities, and the New York companies travelled to other Yiddish communities. But the Lower East Side was the source. Progressive journalist Hutchins Hapgood described the audience at the turn of the century as "poor workingmen and women with their babies of all ages." More prosperous, assimilated German Jews shunned it.[45] Tickets ranged from twenty-five cents to a dollar. One contemporary claimed that "many a poor Jew, man or girl, who makes no more than $10 a week in the sweatshop, will spend $5 of it on the theater, which is practically the only amusement of the ghetto Jew. He has not the loafing and sporting instincts of the poor Christian, and spends his money for the theatre rather than for drink." Social reformer Annie MacLean found in 1910 that a third of Jewish working girls, earning four or five dollars a week, gave theater as their favorite amusement.[46] The theater was so popular that unions, burial societies, political parties, and clubs of immigrants rented it on week nights for fund raising. The lower-salaried actors would present a play with a moral suited to the organization. Every member was expected to buy tickets and bring their family.[47]

The importance of theater to these immigrants was expressed in their fierce loyalty to their chosen actor, referring to themselves as *patriotten* of the actor. They idolized the actor even in the streets. When walking down Second Avenue a star like Jakob Adler might be preceded by *patriotten* saying "this is the great Adler," holding his coat and lighting his cigar. At the funeral procession of Sigmund Mogulesko, a popular comic, some thirty thousand people lined the street, even though he was unknown on Broadway.[48]

The Yiddish audience, like the Italian, was working class, voluble, sociable, and sometimes demanding. Writer and critic Carl Van Vecten described them as an avid, captious, ill-mannered pack whose last-minute rush for seats constituted "figurative biting, scratching, rough handling ... and hard words." Once seated they were unruly, ate peanuts and apples, and opened soda bottles. Actress Bessie Thomashevsky likened the turn-of-the-century Yiddish theater to a noisy beer hall. People commented to each other about every event on stage. A reader of a Yiddish newspaper complained, "Audiences applaud at the wrong places, whereupon someone cries out, 'Order!,' and then a second person yells, 'Order!' to the first one, and a third 'Order!' to the second."[49]

If they were displeased with the performance, they made their feelings known. Despite the outspoken habits of the audience, a star could turn them from hisses to hoorays with the right treatment. In 1891, when Jacob Adler starred in a play, *Siberia,* it was too serious and unfamiliar for the audience, who laughed at the serious scenes. Adler came before the curtain after the second act and chastised the audience for not appreciating "such a masterpiece." The audience behaved themselves thereafter, weeping and laughing in the right places and applauding heartily at the end.[50]

Most of all, the theater was a social center. The Lower East Side provided little public space other than the streets. Apartments were crowded and cramped. Theaters were among the few places where people could gather at little cost; they were commercial substitutes for the piazzas and other places in European villages and towns, where these immigrants had been accustomed to gather and talk. According to Hutchins Hapgood, "It is not only to see the play that the poor Jew goes to the theatre. It is to see his friends and the actors... Conversation during the play is received with strenuous hisses, but the falling of the curtain is the signal for groups of friends to get together and gossip about the play or the affair of the week." They moved about the aisles and greeted each other. The Yiddish newspaper editor, Abraham Cahan, said at intermissions, "the audience reminded one of a crowd at a picnic."[51]

Despite their social predilections, the audience paid close attention to the plays, which expressed their own ghetto experiences. *The Outlook* described one of the fundraising performances in 1905 for the benefit of the "Knee-pants Union." The theater was packed. Small children and women with infants were everywhere. They watched with rapt attention and cried deeply. Children joined in hissing the villain, even at the curtain call. They made little distinction between the character and the actor, to such a degree that actors did not wish to play the villain, fearing it would make them unpopular. When forced to play a villain, Boris Thomashevsky, the star of his own theater and husband of Bessie, diverged from the script and began a speech defending the Jews – to the dismay of the other actors, but the delight of the audience.[52] Sometimes a person became so absorbed in the melodrama, that he or she forsook the boundary between acting and reality and interjected into events onstage. One spectator warned a Yiddish King Lear to "Leave those rotten children of yours and come home with me. My wife is a good cook, she'll fix you up." In another incident, Dina Feinman, wife of Jacob Adler, was playing an abused wife whose husband demanded she pull off his boots. A woman in the audience rose and shouted,

"Don't you do it Dina, don't you do it. You tell that bum where to get off." When a woman was being strangled by her husband in the play, the audience shouted in unison, "Enough, enough!" When the wife died a girl down front fainted.[53]

Italian and Yiddish immigrant audiences at the turn of the century behaved similarly to the working-class audiences of a century earlier. The use of the theater as a social center is reminiscent of early American theater. The camaraderie and socializing with friends described by witnesses at the turn of the century compare closely to that described at the turn of the previous century. The engagement with and interjection into events on-stage also parallel the past. Green'un stories from both periods could be interchanged without any loss of historical accuracy for either period. Likewise the pride of the audience in knowing what was to transpire in a play and policing its performance reflected elements of an earlier knowledgeable audience. On occasion they even exercised the old-fashioned audience sovereignty familiar to the Bowery b'hoys almost a century before and that had been suppressed in "legitimate" theaters, although their exercise of these rights was circumscribed by turn-of-the-century law and less violent than that of the Bowery b'hoys.

The distinctive difference between the early nineteenth-century and the turn-of-the-century immigrant audiences was gender and age. For the most part, the immigrant theaters attracted families, creating an audience with a wider range of ages, rather than a predominance of young men. Correspondingly, there was no drinking or prostitution and less violence.

The family mix also made the audience more representative of the working-class community, more like a public urban space, where all groups had their place. It constituted an autonomous, working-class public sphere, a place where the audience could formulate and rehearse a common understanding of their experience and a common identity. There is no evidence of direct collective action arising in or from these theaters. Instead their effect most likely was to cement community solidarity among these working-class immigrants in facing the world outside. But community building by ethnic theater soon was undercut by Americanization of younger generations. As they learned English, many alternatives opened up to them that were beyond the control of their parents. Their assimilation led to the demise of ethnic theater and community.[54]

On the Road: Ten-Twenty-Thirty

Such audience behavior was not unique to big cities or to immigrants. English-speaking audiences of melodrama across the nation exhibited behavior similar to these ethnic audiences. In small cities and towns throughout the nation, working-class audiences frequented ten-twenty-thirties, that is, theaters charging ten, twenty, or thirty cents admission around the turn of the century. These English-speaking working-class audiences continued the lively audience traditions that would soon transfer to the early movie nickelodeons.

After the Civil War every town in the nation sought to build a theater, even a simple one, as railroads, the spread of combination companies, and the organization of booking agencies created a ready supply of touring plays and performers to supplement minstrels, lecturers, and variety. The big stars and Broadway shows that played cities were only a few of the many touring companies. Small towns were served by regional low-priced drama companies that performed in "opera houses," frequently a second-floor meeting hall with a flat floor used for dances, political rallies, or stage shows, anything that came to town to draw a crowd and sell tickets. The "blood-and-thunder" circuit, as it was called, offered heavy-handed melodrama. Every small town got its one-night stand.[55]

Some troupes performed in tents, and followed the warm weather – the South in winter and the Midwest in summer. Tent drama grew from the Chautauqua movement that brought educational lectures and plays to small towns and rural areas during the summers. Association with Chautauqua broke down rural prejudices against theater. Others toured on showboats along the Ohio, Mississippi, and Missouri rivers. These melodrama circuits thrived in the 1880s and competed with vaudeville as the entertainment of the multitude, until movies and rising production costs killed them in the 1920s.[56]

The ten-twenty-thirty audience was typically made up of small tradesmen, mechanics and laborers, lower-salaried workers, and shop-girls. In the more expensive seats were upper-income tradesmen, young couples, and families. In the gallery were factory workers, blacks, foreigners, and newsboys. Unmarried workers often went to the theater together, as they had in the 1840s. According to testimony before the Senate in 1885, "It is customary for a little group of [workmen] to form something of coterie or an informal club and attend places of amusement together ... at least once a week."[57] The atmosphere was informal and friendly: people knew each other and the manager. Regional troupes would get to know the townspeople in the audiences. Porter Emerson Browne, writing to "legitimate" theatergoers in 1909, wished he could enjoy drama as much as these "mellowdrammer" audiences, unencumbered by taste or intellectual subtlety. Audiences often joined spontaneously in singing the overture; in other cases, managers would organize singalongs and other participatory activities to keep audiences away from more problematic behavior.[58]

They hissed the villain and sometimes the actors. A writer and performer in Worcester, Massachusetts at the turn of the century noted that "the dime audience" would be so vocal in their disapproval of a poor joke that new ones would have "to be written before the next afternoon."[59] In a village outside the small town of Gloversville, New York in the 1890s townsfolk demanded their money back when they were offered a variety show instead of a play. Some ambushed the troupe's wagon with rotten eggs on their ride back to their Gloversville hotel. On another occasion lumberjacks from the nearby Adirondack Mountains intimidated the ticket taker into a free admission.[60]

In a rare complaint about these audiences, actress Mary Shaw in 1911 criticized the puritanical orchestra audience and childish gallery in small towns. She described the orchestra as well behaved, although its disapprobation was chilling. She accused the gallery of making "ribald comments, imitations of kissing and so forth." She once stopped the play in protest over the gallery hi-jinx. "The whole audience knows not when to laugh and applaud. They even missed the incongruity of actor Tom Keene doing a somersault in the midst of a heart-wrenching scene of *East Lynne*." She related several anecdotes of the ignorance of these small-town audiences, usually involving some working-class stiff.[61]

Common also were the "green'un" stories of audience members so enraptured in the play as to take it for reality and try to intervene. In Trenton in 1904 the audience was so "wrought up" by a villain that it appeared some would leap onto the stage to tear him limb from limb. The manager went into the gallery to warn that if better order were not kept he would close the gallery for the season. In Portland, Maine in the 1890s, the wife confronted the mistress in a play. A woman in the audience yelled, "For God's sake, hit her with a dish!" The audience roared and so did the actors. Then the leading lady threw a dish as instructed, making it look like part of the play and the audience applauded even more. Improvisation and accidents were common in these unpolished productions. A common story of these small-town productions was the unexpected event, which distinguished them from the highly polished stage shows of the big cities. In Oswego, New York in the midst of a play someone in the balcony belched loudly. First there was silence, then a titter, then a roar of laughter, which then recurred throughout the play.[62]

It was common around the turn of the century and into the 1920s for commentators to excuse the melodramas of the ten-twenty-thirty as no worse than the poor quality and low morality of plays at "legitimate" theaters. Reformer Raymond Calkins bemoaned the decline of melodrama for the working classes, since although sensational, "often the play presents a very decided ethical lesson... Probably the influence of the higher grade theaters has made itself felt for the worse." Michael Davis similarly considered ethnic theaters of New York a valuable social contribution to their working-class ghettoes.[63] The discourse had changed. Working-class theaters and audiences, rather than being seen as dangerous and degraded, now were characterized as closer to human nature, to "natural man," an antidote to the over-civilized sophisticates.[64]

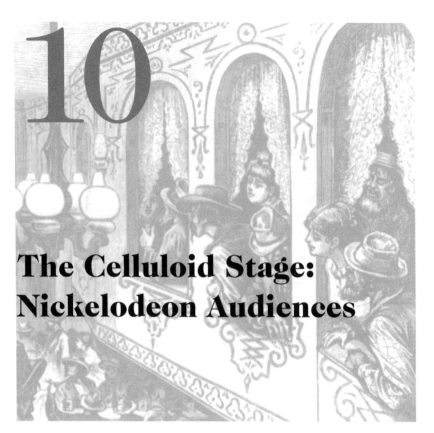

The Celluloid Stage: Nickelodeon Audiences

A decade after their first commercial exhibition, millions of people made movies a weekly habit. But who went to the movies in the early days and what was the character of the early movie theaters were matters of debate. Multiple images of movie theaters and audiences vied for acceptance. Reformers and *flaneurs* described movies as immigrant entertainment, yet small-town entrepreneurs promoted it as an entertainment for the middle class. The working-class nickelodeon was described on the one hand as community center and conqueror of the saloon, and on the other as a school for scandal teaching adolescent boys to steal and girls to be promiscuous. The latter image of endangered children represented a shift from the nineteenth-century concern about women's respectability to a twentieth-century fixation on children's welfare, and from the place to the performance as the cause of the problem. This would give rise in the 1920s to research on the effects on children and the beginnings of a mass communication research tradition. In this chapter I will explore how some characterizations were contradicted by the growth of middle-class attendance, but nevertheless continued to fuel popular worries about and eventual research interest in the effects of the media on children.

From Kinetoscope to Nickelodeon

Movies were first shown commercially as a technological novelty, *moving* pictures. It did not much matter *what* was filmed, just that it *moved*. People were intrigued by films of such simple things as smoke puffing from a chimney or waves breaking on a beach. The earliest commercial exhibition was by kinetoscope, a machine through which one person at a time could view the film. For a penny one could view a film lasting about a minute. By the end of 1895 kinetoscopes were operating in most major cities and even small towns like Portage, Wisconsin and Butte, Montana.[1] While kinetoscopes were installed in department stores, hotel lobbies, barrooms, drug stores, and so on, they became identified with penny arcades. The arcade patrons were primarily men and boys, who came to peep through the kinetoscope, often at sexually suggestive films. Movie historian Benjamin Hampton said patrons of arcades, parlors, and dime museums had an insatiable appetite for these movies and went from place to place in search of films they had not seen.[2]

But the kinetoscope fad was brief; by 1900 projector and screen displaced it.[3] Movie projection was commercially demonstrated first in April 1896 at Koster and Bial's Music Hall, the sporting vaudeville theater near Herald Square in New York. A newspaper lithograph shows an audience of men in tails and top hats engrossed in watching the novel demonstration. That same summer movies were included as a novelty in programs of vaudeville houses, amusement parks, traveling exhibitors and lecturers, legitimate theaters, phonograph and kinetoscope parlors, and church groups around the country.[4]

Soon, the Keith vaudeville circuit began to feature movies and other big-time houses followed suit. Movies became the featured "act" and created a boom in "refined" vaudeville between 1898–1900, during which time vaudeville provided the main exhibition outlet for movies. But this novelty also wore off, and until films with more sustaining interest than waves on beaches were produced, it could not hold an audience. By 1900 continuous vaudeville managers began to use the short films as "chasers" to clear the house before the next performance.[5]

Nickelodeons became the next dominant exhibition form. As early as 1895, a few storefronts were converted into motion picture show-rooms. They held from 200 to 500 people – the number often limited by theater licensing laws or building codes – who were seated on ordi-nary kitchen chairs not fastened to the floor. Enterprising arcade own-ers bought screens and projectors, and opened back rooms to audiences. *Variety* claimed it was "the natural outcome of the Penny Arcade." In 1905, nickelodeons in converted storefronts spread across the country so rapidly that *Billboard* called them the "jack-rabbits of public entertainment" and the *Moving Picture World* said they were "multiplying faster than guinea pigs." By 1910 there were reputedly over 10,000. Even smaller cities had several: Grand Rapids had fifteen in 1908, Youngstown twenty.[6]

Shows ran from morning to night. The films changed each day, encouraging daily attendance. The films were short, about fifteen min-utes, and movie projection was erratic. The picture flickered on the screen, and the projector was hand-operated. Nevertheless, the real-ism was a dramatic change from the sets of cheap melodrama.[7]

Nickelodeon Demographics

Film history tradition has characterized nickelodeon audiences as urban immigrant workers who found in the nickelodeon a place to socialize, and in the movies ideas to negotiate the transition between the old country and their new home. This image derived from a turn-of-the-century fascination with the Lower East Side of New York City by intellectuals who created vivid public images of every aspect of the lives of these poor immigrants, including their attraction to nick-elodeons.[8]

Ample evidence does indicate the presence of a substantial work-ing-class audience and of many nickelodeons in immigrant neighbor-hoods. Nickelodeon was one of very few entertainments affordable to working-class immigrants, and the silent films proved no barrier to their lack of English. In 1910, nickelodeons in Manhattan were concentrated in or on the periphery of tenement neighborhoods filled with immigrants.[9] Progressive reformer Annie MacLean in 1910 found that foreigners preferred nickelodeons over theaters in Johnstown, Pennsylvania. A study of the steel-mill town of Homestead, Pennsylvania, home of many Hungarian and Polish immigrants, describes their situation.

...five cents for a show consisting of songs, moving pictures, etc., which lasts fifteen minutes or so... Men on their way home from work stop for a few minutes to see something of life outside the alternation of mill and home; the shopper rests while she enjoys the music, poor though it be, and the children are always begging for five cents to go the nickelodeon.[10]

One handbook advised would-be entrepreneurs that the ideal location for a nickelodeon was "a densely populated workingmen's residence section, with a frontage on a much-traveled business street."[11]

The image of the urban nickelodeon as an immigrant refuge made it inappropriate for middle-class clientele. Lights, posters, and a barker with megaphone outside gave the theater a circus atmosphere and inside it was dark and odorous. The *Moving Picture World* editor said "any person of refinement looked around to see if [he were] likely to be recognized by anyone before entering the doors."[12] The movie exhibition industry and trade press strove to distinguish movie houses from this disreputable nickelodeon image. *The Moving Picture World* in 1909 cited the neighborhood Audubon Theater of the Washington Heights neighborhood of Manhattan as a family theater attracting children of the "better classes" and the Parkway Theater at 110th and Central Park West as having "high class character of the patrons ... quite a family aspect."[13]

Recent research looking beyond immigrant working-class neighborhoods finds other sites with other audiences. Movies were popular in cities with few immigrants and small working-class populations, such as Kansas City in 1912. In big cities there were a variety of opportunities for the middle class to go to movies, in better theaters, in vaudeville, or in amusement parks. Middle-class shoppers dropped into nickelodeons along Fourteenth Street and Sixth Avenue in New York – although they attended vaudeville or theater at night.[14]

That the audiences were middle class has been inferred from the geographic location of many nickelodeons on retail streets served by mass transportation within major cities. In Boston before 1910 several movie houses had opened in the central shopping district amid the major department stores, vaudeville houses, and legitimate theaters. The Stanley theater chain began in Philadelphia in the city center, next to the largest department stores. Similarly, Milwaukee movie houses were located near transit lines and shopping streets. In New York in 1908, many were located on main thoroughfares or along transit lines. Seven were located around Union Square, near the refined vaudeville houses of Proctor and Keith. Many others were located in other entertainment streets of the city such as 125th Street and along the Second and Third Avenue streetcar lines, near lower-middle- and middle-class ethnic neighborhoods whose residents were somewhat better off than the new immigrants of the Lower East Side. Many of the earlier movie houses in Chicago were located in business districts rather than working-class neighborhoods. The Chicago *Sunday Tribune* said in 1906 that "there is hardly a section of the city that is without this class of show house ... from three theaters in the heart of the shopping district on State Street ... to the more modest establishments well up North Clark Street." In 1913, thirteen movie houses were in Cincinnati's downtown business district, thirty-three in the downtown residential, probably working-class districts, and thirty-five in suburban residential, middle-class districts.[15]

English professor Edward Wagenknecht reminisced that middle-class children attended with glee. The storefronts he described were on commercial streets in the lower-middle-class neighborhood of Lawndale around 1907. It was a German-Irish neighborhood of Chicago with a growing number of Jewish families. The nickelodeons were rather humble places with posters pasted in the windows, no wider that an ordinary city lot, and with ceilings so low that the top of the picture sometimes was cut off. He mentions his favorite nickelodeon doing badly. The owner remedied the problem by opening a saloon in the front and continuing to show movies in the rear. The remaining movie patrons deserted at once and the theater closed. Apparently the saloon was not an acceptable solution, as it might have been in a working-class neighborhood.[16]

Small-town movie houses, which accounted for a substantial part of the audience, also contradicted this shoddy immigrant image.[17] Small-town patterns of moviegoing varied not only from those of big cities but also from region to region. In general, however, the small-town movie house was more dependent on the middle class, as it needed broad approval not only for sufficient attendance but also to prevent attacks from moral crusaders. Here, perhaps sooner and more consistently than in cities, we find efforts to ensure the respectable nature of the movie house. One producer touring the small towns of the Northwest reassured readers of *Moving Picture World* that exhibitors were respected members of their communities and that the best class of people attended. An exhibitor of Pennsylvania in 1910 noted that

small-town houses catered to the "best people" because they needed
everyone's patronage to survive.[18]

All of this indicates an early differentiation of houses: the small,
dark, and crowded neighborhood nickelodeon seating only a couple
hundred people; the larger houses on commercial blocks, some formerly vaudeville or drama theaters; and the spare but respectable
small-town movie theater. The larger houses in downtown shopping
districts were more profitable, but the neighborhood storefront dominated public imagery of movie houses.[19]

The equating of the nickelodeon with the immigrant working class
has been largely a matter of nomenclature. The term "nickelodeon" was
and continues to be used synonymously with a cheap movie house with
a low-income patronage, producing a tautological argument about
patronage. Other movie outlets received little description in the press,
making the nickelodeon by default *the* representative of movie exhibition in public discourse. Film history research continued this reduction
of exhibition to that of cheap houses full of immigrants, perhaps due to
the plentiful descriptions of nickelodeons and the obscurity of others.
Only recently have film historians begun to pay attention to the wide
variety of other exhibition venues with similarly varied audiences.

A more complete description includes movie houses ranging from
frugal to fancy and the clientele likewise. The frugal ones, in poorer
neighborhoods, were called nickelodeons; the fancier ones were called
theaters. Moviegoing included a variety of audiences distributed
across these venues: the middle class, who had not previously patronized stage entertainments because of religious beliefs; more prosperous working-class patrons of melodrama or vaudeville, who
abandoned stage entertainment for movies; and the urban working
class, who seldom spent anything on entertainment until the
movies.[20]

The debate about the class of movie audiences has left in the shadows the consideration of other groups. Blacks, Indians, Mexicans, and
Asians were segregated to galleries or excluded altogether.[21] Such
exclusion constituted a minimal measure of respectability for any
public place in this era. However, a few black-owned theaters offered
an alternative and advertised that blacks were free to sit anywhere.
According to the black weekly newspaper, the Indianapolis *Freeman*,
in 1909 there were 112 "colored theaters" of all types in the United
States, most of them outside major cities and being combination
vaudeville and movie houses. From the first, black-owned theaters in

Chicago's South Side and in the small city of Lexington, Kentucky combined live entertainment, particularly by black musicians, with movies. In both cities they advertised the "high-class" nature of their clientele, distinguishing them from the rougher patrons of black saloons and dance halls.[22] Women were an important part of the audiences, even in immigrant nickelodeons. Low costs and convenient location made the nickelodeons accessible to women workers and shoppers. Their informality meant mothers did not have to "dress up" to attend them. A trade journal in 1907 attributed the growth of nickelodeon to women and children. A photograph of an audience in a Troy, New York movie house shows mostly women and children. Several sources noted baby carriages lining the sidewalk or cluttering the entrances to movie houses. Social reformer Mary Heaton Vorse commented, "Prayers finished, you may see a mother sorting out her own babies and moving on serenely to the picture show down the road" after evening church services.[23]

As with theater sixty years earlier, the image of mother and child in attendance would help to certify the safety and propriety of the nickelodeon.[24] Some exhibitors and producers fostered this image by encouraging women to bring the children. Theaters in Lewiston, Maine in 1907 offered teddy-bear souvenirs, checked baby carriages, and encouraged parents to send their children unattended. Some mothers apparently agreed and let their boys go unattended.[25]

A large percentage of the regular audience were children. Estimates of children in the audience ranged from 20 percent in Detroit and Madison, Wisconsin to two-thirds in Pittsburgh and Portland, Oregon. Reports from New York and Cleveland complained that large numbers of these children were unescorted by adults. The thought of unchaperoned teenage girls in particular raised fears of sexual promiscuity. A Chicago *Tribune* reporter in 1907 observed a downtown nickelodeon at six P.M. "composed largely of girls from the big department stores who came in with bundles under their arms." The reporter's concern was that they made "undesirable acquaintances [men] of mature age."[26]

Young single immigrant working women enjoyed the freedom of going to the nickelodeon on their own. An Italian garment worker from New York's Lower East Side reminisced:

The one place I was allowed to go by myself was the movies. I went for fun. My parents wouldn't let me go anywhere else ... I used to enjoy going to the movies two or three times a week. But I would always be home by 9 o'clock.

An Italian girl met her boyfriend on the sly at the movies in the afternoon.[27]

Recreational surveys by reformers found that location and hours made great differences in audience profiles. Men predominated in downtown houses while women and children were more common in neighborhood houses, especially on Saturday and Sunday afternoons. A survey in Cincinnati characterized the daytime audience as being predominantly men, with an occasional woman, sometimes with children, and a few truant boys and girls; a noon audience was composed of young people from stores and factories and a downtown high school. In evenings, downtown theaters were "evenly mixed", while the residential theaters were attended by mostly women and children. A study of Madison in 1915 reported a similar pattern. Whether movies were a male or female, children or adult pastime, depended on the time and place.[28]

A Mass Medium

Some film historians have claimed that immigrant working-class moviegoers represented a new market for commercial entertainment.[29] Yet, through the late nineteenth century and into the movie era, immigrants supported their own ethnic theaters. As noted in the previous chapter, Lower East Side Jews were avid supporters of Yiddish theater and Sicilians were supporters of puppet shows. Descriptions of their behavior are interchangable with those of ethnic movie audiences. The movies benefited from the entertainment habits nurtured by the stage: avid theatergoers became avid moviegoers.[30]

What distinguished movies from previous stage entertainments was *not* the creation of a new market of immigrants or working-class people. Rather it was the *depth* of saturation of these markets that was new. Actual data on saturation rates do not exist. But commentary and overall attendance suggest that higher proportions of all groups must have been attending movies to achieve such high numbers of admissions and receipts. Clearly more people, especially children, went regularly to nickelodeons than ever went to previous stage entertainments.[31] Places of exhibition were numerous and admission cheap, even compared to cheap vaudeville, so that accessibility was increased dramatically for those with low incomes and those living in remote places.

Nickelodeons blanketed the country far more thoroughly than theater or vaudeville. This, despite the fact that, as we have seen, theater had penetrated into some rather remote places, and vaudeville circuits covered almost every small city. Some vaudevillians claimed that at the turn of the century there were over a thousand vaudeville houses in the United States – the vast majority small-time with ten-cent admission – where a performer could play for years without repeating a house. There were probably not more than that number of theaters for drama, including the many small-town houses that served whatever use was requested in a given week, whether drama, vaudeville, or some local club's gala. By contrast, it was estimated that there were about ten times that number of nickelodeons around 1910. Michael Davis' thorough survey of Manhattan in 1910 enumerated 201 movie houses and 74 theaters for drama, vaudeville, and burlesque. In 1912, Milwaukee had 50 movie houses and 12 stage theaters.[32]

Moreover, movie houses presented more showings than even continuous vaudeville. Theater was seasonal, and touring companies and vaudeville acts were intermittent entertainments for most of the nation, while even in small towns movie houses operated daily and year-round. There was therefore an even greater difference in seating capacity between movie houses and live entertainment than the number of theaters would indicate. Theater historian Alfred Bernheim claimed that the movie audience in 1925 was fifty-six times the weekly seating capacity of all legitimate drama theaters in 1900.[33]

Many went. The *Independent* claimed in 1908 that the movies attracted "thousands who never go to the theater, and particularly [were] appealing to the children." Surveys in the prewar period indicate that weekly attendance was approximately equal to the city's population in most cities. More people went and more went more frequently than they had to other theater entertainments. Most movie shows in the nickelodeon era were cheap, half the price of the gallery for drama theaters or vaudeville, making frequent attendance feasible for lower-income groups and even children. Frequent moviegoers always represented a large portion of the movie audience. Many adults and children went more than once per week.[34]

Working-Class Audiences, Autonomous Publics

In contrast to the extensive literature on the *demographics* of the nickelodeon audience, there is relatively little about their *behavior.* But these descriptions, mostly of working-class immigrants, are intriguing for their resemblance to that of nineteenth-century work-

ing-class audiences, in their sociability and appropriation of nickelodeons as an alternative public space. Contemporary writers
described the nickelodeons as family and community centers, contradicting the fears about unchaperoned children in the audiences. Lewis
Palmer noted in 1909, "Certain houses have become genuine social
centers where neighborhood groups may be found any evening of the
week ... where the regulars stroll up and down the aisles between acts
and visit friends." A 1914 Portland, Oregon study claimed, "Many of
them are family resorts. Community pictures are shown, the people
chat in a friendly manner, children move freely about the house and
the manager knows his patrons personally ... these houses already
take in many a nickel and dime that would otherwise go over the bar
[of saloons] ... people attending all kinds of theaters are orderly, quiet
and courteous."35

For temperance reformers the nickelodeon was a happy contrast to
the "workingman's club," the saloon, because it was free of alcohol
and reunited men with their families. According to the *Willamantic*
(Connecticut) *Journal*, "Men not often seen in the company of their
wives on the street were now taking whole families to the motion pictures night after night." Many surveys noted a diminished attendance
at saloons attributed to men going to movies with their families. In
1914, Presbyterian minister Charles Stelzle asserted that movies were
cutting into the profits of saloons; in a 1916 article in the *Independent*
he favored the movies as a substitute for the saloon. The motion picture house, he claimed, was democratic just as the saloon, where the
working man could feel comfortable and at home. He could come just
as he is, without dressing up. But in addition he could take his family
there, where he could not to the saloon. A few years later a saloon-
keeper of Middletown told sociologists Robert and Helen Lynds, "The
movies killed the saloon. They cut our business in half overnight."36

Observers described audiences, to a significant degree, as determining their own use of the space in the nickelodeon and even in the
small theaters of the silent era of the 1920s. Even though film had displaced live actors, the performance was not yet standardized.
Managers edited movies to fit their audiences' tastes. Sometimes projectionists would change the speed of the film and even run the film
backward for the amusement of the audience. There was a notable
interaction between audiences and projectionists and managers.37

Live musical accompaniment to the film also provided a rich source
of interaction, akin to that for stage performers. Piano players, mostly

women, took pride in their improvisational skills, through which they responded to the audience, especially in neighborhood theaters. When movie producers began in about 1910 to distribute cue sheets for musicians to accompany their movies, many musicians rejected these and continued to play according to their own tastes and that of their audiences. Musicians and audiences could thus entirely alter the mood and intent of a scene. A serious drama could be made into a farce.[38]

Managers of small theaters attempted a delicate balance between acquiescing to their audiences' wishes and "managing" the audience. They were generally supportive of musicians' efforts to please the audience, regardless of the impact on the dramatic effects of the movie, and despite objections of movie producers. Managers also used sing-alongs and sometimes giveaways to modulate and manipulate their audiences. Illustrated songs were often advertised to the less-inhibited working-class and small-town audiences. Almost all nickelodeons had a singer who led the audience, who were guided by song slides. Sing-alongs were familiar from cheap vaudeville. Almost every house used illustrated songs while the projector was loaded with a new reel of film. Reformer Michael Davis said about audience participation in sing-alongs, "no warm-blooded person can watch the rapt attention of an audience during the song, and hear the voices swell as children and adults join spontaneously in the chorus, without feeling how deeply human is the appeal of the music, and how clearly it meets a sound popular need."[39]

But nickelodeons were rarely sites of political activism. A few held benefits for strikers, much as other local merchants would often advance credit to strikers. In 1911, some theaters screened an announcement supporting a campaign against a local gas company.[40] But there is no record of the kinds of crowd actions that had been common in early nineteenth-century theaters, in which working-class audiences often orchestrated the political messages on-stage, objecting to some, demanding others. Working-class audiences exercised some autonomy in controlling the space and defining its purpose to suit their own needs. In doing so they collectively shaped the reading of both the situation and the movies to fit their own working-class experience, and thus used the nickelodeon as a site for producing an alternative culture. But they rarely expressed overt political consciousness or purpose, unlike the saloon that often had been the meeting place for unions and strikers. This perhaps made it reassuring to middle- and upper-class reformers worried about social control.

Changing Habits, for Better or Worse

If people were frequently going to the movies, what had they stopped doing, what had they previously done with this time? The citizens of Middletown told the Lynds that "movies have cut into lodge attendance" and probably the patronage of saloons and attendance at union meetings as well. Saloonkeepers' concern over loss of business was a reason for middle- and upper-class rejoicing. But theater owners worried that people were leaving drama theater for the movies. The galleries were empty, they said, because the boys who had formerly sat there now frequented the movies. Hard times favored the nickelodeon over other entertainments. When people could not afford a theater or vaudeville ticket they could still muster a nickel for the movies. In the 1907–08 recession many theaters closed but nickelodeons were booming. *Lippincott's* magazine said that the movies caused decreases in box office at legitimate and vaudeville theaters and disbanding of theater companies. It claimed the nickelodeon attracted "nearly every class of those we term theater-goers" and that "it is a common occurrence to enjoy amusement by machinery in what was a regulation playhouse." In 1910, *World's Work* cited nine New York theaters from which "the Biograph manager has driven vaudeville and the old-fashioned first-class drama." In 1911 the same magazine claimed movies had replaced theatrical performances in 1,400 former playhouses. Robert Grau claimed that seventy traveling theatrical companies had to fold because of the movies and that movies had "contributed principally" to the decline of melodrama. The *Jewish Daily Forward* commented on the impact of movies on Yiddish performances in 1906. "A year ago there were about ten Jewish music halls in New York and Brooklyn. Now there are only two [while at movies] hundreds of people wait in line."[41]

Business histories of theater indicate that movies did displace drama theater as a popular entertainment form, particularly outside the largest cities. Around the turn of the century, drama outside the largest cities was supplied by stock companies touring from town to town. Touring began to decline, from over 300 touring companies each year to less than 100 by the mid-1910s. Musicals, spectacles, and dramas with literary reputations could still survive on the road. These offered something more than silent movies. But melodramas and average comedies, which had been the bread and butter of many companies, no longer attracted sufficient sales. They had simply been an evening's diversion, which silent movies could as easily satisfy. Price gave a clear advantage to the movies. In the 1910s theater tickets at their cheapest were twenty-five to fifty cents for a seat in the gallery, while a movie cost five to ten cents. George Bevans found that working men who attended theater spent about forty-five cents per week compared to fifteen cents for those who attended motion pictures.[42]

As movies moved out of storefronts into regular theaters, they demonstrated their greater profitability even in drama's own home. Movies provided a greater profit even on Saturdays, the traditional theater night. Drama theaters that traditionally closed for the summer began to show movies instead. Movie companies began aggressively buying and closing theaters or pressuring local governments to tax or restrict licensing for drama productions. The result was a greater difficulty for touring companies to find a theater at an affordable rent.[43] By 1914, movie palaces were being built in Times Square that were equal in comfort and luxury to those of drama theaters, with admission of twenty-five cents instead of two dollars.[44]

Some argued that movies also fatally wounded vaudeville by the 1910s, so that it gradually bled to death through the 1920s. Independent "small-time" vaudeville that included movies in its bills cut significantly into the United Booking Office's big-time market. Once established, small-time gradually metamorphosed into outright movie theaters and continued to bleed big-time vaudeville. Nickelodeons survived while variety and foreign language theaters closed during the 1907 depression, because of the difference in production cost.[45]

Children, Movies, and Reformers

The movies stirred new concerns among moral reformers. Even though children attended theaters in the nineteenth century, reformers directed their concerns toward the dangers to young men and women and to the general moral climate of the community as a whole. The central issue about nineteenth-century audiences had been respectability, which applied to adult behavior and especially to women. The primary focus of criticism was the behavior in the audience, the rowdiness, drinking, and prostitution. Even in the concert saloons the primary concern was not the entertainment, but the alleged licentious behavior of the waiter girls with the clientele.

By the turn of the century, women's respectability was no longer the issue. This older fear was overshadowed by concerns about the safety and socialization of children. Children were being redefined sympathetically as innocent and impressionable, a departure from earlier Calvinist conceptions of children as evil barbarians in need of discipline. Adolescence was being defined as a distinct developmental period, subject to many pitfalls. Charitable organizations began to direct attention to lower-class child abuse and neglect; juvenile delinquency was distinguished from adult crime, and states instituted the first juvenile courts. Children were defined as endangered creatures.[46]

Accompanying the shift in focus from women to children was a shift in attention to class. The primary concern in the era of respectability was its certification of the class credentials of the middle and upper classes. The new concern about children was centered on the lower classes. Society women's charities as well as middle-class professionals focused on socializing lower-class children, especially the growing numbers of urban-dwelling immigrants, who they believed lacked adequate parenting.

Almost from the first, what drew the attention of movie crusaders were the large numbers of unchaperoned adolescents and children in nickelodeon audiences. Reformers feared that moviegoing led to delinquency among boys and sexual immorality among girls. For the first time, reformers concentrated their attention on the effect of the show rather than on the behavior in the audience as the primary concern, although audience behavior continued to be part of the discussion. Previous New York state laws focused on theaters (1839) and concert saloons (1862) as *places* of delinquency, but not on the performance. But in the nickelodeon era the movie itself became a central focus and censorship the means to control its dangers.[47]

Jane Addams, settlement house founder and reformer, in a series of essays published in 1909 as *Spirit of Youth*, worried about the many children who seemed addicted to the motion pictures. She cited a group of young girls who refused a day's outing in the country because they would miss their evening at the nickelodeon; and four daughters of a shopkeeper who would steal movie admission from his till.[48] Addams identified movie *content* as the root cause of the children's misbehavior. She called the nickelodeon the "house of dreams" to indicate movies' inducement of fantasies in children's minds.[49] She told a tale of boys nine to thirteen years old who saw a movie of a stagecoach holdup and mimicked it themselves. They bought a lariat and a gun and, one morning, lay in ambush for the milkman, nearly killing him. Addams was only one among many writers at the time who publicized stories of children imitating movie crimes.[50] As a result, censorship became an early instrument of reform. Chicago enacted the first movie censorship ordinance in 1907, followed by dozens of other cities. By 1913 several states and cities had laws prohibiting children's attendance without an adult after a certain hour. In a cover letter to a report on movies, the mayor of Cleveland in 1913 cited movies of crime as the major evil of movie exhibition and urged censorship in that city. *American Magazine,* citing the Cleveland report, urged industry self-censorship over government censorship.[51] To protect themselves from government regulation the Motion Picture Patent Company, an organization of movie producers, formed a censorship board for New York and enlisted the cooperation of the People's Institute. This soon became the voluntary National Board of Censorship. Producers hoped to counter criticism that might threaten their efforts to capture a middle-class market.

Reformers claimed censorship markedly improved the moral quality of movies. Louise de Koven Bowen, wealthy friend and patron of Jane Addams, claimed the Chicago ordinance of 1911 which her Juvenile Protection Association of Chicago advocated, had made a difference. Similarly, Michael Davis credited the Board of Censorship, with which he was involved, for much improvement from 1908 to 1910.[52]

Censorship blunted but did not stop criticism. Many continued to object to movie content, whether or not censorship had been instituted in their city. In a 1914 debate in the *Outlook,* some letter-writers still worried that girls might be led into prostitution by what they called "white slave" films, which they said did not depict the awful consequences for girls. Another article expressed fear that movies would give immigrant children unrealistic expectations of what they could have and accomplish in America, leading to their disillusion and dissolution: "The version of life presented to him in the majority of moving pictures is false in fact, sickly in sentiment, and utterly foreign to the Anglo-Saxon ideals of our nation. In them we usually find this formula for a hero: He must commit a crime, repent of it, and be exonerated on the ground that he 'never had a mother' or 'never had a chance' – or perhaps that he was born poor."[53]

Fears of the effects of movies were accompanied by a belief that movies were unusually effective in "implanting" – a word often used at the time – ideas in children's minds. In an address to the People's

Institute in New York, Reverend H. A. Jump in 1911 expressed the theory that movies operated through "psychologic suggestion" to put ideas in the viewer's head without his knowing it. He therefore wanted to make sure, through censorship, that these ideas were what he considered good. The same sentiments were expressed at the Conference of the National Child Labor Committee by a Birmingham Alabama Boy's Club superintendent. Making the same claim in more "scientific" garb, Harvard professor Hugo Munsterberg concluded in *The Photoplay: A Psychological Study*, "The intensity with which the plays take hold of the audience cannot remain without social effects ... the mind is so completely given up to the moving pictures."[54] These were the first expressions of what would later be called "hypodermic" theories of media effects.

Critics did not entirely ignore the atmosphere within the storefront theater itself. The two concerns were sometimes intermingled in the same article. They related many "horrors" perpetrated therein, some reading like a tabloid front page. Censorship was no guarantee of the conditions within the theater. Theater ownership was not centralized, leaving each to compete in the market as he chose. Critics were dismayed at the darkness in the storefront theaters, which they saw as encouraging and enabling sexual encounters.[55] Louise de Koven Bowen cited as an example of the dangers a case in which a Chicago proprietor had enticed young girls into his theater and molested them. She claimed that "boys and men in such crowds [outside nickelodeons] often speak to the girls and invite them to see the show, and there is an unwritten code that such courtesies shall be paid for later by the girls," and that "darkness afforded a cover for familiarity and sometimes even for immorality." *American Magazine* reiterated to its nationwide readership the dangers of darkness, "indiscriminate acquaintance," and foul air in the theaters.[56]

Mrs. W. I. Thomas, wife of the Chicago sociologist and prominent women's advocate, also expressed concern about the dangers of the theater environment, including begging outside, admission of children to late shows at reduced rates, darkness in the theater, and, curiously, "audience joining in chorus," presumably of off-color songs. She described it as "a form of amusement which is entirely passive in its nature ... where there is no chance to transmute feeling into social values and in situations where the only outlet for emotion aroused is apt to be through sex experiences or questionable and criminal adventures."[57]

Nevertheless, after censorship, reformers often preferred movies to other entertainments, particularly cheap vaudeville. As a neighborhood and family institution, the nickelodeon was much less threatening than more anonymous entertainments farther from the reach of family and neighborhoods. By contrast, reformers sometimes condemned cheap vaudeville's sexual immorality, in terms reminiscent of the criticisms of concert saloons in the 1860s, except now the attention was on stage acts. The Cleveland study referred to cheap vaudeville acts as "positively degrading", and in describing an audience of one indecent dancer stated, "the ladies in the audience hid their faces … many of the older men turned their heads while the young men and boys stamped their feet, clapped their hands, many of them rising out of their seats, waving their hats, at the same time shouting vulgar suggestions to the performer." A few simply condemned its very low intellectual level and deadening effects educationally.[58]

Reverend H. A. Jump, in his address to the People's Institute, the home of the National Board of Censorship, praised the movies as "the cleanest form of popular entertainment being given indoors today" and thanked the Board for this. He claimed those who thought movies immoral did so on the prejudice that cheap admission implied immorality. Yet movies had a high standard which "would never be allowed to apply to the drama patronized by the well-to-do." He considered movies to have a good educational and moral effect upon the "common people."[59]

A Madison, Wisconsin report in 1915 expressed a definite change in attitude since censorship – "of course there is nothing alarming in children going to movies in the afternoon unattended by elders" – and accepted the claims that movies have "substituted good recreation for many less desirable forms" and "tended to draw families together by giving them a common interest." It too complained of the worst types of vaudeville, the mixed bill of vaudeville acts and movies. A recreation survey of Cincinnati 1913 described the movies as "unobjectionable and provided clean recreation … films of distinctly educational and high recreational value are frequently shown... There can be no doubt that the quality of recreation offered by the moving picture show has vastly improved in the last few years and is still improving."[60]

Later in the 1910s women's groups began to pressure local exhibitors to offer special showings for children in neighborhood theaters.[61] Local civic groups in several cities organized Saturday matinee movies for children in the mid-1910s. While these often were located in movie houses, the theater managers were not the initiators but simply cooperators. The Women's Press Club of New York sponsored Saturday morning movies in two commercial theaters in 1916–17. The Club selected the films for moral education. They excluded films that depicted crimes, convicts, fighting, saloons, gambling, and sex. They also chose films with an eye to their entertainment value to ensure the theater owners of some profit. A women's club of Chicago organized a Better Films Committee to advise local groups on how to organize children's or family programs and what films to show. If local exhibitors would not cooperate they advised groups to buy a projector and show films in schools. Such programs were not commercial but reform efforts, often directed at working-class children. Organizations and businesses sometimes bought blocks of tickets to distribute free to poor children or to their employees. Programs were "planned for clean entertainment, making education secondary." However, the results were mixed, as some children still preferred to see the more exciting adult movies.[62]

The thrust of almost all of the discussion, although ostensibly about children, when examined more closely, is about class. Middle- and upper-class reformers worried about the lower classes absorbing dangerous ideas from movies, many made by immigrants themselves. Lists of topics to be avoided in movies included workers' strikes. The recreational surveys quoted above were sponsored by private elite groups and directed primarily at gathering data on working-class neighborhoods and working-class children. Michael Davis looked in depth at three tenement districts in Manhattan, and the Cincinnati study targeted similar districts for closer examination. Cover letters, introductions, conclusions, and recommendations typically reveal a fear of working-class juvenile delinquency. They proposed funding public recreation facilities for these working-class neighborhoods, since such neighborhoods could not afford private clubs. There is almost complete absence of comment about middle- and upper-class youths' recreation. Such attention might have raised questions about the surveyors' own child-rearing practices.[63]

Magazine articles also reveal the same concerns. In one expression of this attitude, some reformers equated uneducated adults with children, claiming they could not discern reality from fiction and were more susceptible to movies than the better educated. One reformer in 1909 claimed "the constant picturing of crime ... is a harmful and degrading thing, especially when a large percentage of the patrons of such theaters is made up of minors, or adults without education." The *Outlook* stated, "Undeveloped people, people in transitional stages [i.e., immigrants] and children are deeply affected [by movies]." The quote reveals what lay behind these fears of the movies, that these immigrants would not learn to behave like the middle- and upper-class "Anglo-Saxon" reformers. It considered sympathy for the circumstances of the poor to be misplaced and not a suitable explanation for crime.[64]

More optimistic reformers saw movies as potentially being a great educator for adult poor and immigrants. Mrs. W. I. Thomas considered movies not inherently bad but "an educational medium that is historic" in its potential, which had been "turned over to these mere 'promoters of pleasure.'" The *Outlook* similarly contended that movies "could be made as effective a means of instruction in such social problems [as white slavery] as either fiction or the stage." They hoped to harness this great resource and use it as a tool of social control.[65]

But whether pessimists or optimists, their concerns were often rooted in class-based fears of lower-class disorder, the underlying concern of much Progressive reform and the overt fear of conservatives in efforts such as the eugenics movement. While the subject was ostensibly children, this discourse was part of the larger concern about the huge wave of lower-class immigration into the nation in this era.[66]

Storefronts to Theaters: Seeking the Middle Class

Almost from its beginning the movie industry had sought a middle-class audience. Producers hoped to attract the "better classes" by publicizing their efforts at regulation and their responsiveness to reformers' criticisms. Some studios produced films of literary and dramatic classics and avoided the histrionic acting associated with cheap melodrama and lower-class audiences.[1]

Exhibitors in smaller towns were among the earliest to seek a middle-class clientele, since they had to cater to a broader market. A Lexington, Kentucky nickelodeon advertised "polite, fashionable moving pictures ... a nice place to spend a half-hour: With the children! With your wife! With your girl!" Another employed uniformed doormen and ushers to ensure order and encourage women and children to attend. A show in Milwaukee gave away a bottle of perfume to women attending matinees; they offered baby sitting as well.[2]

But the major change and the major investment was moving toward regular theaters. There were many more storefront movie shows, but theaters quickly became an important part of the business and increased the visible middle-class clientele. The trade press from 1907 to 1913 urged exhibitors to attract a middle-class audience by refurbishing storefronts into "handsomely decorated and well-equipped little theatres." Nickelodeon owners who made good profits – not all did – soon began looking for ways to invest their profits and heeded such advice. One owner in a modest residential neighborhood of Denver added a raked floor, a new screen, and fans for cooling air and renamed it the Family Theatre, a "place of charming recreation" operated in a "moral way."[3] Others bought or built regular theaters for movie exhibition. Vaudeville and drama theater owners began to show movies to boost sagging incomes. Some offered a bill solely of movies; others interspersed vaudeville acts between the movies. The latter bills were called "small-time vaudeville" because of the admission price of ten to twenty-five cents was inexpensive compared to refined vaudeville, and because they did not book talent through Keith's United Booking Office, which controlled most of vaudeville at the time.[4]

Marcus Loew exemplified the transformation. In 1904 he invested in penny arcades in Manhattan and downtown Cincinnati. Soon he had removed the penny machines and turned his arcades into nickelodeons. He added illustrated songs and then live entertainers to raise his admission to a dime. By 1907 he saw that the small size of the stores limited his profits and began looking for a larger place, since a smaller house limited what he could spend on vaudeville acts. He converted a deserted burlesque house in Brooklyn into a combination movie and vaudeville entertainment. He pitched his theater to the "family trade," hoping to sell tickets to the entire family instead of a few "leering males." By 1911, with the silent backing of the powerful theatrical firm of the Shuberts, he had forty such theaters throughout New York City.[5] These were converted theaters with a mixed bill, but they charged a higher admission, ten to twenty-five cents, and sought a middle-class clientele, preparing the way for the movie palace.

The small-time mix of movie and vaudeville drove nickelodeons out of business. Distributor William Swanson claimed that small-time vaudeville had closed 200 Chicago nickelodeons in 1909. About the same time, *Variety* said that half the nickelodeons in New York were closed and only one in six were making "any considerable profit." Storefronts with limited capacity to spread the cost could not afford the vaudeville acts that were needed to compete. Vaudeville businessman Robert Grau noted in 1910, "In greater New York alone no less than twenty modern and fully equipped theatres have been transformed into the type of amusement resort where a combination of pictures and vaudeville may be seen at prices ranging from 5 to 25 cents," compared to the dollar vaudeville of Keith a decade earlier. Nor was this confined to New York. In 1913 in Lexington, Kentucky an eight-act program booked through Keith was combined with a feature-length film.[6]

Some stage theaters converted directly to an all-movie bill. Even before nickelodeons spread, movie promoter Archie Shepard organized several traveling companies of projectionists and movies that played "in the first-class theaters of all the principal cities throughout the United States and Canada" to turn profits from drama theaters that were empty on Sundays and after failed plays closed. In New York Shepard leased a Broadway theater and showed movies exclusively. Soon Proctor's Twenty-Third Street and Keith's Union Square big-time vaudeville houses also converted to all-movie bills. In 1909 Lewis Palmer described Union Square, formerly New York's theater district, as "the hot bed of moving picture shows."[7]

Converted theaters and even theaters built specifically for movie exhibition were rapidly becoming an important sector of the movie business. By 1910 Boston had at least two luxury movie theaters, including the Scenic Temple, a movie theater with 1,444 seats and only three showings daily. By 1910 Robert Grau declared Philadelphia had "no less than twenty five beautiful theatres with a seating capacity in excess of 1,000 [built since 1905] ... the city is virtually moving picture mad." By 1914 Chicago had thirty theaters with seating capacity of a thousand or more, "practically all" devoted exclusively to feature films. Movie theaters were replacing nickelodeons in smaller cities as well. In Lexington, Kentucky, in 1915 a 1,500-seat legitimate theater converted to an all-movie bill, and in 1916 a 1,600-seat theater built expressly for movies opened, with all the luxury of a big-city "palace."[8]

These large, luxurious theaters opened a decade earlier than is traditionally thought of as the movie palace era. Fox's Dewey Theater had uniformed ushers in 1908 and an audience "of real 'class' ... dinner coats were in evidence in the auditorium." The Saxe Brothers opened the first movie palace in Milwaukee in December 1909, with ushers, cushioned opera seats, and flowers and palm trees in the lobby. The façade was lit with 1,200 lights. The Bijou Dream in Boston in 1909 had a huge Art Deco proscenium, a grand piano in the orchestra pit, and palm trees at each side of the stage. Movie theaters grew even more grand in the 1920s, with elaborate and exotic decorative motifs, huge lobbies, scores of uniformed doormen and ushers, multiple balconies, and as many as 5,000 seats. By 1929 theaters were so lavish that a *New Yorker* cartoon depicted a child in a lobby saying, "Mama – does God live here?" These movie palaces recapitulated on a larger scale the palaces of Keith era vaudeville.[9]

Film historian Douglas Gomery argues that the movie palaces of the late 1910s and the 1920s were built on the shopping streets of middle-class neighborhoods, with services and decor suited to this class. In 1917 the Central Park Theater opened in Chicago with a domed ceiling painted with frescoes, and a huge glass chandelier suspended from the center. Elaborate molded plasterwork made the theater look like a first-rank opera house. The orchestra included a grand piano and a large harp. Some theaters had smoking lounges, art galleries, and organ music for those waiting to be seated. Male college students in uniforms with epaulets and white gloves served as polite ushers and doormen. Restrooms were staffed with attendants. Sociologists Robert and Helen Lynd found that it worked: "business-class" families went more often than working-class families to the movies in Middletown in the mid-1920s.[10]

The movie palace represented a different marketing strategy from the first efforts made by nickelodeons. Nickelodeons sought to shed the disreputable image created by critics and to gain modest respectability. Like nineteenth-century theaters, they promoted the safety of women and children in their environs. Movie palaces, on the other hand, were not the target of such criticism and respectability was not an issue. They instead offered the consumption of luxury, much as the late-nineteenth-century theaters had promoted fashion.

The essence of the picture palace was luxury at moderate prices, more expensive than the nickelodeon or the neighborhood house but less than big-time vaudeville or legitimate drama theaters. It represented a special night out when a couple might play at being fashionable, rather than a time-filler or a show for the children at the neighborhood house. It lured, then awed and silenced the audience. It shifted the predominant class of the movie audience upward and changed the relationship of working-class patrons to the theater. While the middle class may have been attracted by the luxury they aspired to, working-class people felt out of place. Movie palaces were not located in their neighborhoods; admissions were high; and the formality and the dress were not to their taste. This was not the comfortable, familiar neighborhood show. They could attend but had to abide by middle-class rules. Informal sociability was restricted, even before talking movies arrived. While young working-class couples might go for a night on the town, their parents stayed in their familiar neighborhood houses.[11]

Audiences momentarily inhabited a house of luxury, but they did so at the price of self-expression. The exotic environments and management policies both suppressed audience expression. The decoration as well as an army of ushers emphasized the formality of the occasion, a situation calling for silence and whispers rather than shouts and socializing. Darkness further enforced the silence and made the experience less collective and more a dialog between individual viewer and film.

Low-Brow/High-Brow

The growth of upscale movie theaters unnerved supporters of drama, who feared further loss of drama patrons to these luxury houses. Drama critics showed little concern for the cheap melodrama theaters closed by competition from nickelodeons; these had tainted the image of drama. With their demise, drama could more readily claim a place in high culture. Movie palaces, however, attracted some of the same audience as "legitimate" theater. These defenders of drama did not object to the luxury of movie theaters, but rather to the low-brow aesthetics of the movies themselves. They argued movies degraded people's tastes. They wanted instead to nurture the tastes of the middle brow and protect "Art" from low-brow competition. *Harper's Weekly* claimed that for movies "no degree of intelligence is necessary ... good eyesight being indeed the only requisite," and described movie audiences as "dull-eyed," "mental oysters," and "shallow-brained." *American Magazine* worried that "some ruts and grooves must be formed in the brain, to no good purpose."[12]

Joining the chorus, the *Literary Digest* in 1915 reprinted the claim of a St. Louis magazine editor, Marion Reedy, that movies ruined people's taste. Anticipating latter-day criticisms of television, the article claimed that movies needed an aesthetic censor: "All the meaning there is in [Ibsen's play] *Ghosts* is utterly killed in its movie form. It is debased to the most sensational kind of yellow drama." The low-brow movies were "making the taste of the millions. They are making it bad, execrable taste – bad and execrable because it is based solely on sensation, and is to that extent wholly animalistic."[13]

Walter Prichard Eaton, who had not been concerned in 1913 about the nickelodeon, had become by 1920 more pessimistic, dismayed by the displacement of drama on Broadway with movies. In 1926 he summarized a symposium of articles published in *Vanity Fair* on the war between stage and films. Contributors included play producer Brook Pemberton, theater owner Lee Shubert, drama critic and staff member for Famous Player movies Ralph Block, and Actors Equity president John Emerson. They agreed that movies had diverted audiences from theater, and that small-town theaters and ten-twenty-thirtys had closed. But symposium contributors disagreed about the consequences. Some claimed movies had degraded tastes, while others argued that those who deserted to the movies had been fans of melodrama, not the "spoken drama." Some expressed concern that movie companies were buying control over play production and hiring away actors. Eaton concluded that "fine dramatic art" – excluding melodrama theaters – was not widely popular even before movies, and had to be subsidized to survive.[14]

Where Did the Working Class Go?

But movie palaces did not make up the majority of houses or of seating. This was still a nation of farms and small towns. Simple country theaters (outside the largest 190 cities) accounted for most movie theater seats in America. William Johnston, editor of *Motion Picture News*, claimed in 1926, "The picture house of 1914 that cost above $50,000 was the exception. A house that cost $5,000 dollars in a town of five thousand population was considered quite good enough and perhaps better than the village could afford." In cities there were many levels of houses from the first-run to fifth-run, downtown palaces to neighborhood houses. Contemporary sociologist Alice Mitchell estimated that ten of every eleven movie houses in Chicago were located in residential neighborhoods, within walking distance for most people, rather than in the central business district of the Loop. Some were palaces, but most were not.[15]

Modest neighborhood houses were the norm in urban working-class districts. Nickel-theater owners spruced up their theaters with prefabricated façades and interior ornamentation. Some nickelodeon owners moved into abandoned neighborhood theaters, but they were still cheaper (10 to 25 cents vs. $1.00), smaller (300 vs. 1,000 seats), and less imposing than the palaces. Patrons were more likely to know the

ticket taker, the usher, or even the owner, in contrast to the anonymous corporate owner and numerous faceless employees of the
palace. This is where working-class adults and children went to see
movies in the 1920s. Memories of palaces are mostly urban, middle-
class memories.[16]

Blacks too did not share the movie palace experience. Some theaters refused admission to all blacks; others confined them to the
gallery with a separate entrance. A survey of recreational facilities
open to blacks in fifty-seven cities found that in four of seventeen
southern cities blacks were excluded altogether from movie theaters.
Ten other cities had segregated seating, and blacks were required to
enter from alley doors instead of the front of the theater. Of forty
northern cities thirty-three had segregated seating, though they did
not require blacks to use a separate entrance.[17]

In many northern states segregation was illegal and some blacks
brought suits against theater owners. In 1913, a black woman in
Rochester refused to sit in the balcony and filed a civil rights suit against
the theater. Suits, however, did not stop *de facto* segregation. Theater
owners and black patrons played cat-and-mouse to enforce or circum-
vent segregation. Sometimes a black person would hire a white boy to
buy his ticket. Ushers were instructed to "lose" those tickets when given
to them and instead substitute tickets for the black gallery.[18]

Other factors in addition to discrimination discouraged black attendance at movie palaces. First-run white movie palaces were expensive
for most blacks. Moreover, their white upper-class ambiance probably
did not appeal to many blacks. There were some black theaters, and
these seem to represent a distinct style of movie theater. The South
Side black ghetto of Chicago featured a vibrant, black-oriented entertainment culture that included movie houses. Most of these houses
featured stage shows with the movies. The movies were usually the
same as shown in white movie houses, but the stage show featured
outstanding black performers, including many big-name blues singers
and musicians. Audiences attended for the music as much as or more
than for the movie. They were very lively featuring shout-and-
response-style participation and dancing in the aisles.[19]

A typical southern town, Lexington, Kentucky, had several black
movie theaters through the 1910s and 1920s. These theaters were
remodeled storefronts, attempting a modest luxury and presenting
themselves as respectable and fashionable within the black community. They offered second-run movies with a few vaudeville acts. They

did not, however, flourish. All closed within a short time. Yet black dance halls did very well. Apparently the white movies shown were not as appealing as black music and dancing; and they were not affordable enough to draw a sufficient children's audience.[20]

Just as among whites, there were strains among blacks of different classes concerning appropriate audience behavior. Middle-class blacks tried to distance themselves from boisterous behavior. In Chicago middle-class blacks attended the same theaters, but objected to "distasteful" behavior such as dancing in the aisles. Black professionals objected to the dance halls in Lexington, and one black newspaper writer accused black professionals of attending the segregated white theaters instead of their own.[21]

The 1920s Movie Audience: A Nonissue

Nickelodeon audiences had been the subject of lively discourses in the 1900s and 1910s among reformers, the trade press, and writers for upscale magazines such as *Harper's* and *Theatre Magazine*. They gave considerable attention to the behavior of the audiences and to the physical and social conditions of the theater, providing some rich descriptions of the people who went and what they did while they were there.

By contrast, the palace era of the 1920s produced few commentaries on audience behavior. Almost no magazines for the general reader touched on the subject of behavior. In one of the very few articles commenting on the audience of the movie palace, movie director Robert Wagner noted that American movie audiences sometimes hissed an unpopular figure in a newsreel but never a bad movie or play, that "if they can't applaud they keep still." He commended the audiences "for good humor and kind behavior." There was a similar absence of comment on movie audiences in the *New York Times* during the 1920s. Only two very brief reports late in the decade – totaling three column inches – described their behavior. One reported a traveling salesman's suit against B. F. Keith's Hippodrome for being beaten by another patron when he told that patron to stop reading subtitles aloud; the other noted the revival of stamping feet in unison by audiences to signal to the projectionist that something was wrong with the sound or the picture – such a contrast to the descriptions of the voluble immigrant audiences in nickelodeons![22]

The earlier descriptions of nickelodeon audiences had been part of the turn-of-the-century interest in the great flood of immigrants into urban ghettos that had disturbed upper-class racists and reformers alike. Changes in immigration laws in the 1920s reduced the flood to a trickle, and the second generation of immigrants was less fearsome to observers. By this time too, movies were no longer a newsworthy novelty. The popular press turned elsewhere for grist. The neighborhood theaters that replaced nickelodeons slipped into oblivion and their adult audiences with them.

There is little evidence of active audiences in this period. The public sphere of the immigrant nickelodeon and small-town working-class theater had melted into quietude, at least among adults. Kids apparently continued their irrepressible antics into the 1920s. This seems to have been a preadolescent audience, younger than that of the nickelodeon era. A dozen studies found children attending movies once or twice a week, on weekends and during evenings. One theater manager in the late 1920s said, "85% of my audience is made up of them." Children attended inexpensive neighborhood theaters within walking distance of their homes, mostly without their parents. A photo outside a neighborhood house (ironically, named the Palace) in November 1920 showed mostly unchaperoned children and was captioned "waiting patiently for the 'next show' … a common sight in scores of American cities." In contrast to nickelodeon days, there was no moral panic about unchaperoned children, although the Lynds expressed a concern about a "decentralizing tendency" upon the family.[23]

The Saturday matinee was a favorite of children. Saturday matinee serials began early on and were effective in bringing children back every week. A man remembered the serials of the 1920s, "practically all of our friends and, of course, all of my brothers and sisters, went religiously … we used to stamp, whistle, holler, cheer, clap and do everything possible to urge on our hero or heroine." Another said, "The end of each part always put you in so much suspense that if you missed the next week, you had to ask one of your friends how it ended, or what happened… [When] the movie camera would break down [a]ll the kids would start hollering and booing the camera operator."[24]

Reform Discourse in the 1920s

Discussion about movie audiences in the late 1920s faded from newspapers and magazines, withdrawing to books and research reports. Reformers turned to social research, employing some of the most well-known social scientists using newly developed survey techniques. The primary force shaping the new research was the Payne Fund, founded in 1925 to study juvenile reading and expanded in 1927 to include the effects of movies and radio on children. The movie studies became more influential than the rest. To reach a broader market and have greater impact, several of these reports were published as books marketed to the general public, including *Motion Pictures and the Social Attitudes of Children, The Emotional Responses of Children to the Motion Picture Situation, Movies, Delinquency and Crime,* and *Motion Pictures and Youth.*[25]

The concern about movies was part of a general debate about children's behavior and child-rearing in the 1920s. The press was full of articles expressing shock at the behavior of teenagers and young adults in the 1920s, labeling them the "lost generation." Exemplifying the shock were the comments of sociologist E. A. Ross, who saw movies as the culprit, making young people prematurely "sex-wise, sex-excited and sex-absorbed." He blamed movies for "less-concealing fashions, pornographic literature, provocative dances, and briefer bathing suits."[26]

Many critics complained that movies drew children away from more constructive activities. Researcher Alice Mitchell reported grade-school children preferred movies over reading, but not other play activities. The problem according to Mitchell was not an uncontrollable addiction to movies, but their wide availability. Children could go to movies almost anytime. Other activities, although preferred, were less accessible and required the cooperation of others.[27]

The Payne Fund research provided almost no description of people's actual behavior in the theater. The research typically conceived moviegoing as an individual psychological experience, and concentrated on the psychological impact on young viewers. This psychological approach is surprising given that many of these researchers were prominent sociologists who had pioneered methods of observing social interactions in natural settings and could have readily built on the ethnographic observations of reformers in the 1910s. Yet their research on movie audiences did not utilize observations of actual audiences or examine social interaction.[28]

University of Chicago sociologist Herbert Blumer, in his studies for the Payne Fund entitled *Movies and Conduct* and *Movies, Delinquency and Crime,* concentrated on children's reactions to the movies and made no mention of audience behavior. Using survey methods rather than attending theaters to observe the audience, he asked children to state what movie scenes were memorable and what effect they had on the children's fantasies, fears, goals, and attitudes toward parents, reading, school, sex, and crime. He took pains to understand how movies "implanted" ideas. He claimed that the viewers had no control over their reactions, and he coined the term "emotional possession" to describe what he saw as a loss of self-control: "the individual identifies himself so thoroughly with the plot or loses himself so much in the picture that he is carried away from the usual trend of conduct ... impulses usually latent or kept under restraint gain expression."

The loss of self-control was repeatedly asserted to be worse among the less-educated lower classes. Blumer stated, "the degree of influence of motion pictures is less in the cultured classes than it is in the case of others," and philosopher John Dewey and his colleagues at the University of Chicago considered the effect to be mediated by the child's surroundings, those of the tenement child leading to greater effects. These researchers were concerned specifically about lower-class children, who, in being influenced by movies, "raised problems of social control."[29]

The Payne Fund studies established an "effects" approach as the dominant paradigm for researching movie audiences. This was the first time that a preoccupation with reception dominated the discourse about audiences. The reform discourse on the nickelodeon expressed worry about the effects of movies on the morals of children, but concern about the movie house itself and about children's behavior in and about the theater continued as a theme of criticism. Moreover, the discourse was based upon actual visits to the theaters. This new movie research, by contrast, concentrated solely on the effects of mass media content, ignored the social context of viewing, and was premised on the notion that viewing was an individual and psychological experience. Consequently, observations in theaters and discussions of audience behavior disappeared from the discourse. From this time, media effects would dominate public and scientific discourse about audiences.

Sound Silences the Audience

Between 1926 and 1930 almost all movie theaters were fitted with sound systems. Live music was displaced in all except a few deluxe downtown houses. Recorded sound and music standardized mood and message, eliminating audiences' control over that aspect of the entertainment. One old moviegoer said, "After that, everything seemed to change with the movie business. Even the prices started to go up." Sound also changed behavior. As one report phrased it, "the talking audience for silent pictures became a silent audience for talking pictures."[30]

Sound at first received an uncertain welcome. Early sound tracks and the acoustics of early theaters did not produce good sound quality. In small theaters, where musicians often played poorly, even a limited-quality recording might be an improvement. But at downtown theaters with dollar admissions, where the stage shows and orchestras had been quite elaborate, attendance dropped precipitously when musicians were fired and the shows ended. Surveys found that most people preferred talking movies but live music.

Movie and culture critics differed in their opinion about "canned music." Some considered it degraded and feared that "evaporated music" – a reference to canned milk – would discourage students from training to become the next generation of musicians. There would be fewer music makers, even if there were more sophisticated listeners. Others, however, saw talking movies, along with radio and phonograph, as new means to deliver top-quality music to the masses and thereby elevate the general level of American musical taste.[31]

Sound changed people's attitude about talking and socializing in movie theaters. Talking in the audience now interfered with listening to the movie dialog. Silence was self-enforced, with audiences shushing talkers. The sole remaining evidence of assertiveness occurred when there were problems with the projector. When the sound was unsatisfactory it became customary for audiences to stamp their feet and clap in unison until something was done. Projection problems broke audience absorption in the story and reengaged them with their fellow viewers, momentarily uniting them in common interest and action.[32]

Depression Cutbacks and Audience Construction

Sound spurred a new growth in moviegoing. Movie attendance rose steadily from 1929 through World War II, faltering only momentarily in 1932. Moviegoing became the second most frequent away-from-home activity after pleasure driving. During the 1930s admissions accounted for 20 percent of all recreational expenditures and 80 percent of spectator amusements.[33] The Depression took hold just as a few Hollywood studios had established firm control of the industry. These studios were vertically integrated from production to exhibition. Their response to the Depression was to shift investment from large and lavish movie palaces to less costly neighborhood houses. They instituted a new wave of theater construction after 1932, building smaller, modern theaters with sound systems in working- and lower-middle-class neighborhoods and in smaller towns to try to expand the market.[34] Staffs were reduced and jobs redefined. Ushers were trained less for courteous assistance and more for crowd control. Exhibitors hired lower-wage high-school boys and young women instead of college men. They turned up lights so patrons could seat themselves. They ended the ban on food and drinks in the theater and opened refreshment stands to supplement income. Popcorn was introduced for the first time and found to be very profitable.[35]

To compete with the integrated chains and to counter the hard times of the Depression, many of the smaller independent houses began to give door prizes and hold bingoes along with the movies. A *New York Times* article claimed that over 2,000 theaters, mostly independent and in small towns, were using premiums to entice customers. Premiums such as "Depression-ware" dishes were designed to appeal to women and make them regular customers who would return each week (for as many as 86 weeks) until they had a complete set of dishes. For forty cents she got an article that would have cost twenty cents or more at a store and also saw a double feature. These giveaways filled many theaters. The better movie houses of Middletown in the mid-1930s were frequented heavily by adult women, one exhibitor estimating the audience to be 60 percent women.[36]

The Hollywood studios opposed these promotions. Warner Bros. released *Robin Hood* with the condition that no games or giveaways be used when the film was shown. Instead they preferred promotions that built audience allegiance to the studio, not the theater. Shifting focus from the theater and its features, movie studios promoted their movie stars under contract. Pioneering such efforts was Walt Disney, who was a master of studio promotion. In 1929 Disney formed Mickey Mouse Clubs with weekly meetings scheduled for Saturday matinees in specific theaters. The clubs promoted Disney characters and movies as well as tie-ins for a range of Disney toys. Disney made efforts to link community organizations into this activity as well, adding a veneer that would appeal to reformers and also further enhance his product image. Loews and Warner Bros. circuits also organized children's clubs, as did many local theater managers.[37]

Whether for the clubs or other reasons, children flocked to neighborhood movie theaters. In Middletown, Saturday matinees were popular with preadolescent children, at least half staying for five to six hours. Children from a working-class district of New Haven attended movies frequently, over half going twice a week or more. Movies were overwhelmingly the first preference of leisure activities of Italian working-class teenage girls in East Harlem in 1930. Two-thirds reported that they went to movies at least once a week, and another fifth went twice a week, usually alone. This pattern matched that of Alice Mitchell's study, discussed earlier. It was also similar to what high-school students from a range of social classes in Chicago reported, and similar to findings in Philadelphia in 1935 among junior-high students. Movies were overtaking all other activities in children's preferences, including outdoor games for boys and shopping for girls, that had previously retained their attraction.[38]

Unlike adults' behavior, children's behavior didn't change much with the coming of sound. Reminiscent of reformers' fears in the 1910s, the mayor of Chelsea, Massachusetts in 1930 closed a theater because "the actions of many juvenile spectators were such as to endanger their morals," apparently a reference to necking. Just north of the Bronx a cheap theater attracted a mix of black, Italian, and Jewish children for Saturday serials. One of them reported years later that the film broke regularly and the children "booed, stamped feet and often had fist fights."[39]

During the late 1930s the *New York Times* published several articles and letters complaining about adult audience behavior. Letters in 1936 complained of women not removing their hats and of people talking or crumpling candy wrappers. In 1938 one man complained of unemployed men spending their time at the movies instead of looking for jobs. But another came to their defense saying these unemployed men needed a relief from their troubles. In 1938 and again in 1940 letters to the drama editor complained of people in the audience hissing President Roosevelt in newsreels. The Mayor of Bronxville, New York, asked theater managers to put on the screen an announcement that the President should not be booed and that the audience should stand for the national anthem. In 1939 a New York court upheld the right of audiences annoyed by talkers in the audience to give them a Bronx cheer.[40]

During the 1930s moviegoing settled into a form familiar to us today. The movie, not the place, and comfort and convenience, not luxury, were the attractions. At the same time it had transcended its tawdry early reputation and had become acceptable entertainment to the middle class. It became an activity predominantly of children and young adults. Behavior too had settled into a familiar pattern. Talking and other noises became annoyances to adults in the audience, while youth continued to challenge the rules of decorum at Saturday matinee, drive-ins, and other youthful gatherings.[41]

Voices from the Ether: Early Radio Listening

O nly two decades after movies created a historic juncture from live to recorded entertainment, radio instituted another great transformation, bringing into the home entertainment previously available only in public theaters. Broadcasting changed the collective dimension of public audiences, dispersing them to their homes. The phonograph had this potential, but it spread very slowly. For decades it was expensive and severely limited as a music instrument.[1] The phonograph was quickly overshadowed by the much less expensive, more versatile, and fascinating technology of radio.

Radio broadcasting was born in the 1920s, a decade that, in many ways, divided the nineteenth century from the twentieth. Technologies such as the automobile, telephone, and household electrification took hold. Changes in sexual mores, gender roles, and child-rearing practices that had been brewing for some time gelled into "modern" middle-class culture. Reactions to radio can be appreciated within this context.[2]

Radio's first incarnation, however, was not as entertainment broadcasting, and radio listening was not the first leisure use of radio. Radio
began as a wireless telegraph, transmitting dots and dashes through
the air. The signals were broadcast, rather than transmitted point to
point, but the purpose was two-way communication, as with wire
telegraphy. In the early 1900s a hobby of amateur wireless operators
sprang up, mostly middle-class schoolboys. Local clubs and a larger
informal network of amateurs quickly evolved into a national organization, the American Radio Relay League, to promote communication
among amateurs. The hobby by its very nature lent itself to enthusiasts discussing their common interests and forming activist groups
nationally as well as locally. It is not surprising then that radio hobbyists, particularly amateur broadcasters committed to greater skill
development and investment, formed a strong opposition to forces
threatening to change radio.[3]

During World War I amateurs were prohibited from transmitting, to
avoid interference with military communications. At the end of the
war they began again, with new equipment developed during the war
that made voice transmission more feasible, which stimulated interest
in the amateur hobby. By 1920 over 6,000 licensed amateurs were
active. Moreover, voice transmission provided the basis for radio to
move from hobby to entertainment, with a considerable push from
radio manufacturers.[4]

The Euphoria of 1922

Some amateurs not only used the wireless to talk to each other but
also to make announcements and play music recordings for anyone
listening. Commercial broadcasting began in November 1920 when
Westinghouse executives recognized an opportunity to foster a
broader market for their radio equipment. People not interested in
talking via radio might be interested in *listening* to something more
entertaining. Frank Conrad, an amateur employed by Westinghouse,
was broadcasting music regularly from his own radio transmitter.
Local Pittsburgh newspapers even began to announce his broadcast
schedule. Westinghouse directed Conrad to establish the first commercial radio station, KDKA. Numerous others soon followed.
Broadcasting mushroomed in 1922. *Wireless Age* wrote, "Churches,
high schools, newspapers, theaters, garages, music stores, department
stores, electric shops installed sending sets" and began broadcasting

phonograph music, talk, and anything else. The number of licensed stations rose from 77 in March to 524 by September 1922.[5] This blossoming of broadcasting spawned a craze among people previously uninterested in radio that was called the "euphoria of 1922." People were amazed at this new phenomenon of "pulling voices from out of the air" as they termed it. Broadcasts were something entirely new, far more strange and mysterious in the early 1920s than the first regular television broadcasts in the late 1940s. Radio was hailed as a triumph of science. At the same time, radio was referred to as unnatural. Listeners accused radiowaves of hitting and killing birds, causing rain and drought, vibrating metal springs of a mattress, making floorboards creak, causing a child to vomit, and conjuring ghosts.[6]

Broadcasting changed radio suddenly from a hobby of a few thousand operators to a fad of hundreds of thousands of listeners. With something to listen to, other than amateurs talking to each other, radio sales soared. Retailers and manufacturers could not meet the demand for radios and parts. A letter to *Radio News* called it a "popular craze"; another to *Radio Broadcast* used the term "epidemic."[7]

Saturating the Market[8]

Estimates of radios in use vary, but all sources agree on the overall trends: the diffusion of radio was far more rapid than the growth of telephone or automobile during the same period. *Radio Retailing* estimated a twenty-five-fold increase from 60,000 sets in January 1922 to 1.5 million in January 1923. In 1924 the balance of sales shifted from parts for home-made sets to factory-built sets. By 1926, 18 percent of U.S. homes had a radio; by 1931, over half had a radio[9] (see Table 12.1).

Saturation varied significantly by region, race, and rural versus urban areas, all of which reflected differences by income. In 1930 saturation was 51.1 percent in the North, 43.9 percent in the Rocky Mountain and Pacific States, but only 16.2 percent in the South. Rural saturation nationwide was 21.0 percent, compared to 50.0 percent for urban areas; 44 percent of white families had a radio compared to just 7.5 percent of Negro families.[10] Price was an inhibitor. Lower-priced radios had a limited range, presented much greater problems of interference, and required much more skill to operate.[11]

Table 12.1. Families with Radio Receivers, 1922–1940

Year	Families (1,000s)	Percent of all Homes	Average Price	Percent of Autos with Radio
1922	60		50	
1923	400		60	
1924	1250	11.1	67	
1925	2750	14.6	82	
1926	4500	18.0	114	
1927	6750	23.0	125	
1928	8000	26.3	118	
1929	10250	31.2	133	
1930	13750	40.2	87	0.1
1931	16700	55.2	62	0.4
1932	18450	60.6	48	1.2
1935	21456	67.3	49	8.9
1940	28500	81.1	40	27.4

Sources: U.S. Bureau of the Census, *Historical Statistics of U.S.* (Washington, DC: USGPO, 1975), Series R90–98, p. 491; percent of U.S. households from Thomas Eoyang, "An Economic Study of the Radio Industry in the USA" (Ph.D., Columbia University, 1936), 67, and Christopher Sterling and Timothy Haight, *The Mass Media: Aspen Institute Guide to Communication Industry Trends* (New York: Praeger, 1978), 360, 363, 367; auto data from Sterling and Haight. Average radio prices for 1922–32 from Eoyang, 89, 1935 from "Are New Radios Good Enough?" *Radio Retailing* (March 1939), 19; 1940 from *Radio Retailing* (January 1941), 15.

Amateurs, DXers, and Simple Listeners

Radio amateurs felt threatened by the flood of new radio fans. Many broadcast listeners in turn blamed reception interference on the amateur next door. *QST,* the magazine of the amateurs' American Radio Relay League, published an editorial titled "Girding Up Our Loins," expressing the beleaguered feeling and bracing for a fight. The editorial stated, "We hope we're not going to have to scrap to retain a place in the ether for amateur operation.... We amateurs must not let ourselves be crowded out of existence by a horde of listeners-in." It proposed a division of time, giving broadcasters time before 10 P.M., and leaving the night to amateurs.[12]

In October 1922 Hugo Gernsback, editor of *Radio News,* offered a contest, with $200 for first prize, for essays to answer the question, "Who Will Save the Radio Amateur?" A cartoon accompanying the explanation of the contest depicted an amateur sitting in a chair listening to his set. He is on a beach, and a large wave labeled "Radiophone Popularity" is about to crash down on him. The contest was introduced by Armstrong Perry, a well-known writer on radio, with an article titled "Is the Radio Amateur Doomed?" Perry claimed that before 1922,

practically one hundred percent of the American radio users, aside from people in government or commercial radio services, were "radio amateurs"… Today the percentage of "radio amateurs" as compared with other radio users has nearly or quite lost its two ciphers, dividing it by 100. The amateur, once alone in his fascinating field, finds himself jostled and trampled upon by a horde of common folks who want to hear a concert or something.

Soon amateurs would have little influence in shaping radio use. The vast majority of Americans listened, at first for the novelty of receiving signals from great distances but increasingly simply for entertainment. The prize essays expressed desires of amateurs to make peace with this new world, offering to help with problems of interference and to provide other community services with their transmitters.[13]

DX Hounds

Early listeners had little to attract them beyond the sheer novelty of "capturing voices out of the air." Broadcast schedules were limited to a few hours a day; most of this was not very entertaining, interference was a chronic problem, and tuning was constant. Even the listener who was not enamored of distance spent much time trying to "capture" any broadcast that offered something entertaining. People commonly listened to stations hundreds of miles away. Even in major cities people supplemented local stations by tuning in distant ones.

Early listeners were therefore often DX fans; they sought to tune in stations from ever-greater distances. Unlike the amateur, who wanted to send as well as receive signals, the DX "hound" was preoccupied only with receiving distant stations and identifying their call letters. DXing was humorously described as an addiction. One writer used heroin as a metaphor; others likened it to alcoholism. Magazines frequently referred to men being "bitten by the radio bug," shamed by their "lust" for DX, and hiding their "addiction."[14]

For the benefit of DXers, newspapers printed radio schedules not only for their own city but for stations across the nation. Schedules for even the largest stations as late as 1926 required no more than two column inches. Many stations broadcast only two or three programs during the evening. Such abbreviated schedules made nationwide listings feasible, requiring about a half page to list the major stations from east to west coast, Canada to Cuba.

As more and better entertainment was broadcast, the interests of the DX hounds and big-city listeners satisfied with their local stations began to diverge. The conflict depended upon the balance in a particular city between what broadcast programs were available locally and what had to be received from a distance. While typically the two pursuits were characterized as separate and opposed, sometimes the same person engaged in both. City DXers were described as men whose first priority was distance and who stayed up all hours after local stations ceased broadcasting and distance reception was better. These same men joined their families to listen to local stations' broadcasts of cultural events earlier in the evening as part of their familial responsibilities. Attitudes varied from place to place. A Connecticut respondent to a *Radio Broadcast* survey in 1927 noted, "DX in itself is not sought except when experimenting with a new hook-up or new parts. There is still a thrill in DX," which this man engaged in late at night when he couldn't sleep. But a Washington state respondent to the same survey was more enthusiastic, claiming, "Every radio fan likes to fish for DX." DXing necessarily was more popular and survived longer in more remote regions. As late as 1927 *Radio Broadcast* claimed that 80 percent of the geographic area of the United States still required DXing to receive stations. But more people were beginning to listen rather than tune. In 1928–29 NBC's market researcher Daniel Starch found that about one-fifth of families continued to seek distant stations, but three-fourths listened regularly to one or two favorite stations with good reception.[15]

"Listeners-in"

Even the simple broadcast listener needed some knowledge to install and operate his set. Batteries for tube sets ran down and had to be tested and charged or replaced. As tubes wore out, reception weakened. Owners had to figure out which tubes needed replacing and do it themselves. Only expensive radios had speakers and could be heard without headphones, restricting family listening. Newspapers and magazines published many articles about buying, assembling, and operating radio sets. One such article referred to "this intriguing sport called radio." Even as late as Christmas 1926, when Crosley Radio Company announced a free instruction booklet, thousands wrote in requesting it.[16]

Tuning involved several dials, and the more tubes, the more dials. Sets with vacuum tubes required two separate batteries. Voltages from the two batteries had to be carefully adjusted to obtain good reception and to avoid burning out tubes. Before the neutrodyne was introduced in 1924, one could not reliably receive a station by adjusting the dial to the same position that had succeeded before. Rather, one had to scan the dials until some station was tuned in, then listen for the call letters to discover what station one had tuned.[17]

Tuning was typically depicted as a masculine skill. It was usually the role of the father or son to be the "operator." One wife from Pennsylvania complained that the quiet necessary for tuning was destroying family discussion, as a "deathlike silence must prevail in the family circle ... prattle of the children is hushed, necessary questions are answered in stealthy whispers."[18] Such limitations sustained the idea of radio as a hobby of tuning rather than a relaxing practice of listening. Not being able to reliably tune to a particular station deterred interest in specific programs and encouraged random scanning to receive any station as long as it was a distant one.

The distinctions between amateurs, DXers, and simple listeners meant that the name of the radio audience underwent an evolution. Since radio required more than listening, in the early 1920s it was not customary to refer to those using radios as simply "listeners." "Fan" was most common during the craze of 1922. A fan might build his or her own receiving set and engage in DXing, but not in transmitting signals like the amateur operator. "Listener" or "listener-in" began to replace "fan" as more and more people acquired radios. *Radio News* began a column in 1923 titled "Broadcast Listener," offering technical information in terms understandable to the radio novice that offered help in building or operating a radio set. *Radio Broadcast* had a high-brow program critic's column titled "The Listeners' Point of View," beginning in April 1924. In June 1925 *Popular Radio* began a similar but somewhat more relaxed program critic's column, titled "The Broadcast Listener," and another column in January 1926 titled "Listening In."[19]

These columns, despite their titles, reflected a shift of attention away from the listener to programs. "Listener" implied inactivity. *Radio Broadcast* articles in 1927 used the term "passive listener" to describe the average radio listener who accepted whatever was broadcast, and complained of the failure of listeners to speak up. Amateurs derided those who merely "listened." As we will see, some thought passive radio listening was de-masculinizing.[20]

Gendering the Listener

With the introduction of broadcasting, radio magazines sought to enroll the new radio fans as readers. Wireless magazines that had served hobbyists began to change, and new magazines were conceived specifically for broadcast listeners.[21] These makeovers were obvious attempts to attract a new female readership, mixing messages of domesticity and women's equality with unflattering images of men fumbling with radio technology. *The Wireless Age* had been published for amateur wireless enthusiasts since 1913 by American Marconi Company, holder of many radio patents.[22] It was a slim monthly of about 50 pages per issue, most of it advertising radio parts and accessories. A column called "World-Wide Wireless" chronicled new breakthroughs in radio technology. The "Experimenters' World" column and "Queries Answered" offered solutions to readers' technical problems. The cover pictured technical facilities such as giant aerial emplacements.

Beginning in May 1922, the magazine presented an entirely new face, without any explanation to its readers. It was clearly an effort to appeal to a broader, less technical readership. The covers featured Norman Rockwell–style color illustrations of people listening instead of black-and-white photographs of equipment. The May cover depicted a well-dressed woman sitting listening with headphones, radio wires and batteries hidden in a furniture cabinet, and "air conducting" the music with her hands. On the August cover, sophisticated couples danced on a verandah under Japanese lanterns to music from a radio loudspeaker. In January 1923 a young couple was depicted visiting their parents, the men in suits and ties with cocktails in hand, the women sitting next to each other holding hands before a roaring fire in a large stone fireplace. A large loudspeaker is situated just next to the fireplace, competing with it as the new hearth.[23]

These covers were part of a larger discourse in radio magazines constructing the new radio audience. The people were affluent, as indicated by their houses, dress, and expensive radios with cabinets and loudspeakers. Radio listening was problem-free enjoyment, slightly romantic, and family oriented. All the covers, even the dance, were set at private homes. Romance and family were icons of gender that softened the previous masculine image of radio as technology and broadened the appeal beyond middle-age men and their teenage sons.

A pictorial rotogravure section of several pages was introduced, showing all types of people using radio almost everywhere. Each monthly issue included a page of children, another of movie actresses, another of women outdoors, all listening without men's help. Feature articles concentrated on broadcasting rather than telegraphy and equipment. Two pages of cartoons reprinted from newspapers and other magazines, and another two pages of "radio humor," were introduced. A "Letters from Readers" column printed "applause cards" from readers expressing appreciation for various broadcast programs.

Several articles appeared concerning women in radio, and many pictures showed women listening. Technical matters were pushed to the back of the magazine, which had doubled its length to about 100 pages, the first half reserved for the new look and broadcasting, the second half retaining the older, technical departments for hobbyists.

Radio News underwent a less thorough makeover, but male readers nonetheless objected. When the editor tried a new cover style in 1920, one reader complained about their light-hearted nature. In 1922 the magazine was still predominantly technical, and a husky 200 to 300 pages per issue, but added a few whimsical covers, melodramatic fictional stories about radio amateurs, cartoons about radio, and occasional pieces on women using radio.[24] Yet some readers felt betrayed. A Philadelphia reader objected strenuously to changes that suggested anyone other than the amateur operator as reader. He wrote,

in the editorial of the first issue [July 1919] you stated that the magazine was for and by the AMATEUR, and you signed off H. Gernsback – *your editor.* The issue of August, 1922 is nothing more than the average broadcast magazine, great numbers of which have recently sprung up, and you signed the editorial with a plain H. Gernsback.

...if you canned those silly [fiction] stories and the articles on scarfpin radio sets you would have room to admit some of the amateur stuff you were so glad to start with.

do you know Mr. Gernsback that there are two general classes of broadcast fiends? 1. The rich bird who buys his stuff outright and wonders why he can't get long distance telephony, especially in summer [season of greatest interference] by simply turning the knob. 2. The fellow who builds his set according to directions and if it doesn't come up to his expectations tortures his paper with fool questions such as "Why can't I get the music from Hokem with my $3.75 set?"[25]

The letter writer was insulted that his technical knowledge was pushed aside in favor of the effeminate know-nothings who preferred broadcast listening. He was not "a kid" or a "silly" woman with a "scarf-pin radio." He was a master of technology. The technical and serious nature of the magazine was an affirmation of his manhood. Tinkering with its content betrayed his manhood.

Foolish Father and His Radio

This sentiment of insulted male pride in the letter was mixed with a hint of lower-middle-class resentment. The "rich bird" was pushing aside the hard-working amateur unafraid to dirty his hands with radio technology. Images in the magazines probably furthered such class resentment. Broadcast listeners depicted elegantly on the magazine covers and in radio ads were quite affluent. Inside, cartoons typically depicted lower-middle-class men, neither a manual worker nor affluent. For these men especially, masculinity, unproven by physical labor or success, was a sensitive issue, part of the larger shift in masculinity of the Progressive era.[26] The male bastion of radio technology was being breached by women, with the help of turncoat magazine editors. To make matters worse, their unsure hold on the world of radio technology was made the butt of humor. In 1922–23, newspapers were filled with cartoons about radio, enough to fill pages of reprints each month in *Wireless Age* and *Radio News*. Many popular comic strips such as "Mutt and Jeff," "Simeon Batts," "Cicero Sapp," and "Out Our Way" took up the theme of radio high jinks. The men in these cartoons were typically lower-level white-collar workers pushed around by their bosses.

The most prevalent theme in these cartoons was the ignorance, ineptness, and foolishness of men who succumbed to the radio craze. There were several versions of this view of the foolish white-collar man. One was the father pretending to buy the set as a toy for his son, but in fact using it himself. More common was the man who knows little but pretends to know. The man offers to help fix someone's set, and of course destroys it. A husband explains how radio works to his wife: "They sing into the horn and it goes out of the box and up a wire to the roof, see? Then there's something they call vitamins or kilometers or whatever it is and they grab it and the next minute those wires of ours grab it and down it comes through the box." Another man tries for hours to tune his radio with no success, when his son or daughter or wife sits down and in seconds tunes in a station.[27] The success of the wife or daughter was not portrayed as skill, but simply dumb luck, the son more often as skill. The point, however, was about the man rather than the wife or children. Another theme that depicts the man's loss of his domain is the domineering wife who monitors her husband's activities by sending him messages via radiophone, or who decides what show they will tune in.

Women's Equality in Radio

The gender references in stories and cartoons about radio were not coincidental. The 1920s was a distinct turning point in gender roles. The early years of the decade were an era of triumph, riding on the exhilaration of the passage of the nineteenth amendment. In 1922, when broadcast radio began, there was much discussion and hope of extending women's rights to other areas, including assertions of women's competence with technology. But soon the political mood of the country began to shift to the right, and feminists were attacked as communists or labeled unfashionable. Conservatives mounted a campaign against women's organizations in 1923–24, and magazines began writing about the ineffectiveness of women's votes. In 1925 the child labor amendment that feminists had advocated was defeated.[28]

Popular interest too shifted from politics to pleasure. Emancipation from patriarchal control and greater freedom in social behavior were for some more significant than political freedom. Younger women diverted their attention from political goals to a fusion of sexuality and consumerism, emphasizing fashion and cosmetics, fostered in popular media. The Ladies' Home Journal called it the "cosmetics revolution." Magazine articles emphasized the modern woman defined in personal terms, while the numbers of newspaper article about women's rights and the women's movement dropped precipitously. By mid-decade the flapper replaced the suffragist as the image of the modern woman.[29]

As radio changed from a hobby to a domestic furnishing, the gender of radio use underwent similar metamorphoses. The changing discourses on women and radio in the 1920s radio magazines reveal the nature of such process submerged in popular discourse rather than in more overt political debates, and thus help us understand broader cultural changes. Radio had become a fixture in the living rooms of millions of homes. This "domestication" of radio effectively moved the radio from the traditional masculine sphere of technology to the feminine domestic sphere.

But before domestication, there was a brief period in which a case was made for the equality of women within the *technical* sphere of radio. Articles, pictures, and cartoons in radio magazines suggest a more complicated picture of gender issues during the early stage of crystal sets and DXing than is typically recognized.[30] Two discourses coexisted in the same magazines: one asserting women's technical prowess and "rights" to radio; the other depicting their ignorance and ineptness. The peak in women's advocacy was 1922. It gradually withered until 1924, when magazines turned again to more masculine formats.

Broadcast magazines included some surprising assertions of women's equality, which demanded access to the already masculinized activity of radio use. A speech advocating women in radio was printed in the third issue of *Radio Age,* a magazine for teenage boys. *Radio Broadcast* told of a woman who had made and installed 37 receiving sets, including stringing the antennae wires outside. She began when her husband brought home parts to build a set. But while he was at work she put it together herself.[31]

From its inception in 1922 to about mid-1924, *Radio World* gave marked attention to women. Pictures, stories, and cartoons presented images of women in control of this new technology. The predominant message was one of women successfully using and enjoying radio. Numerous pictures showed women listening and operating radios, for radio telegraphy as well as broadcast listening. A woman in New York was pictured playing chess via radio telephone with a female friend in Chicago. One cover featured the first woman graduate of a radio school.

Many of these pictures appeared as part of a regular column, titled "Radio and the Woman," which began with two pages in 1922. The columnist's pseudonym, Crystal D. Tector, alluded to the crystal set, suggesting that the author was something more than a passive listener. She was a weekly booster of women, sprinkling her column with examples of women's technical feats with radio, and generally advocating women's equality.[32] She said such things as "women are equally as capable and as practical as men," as evidenced by the use of a hairpin to fix a radio; "there will be many positions which [women] will fill to better advantage than men"; "promising girl student among those taking the wireless course at the Radio Institute of America, spiritedly contradicts all masculine statements which infer that women in general appear dazed when technical terms are mentioned"; "Most any department store will tell you ... that at least half the inquiries for sets and parts are made by women, and that their knowledge of the science is equal to that of the men."[33]

But the outright assertions of women's equality ended in 1922. After that the column occasionally mentioned what women did, but not as frequently and not tagged with feminist alarums. The "Radio and the Woman" column gradually shrank to one page in 1923, to intermittent quarter-pages, and then disappeared in 1924. In mid-1924 the message of the magazine changed. Covers frequently pictured young women in bathing suits or dancing, legs exposed, while listening to radio. Beauties posed beside radios, but did not operate them. Cartoons depicted women as ignorant of the technology. One showed a housewife who tells her husband she cleaned his radio – but could not put it back together. Another showed her using the radio aerial as a clothesline. By the end of 1924, *Radio World* had shifted to a more technical, masculine readership, publishing almost exclusively sober, technical articles and eliminating the humor and women's columns altogether.

A similar but less pronounced pattern appeared in *Wireless Age*. In 1922 in the magazine's pictorial section there were plentiful pictures of women using radios in almost every conceivable setting. By 1924 pictures of pretty young women in swimsuits listening to radio predominated. The magazine published a few articles in 1924 and 1925 whose very faintness in advocating women's place in radio simply echoed the decline. One article about Eleanor Poehlor, the first director of a broadcast station, emphasized her skills as a saleswoman for her station, not her technical know-how. Another about Christine Frederick, who broadcast home economics programs, actually highlighted the domestication of radio. Even an article that asserted a girl was "just as good as father or brother!" acknowledged radio technology as a masculine sphere and males as the standard of skill.[34]

The trend was decidedly away from advocacy of women's equality in radio technical skill. *Radio Age* soon pictured a mother hanging wash on a boy's aerial, and pretty young women in the kitchen following a recipe from the radio, stringing an aerial on a rooftop in an evening gown and high heels, and listening to the radio on the beach with prominent nipples showing through their bathing suits! These and a goodly number of other pictures of attractive young women suggest that, by 1924, the magazine was courting not-so-young boys as their market, and considered women not a market but bait.[35] Magazines frequently referred to women listening while the man or boy did the building and operating. One *Radio Broadcast* article, to indicate the contribution of women, described their role as interior decorators. The women made suggestions as to where to place the radio, but the boys solved the technical problems to achieve these. A wife demanded a radio, but the husband was expected to buy the parts, set it up, and make it work.[36]

Ads continued to feature women operating a radio set. Such ads, however, were not suggesting women's skills. Quite the contrary; ads used the image of women as technically inept to demonstrate how easy it was to use the featured brand of radio. A 1925 Atwater Kent pamphlet pictured a woman in evening dress tuning a set with one hand. The ad copy read, "Any child can do it!," equating women to children.[37]

These disparaging images of women's competence in ads and cartoons were part of the larger backlash against women's equality that gained ground in the mid- and late 1920s. Between the wars, advertisements, information, and advice articles in women's magazines emphasized women's domestic role as a labor of love for her family. She was also depicted as needing experts like Christine Frederick to tell her how to be the perfect wife and mother, and to use domestic appliances she did not understand, like the radio. The voices of these experts were also brought to her by the radio in the first daytime programs in the mid-to-late 1920s.[38]

Listening Habits

Letters and cards from early listeners indicate they did not experience themselves as passive eavesdroppers listening to something happening far away.[39] For them radio was a form of imaginative yet real *interaction*, what television researchers would later call parasocial interaction. People often wrote that they felt like the person on the radio was actually in their home, and wrote to welcome them. Letters from all over, large cities and small, east and west, are filled with open-hearted responsiveness to announcers and entertainers they heard on the radio. Listeners of the 1920s looked upon the radio announcer as a friendly good Samaritan to whom they turned for help in resolving problems and mysteries of their lives, to find a lost loved one, to

announce over the air calls for missing persons, and so on. Some even
visited stations to ask announcers to broadcast personal messages.[40]
Such responses were encouraged by the practices of live broadcasts. Announcers intentionally addressed listeners as if they were
speaking to old friends. Broadcasts consisted largely of direct address
to listeners and relatively little drama or even conversation among
announcers and guests at the station. The style elicited strong attachment by listeners to announcers and performers, and the "location" of
the interaction in their homes domesticated the relationship.[41]

One of the consequences of this social orientation to the radio
voices was that listeners often talked back, and listening was lively. A
Nebraska "traveling man" claimed in a letter to the editor that, of at
least 200 homes he visited each year, he could not remember a single
place where the broadcasts were listened to quietly: "Even the prayers
in the [broadcast] church services were interrupted with bright
remarks, and other irresponsible and extraneous material." Robert
and Helen Merrill Lynd described Middletown radio listening in 1924
as an active pursuit.[42]

Communal listening also was a widespread and viable institution in
the 1920s. Public listening occurred in many places. Pictures showed
crowds listening in streets by stores that had placed a loudspeaker
outside. Major radio stations mounted radio sets with public address
loudspeakers on trucks that parked and turned on the sets in parks
and other places of public gathering for major sporting and political
events, as a means of promoting the station. "Radio and the Woman"
mentioned that "several of the better class tea shops [along Fifth
Avenue, New York City] were equipped with radio sets." Another column mentioned a radio in a barbershop.[43] However, such listening
was among anonymous crowds that were unlikely to foster a sense of
commonality and collective action, as in nineteenth-century theater
audiences.

Before radio was commonplace, homes with radios also became
centers of social gatherings, much as the first television homes would
in the early 1950s. Those with a radio, whether in their home or store,
often found themselves hosting an audience of friends, neighbors, and
relatives who were eager and curious to experience the new invention.
A New Jersey woman wrote to *Radio World* that "Every night our
home is crowded with neighbors." A Tennessee farm wife wrote to
Radio Broadcast in 1924, "There are only six radios in our area of
thirty square miles. So quite often, we invite our friends in to enjoy a

good program of music or lecture of some special interest."[44] This listening was not just collective, as in public places, but communal.

In the early to mid-1920s such socializing centered around the radio was common even among the affluent, as attested to by the many references in magazine columns and ads to "radio parties" at which curious guests could enjoy the new marvel of radio. A Connecticut respondent to a *Radio Broadcast* survey in 1927 said, "When any particular event of outstanding interest is advertised we generally plan to invite a few friends and make an evening of it." The "Radio and the Woman" columnist mentioned a friend who ensured everyone would come to her parties by writing on the invitation, "Radio Party and Tea." A "Radio Supper Club" met every Friday evening for dinner and dancing to radio at another friend's house. She said that, since installing a radio speaker, "all my friends want to do is come over and dance." In another column she exclaimed, "Heaven help you if you should forget to invite [your neighbors] to your house every evening for that radio entertainment."[45]

By the late 1920s these "radio parties" were waning. The *New York Times* described an incident in the late 1920s where the etiquette of listening together was unclear, apparently already becoming less familiar. Another *Times* article characterized the radio audience as individuals "without a group mind," referring to the habit of listening in their separate homes.[46] The communal use of radio lasted longer in working-class and rural communities, where radio was slower to become a fixture in every home, especially under the financial stress of the Depression. In working-class Chicago homes in 1930, people listened together in shops and neighbors' parlors; most families listened together. Even in 1931 a radio attracted visitors to a rural Virginia home.[47]

The shift from communal to family listening was implicit in the domestication of radio, which presumed that each family would listen separately in the privacy of their home. As soon as radio was defined as a household appliance, privatization was just a matter of time. But group listening did not disappear entirely; in the 1930s it became formalized. Various organizations established listening groups for educational purposes, supplanting the grassroots communal listening of the 1920s. Participants were from all backgrounds, although housewives and students predominated and they had more than average education. They met in private homes to listen to and discuss public affairs or family guidance programs (child-rearing, homemaking, education).

Some listened to high culture, such as classical music or plays. Extension services of land grant colleges in Ohio, Iowa, New Jersey, and Kentucky began to offer courses via radio, for which people were encouraged to listen in groups. Many other types of organizations formed listening groups, among them the National League of Women Voters, local PTAs, YMCAs, and libraries. The Civilian Conservation Corps and the Works Progress Administration organized groups to listen to NBC's *American Town Meeting of the Air*, which began broadcasting in 1935 to foster group discussions of current public issues. An estimated 3,000 groups across the country listened to the program in 1938–39. Another program, *Great Plays*, reported a thousand groups listening. Several other radio programs were designed specifically for such voluntary group listening, announcing availability of information or mailings to help.[48]

Listeners Organize!

Some listeners went beyond communal listening and acted collectively to shape radio. This represents some of the most significant collective actions by twentieth-century audiences, short-lived and different from, yet equal in ways to the actions of theater audiences of the early nineteenth century. Listeners organized to solve problems of interference in receiving broadcast signals.[49] Most significant was the movement for "silent nights," when local stations agreed not to broadcast so listeners could tune in distant stations without local interference. This movement arose and faded with the shift from DX to program listening and the growth of broadcasting from an experiment to a profitable commercial venture.

The first silent nights were established sometime in 1922. At that time broadcasting was sufficiently experimental and unprofitable that broadcasters voluntarily agreed not to broadcast one night a week in several cities, among them Kansas City, Cincinnati, Dallas, and San Francisco. Chicago stations agreed to silent Monday nights in 1922 when the Department of Commerce radio inspector suggested it "in response to a demand from many fans," and after a poll taken by the *Chicago Daily News* indicated listeners were 11 to 1 in favor of a silent night. The radio inspector also obtained agreement by the American Radio Relay League for amateur operators to be silent that night.[50]

Chicago's silent night continued through 1924 without controversy. In 1925, however, some stations began to construct powerful transmitters in suburban areas. The original agreement applied to stations within Chicago, so these stations claimed exemption. In August a local organization, the Broadcast Listeners' Association, called for a boycott of stations violating silent night. Within three weeks two such stations agreed to adhere to silent night; another agreed in September; and the last capitulated in late November. In the midst of this the city broadcast stations reendorsed silent nights, supporting the boycott.[51]

Silent nights continued through 1926 and 1927, accompanied by "a more or less animated discussion." In March 1927 a major Chicago station ceased silent Mondays in order to broadcast an NBC network program from New York. This raised the question anew whether to abandon silent nights. A poll indicated a five-to-one support for silent nights and the broadcasters' association decided to retain the practice. Then in November 1927 Chicago stations announced they would end silent nights. The trend toward commercial broadcasting made Monday nights too valuable as advertising time to remain silent. Chicago broadcasters claimed in the *Daily News* that silent nights were no longer necessary for DXing and that they deprived other listeners of a night's radio. As if to close the story of silent nights in Chicago, a radio writer in the *Daily News* claimed that the DX fan had settled down to enjoy programs on local stations.[52]

As the need for distance reception varied with location, the demand for silent nights differed from place to place. During this same period, silent nights were debated in New York City with different results. In a 1925 discussion of the topic, the *New York Times* wrote that "New York has heard less agitation for one silent night a week on the radio than any other big city." It claimed that this was because New York was the radio entertainment center, so anyone seeking entertainment need not seek distant stations, and that the majority had given up DXing until late at night.[53] Nevertheless, in October 1925 a Citizens Radio Committee, coordinating its efforts with the Chicago boycott, mounted a campaign for the first silent night in New York City. A week later another organization, the National Radio Service League, announced its opposition to a silent night, arguing that New York programs were much better than in the past and "the distance craze" had been replaced by "a desire on the part of listeners for genuine entertainment... A radio set is no longer a scientific plaything for the mechanically inclined man; it is a source of amusement for the whole family." The organization had offices in Aeolian Hall, the location of classical music concert broadcasts. So it would appear that this was likely the voice of cultural elites and/or broadcasters. "The Broadcast Listener" column in *Popular Radio* also opposed the idea, referring to DX fans as "animated by some sort of kid passion" in whose hands "A radio receiver becomes a mere toy." It referred to the Chicago strike as "foolish." The same column in December 1925 used harsher terms, calling DX fans "long distance cranks" and "a bunch of idiots."[54]

Such belittling of DX fans was a notable change. Metropolitan listeners had lost interest in DXing as broadcast programs and tuning capabilities of radio sets dramatically improved. The loss of interest was greater and occured sooner in New York City, so that support for silent nights was never sufficient. In Chicago support remained into 1927, yet by the end of that year no protest arose when broadcasters abandoned silent nights. Newspapers and others claimed DXing was no longer popular and that most people just wanted to receive a good program and, in cities like New York and Chicago, could do so without DX.

As circumstances shifted, so did listener concerns, from support of DX to objections to interference in tuning in local stations. There were more complaints to city officials and radio inspectors in New York City about interference from nearby transmitters or cheap regenerative radio receivers than about silent nights.[55] In 1925 and 1926 listener organizations formed in several cities. Little information beyond brief mention in newspapers and magazines exists about these groups. Many organizations, often formed by local elites, planned to put a stop to cheap radio sets that interfered with local station transmission. The United States Radio Society was formed in Cincinnati in February 1926. The National Broadcast Listeners' League in Indianapolis organized "to fight all forms of outside interference" from "blooping" regenerative sets. Another antiblooping organization was formed in Chicago by several prominent Illinois politicians.[56]

An example of these elite organizations, The Listeners' League of Greater Cleveland was founded in March 1926 at a meeting at the Cleveland Chamber of Commerce. It had as its board of directors the trust officer of the Central National Bank, the secretary of the Lake Erie Trust Company, a superintendent of roads for the Cleveland Railway Company, the agent for the American Railway Association, an attorney, and a consulting engineer. Its expressed goal was "first to campaign against avoidable interference with reception."[57]

There were a couple of organizations that seemed more concerned about the rights of listeners versus broadcasters, but there is little to suggest they were successful. A Boston group named the Association of Broadcast Listeners, begun in summer of 1925, composed of about 300 "storekeepers, accountants, ministers, mechanics, chauffeurs, trolley conductors and motor men," proposed creating a national system of powerful broadcast stations owned and controlled by listeners. Nothing came of the proposal.[58]

Radio Broadcast briefly mentioned receiving information from the Iowa Listeners' League and other Midwest groups attempting to organize listeners. The magazine supported the idea, but doubted "very much if the radio listener can ever be organized." The president of the Iowa League published a criticism of Henry Field's use of his radio station in Shenandoah, Iowa, as a "home shopping" station, announcing his products and prices and giving the address to send money and orders. This appears to be a different and more critical stance than that taken by those organizations concerned with interference from cheap radio sets. However, a hint of elitism bleeds through the criticism here too. He bemoans the station's entertainment as "not of a high-class nature [but] common music for common people." He claimed that "letters from opponents of the principles of direct selling are on excellent paper and represent a highly educated class, while those from supporters of the direct seller are for the most part extremely hard to read, are not noted for cleanliness and usually avoid referring to the real subject of debate."[59]

Class issues underlay these contests over silent nights and interference as well as between DX hounds and other listeners. More powerful, richer stations opposed silent nights. Upper-class listeners with more expensive, powerful receivers were more concerned with interference from cheaper sets, likely owned by lower-income listeners. In a range of ways the debates over broadcasting were struggles between unequal economic forces or classes over whose interests would prevail. By the end of the 1920s the more powerful corporate forces had prevailed in broadcasting, while for listeners issues of silent nights and interference faded away as better technology and programming became accessible to a broader spectrum of classes.

13

Radio Cabinets and Network Chains

I n the early 1920s radios were purchased in pieces, not just by those ambitious to build their own set, but by everyone. People purchased tubes, dials, headphones, batteries, and aerials, and wired them together at home. The challenge for the middle-class homemaker was to make this mess of wires and parts invisible or at least presentable, and to prevent leaking batteries from ruining furniture and carpets. Christine Frederick, a popular home economist and magazine writer, provided extended interior decorating advice on the appropriate place in the home for a radio. She chronicled the change.

...for the first couple years of radio [1922–23], no body seemed to think it strange to pile the library table with mechanical paraphernalia... Until this current year radio was the toy and the joy of men rather than women. It has been only since women have taken a practical home making interest in radio that ... has resulted in demand for higher class, more beautiful and more artistically designed sets... She is thoroughly through with all the original radio messiness.

193

Frederick suggested putting the radio in a room where the family gathered, and hiding the "ungainly horns and instruments" in a cabinet or wall recess. More direct, an Atwater Kent ad in *Ladies' Home Journal* of December 1925 reassured middle-class housewives that "radio needn't disturb any room."[1]

Soon the whole task was made simple by manufacturers offering factory-built radio sets mounted in fine wood cabinets. In 1923, *House and Garden* announced the appearance of the first radio "desk cabinets" in which to hide the mess, but still located the radio room, "a room of masculine character," in the attic. A few months later *Radio Broadcast* noted, "While there are still in use plenty of unprepossessing and shy crystal receivers ... an aristocracy of receiving sets is emerging." This "aristocracy" was radios in wood cabinets designed to blend with the parlor decor, much as had been done with phonographs earlier. But these were not yet commonplace.[2]

To fit a radio into a cabinet meant replacing headphones with a loudspeaker and batteries with house electricity. Loudspeakers were becoming affordable, and electric service was becoming a standard feature of new, upper middle-class homes by the late 1920s.[3] The year 1927 marked a significant shift in marketing radios as furniture. The January issue of *Radio Retailing* noted that manufacturers would be offering far more console models than in 1926. A February article noted that manufacturers were concentrating on cabinet design and making tuning easier, using two dials instead of three. Radio dealers were giving up the parts business and selling only factory-built sets. By 1929, only 3 percent of families still used home-made crystal sets.[4]

The radio was now within the upper-middle-class woman's realm of home decoration.[5] With the domestication of the radio, *Radio Retailing* said, "no longer can the radio dealer slight the artistic appeal when selling the woman prospect." Another ad in the upscale *Saturday Evening Post* said,

The men have had their turn at radio. They've fiddled and fussed with a thousand-and-one hook-ups, amplifiers, relays and what-nots in their efforts to get "distance" and "volume" until our living rooms resemble the workshop of a boy inventor. The ladies' turn has come and here is the instrument built expressly for them. It's a smart little *personal* writing desk all the time and a wonderful radio whenever you switch on.

The ad pictured an affluent woman in high heels and evening dress, with a pull cord behind the $120 radio desk to call the maid.[6]

Radio Retailing announced that dealers needed to sell the radio as a fine piece of furniture rather than as a technical instrument, in order to please their new market of women. *New York Times* radio columnist Orrin Dunlap, Jr. claimed housewives' desire for a radio built as a fine piece of furniture that was compatible with the living room decor also fueled this shift.[7]

The year 1927 was also significant in advertising's shift to emphasize the entertainment delivered into the home by radio. Many ads and articles referred to radio as a "musical instrument." *Radio Retailing* told dealers, "You are selling music, not radio." The magazine claimed that radio needed to be marketed to the three-quarters of American homes without a radio at that time as "music and entertainment, not as a technical instrument." An ad stated, "RCA Victor introduces a master built musical instrument."[8] Such marketing suggests listeners who cared not for technical wonders but convenience, something easy to use that would blend into the rooms' furnishings.

No Place Like Home

Radio was being redefined as a domestic appliance. Early communal uses and public listening places, under other circumstances, could have become the standard for radio. Amateurs, crystal set hobbyists, and DX fans, even while operating from their homes, were oriented to a community of fellow hobbyists. But domestication of the radio implied privatization within the home. Making radios affordable for the single family was a prerequisite for this "ideal" to be realized. But the symbolism of the time also strongly reinforced this idea of radio domesticity. The association of radio with the home was part of a larger movement in advertising to depict products and center consumption in the home by creating a domestic ideal.[9]

Ads deployed many metaphors of domesticity and domestic tranquillity. An RCA ad circa 1927 showed a little cottage and was captioned, "When you own a radio there is no place like home." Another RCA ad in *Saturday Evening Post* was captioned, "Make your home life richer with the magic of Radiola." It went on, "A world of entertainment ... in your home." The family gathered around the radio was a common picture.[10]

Ads claimed the radio eliminated the need to go out for entertainment. A Stewart-Warner radio ad claimed the radio "cuts your entertainment cost in half" since it provided good entertainment in the

home, and people therefore went out less. An ad for Herald loudspeakers stated, "Dine out – at home! A famous restaurant, a great orchestra ... right in your own dining room." Many ads featured an
upper-class couple entertaining another couple in their home, using
radio to provide high-class background music for an intimate evening
of dinner and conversation.[11]

Radio Comes of Age in the Depression

Despite the Depression, radio saturation continued to rise. Radio set
prices dropped precipitously to an average of $34 in 1933. Income
became less a factor in radio ownership, and radio use was no longer
skewed upscale. By the late 1930s, lower-income groups listened more,
preferred local over network programs, and preferred radio to reading.[12]

In the late 1920s and early 1930s, practices of broadcasters and listeners became institutionalized. Broadcasting settled into its commercially sponsored form, dominated by networks. Networking, or what
was then called "chain broadcasting," made radio attractive to
national advertisers with budgets large enough to sponsor more elaborate programs. NBC began the first network programming in 1926 and
CBS began in 1929. Soon higher-cost drama and variety programs
began to make inroads into music as the principal form of programming. Regular commercially sponsored programs, broadcast at the
same hour each day or week, began in the early 1930s.[13]

Market Research Constructs an Audience

Since radio listening was rapidly becoming a familiar daily routine, it no longer warranted discussion in magazines. Radio magazines themselves disappeared, became simply program listings (e.g.,
Radio Broadcast became *Radio Digest*), or shifted their market from
the general listener to retailers, repairmen, or hobbyists (e.g., *Radio
World* reverted to an all-technical format). About the same time,
radio stations and networks were beginning to conduct systematic
surveys of their listeners.[14] From the earliest days of radio, stations
wanted to know who was listening. At first they distributed
"applause cards" and encouraged people to write in.[15] By the late
1920s the audience had become a product for sale to advertisers,
who wanted more accurate measures to price the product they were
buying. They turned to the nascent fields of market research and
academic radio research.

One of the earliest market researchers was Daniel Starch, whom NBC contracted in 1928 to measure its national audience. CBS also began its own research in 1930, contracting with Price Waterhouse. Many stations and organizations soon conducted or commissioned their own surveys.[16] Broadcasters hired business professors at prestigious universities, such as Robert Elder at MIT and Herman Hettinger at the University of Pennsylvania, to conduct surveys.[17] These one-shot surveys were quickly displaced by regular ratings services. In 1930 the Association of National Advertisers and the American Association of Advertising Agencies, representing the sponsors and ad agencies for most of the network programs at the time, formed the Cooperative Analysis of Broadcasting and appointed Archibald Crossley, former pollster for the *Literary Digest,* as head, starting what quickly became known as the Crossley ratings. Crossley conducted monthly telephone surveys asking people to recall what programs they had listened to. In 1934 Claude E. Hooper, a former researcher for Daniel Starch, began his Hooper ratings to compete with Crossley. Hooper also used telephone surveys, but asked people what they were listening to at the moment, rather than asking them to recall.[18]

Market research and ratings described the size and demographics of the audience, when and how much they used their radio and types of programs they preferred. Absent from these studies is any information on what people did with radio, other than selecting programs. We cannot reconstruct from them a picture of a family's daily life and how radio fit into it. But the surveys and other studies of the 1930s do provide basic information helpful in picturing the radio audience.

Radio audience habits, which carried over to television viewing, were established around 1930 with the regularization of radio schedules. Listening quickly became routine, fitted to people's daily schedules. Housewives were the primary listeners in morning and afternoon, children after school, and men and women equally in "prime time" between 7 and 9 P.M. Surveys indicated household averages of two to three persons listening per set during evening hours in households in the late 1920s and early 1930s. Families listened together in 85 percent of households. Most people preferred popular music, and secondly comedy over other programming. As early as 1928 almost three-fourths of listeners preferred network programs over local programs.[19]

A handful of studies offered richer images of the radio audience. When the Lynds returned to Middletown in 1935, they found radio a "mild cohesive element in family life." But they believed that radio "carries people away from localism," while "binding together an increasingly large and diversified city." In other words, radio was eroding civic engagement and participation in community activities, making families more insular and orienting them, as described by mass society theories, to national elites, instead of to their local community peers. The Lynds' expression of concern was one of the earliest of what would become in the 1950s a small industry of criticism of radio and television for causing the breakdown of community and the "atomization" of society. The local radio station linked Middletowners to cultural elites in New York, and substituted sport spectatorship as the basis for civic identification over civic participation. In both cases the participation in community that mass society theorists considered important to integrating people into the national fabric, was supplanted by a superficial identification via centralized radio programming.[20] The Lynds also characterized radio as "almost entirely a passive form of leisure," in contrast to what they had noted as an active involvement in the 1920s. The change from DXing to listening struck them as a change from the active to the passive, and foreshadowed mass culture critic Theodor Adorno's claim that radio induced passivity and the common criticism in later years of television "narcotizing" viewers.

Perhaps reflecting the change from civic engagement to radio listening is the importance some listeners placed on the radio rather than on friends and neighbors to help them through hard times. For the unemployed during the Depression, listening filled the long idle hours. One unemployed listener in Chicago in 1935 wrote, "I feel your music and songs are what pulled me through this winter. Half the time we were blue and broke. One year during the Depression and no work. Kept from going on relief but lost everything we possessed doing so. So thanks for the songs, for they make life seem more like living." Destitute families who had to sell their radio described the loss as a considerable hardship.[21]

Other descriptions of radio listening portrayed a much more innocuous device, providing aural wallpaper for the family's activities. These were the frequent comments on radio's use as background and the inattentiveness of listeners. Inattentiveness contradicted the fear of radio's power to induce passivity. In 1928,

13 percent of respondents to a national survey said that no one in the family was listening when the radio was on. During the day housewives frequently listened while doing chores. A 1931 study found that only 13 percent of housewives were giving radio their full attention in the morning, 22 percent in the afternoon, and 55 percent in the evening. The author of a Minnesota survey commented that "No one who has heard his neighbor's radio blaring away constantly day and night can doubt that many radio owners fail to give full attention to their instrument."[22]

Send in Those Letters!

One of the few remaining examples of listener voices from the 1930s is fan mail, which tells us how listeners used radio and what it meant to them. Lower-income and rural people were more likely to write. The class of letter-writers, however, varied with the program. For example, an upscale audience wrote to the *American School of the Air*.[23]

Personal attachments to announcers and entertainers survived the shift from local stations to national network broadcasts. Listeners expressed the same un-self-conscious openness toward national radio stars as they did to local radio station announcers. One indicator of this is the ease with which performers prompted gifts from listeners. When Guy Lombardo mentioned strings on his violin, he received 193 yards of violin strings. When Amos and Kingfish decided to start a bank, hundreds of listeners sent in dollar bills to deposit! Listeners sent hams, sugar cane, maple syrup, peaches, sombreros, oranges, linen, cats, dogs, pencils, shoes, tires, and so on.[24]

Fan mail to Lowell Thomas, who began a fifteen-minute nightly news broadcast in fall 1930, also suggests at least some listeners constructed a personal relationship with him. One writer castigated Thomas for making a remark about thick ankles because a young woman with thick ankles happened to be listening at the writer's home and left the table in tears. Another wrote, "Last night you mentioned that women use rouge. I myself never use any and certainly think it a most disgraceful remark to make over the radio." And another, "You embarrassed me so this evening in your talk about the dude hunters that if I live to be a hundred years old I will never be myself again."[25] They reacted to his behavior as if he were physically present in their home and had insulted them to their face. They showed no awareness of him speaking to thousands of others at the same time. Others saw him as someone to turn to for help and asked him to intervene for them to help along a romance, promote some invention or idea, or pass along messages, as was common on local stations in the 1920s. They wrote as if he were likely to know their neighborhood and even their friends and family.

Such personal responses were not confined to simple folk. Letters to the Baldwin piano company for their broadcasts of classical music in 1929 reveal similar responses, except these listeners felt themselves guests in the "home" of the performers. One letter-writer from Staten Island phrased it, "our whole family greatfully [sic] accepts your invitation to listen in again.... We felt very much at home during your *Concert At Home* tonight." Another from Colorado said, "thanks for the pleasure in being a guest in that delightful music loving home yesterday." And another from Bay City, Michigan wrote, "I almost felt as if I were in the room too – it seemed so delightfully informal." The inversion of listeners from "hosts" to "guests" eliminated the feeling of radio performers invading their homes. It meant too that they were less likely to write about their own families and their use of radio.[26]

Daytime Listening

Radio stations at first concentrated their broadcasts in the evening, when the largest audiences were available. But soon some began to identify daytime as the "women's hours."[27] The first daytime programming was primarily informational homemaking and childcare programs for housewives. Broadcasters believed that the daytime schedule should look "like the non-fiction features of *Good Housekeeping*."[28] There was no criticism of these homemaker programs or their effects on the women listening.

This contrasts markedly to the attitudes of cultural elites toward the soap operas of the 1930s and 1940s. The first daytime serial began in 1929 when WGN in Chicago began daily broadcast of Irna Phillips' *Painted Dream*. Proctor & Gamble soon became the major sponsor of daytime serials in the 1930s, including *Ma Perkins, Home Sweet Home, Dreams Come True, Song of the City, The O'Neills, Pepper Young's Family, The Guiding Light, The Couple Next Door, Road of Life,* and *Kitty Keene*. The number of network daytime serials peaked in 1941 when at least one serial was broadcast in fifty-nine of the sixty quarter-hour segments between 10 A.M. and 6 P.M. on weekdays, on CBS, NBC Blue, and NBC Red networks.[29] By the 1940s half of

American women listened regularly to at lease one serial; 10 percent listened regularly to seven or more serials.[30] As the soaps grew in numbers and popularity, they came under attack from social and cultural elites. Serials were first criticized for crowding out valuable programming. A New Rochelle woman's club in November 1939 began organizing an "I'm Not Listening" boycott, which by the spring had supporters in thirty-nine states. The boycott had little effect, however. The vice president of WHN chastised these affluent women for campaigning against serials that meant so much to "women not so fortunate as you club ladies." In 1942 more such "club ladies" mounted a campaign against soaps for their "insipid stories" and "belittling attitude" toward women. Mme. Yolanda Mero-Irion, the founder and president of the National Radio Committee, lambasted advertisers for "feeding women soap operas" that she described as "ridiculous, sentimental bunk which has no relation to any of the realities of our lives." She accused advertisers of handling women as if they were imbeciles; "The picture of the little woman with her hands in soapsuds, rapturously listening to Joe and Mary's imaginary trials and tribulations when the world is burning has something sickening in it."[31]

James Thurber caricatured soaps as "a kind of sandwich… Between thick slices of advertising spread twelve minutes of dialog, ad predicament, villainy, and female suffering in equal measure, throw in a dash of nobility, sprinkle with tears, season with organ music, cover with a rich announcer sauce, and serve five times a week." Thurber went beyond criticizing the shows to caricaturing the women listeners. He ridiculed those who "confuse the actors with the characters." He cited listeners in 1935 who sent hundreds of gifts to a character who was going to have a baby, and again in 1940 when two characters were to marry. Actors playing other characters received soap, live turtles, flowers, and get well cards. Thurber was not alone in deriding women soap opera fans and in characterizing them as mentally unstable. He cited a Buffalo doctor who in 1942 claimed that soaps caused an "acute anxiety state" in women listeners. The doctor's claims received much attention from the press.[32]

Attacks on soaps continued a tradition in which, film theorist Tania Modleski argues, critics consistently have denigrated women's mass media and their readers, listeners, and viewers. The Buffalo doctor's reference to "acute anxiety state" echoed a very similar claim in 1901 by a Milwaukee doctor that drama matinees were harmful to young women, causing "nervous prostration." A 1951 *Sponsor* magazine article suggested magazines and novels afforded women with sources of romance and adventure, but not companionship.[33]

In the 1940s women researchers began to investigate charges that serials made women listeners psychologically unstable.[34] Although some critics suggested fans were lower class, studies consistently found no differences between listeners' and nonlisteners' educational or class strata. Women claimed radio helped the time pass while doing repetitive work like dishes or ironing, echoing the same sentiments expressed by women in the 1920s. In 1946, sociologist Ruth Palter conducted an in-depth study of white lower-middle-class women who were heavy radio listeners. They said radio took the drudge out of housework; "the ironing goes much faster," "it breaks the monotony and I don't even think about what I'm doing," "If a woman has the radio ... She ain't stuck in the ol' house." They described radio as a companion that warded off loneliness in an empty house.[35]

Palter also described listeners relating to the speaker on the radio as someone with whom they interact. This "parasocial interaction," as it came to be called, was characterized in magazines and research of others as an unhealthy blurring of reality. But such involvement, reminiscent of the nineteenth-century tales of green'uns in theaters, has been given more positive interpretations by other writers that imply no loss of a sense of reality.[36]

Psychologist Herta Herzog analyzed the results of four surveys conducted in the early 1940s to construct a picture of the daytime listener, and concluded women enjoyed serials for escape from their own problems and for an emotional release – a "good cry." Iowa listeners surveyed by sociologist Leda Summers in 1942 stated that serials helped them to solve their own problems. This was true for women with a college education as well as those with less education. Women in Pittsburgh and New York corroborated the statements of Iowa women, describing in their own words how serials helped them in their own lives. Respondents to a CBS national survey similarly said the stories were "true to life" and enabled them to extract "lessons in living."[37] The "true to life" comments suggest an explanation for talking about the characters as if they were real. Such talk would seem to make sense as part of the practice of extracting "lessons," rather than indicating confusion about the boundary between reality and fiction.

The research suggests more complex responses to radio than housewives becoming dangerously lost in the fantasies of the soaps.

More recent researchers argue that women have constructed positive readings from women's fiction and drama. Fiction writer Helen Papashvily claims the domestic or sentimental novel of the 1830s to 1880s lent themselves to a reading more supportive of women, glorifying the home and women in it and portraying men and the world outside negatively. The novels were a sort of subtle revolt, portraying men in uncomplimentary terms and focusing on the tribulations of the heroine. Yet men did not read them and accepted the novels as harmless pastimes for their wives and daughters. The soap opera is in some ways the twentieth-century equivalent of the nineteenth-century novel. Researchers interviewing television soap opera viewers in the 1980s similarly have documented alternative positive readings that viewers construct. So, we might suspect, did serial listeners of the 1940s.[38]

Fan mail confirms this "lessons for life" orientation on the part of many devoted listeners. Letter-writers tended to be more regular listeners than the average, yet their letters suggest a helpful side to their habit. Letters to the creator of *The Guiding Light,* Irna Phillips, contain less talk of the listener's own activities and more focus on the show than did earlier fan mail.[39] They do not exhibit much absorption in the lives of the characters, the usual stereotype of the soap opera fan, but rather responses to the serials as morality plays from which they can draw lessons applicable to their own lives. Most of these letters are either asking for copies of dialog that they can use in their own work with children as mothers, teachers, and advisors; or they express concern about the fates of characters. Some write about characters as if they were alive. But this represents a conversational shorthand more than an actual belief. They talk about the characters as models.

Letters as well as interviews conducted by researchers then and more recently emphasize a more positive and autonomous use of radio text than critics warned of. What they do not reveal is more details about their behavior, details that would tell us something about the public or private, individual or collective nature of the audience. Did they listen together? Did they talk with each other about their readings? Did this lead to collective applications to their lives, or did these "lessons for living" promote an individual orientation to problem solving, a "reading" of life as interpersonal problems? Did the readings encourage or discourage the kind of collective action that was at a high mark at the dawn of broadcasting in the early 1920s, just as women gained the right to vote? What is important is not only whether women were able to construct positive readings that might aide their self-esteem and individual autonomy, but also whether these listening practices fostered or interfered with their responding collectively beyond their circle of family and friends.[40]

"Other" Audiences

It is difficult to ascertain anything about black audiences in the 1920s. In radio magazines, for example, they are simply nonexistent. With few exceptions radio programs of the 1920s were directed to white audiences. The percentage of blacks owning radios was much smaller than that of whites. But, much like whites, when there was something broadcast that attracted them, they gathered together in large numbers to listen. Writer Maya Angelou related her childhood memories of the crowd that gathered at a small black-owned grocery in Stamps, Arkansas to listen to a Joe Louis fight in the 1930s: "The last inch of space was filled, yet people continued to wedge themselves along the walls of the store ... youngsters on the porch... Women sat on kitchen chairs, dining room chairs, stools and upturned boxes. Small children and babies perched on every lap." Clearly this event was exceptional enough to make a deep impression on the young Maya, but it is also reminiscent of similar scenes described in 1920s rural stores with white clientele, a customary way of listening to radio that survived longer in poor black communities where radios remained scarce.[41]

Another form of programming that may have attracted a black audience was the frequent broadcasts of "jazz." Radio magazines frequently complained of the many hours of radio time "wasted" on jazz, the favorite music of the "lost generation" of young, white middle-class listeners in the 1920s. Magazines frequently described generational conflicts in white homes between teenagers wanting to listen to jazz and parents and youngsters who wanted to tune in something else. No mention is made in the magazines, but it is probable that these programs also appealed to black fans of jazz.

Record sales indicate heavy black consumption of *recorded* music. Record companies began race records, including most jazz, shortly after World War I, and race records sold well during a severe drop in record sales in the early 1920s when the radio craze hit. Okeh Records sold a million copies of its first blues recording. Black vaudeville singers were widely recorded, and vaudeville blues sold well to blacks in the 1920s. By 1927 blacks were purchasing an estimated 10 million records a year, or one record for every black American. Twenty percent of Victor's catalog in 1928 was race records. The keen interest in recorded music on the part of blacks suggests that they probably also listened to radio broadcasts of jazz. Nevertheless, the first explicitly black-appeal radio program did not appear until 1929, when a small Chicago station, WSBC, began a black variety hour.[42] Few stations broadcast exclusively for any nonwhite or ethnic market. In the 1930s and 1940s, most such broadcasts were confined to specific programs on stations that either tried to supplement their mainstream market or tried to serve many different groups with programs tailored to each. In 1925 WSBC began to broadcast a variety of foreign-language programs to reach the one in four Chicagoans who were foreign-language speakers. By 1942, 205 stations offered foreign-language broadcasts in twenty-six languages, most commonly Polish, Spanish, Yiddish, and German.[43]

Ethnic broadcasts sentimentalized the old country. The audience was predominantly elderly and housewives who were confined largely to the home and thus slow to learn English and American norms, and who consequently continued to be oriented and attached to their native culture and language.[44] Second-generation youth were assimilating to American ways and listening to mainstream American broadcasts. Radio served to widen the gulf between foreign-language-speaking parents and English-language-speaking children that has been chronicled in immigrant studies such as that by William I. Thomas and Florian Znaniecki on Chicago Poles. Thus, while in the short run it may have provided a sense of ethnic and working-class community, it did so in a manner doomed to disappear with its aging audience, much like ethnic theater.[45]

Individuation

Privatization, which was part of radio listening early on, refers to the process in which people consume a significant part of their entertainment within the household rather than in public spaces. Once the household market began to reach saturation, however, manufacturers reversed their domestication strategy and began to associate radio with individuals rather than the family and home.[46] One such effort was to promote radios in automobiles. Magazine ads for car radios began to appear in 1930. By 1933 the *New York Times* identified a "craze" for car radios and attributed it to young people. NBC published a promotional booklet in 1936, "Radio Takes to the Road," telling advertisers that the car radio audience was already large and would eventually be almost as big as the home audience. The booklet reflected the change from domesticity in a sentence; "No longer is listening confined to the fireplace." In a similar 1937 booklet directed to advertisers, CBS promoted advertising sales in a graph that depicted the sharp rise in car radios. *Radio Retailing* reported that half of new cars sold in 1941 were equipped with a radio, and 30 percent of all autos had a radio.[47] Car radio advertising abandoned domesticity for other themes, particularly romance and sex.

A second strategy was to replace ads picturing families listening together with ads picturing them quarreling over what to listen to. The advertised solution was multiple radios in the home. The earliest experiments with such a strategy were initiated in the late 1920s. *Radio Retailing* called it "the 'radio in every room' plan." An Atwater Kent ad of 1929 illustrated this new theme, showing four hands reaching for the radio dial, each wanting to listen to something different. Crosley Radio introduced a new slogan, "A radio receiving set for every member of the family," allowing dad to hear "the baseball series, while the children tune in the bedtime stories and the young folks have dance music."[48]

A third strategy to expand the market was launched in the late 1930s with widespread manufacture of portable radios. By 1940, over 80 percent of American households had a radio. Radio had far exceeded saturation levels of all other electric appliances except the electric iron. Only 56 percent of homes had a refrigerator, only 60 percent electric washers. Selling to the individual was a response to household saturation. Portable radios were the ultimate individuation, sold as an individual's accessory to enhance one's appearance and attractiveness, equivalent to a pocketbook, rather than a fireplace. In fall 1939, Majestic introduced a portable with shoulder strap weighing less than four pounds. The change in retailing was expressed in the 1941 headline by *Radio & Television Retailing* that the "Important statistic in the future will be the number of *people* with receivers rather than the number of *homes*." This article was illustrated with a photo of portables owned by an airplane pilot, a champion ice skater, and a fisherman, and small tabletop radios in a bedroom, cars, a piano studio, a lawyer's office, and a fire station. A photo in the August 1941 issue showed a bootblack with a portable radio under his chair, played to entice trade and increase tips.[49]

Ads associated portables with sex appeal (a girl's dress blown up by the wind as she carries a portable radio) and romance (a couple holding hands while they walk with a portable radio.)[50] In contrast to the mid-1920s association with the home and family, these ads emphasized fun and going places. This shifted focus to individuals, particularly young people without spouses and children and household responsibilities. Such a change suggested significant reconstructions of the radio audience, or at least the construction of an additional new radio audience segment.

Young listeners were themselves expressing a desire for individuation of radio listening. A 1935 study found that California high school students were already listening alone or with friends, rather than with their families. A striking difference from earlier listeners was the desire to listen alone and not to be interrupted. As radio programs became subjects of interest, and as drama and comedy became increasingly significant forms of programming, attentive listening became more important than interaction with family and friends. Listeners were especially concerned not to miss a word of daytime serials. One researcher quoted women as saying, "I can't stand no talkin' while I'm listening"; "[if someone phones] I just say, 'Kid, I'm listening to so-and-so. I'll call you back'"; and "Naturally when you're with others they start to talk and they interrupt your listening ways."[51]

Listening was becoming an individual experience, each person attuned to the radio and insulated from every other. This was similar to the effect of dimming the lights in theater in the nineteenth century, which focused attention on the stage, discouraged conversation, and isolated audience members from each other. Radio both removed people from the crowd of the theater and isolated people from each other in – and out of – the home. Radio announcers began to foster a one-to-one intimacy between individual listeners and themselves. No longer did the announcer enter the listener's home. Rather the announcer drew the listener out of the family into a personal conversation in "radioland." This practice removed audiences further from the ground of collective action and provided grounds for critics to decry "hypnotic," "narcotic" effects of broadcasting on individuals.

Rural Radio: "We Are Seldom Lonely Anymore"

Radio had a dramatic impact on rural life. The United States was a rural nation when radio broadcasting began. In 1920, 49 percent of Americans lived in rural areas; in 1940, 43 percent were still living in rural areas. Before radio, few rural people had daily contact with the "outside world." Most had no telephone or newspaper. News mostly came from neighbors and mail. They did not have daily weather forecasts that would enable them to prepare their crops and animals for a frost or storms. They sold their crops with no knowledge of current prices on commodities markets, the prices at which the buyer could sell them. In bad weather they were often isolated even from their neighbors. Paved roads were rare; dirt roads turned into muddy quagmires whenever it rained. Snow made them impassable. Often farmers could not get to town for weeks, sometimes not even to their own mailbox.

Radio changed that. It would bring timely weather and market reports, news and entertainment. Far more than city dwellers, rural people were most grateful. In numerous letters to stations, entertainers and magazines and in conversations with agriculture agents and radio dealers, they expressed the value of the information and the great relief to isolation and loneliness. As soon as they could afford it, farmers purchased radios. But many could not afford it. Low rural income and high cost of radios restricted the spread of rural radios. During the Depression, which started in the 1920s in agriculture, some farmers could not afford even the seventy-five cents to recharge the six-volt battery most farm radios used.[1] Regional differences in radio saturation rates in rural areas reflected differences in income. Only about 5 percent of southern farmers had a radio in 1930, while about 40 percent of farmers in mid-Atlantic and North Central States had one. Despite the lack of electricity, most farmers in Montana, Idaho, and Wisconsin had radios, yet in Missouri, "not one farmer in twenty can afford and maintain a radio," according to William Hirth, publisher of *Missouri Farmer.*[2]

Despite the financial difficulties, by 1938 two-thirds of rural families had radios. Sociologist James West's study of a small Midwestern farm town found that by 1939–41, "Over half the townspeople and nearly half the farmers owned them. Most of the town sets are operated electrically, but nearly all of the country sets are battery-run. A few crystal sets are still in service." As West put it, radios were considered a necessity.[3]

"An Essential Marketing Tool"

The principal incentive for farmers to purchase a radio and the reason the U.S. Department of Agriculture and many state agriculture colleges fostered the development of radio broadcasting was its value for the business of farming. Weather and market price reports were invaluable. Farmers had been at a great disadvantage in selling their crops, since they had no independent information about market prices other than what wholesale buyers told them. Congress in 1913 created the Federal Bureau of Markets in the Department of Agriculture specifically to provide price information to farmers. The agency at first relied on telegraph to collect and distribute reports of prices to newspapers, post offices, and country stores in rural areas across the country. Farmers went to town for the latest report at their local store or post office. Radio greatly enhanced the distribution of this information. The USDA sent its first report by radio in 1920. By 1922 reports were being sent to over fifty radio stations to broadcast. The Weather Bureau also sent its reports by radio beginning in 1921. By 1923, USDA weather reports were broadcast by 140 stations.[4]

Some of these stations were operated by state agricultural extension services and by state universities. Kansas State Agricultural College began the first "farm school of the air" in January 1923. By 1925, twenty-four of the nation's land-grant colleges had established radio stations, and a dozen were broadcasting regularly on commercial stations. The University of Kentucky even purchased radios and set up community listening centers in poor mountain counties where farmers could not afford their own radios.[5]

Farmers remarked on the dramatic change they experienced in the 1920s with the arrival of these radio reports. A letter-writer to *Radio Broadcast* remarked, "The weather forecasts were broadcast last spring when almost everyone around had large numbers of little chickens. If there were to be bad weather I would call to my nearest neighbors and telephone the others. In that way we could get our chickens up and save much work and worry."[6]

Radio salesmen focused their sales pitch on the business value of radios for farmers. A *Radio Retailing* article recommended using the radio reports of prices as a way of convincing farmers of the value of an investment in a radio. A dealer kept records of the rise and fall of farm product prices, would ask farmers what they had gotten for their sale, and then point out how they could have done better if they had followed the prices reported on radio. Of course the dealer neglected to point out that, even with the radio, one could not predict when the price would peak.[7]

An Ear to the World

Radio continued to be important to rural people through the 1920s, 1930s, and 1940s. Farm men listened to market reports at the noon meal. Women listened in the morning while they worked around the house. Teenagers used it for music and parties. All listened in the evening. But the device was still too expensive and too "worldly" for children. Parents restricted children's listening in rural areas more than in cities.[8]

Initially rural listeners valued radio primarily as a source of information. But they soon began to value it for entertainment and as a companion. Urban radio stations discovered the potential rural market of listeners surrounding them. WEB in Atlanta and WLS in

Chicago were the first stations to offer regular country programs beginning in the mid-1920s. Many stations instituted "barn dance" programs when swamped with cards and letters in response to some incidental country musician who had performed on the air.[9] The radio introduced farm listeners to new music styles. A professor at the University of Wisconsin remarked, "I have been really amazed at the number of musical instruments found in country homes and the ability of some of the youngsters to play… It is surprising how quickly these youngsters improve their rendition *as a result of hearing radio music* [emphasis added] and picking up the modern tunes." Both white country and black blues musicians mentioned listening to and borrowing ideas from music on radio.[10]

More important than novelty, however, radio helped to curb the loneliness and isolation of rural life. A Kansas writer indicated that, before radio, trains were the principal source of information from the outside world, even from nearby towns. She said, "The arrival of the local train was once an event in the country town," bringing news, gossip, and entertainment, until radio replaced it. Another writer referred to the different circumstance before radio, "when the traveling circus, the home talent play and the church social afforded the principal forms of entertainment." One Iowa writer described the early 1920s, "During the long winter evenings, after the newspaper had been gone through thoroughly, the only other entertainment was to listen in on the telephone lines to the conversations of neighbors, or play the same records over and over again on the phonograph."[11]

L. L. Longsdorf of the Kansas agricultural extension service described radio as breaking the isolation of long winters homesteading, finding its niche in "a formerly vacant corner of the lives of rural people." *Radio Retailing* referred to the winter as "shut-in" season, the best time for radio dealers to mount a sales campaign directed at farmers. The impact was expressed in a poem by Ethel Romig Fuller, published in 1935 in *Good Housekeeping:*

And so you think us lonely when the snow
is piled up to the eaves? We used to be –
the one road blocked by drifts, no company.
How stillness hurts, you town folks cannot know!
The chores and housework done, time dragged along.
It's different now. Of course we're shut in still,
But we've a radio with which to fill
The ice-bound chinks of silence with song.

The while we sit beside our own hearth fire,
We hear the news and plays and symphonies;
Dance orchestras; chimes in a London spire;
A jungle's turmoil; waves of arctic seas...
Oh, we are seldom lonely any more –
A winter brings the whole world to our door.

Of course, *Good Housekeeping* was not a farmer's magazine, and few farmers chose plays and symphonies when they did acquire a radio. Nevertheless, the poem did express the relief from winter isolation that radio brought to farm families.[12]

The same sentiments were expressed by farmers, farm agents, rural magazine editors, radio executives, and advertisers. Agricultural officials and educators declared: "Radio is the greatest boon to isolated rural life since man's advent on earth"; "Radio has been one of the greatest blessings that the farmers of my part of the country have received during my lifetime"; "Rural life without the radio, especially since we have had the radio, would be unbearable."[13] Most frequently mentioned was the loneliness of the farm wife. The editor of the Lambertville, New Jersey *Record* stated that "a majority of the housewives turn on the radio in the morning 'Just for company' – and let it rattle away with whatever comes," evaporating "the solitude of the farm house, when the men are in the field." Another said, "Before the advent of the radio she spent most of her life in loneliness."[14]

Radio's importance to ward off loneliness continued into the 1940s. A 1945 USDA report on rural radio asked how farmer families would feel if their radio were broken for over a month. Respondents answered: "I am alone so much of the time, I look upon my radio as my companion." "I am just lost when the radio is broken." "We need the radio very much... We have a mile of bad road between the house and mailbox, and sometimes only get the mail once a week." When in the mid-1930s Oregon considered eliminating funding for a rural radio station, there was a quick outcry and the proposal died.[15]

People spoke of the radio "voice" as a substitute for real human company. Rural radio stations began to refer to "neighboring," where the radio announcer actively took on the role of neighbor and friend to his or her listeners. Often this was homemaking conversation directed to farm wives. Among the earliest and most long-lived were "neighboring" programs at KMA of Shenandoah, Iowa. The station owner, Earl May Seed & Nursery Company, used the programs to sell its seeds to farm wives, who planted vegetable and flower gardens for household consumption. From its first broadcast in 1925, KMA offered programs by and for women on singing and inspirational messages, growing and arranging flowers, beauty tips and home-made cosmetics, fashion and recipes, and religious broadcasts which included weddings on the air.[16] These "homemakers of the air" projected sincerity, enthusiasm, and optimism. They shared their personal lives with their listeners as close neighbors would. And they responded to letters from listeners. Listeners got to know them and their families and to follow the events in their lives, not unlike a soap opera. This feeling of community extended beyond the programs to an annual Fall Jubilee, begun in 1926, at which listeners could meet announcers, talk with each other, eat free pancakes, and not incidentally buy seed from the Earl May Seed Company. The jubilees continued until World War II.[17]

An Iowa competitor, Henry Field Seed Company, also used this neighboring style on its KFNF station, with Henry himself as announcer. He presented old-fashioned music and homey talks on farming and homemaking, mixed with direct selling over the air of Field Company products. Henry presented himself as just one of the plain rural folks, in contrast to the more middle-class tastes expressed by the KMA homemakers. He even used the station to rally his loyal listeners, reportedly numbering hundreds of thousands across the plains, to lobby for less Federal Radio Commission regulation and against increases in postage rates, which would significantly affect his mail-order seed business.[18]

My Friend on the Radio

Fan mail provides a rich picture of what the radio meant to rural people in the 1920s. One example is the fan mail of one of the favorite performers of the time, Wendell Hall. Hall was an itinerant musician who first broadcast from Chicago and then toured from station to station in the Midwest and Central Plains in the days before network radio. Hall was the first radio star to be sponsored (by Eveready Battery) and a prolific popular music writer. His hits included "It Ain't Gonna Rain No Mo," and "My Carolina Rose." He had a folksy appeal to listeners, many of whom tuned into distant stations to follow him on his tour of stations, some staying up late into the night to pick up his broadcasts.[19]

Hall encouraged people to send in applause cards and letters, so stations and his sponsor would know the size of his audience. Over the years he claimed to have received a million letters.[20] Many letters were personal, like correspondence with a friend. They reveal a more sincere and personal relationship to the broadcast than that which developed once broadcasts were a fixture of everyday life. Hall invented the method of talking and singing directly to the audience as if to someone in the room, a method that later was claimed to be the source of success of network stars Rudy Vallee, Bing Crosby, and Arthur Godfrey. This was especially effective in this era when people thought of the voice from the box as someone talking to them face to face. Unaccustomed to broadcasting or even the telephone, they thought of the performer as actually in their home. They answered back through their letters.

Fan letters repeatedly expressed feelings of friendship: "it seemed as if you were in the same room and had heard me laugh"; "It seems as though we were writing to an old friend when we write to you, as we surely have enjoyed many an evening with you"; "When you said 'good bye' it seemed as if an old friend was leaving us. Please come back"; "a friend of the family who has been kind enough to drop in and entertain us"; "You are a great favorite at our house and we missed you and your clever entertainment while you were away."

They often talked about what was happening to them as if writing to a confidant. A boy wrote that he didn't do his homework in order to listen in, and suspected his teacher had listened as well. A young Iowa woman wrote, "my [boyfriend's] mother just phone [sic] about fifteen minutes ago and told him it was time to come home, and just like a 'Mama's Model Lil' twenty-one year old Man' he obeyed her and left me! Now just isn't that 'the eye's pupil'? Well, since your kind, gentle and lamb-like voice sounded sorta lonesome and since I am, I'm going to write you."

They spoke openly and un-self-consciously about themselves and what they thought. One, who claimed Hall's singing about sleepy people put him to sleep while smoking his pipe, said his wife "lit into me and now I've got a set of black eyes and me back's nearly bursted" for burning the carpet with his pipe. One spoke of falling asleep with the headphones on, while another was pleasantly awakened at midnight by the sound from the earphones at the head of her bed. A Texas woman wrote of a three-year-old boy greeting his daddy coming home from work, saying, "Daddy, I guess we ain't goina have no supper tonight, Ma is yonder listening to Red." An eleven-year-old boy wrote in 1924 as if to a distant uncle, telling about his move to the country, his fondness for the country, the kind old German couple who lived nearby, and on for eight pages. They related their personal tragedies and hardships. In a heart-rending letter a Pennsylvania mother related how her twenty-one-year-old son was killed in a tractor accident, and the radio was the only thing that took the father's mind off it. Another spoke of his wife recovering from knee surgery, "But when she listens to you she forgets the pain and everything but the Red-Headed Music Maker ... all cares are sung away and we are ready for a good night's sleep." A farm couple wrote, "we've only had our radio a short time. We are farmers and it surely rests one after a hard day's work, to sit down and listen to such wonderful music of all kinds and the splendid sacred music without having to "dress up" and ride 8 ½ miles to church – on Sunday."

Several letter writers wrote of introducing him to their friends and neighbors. One said, "Mother [who was 76 years old] ... was very proud to show you off to some visitors last night." A Missouri woman spoke of having a couple and their children visit them to listen in and coming back for a second night. A boy wrote in 1924, "If the roads are better this week [his teacher] will come and hear you sing [on his radio]." Another wrote, "At a radio party at my house tonite your program came in as usual 100%." One young man wrote, "I had a gang at the house especially to get your stuff ... and the same gang threaten to camp in my room tonight, Friday and Saturday." An appliance store owner wrote, "I had a store full of customers and they stuck around until you signed off."

Letters frequently talk of parents and children together enjoying his music. One recalled, "as the different ones of the family heard your voice and uke they rolled out of bed to appear at the door of the radio room. Tonight your voice was soon recognized by even the 5 year old twins who were soon on the stairs to listen to your program." One girl wrote that her mother "persuaded the rest of the family to take a night off and spend the evening at home 'listening in' ... not one of us considered that evening wasted."[21]

The consistent and overwhelming tone of the letters was the treatment of Hall as a new friend visiting their home, bringing them pleasant diversion, relaxation, contentment. Hall on the radio was a welcome respite from their work and worries, and someone they could talk *to*. The letters vividly indicate that the neighboring was not just a marketing strategy of stations but was the way in which these farm families actually felt about radio and the people it brought into their homes. There could hardly be stronger testimony to the personal importance of radio than the sentiments in these letters.

A Community Resource

While a personal and even intimate experience, rural listening in the 1920s and 1930s was not a private experience. More than in urban areas, radio encouraged communal participation. Morse Salisbury, chief of radio service for the U.S. Department of Agriculture, noted that even as late as 1935, "especially in the South, many farmers not owning radio receiving equipment gather in central places of the community such as the store or cotton gin, to listen to farm and other broadcasts" and that persons that do own sets "exert strong leadership within their communities." He cited Arkansas, where only 2.4 percent of farmers owned sets, yet many more learned of government programs through radio. Tenant farmers of Arkansas listened in stores and garages, which "were the noonday daily centers of interest when cotton news was broadcast."[22]

Letters from farmers confirm Salisbury's claim. Two letters quoted in *Wireless Age,* one from Iowa, another from Missouri, refer to their sharing market reports via telephone with their neighbors who do not have radios. A letter from an Indiana farm wife published in *Farming – The Business Magazine* stated, "we are on a party telephone line and our neighbors often keep posted through our radio, about markets and prices."[23]

Extending this logic a step further, some enterprising Carolina farmers without electricity or telephone purchased loudspeakers and linked them to a cooperative neighbor's radio by wires strung on trees and fence posts across fields and woods, in an early nonprofit version of cable systems. The farmer with the receiver would tune in programs popular among the "subscribers," usually country music. These systems sometimes served several hundred homes and involved a similar number of miles of wire.[24]

Radios in public places in farm towns were particularly important before radio was more affordable and ownership more common. The "cracker barrel circle" in general stores began to include a radio. The St. Louis *Post-Dispatch* reported from a survey in fall 1922 that nearly all the country banks in the mid-Mississippi Valley had radio sets to receive news and market reports. Banks installed radios to receive market reports from stations in Chicago and other large cities several times a day, which were then posted on bulletin boards.[25] Community radios were set up for other purposes as well. One photo showed about 100 to 150 people listening to an agricultural lecture on radio in a local schoolhouse. A survey of Illinois farmers stated that radio sets were frequently used for community gatherings in schools, churches, and other public places for lectures and music. Rural schools and churches in 1927 held community gatherings for special educational broadcasts. Radio continued to be used for community gatherings in rural areas through the 1930s. Even in the late 1930s Midwest, men gathered in local stores and town squares to listen to famous prizefights and the world series.[26]

Out in the countryside, informal groups gathered to listen together, especially for musical entertainment. Elmer Bird, a well-known banjo player of the 1940s and 1950s, recalled radio listening when he was a child. In 1930 West Virginia, his family of local musicians climbed to the top of a ridge where there was good reception to set up their radio run on a car battery. Other people joined them, walking as much as three or four miles. At nine o'clock the Grand Ole Opry began broadcasting. They listened until it ended at midnight; then they walked home in the dark.[27] For Elmer and his family to hear their own kind of music broadcast from a city 300 miles away was a validation of their own music and culture.

A 1931 study of illiterate Virginia mountain people reported one family with a radio whom neighbors visited almost nightly. A letter-writer in North Dakota wrote in 1936, "Saturday night is the affair of affairs up here. Those who have no radio congregate at the homes of those who have and what an enjoyable evening! Yes, enjoyable to the superlative degree. The only amusement we have is a show house 20 miles away and an occasional dance. So radio folks can't possibly know what glorious entertainment you render to us 'shut-ins.'" The president of the Wyoming Farm Bureau stated that radio had "taken the place of the phonograph in giving dance music to little parties." A letter-writer from Ontario in 1938 said, "Radios are not too plentiful here. I have seen as many as twenty or thirty gathered in our home on Saturday night to enjoy the Saturday Night Barn Dance."[28]

Community listening was a response to the scarcity of radios. Even in the mid-1930s in many areas, radio was still not common in farm households, and they continued to practice the community listening that had by then disappeared from the radio habits of urban listeners.

Community or Privatization?

Radio was one of several new technical innovations in the 1920s. Automobiles, telephones, rural mail delivery, and in the 1930s, electrification all helped to reduce isolation. But radio was considered the most significant by almost all commentators. The automobile could not negotiate muddy or snow- and ice-covered country roads in bad weather. Many could not afford a telephone. A study of farm families in Illinois and Nebraska in the late 1930s found that, when forced to choose between radio and telephone, some families gave up the telephone or shared the cost of a phone with several neighbors, using the savings to buy their own radio. When the radio arrived, often it was preferred over the phonograph for spontaneous dancing groups.[29]

Many sociologists blamed radio and the auto for weakening community because it led to people staying at home rather than visiting neighbors or attending meetings. Rural sociologist Howard Forsyth argued that radio was reducing social contact outside the family. Edmund Brunner said, "many families have more than paid for their radio by attending fewer picture shows." Another researcher quoted a 1925 letter from an Illinois farmer who wrote that radio "keeps young people at home at night." Sociologists John Gillette and the Lynds blamed radio for drawing people's attention from the local community by their listening to national network programs.[30]

But not all sociologists agreed about radio's effect on community. Brunner and co-author Irving Lorge attributed the decline in the numbers and memberships of social organizations to "the leaner purses of rural folk during the Depression," and William Robinson concluded that owning a radio had little effect on reducing membership and attendance, or on visiting or social telephoning.[31]

If radio relieved "isolation," it filled a void rather than replaced some more community-oriented activity. If it had an effect on community, it was indirect, on attitude and values concerning community. During this "community" phase, radio enhanced community ties as people shared scarce radios. But as more households acquired radios, the "boon" to the rural family did not strengthen community ties. Rather it contributed to privatization, as it did in urban areas.

15

Fears and Dreams: Public Discourses about Radio

I n the early years of broadcasting almost everyone had some opinion about the future of radio, its promise and dangers. Theater managers, newspaper and music publishers, even preachers debated its effect on attendance. Some early commentators expressed great hopes for radio as a source of cultural uplift for the masses. Others feared the degenerative social, psychological, and aesthetic effects of commercial radio. How would it affect other cultural institutions, the family and children, education, political campaigns?[1]

Commerce clashed with aesthetic interests in these discourses. In the 1920s owners and managers of other entertainments worried whether radio might woo away their audiences. When these fears proved unfounded, they accommodated themselves to the new medium and it to their own needs. Cultural elites, on the other hand, soon realized that commercial radio would not fulfill their dreams for educating the masses. Rather than become accommodated to this unfortunate conclusion, they assailed radio's content and motives, and mounted campaigns to restrict or reform it.

The conflict between commercial and cultural interests recapitulated earlier struggles over leisure between commerce and social reformers.[2] Through the nineteenth century, elite reformers worried about working-class pleasures and attempted to shape them through public regulation and facilities. They met with little success in either forcing or persuading working-class adults and children to follow their instructions. Newly forming commercialized leisure, on the other hand, offered release from work and from reformers' controlling instincts. Commercial interest made profits satisfying working-class demands, while reformers found themselves trying to force alien tastes upon an unwilling class. Radio repeated the contest and the outcome.

With radio, intellect replaced morality in the battle against commerce. The voice of the moralizer, so prominent in nineteenth-century debates, was muted; few worried about the moral ramifications of radio. The 1920s were a decade in which cultural aesthetes and social science experts spoke louder than moralists. Advertising executives considered themselves "apostles of modernity," who used and promoted radio as a tool of cultural uplift. The upper middle class turned to experts like psychologist John Watson and home economist Christine Frederick, rather than to their preachers, for advice about home and family. The behavior of the younger generation, so shocking to some, was an expression of this modernity.[3]

Commercial Concerns

Initially, theatrical professionals were delighted to appear on radio which they saw as a wonderful new form of publicity. Press agents for theaters and music publishers busily arranged performances. But attendance at Broadway and vaudeville theaters and sheet music and record sales dropped off slightly, and they panicked. The playwright Augustus Thomas testified at the 1923 Congressional hearings on copyright that radio was the cause of cancellations of several road-company plays because the plays had been broadcast on radio. Producers of musical comedies, the most successful genre of the time, feared that radio would empty theater seats. The Keith and Orpheum vaudeville agency forbade vaudevillians to perform on radio.[4]

Once over the panic, however, theaters adapted radio to their own needs and used it to promote their plays. A turning point was when Arthur Hammerstein broadcast the first act of his new musical comedy, *Wildflower,* on WEAF, New York City in 1923. Box office receipts for the play jumped considerably, and many who attended the theater performance said they came as a result of the radio broadcast. After that, New York producers ceased to frown on radio and even encouraged broadcasts of plays. In order to use radio to promote musical comedies, producers joined radio broadcasters against the American Society of Composers, Authors and Publishers (ASCAP) in a dispute over the right to broadcast copyrighted music. Thomas Gozzola, manager of the Studebaker Theater in Chicago, adopted Hammerstein's strategy, permitting broadcast of the play *Abie's Irish Rose* that was being staged at his theater. The result was a flood of requests for tickets to the play. Gozzola said, "Never in my twenty years' experience as a Chicago theater manager has any one feature helped patronage like the broadcasting of *Abie's Irish Rose.*"[5]

Nevertheless, fears remained. A broadcast may have benefited a particular play but also weakened the general habit of regular theater-going. Big hits could still draw, but the run-of-the-mill play at most theaters was hurt. The radio was more likely a substitute for the ten-twenty-thirty than for the high-priced Broadway play. The same article that proclaimed the success of broadcasting *Abie's Irish Rose* also claimed that when famous opera stars sang on the radio, people stayed home to listen and theaters remained half-filled. Arthur Hornblow, editor of *Theater Magazine,* claimed that "common sense tells anyone that broadcasting plays cannot possibly do theatre any good" and that most producers were "bitterly opposed to it." Producers' fears certainly were not abated by radio manufactures' ads that equated radio with theater. An ad in *Saturday Evening Post* for Stewart-Warner radios claimed it "Cuts your entertainment cost in half" and showed a couple's handwritten budgets for 1925 before their radio purchase and for 1926 after their purchase – the couples' attendance of movies was reduced from four to two and concerts from one to none each month.[6]

The music industry feared the effects of radio much more than theater producers. Phonograph record sales declined for ten years after peaking in 1922 at 100 million. Phonographs shipped by manufacturers dropped from a peak of 2.2 million in 1919 to 600,000 in 1921 and stagnated around a million per year until rock 'n' roll began in the 1950s. Musical instrument production went from $175 million in 1923 to $80 million in 1929. For pianos, the quintessential musical instrument for middle-class homes, sales dropped from $111 million to $42 million. ASCAP published a leaflet, titled "The Murder of Music," blaming radio for the shrinking sales of pianos, phonographs, and sheet music between 1925 and 1932.[7]

Victor Herbert and John Phillip Sousa feared radio would reduce sales of their sheet music and recordings. Alma Gluck, famous operatic star of the 1920s, claimed that radio broadcasts of her recordings had reduced her royalty income "precipitously." ASCAP controlled copyright permission for most of the popular music of the day and was adamant that broadcasters pay for use of their music. In 1923, ASCAP served notice on radio stations that they would be required to pay license fees for use of ASCAP music, including record playing as well as live performances.[8]

While ASCAP battled for payment of royalties, the American Federation of Musicians (AFM), the musician's union, opposed the broadcast of recordings. Even the Department of Commerce recognized the heavy use of recorded music by early radio stations, stating, "During the early days, the programs of a majority of the stations consisted almost entirely of phonograph records." AFM hoped to create jobs for musicians at each station.[9] But the creation of networks in the late 1920s enabled a few musicians employed at one station to be broadcast across the country. Networks circumvented the need for every radio station to hire their own musicians.

Victor Talking Machine Company and Brunswick Records at first restricted radio performance by singers and musicians under contract to them. Both Victor and Brunswick were known for their classical and operatic music records. They claimed that radio broadcasts were poor reproductions and detrimental to their artists' reputations.[10] But, as did Broadway producers, they changed their tune. In January 1925, Victor relented and arranged a concert series for its operatic stars on WEAF in New York. The Brunswick Records Hour followed shortly thereafter.[11]

The movie industry seems to have been less concerned, despite the fact that some believed people were staying home from the movies because of radio. In 1933 Minneapolis respondents said that radio resulted in a 19 percent reduction in their theater and movie attendance. The president of the Wyoming State Farm Bureau claimed that radio paid for itself in rural areas in the savings of fewer visits to the movies.[12]

Among newspapers, initial reaction was mixed. Associated Press banned the use of its service on radio, but United Press International gladly sold its service to radio. AP soon relented. Many early broadcast stations were owned and operated by newspapers. Some, however, believed that radio would supplant newspapers. An article in *Radio Broadcast* claimed that radio was responsible for the demise of the "extra edition" and of small newspapers who relied on reprinting stories from metropolitan dailies. Others, whether bravely whistling in the dark or genuinely unafraid, were more optimistic. M. E. Tracy of Scripps-Howard Newspapers, speaking to the Radio Manufacturers convention in June 1928, said that Scripps viewed radio "as a great advantage to them." The American Newspaper Publishers Association declared that radio was helpful to newspapers rather than a threat.[13]

Cultural Uplifters

Many believed radio was a tremendous tool in raising the cultural and educational level of the population. In the early 1920s, radio was claimed to be a godsend to all, bringing the world to every American's door. An editorial cartoon in the *San Francisco Examiner* showed a "Mr. Everybody" with headphones connected to a broadcast station atop a little globe in the palm of his hand. The caption reads, "How you have shrunk!" A very similar cartoon in the *Chicago News* showed the public sitting in an upholstered chair listening to radio and saying to a very small world on the floor, "Isn't he a cute little fellow?" *Wireless Age* phrased it, "in whatever direction you please, radio does make a bigger world."[14]

The early promise and, more so, the later disappointments were founded on beliefs about the cultural potential of radio. Classical music elites advocated the use of radio to elevate the musical taste of the nation. A writer in *Radio Broadcast* boasted, "Grand opera, news expensively and quickly gathered, the words of political and religious leaders, instrumental music by great artists – all these are carried by the house-top antennas down into dingy rooms for the comfort of persons for whom such things simply did not exist a year ago... It is hard to imagine the splendor of the vistas which radio must have opened to many of these people [in Chicago's west-side tenements]." They assumed that everyone naturally would prefer classical music, once they had the opportunity to hear it regularly. They were especially opposed to jazz music played on urban stations, to which they reacted much as some did to rock 'n' roll in the 1950s.[15] Anxieties about the dangers of jazz could be counterbalanced by the reassuring, immutable standards of classical music.

Even commercial interests promoted radio as a cultural tool. Cultural historian Roland Marchand observed that radio in the mid-1920s "enjoyed an aura of cultural uplift, unlike that of any other medium." Radio manufacturers cultivated this image in their ads, associating radio with elegance and high culture. Magazine ads featured luxurious interiors and wealthy men and women in formal attire listening to opera and orchestra. The trade magazines *Advertising and Selling* and *Judicious Advertising* claimed radio elevated popular tastes. *Radio Retailing* said that "the average listener wants good music," by which was meant opera and orchestral music. The magazine recommended illustrations of orchestral music to sell radios. Advertisers in radio magazines hailed their equipment as educational tools and musical instruments. RCA's broadcast arm, NBC, complemented such ads by funding many classical music programs – until they found advertisers to pay for programs.[16]

In the battle over interference, cultural uplifters equated the major and most powerful stations, such as those owned by Westinghouse and General Electric and affiliates of the NBC chain, with fine programming of classical music and the smaller stations as offering inferior "jazz." *Radio Broadcast* claimed that its readers favored "wholesale elimination of mediocre stations." "Little, willful broadcast stations" were accused of degraded programs and of interfering with good programming of the major stations. A cartoon in the New York *Daily Mirror* theater newspaper read, "Cheap radio stations, built solely for profit, are cluttering up New York City – Great artists who could entertain millions play at the better class stations, but – "honky tonk" performers at the cheap stations fill the air with their awful noises."[17]

In the 1920s radio magazines generally favored classical music programming, perhaps to justify radio's worthiness. They argued that listeners *wanted* classical music. *Wireless Age* claimed radio broadcasts had improved student knowledge of classical music in over 500 cities and towns by promoting contests of musical memory of what was broadcast. The magazine included a series of articles in 1922 and 1923 by famous musicians, opera singers, and educators that predicted great benefits of radio to American musical education and taste.[18] *Radio World* regularly published articles claiming that radio's audience was superior to theater's in preferring classical music; that radio cultivated better taste in music and even improved jazz, making it more "refined and harmonious" and less "barbarous"; and that it enriched the English language with 5,000 new words. One article claimed that KDKA of Pittsburgh had gradually lifted its audience's taste from jazz to folk music to light opera to Bach.[19]

Radio Broadcast reported from surveys by Atwater Kent, manufacturer of expensive radios, and WJZ, the Westinghouse Station in New York, and from its own readers that listeners wanted more classical music and less jazz.[20] These surveys were cited in the column "The Listeners' Point of View," written by Jennie Irene Mix and then John Wallace, in which they persistently advocated classical music programming. The masthead declared it was "conducted by" rather than written by the columnists. Irene Mix, a music critic who had published a book to introduce the layperson to classical music, originated the column in 1924. She cited her own acquaintances, letters to the editor, and other anecdotal evidence to support her contention that many people wanted to hear classical music and objected to what she considered a preponderance of jazz. In June 1924 she claimed the public wanted orchestral music, basing her conclusion on the attendance at and support of symphony orchestras in the United States. Mix argued that stations should broadcast high-quality music and avoid "trash," for they had a "responsibility of using for a constructive purpose this greatest musical opportunity [radio] that has ever been available to the public." In January 1925 she noted that "quite a bit of good music [i.e., classical] is broadcast each week. But it is insignificant in quantity when compared with the cheap and tawdry stuff." She quoted a *New York Times* editorial, saying, "there is no imaginable excuse for giving [radio audiences] jazz, hour after hour, every evening from nearly all the stations." In February 1925 she again complained that "with some few and notable exceptions, all the stations put on the same character of program, cheap enough ... for the purpose of reaching the largest number of people possible, rather than with the desire ever to make an appeal to a discriminating public." She referred to the "accustomed dullness" of usual radio music. Mix expressed a recurring theme of the time, equating low-brow "jazz" to taste of the masses and commercial success, while portraying high-brows as superior and embattled in defense of taste against commercialism.[21]

By the time John Wallace succeeded Irene Mix in 1926, the glorious praises that cultural high-brows lavished on radio in 1923 had turned sour. Wallace complained that stations who had earlier been responsible for the high-brow programs had now abandoned that for fear of losing their audience, a fear he claimed was unfounded. He believed that radio had elevated the public taste during the early years until 1927 when the amount of orchestral music had drastically declined. He complained that stations that had maintained their own orchestras had now disbanded them. He described programs in January 1928 as "a lot of inanities that only the veriest imbecile, with the meagerest amusement resources conceivable, could dignify with the name of worthwhile entertainment." Sponsored programs he described as "all alike as peas in a pod." In August 1928 he said, "There is not the slightest danger that the masses will ever be neglected by the entertainment purveyors. They present far too large a potential market for cleansing powders, tires, tooth paste, hair tonic and linoleum."[22]

As the 1920s wore on, magazines wrote less about uplifting the masses and some became hostile both to the masses and to radio stations, whom they blamed for reducing the number of classical music broadcasts and for the success of jazz. Wallace, perhaps frustrated with what he saw as the deleterious effects of commercially sponsored programming, lashed out viciously at the "masses." In April 1926 he remarked that "the [cultural] taste of the American nation is incontrovertibly low. It could adorn itself with a parasol and still walk under a dachshund." In November 1927 he referred to the average listener's "unimaginative and uncritical mind." In another issue he claimed that no more than one in a thousand listeners had the "latent capacity" to be educated.[23]

Wallace may have been reacting to the declining class of the radio audience. As more people purchased radios, the average income of radio homes declined. By the end of the decade there was less of the high-brow programming that Wallace advocated. Radio was shifting from a diversion of the affluent to an entertainment for lower- and middle-income families.[24]

A few advocates of cultural uplift persisted through the 1930s. The conductor Walter Damrosch remained a true believer in cultural programming and in the "masses." Damrosch had retired as conductor of the New York Symphony in 1928 to broadcast on NBC a series of concerts with explanations for elementary and high school students. In 1934 he claimed his classical musical series had had benefits and that "The radio is revolutionizing our national approach to music." He claimed his audience "represents a fair cross-section of the American nation" and that "the public seems to like what I give it – and I give it only the best." An article in *Atlantic Monthly* blamed people like Wallace, with their low opinion of the American audience, for causing low-grade programming. It cited a memo circulated by the Federal Bureau of Education on how to write a radio script: "Present your specialty on the level of thirteen-year-olds. Do not overrate the intelligence of your listeners" as an indicator of the guideline used to produce *educational* programs and therefore the reason for the low quality. But it agreed with other elitists that commercialism was the main culprit. Advertising squeezed out the sustaining programs that "furnish practically all material of genuine cultural or educational value." As station owners and networks realized they could make money through advertising, they stopped the high-brow programs they had been supporting from their own pockets.[25]

The American Association for Adult Education founded the National Advisory Council on Radio in Education in January 1930 to promote "good" programming. Levering Tyson, head of the Council, admitted that most educators were disappointed that radio's great potential was being wasted. However, he argued there were many "first-class programs" on the air, and committed his Council to increasing the educational value of programming.[26] In the 1940s critics still talked of the great cultural and educational potential of radio, but now they lowered their expectations. Sherwood Gates, a professor of education representing the National Recreation Association, reiterated the phrases of the 1920s, calling radio the greatest cultural medium since print, providing "opportunity for cultural enlargement" to those who do not read serious books or cannot attend concerts. He advocated using radio in recreation facilities and other group settings for educational purposes. The Women's National Radio Committee, instead of demanding classical music and Shakespearean plays, awarded certificates of merit to the *Fibber McGee and Molly* and Fanny Brice shows.[27]

Against Uplift: Leave Us Alone

Average listeners preferred middle-brow entertainment to the ones advocated by cultural elites. Audience researcher Frederick Lumley created a composite from ten surveys from 1928 to 1932, which indicated a strong preference for popular music, including jazz, Tin Pan Alley, and old-time, over classical. Popular music was the first preference in his composite rankings, classical music fifth after comedy, drama, and sports, and before general talk, religious, news, and educational programs. "Old-time" music, turn-of-the-century popular songs such as *Let Me Call You Sweetheart*, *My Wild Irish Rose*, and *When*

You and I Were Young, Maggie, especially had a wide appeal in small towns and rural areas.[28]

Most people simply ignored classical music advocates; many thought uplifters took themselves, radio, and life too seriously. A respondent to a *Radio Broadcast* 1927 survey from Saranac, New York said, "the average family about the fireside wants to be entertained, not forcibly educated ... relief when one is tired." The editor, introducing an article that parodied uplifters' complaints, said, "So much piffle has been written about the great mission of broadcasting that it is a relief to find a real authority laying about him with a club at many of the fundamentals in the radio Credo."[29]

Such debunking appeared regularly in the *Popular Radio* column "The Broadcast Listener," which first appeared in June 1925. Written by Raymond Francis Yates, it spoke for those middle-brows who were not overtly antagonistic to cultural uplift but simply wanted to enjoy radio, not be educated by it. Suggesting a democratic ethos, it urged readers to send in their own ideas about radio programs. The subtitle of the column was "From the Point of View of the *Average* Fan" [emphasis added] – in marked distinction to the tone of Mix and Wallace. The column was also more free ranging, including, as the subtitle indicated, "comments on radio programs, methods and technique." Yates' column was a conventional middle-brow discourse. He disliked jazz. In July 1925 he was already complaining, "For three years now we have been ranting semi-frantically about the unmitigated employment by the [radio] studios of the zoological brand of music ... jazz is a bankrupt art... Radio has made jazz so hopelessly common that it is hurting both itself and broadcasting."[30]

On the other hand, Yates also debunked high-brow snobbery. He was a deflator of the snob and the righteous. He remarked sarcastically about a wealthy wife who was "one of the first to discover radio as a means of lifting the literary tastes of the masses." He objected giving such persons broadcast time for a dramatic reading that was dreadful. He distanced himself from the uplifters and identified with his "average listener" readers, by admitting his own cultural limitations. He described himself as "perhaps one of the worst listeners that ever fell into applauding with the rest of the pretenders at Carnegie Hall" and his operatic education as "so incomplete and plebeian that we are cold to the demands made by the more erudite students." Contradicting the listener surveys quoted by Wallace and others, he reported that letters from readers indicated that broadcasters were offering pretty much what readers wanted, as he phrased it, "noodle soup" rather than the taste for *pate foie gras* he had expected. He crisply expressed the irritation with uplifters, complaining, "What we object to is the persistent effort to make of radio one vast institution for musical discussion and analyzing. We want to enjoy music ... without the interference of a flock of long-hairs who would have us listen with furrowed brows and eardrums straining for the slightest imperfection."[31]

Others were more hostile in their reactions to cultural elites. In the mid-1920s Henry Ford began a campaign for "old-time music" that expressed traditional values over the snobbery of classical music, and even more against jazz. Ford was widely praised in rural areas for his support of country music. Broadcasters frequently received requests in 1926 to play a song, *Let's All Henry Ford*, in his honor. Ford contrasted his old-time music to the jazz of the commercial music industry that he described as a "Jewish trust." He attributed the rise of jazz to Jews, blacks, and communists.[32] Ford's appeal was strong among farmers who, in letters to editors and radio stations and in surveys of their radio program preferences, consistently expressed a preference for "old-time" country music over classical, orchestral, or jazz. Their reaction against high-brow tendencies was captured in the comment of W. S. Porter of Utah's Agricultural College, that rural people are "eager for knowledge provided it is not made self-evident that someone is trying to educate them."[33]

Classical music, jazz, and old-time music represented high, commercial, and folk cultures in the debates over cultural hierarchy and mass culture. Cultural elites criticized jazz and old-time music as devoid of aesthetic quality; fans of old-time music, who tended to be populists, resented the superior attitudes of elites, while joining them in condemning jazz, though for reasons of morality – and racism.

Popular criticisms of jazz paralleled the turn-of-the-century elite criticism of mass culture as a feminine influence destroying art, but attached the problem to blacks instead of women. Jazz did not have the narrower definition of today, but referred perjoratively to many popular musical forms of alleged black origin. Jazz was characterized with all the usual racist stereotypes of blacks as oversexed and out of control. Radio jazz was seen by uplifters and the old-time movement as a commercial conspiracy to degrade America aesthetically and morally. Meanwhile, however, most people ignored the debate and tuned in their radios to relax and enjoy themselves, much as a generation earlier, working people had enjoyed cheap vaudeville and nickelodeons and ignored Progressive reformers' efforts to dissuade them.

The High-Brow Listener Speaks, 1930

Uplifters placed much faith in the benefits of high-culture programming. What did the actual listeners have to say about such programs? From a sample of about a hundred fan letters we can glimpse an audience in 1930 who were loyal listeners to two early high-brow NBC drama programs. A Wednesday matinee of the air titled *The Radio Guild* offered high-quality dramas performed by an NBC repertory company. On Sunday nights *An Hour with Shakespeare* presented his plays performed well.[34] These listeners were themselves believers in cultural uplift. But their expressions also tell us about their orientation to radio, how it affected their lives and homes, and how they differed from other listeners.

In contrast to the folksy letters to Wendell Hall in the mid-1920s from people who preferred old-time music, these culturally sophisticated listeners tell us relatively little about themselves. They don't share their lives the way Hall's listeners did. Their comments concentrated on the performance. Sometimes they echoed the cultural uplifters concerning the value of radio. One letter from Cleveland said, "More and more and more power to you for your *Hour with Shakespeare*. It is a welcome oasis in a world of blah."

Some mentioned group listening and discussions among their friends. One wrote, "If you knew how much the dramas and [Shakespeare] plays are talked about, looked forward to, and listened into I feel sure you would put more on." A New York wife wrote on her own letterhead, "I had a porch party to-day and at 4:00 pm we tuned the radio in to your station to hear one of your wonderful radio dramas.... All exclaimed at the magnificent performance. They enjoyed it as thoroughly as if it were a visible performance on the stage."

Several letters noted that they would allow no other obligations to interfere with their date with the broadcast. One noted that "many of my friends ... also await eagerly, every Wednesday, the hour of 4 to 5." Another wrote they spend "all spare time each Sunday out-of-doors reading up the play from Shakespeare, so as to thoroughly enjoy the 9:45 broadcast." One from Georgia said, "My fifteen year old son and I sat with the book in our hands, following you, and I enjoyed it as much as tho I were seeing [*Hamlet*] played."

This is as personal as these letters got. There are no confessions of deaths or other heartbreaks, no talking about mom and dad and the children, and no expressions that it was almost like having friends into their living room. There were some references to group listening, mothers and daughters and sons, and a party. But there was more frequent reference to people talking about the shows after performances, while they listened separately. Presumably the spread of ownership played a part in this change from the 1920s letters. What comes through consistently is that these were selective listeners. They planned what they were going to listen to. They did not use radio as background, nor did they weave listening into whatever they were doing. They paid close attention to the radio, listening to every line of the play, immersed in the conjured fantasy.

The two collections of radio letters, to Wendell Hall and to NBC, reveal patterns of behavior and radio use that foreshadow recent typologies of family uses of television. We will see that the television audience typologies have roots that reach back into the early days of radio. The high-brow listeners of 1930 were the precursors of more recent middle-class television viewers, just as Hall's listeners of the mid-1920s presaged the working-class style of television use in the 1950s and after. What these letters tell us is repeated in the observations by television researchers from the 1950s on. In some, the focus was on adult use or family habits; in others, the focus was more specifically on child-rearing practices. In all, however, the same patterns of working-class and middle-class styles recur.[35]

From Culture to Counting: Early Effects Research

As the cultural uplift debate of the 1920s waned, concerns about the effects of radio programs on children waxed in the 1930s. At first glance this appears to be an extension of the concerns about movies in the early 1920s and the more general disapproval of that decade's youth culture. But these other concerns focused on teenagers and young adults and their loosened sexual mores, while concerns about radio focused on the effects on younger children. In contrast to the fears in the 1920s that movies corrupted adolescents, the principal concern in the 1930s was that thriller radio serials caused anxiety and nightmares among preadolescent children. While movie reformers had worried about the wayward effects on working-class children, radio reformers worried about their own middle-class children.[36]

Concerns arose with the rapid growth in children's programming, which increased in New York City from three programs in 1928 to fifty-two programs in 1934. Parents in Scarsdale, New York in 1933 protested that certain radio drama programs caused their children to have nightmares. They surveyed network programs for children broadcast between 4:45 and 8:00 P.M., rating many of them as harmful, offering "nerve-racking stories to children just before bedtime." They expressed concern about the steady diet of such programs each night. The parents were sufficiently well connected to gain support in publications such as the *New York Times, Time,* and *Literary Digest.* The National Association of Broadcasters responded by offering to produce more wholesome programs like *Tom Mix* and children's classics like *Robin Hood* and *The Wizard of Oz.*[37]

Through the 1930s various groups continued to express concern about the dangers of radio programs to preadolescent youths and to pressure broadcasters for change. The National Advisory Council on Radio in Education held a conference in 1934 on the topic of parents, children, and radio, after which representatives of several national organizations met to establish a clearinghouse for information on the topic. The *New York Times* periodically published reports critical of children's programs. In 1935 Mme. Yolanda Mero-Irion, president of the Women's National Radio Committee, condemned crime stories as "the most pernicious of all broadcasts." In 1938 a physical education professor at Columbia University denounced children's programs, saying, "it's the moronishness, the stupidity, the inactivity of it rather than the badness, that gives us the greatest concern." He called for parents to mount a letter-writing campaign to advertisers who he believed "would instantly turn somersaults in an effort to right the programs." The *New York Times* publicized a University of Chicago sociology dissertation that supported parents' concerns about the frightfulness of radio programs, stating that "boys and girl in the 6 to 8 age group respond by gripping some article of furniture tightly, gasping, chuckling involuntarily, sobbing, laughing and weeping quietly." In 1939, the General Federation of Women's Clubs, the American Legion Auxiliary, the National Society of New England Women, the United Parents Association of New York City, and the Parents League of New York City joined to oppose programs that they believed frightened or "overstimulated" children. In January 1940, Reverend Ralph Long, executive director of the National Lutheran Council, scored radio "thrillers," which he said "make neurotics of children."[38]

Only after a decade of such criticisms did the *New York Times* publish an article that disputed the dangers of radio thrillers to children. In 1943 John Hutchens stated the dangers were never proved, and that as a result of protests, broadcasters withdrew objectionable programs without replacing them with other children's fare, "leaving the children to listen to the even more exciting adult programs ... the would-be reformers [having] defeated their own purpose."[39]

These public expressions of fears about radio's danger to children reinforced the "effects" approach in mass communications research on audiences. Education researcher Azriel Eisenberg noted the influence of public opinion on research agendas: "increasing numbers of investigations have been set up in various parts of the country to study the activities of children in listening to the radio at home and the effects of the radio upon them." The most influential radio research through the 1930s and 1940s was funded by foundations that had explicit reform agendas and were seeking scientific support for them.[40]

The Payne Fund of Cleveland funded radio research at Ohio State University, the University of Chicago, and Columbia Teachers College. The Payne Fund in 1930 set up the National Committee on Education by Radio to promote cultural and educational uses of radio. In 1931 it proposed an agenda for radio research and began supporting radio research at Ohio State in 1933. W. W. Charters, who had been involved in the Payne movie studies, added a Radio Division to his Bureau of Education Research at Ohio State University with the Payne money. The first study surveyed program preferences of Ohio children. The Bureau also funded Frederick Lumley's 1934 survey of radio listener research.[41]

Charters partly supported with Payne funds a dissertation at Columbia Teachers College by Azriel Eisenberg. Eisenberg defined his purpose as documenting "habits, preference and reactions of children ... reactions of the parents to the listening activities of their children ... and the role of the radio in the home." He examined radio's effects on the family and on other activities. A third of children listened while engaged in another activity, most often reading or doing homework. Such divided attention would become a staple finding of later research.[42]

By the mid-1930s the Payne Fund had succeeded in shaping radio audience research, even as memories of its role faded. It had established "effects" research as the core of academic study of radio. As the

Payne Fund waned, another much larger fund, the Rockefeller Foundation, began to replace it. John D. Rockefeller, Jr., in charge of the Foundation, was among those interested in improving radio programming and presumably was supportive of the Foundation's plan in 1933 to support radio research. John Marshall, associate director of humanities at the Foundation and, like Rockefeller, an advocate of using radio for cultural uplift, began to work on a proposal to provide research that would convince radio executives to raise the level of their programming. Marshall was impressed by Hadley Cantril and Gordon Allport's book *The Psychology of Radio,* published in 1935, which summarized research to that date within a psychological effects framework and presented the results of a series of controlled experiments on the effects of radio. The book persuaded Marshall to recruit Cantril, another believer in cultural uplift, for the Rockefeller project. The two fashioned a proposal for a Radio Research Project in 1936. However, Cantril became too busy with other projects and, at Robert Lynd's suggestion, he appointed recent European emigre Paul Lazarsfeld to head the project. Lazarsfeld had no cultural uplifting agenda, but he was intrigued with research methods. Consequently, the project shed its reform agenda, but retained the young tradition of "effects" research as its guiding purpose.[43]

Lazarsfeld's approach, while eclectic in method, presumed a psychological model of communication between broadcaster and individual listeners, isolated from historical and social context. Effects were narrowly conceived, as the immediate and direct effect on individuals of a single program.[44] The approach tells us almost nothing about the context of listening in the family, home, or group, about the place of radio in people's daily routines. But Lazarsfeld's prodigious fund-raising, research, and publishing made his approach the standard and shaped audience research for years to come.[45]

16

The Electronic Cyclops: Fifties Television

Television inherited the practices of radio listening. It was born within the institution of radio and when it appeared, it appeared within the preexisting, fully established context of advertising-supported network broadcasting. The television set arrived on the market as a fully developed appliance. There was no period of amateur experimentation and no crystal-set phase. It moved immediately into the living room, becoming the new hearth around which the family gathered. While people were intrigued by television, the level of amazement in no way approached that of the 1920s. Television was simply radio with a picture.

Nevertheless, it moved in quickly. NBC estimated there were 60,000 television sets in the United States in July 1947. By 1950, 9 percent of all U.S. households had a television; by 1955, 64.5 percent. It spread faster than radio. In the first ten years, 1948–58, there was one television set for every four Americans, versus one radio for seven Americans in the comparable decade of 1922–32.[1]

As with radio, the early television audience was skewed upscale. High prices for early televisions retarded sales and restricted it to the affluent. The cost of televisions ranged from $100 to $4,100 in late 1948 with an average sale price of $375. Short supply of all but the most expensive sets also restricted sales to high-income groups.[2]

Saturation rates corresponded to the arrival of broadcast stations in each region. Saturation rose more rapidly in the largest cities with more stations. Whereas with radio, government agencies and agricultural colleges provided early rural coverage, there was no equivalent early television presence in rural areas. Saturation was highest and increased soonest in the Northeast, where more stations began broadcasting in earlier years. By spring 1955 it had reached 84 percent in Chicago, 85 percent in Los Angeles and Pittsburgh, 92 percent in Cleveland and Philadelphia, and nearly 100 percent in many suburbs. Saturation in the South was slowest, lagging behind the rest of the nation, similar to the pattern with radio.[3] (See Table 16.1.)

Table 16.1. Market Saturation by Television

Year	Price Index for TV Sets 1967 = 100	Saturation % U.S. Households	Average Hours Household Viewing Per Day
1950		9.0	4.6
1951		23.5	4.7
1952		34.2	4.8
1953	147	44.7	4.7
1954	142	55.7	4.8
1955	136	64.5	4.9
1956	130	71.8	5.0
1957	135	78.6	5.1
1958	131	83.2	5.1
1959	127	85.9	5.0
1960	124	87.1	5.1
1961	120	88.8	5.1
1962	118	90.0	5.1

Source: Price index from *Consumer Electonics Annual Review, 1985* (Washington, D.C.: Electronic Industries Association, 1985), 7; saturation 1950–1962 from *1975 International TV Almanac* (New York: Quigley, 1975), 16A; hours viewing from A.C. Nielsen Co.

The average number of hours of television use in households has grown gradually but continually from the early 1950s through the 1990s.[4] A 1950s parody in *Newsweek* described a well-educated family who failed to get out of the house on weekends because they found themselves glued to program after program offering current affairs and culture.[5] Television's great appetite for viewers' time, and viewers' great appetite for television, have long been concerns of critics. Very early in its development, people frequently talked about how television changed their household schedules when it arrived in their homes. Advice magazines discussed how "you may have to change your schedule around," and how important it was to set rules for children's use, so it did not displace eating, sleeping, homework, and just about everything else.[6]

An article in *American Mercury* in February 1952 called television the "giant in the living room," saying fear of its impact was "an almost universal reaction among thoughtful people." *Business Week* published a fifteen-page special report on television, "The New Cyclops," claiming it caused declines in movie attendance, radio listening, and reading, and consumed more time than any other activity than sleep.[7] Articles in a wide range of magazines in the early 1950s worried about the effects of television on the radio, movie, publishing, and other industries; on culture, libraries, and education; on the family; and on children's reading, homework, play habits, even on their eyes. All of these public worries attest to the belief that television was very powerful and would turn the worlds of leisure, culture, and education upside down.

Television seems to have narrowed the audience to the family and reduced activities outside the home, increasing privatization. The clearest impact was upon radio. Television recapitulated the phases of radio audience development: from communal to domestic viewing, from rapt attention to use of television as background, from family hearth to individual use, and from early fear and promise to disappointment. This chapter focuses on these processes in the 1940s and 1950s.

Market researcher Leo Bogart summed up the early development of television viewing habits in three phases: the tavern phase, the pioneer phase, and the mature phase. The first two constituted a brief, transitory period of communal "public" use of television in the 1940s and the earliest years of the 1950s, when television was still a novelty and few homes had one. "Tavern TV" involved mostly men crowded in bars to watch this new phenomenon. The "pioneer phase" involved the early owners of TVs who often had guests in their house to watch with them. This pattern of neighborly viewing rapidly disappeared among adults, as more families obtained their own television sets. With the "mature phase," viewing reverted to the radio pattern of listening at home with the family and without visitors. With "maturity" it became private, an electronic hearth. The rapid spread of television meant that people were spending time at home watching, time that previously they had spent doing something else.[8]

Watching Together: The Communal Phase

When television first arrived, scarcity and curiosity pushed people to watch together. Bars, restaurants, private clubs, schools, and hotels installed televisions. Boxing and other sporting events drew crowds into bars to watch. *Radio and Television News* estimated 10 percent of televisions in November 1948 were located in public places. *Televiser,* a magazine for broadcast stations, estimated that 17 percent of receivers were located in public places in March 1948, dropping to 4 percent by September 1949 as families began to buy sets.[9]

The numbers of people watching in public places, however, continued to be robust. People gathered in bars and in front of store display windows to watch this fascinating new instrument. A national survey conducted in November 1950 by Batten, Barton, Durstine, and Osborn advertising agency found that on a typical day 11 percent of those without a TV and 9 percent of those with a TV at home watched TV away from home, and both spent about two hours a day doing so. The study showed little difference between non-TV homes and TV homes or between housewives who more likely watched at a neighbor's and husbands who might have gone to a bar![10]

By far most common public place to find a television in the early 1950s was in a bar. Saloons have long used free entertainment as a means of attracting a clientele for drinking. In the nineteenth century this spawned the concert saloon, birthplace of vaudeville. Frontier saloons were the principal site for entertainment in cattle and mining towns. In the early twentieth century, some saloons installed kinetoscopes and a few years later replaced the kinetoscope with a backroom theater for movies. Saloons seem to have skipped the radio; few sources mention radios in bars during the communal phase of radio in the early 1920s. But with the advent of television the saloon's pioneering role of adopting new entertainment forms revived.

Chicago's only television station in March 1947 reported that two-thirds of its audience watched at the 250 bars with TV. Bar owners reported business improved dramatically when they installed a TV. For a fight telecast, a New York bar accommodated 70 customers at "ringside" seats in front of the television, 50 in booths, another 200 standing at the bar, and several dozen "nonpaying" viewers on the sidewalk watching through the window. Waiters served drinks during commercials. A "viewers credo" in *TV Guide* characterized the bar as a backup to the home television; "Strengthen me for the moment when my first tube blows out and I have to rush to the nearest bar and grill."[11]

Several *New Yorker* cartoons and articles in 1949–50 commented on tavern television. One cartoon depicted a bartender engrossed in watching a football game on television while the whiskey he is pouring spills all over the bar. In another cartoon a bar advertised in its window, "Television: U.N. Session Today, Vishinsky vs. Austin," referring to debates between the Soviet and American representatives to the founding sessions of the United Nations and alluding to the popularity of watching boxing on television in bars. A "Talk of the Town" comment noted a sign in a Second Avenue bar advertising the "largest life-size television screen in the world." Its first "Television" column referred to "people standing four deep at the bar, laughing, nudging one another, and neglecting their warm beers."[12]

Television may have fit in with some taverns' function as an autonomous public sphere. The neighborhood bar was the working man's club, a place where patrons engaged in public discussion of a wide range of issues. *Business Week* described tavern audiences as favoring sports and news. When few working-class families could afford their own television, the husband might be able to watch his favorite shows at a corner bar. However, the specific television taverns identified in magazine reports tended to be located in commercial districts rather than neighborhoods. A perceptive bartender in New York noticed that neighborhood bars could do without TV, but the commercial bars could not compete without one. Historically, saloons that offered entertainment have been those in commercial districts, not corner taverns. Many contemporaries complained that television also suppressed that aspect of the bar most vital to a public sphere, conversation among equals. In commercial bars, where people were more likely to be strangers, conversation was already less expected; in other bars television may have drawn outsiders who came to watch but not socialize or converse. So the influence of television in briefly fostering a public sphere was at best limited.[13]

"Come-ona My House"

The other communal audience was in the homes of the pioneer owners of television sets, the "first on their block" sprouting an aerial on their roof, in response to which neighbors often invoked an open-door policy. Many people watched their neighbor's television. A 1947 Los Angeles survey reported average family size of owners of home television sets to be 3.6, but the average evening audience in these homes to be 5 persons. The "Videotown" survey of New Brunswick, New Jersey found that in 1948–49 TV ownership increased family entertaining, even of uninvited guests, who came to share the new medium. Atlanta TV owners in 1950 reported receiving more visitors than before they bought a TV. Interior decorating magazines recommended living room chairs with casters to easily rearrange furniture when guests came to watch.[14]

Magazine articles characterized the "communal" nature of this group viewing as superficial. A common theme was the irritation with television guests who insisted on their own choice of program, helped themselves to refreshments, burned holes in the rug, and left without helping to clean up. Jack Gould, radio editor for the *New York Times* sarcastically offered "rules of behavior" for guests and hosts. Hosts should stock their refrigerator full of refreshments, leaving no room for staples such as milk, and display "patience and fortitude" when guests are obnoxious or boring. Guests should forget about finding a comfortable seat in the crowded room; "keep cool" when the owner adjusts the set at a crucial moment in the prizefight; and never show boredom or fall asleep. Both should refrain from talking.[15]

Comic writer Paul Ritts wrote that for TV owners, "being alone was something of a rarity. Having a television set, one automatically becomes the proprietor of a free theatre, free snack bar and public lounge. Nobody in the neighborhood is just a casual acquaintance. They are all *friends* – the 'just-thought-I'd-drop-in' variety. People who merely nodded to me on the street before now made it a point to wave cheerily and shout, 'Hello, *neighbor!*' They were especially friendly just before big football games, boxing matches and vaudeville reviews."

Ritts placed these obnoxious neighbors into seven categories: the amateur engineer who likes to toss around technical television terms, without knowing what they mean; the station switcher "with his hand constantly on the automatic station switch"; the conversationalist who talks continually during the program; the screen hog who blocks the view; the critic who gives a running commentary of the poor quality of the program; the moocher who eats continually; and the ideal viewer whom Ritts claimed to have never had at his house.[16]

Such negative stereotypes have no equivalent in the descriptions of 1920s radio listening guests. They described television guests who gave priority to watching over socializing, and joked about guests of guests who didn't even know the hosts. The only positive description was one of the very first published about television visitors. An affluent family lived in a posh apartment on the Upper East Side of Manhattan and had purchased a television in 1941, making them among the very first owners. The family regularly had guests over to watch together, but unlike many other descriptions, these guests seem always to have been invited. The couple mentioned that they went out less than previously and entertained at home more, inviting large groups of twenty-five or thirty for special events on television, such as a Joe Louis boxing match. This is reminiscent of the radio parties common in the early to mid-1920s among affluent couples.[17]

But even in this article some negative tone appears. The author described a night when a visiting couple "emphatically chose to view the wrestling" although the host wanted to watch boxing. The host and hostess fetched drinks and snacks rather than watched with their guests. Their fourteen-year-old son similarly served his friends who watched an afternoon baseball game. The boy and his mom provided a veritable conveyor belt of food. The friends abruptly left at the end of the game.

Neighborhood children, as well as adults, availed themselves of their neighbor's television. Jack Gould, radio editor for the *New York Times,* described the television party as having two shifts, afternoon for the neighbors' kids, and after dinner for their parents.[18] Commentary on group viewing by children vacillated between positive and negative descriptions, and was to be found more in parental advice articles rather than in humorous ones.

Magazines described the inevitable crowd of youngsters sprawled in front of the TV each afternoon, alternately sedated and electrified by television. *Architectural FORUM* described a group of children who "assembles outside just before the broadcast schedule is to begin, files in, and settles down on chairs and floors for two hours of somber, intent appraisal of some adult's foolish ways on the screen. These children are the source of no trouble, but come and go like a harmless swarm of bats. Almost no talking interrupts their vigil." On the other hand, a mother wrote to TV Guide complaining about her children's TV guests, and Ritts described his son's friends crowding the living room to watch westerns.[19]

Early research studies of children and television cited the group-viewing phenomenon. Over 60 percent of Atlanta children in 1950 watched TV in groups, and this was more common in higher-income homes. A 1951 survey of Los Angeles school children revealed that almost 60 percent of children without TV watched at a friend's house.[20]

But, as with adults, the bonds of the children's television gathering did not outlast their convenience. As soon as most kids got a TV they ceased to gather at one another's house. Psychologist Eleanor Maccoby commented that, "When most or all of a child's friends have TV sets, TV seems to make him more solitary rather than more social, for when a program is on that they want to see, children usually separate and go to their own homes, instead of watching the program together."[21]

But why separate? There is no necessary reason for the separate viewing. If they were all watching the same show and before had watched together, why then switch to isolated viewing? Perhaps parents discouraged group viewing. Parents did complain of the trouble of the little visitors eating and making a mess. Together children were more active; alone they were quiet and less restless. Maccoby's mothers appreciated the sedating effect of television. There was less rough-housing and fewer questions; it kept children at home and off the street; one mother said, "It's much easier – it's just like putting him to sleep."[22] The contrast in descriptions suggests mothers soon discouraged visitors.

Whatever the reasons, the inversion of the effect of television, first encouraging communal viewing, then abruptly privatizing viewing, is an exaggeration of what happened with radio. Radio listening too shifted from group to family to individual, but not so suddenly, or so starkly. But such irritated descriptions of television parties contrast with the more positive construction of group listening to radio, which did bring people together. There was no talk of intrusive neighbors in the 1920s; descriptions emphasized owners sharing information and inviting people in to listen. One difference between the 1920s and the 1950s was darkness. It was a common practice in the 1950s to watch television in the dark, to avoid any sun glare on the screen and improve viewing. Lights were switched off at night, the shades pulled during the day, like a darkened movie theater. The habit of darkened viewing apparently continued into the mid-1950s, as a 1955 *New Yorker* cartoon depicted a child watching a baseball game on TV in his dark living room and a doctor telling his mother to discourage his interest in sports and get him out into the fresh air. Maccoby concluded that semidarkness and the demand for quiet from viewers inhibited conversation and play, even among family members. The TV audience may have imported their moviegoing habit of suspending conversation while viewing in the dark. The dark focused attention on the lighted television screen and reduced sociability, compared to that with radio listening.[23]

By January 1953, 68 percent of homes had their own TV, and communal viewing waned. By then McGeehan reported that Lexington, Kentucky residents seldom visited others to watch TV, though many had done so only a couple of years earlier. The "communal phase" for children may have persisted longer because of its "baby-sitting" function, but it did not retain the mesmerizing hold on children that it had when it was new.[24]

Watching versus Listening to Jack Benny

Already evident in the home during the "pioneer phase" was the impact of television on radio. Shortly after regular television broadcasting began, Americans were spending their evenings watching television rather than listening to the radio. The change occurred rather abruptly between 1950 and 1953 when radio use in all homes, with or without television, dropped from about five to three hours per day. (See Table 16.2.) Once families had a television they effectively eliminated radio as an evening entertainment. Television homes using radio at 8 P.M. dropped from 40 percent in 1950 to 5 percent in 1952. Average radio network audience ratings dropped from 13 in 1948 to 1 in 1956. Even the popular Bob Hope show experienced dramatic shrinkage from 24 in 1949 to 5.4 in 1953.[25]

Radio was losing in part because the networks bled radio to feed television, using profits from radio to fund television and, more importantly, transferring the most popular evening radio programs to televi-

Table 16.2. Average Radio and Television Use (Hours/Day)

Year – January		Radio hrs/day	TV hrs/day	Radio % at 8 PM	TV % at 8 PM
1946	Radio homes	4.79			
1948	Radio homes	5.20			
1950	Radio homes	4.73		40.4	
1951	Radio homes	4.07	1.39	30.8	17.8
1951	TV homes	2.33	5.49	7.5	70.5
1952	Radio homes	3.54	2.11	26.1	25.6
1952	TV homes	1.85	5.76	5.4	69.8
1953	Radio homes	3.16	2.71	21.8	31.4
1953	TV homes	1.71	5.76	5.8	66.7

Source: *Nielsen Radio Index Reports* (1946 and 1948) and *Nielsen Television Index Reports,* 1951–3, A. C. Nielsen papers, boxes 22–4, State Historical Society of Wisconsin.

sion. Over 150 prime-time network radio shows appeared on television during these transitional years. Many shows were aired on both radio and television at the same time: 1 in 1947, 15 in 1948, 25 in 1949, 24 in 1950, 13 in 1951, 17 in 1952, 5 in 1953, and 4 in 1954. But the formats were changed to make them suitable for television and thus less suitable for radio, often leaving radio listeners in the dark. Some predicted the death of radio.[26]

The advantages of television over radio were not universal, however. In the late 1940s magazine articles frequently observed that television watching could not be combined with other activities as people were accustomed to do with radio. News commentator Clifton Utley said that "you can easily do a lot of things while the radio is on ... With television you can't do both at once. You've got to be where the television receiver is, and look at it."[27]

Thus conceived, television created a conflict between viewing and other activities such as dinner, homework, reading, even conversation. People felt forced to choose, whereas with radio they did not. Housewives often listened to radio while doing their housework, but in weighing the decision to buy a television, most believed that they would have to choose between watching television and doing housework. Children who had become accustomed to reading or doing homework while listening to music on the radio could not do this with television. Clifton Utley cited how his son could not even dry the dishes while watching, instead sitting there mesmerized, oblivious of the dish and towel in his hand.[28] TV easily displaced radio in the evening when people could give it their full attention. But radio remained more resistant to television's incursion during the day when people were busy doing other things or on the move outside the home. Two new patterns of radio listening emerged, random listening and reference listening. Random listeners used radio wherever they had a few minutes, turning it on without regard to the program or station, and using it as background. Reference listeners turned on the radio for a specific purpose, such as news, weather, or a wakeup alarm. In both patterns there was little loyalty to a particular program or station, which were perceived as not much different. This contrasted sharply with previous nighttime listening patterns and the current TV viewing patterns.[29]

Radio became a daytime activity, often outside the home and along with other activities like work. Nielsen television index reports showed daytime radio listening dropped only slightly when nighttime ratings plummeted. In 1948 the highest-rated radio programs were evening programs, but by 1955 they were almost all daytime serials. A quarter of the radio audience in 1953 listened outside the home, mostly during the day. A 1955 NBC survey found that people used radio heavily as background, while doing other things like housework or driving. Quotes from housewives duplicated statements made about daytime listening in the 1930s. Now, however, this was the predominant form of listening, as television took the nighttime audience. By 1954 television had displaced radio from the living room; 85 percent of TVs but only 25 percent of radios were located in living rooms. Radios were as likely in autos or bedrooms or kitchens. The locations reflected the conception of television as a group family activity while radio was individualized and accompanied other activities.[30]

The daytime preference for radio may explain why the networks were slower to transfer *daytime* radio programs to television. They held back these radio programs for fear of undermining their profit center. ABC, CBS, and NBC did not begin daytime programming until 1951 when the demand for TV advertising outgrew nighttime slots available.[31]

Let's Stay Home and Watch TV

More significant than people's changed use of radio was that people seemed to go out less for entertainment once they bought a television. Industry statistics showed a strong correlation between television's rise and the decline in movie attendance.[32] Movie attendance reached its all-time peak of four billion admissions a year just as regular television broadcasts began right after World War II. From that peak it declined steadily until it leveled off in the early 1960s to one billion. (See Table 16.3.) The first years of decline might have been explained as a postwar adjustment, but the continued decline indicates some long-term change.

Almost from the beginning of the decline people pointed their finger at television as the cause. Surveys at the time, based on respondents' statements about their behavior, cited a correlation between television ownership and movie attendance. People consistently stated that they were going out less, to the movies and elsewhere, once they purchased a television. Cartoons and newspaper and magazine articles expressed a widespread belief that television deeply eroded moviegoing habits. A book of magazine cartoons about television included a section titled "Remember the Movies?" One cartoon reprinted in several publications showed a movie theater empty except for two couples. The one wife says to the other, "ours is out for repair too."[33]

Movie industry executives tried to downplay the widespread belief about the effect of television on movie admissions. Charles Skouras,

Table 16.3   U.S. Annual Movie Admissions (in billions.)

Year	Tickets (billions)	Year	Tickets
1946	4.1	1955	2.1
1947	3.7	1956	1.9
1948	3.4	1957	1.7
1949	3.2	1958	1.5
1950	3.0	1959	1.5
1951	2.8	1960	1.3
1952	2.8	1961	1.2
1953	2.6	1962	1.1
1954	2.3	1963	1.1

Source: "United States Theatrical Film Admissions," *Variety* (June 24, 1981), 6.

owner of a movie theater chain, stated in a speech to a meeting of Hollywood movie executives in December 1950 that movie attendance was off 10 to 15 percent in television areas, but also 2 to 4 percent in areas without television stations. Paul Raibourn, vice president of Paramount Pictures, also claimed that television had taken about 10 percent of the movie audience, saying the additional losses were due to cyclical economic factors. Some claimed that movies and television would work together to the benefit of both.[34]

But they could not deny the steady decline in movie attendance. The surveys, the public discourse, and industry statistics establish an association of declining movie attendance with rising television use. People who had televisions did go to movies less. The only question is whether it was *because* of television. Both purchasing a television and reducing moviegoing may have been simply two among many factors in a larger social and cultural shift reflected in leisure choices toward home and family and away from community and public. The shift represented a withdrawal from public space, a privatization which had ramifications for the decline of community and the public sphere. These concerns about community and mass culture were widely discussed in the 1950s and 1960s among social scientists, and have recently returned to the social science agenda.[35] The issue is television's place in this broader process.

Television and Suburbia

The audience shift from movies to television was an aspect of a broader cultural and social transformation that took place after World War II. The change has often been labeled with the vague and misleading term, suburbanization. This change in American living means more than simply a population shift. It means a substitution of the car for walking and mass transit. It means increased affluence for the postwar working and middle classes that allowed a much broader participation in the consumer culture of home, auto, and appliance purchasing. It means changes in household design and use that emphasize the home as a place of family leisure. It means a cultural shift in the importance given public life versus privacy, community versus nuclear family.

Several researchers in the 1950s suggested suburbanization as the cause of the decline in moviegoing. But communication researcher Frederick Stuart dismissed the numbers of families who had moved to the suburbs as insufficient to account for the three billion drop in moviegoing.[36] Historian Kenneth Jackson, on the other hand, described the postwar home-building boom as being "of enormous proportions." From 1946 to 1962, 23 million new homes were built in the United States, at least two-thirds in suburbs.[37] At three residents per suburban home, this is approximately 50 million people. If they reduced their moviegoing from once every other week (the average per U.S. resident in 1946) to once a month (the average in 1962), they would represent a loss of two billion tickets annually. So the effect of the move to the suburbs cannot be dismissed simply on the basis of its size.

Recently, film historian Douglas Gomery has revived the suburbanization explanation. He claims the television audience was too small to account for the 25 percent drop in annual movie attendance by 1950 when only 9 percent of households had a television. Gomery emphasizes the growth in family size and the looming importance of raising children in the late 1940s and 1950s as a factor in this audience shift.[38]

Gomery's shift of attention to demographic changes moves us closer to an approach that considers television and movie trends in a broader context of cultural change. Television developed at the same time as the great postwar migration to suburbia. This involved geographical and social structural changes such as shopping at malls, the decline of downtown and old established neighborhoods, the building of highways to support the relocation, and the general sprawl and attendant dependence on the automobile. It involved the dismantling of institutions that sustain community, public places that foster unplanned socializing among community members.[39]

But the structural changes are not the sole explanation; cultural forces also played a part. This was a migration of the mind as well as a geographical migration. It was a change in the conception of living and of the value of community. The end of the war meant an end to separation of loved ones. When husbands and fathers came home from the war, the nationwide response seems to have been an intense desire for reuniting the nuclear family. Historian Elaine Tyler May coined the term "domestic containment" to describe this relocating social identity within the home. The focus on marriage and children and home meant less going out to the neighborhood bar or to movies, where lonely spouses spent time during the war. Suburban homes were made to order, with yards for play, windows for sunlight, even air conditioning for a few. Reflecting the turn inward, new houses shed the old front porch in favor of the reclusive rear patio. This was a cultural choice, not a structural necessity; a change in values, not an economic substitution.[40]

Television complemented these trends, providing diversions within the home to compensate for their disappearance from the neighborhood. Television was not so much the culprit as an accomplice of a great change in American lifestyle. What is notable about television is its immense *cultural* contribution to this *cultural* change from community to family, public to private. The imagery of television was familial and private. It enhanced and encouraged the cultural preference for the private by what it offered in the home. The choice of television over movies was not a narrow *economic* choice between media, but a larger *cultural* choice between public and private.

The Electronic Hearth: The Constructed Family

Television was well suited to the nesting habit. From its beginning it was presented as the new hearth. Magazines offered advice on how to arrange seating around the television. The image of the hearth resonated a need for reassurance amid threats to family security. Rock 'n' roll and street gangs, in ominous newspaper articles, threatened to steal teenage children's allegiance from their parents. Nuclear bombs and the cold war were an even graver threat. According to May, "Americans were well poised to embrace domesticity in the midst of the terrors of the nuclear age" and, I might add, in retreat from the collective effort of World War II to the insular concentration on raising a family.[41] Around the electronic hearth the family was turned in on itself, to the television, and its back to its neighbors and community. Domesticity was an anticommunity message. Privacy was juxtaposed to public, while public was reconstructed not as the community of friends and neighbors outside the door who shared the same interests and fate, but as a dangerous and alien place. The nineteenth century echoes in these images of the world outside as a dangerous place. In the 1850s the danger was to the virtue of women; in the 1950s the danger was to the welfare of children.

The domestic image of the hearth emphasized television drawing the family together. Magazine articles often referred to how television kept the children at home or brought the family together. Researchers too examined whether families gathered together around television, like they presumably did around the hearth. Two of the most influential early studies contradicted each other on this point. Sociologist John Riley described television as "a new focus for family interest" creating "a bridge between adults and children" and "new ties between family members." Psychologist Eleanor Maccoby, on the other hand, concluded that families did watch together, but silently. Watching inhibited other interaction. The amount of conversation was "very small," and TV cut into the amount of non-TV joint family activity.[42]

From Hearth to Rec Room

The hearth image would serve manufacturers' purposes for a limited time only. As the market rapidly reached saturation, manufacturers changed their strategy, as they did with radio, to create a demand for more than one television per household. Soon the emphasis on family viewing was interspersed with messages to buy another television. By 1952 ads were showing family members dispersed, viewing alone or in separate groups.[43]

Before the mid-1950s, small portable sets were marketed as an economical first set. Motorola advertised a 1948 table model television "so light (26 $\frac{1}{2}$ lbs) you can move it from room to room and ... at a price all can afford." It sat on a table next to the Christmas tree while the wife kissed the Santa-dressed husband and her son pulled on dad's sleeve to come and turn it on. Even the cat looked up at it admiringly. It was promoted as an "affordable" first set for the whole family rather than a second set that would pull the family apart.[44]

But soon the message changed. Already in 1950, *TV Guide* recommended a second set for Dad, and RCA urged parents to buy another set for the children, saying "America's children learn by seeing." *Business Week* suggested the two-set marketing strategy to counter a slump in TV sales. Dumont advertised a two-set home, depicting parents watching the console in the living room while the teenagers watched the table model in another room with friends. By 1960 the major manufacturers were aggressively promoting the portable.[45]

Conflicts among family members over what to watch occurred from the beginning, a problem familiar from radio. Cartoons humorously showed family members dispersed to their individual sets. Manufacturers promoted a second set as the solution. Dumont even manufactured a television with two screens, so husband and wife could sit together and yet each watch their own program. Ironically, individuation was presented as a way to preserve family unity.[46]

Impact on Activities Outside the Home

It has been persistently argued that television has a strong magnetic pull on people, keeping them home and drawing them away from activities outside the home. Early surveys found that families with televisions spent fewer hours outside the home.[47] Later studies indicate the impact was not temporary, nor due to the novelty of television. Television use increased steadily over the next forty years. Average weekly use based upon Nielsen surveys indicate a rise from thirty-two hours per week in the early 1950s to fifty hours per week in the mid-1980s. Television, in other words, has increasingly "colonized" free time, taking an increasing share of time from other activities. A comparison of leisure time data for 1965 to that for 1975 revealed that hours of television use was most strongly and negatively correlated with activities away from home, including socializing, travel, going to bars and parties, and going to church. It has become, in other words, the leisure activity of least resistance and last resort.[48]

Television has colonized children's free time as well. Comparisons of time budgets of teenagers from the 1930s and the 1980s indicate that media use grew from 38 percent to 51 percent of leisure time. Television accounted for the lion's share, 46 percent of all leisure time, in the 1980s. Social interaction in the form of team sports and visiting/talking with friends dropped from 39 percent to 28 percent.[49]

Growing television use has been cited as causing a decline in civic participation and the public sphere. Most recently, political scientist Robert Putnam has reiterated this claim. Both the claim that participation has declined and that it is caused by television have been disputed. But Putnam and his critics alike chase a chimera in trying to establish the effect of television. The part played by television cannot be separated from the cast and props that together create the American drama.[50]

As with the impact of television on moviegoing, it is difficult to determine cause and effect, but clearly television is related to a decline in civic participation. Both are part of a general trend that began after World War II and originated with surbubanization and the Baby Boom of the 1950s. But its continuation indicates deeper changes.

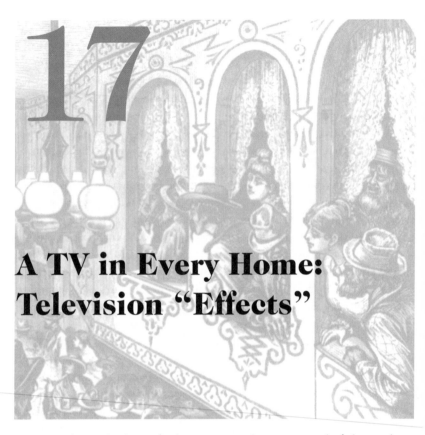

A TV in Every Home:
Television "Effects"

I n the early days of television people were proud of their television set and placed it in the living room to entertain guests. They considered it a wonderful and entertaining new addition to their homes and even felt gratitude for it. But by 1958 television viewing was no longer novel. Television use had settled into a routine. Market researchers Ira Glick and Sidney Levy described the change as a shift from excitement and widespread acceptance to uneasiness, dissatisfaction, denial, and criticism. By the late 1950s it was not considered appropriate among college-educated people to admit that one watched television much. They no longer turned on television when visitors came. Instead they placed the television where it could be viewed privately, by children or the family without company, in the recreation room or in the parents' bedroom.[1]

From that time the negative characterizations of television would persist for decades as conventional wisdoms. Culture critics, communication researchers, and viewers asked whether television was a good thing and what was it doing to viewers. This chapter examines how the discourse on television defined cultural capital and reinforced class distinctions. French sociologist Pierre Bourdieu used the term "cultural capital" to refer to the possession of cultural knowledge, abilities, and tastes that allowed one to claim higher status in a social hierarchy, distinguishing higher from lower classes by their tastes. The discourse on television demonstrates that one's attitudes toward and use of television have been a common basis for such distinctions.[2]

Cultural Critics

The wide-eyed utopian optimism in the early to mid-1920s about radio was not duplicated for television in the late 1940s and early 1950s. While early viewers were excited by this new medium, even in the early 1950s television columnists were often harsh critics. There were two major categories of criticism: television viewing's alleged displacement of more valuable activities, and the negative impact of television programs, aesthetically, socially, or morally, upon viewers. The first category was buttressed by the belief in the early years that people could not combine television viewing with other activities. Television was blamed for destroying conversation; interfering with children's homework, eating, and sleeping; distracting wives from preparing dinner; and wrecking the radio industry and running neighborhood movie theaters out of business.[3]

On the matter of content, arts and entertainment critics quickly labeled the programming "low-brow." The *New York Times* television columnist Jack Gould, likened it to "a cut-rate nickelodeon." Arts critic Gilbert Seldes, who had championed the "popular arts" in the 1920s and 1930s, described early programming as "rather bad vaudeville ... unimaginative and tasteless." *Saturday Review* editor Norman Cousins condemned television as "such an invasion of good taste as no other communications medium has known."[4]

The *New Yorker* television columnist Philip Hamburger regularly skewered the "best" programs. He disparaged Milton Berle as "doing nothing that is not being done in third-rate night clubs and second-class summer hotels." The humor of Dean Martin and Jerry Lewis on the Berle show "consisted of behaving like delinquent children." This was the show that network executives boasted brought the best of vaudeville into every home! In another column he condemned what was promoted as great television drama, calling it crass melodrama with saintly heroes and "unmitigated swine" for villains. He was appalled by the butchering of *A Comedy of Errors* to fit a one-hour for-

mat, described a satire as so bad he could not figure out what was
being satirized, and criticized the poor camerawork of a third drama.
He did approve of coverage of the San Francisco conference that laid
the foundation of the United Nations.[5]

Commercialism was blamed for reducing programming to the lowest common denominator. They revived arguments from the turn of
the century when theater critics blamed the woeful state of American
drama on the rise of the Theater Syndicate turning theater into big
business. They blamed broadcasters for "selling their souls" to advertisers and placing business above aesthetics. Others blamed the more
anonymous marketplace, and recommended providing better programming outside the discipline of the market, through public television of some sort, much as earlier advocates of the Little Theater
movement had advocated various means of subsidy to free drama theaters from the market.[6]

Broadcasters and advertisers countered critics with what they promoted as quality programming. As it had done in the 1920s with radio,
NBC justified its nationwide dominance in television by claiming to
"elevate tastes" and "make us all into intellectuals." ABC announced
in spring 1949 that it would broadcast the Metropolitan Opera each
Saturday afternoon that fall. But most often they selected an art better
suited to a visual medium, drama. The "tasteful" television programming tended to be legitimate drama anthologies sponsored by large
corporations as institutional advertising: *Ford Theater* (1949–57),
United States Steel Hour (1953–63), *General Electric Theater*
(1953–62), *Dupont Cavalcade of America* (1954–57), and *Armstrong
Circle Theater* (1950–63). They commissioned legitimate plays from
respected playwrights. Three of the programs were created by the
advertising agency Batten, Barton, Durstine and Osborn (BBD&O),
which had a history of such high-culture associations in its advertising
campaigns.[7] These programs were introduced with voices and music
that cast them as serious, almost sacred, television, as contributions
to culture and education that warranted careful and thoughtful attention. Broadcasters and sponsors used the shows to promote themselves as supporters of culture and good corporate citizens. At the
same time they offered viewers a chance to enhance their cultural
capital by watching.

But concerns about the low-brow tastes of television prevailed over
industry promotional efforts. Rather than subsiding, the criticism
seemed to increase and peaked in the late 1950s. The quiz show

scandal in the fall of 1959 stripped away the public relations image of good will, of concern with the public interest, and of honesty that the networks had constructed, making their protestations of offering what America wanted and needed seem a hollow lie.

Aesthetic criticism continued to be harsh. In 1960–61, *Harper's* magazine published several articles on the quality of high-brow programs such as operas, legitimate drama, and current-events documentaries. After surveying programs aired during the 1959–60 season, critic Martin Mayer concluded that most public affairs programs "contained moments that were little less than infuriating," and that the dramas were "artistically lightweight semi-documentaries." These comments were matched or exceeded by other prominent writers about the same time. Arthur Schlesinger, Jr., historian and adviser to President Kennedy, said, "From its inception television has been in a downward spiral as an artistic medium." Thomas Griffith of *Time* worried we had sold our souls "for a mess of pottage"; television producer David Susskind described programming as "oceans of junk."[8]

The dour picture of television was part of a larger disdain for mass culture that reached high tide in the late 1950s and early 1960s. Television was *the* prime example of this debased culture.[9] Unique among household objects, television was demonized as powerful, dangerous, and low-brow. In the words of literature professor Cecilia Tichi, the choice was between "puerility versus maturity, low culture versus high, entertainment versus intellectual engagement, frivolity versus seriousness, contamination versus purity, robotry versus critical imagination, sickness versus health." The low-brow argument frequently charged television with undermining the good habit of reading. Reading, and by extension literacy, conferred positive cultural capital. The issue of literacy made television not only low brow, but a danger to children.[10]

Worries about Children

Much criticism of television was expressed in terms of its dangers to children. Expressing concerns in these terms moved them beyond mere cultural snobbery to a ground where many people would begin to question the value of television, making the cultural devaluation of television widespread. Around 1950 numerous articles appeared in magazines about the effects of television on children and gave advice about television in the rearing of children. Most of these were concerned about television's displacement of other activities, rather than the content of programs. Early articles in fact tended to describe television programs as positive, just requiring some ground rules like limiting how much time children could spend watching. They agreed with the industry promotion that television "widens horizons" of children. Even the *Christian Science Monitor* expressed confidence that television stations would do the right thing and provide good programming for children. In *Parents Magazine,* Dorothy McFadden, president of Junior Programs Inc., promoted the industry, saying television was an asset to children and that television officials welcomed good ideas and programs for children.[11] Writers were much more inclined to be concerned about the amount of time children spent in front of television sets, reducing the time spent in more constructive activities that were active, social, educational, and physically healthful.

A few "hysterical" articles appeared, written mostly by child professionals, educators, and recreational specialists. But the tone of many of the advice articles in women's magazines was to calm and reassure mothers that television simply needed to be handled properly. They proposed rules for its use so that it did not displace homework, eating, and sleeping, and that it even be used as a reward or incentive for children to finish their chores. An article in *Library Journal* dismissed the fears of television viewing endangering the practice of reading, by reprinting an article from 1924 expressing such a fear about radio, with the implicit conclusion that of course this doomsday prediction did not come true, and neither will dire predictions about television. In *Harper's* a housewife chronicled her children's first total absorption with television followed in short order by disenchantment and boredom with it.[12]

By the mid-1950s the balance of concern had shifted from television *use* to television *content*. In contrast to the advice articles of 1950, an article in *Parents Magazine* in December 1954 marshaled the expertise of "eighteen prominent authorities [for a] guide to help regulate your child's TV viewing." The bulk of advice was directed to concerns about the effects of crime shows, westerns, and adult programs, causing emotional upset, anxiety, juvenile delinquency, even "bad taste."[13]

Unlike the 1930s, when broadcasters did little to dispute what critics said about programs, the television industry in the 1940s and 1950s went on the offensive. Broadcasters answered the criticisms with "science," financing audience research in the days before plentiful federal funding, and publicizing the results beyond the research community. CBS funded major academic research projects. They funded the 1948 Riley study, the first influential study on children and television and the classic summary of effects research by Joseph Klapper, *Effects of Mass Communication,* a revision of his 1949 dissertation at the Columbia University Bureau of Applied Social Research. (Klapper himself worked for GE, a major television manufacturer and program sponsor.) They also funded an influential national 1960 survey by Gary Steiner which was also funded through the Bureau. Many surveys had market research origins: the ten-year Videotown study by Cunningham and Walsh advertising agency; Leo Bogart's 1955 review of survey research sponsored by McCann Erickson advertising agency; and Ira Glick and Sidney Levy's synthesis of the results of dozens of surveys they conducted for Campbell-Ewald advertising agency from 1957–61.[14]

Manufacturers' response to television criticism was to claim television was educational, bringing the "best of the world" into people's homes. A Dumont ad showed a young girl at Christmas watching a television with her teddy bears. On the screen is a fairy godmother talking to the child, describing the television as "an Enchanted Mirror... Through it, skilled musicians will play for you and learned men will speak to you. This Enchanted Mirror will bring to you much pleasure and deeper understanding, so that you may live your life in wisdom and happiness."[15]

They overstepped the bounds, however, in 1950 when the American Television Dealers and Manufacturers (ATDM) Association placed full-page ads in newspapers and on radio across the country, suggesting children without a television were outcasts. Ad copy described a boy who came home early to his parents' surprise because all the other children were talking about television and he was left out because his family had not bought one. The ad then quoted a psychologist as saying, "children need home television for their morals as they need sunshine and fresh air for their health." A magazine ad in the same campaign claimed children without TV felt ashamed not knowing about the television shows other children talked about and humiliated to have to "beg" to watch the neighbor's television.[16]

The campaign triggered an immediate widespread reaction from Eleanor Roosevelt, the Family Service Association of America, and the National Assembly of the United Council of Church Women. Middle-class parents sent letters to the editors of magazines and newspapers who printed the ads. Newspapers received a wave of phone calls denouncing the ads, greater response than to any other ad according to *Editor and Publisher*. The ATDM canceled the negative ads – claiming they had planned to anyway as part of a two-phase campaign – and substituted some more positive ads, which still focused on the value of TV for children.[17]

The reactions were so widespread that book publishers took advantage of them to promote their books. Harper Brothers placed an ad for children's books that poked fun at the ATDM ads.[18] The publishing industry itself promoted attacks on television as a threat to reading and, by extension, education. At the same time, the industry carefully followed surveys that indicated reading was, or was not, displaced by television.

The low valuation of television was set in place. Its use must be guarded. Anyone who did not use it selectively for themselves or their children were labeled as wanting.

Negative Cultural Capital

By the late 1950s critical attitudes toward television had sedimented into American culture, a measure of whether one was educated or ignorant. Magazines published fewer positive treatments about its novelty and pleasures. People described TV programs as low quality, unimaginative, and repetitive. Reflecting this devaluation was a trend in interior decorating to make television's presence more discrete, no longer making it the centerpiece of the living room. Ads for high-end TVs featured doors to hide the screen when not in use.[19]

These attitudes presented television as a "reverse status symbol," a term coined by *Time* magazine.[20] Watching television became an admission of low-brow taste. Family television viewing patterns thus became a measure of cultural capital. Heavy viewing, indiscriminate viewing, leaving the television on even when not attending, providing little or no parental control of children's viewing and using television as a baby sitter were all associated with being lower class. All of these constituted a syndrome of "passive viewing." To avoid tainting one's cultural capital with television, a person had to demonstrate characteristics of an "active" viewer by placing the television in a room not used for entertaining guests or discretely hiding the television behind cabinet doors; selectively using television only for informational and culturally uplifting programs; and limiting children's

use in time and program selection for educational value. The preferred middle-class style was juxtaposed to detrimental working-
class/lower-class viewing patterns.

The attitudes were captured in a satire in the *Saturday Evening
Post* titled "Oh, Mass Man! Oh Lumpen Lug! Why Do You Watch TV?"
The writer confessed his attraction to television viewing and grum-
bled, "why do I have to dissemble and explain and justify and tell outright lies" about his watching television too much. When he bought
his first TV his friends needled him with "sell out!," "cop out!" and
threw him a "middle-brow party," bringing old copies of *Readers
Digest*. The whole tone of the satire was the guilt shared with his readers that watching television was a lower form of pleasure in which
they all secretly indulged.[21]

Audience Research and the Construction of Cultural Capital

Television audience research was itself driven by these criticisms
and attempted to provide "scientific evidence" to decide the case on
television. This was especially true of studies published in book form
rather than in obscure academic journals. Even as these studies contradicted the more extreme claims about television, they confirmed
the definition of television as a cultural problem to be contained
rather than as a cultural asset. Market researcher Leo Bogart organized his survey of 1950s research around popular concerns about
television and bluntly stated the class prejudice of the discourse, that
"better educated and wealthier persons, with their greater resources,
are best able to take television in their stride." Psychologists Wilbur
Schramm, Jack Lyle, and Edwin Parker, authors of one of the most
influential studies of television and children, organized their conclusions in terms of answers to popular claims and questions about television and children and initiated a veritable industry of research on
the effects of television violence.[22]

Researchers affirmed the relationship between social class and patterns of television use. They helped to define upper-middle-class patterns as normal and working-class patterns as deficient. One of the
first and most systematic elaborations of class-differentiated viewing
patterns was market researchers Ira Glick and Sidney Levy's report of
surveys they conducted from 1957 to 1961 for various advertisers.
From these they constructed three types of viewer orientations to
television, Embrace, Accommodation, and Protest, which they associ-

ated with working-class, lower-middle-class, and upper-middle-class families, respectively.[23]

Working-class Embracers were the stereotypic TV fans. These were heavy viewers; they watched television in "large blocks of time." Watching was integrated into their daily routine, something they did at specific times of every day. Their choice of program was secondary to watching at certain hours. Referring specifically to working-class families, Glick and Levy said, "Television for these people functions as a readily available companion and activity – a thing to do – in a world in which there are not too many alternatives."[24]

Glick and Levy described Embracers as "people with few inner resources that would lead them to cultivate other 'outside' interests" who expect immediate gratification and want programs which are "obvious," "not too complicated or involved" and do not make them "work at watching." In this category they grouped children, the home-bound elderly, and the working class. They further stated that the stereotype "fits the working-class viewer more than others, as less motivated to act in an energetic, censoring or selective fashion." Such descriptions contributed to the larger discourse that used television use as an indicator of status.

Opposite to Embracers were upper-middle-class, college-educated Protesters, the writers and readers of those critical articles about TV. Protesters objected to television's detrimental effects on child-rearing, to its low aesthetic standards, and to the waste of its potential for social good. They watched fewer hours and confined their use to self-improving, educational, informational, and culturally uplifting goals. They restricted use for themselves and their children and expressed guilt about overstepping these principles. They excluded television from the living room and placed it where it would be less conspicuous. Glick and Levy specifically describe the upper-middle-class attitude as more "active and self-directing [while] selection, discrimination and planning are the keynotes of their viewing." They looked for "worth-while" programs and had "little room left for self-indulgence." Glick and Levy attribute to them praiseworthy goals by the standards of the dominant culture, that is, goals that represent high cultural capital, but also depict them as a bit puritanical and stiff.

Glick and Levy wrote disapprovingly of elitist television critics, such as John Crosby (*Life*), John Fischer (*Harper's*), Marya Mannes (*McCall's, Vogue, Glamour, New York Times*), Paul Molloy (*Chicago Sun Times, Time*), and Frederick Wertham (author of *Seduction of the Innocent,* a harsh critique of comic books), who epitomized these Protesters. Glick and Levy's tone and conclusions favored instead a reasonable "accommodation" rather than "protest" or a too obvious "embrace."

They described Accommodators as making an "attempt to balance" the oppositions of the other two types. Accommodators made an active decision to watch. Television was not simply part of the daily routine. Watching varied from day to day depending on what programs they decided to watch and what other activities they chose to do instead. They planned and selected like Protesters, but watched for enjoyment as well as self-improvement, giving entertainment greater ground. Also like the Protester, what the Accommodator did watch he watched intently. Accommodators were thus characterized as a "reasonable" compromise between the indiscriminate indulgence of the working class and the overly critical and puritanical upper middle class.

"Children are Watching": Class Patterns of Child-Rearing

These class distinctions extended to children's viewing as well. A series of influential studies of child viewers from the late 1950s to the late 1970s distinguished between good and bad parenting in controlling children's television use.[25] In this work, the lower class or less educated are repeatedly identified as inadequate parents as measured by their lax attitudes toward television. Leo Bogart's summary of 1950s research concluded that parents of below-average income were overwhelmingly favorable toward television; while middle-class parents were concerned about loss of other activities to television and about television content. Bogart believed they were better equipped to handle the problems.[26] Professor Gary Steiner noted parents with grade school education were more likely to mention TV's "baby sitting" function positively, and criticized this as relegating the young to the television set "in the service of their own freedom."[27]

Psychologists Wilbur Schramm, Jack Lyle, and Edwin Parker opened their book with a cautionary statement that what television does to a child depends upon the child and by extension the parents, that is, it was a problem of parenting. They concluded with a guide to parents, listing "danger signals" that might indicate an undesirable influence of television. "Every time a parent finds himself using television as a baby sitter, he could well examine his practice and whether it is really necessary."[28]

Social researcher Robert Bower's 1970 follow-up to Steiner's study contrasted more- with less-educated parents, noting they were "quite divergent." More-educated parents monitored their children's television use more carefully. "The child with less-educated parents is more apt to be actually encouraged to watch in order to keep him occupied." Bower stated that more-educated parents regulated the amount and content of viewing and did not use television as a baby sitter, and went on to state approvingly that such a parent acted responsibly, being "more willing to take action against whatever potential dangers he sees for his children in watching too much or the wrong kinds of programs." Bower criticized less-educated parents for giving children too much autonomy in choosing their programs.[29]

In a widely cited article, Elliot Medrich coined the term "constant television households," in which parents are less likely to regulate their children's viewing and don't question the message, and where TV dominates the children's out-of-school lives. About half of the lowest income and least educated families were "constant" households and the same held true for 20 percent of the highest income and education families. Medrich contrasted "constant television" to "parentally controlled television" and concluded the latter occurred primarily in middle-class families, again affirming television use as a measure of class superiority.[30]

Study after study from the late 1950s through the 1970s constructed a discourse that distinguished between the negligent lower-status parent who did not monitor TV use and the responsible higher-status parent who did. By the 1980s the ideas had so melted into general consciousness that researchers moved on to other issues, but the ideas had become part of standard advice of doctors and other sources of child-rearing guidance. In 1976 the American Medical Association decided to publish a booklet for physicians to distribute to patients "emphasizing parental responsiblity for children's viewing." In 1982 the AMA reaffirmed their 1976 "action program" to advise patients on children's use of television. In 1996 the AMA distributed a new booklet to 60,000 physicians to advise parents to control children's viewing.[31] In 1995 and again in 1999 the American Academy of Pediatrics encouraged physicians to tell parents to carefully monitor children's use of television.

The logic underlying the negative valuation of television viewing, however, was based upon questionable assumptions. Common to all the literature on children and television, scholarly and popular, past and present, are the assumptions that television is detrimental if overused (displacement) or misused (dangerous content). These assumptions were rarely applied so consistently to other children's toys or activities. Concerns about doing too much of other activities (e.g., like sports or sleep) presumed a pathology of the child, not of the activity. Even heavy use of the telephone has been seen as a trait of adolescents rather than the phone. Television, by contrast, was constructed as an ever-present menace that might ensnare any child and that parents must guard against, regardless of their child's own personality.[32] In this context, discussions of parental control of this "beast" were all the more loaded with significance. Yet the assumptions linking heavy or indiscriminate use, passivity and control *by* television are at best questionable.

The Passive Viewer and Inatttentive Audiences

Underlying the concerns about television use has been an image of viewers as passively succumbing to this "plug-in drug."[33] The drug metaphor for television was based upon a presumption that the television addict had lost control and was passively consuming. If television was conceived as all-powerful, then viewers necessarily became powerless (i.e., passive), if not careful in its use. Passivity caused capabilities to wither in adults and to fail to develop in children. The passive viewer was susceptible to whatever television offered. If content was low-brow, the viewer became low-brow; if demagogic, the viewer fell into line.

Passivity was the focus of public concern and the question around which research was formulated. Regardless of the stance of the particular researcher, public issues and research questions have been couched in terms of the issue of the passive viewer.[34] Public criticism has focused primarily on the quantity of television use, with public debate castigating as self-indulgent the working-class viewers who turn the television on for many hours. The main criticism of heavy viewing was the assumption that it was indiscriminate and that the viewer would be susceptible to whatever messages were conveyed by programs. Researchers assumed a correlation between amount of viewing and susceptibility. Hidden in this is a prejudice that heavy viewers, who tend to be working class, are dumb, naive, gullible, and thus susceptible.

The presumed connection between heavy indiscriminate viewing and susceptibility hinges on the amount of attention viewers actually give to the program. However, researchers from a variety of theoretical camps have found that heavy viewers often give *less* attention to program content. Working-class families, who were typically identified as heavy users of television, at the same time were not intensive viewers. They did not devote complete attention to the program. Rather, their pattern was typically to leave the television on regardless of the program and regardless whether they were still watching. Interruptions were not prohibited and were not an occasion to turn off the television. Instead, they attended to other matters and returned to viewing when they were done. Such viewing patterns meant they were not likely to choose shows that required continuous attention. An obvious, but un-noted alternative conclusion is that such people are *less* susceptible to television.

By contrast, middle-class "selective" viewers, who are more discriminating in what they watch, give such programs their fullest attention and thus could be most susceptible. One could easily claim that selective viewers are duped by the cultural hegemony represented by the programs they select. Yet the predominant interpretation condemns "constant television" and praises selective viewing. Underlying this is a deeper assumption that what the middle class chooses to watch is good and what the working class chooses is detrimental.[35]

The negative evaluation of passivity then is implicated in the question of attention. Concern about effects, in fact, hinges on the question of attention. Inattention has been a long-standing complaint about entertainment audiences. Before the twentieth century, the *upper* class had a reputation for inattention. Working-class audiences also combined talking and watching in cheap theaters and later nickelodeons. Radio quickly became background while women did their housework. With television, however, for the first time working-class inattention was turned into a negative. Working-class viewers were labeled as inattentive, leaving television on even while not watching. This was interpreted as a sign of their irresponsible use of television, an indicator that they were not selective in the programs they tuned in and did not properly limit their children's television use. The appropriate use was to select a beneficial program and then to sit and watch attentively.

Engaging in a collateral activity while watching soon became a standard practice of viewing, as it had with radio, despite the initial beliefs that one could not do so with television. A study in 1955 reported that two-thirds of those with a television on during the day were doing something else simultaneously, most times housework. During the evening (6–10 P.M.) half were doing something else as well. In 1970, researchers for the Surgeon General's report on television videotaped twenty families in their homes while their televisions were on. They found that family members spent 24 to 45 percent of the time *not* watching while the television was on. People engaged in many collateral activities while watching, including doing homework, reading, sorting wash, preparing meals, setting the table, dressing and undressing, exercising, playing cards and board games, and conversing.[36]

Resistance in the Era of Conformity

Passive viewing is not what working-class community studies of the 1950s and 1960s reported. Ethnographers observed working-class viewers actively reconstructing media messages, classic examples of what later would be called cultural resistance. Sociologists Herbert Gans, Bennett Berger, and Alan Blum described working-class men in the late 1950s interacting with and interpreting programs within their own subcultural values.[37] Bennett Berger interviewed working-class suburbanites in 1957. The men rejected "middle-class" shows with high ratings, such as *Perry Como, Ed Sullivan, Steve Allen,* and even *I Love Lucy.* This was consistent with Berger's general conclusion that, in their move to the suburbs, working-class people did not adopt middle-class values and lifestyle. Their favorite drama series were *Cheyenne, Sergeant Bilko,* and *Meet McGraw.*[38]

Herbert Gans observed working-class families in 1957–58 in the West End of Boston and in 1958–59 in a Levitt development in Willingboro Township, New Jersey. In both communities he found early examples of "constant television." Television was used as background. It was kept on when company came, with people turning to it during pauses in the conversation or when something "important seems to be happening." The urban villagers of Boston's West End sustained an us-them distinction between their Italian working-class subculture and the dominant middle-class American culture. Gans said they "accept themes that mirror their own values, and reject others as illustrating the immorality and dishonesty of the outside world." He described the men in particular as using TV to "justify both the peer group society and its rejection of the outside world." Among the men he observed a combative attitude toward television. One of Gans's informants said, "We heckle TV just like we used to heckle the freaks

at the circus when we were kids." They watched commercials attentively but bombarded them with sarcasm. They vocally rejected statements that contradicted their own beliefs. If a show was not
entertaining they entertained themselves by making fun of the show.
They disliked Sergeant Friday of *Dragnet* because of his hostility to
working-class characters and preferred instead *Meet McGraw* because
he was friendly to working-class types. Similarly they favored portrayals of men as powerful and rejected portrayals of men as weak or
dumb, such as Ralph Kramden and Chester Riley, the working-class
husbands in situation comedies of the time. In *Levittown,* Gans also
found that mass media were "filtered through a variety of personal
predispositions so that not many messages reach the receiver intact."
(Gans's language here is prescient of cultural studies.) He observed
here the same skepticism about advertising claims and readiness to
point out flaws in plots.[39]

Alan Blum found black working-class men "carry on a continuous
joking dialogue with the television," which he interpreted as indicating an underlying hostility to the white performers on TV, similar to
the "us-them" attitude Gans found among working-class Italian-
Americans.[40] Such "talking back" to the TV was not unusual. In
taping families watching television in their homes, Bechtel and his
associates found it a sufficiently common practice to require a distinct category.[41]

Surveys of audience reactions to *All in the Family* in the 1970s suggests a similar phenomenon.[42] Viewers with prejudices similar to
Archie Bunker tended to see him in a positive light, even winning
arguments with his college-educated son-in-law, Mike. Given the correlation between class and scores on measures of prejudice, this audience was probably working class. One can see here the identification
with the working-class father and rejection of the upwardly mobile
son, much as Gans described working-class viewers rejecting the educated man who displays his education.

Home Video: Viewer Autonomy?

For three decades cultural critics railed at television and researchers attempted to demonstrate precisely what were the social, psychological, and political consequences of watching. Television was so alarming perhaps because it loomed so large in American life. From the 1950s through the 1970s the three commercial networks, ABC, CBS, and NBC, had commanded control of television through their 90 percent share of the nighttime audience. The *average* primetime show could guarantee entry for advertisers any night into nearly 30 percent of all American households. Primetime network programs had become the most widely shared cultural experience among Americans. It was taken for granted in most American families that they would watch television after dinner, separately or together – a national domestic ritual of tens of millions. For the vast majority, their choices of what to watch were limited to little more than the three major networks or reruns from those networks on independent stations not affiliated with any network.

The ritual began to unravel during the 1980s, however, as cable television multiplied the numbers of channels delivered to homes and videocassette recorders (VCRs) introduced time-shifting, commercial-zapping, and movie rental. The number of independent stations not affiliated with a network also increased, adding even more channels from which viewers could select.[1] Remote control devices (RCDs) became desirable in this TV environment of proliferating channels and soon became standard equipment with new TVs, VCRs, and cable hookups. These changes dramatically increased viewers' options and flexibility in using television. They would reopen questions of audience behavior and activism and create opportunities for new habits to form.

Cable versus Broadcast

Cable had originated in the early days of television as community antennae for rural areas where broadcast signals were difficult to receive. For a monthly fee, a local company connected homes by coaxial cable to a large antenna atop the highest peak for optimum reception. The cable business was a minor part of the industry until the mid-1970s, when it was transformed by the first commercial communication satellites. The networks had long sent their signals to local stations by phone line, rented at a bulk rate, but this was prohibitively expensive for other program suppliers on a show-by-show basis. Satellites made it economically feasible for new "cable network" companies to supply programming via satellite directly to cable systems and bypass broadcast stations and networks entirely. Cable systems installed satellite receivers and old programming not available on broadcast television, such as first-run movies. Home Box Office became the first such cable network in 1973, but quickly many other programmers began to supply cable systems. The availability of programming alternatives changed cable from a small part of the broadcasting industry into a distinct and competing industry. It stimulated the construction of cable systems in urban and suburban areas. Cable offered the local broadcast stations *plus* a wide variety of other channels to lure viewers away from the networks that dominated broadcast television. From that time cable spread steadily.

It did not spread as fast as radio or television had in their initial decades, since it required investing billions of dollars to construct a new house-to-house wire network. Nevertheless, by 1987 half of U.S.

households were cable subscribers. (See Table 18.1.) From 1979 to 1987, as cable penetration rate rose from 20 percent to 50 percent of TV households, the major networks' share of the audience fell from 90 percent to 75 percent. This was due in part but not solely to cable, since the VCR penetration rate rose during the same years from 2 percent to 50 percent.

Table 18.1   The Shift to Homevideo

Year	TV Households with VCR[a] (%)	TV Households with Cable[b] (%)	Three-Network Primetime Rating[c] (%)	Three-Network Primetime Share (%)	Basic Cable Primetime Rating (%)	Basic Cable Primetime Share (%)	Daily TV Use[c] (hrs/day)	Movie Admissions (billion/yr)
1975		13.2	57.3				6:07	1.03
1976		15.1	56.3				6:18	0.96
1977		16.6	58.5				6.10	1.05
1978		17.9	57.6				6.17	1.17
1979		19.4	56.7	91			6.28	1.16
1980	2.4 MPAA	22.6	56.5	90			6.36	1.02
1981	3.1	28.3	54.6	85			6.45	1.06
1982	5.7	35.0	52.3	83			6.48	1.18
1983	9.9	40.5	51.0	81			6.55	1.20
1984	12.4 Nielsen	43.7	50.1	78			7.08	1.20
1985	23.2	46.2	48.5	77	3.6	6	7.07	1.06
1986	39.0	48.1	49.1	76	4.1	7	7:10	1.02
1987	49.7	50.5	47.7	75	5.2	9	7:05	1.08
1988	59.0	53.8	43.1	70	6.6	11	6:59	1.08
1989	65.5	57.1	41.3	67	7.9	14	7:02	1.13
1990	69.4	59.0	39.7	65	9.6	17	6:55	1.06
1991	72.5	60.6	37.5	63	12.5	22	6:56	.98
1992	74.8	61.5	38.3	63	13.1	22	7.04	.97
1993	77.3	62.5	36.7	60	13.7	23	7:12	1.18
1994	79.2	63.4	37.4	61	14.5	24	7:16	1.21
1995	80.9	65.7	34.6	57	16.9	29	7:15	1.23
1996	82.3	66.7	31.9	53	18.5	32	7:17	1.26
1997	84.0	67.3	29.3	49			7:12	1.25

[a] For 1980–83 as of December and for 1984–97 as of May; [b] as of November; [c] for season (i.e., 1979 means September 1978 to April 1979).

Sources: Cable households, network primetime rating, basic cable ratings, and hours of daily use compliments of Nielsen Media Research. VCR households for 1980–83 from "1985 U.S. Economics Review" (New York: Motion Picture Association of America, 1986), 8; for 1984–97 from Nielsen Media Research. Theater admissions from *Variety*'s January annual summary issues.

VCR and Consumer Power[2]

Like cable, VCR had a long prehistory. CBS built the first video tape recorders in the 1950s as an industrial technology to record programs for broadcast and syndication. Sony used some of CBS's early patents for the first consumer videotape player in 1975.[3] Sales grew slowly at first, but increased so fast in the mid-1980s that it quickly surpassed the penetration rate of cable.

VCR sales were slow in the 1970s due to the simultaneous introduction of cable programming, the limited range of entertainment available on prerecorded videotape (predominantly X-rated), competing VCR recording formats, and the high prices of VCRs.[4] Less than 3 percent of U.S. homes had a VCR in 1980, five years after their introduction. Then VCR prices dropped from about $2,000 in 1976 to around $200 in 1985.[5] VHS became the dominant format, removing the confusion of incompatible technologies.[6] Probably the most important factor in boosting VCR sales was the availability of movies on videotape for rental fees of two to three dollars. By the end of 1987 more than half of U.S. households had a VCR. Americans had adopted the VCR as a common household product almost as quickly as they did television in the 1950s. Embedded in this rapid adoption are two dramatic examples of the power exercised by audiences: the rental rebellion against the movie studios, and the failure of videodisc despite the backing of the largest consumer electronics corporations.

Around 1980 the major movie studios recognized that videotape gave them a new way to turn the family television into an exhibition medium for movies and supplement theater admission profits. Hundreds of titles were licensed for release by 1980 as the major studios created distribution subsidiaries to market their film libraries on videotape.[7] At first the major studios only offered the cassettes for sale and explicitly prohibited retailers from renting them. But at $50, the retail price for movie tapes was prohibitively high and stunted sales. Faced with an inventory that did not sell, a few small retailers began to violate the sales agreement and started renting the tapes to their customers.[8] Consumers responded enthusiastically to this new option. By 1982 three-fourths to 95 percent of movie tape transactions were rentals. In 1983 VCR owners averaged three rentals a month.[9]

The major movie studios unsuccessfully attempted numerous schemes to regain control of their product. Rental was legally possible as a result of the First Sale Doctrine of U.S. copyright law. The movie studios sold the movie tapes to wholesalers and retailers instead of leasing to them, as they did to theaters. Having sold the cassettes, the movie studios could not legally prohibit the buyers from renting the cassettes to their customers, nor demand a share of rental revenue.[10]

The rental rebellion succeeded in part because retailers organized and took concerted action to protect their interests and because video retailers' interests coincided with those of consumer electronics companies. When the Motion Picture Association of America lobbied Congress to repeal the First Sale Doctrine, the Electronics Industry Association joined retailers to oppose repeal, since rental had dramatically boosted VCR sales.[11] Yet it was the day-to-day decisions of customers at thousands of mom-and-pop stores that had the greatest effect. Audiences acted in their own interest, not collectively but as individual consumers. Nevertheless, they had their way despite the wishes of the major movie studios.

The Videodisc Fiasco

One of the attractive features of the VCR was its capacity to record as well as play tapes. Recording enabled viewers to watch television programs at times convenient to them, giving them new flexibility and control over their use of television. This capability of VCRs distinguished it from an alternative technology introduced at the time, videodisc, which could play prerecorded movies but lacked recording capability. Videodisc had the backing of the world's largest consumer electronics manufacturers, including RCA, Zenith, Philips, General Electric, Thorn/EMI, and Matsushita. In 1979, these companies formed three consortia to manufacture and market different videodisc systems in the United States.[12] RCA, the principal company in videodisc development, expected videotape to remain an expensive specialty item for a select market. They hoped to produce an inexpensive videodisc player that would undersell VCRs.

RCA's expectation about VCR prices proved wrong, giving no price advantage to videodisc. Moreover, the videodisc arrived too late. Technological problems slowed development.[13] The rental rebellion also played a central part in its failure. Just as videodisc began to be marketed, hundreds of movies became available through rental to VCR owners. This combined with the advantage of the VCR's recording capability made VCRs a better buy than videodisc players.

RCA quickly dropped its player price to no avail. In February 1982, the videodisc plant for the Philips system closed; in November, GE and its partners put their system on "indefinite hold." RCA held on until 1984 when it shut down its player production. The companies involved reported losses over $1 billion on this failed consumer technology.[14]

People chose VCR, the more liberating technology, and defeated corporate efforts to substitute videodisc players as the mass-market product. Again, audiences as individual consumers determined the prevailing technology and shaped how they could use their television. It was the combined effect of their millions of purchasing decisions arrived at individually that created a product and market to serve their needs and to realize new uses of television and new control of what and when one could watch.

In both instances, viewers held sway. But they did not do this through collective action. Moreover, the advantages they gained they also exercised individually in the privacy of their homes. These cultural victories did not change the trend toward privatization that had been the mark of radio and television.

Culture Wars over Viewer Time and Attention

VCRs enabled viewers to regain control of their leisure time through time-shifting[15] and to enhance their program selection through movie rentals. VCRs also increased the use of remote control devices (RCDs) not only for the VCR but also to increase the flexibility of television viewing through "grazing." Time-shifting and grazing were in turn countered by network programming strategies to retain audiences. Corporate efforts to control viewer behavior and viewers' desires to resist such control well illustrate the conception of culture as an arena of struggle between domination of and resistance by audiences.

Two minor changes in audience behavior that accompanied the new technology are similar to those attendant upon the introduction of other new entertainment technologies. One consequence of the increased number of program choices from cable and VCR was increased use of television. Daily household television use had plateaued in the 1970s at about six hours. From about 1979 to 1984 average use again began to rise to about seven hours and has remained at this level since (Table 18.1). More viewing has meant less time at other activities, especially those outside the home. About 15 percent of cable subscribers reported spending more time at home and driving fewer miles weekly.[16] However, there was no substantial drop in going out to the movies. At the same time that the movie studio profits from tape rental surpassed those from domestic theater exhibition, theater admissions did not significantly drop.[17]

A second change was a limited renaissance of group viewing. In the early days of VCRs, the first owners invited friends over to watch movies with them, similar to the communal viewing phase of television in the early 1950s. A study in 1985 found that ninth- and tenth-grade children whose families owned VCRs were more likely to watch TV with friends.[18] More long term, the VCR enhanced college students' habits of watching television in groups. In dorms and apartments, students taped their favorite programs or rented movies and watched together at times convenient to them. Female dorm students watched taped soaps or evening serials like *Northern Exposure* or *Melrose Place* after studying, or male housemates watched taped episodes of *Seinfeld* or *Cheers.*[19]

Time-Shifting: Consumer Programming

VCRs made it possible for the first time for television users to watch programming at times of their own choosing, instead of at the will of the broadcaster or cable system.[20] The long-standing reason consumers have given for purchasing VCRs has been the time-shifting capability: three-fourths of consumers in 1978 and again in 1984 gave this as their primary reason for buying a VCR. This is also borne out in owners' use of VCRs. Even after movie rental was widely available, time-shifting remained an important use. In 1985, Nielsen found households spent almost three hours per week watching playback of taped programs and less than one hour per week watching prerecorded cassettes. Nielsen also found that viewing rented movie tapes dropped by half after two to three years of VCR ownership, while playback of taped programs remained stable.[21] About three-fourths of taping has been of network programs, with a heavier emphasis on the fall and winter primetime season. Television series, and particularly daytime serials, are the programs most frequently time-shifted, followed by movies. VCR owners who were also cable subscribers tended to use their VCR even more for time-shifting.[22]

Time-shifting has added flexibility to people's leisure, giving people some independence from the control of their time by broadcasters and cablecasters. With this new flexibility the viewing audience has begun to act in ways that have created some difficulties for advertising-based television. Time-shifting contributes to audience fragmentation, making it more difficult to measure, predict, and deliver an audience of specific demographics to advertisers. Audience demographics previously could be predicted by what groups were at home during certain hours. Advertising could be matched to these groups. Time-shifting eliminates the connection between the time of broadcast or cablecast and the demographics of the audience.

Zapping: Nightmare for Advertisers

More threatening to television advertising is the VCR's enabling viewers to skip or "zap" commercials. Audiences have traditionally switched stations or left the room during commercial breaks, but the VCR carries this a step farther. For the first time viewers can separate commercials from the entertainment. In 1984, Neilsen found 5 percent of the total audience of any given commercial was lost through VCR zapping. Some in the industry considered this loss significant. One ad agency claimed that General Foods lost $1 million in paid advertising time in 1984 due to zapping. Yet only 10 percent of television homes had VCRs at the time. In 1985, with VCRs in 28 percent of homes, 44 percent of VCR users always fast-forwarded commercials. This could mean that 12 percent of the audience of a given commercial was lost in 1985 to zapping. Another Nielsen study in 1990 again found 40 percent of VCR users skipped commercials.[23] The spread of VCRs makes zapping a very real danger to broadcast and cable television based on advertising. An obvious solution for advertisers is to embed commercial material into the entertainment itself so that it is not separable. This is already done with children's programming, with programs built around a toy; and with movies, with products prominently displayed in scenes for a fee.

Remote Control versus Audience Flow

The growth in the number of channels offered through cable and independent stations and the flexible capabilities of VCRs led to the rapid spread of television remote-control devices. Proliferating channels complicates viewers' program choice, which RCDs help to resolve. As with the other technologies, the remote control had a long prehistory and then a rapid spread. Zenith offered an RCD as a optional extra for some of its televisions in the 1950s. But the RCD did not become a standard part of television and VCR purchase until the 1970s.[24]

Remote control devices made channel changing easier for viewers. This gave rise to the phenomenon called "grazing" or "surfing" from channel to channel, which directly interfered with programmers' efforts to retain audiences from one show to the next, a phenomenon called "audience flow." It also made it easier for viewers to switch channels in an effort to avoid commercials.

Researchers of RCD use have reported widely varying results. A 1996 survey of research results concluded that remotes substantially increase (by approximately 70%) channel changing and zapping of commercials by changing channels (5–20% of commercials) or skipping commercials in recorded programs (20–80% of commercials). Most remote use is accounted for by about a fifth of all viewers. The most robust research results replicated across many studies indicate that younger male viewers are the most frequent remote users. RCD use is also more frequent among those viewing alone, presumably since it does not disturb anyone else's viewing. Moreover, zapping tended to be more common among those who do not plan their viewing and use television more for background (i.e., are inattentive).[25] Researchers found no correlation between education and income and RCD use.

Concerning the relation of RCD use to active audiences, research reports that RCD use is more related to "passive" use of television for escape and diversion than for more active cognitive learning and personal identity.[26] This mitigates the interpretations that the new technologies are enabling a more active audience.

Grazing, which RCDs have made easy, has caused enough concern among programmers that they have developed a variety of strategies to hold viewers' attention between shows. They have shortened the credits at the beginning and moved ads to midprogram instead of between programs; and they have enlivened the credits by offering further entertainment while the credits run.[27]

The Decline of Mass Medium Television?

VCRs, remotes, and the new television program sources of videotape, cable, and independent stations had two consequences for audiences. First, they increased household television use from about six hours per day to about seven hours. At the same time they unleashed audiences from the control of the three commercial networks, unraveling the national nightly ritual of Americans together in their separate homes watching network television shows.[28] The audience spread itself across a much broader range of programs and uses in the 1990s compared to the 1970s. The three commercial networks' share of the primetime audience (the percent of households with the television on that are tuned to a network-affiliated station) dropped steadily from their 90 percent share in the 1970s to 49 percent for the 1996–97 season (Table 18.1).[29]

The erosion of network audience share has made network executives desperate to retain whatever viewers they have and to appeal to those they previously ignored.[30] Consequently, for the first time in American history blacks became an important audience for mainstream media. As a higher percentage of whites subscribed to cable, blacks, who were already significantly heavier TV viewers, became disproportionately represented in the network audience. According to ratings analysts, blacks could add 1 to 2 $\frac{1}{2}$ points to a show's rating and change it from average to successful. Black viewers were credited with saving primetime programs through their disproportionate support. Networks began offering more programming for black audiences, including shows directed specifically to blacks. In the 1990s this trend ironically has resulted in increasing segregation of audiences and shows. Nevertheless, networks continue to program black situation comedies, since they cannot afford to ignore any segment of their audience, as their ratings continue to decline.[31]

Another side effect of the networks' desperate attempts to counter slipping ratings was to rediscover television viewing outside the home. They commissioned studies by A. C. Nielsen in 1989 to measure it. Nielsen concluded that it represented about 2 percent of the total television audience, although it represented a much larger proportion of the audience for particular programs. ABC's *Monday Night Football*, for example, increased its audience by 7 percent or 1.5 ratings points – a significant increase. Nielsen found a third of the out-of-home audience at workplaces, a fifth at colleges, and a sixth in hotels and motels.[32]

A similar study by Nielsen in March 1993 found the out-of-home audience to be about 4 percent of the total audience. A fourth of the network out-of-home audience was at work, another fourth at colleges (including dorms, which are not in Nielsen's ratings), a fifth in hotels and motels, a tenth in bars and restaurants, and the rest in places such as hospitals and waiting rooms for doctors, airports, buses, and so forth.[33]

However, this out-of-home viewing was not a return to communal viewing. Viewing in public places like waiting rooms is distinctly individual and alienating. For example, students watching television in a student center lounge were strikingly alienated, with people not acknowledging others outside their dyad, using the television as a distraction to kill time for a few minutes while they ate lunch alone or waited for their next class. Many viewers, a mix of men and women coming and going, were doing other things such as eating, reading, writing, looking around the room, and talking. One would expect that viewing at work also accompanies working.

Student viewers in college dorms, on the other hand, used TV to enhance their relationships to each other, cementing community that already existed. They conversed with each other, relating their own experiences to that of the characters. I employed a student assistant to observe other student viewers at an Eastern private college. Three white female students gathered one evening in a dorm room to watch *Melrose Place,* a romantic serial. None of the girls paid close attention to the show. They talked most of the time. Food was the major topic of conversation. They discussed the show more than watched it. An added distraction was the traffic of friends coming and going. It seems the TV program was merely an occasion to get together rather than an end in itself. A group of male roommates gathered regularly to watch *Cheers.* They paid more attention to the show. The men would repeat lines or jokes from the show, making a running commentary on the show's events and characters. Like the women, these male viewers also *used* the show for their own purposes, a peg on which to hang their conversation and to support their interaction with each other.

These student viewers used television as a source of conversation, discussing and commenting on the shows, and as a bridge between conversation, watching when conversation stopped but readily interrupting their viewing for brief conversations. It is reminiscent of the working-class viewing habits described in Chapter 17. And it's not unlike those distracted young bucks whom Washington Irving described at the theater in 1803, who were there to socialize with their friends. *Plus ça change, plus c'est la même chose.*[34]

Conclusion

The VCR and RCD have brought a new level of independence to people in their primary leisure activity, television viewing. This new era of "second-generation" television has been dubbed a time of active television *use* in contrast to previous passive television *viewing.* There has been much debate about how much change this represents in the balance of power of cultural hegemony, whether audiences have gained actual power or simply more maneuverability in consuming what is still determined and offered to them by media monopolies. The stark phrasing of active use versus passive viewing does tend to exaggerate the conditions both before and after home video: audiences were neither so passive before, nor so active today as to suggest any return to audience sovereignty. Nevertheless there does seem to have been an *incremental* improvement of the position of the audience vis-à-vis media and advertisers' control of them.

Certainly home video and the new era has not improved the prospects of collective action on the part of television audiences. VCRs and cable have increased television use and lessened time spent in other activities outside the home. And they have increased privatization of the family, since TV use is still overwhelmingly in the home. Consumers have been victorious in making their choice of technology, the VCR, dominant, which improved individuals' abilities to select what to see and when to consume television programming, but these new technologies have done nothing to assemble audience members into collectivities and therefore are unlikely to produce more significant changes in the power of audiences.

At the same time, lower ratings for programs, the habit of grazing, and the use of movie tapes all indicate a greater independence and less loyalty of viewers to television programs. Recent evidence indicates that people no longer make a point of seeing every episode of even their favorite series. Half the audience of even popular series watch only once a month.[35] Children too began to discover other uses of television, with home video games such as Nintendo as well as videotapes of their favorite movies.[36] People so far have not reduced television use, as they had with movies and radio when new technologies arrived, but they do use it in different and less predictable ways than had been customary for three decades. However, in the late 1990s, there are some suggestions that the trend may be changing and people may be reducing their television use for the first time. Some have claimed that younger viewers seem to be abandoning television altogether, perhaps for the Internet.[37] But it is too soon to tell where this will lead.

In the meantime, worries about TV continue among critics and researchers. A *New York Times* article argued that "television is our most underappreciated medium" and complained about the continued casting of television as the opposite of education, health, and taste. Concerns about effects on children were restated in a 1998 issue of the *Annals of the American Academy of Political and Social Science*.[38] And the potential next-generation technology that may curb television – computers and the Internet – is generating the same familiar hopes and fears that radio and TV had, that it has great educational potential, but that it may promote passivity, limit socialization, displace more valuable activities, and even be addictive.[39]

19

Conclusion: From Effects to Resistance and Beyond

S
urveys of communication research have characterized the history of the field as a movement from conceiving audiences as passive to seeing them as active.[1] As we have seen, the image of audiences as passive victims arose from countless articles in the popular press expressing fears about new mass media. Reformers, educators, clergy, and other human service professionals wrote extensively about the dangers of movies, radio, and television, as each became popular. Intellectuals and cultural critics blamed these media for the decline in culture. They expressed little faith in the average person's ability to manage mass media and, in the spirit of mass culture criticism, characterized the masses as in danger of becoming helpless victims.

Communication researchers typically have shaped their agenda to answer and allay these public concerns. Research reports often began by quoting magazine claims of the dangers of mass media and then proceeded to answer these fears with reassuring research results that the effects were not so serious.[2] The Payne Fund researchers in the 1930s began with their benefactor's fears about effects of movies on children, but reported less extreme results, and even objected to stronger statements made in the project's final report. Early propaganda studies similarly were prompted by a popular "hypodermic theory" that propaganda simply injected ideas into its audiences.[3] Paul Lazarsfeld's work in the 1940s solidified researchers' rejection of the paradigm of powerful media and passive audiences. This began with *The People's Choice,* a study of the short-run effects of radio on the 1940 presidential voting. In this study, Lazarsfeld introduced the idea of a "two-step flow of communication," with local opinion leaders as mediators between media and listeners. *Personal Influence,* coauthored with Elihu Katz, emphasized the significance of peers in constructing the meaning of media messages. Lazarsfeld was not only saying audiences were active in the face of media effects; he was moving toward a paradigm that focused on these audience activities instead of media effects.[4] But this development was cut short by television.

With the arrival of television a new generation of researchers, trained in experimental social psychology rather than Lazarsfeld's radio research paradigm, returned to the "effects" approach to answer popular fears about the dangers of television to children.[5] Congressional hearings led to federal funding of numerous studies in the 1960s and 1970s meticulously documenting specific but limited effects, confirming but reducing the feared dangers. The underlying model of "effects" research presumed a passive viewer, acted upon, not acting. The communication model, sender-message-receiver, was one-way with a fixed message. In the behaviorist frame of experimental research, media stimuli caused viewer response. The living, acting viewer was reduced to behavior determined by television messages and modified by other environmental stimuli.

Lazarsfeld's emphasis on mediating factors and his nascent consideration of an active audience were kept alive during this time by those who advocated a "uses and gratifications" approach.[6] In the early 1970s Elihu Katz, himself a student and coauthor of Lazarsfeld, explicitly formulated the premises of this approach and a school of researchers began to coalesce around them. The approach was captured in a motto coined by Katz, to pay "less attention to what media do *to* people and more to what people do *with* the media."[7] It had the virtue of recognizing audiences as active agents.

But this approach did not so much reject the "effects" model of communication as sidestep it. It did not address the question of power of media, implicit in the "effects" model. While granting viewers' agency, it limited this agency to the apparently innocuous choice of what to do with one's leisure time. Uses were formulated as individuals gratifying their personal needs and desires, as if power and inequality did not constrain these pursuits. Nor did this approach explore such issues as audiences constituting autonomous cultures or engaging in collective action.[8]

In the 1980s, American ethnographic audience studies expanded the idea of active audiences, while not yet including the factor of power. A new generation of young researchers sought to document people's television "uses" by observing them within their homes.[9] They wedded two previously segregated fields of research, mass communication and family communication. Drawing upon various social contructivist theories then popular in sociology and anthropology, they developed an "interpretive paradigm" that replaced the motive of viewers gratifying needs with one of viewers using media text to construct "fields of meaning." They also reconceived viewing as one among a constellation of family activities, rather than as the determining activity. They saw that, unlike watching in theaters, television viewing is embedded thoroughly in daily routine and involves activities simultaneous with or interrupting television. Television is merged into these activities and the daily schedule.[10]

This approach not only granted viewers agency, but grounded their agency within the social relations of the family. This had the potential of placing the family within the larger frameworks of power and inequality in the society, and it framed their viewing in these terms. Unfortunately, like its predecessors in "uses and gratifications" research and many of its adopted social constructivist theories, this research tended to ignore questions of power.

Reconsidering Resistance

The other new type of television research that developed in the 1980s, cultural studies, also grew out of an ethnographic approach, but it placed power at the center of its concern.[11] Explicitly rejecting the idea of the passive viewer, it conceives viewers' relationship to media specifically in terms of power. It starts with an assumption that subordinate groups use television and other commodities to construct their own culture, documenting what Raymond Williams had called oppositional cultures and what has come to be called cultural resistance.[12]

Audience research in cultural studies can be traced to the University of Birmingham's Centre for Contemporary Cultural Studies (CCCS), birthplace of cultural studies, and to its director, sociologist Stuart Hall's "Encoding/Decoding" paper, which used the poststructural idea of multiple readings of a text. Hall replaced the model of the passive viewer ingesting a fixed media message with one who actively created his own interpretations of media messages grounded in his own social experience. According to Hall, the flaw in the "effects" approach that led to a presumption of powerful media and passive audiences was the presumption of a fixed message. He instead presumed the polysemy or openness of television text to variant readings. David Morley and other students of Hall at the Centre asked working-class Britons about their television viewing to test Hall's model.[13]

Others at the Centre were engaged in ethnographic research documenting working-class youth subcultures.[14] They conceived popular cultural consumption, exemplified in style cultures of the 1960s and 1970s, as evidence of active resistance to hegemony, contradicting those who defined people as passive victims of mass culture. The CCCS subcultural studies emphasized how working-class youth transformed the meaning of popular cultural commodities to construct their own subcultural styles through a process called *bricolage*. This approach too presumed the openness of the text, in this case the meaning of a wide range of objects, from music to motor scooters. At the core of both audience and subcultural studies was a presumption of active consumers engaged in power struggles over meanings with purveyors of mass culture. Mass culture consumption was seen as a site of resistance to domination. One difference was that the subcultural studies intrinsically emphasized collective action, while audience studies did not. We will return to this later.

What distinguished cultural studies approaches from American ethnography, "uses and gratification" and even "effects" research, was counterposing the power of media against active audiences. Subordinate groups construct variant readings of television and other mass-produced commodities that express opposition to the dominant culture. Cultural resistance has been the core concern.

In the 1990s, there has been a growing backlash among researchers against overextended ideas of resistance. Some see conceptual vagueness or epistemological problems.[15] More pertinent to the issues here is criticism, even by cultural studies advocates, for attributing political significance to trivial, individual acts.[16] They protest indiscriminate

celebrations of almost any creative consuming as politically significant. As Australian interpreter of cultural studies Graeme Turner
phrased it, "making over the meaning of a television program may be
much easier than climbing out of a ghetto, changing the color of one's
skin, changing one's gender, or reducing one's dependence on the varied mechanisms of state welfare."[17]

Another important figure in cultural studies, Australian Meaghan
Morris, complained about what she calls the *voxpop* version of cultural studies, characterizing resistance as light-hearted and light-
headed, disconnected from any concrete struggle, and without
qualifying the extent of such "liberation." Morris also objects to
describing popular culture as "a terrain of struggle" since it implies
that such featherweight acts as playing with the meaning of a television show constitutes "struggle" against hegemony. Morris prefers
French theorist Michel de Certeau's idea of "making do" to characterize these little acts of getting through the day. She refers to them as
"fleeting appropriations." She also criticizes the tendency in the *voxpop* version of cultural studies to erase the negative, failing to "articulate loss, despair, disillusion, anger, and thus to learn from failure." In
other words, she wants to place the little victories within the larger
context of hegemony, to balance populism with pessimism.[18]

Originally within cultural studies, resistance was conceived not as
triumphant, or even as liberating, but as simply a recognition that
hegemony was not total, that there was contestation, even though the
dominant culture remains dominant and even politically victorious.
The godfather of cultural studies, Raymond Williams, formulated the
original idea as a limitation on the total domination implicit in overde-
termined concepts of base and superstructure and ideology. He conceived of alternative and oppositional cultures as part of an
ever-incomplete hegemony, which has "continually to be renewed,
recreated and defended [and is] continually challenged."[19] Early cultural studies' use of Williams's idea considered cultural resistance not
as an end in itself but as a step to collective action. Sociologist Stuart
Hall concluded his "Notes on Deconstructing the Popular" with the
point:

[Popular culture] is one of the sites where this struggle for and against a
culture of the powerful is engaged: it is also the stake to be won or lost
in the struggle. It is the arena of consent and resistance. It is partly
where hegemony arises, and where it is secured. It is not a sphere where
socialism, a socialist culture – already fully formed – might be simply

"expressed." But is one of the places where socialism might be constituted. That is why "popular culture" matters. Otherwise, to tell you the truth, I don't give a damn about it.[20]

Hall describes resistance as *potential*, not inevitable, and as the *beginning*, not the end. It is of interest only because of its "capacity to *constitute* classes and individuals as a popular force," not as examples of the *exercise* of that force. This is echoed in audience theorist Ien Ang's remarks that a concept of active audiences should not romanticize people's efforts to "make do" by calling them "resistance." Ang points out that viewers giving oppositional meanings "should be understood not as an example of 'audience freedom' but as a moment in that cultural struggle, an on-going struggle over meaning and pleasure which is central to the fabric (ation) of everyday life."[21]

Williams's concept of incorporation, how dominant forces act to incorporate alternative and oppositional cultures into the dominant culture, is necessary to balance the concept of resistance. Subcultural studies, most notably Dick Hebdige's *Subculture* which emphasized the aspect of *bricolage*, of consumers using commodities in distinctive ways with new meanings, have also noted how such uses and groups have been incorporated back into the nexus of consumption and profit. Hebdige's analysis of *bricolage*, however, was more elaborate and brilliant than his examination of incorporation. Cultural studies of audiences have tended to neglect incorporative aspects.[22]

Some studies of resistance that have been criticized as trivial have forgotten that resistance is necessarily *collective*. Individual acts are trivial if they are not part of a collective stance. In describing resistance as culture, Williams implicitly recognized that it was collective. Egoistic individual viewers giving idiosyncratic interpretations of a television program, without consciousness of being part of a collective enterprise, do not qualify as resistance. Resistance is constituted of acts expressing the shared culture of a subordinate group. Before applying the term "resistance," researchers need to gauge the degree to which acts are collective and thus may promise political significance beyond the immediate moment's pleasure.[23]

Women Viewers

To further explore the idea of resistance I will consider two fields of inquiry into resistance, that of women television viewers and that of fandom. Feminist audience studies emerged from the 1970s and early 1980s studies of film and television text. Content analyses, mostly of television programs, and textual analyses of the subject position of the "male gaze" inherent in film text, both conceived the "women viewer" as a passive receiver of the messages inscribed in the text, and thus a passive victim of patriarchal propaganda.[24]

By the late 1980s others challenged this conception of the woman as passive victim. This was part of a larger shift in feminist scholarship toward a more positive, activist, and resistant construction of women.[25] Within film studies, earlier feminist theorists were criticized for textual reductionism, conflating subject position and real women viewers.[26]

Cultural studies researchers focused on actual viewers, presuming active female audiences interpreted text to suit their own needs within the framework of domestic gender roles.[27] Many of the studies focused on the women's genre, soap operas, so debased by aesthetic critics and criticized by earlier feminists. Cultural studies researchers reinterpreted them as ground upon which women constructed positive identities and other forms of cultural resistance.

Ellen Seiter and her team of researchers from the Tübingen (Germany) Soap Opera Project found working-class women tended to be hostile to the heroines with whom they were supposed to sympathize and to cheer on the villainess who violated norms of femininity and motherhood. The villainess expressed their class resentments. The working-class viewers saw the "sympathetic" female leads as whiners or wimps who had comfortable, privileged lives compared to their own. They felt no sympathy but rather resentment and anger, which they sometimes expressed out loud at the screen. They similarly yelled at male characters and even the scriptwriters whom they saw also as privileged. Watching allowed them to express this anger about their own economic straits.[28]

The women observed by Ellen Seiter's team, by Andrea Press, and others are remarkable for their similarity to working-class men observed thirty years earlier by Herbert Gans and Alan Blum, discussed in Chapter 17. In those studies, working-class men identified with the "wrong" characters too, and vented their anger at the middle and upper class and about their own position by spitting remarks at the screen, making fun of or despising middle- and upper-class characters cast as the heroes. Then as now, watching was one of the few occasions that afforded lower-class viewers an opportunity to vent their class resentments. In public situations, at work, while shopping, or at leisure, such venting typically would have serious repercussions. But in their home they could let out these feelings otherwise suppressed.

Embeddedness and Inattention

Another thread of these studies of women's viewing of daytime television was the embeddedness of television in family activities. For women, embeddedness means viewing that is regularly interrupted. In the words of writer and poet Tillie Olsen, "motherhood means being instantly interruptable... It is distraction, not meditation, that becomes habitual; interruption, not continuity." Soaps have long been written to fit this domestic situation of women. Multiple plot lines of soaps interrupt each other from day to day, mimicking the skipping of attention of the housewife, while repetition allows viewers to catch up on what one missed when away from the television.[29]

Embeddedness means that television, not only for women viewers, is simply one among other simultaneous activities in homes. Inattention is an inevitable aspect of this fact. Television is not *the* feature of the home landscape; it is simply "there," an ever-present part of the household. Not that it is unnoticed, but that it does not warrant full attention, except at moments when something "interesting" appears on the screen. Moreover, this reduced salience has become a characteristic of television generally, even outside the home. Interruption is no longer characteristic of viewing in the home or of women in the home but of viewers anywhere in the United States.

At the same time, television has come to saturate our environment. TV sets have proliferated from one to several in a home, from the home to the car, to the beach, to public places like waiting rooms and lounges. Public viewing no longer has the communal property it once had in the "tavern phase" of television. One reason television can be included in so many different environments and activities is because it is no longer intrusive, the center of attention. People can "take it or leave it."

Both the lack of salience and the saturation with television have gradually evolved. Therefore, we may learn a great deal about the significance of this saturation if we explore how it has arisen historically. Television in the 1950s, 1960s, and even 1970s did not yet saturate life. It was the focus of attention for a wide range of people and occasions, to a degree not now true. People paid attention more then than now. Television was foreground, not environment. The working-class viewing patterns of the 1950s, of "constant television," leaving television on even when not intently watching, actually pioneered this phenomenon of television as wallpaper. The inattentiveness that researchers attributed to working-class viewers in the 1960s and 1970s revisits us in the 1990s with a new significance.

Inattention demonstrates viewers' independence from and yet familiarity with television text. People's ability to interpolate the gaps in their viewing reveals their knowledge of television forms.[30] Facility allows also for a certain distance from the text, and for extracting pieces from the text as suits the viewers' momentary needs. It allows us to toy with the meanings of television (*bricolage*). Thus embeddedness, saturation, and inattention facilitate cultural autonomy. It now appears difficult to say who is the puppet and who the puppeteer. But autonomy is not resistance, and toying is not collective action. One must distinguish between bread and circuses and the exercise of power, and how one may or may not lead to the other. What do viewers do with this autonomy? Does the saturation counteract this autonomy by its very pervasiveness?

Embeddedness and the Disappearing Audience

David Morley, in his second study, *Family Television,* emphasized the context of viewing television within the home. He rooted interpretation of viewers' responses in terms of the relevance to their everyday life, disconnecting the analysis from the text. This in turn also shifted the critical definition of people's role from that of viewer to that of family member or some role other than that of viewer. In doing so, Morley effectively eliminated the category of "audience" from his analysis, substituting instead the category "family." Two other cultural studies researchers, John Hartley and Ien Ang, also argue that viewers in homes do not experience themselves as members of a television audience, like people in a theater might, but rather as members of a family, others of whom may or may not be viewing.[31] The fact that one family member is watching television is no different than if that person were playing with a toy, or fixing dinner, or combing his or her hair. These activities are not constitutive, but merely aspects of being part of the family.

The emphases on embeddedness of viewing in other domestic activities has raised the question whether television audiences constitute groups. An audience constituted as a self-conscious group may act collectively and thus offer politically significant resistance to domination, cultural or otherwise. Is the television audience a group? The "classic" works of Morley's *Nationwide* study and Janice Radway's study of romance readers looked at individual viewers gathered together by the researchers. These were not groups with preexisting relationships and shared norms, such as were the focus of subcultural studies or of earlier community studies. They were simply samples of collectivities (classes, races), not even of communities. The families that Morley and others observed, on the other hand, while groups, were not groups of *viewers*.[32]

This question of whether television audiences constitute groups is central to evaluating whether their cultural resistance is politically significant. The concept of "interpretive community," the emphasis on group rather than individual response, has highlighted the importance of collective response to television as necessary to constitute noteworthy cultural resistance.[33] It is even more relevant for any forms of collective action beyond that. Also this bears on the degree to which television has, according to an older debate, privatized, isolated, and thus pacified people, so they no longer engage in group activities that are prerequisites for learning to take collective action.

Historical comparison helps to highlight these matters. As we have seen, theater audiences existed – and acted – as self-conscious groups in two senses. First, in live theater the meanings from text (the play) and from social interaction (performers with audience) merged, since audiences interacted with actors as both text (the characters) and as social beings (actors). There was no segregation here of text from context. In theater before the mid-nineteenth century the recognition of audience sovereignty, the right to intervene, implicit in the rhetorical style of acting at the time, ensured the significance of this interaction. Such interaction has continued to be asserted and holds a central place in other entertainments such as rock music concerts, although in attenuated form. These still exhibit collective interaction by the audience with live performers and performance.

Second, the audience was local and a microcosm of the community, or of sectors within the community. The theater was an arena for public discourse. It is a change of major political significance that "the television audience" exists only with the text of a program. Beyond that, "the audience" does not exist; rather the individuals or households exist as entities unrelated to each other. In contrast to "the audience," these individuals are defined by environmental artifacts beyond the program, and TV is merely one of these artifacts.

Since most television viewing is done within households, any response encompassing a larger group would seem to inevitably arise through, to be orchestrated by the medium, as independent and simultaneous responses by viewers in separate households and as a response *after* the fact, rather than one that bears directly and immediately upon the entertainment/situation to shape it – that is, unless these families' shared responses are mediated by their participation in some community, interpretive or otherwise. The communities to which these families belong have been almost ignored in research.[34] Instead of rooting viewers' social identities of class, race, or gender in such communities, they have been taken simply as demographic labels.

In lieu of such communities, the entertainment itself becomes the intermediary for group action; and as privatization dismantles the public sphere where unmediated interaction might have taken place, such communities fade. Reception theory is perfectly adequate to grasp this sort of resistance orchestrated by reception, but not to explain/document the community bases of autonomous resistance unmediated by the entertainment, which is the strength of a broadened ethnographic approach.

Fandom: Resistance or Incorporation?

Let us now consider a more promising circumstance for resistance, an audience that is self-consciously organized into groups, fans. Recent research on fandom has reconstructed fans, like women viewers, not as passive dependents of media, but as active viewers using media products to create their own world.[35]

Media researcher Henry Jenkins notes five ways in which fandom constitutes an active presence, appropriating television to construct a subculture. Fans develop refined critical and interpretive practices, actively reinterpret text while viewing, lobby producers to shape programs, create their own products, capture a segment of the "spin-off" market for themselves, and function as an alternative community. John Fiske similarly described fans as discriminating and productive in much the same sense as Jenkins. This is a step beyond *bricolage*. These consumers are taking not only pieces but the whole product and making it their own. Jenkins is careful not to claim that fan subcultures are progressive, nor to exaggerate their numbers. He does, however, see their "work" as politically significant by virtue of their recapturing cultural production from mass media.[36]

Fandom exhibits two characteristics absent from many examples of cultural resistance, that of community action and that of collective action. Audience resistance studies have tended to focus on the creativity of immediate reception, what Fiske called semiotic productivity. Such studies often focus on individuals. Even those studies that examine group viewing and conversation still depict a rather narrow circle of family and close friends who view and share with each other.[37] Such resistance does not extend much beyond the purchasing decision as consumers. There is no organized resistance. Fans, on the other hand, are discovered and noticed by virtue of the very fact that they do create communities and organizations beyond the small circles. They do constitute communities, and they even engage in collective actions such as campaigns aimed at producers and executives to keep their shows on the air.

Yet fandom highlights another problem of resistance studies. Fan subcultures are typically inward looking. Their shared interest in the show is an end in itself and seldom leads to some action beyond that interest, some larger political purpose. Their collective consciousness does not become the foundation for collective action, except as narrowly related to protecting or changing their favorite show. This insularity is reinforced by the fact that fan communities are rhetorical; that is, they sustain themselves through rhetorical forms. Their primary activity is discourse among themselves concerning their chosen show.[38] Despite the positive aspects that recent ethnographers have pointed out, the original critique of fans still holds: fandom easily becomes a form of escape from, rather than a challenge to the conditions of everyday life, possibly diverting energy from substantial political action.

Fandom might better be conceived as an alternative rather than oppositional culture, an attempt by subordinate individuals to carve out an alternative social space for themselves and construct their own positive identity, where they can "make do" in the words of de Certeau.

Fans are not always insular and irrelevant, however. The development of "zines" clearly marks an extension into the larger world and even overt efforts at organizing and acting collectively.[39] Perhaps as early as the 1970s "fanzines," small-scale magazines, often no more than a few typed, xeroxed pages, became a means of communication among fans, first in science fiction. Gradually this form broadened into "zines," which have the same format but extend beyond fandom to a wide range of issues from personal expression to political action. Fanzines' significance lies in their contribution to a self-conscious collectivity, or public. Zines add more overt political issues to such groups. Many zines are produced by women and perhaps they constitute the most activist zine genre.[40] Some zines constitute a modern form of pamphleteering, much in the tradition of the era of the American revolution and early republic, with the same political goals of arousing people to act. What seems to be missing as yet, according to the description of this movement by sociologist Stephen Duncombe, is the formation of action groups, or parties, or otherwise to carry out political actions collectively rather than individually.

An Array of "Resistances"

Underlying this chapter's discussion of resistance is the question of how we should characterize these audience behaviors. Researchers have offered a wide range of examples of resistance with little effort to distinguish them. Preoccupation with documenting audience resistance to powerful media has resulted in broadening the concept of resistance. This has led some critics like Meagan Morris to draw a boundary, accepting some, excluding others. They would place women viewers' "resistive readings" outside the category of "real" resistance, on the grounds that these are politically insignificant, "fleeting appropriations" as Morris calls them. But drawing such a boundary has precluded further exploration of the differences among the many types of actions labeled "resistive".

Obviously some acts effect more dramatic changes than others, have more potential to do so, or are more likely to lead to such actions. But even seemingly private "resistive" readings are "political." Indeed, *all* actions (and inaction) are inescapably political, in the sense that every act inevitably contributes to recreating existing conditions or to changing them. Women viewers' and fans' "resistive readings" clearly demonstrate characteristics crucial to the making of audience resistance. First, they demonstrate the limits of hegemony, that people are *not* taken in, not incorporated into the dominant culture. This was the original purpose of resistance studies, to demonstrate this basic fact. They exhibit what may be usefully labeled "autonomy," a term that recognizes the refusal of or independence from domination, and at the same time reserves the label "resistance" for something else. Autonomy is a theme underlying the entire research tradition of disputing passivity in audiences, including "effects" and "uses and gratifications" research as well as cultural studies, which would seem to demonstrate its conceptual importance. The tradition has talked about "active" audiences, and indeed autonomous audiences are active in constructing their own readings by which they express their autonomy from the dominant culture.

The labels of "resistance" and "opposition" imply something other than autonomy. "Autonomy" carries the baggage of individualism, as in the phrase "autonomous individual." It suggests individuals acting alone, independent not only from the dominant culture but from each other as well. "Resistance" and "opposition" have been characterized in resistance literature as actions of *groups,* and specifically subordinate groups whose power resides in their group *solidarity* and *collective* action. The b'hoys of the 1840s, the immigrant audiences of turn-of-the-century ethnic theaters and nickelodeons, and even neighborhood children at Saturday matinee movies in the 1950s exhibited such solidarity that often was troublesome to theater managers.

"Autonomy" and "resistance" both imply self-conscious acts or intentionality. Yet un-self-conscious acts, if done by many people together, can produce change, even though the change may be unintended. The latter may inadvertently produce changes favorable to a group, but such outcomes are serendipitous. The aggregate of consumer decisions in favor of purchasing VCRs instead of videodisc players is a good example. The limitation is that such actions may also inadvertently produce changes *un*favorable to the group.

"Making do," making space for some personal autonomy even while accepting the overall conditions of subordination, is qualitatively different from "making changes," in the sense of social movements with explicit, if informal agenda. Youth subcultures of the 1960s that were the subject of the original resistance studies intentionally used their consumption styles to express collective identity and solidarity and to reject the dominant culture.[41] In the words of singer Neil Young, young men wearing their hair long were letting their "freak flag fly." The 1960s "counterculture," though amorphous, was nevertheless insistently collective, self-conscious, and intent on making big changes in society. Fans, while collective and self-conscious, seem intent on making more circumscribed changes in their favorite TV series or movie. The simple matter of talking back to your television and the whole concept of the television audience have been criticized because they are not collective, part of a shared subculture, and they are not demonstrably intent on making changes. This last example, however, of disaggregated audiences, is a point of disagreement. A subordinate group might collectively express their rejection of the dominant culture, even doing so in the privacy of their homes, though such separate actions need to be linked with some kind of rhetorical support in order to sustain a shared subculture; that is, talking back to television cannot alone represent resistance, but must be part of some set of collective practices.

Not only may we distinguish different types of audience "resistance." An audience practice may be at one level resistant and another incorporative, at one level active and another passive, at one private and individual and another public and collective. Williams spoke of the intimate dialectic between resistance and incorporation, how dominant and subordinate groups engage in a dance in which resistance is turned into incorporation and vice versa. Sometimes the very efforts to resist become a means to subvert that very resistance, or reinforce the subordination, or are leveraged into incorporation. The b'hoys of the 1840s and 1850s affirmed their solidarity through their knowledge and support of their favorite actors, yet this very practice became the means to undercut their control of the theater.

Despite their qualititative differences, various forms of "resistance" may become linked to each other, combining in ways that increase their impact. What may seem insignificant may develop into or prepare the ground for other more significant types. Subordinate groups gathering for fun may turn to an overt revolt. Nineteenth-century theater riots and twentieth-century rock concert riots may be examples. The simple matter of groups having customs of acting collectively in innocuous ways, for example, as active audiences gathered in theaters, may serve to train them for and incline them to collective actions in more serious circumstances. This history's exploration of audiences as active, public gatherings has been motivated by the significance of such potential.

1. Box at a New York theater, 1830, from Frances Trollope, *Domestic Manners in America* (London: Whittaker, Treacher, 1832). Photo courtesy of Rider University.

AMERICAN THEATRE BOWERY NEW YORK

View of the Stage on the fifty seventh night of Mr T.D.RICE of Kentucky in his original and celebrated extravaganza JIM CROW on which occasion every department of the house was thronged to an excess unprecedented in the records Theatrical attraction — New York 25th November 1833

2. Bowery Theater, T. D. Rice performance of "Jim Crow," 1833. Photo courtesy of Harvard Theater Collection, Houghton Library, Frederic Woodbridge Wilson, Curator.

3. Broadway concert saloon, 1859, from "Sketches of the People Who Oppose Our Sunday Laws," *Harper's Weekly* (October 8, 1859). Photo courtesy of Morris L. Parrish Collection of Victorian Novelists, Department of Rare Books and Special Collections, Princeton University Library.

4. Interior of a concert saloon, 1869, from George Ellington, *The Women of New York* (New York: New York Book Co., 1869). Photo courtesy of Rider University.

5. Audience throwing things at a minstrel troupe. Photo courtesy of Rider University.

6. Box house in Cheyenne, Wyoming, circa 1870s, from *Frank Leslie's Illustrated Newspaper*. Photo courtesy of Rider University.

AN EXCITING SCENE LAST SATURDAY EVENING AT THE BOWERY THEATRE, NEW YORK CITY.   1878

7. Bowery Theater, protesting audience, 1878. Photo courtesy of Harvard Theater Collection, Houghton Library, Frederic Woodbridge Wilson, Curator.

8. Italian puppet theater, circa 1890s, from *Scribner's* (August 1899). Photo courtesy of Morris L. Parrish Collection of Victorian Novelists, Department of Rare Books and Special Collections, Princeton University Library.

9. Uptown American theater and downtown Yiddish theater, 1909, from *Groyser Kundis* (*The Big Stick*) comic newspaper. Photo courtesy of Rider University.

10. Baby carriages outside a nickelodeon, circa 1910. Photo courtesy of Rider University.

11. "Can you guess who's on the stage?" 1920, Harriet Fish cartoon from Dorothy Parker, et al., *High Society* (New York: Putnam's Sons, 1920). Photo courtesy of Rider University.

The Wireless Age

"America's Foremost Radiophone Review"

May·1922 25 Cents

WIRELESS AGE

Getting Acquainted With the Entertainers of the Air

Their Impressions of the "Unseen Audiences" Given In a Series of Intimate Interviews

The Radio Pictorial

News—Humor—Visions of Radio's Future
Radio In World-Wide Review

The Permanency of Radio---By H. P. Davis

And Scores of Exclusive Articles
Amateur--Commercial--Engineering

12. Listening and "air" conducting, 1922, from *Wireless Age* (May 1922). Photo courtesy of Morris L. Parrish Collection of Victorian Novelists, Department of Rare Books and Special Collections, Princeton University Library.

The Coming of Cold Weather and Revival of Interest in

WEEKLY RADIO RAVINGS

—N. Y. Evening Mail

13. "Weekly Radio Raving," from *Wireless Age* (November 1922). Photo courtesy of Morris L. Parrish Collection of Victorian Novelists, Department of Rare Books and Special Collections, Princeton University Library.

Women in Radio

Miss Mimi Palmeri, the beautiful star in "Ragged Edge" takes a dip and listens in

With the most popular orchestras to furnish the music these terpsichorean damsels can't miss the chance to dance even though the floor is "terrible"

Vacationists this year took their radio sets along and were suprised at the pleasure it afforded them—and some of the ladies did their own installing

New York society finds pleasure in "listening in" to radio broadcasting while enjoying afternoon tea

14. "Women in Radio," 1924, from *Wireless Age* (September 1924). Photo courtesy of Morris L. Parrish Collection of Victorian Novelists, Department of Rare Books and Special Collections, Princeton University Library.

15. "Go to the 'theatre of the air' via Radiola," RCA ad, 1925. Clark Collection, Archives Center, National Museum of American History.

16. Movie matinee audience holding door prizes, San Diego, 1935. San Diego Historical Society Photograph Collection.

17. Crowd watching television in a bar, New York City, 1947. Reprinted from *Business Week* (September 13, 1947) by special permission, copyright 1999 by McGraw-Hill Companies. Photo from Morris L. Parrish Collection of Victorian Novelists, Department of Rare Books and Special Collections, Princeton University Library.

18. Separate television, *New Yorker* cartoon, 1948. Copyright New Yorker
Collection 1948, Allan Dunn from cartoonbank.com. All rights reserved.

Appendix:
Availability, Affordability, Admission Price

R
emarkable as it may seem, Americans spend more of their lifetime being an audience than working or sleeping. This reflects the cornucopia of entertainment and communication that surrounds us in the latter part of the twentieth century. Its pervasiveness makes it central to understanding our culture and our society today.

This was not always the case. We did not consume as many hours of our lives with radio and movies, even at their height of popularity, as we do with television. In the nineteenth century, theatergoing was far more popular than it is today. Nevertheless, it did not reach the same proportion of the population, with the same regularity, as movies, radio, and television have in the twentieth century. Nor was it an everyday, or even weekly, source of entertainment for the vast majority of the population as the mass media became. Attendance records confirm the difference. Compare the estimated 36 million tickets sold annually for theater in the last half of the 1860s, about one ticket per person per year, to the approximate 4 billion tickets annually for movies in the late 1940s, about twenty-seven per person per year, or the audiences of approximately 20 million for the average primetime network television program every night. While in the nineteenth century some Americans were weekly audiences, by the mid-twentieth century, being an entertainment audience was a daily activity for almost everyone in the United States.

To appreciate the place of the various entertainments in the lives of people and how many people could afford it, it will be helpful to compare admission prices and wages during different eras. (See Tables A.1, A.2, and A.3.) During the colonial period, theater was too expensive for artisans and laborers, although they might have attended on rare occasion. The cheapest seats in the gallery cost a half-day's wages for an artisan and more than a full day's for a laborer. During the early republic, admission became more affordable, the gallery being about a third of a laborer's daily wage. The pit where an artisan might be expected to sit cost about a third of his daily wage. General admission to minstrel shows in the 1840s and 1850s was twenty-five cents, a little less than a third of a laborer's wage and about a sixth of a day's pay for an artisan. General admission to minstrel and variety shows (usually in concert saloons) remained at twenty-five cents through much of the rest of the century, while wages rose during the Civil War and remained above prewar wages. Laborers' wages rose to $1.50 and artisans' to $2.60 in 1870, lowering admission price to a sixth of a laborer's and a tenth of an artisan's wage. During the 1880s, prices for some popular entertainments dropped further. The ten-cent ticket for the ten-twenty-thirty melodrama theater represented about one-twentieth of a day's pay for an artisan and a thirteenth of a laborer's. Cheap vaudeville had similar prices, ranging between ten and twenty-five cents for balcony seats.

The drop in costs helps to explain why popular entertainments thrived in the last half of the nineteenth century. The prices for vaudeville and melodrama in particular were within affordable limits for much of the working class, although workers could probably not afford to go more than once a week. It also explains how these entertainments could become "family entertainments." Workers could afford to take the whole family instead of just themselves; mothers could afford to take the children.

Mass media in the twentieth century reduced prices and broadened access even further. The nickel admission for the nickelodeon around 1910 represented only about one-fortieth of a day's pay for a laborer. Prices rose in the 1910s as theaters replaced storefronts for movie exhibition, but still cost only about ten cents in neighborhood theaters in 1920, an increase less than that of laborers' wages. Broadcasting reduced the price of entertainment much further and made entertainment accessible to almost everyone regularly, even in remote rural areas. A television costing around $200 in the 1960s had a life of about fifteen years, for a cost of less than five cents a day, or about one three-hundred-sixtieth of the average family daily income. Television costs one-ninth the price of nickelodeons and is roughly one two-hundredths the cost of colonial theater. In other words, the economic demand for commercial entertainments steadily increased through U.S. history.

The supply of entertainment also increased in quantity and frequency. Before the 1850s regular stage entertainment was urban. Troupes traveled to remote places and played in small towns, but appeared infrequently in any given place outside cities. In the second half of the century, such touring increased, brought by the railroad, but was still in most places an infrequent and intermittent treat. Stage entertainment in the nineteenth century was largely an urban phenomenon. The lion's share of theater attendance was concentrated in cities and even more so in the largest cities. Here it was a regular entertainment, available year-round and in myriad forms for different tastes and budgets. The five largest theater markets in the 1860s, New York City, Boston, Philadelphia, Chicago, and San Francisco, accounted for more than half the total national box office receipts. The top fifteen accounted for 70 percent of the nation's box office. The surprisingly low rate of one theater visit per year per person in the 1860s, mentioned before, perhaps is explainable by the fact that, while most entertainment was urban, the large majority of the population was still rural (75%) and had only infrequent access to theater of any sort. Many in rural areas never went to theater even while many working class people in large cities attended frequently.[1]

Radio changed this. As radios became affordable, they brought into even the most remote homes an unending flow of professional entertainment. Television, and recently VCR, cable, and direct-broadcast satellites, have increased this flow, beckoning everyone to be an audience, not for an evening, but anytime, anywhere.

Table A.1 Admission Prices for Stage Entertainments

Year	Theater				Minstrelsy		Variety-Vaudeville			
	City	Box	Pit	Gallery	City		City	Box	Pit	Gallery
1754	Philadelphia	6s	4s	2s6d						
1760	Maryland	7s6d	5s							
1767	Albany	6s	4s	2s						
1773		7s	5s							
1782	Baltimore	$1Sp	5s							
1786	Baltimore	$1Sp	6s							
1791	Philadelphia	7s6d	5s	3s9d						
1795	Boston	6s	2s	1s6d						
1801	Boston	$1.00	.50	.25						
1805	Charleston	4s8d	2s4d							
1811	Pennsylvania	.50	.25							
1815	Baltimore	1.00	.75	.50						
1821	Philadelphia	1.00	.75	.50						
1828	Philadelphia	.50	.25	.18						
1835	Philadelphia	.50	.25	.25						
1841	Boston		.25							
1844	Philadelphia	.50	.25	.25	Baltimore	.25	Philadelphia	.50	.12	.12
1852	Louisville		.50	.25	Various	.25	Philadelphia '54		.25	

298

1857					New York	.25	New York		.12	
1860	Philadelphia	.50	.37	.25	Various	.25	Various		.15	
1862					Philadelphia	.25	Philadelphia '61–3	.50	.25	.15
1872	Minneapolis	.75		.50			Philadelphia '73		.25	
1874							Various		.25	
1881							Albany	.75	.35	.15
1888							Brooklyn	.75	.50	.20
1893							New York		.50	.15
1902							Seattle		.25	
1910	New York	$1–2		.25–50			New York	.20	.10	
1927	New York '28	$4–6					New York	3.30	1.25	

Sources: For theater: various playbills and Hugh Rankin, *The Theatre in Colonial America* (Chapel Hill: University of North Carolina Press, 1965), 88, 133; Michael Davis, *The Exploitation of Pleasure* (New York: Russell Sage Foundation, 1910), 25, 26; Jack Poggi, *Theater in America: The Impact of Economic Forces* (Ithaca, NY: Cornell University Press, 1968), 71; Zachary Bloomfield, "Baptism of a Deacon's Theatre: Audience Development at the Boston Museum, 1841–1861" (Ph.D., University of Missouri, 1991), 180; Lawrence Hill, "A History of Variety-Vaudeville in Minneapolis, Minnesota" (Ph.D., University of Minnesota, 1979), 84. For minstrelsy: various playbills and Frank Davidson, "The Rise, Development, Decline and Influence of the American Minstrel Show," (Ph.D., New York University, 1952), 88, 93; George C. D. Odell, *Annals of the New York Stage* (New York: Columbia University Press, 1927), VI–591. For variety-vaudeville: various playbills and Odell, *Annals of the New York Stage*, VI 591, VII 93, 285; Lawrence Hill, "A History of Variety-Vaudeville in Minneapolis, Minnesota" (Ph.D., University of Minnesota, 1979), 75, 89; Parker Zellars, "Tony Pastor: Manager and Impressario of the American Variety Stage" (Ph.D., University of Iowa, 1964), 161, 309, 329; William Marston, *F. F. Proctor: Vaudeville Pioneer* (New York: Richard R. Smith, 1943), 46, 64–5, 97–9; Eugene Elliott, "A History of Variety-Vaudeville from the Beginning to 1914" (Seattle: University of Washington Press, 1941), 27, 50, 56; Michael Davis, *The Exploitation of Pleasure* 25; Robert Snyder, *The Voice of the City* (Oxford University Press, 1989), 88; Frederick Snyder, "American Vaudeville: Theater in a Package" (Ph.D., Yale University, 1970), 136.

Table A.2   Movie Admissions, Radio, and Television Set Retail Prices

Year	Movie Admission	Radios	Televisions B&W	Televisions Color	VCRs	Cable Monthly Basic Rate
1905	$0.05					
1910s	.10					
1922	.25	$50				
1925		83				
1930	.16	78				
1935	.13	55				
1940	.18	38				
1945/46	.33	40	$279			
1950	.44	26	190			
1955	.55	20	138			
1960	.46	20	137	$392		
1965	.41	10	104	356		
1970		11	81	321		
1975					$2,100	
1980	2.69				750	
1983					600	$8.61
1985	3.55				200	9.73
1990	4.22					16.78
1995	4.35					23.07
1998						27.43

Sources: Douglas Gomery, *Shared Pleasures: A History of Movie Presentation in the United States,* (Madison: University of Wisconsin Press, 1992), 180; Richard Kosarski, *An Evening's Entertainment* (Berkeley: University of California Press, 1990), 13, 15; Motion Picture Association of America, *U.S. Economic Review, 1997; Historical Statistics of the United States, Colonial Times to 1970,* (Washington, DC: U.S. Bureau of Census, 1975), 400; Lawrence Lichty and Malachi Topping, *American Broadcasting: A Sourcebook on the History of Radio and Television* (New York: Hastings House, 1975), 521, 522; Paul Kagan Associates, Inc., *Cable TV Investor* (August 10, 1998), 4; "VCRs: Ogre or Opportunity?" *Marketing & Media Decisions* (September 1984), 50.

Table A.3   Population and Income

Year	Population (millions)	Daily Wages Artisan	Daily Wages Laborer	Family Income	Consumer Price Index
1750	1.17		10s/wk		
1760	1.59	(1762) 4s			
1770	2.15				
1780	2.78		(1785) $.70		
1790	3.93	$1.01	.50		
1800	5.30	1.64	1.00		51
1810	7.22	1.72	1.00		47
1820	9.62	1.55	1.00		42
1830	12.90	(Phila) 1.73 (Erie) 1.25	(Phila) 1.00 (Erie) .75		32
1840	17.12	1.50	.88		30
1850	23.26	1.50	.88		25
1860	31.51	(Erie) 1.75 (manf) 1.65	(Erie) 1.00 (manf) 1.03		27
1870	39.90	2.64	1.52	(1874) 763	38
1880	50.26	2.15	1.32		29
1890	63.06		1.74	573	27
1900	76.09		1.77	(1901) 651	25
1910	92.41		2.13		28
1920	106.46		5.20	(1919) 1505	60
1930	123.19			(1934) 1518	50
1940	132.12				42
1950	151.68			3923	72
1960	180.67			6509	89
1970	204.88				116

Source: U.S. Bureau of the Census, *Historical Statistics of the United States, Colonial Times to 1970* (Washington, DC: U.S. GPO 1975), 8, 163–5, 168, 210–11, 320–3, 1168; Billie G. Smith, *The "Lower Sort": Philadelphia Laboring People, 1750–1800* (Ithaca, NY: Cornell University Press, 1990) 109–10, 120.

Notes

Introduction: Participative Public, Passive Private?

1. *Physician Guide to Media Violence* (Chicago: American Medical Association, 1996); AMA News Release, "AMA Survey Shows 75% of Parents Disgusted with Media Violence" (September 9, 1996).
2. Joan Scott, *Gender and the Politics of History* (New York: Columbia University Press, 1988), 7.
3. On mass culture theories see Alan Swingewood, *The Myth of Mass Culture* (Atlantic Highlands, NJ: Humanities Press, 1977); Patrick Brantlinger, *Bread and Circuses* (Ithaca, NY: Cornell University Press, 1983); Bernard Rosenberg and David White, *Mass Culture: The Popular Arts in America* (New York: Free Press, 1957). For recent revivals see Michael Denning, "The End of Mass Culture" and responses, *International Labor and Working Class History*, 37–39 (spring 1990 to spring 1991); David Grimsted, "The Purple Rose of Popular Culture Theory," *American Quarterly* 43:4 (December 1991), 541–78; Robert Putnam, "The Strange Disappearance of Civic America," *American Prospect*, 24 (Winter 1996), 34–48, and responses in 25 (March–April 1996), 17–28, and 26 (May–June 1996), 16–21, 94.
4. On active audiences see, e.g., Andrew Gurr, *Playgoing in Shakespeare's London* (Cambridge, UK: Cambridge University Press, 1987); John Lough, *Paris Theatre Audiences in the Seventeenth and Eighteenth Centuries* (London: Oxford University Press, 1957); John Rosselli, *The Opera Industry in Italy from Cimarosa to Verdi* (Cambridge, UK: Cambridge University Press, 1984). On definition, see Ann Cook, *The Privileged Playgoers of Shakespeare's London, 1576–1642* (Princeton, NJ: Princeton University Press, 1981), 16–17, 218.
5. Peter Burke, *Popular Culture in Early Modern Europe* (London: Temple Smith, 1978); also Peter Stallybrass and Allon White, *The Politics and Poetics of Transgression* (Ithaca, NY: Cornell University Press, 1986), 86; Robert Malcolmson, *Popular Recreation in English Society, 1700–1850* (Cambridge, UK: Cambridge University Press, 1973), 68.
6. Cook, 135, 150–5; Gurr, 72.

7. Carl Thomas, "The Restoration Theatre Audience" (Ph.D., University of Southern California, 1952), 17; Sheldon Zitner, "The English Theatre Audience: 1660–1700" (Ph.D., Duke University, 1955), 133–4, 144.

8. Harry W. Pedicord, *The Theatrical Public in the Time of Garrick* (New York: Columbia University Press, 1954), 23–4; James Lynch, *Box, Pit and Gallery: Stage and Society in Johnson's London* (New York: Russell & Russell, 1953), 203, etc.; Jerry Roland Bailor, "The late eighteenth century theatrical public of London" (Ph.D., University of Southern California, 1974), 102–15, esp. 111, 113.

9. Major theater riots occurred periodically in London in the mid-eighteenth century. See Richard Moody, *The Astor Place Riot* (Bloomington Ind: Indiana University Press, 1958), 13–24; Stephen Tait, "English Theatre Riots," *Theatre Arts* 24 (1940), 97–104; Pedicord, 52.

10. On artists and patrons, see Raymond Williams, *Sociology of Culture* (Schocken, 1982), 38–44.

11. On court theater, see Cook, 113–17; James Johnston, *Listening in Paris* (Berkeley, Cal: University of California Press, 1995). On English private theaters, see Cook, 139–142; Steven Mullaney, *The Place of the Stage* (Chicago: University of Chicago Press, 1988).

12. See Marc Baer, *Theatre and Disorder in Late Georgian London* (London: Oxford University Press, 1992) on theater riots and class; Stallybrass and White, 16, 59–79 on carnival as politics.

13. There have been many descriptions of American theater rowdyism. For an early and thorough treatment, see Ben Henneke, "The Play-goer in America" (Ph.D., University of Illinois, 1956), 114–156. Histories of rowdyism have tended to focus exclusively on males. On young male violence, see David Courtwright, *Violent Land: Single Men and Social Disorder* (Cambridge, MA: Harvard University Press, 1996). Feminist history has written women into this "disorderly" movement too. See, e.g., Christine Stansell, *City of Women: Sex and Class in New York 1789–1860* (New York: Knopf, 1982). Carroll Smith-Rosenberg, *Disorderly Conduct* (New York: Knopf, 1985).

14. Paula Fass, *The Damned and the Beautiful: American Youth in the 1920s* (London: Oxford University Press, 1977), ch. 2; Christopher Lasch, *Haven in a Heartless World* (New York: Basic Books, 1977).

15. On mass society theories, see William Kornhauser, *The Politics of Mass Society* (New York: Free Press, 1959); Salvador Giner, *Mass Society* (New York: Academic Press, 1976).

16. On left versions of the theory, see Alan Swingewood, *The Myth of Mass Culture* (Atlantic Highlands, NJ: Humanities Press, 1977); Martin Jay, *The Dialectical Imagination: A History of the Frankfurt School and the Institute of Social Research, 1923–1950* (Boston: Little, Brown, 1973).

17. Gurr, 121–7 on Tarlton. On Restoration, see Zitner, 114–15, 120; Thomas, 173.

18. Barnard Hewitt, *Theatre U.S.A., 1665 to 1957* (New York: McGraw-Hill, 1959) 37.

19. Since the 1960s, experimental theater groups removed this fourth wall by moving into the audience rather than the reverse. See Don Smith, "Audience Participation," *The Stage in Canada* 4:9/10 (December 1967), 14; Robert Brustein, *The Theater in Revolt* (New York: Ivan R. Dee, 1991); Elinor Fuchs, *The Death of Character* (Bloomington: Indiana University Press, 1996), on other aspects of audience/performer relations.

20. John, Dizikes, *Opera in America* (New Haven: Yale University Press, 1993), 284ff on habits of the Diamond Horseshoe.

21. On contrasting groups accustomed and unaccustomed to television, see Tannis Williams and Gordon Handford, *The Impact of Television* (New York: Academic Press, 1986); Robert Kubey and Mihaly Csikszentmihalyi, *Television and the Quality of Life: How Viewing Shapes Everyday Experience* (Hillsdale, NJ: Erlbaum, 1990), 77–8.

22. Charles Tilly, *From Mobilization to Revolution* (Reading, MA: Addison-Wesley, 1978), 151–9, 232; Craig Calhoun, *The Question of Class Struggle* (Chicago: University of Chicago Press, 1982), 174.

23. Chapter 4; Ron Eyerman and Andrew Jamison, "Social Movements and Cultural Transformation: Popular Music in the 1960s," *Media, Culture and Society* 17 (1995), 449–468; Thomas Strychacz, "American Sports Writers and 'Unruly Rooters': The Significance of Orderly Spectating," *Journal of American Studies* 28:1 (April 1994), 84–9; Football hooliganism issue, *Sociological Review* 39 (August 1991), 423–46.

24. Stallybrass and White, 80–94, compare carnival and eighteenth-century English theater to the public sphere.

25. Patrick Joyce, *Visions of the People* (Cambridge, UK: Cambridge University Press, 1991), 222–5, similarly argues that entertainments of the common people of England in the late nineteenth century were public, participative, and collective.

26. On the town metaphor, see Peter Buckley, "To the Opera House: Culture and Society in New York City, 1820–1860" (Ph.D., SUNY – Stony Brook, 1984), 120–1; Pedicord, 55, 118–19.

27. Sports spectators still exhibit collective interaction by the audience with live performers; night club audiences interact but typically individually.

28. On depoliticization of public space, see Leonore Davidoff, "Regarding Some 'Old Husbands' Tales': Public and Private in Feminist History," in *Worlds Between: Historical Perspectives on Gender and Class* (New York: Routledge, 1995); Frances Olsen, "The Family and the Market," *Harvard Law Review* 96 (1983), 1497–1578. On lighting, see Henneke, 56–63.

29. Mary Ryan, *Women in Public: Between Banners and Ballots, 1825–1880* (Ballimore: Johns Hopkins University Press, 1990), ch. 2 on geography of public space; David Scobey, "Anatomy of the Promenade: The Politics of Bourgeois Sociability in Nineteenth Century New York," *Social History* 17 (May 1992), 203–28; Elinor Fuchs, "Theater as Shopping," in *The Death of Character* (Bloomington: Indiana University Press, 1996), 128–143, for a postmodern treatment of audience as consumer.

30. On loss of community, see Kenneth Jackson, *Crabgrass Frontier: The Suburbanization of the United States* (Oxford, 1985); Robert Fishman, *Bourgeois Utopias* (New York: Basic Books, 1987); on going out, see David Nasaw, *Going Out* (New York Basic Books, 1995). See David Morley, *Television, Audiences, and Cultural Studies* (London: Routledge, 1992), 164, 237, on privatization.

31. Similarly Joyce, 317–20, argues that English popular entertainments successively incorporated similar forms of expression, and particular dialect, and reveal a continuity from the 1880s to the 1950s, i.e., music hall through movies and radio to television.

Chapter 1. Colonial Theater, Privileged Audiences

1. While occasional amateur performances preceded them, the first permanent troupe, apparently a mix of professionals and amateurs, was formed in 1749 and dissolved in 1753. A second, more experienced troupe of English actors, under the direction first of Lewis Hallam and then David Douglass, played in the colonies from 1752 until 1775. See Hugh Rankin, *The Theater in Colonial America* (Chapel Hill, NC: University of North Carolina Press, 1960), 30–50; George C. D. Odell, *Annals of the New York Stage* (New York: Columbia University Press, 1927) vol. I, bk. I.

2. Gordon S. Wood, *The Radicalism of the American Revolution* (New York: Knopf, 1992), ch. 1. The culture of deference was never completely secure (Wood, 145, 275–6). The Great Awakening of the 1740s awakened egalitarianism as well as religious feelings, and elite hegemony was at times precarious. See Gary Nash, *The Urban Crucible* (Harvard University Press, 1979), 262–8.

3. Wood, 29–35, 277, and 281 on North-South differences. Merchants, many of whom strove to become gentlemen, did not qualify until they could seem to be leisured. See Wood, 38–39. Yet once secure in genteel status, a man could safely mingle with the lower sorts in manly pastimes of taverns, blood sports, and theater. As with Europeans they were not put off by lower-class behavior but rather participated heartily in popular culture. See Wood, 41–42; and Peter Burke, *Popular Culture in Early Modern Europe.* (London: Temple Smith, 1978)

4. In 1750, Boston, the largest city in the American colonies, had a population of 17,000. Only six cities had over 5,000 inhabitants by 1760. English visitors of the mid-eighteenth century likened the largest colonial towns to small provincial English towns that were served by strolling troupes, not resident companies. Nash, 313, 409; Wood, 12, 58.

5. The Licensing Act of 1737 had closed many theaters, put actors out of work, and classified strolling players as vagabonds. See Oscar G. Brockett, *History of the Theatre* (Boston: Allyn & Bacon, 1968), 266–8; also Sheldon Zitner, "The English Theatre Audience: 1660–1700" (Ph.D., Duke, 1955), 114–15, 182, on the resulting poverty of players.

6. Wood, 20, 60, 130, on strangers.

7. Charles P. Daly, *First Theater in America* (New York: Burt Franklin, 1896), 10; Odell, I 46, 66, for other examples.
8. Odell, I 41; Odell, I 80, facing page.
9. On patronage, see Raymond Williams, *Sociology of Culture* (New York: Schocken, 1982), 41–54; Steven Mullany, *The Place of the Stage*, (Chicago: University of Chicago Press, 1988), 53–54.
10. Rankin, 31 on "genteel." George Washington was a frequent theatergoer. See Rankin, 90, 159.
11. On ladies' attendance, see Rankin, 31, 65, 90–91; Odell, I 66, 91, 148–49. On servants holding seats, see Odell, I 114; Rankin, 159–60.
12. Quote from Odell, I 126; Rankin, 30, 81.
13. Rankin, 64, on 1754 playbill; William Dunlap, *History of the American Theatre* (New York: Burt Franklin, 1963), I 46–47; Rankin, 87, 97. On restricting access to backstage, see a playbill for the John Street Theater in 1768 from Harvard Theater Collection, and another for the West Street Theater in 1773 from the Historical Society of Pennsylvania.
14. See Appendix on ticket prices and wages. See Steven Rosswurm, *Arms, Country and Class* (New Brunswick, NJ: Rutgers University Press, 1987), 37–38, on difference of values of middling sort from those above and below.
15. Odell, I 113, 123–24; Rankin, 61–62, quotes a similar comment in 1753 New York, and Charles Durang, *The Philadelphia Stage, 1749–1855* (Ann Arbor, MI: University Microfilm, 1868), I 13, quoted another 1759 complaint in Philadelphia; William Dye, "Pennsylvania vs. Theatre," *Pennsylvania Magazine* 55 (1931), 356, quotes a law that "the weak, poor and necessitous have been prevailed upon [by theater] to neglect their labor and industry."
16. Odell, I 92. Oral Coad, "The American Theatre in the Eighteenth Century," *South Atlantic Quarterly* 17 (July 1918), 192, characterized the gallery as already vociferous and in the habit of throwing things, but provides no specific dates or evidence.
17. Eola Willis, *The Charleston Stage in the Eighteenth Century* (Columbia, SC: The State Company, 1924), 48.
18. On spikes see Rankin, 53; and Brooks McNamara, *The American Playhouse in the Eighteenth Century* (Cambridge, MA: Harvard University Press, 1969), 41, 55. See Rankin, 57, on the incident in Williamsburg, and 53, on class division. The use of spikes disappeared after the Revolution. See McNamara, 112.
19. Rankin, 90, on letters of reference in the South.
20. David Grimsted, *Melodrama Unveiled* (Chicago: University of Chicago, 1968), ch. 2; Arthur Hornblow, *A History of the Theatre in America* (New York: Benjamin Blom, 1965), I 24; also Rankin, 22, 31, 190. On Philadelphia, see Rankin, 67–70; Thomas Pollock, *The Philadelphia Theatre in the Eighteenth Century* (Philadelphia: University of Pennsylvania Press, 1933); Dye, 333–72. Religion, politics, and class were intertwined in Pennsylvania of the 1750s and it is likely that the dispute over theater involved complicated class divisions. See Nash, 257, 267–71.

21. Rankin, 22, on Hallam; 60, on New York; 81–82, on Philadelphia. About sympathetic governors, Barnard Hewitt, *Theatre U.S.A., 1665–1957* (New York: McGraw-Hill, 1959) 3, cites Robert Hunter, governor of New York in 1710, as author of the first play to be published in America.

22. Odell, I 85; Rankin, 116, on Douglass. See also Rankin, 67, for 1753 complaint on character of actors. On "house of the devil," see Rankin, 81, 114, 115, as well as Royal Tyler's 1787 parody *The Contrast* quoted in Arthur Hobson Quinn, *A History of the American Drama*, 2nd ed. (New York: Appelton-Century-Crofts, 1943), I 67–69. Rankin, 96, on modesty; Hornblow, I 110, on outside theater. On religious opposition to theater see Dye; Abe Laufe, *The Wicked Stage* (New York: Frederick Ungar, 1978). When fire destroyed a theater in Richmond, Virginia in 1811, killing some seventy men, women, and children, including many respected citizens, some called it the wrath of God. See John Witherspoon, *A Serious Inquiry into the Nature and Effects of the Stage* (New York: Whiting and Watson, 1812). Religious objections to theater lasted well into the nineteenth century. See "Theater and Its Friends," *Harpers Weekly,* January 31, 1857. But religious objections rarely prevailed against theater in eastern cities after the eighteenth century.

23. Before the English civil war Puritans equated Elizabethan theaters with the brothels near which they were located. See Jean-Christophe Agnew, *Worlds Apart* (New York: Cambridge University Press, 1986), 125–28; also Edmund S. Morgan, "Puritan Hostility to the Theatre," *Proceedings of the Americal Philosphical Society* 110 (1966), 340–47.

24. Wood, 145, 275–6; Nash, 246–8, 300, 304. See also George Rude, *Ideology and Popular Protest* (Pantheon, 1980), 96–97.

25. Playbill reproduced in Quinn, I 17; Nash, 292–3, on protests; Peter Davis, "Puritan Mercantilism and the Politics of Anti-Theatrical Legislation in Colonial America," in Ron Engle and Tice Miller, eds., *The American Stage: Social and Economic Issues from the Colonial Period to the Present* (New York: Cambridge University Press, 1993), 18–29. Davis claims that the ban of theater by the Continental Congress in 1774 was also a boycott of British products.

26. Nash, 297, on attack on wealth; also Durang, I 13, Rankin, 61–62, 120, Odell, I 123–4.

27. This change in attitudes toward work and leisure deepened after the Revolution. Anti-federalists considered productivity the mark of worth and idleness the mark of aristocracy and British sympathy. See Wood, 277, 283.

28. George C. D. Odell, *Annals of the New York Stage* (New York: 1927–1949), vol. I, 93–95. Rankin, 109 and 110, for quotes. Also see Paul Gilje, *The Road to Mobocracy* (Chapel Hill, NC: University of North Carolina Press, 1987), 48–51.

29. Rankin, 170–71, interprets the theater incidents as anti-British protest. Rosswurm, 34, and Nash discuss the relative strength of protests in Boston, New York, and Philadelphia.

30. Rankin, 171–72, on Douglass reward offer. Odell, I 163, and Rankin, 176, on threat to close the gallery.
31. E. P. Thompson, "The Moral Economy of the English Crowd in the Eighteenth Century," *Past and Present* 50 (February 1971), 76–136. Thompson focuses on bread riots. George Rude and Charles Tilly have looked more broadly at crowd actions in this period. See George Rude, *The Crowd in History: A Study of Popular Disturbances in France and England, 1730–1848* (New York: Wiley, 1964), and Charles Tilly, *From Mobilization to Revolution* (Reading, MA: Addison-Wesley, 1978); John Bohstedt, "The Moral Economy and the Discipline of Historical Context," *Journal of Social History* 26 (Winter 1992), 265–84.
32. George Rude, *Ideology and Popular Protest*, 138–144.
33. For example, the Doctor's riot of 1788 closed many businesses including the theater. See Gilje, 81.

Chapter 2. Drama in Early Republic Audiences

1. Brooks McNamara, *The American Playhouse in the Eighteenth Century* (Cambridge, MA: Harvard University Press 1969), 69, on new theater construction; on population see Gordon Wood, *The Radicalism of the American Revolution* (New York: Knopf, 1992), 125.
2. For congressional resolutions, see *Journals of the Continental Congress* (Washington, DC: Government Printing Office, 1908), I 24; XII 1001, 1018.
3. Thomas Pollock, *The Philadelphia Theatre in the Eighteenth Century* (Philadelphia: University of Pennsylvania Press, 1933), 40, 132–3; George Seilhamer, *History of the American Theatre* (Philadelphia: Globe Printing House, 1889), II 53, on Baltimore and Annapolis.
4. George C.D. Odell, *Annals of the New York Stage* (New York: Columbia University Press, 1927), I 184–231; Jared Brown, "A Note on British Military Theatre in New York at the End of the American Revolution," *New York History* 62 (April 1981), 177–87.
5. McNamara, 69, 72, on theater building. On "fondness," see William Priest, *Travels in the US of A Commencing in the Year 1793 and Ending in 1797* (London: Printed for J. Johnson, 1802), 17, 30, 157.
6. On changes in theater size and seating, see McNamara, 31, 48, 75, 79, 103, 108, 115, 121, 124–5, 128, 135; John Melish, *Travels through the US of A in the Years 1806 & 1807 and 1809, 1810 & 1811* (Philadelphia: John Melish, 1815), I 185; II 186.
7. Bruce McConachie, "Pacifying American Theatrical Audiences," in Richard Butsch, ed., *For Fun and Profit: The Transformation of Leisure into Consumption* (Philadelphia: Temple University Press, 1990), 49; and Alfred Bernheim, *The Business of the Theatre: An Economic History of the American Theatre, 1750–1932* (New York: Benjamin Blom, 1932), 8, 12–13, on subscription financed building; quote in William Dunlap, *History of the American Theatre* (New York: Burt Franklin, 1963), I 271. Dunlap said mechanics took shares for their labor. But other than the

anti-Federal Haymarket Theater in Boston, there is no evidence of artisan stockholders. Providence, Rhode Island carpenters "labored without fee or reward" to build a theater in 1795, but there is no indication of their being stockholders. George Willard, *History of the Providence Stage* (Providence, RI: Rhode Island News Co., 1891), 26.

8. Pollock, 50, on actors receiving salaries. David Grimsted, *Melodrama Unveiled: American Theater and Culture, 1800–1850* (Chicago: University of Chicago Press, 1968), ch. 3, on wealthy supporting playwrights, etc.

9. Urban theaters expanded their fare to four or more nights of entertainment from the customary two or three. Bernheim, 14; see Appendix on wages and admission prices; Boston mechanic in "For the Centinel, Mr. Russell [editor]," *Columbian Centinel*, (December 8, 1792), 2.

10. The term "fashion" referred to the upper classes until the mid-nineteenth century, when ready-made clothes made fashion affordable and ladies' magazines like *Godey's* began to print "fashion plates" for their middle-class readers. See Chapter 4.

11. For example, Willard, 38–39.

12. Ben Graf Henneke, "The Playgoer in America" (Ph.D., University of Illinois, 1956), 57, for quotes; 56–63, on lighting. Lights were dimmed until the late nineteenth century. See McConachie, 63.

13. Herbert Brown, "Sensibility in Eighteenth Century American Drama," *American Literature* 4:1 (March 1932), 47–60; William Wood, *Personal Recollections of the Stage* (Philadelphia: Henry Carey Baird, 1855), 105, and Julian Mates, *The American Musical Stage Before 1800* (New Brunswick, NJ: Rutgers University Press, 1962), 64–67, on "woman's plays." Sentimental plays from 1760 to 1800 were designed to appeal to women, although it is unclear how many actually went to see plays compared to those who read them at home.

14. Charles H. Sherrill, *French Memories of Eighteenth-Century America* (New York: Charles Scribner's Sons, 1915), 140–1, on Frenchman; Odell, I 267, for "Friend of Decency"; Henneke, 83, on New York ad; McNamara, 122, on Federal Street; Mates, 65, on boxes set aside for prostitutes.

15. Sherrill, 139; Isaac Weld, Jr., *Travels Through North America: 1795–97*, vol. I, 4th ed. (New York: Augustus Kelley, 1969). On tobacco and alcohol, also see Henneke, 147. Odell, I 426, quote on allowing liquor.

16. Linda Kerber, *Women of the Republic* (Chapel Hill, NC: University of North Carolina Press, 1980), 7, 9, 26, 35. On the exclusionary male character of the Enlightenment public sphere, see Joan Landes, *Women and the Public Sphere* (Ithaca, NY: Cornell, 1988).

17. Henneke, 144–9; William Clapp, *A Record of the Boston Stage* (Boston: James Munroe, 1853), 22–3, 26.

18. Washington Irving, *The Letters of Jonathan Oldstyle*, Bruce Granger and Martha Hertzog, eds. (Boston: Twayne Publishing, 1977), 12–25.

19. Irving, 13.

20. "Gentlemen," Philadelphia *General Advertiser* (October 25, 1794), 3. On the efforts to control the gallery, see Henneke, 145; Odell, I 370–3. For

examples of rowdiness, see Patricia Click, *Spirit of the Times: Amusements in Nineteenth Century Baltimore, Norfolk and Richmond* (Charlottesville, VA: University of Virginia Press, 1989), 40–1; "For the Centinel, Mr. Russell [editor]," *Columbian Centinel* (September 15, 1793), 3.

21. Odell, I 247.
22. Odell, II 309, on standing; II 464, on redecorating; I 381, on John St.; Grimsted, 54, on another complaint about the gallery.
23. Odell, II 29, on Park Theater; Bedlow ad in New York *Morning Chronicle* (December 8, 1804), 2.
24. Odell, II 163; also II 128.
25. James Sharp, *American Politics in the Early Republic* (New Haven, CT: Yale University Press, 1993), 92–112.
26. Republicans labeled Federalists, "Anglo-Federalists." See Sharp, 251.
27. On resistance to reserved seating see Henneke, 33–40; John Dizikes, *Opera in America: A Cultural History* (New Haven: Yale University Press, 1993), 62–63; and Olive Logan, *Before the Footlights and Behind the Scenes* (Philadelphia: Parmalee, 1870), 526–30.
28. Ruth Harsha McKensie, "Organization, Production and Management at the Chestnut Street Theatre, Philadelphia, 1791–1820" (Ph.D., Stanford University, 1952), 271–8.
29. William Clapp, 22–23, 26; Henneke, 145–46. When pelted with "apples, stones, etc.," musicians used artisan Republican rhetoric to plead in the newspaper for mercy, citing themselves as workers in a free country, like those in the gallery. See Arthur Hornblow, *A History of the Theatre in America* (New York: Benjamin Blom, 1965) [orig., Lippincott, 1919], I 229.
30. "Dramatic Reminiscences," *New England Magazine* 3 (November 1832), 38–39; Clapp, 35–36.
31. Hornblow, I 237–40; Clapp, 36–37.
32. Clapp, 50–51.
33. "Scene," *Boston Gazette* (March 12, 1801), 1. For discussions, see Clapp, 74–75; Hewitt, 47–48; and Hornblow, I 227–31, 237–42. The year 1794 mentioned in the dialog was the high point of opposition to the federal government. See Sharp, 92–112.
34. Pollock, 63.
35. Reese James, *Cradle of Culture, 1800–1810: The Philadelphia Stage* (Philadelphia: University of Pennsylvania Press, 1957), 19, 39–40, 51; also see Charles Durang, *The Philadelphia Stage from the Year 1749 to the Year 1855*, scrapbook from the Philadelphia *Sunday Dispatch* arranged and illustrated by Thomas Westcott, 1868, Historical Society of Pennsylvania. I 64, 70. On Cooper, see John Bernard, *Retrospections of America, 1797–1811* (New York: Harpers, 1887), 164–8.
36. Clapp, 82–3; James, 96–7. On English embargo, see Durang, I 84.
37. Marvin Carlson, *The Theater of the French Revolution* (Ithaca: Cornell University Press, 1966), and Laura Mason, "'Ça ira' and the Birth of the Revolutionary Song," *History Workshop* 28 (1989): 22–38.

38. Dunlap, I 204–5.
39. Dunlap, I 317–21.
40. Dunlap, II 20–21.
41. On an ethnic riot in 1808 unrelated to the political debate and more typical of the Jacksonian era, see James, 97; Durang, I 83; Paul Gilje, *The Road to Mobocracy: Popular Disorder in New York City, 1763–1864* (Chapel Hill, NC: University of North Carolina Press, 1987), 123. On a riot by French seaman in Charleston in 1794, see Eola Willis, *The Charleston Stage in the Eighteenth Century* (Columbia, SC: The State Company, 1924), 205, 207.
42. On the defeat of the Federalists see Steven Watts, *The Republic Reborn* (Baltimore: Johns Hopkins University Press, 1987), 13.

Chapter 3. The B'Hoys in Jacksonian Theaters

1. Gustave De Beaumont, *Marie, or Slavery in the United States* (Palo Alto, CA: Stanford University Press, 1958), trans. Barbara Chapman, 231.
2. See appendix for wages and ticket prices. Arthur Quinn, *A History of the American Drama*, 2nd ed. (New York: Appleton-Century-Crofts, 1936), I 199, on reduction of prices in 1823.
3. Henry Bradshaw Fearon, *Sketches of America* (New York: Augustus Kelley, 1970; London: Longman, Hurst, Rees, Orme, and Brown, 1818), 86–87; see also Fanny Kemble, *The Journal of Frances Anne Butler* [1835] (New York: Benjamin Blom, 1970), 100.
4. Arthur Hornblow, *A History of the Theatre in America* (New York: Benjamin Blom, 1965), II 11–12, and Peter Buckley, "To the Opera House" (Ph.D., SUNY Stony Brook, 1984), 143, on Chatham Garden; Bruce McConachie, *Melodramatic Formations: American Theatre & Society, 1820–1870* (Iowa City, IA: University of Iowa Press, 1992), 25, on Arch St; 93 and 121, on Walnut St.; 61, 120, and 253, on Boston.
5. James Dormon, *Theater in the Antebellum South, 1815–1861* (Chapel Hill, NC: University of North Carolina Press, 1967), 224, 232, 235–36.
6. Theodore Shank, "The Bowery Theater, 1826–1836" (Ph.D., Stanford University, 1956), 242ff.
7. Shank, 242–3, 304, on new name; 340, on melodramas as popular and cheap to produce; 299, on long runs; Walt Whitman, "The Bowery," in Justin Kaplan, *Walt Whitman: Prose and Poetry* (New York: Library of America, 1982), 1186, 1189, on Booth and Forrest.
8. Whitman, 1189–90.
9. Shank, 245, on *New York Mirror*; Francis Hodge, *Yankee Theatre: The Image of America on the Stage, 1825–1850* (Austin, TX: University of Texas Press, 1964), 32–37, on the *Mirror* as advocate of cultural taste. Whitman, 1190, on change.
10. George Foster, *New York by Gaslight* (New York: Dewitt and Davenport, 1850), 87, quote on Bowery.
11. On New York working class culture, see Richard Stott, *Workers in the Metropolis: Class, Ethnicity and Youth in Antebellum New York City*

(Ithaca, NY: Cornell University Press, 1990), 201–11, 247–8; Christine Stansell, *City of Women: Sex and Class in New York, 1789–1860* (New York: Knopf, 1982); Sean Wilentz, *Chants Democratic: New York City and the Rise of the American Working Class, 1788–1850* (New York: Oxford University Press, 1984). On Philadelphia, see Bruce Laurie, *Working People of Philadelphia, 1800–1850* (Philadelphia: Temple University Press, 1980). Stott, 223, on the term "b'hoys."

12. Many classes lived in New York boarding houses before 1850, but after that they became a feature of working-class life. On New York boarding houses, see Stott, 214–16; Wilentz, 52–53; William Northall, *Before and Behind the Curtains* (New York: W. F. Burgess, 1851), 7; and Thomas Butler Gunn, *The Physiology of New York Boarding-Houses* (New York: Mason Brothers, 1857). For a fictionalized description of boarding houses set in Pittsburgh later in the century, see Thomas Bell, *Out of this Furnace* (Pittsburgh: University of Pittsburgh Press, 1976).

13. On class and subculture see John Clarke, Stuart Hall, Tony Jefferson, and Brian Roberts, "Subcultures, Cultures and Class," in Stuart Hall and Tony Jefferson, eds., *Resistance Through Ritual: Youth Subcultures in Post-War Britain* (London: Hutchinson, 1976), 35–37.

14. Stott, 251; Wilentz, 300; Charles MacKay, *Life and Liberty in America* (New York: Harper & Bros., 1859), 25; "The Italian Opera House and the Bowery, New York," *Spirit of the Times* (February 6, 1847), 590; John Kasson, *Rudeness and Civility: Manners in Nineteenth-Century Urban America* (New York: Hill and Wang, 1990), on middle-class dress.

15. Laurie, 58–60, and 153–7; Wilentz, 259–64; Stott, 229–31.

16. Laurie, ch. 3; David Edelstein, *Joel Munsell: Printer and Antiquarian* (New York: Columbia University Press, 1950), 75–76, 106–7; Fearon, 209. By his mid-twenties Munsell was too busy with his work and courting.

17. Buckley, 368–80, for a fine discussion on contemporary images of b'hoys.

18. "Chatham Theater," *Spirit of the Times* (April 22, 1848), 108; Stott, 223–6; B. Hewitt, 146–7; Quinn, I 303–8; Allen, 65–66. See Quinn, I 305–307, 466, for the names of some of the numerous plays featuring Mose.

19. On danger and geography, see Stansell, 96–9, Kasson, chs. 3 and 4, and Mary Ryan, *Women in Public* (Baltimore: Johns Hopkins, 1990); Wilentz, 263, on "Boweriness"; Pamela Adams, 41–2, on "Boweryisms."

20. On the "light and shadow" genre, see Kasson, 74–80. For examples of lurid and fear-inspiring newspaper reports, see Patricia Cline Cohen, "Unregulated Youth: Masculinity and Murder in the 1830s City," *Radical History Review* 52 (Winter 1992), 33–52, and Timothy Gilfoyle, *City of Eros: New York City, Prostitution, and the Commercialization of Sex, 1790–1920* (New York: Norton, 1992), 92–101, on the Helen Jewett murder in 1836.

21. Foster, quoted in Stott, 253. See also George MacMinn, *Theater of the Golden Era in California* (Caldwell, ID: self published, 1941), 110–15, 126, and Malcolm Rohrbough, *Days of Gold: The California Gold Rush and the American Nation* (University of California Press, 1997), on divide

between miners and "respectability"; Hodge, ch. 3, on the yankee; Richard Slotkin, *The Fatal Environment: The Myth of the Frontier in the Age of Industrialization, 1800–1890* (New York: Atheneum, 1985), on frontier myth.

22. Emmet, quoted in Shank, 310. See also, "The Italian Opera House and the Bowery, New York," *Spirit of the Times* (February 6, 1847), 590.

23. *New-York Mirror* 10 (December 29, 1832), 206. See Plate 2.

24. Trollope, 233–4.

25. Rorabaugh, *The Alcoholic Republic,* on high consumption; Francis J. Grund, *Aristocracy in American: From the Sketch-book of a German Nobleman* (New York) 81; George W. Pierson, *Tocqueville and Beaumont in America* (New York: Oxford University Press 1938); see also Kemble, II 61; Benjamin French, *Witness to the Young Republic: A Yankee's Journal* (Hanover, NH: University Press of New England, 1989), 64.

26. Shank, 245, quote of *New-York Mirror;* Grimsted, 64, on Boston quote: also Trollope, 134, on 1828 Cincinnati.

27. John Kendall, *The Golden Age of the New Orleans Theater* (Baton Rouge, LA: Louisiana State University Press, 1952), 61, on Forrest; George Willard, *History of the Providence Stage* (Providence: Rhode Island News Co., 1891), 106–7, on Booth; Buckley, 55, 58–60, on Macready.

28. Northall, 38, 177; also Hornblow, II 132. Sean Wilentz, *Chants Democratic,* 266, 299, fn 1, on Panic of 1837.

29. Sol Smith, *Theatrical Management in the West and South for Thirty Years* (New York: Harper & Bros., 1869), 118–20.

30. On "Goths," see Odell, II 517, III 693, IV 63; editorial, *The* [NY] *Evening Post* (May 28, 1838), 2; on "rabble" see Allan Nevins, ed., *The Diary of Philip Hone* (New York: Dodd, Mead, 1927), 1309.

31. In general, audiences expected subordination from performers. In 1831 Philadelphia, when someone threw a piece of plaster onto the stage, an actor threw it back. This was taken as an offense to the audience. A "general row ensued, in which stoves were overturned"; Esther Dunn, *Shakespeare in America* (New York: MacMillan, 1939), 171.

32. Richard Butsch, "American Theater Riots and Class Relations, 1754–1849," *Theatre Annual* 48 (1995), 41–59.

33. Hornblow, I 308; William Clapp, *A Record of the Boston Stage* (Boston: James Munroe, 1853), 185–93. H. P. Phelps, *Players of a Century: A Record of the Albany Stage* (Albany: Jos. McDonough, 1880), 90, estimated three-fourths of the audience supported Kean. On other cities, see Patricia Click, *The Spirit of the Times: Amusements in Nineteenth Century Baltimore, Norfolk and Richmond* (Charlottesville: University Press of Virginia, 1989), 42; Joseph Cowell, *Thirty Years Passed Among the Players in England and America* (New York: Harper, 1844), 70–1.

34. Roger Lane, *Policing the City: Boston, 1822–1885* (Cambridge, MA: Harvard University Press, 1967); James Richardson, *The New York Police: Colonial Times to 1901* (New York: Oxford University Press, 1970).

35. There had been a competitive relationship between the two actors going back to 1826 when Forrest at the Bowery competed against

Macready at the Park. Competition eventually grew into open hostility, with Forrest hissing Macready in an Edinburgh performance in 1846, claiming Macready had hissed him in London. The stage was set for confrontation when Macready returned for another tour of America in 1848. The public delighted in the gossip of the personal quarrel that ensued.

36. There are several thorough accounts of this riot. See Moody; and Buckley, 45–75, 306–307. Moody says that thirty-one persons were killed.

37. Ben Graf Henneke, "The Playgoer in America" (Ph.D., University of Illinois, 1956), 156, on 1911 Irish riot in New York; Allston Brown, *A History of the New York Stage* (New York: Benjamin Blom, 1964) [1903], II 323–4, on O'Connor, 1888; Odell, XV 401, on Yiddish protest at the Thalia in New York, 1892; Howard Goodson, "South of the North, North of the South: Public Entertainment in Atlanta, 1880–1930" (Ph.D., Emory University, 1995), 66–67, on 1896 Atlanta; James Dunlap, "Sophisticates and Dupes: Cincinnati Audiences, 1851," *Bulletin of the Historical and Philosophical Society of Ohio* 13:2 (April 1955), 96, on 1851 Cincinnati; "A Touching Incident," *Spirit of the Times* (March 15, 1851), 41. See Chapter 6 for riots in the 1870s.

38. Robert Wiebe, *The Opening of American Society* (New York: Knopf, 1984), chs. 3 and 16, contrasts the politics of character, a remnant of the culture of deference among the elite in the early republic, to that of respectability in the Jacksonian era. On the culture of respectability, see Chapter 5.

Chapter 4.   Knowledge and the Decline of Audience Sovereignty

1. William Alger, *Life of Edwin Forrest* (Philadelphia: Lippincott, 1877), II 477–8; on Baltimore see John Hewitt, *Shadows on the Wall* (New York: AMS Press, 1971) [orig., Baltimore 1877], 105. For many other stories see Joseph Roppolo, "Audiences in New Orleans Theaters, 1845–1861," *Tulane Studies in English* 2 (1950), 132–3; "The Drama: Theatrical Catastrophes," *New York Mirror* (December 29, 1832), 206; James Dormon, *Theater in the Antebellum South, 1815–1861* (Chapel Hill, NC: University of North Carolina Press, 1967), 241–2; David Grimsted, *Melodrama Unveiled: American Theater and Culture, 1800–1850* (Chicago: University of Chicago, 1968), 60; Sol Smith, *Theatrical Management in the West and South* (New York: Harper and Bros., 1868), 47–8, 109–10, 206; Herbert Brown, "Sensibility in 18th Century American Drama," *American Literature* 4:1 (March 1932), 49; "Editor's Easy Chair," *Harper's Magazine* 28 (December 1863), 133; Olive Logan, *Before the Footlights and Behind the Scenes* (Philadelphia: Parmalee & Co., 1870), 309. On audiences reading performances differently from performers, see the concept of disjuncture in Marvin Carlson, "Theatre Audiences and the Reading of Performance," in Thomas Postlewait and Bruce McConachie, eds., *Interpreting the Theatrical Past* (Iowa City: University of Iowa Press, 1989), 85.

2. On fandom, knowledge, and cultural capital, see Joli Jensen, "Fandom as Pathology," and John Fiske, "The Cultural Economy of Fandom," in Lisa Lewis, ed., *The Adoring Audience: Fan Culture and Popular Media* (London: Routledge, 1992), 9–29 and 30–49.

3. William Northall, *Before and Behind the Curtains* (New York: W.F. Burgess, 1851), 72; also New York *Herald* quote in Buckley, 387. On stories of auditors knowing the script, see Sol Smith, 119–20; William Wood, *Personal Recollections of the Stage* (Philadelphia: Henry Carey Baird, 1855), 108; Levine, "Highbrow/Lowbrow," 13–30, on the common familiarity with Shakespeare.

4. Arthur Hornblow, *A History of the Theater in America* (New York: Benjamin Blom, 1965), II 131–2, on Mitchell; also MacMinn, 110–26, for frontier example; examples from music hall, see Patrick Joyce, *Visions of the People: Industrial England and the Question of Class, 1840–1914* (Cambridge, UK: Cambridge University Press, 1991), ch. 13; Peter Bailey, "Conspiracies of Meaning: Music-Hall and the Knowingness of Popular Culture," *Past and Present* 144 (August 1994), 138–70, quote from p. 155. See Introduction on earlier European traditions of audience knowing.

5. Peter Buckley, "To the Opera House," (Ph.D., SUNY, Stony Brook, 1984), 393–4. The Mose plays offered a subject position for the b'hoys in the audience to fill. See Bailey, 146.

6. Northall 73, 71.

7. On subcultures, resistance, and incorporation, see John Clarke, "Style," in Stuart Hall and Tony Jefferson, eds., *Resitance Through Rituals: Youth Cultures in Post-War Britain* (London: Hutchinson, 1976), 185ff; Dick Hebdige, *Subculture: The Meaning of Style* (London: Methuen, 1979), and *Hiding in the Light: On Images and Things* (London: Routledge, 1988).

8. On the promenade as an example, see David Scobey, "Anatomy of the Promenade," *Social History* 17:2 (May 1992), 203–28.

9. Dizikes, 269ff, on small-town opera houses. On civic boosterism, see Lawrence Larsen, "Frontier Urbanization," in Roger Nichols, ed., *American Frontier and Western Issues: An Historiographical Review* (Westport, CT: Greenwood Press, 1986), 69–88. On efforts in small-town and frontier theaters, see MacMinn, 259; Carson, 279; William Gates, "The Theatre in Natchez," *Journal of Mississippi History* 3:2 (April 1941), 110; Harold and Ernestine Briggs, "The Early Theatre in the Upper Mississippi," *Mid-America* 31:3 [new series 20] (July 1949), 140, 154; Dormon, 235–6.

10. The distinction between cultivation and fashion is similar to that between social and cultural capital. See Pierre Bourdieu, *Distinction: A Social Critique of the Judgement of Taste,* trans. Richard Nice (Cambridge, MA: Harvard University Press, 1984), 114–15.

11. Maud and Otis Skinner, *One Man in His Time: The Adventures of H. Watkins, Strolling Player, 1845–1863, From His Journal* (Philadelphia: University of Pennsylvania Press, 1938), 3, on New Orleans; Trollope, 133, n5, on a similar poster in Cincinnati.

12. Joseph Cowell, *Thirty Years Passed Among the Players* (New York: Harper and Bros., 1844), 81; *The Knickerbocker* 16:1 (July 1840), 84; *Harper's Weekly* (November 12, 1859), 740; "Editor's Easy Chair," *Harper's* 28 (December 1863), 131–3. William Carson, *The Theater on the Frontier* (New York: Benjamin Blom, 1965), 279–80, noted that in St. Louis in 1839 the elite preferred foreign actors over Forrest.

13. Cowell, 86; similarly Allan Nevins, *The Diary of Philip Hone* (New York: Dodd, Mead, 1927), 272.

14. "The Italian Opera House and the Bowery, New York," *Spirit of the Times* (February 6, 1847), 590; "Things Theatrical," *Spirit of the Times* (December 21, 1839), 504. See also Trollope, 131–2, Carson, 279–80, and Gates, 110, on Americans assuming English actors necessarily superior, but unable to distinguish good from bad acting.

15. Walt Whitman, "Miserable State of the Stage," in Montrose Moses and John Brown, eds., *The American Theater as Seen By Its Critics* (New York: Cooper Square, 1967), 71–72; George Foster, *New York by Gaslight* (New York: Dewitt & Davenport, 1850), 86–87. Also, on upper-class withdrawal, see Hornblow, II 154; Beaumont, *Marie*, 231; George Willard, *History of the Providence Stage*, 114; Hodge, 38. Mixed audiences persisted in smaller towns. See Dormon, 232–3; Robert Toll, *On with the Show* (New York: Oxford University Press, 1976), 141–6.

16. John Dizikes, *Opera in America: A Cultural History* (New Haven: Yale University Press, 1993), 50–51; Karen Alhquist, "Opera, Theater and Audience in Antebellum New York," (Ph.D., University of Michigan, 1991), 148; Tyrone Power, *Impressions of America* (London: Richard Bentley, 1836), I 171, on pit prices.

17. Jay Teran, "The New York Opera Audience: 1825–1974" (Ph.D., New York University, 1974), 1, 9, 13; Ahlquist, 161, 163–4.

18. Teran, 7, 27; Ahlquist, 93, 148, 155, 165.

19. Dizikes, 163–67; Bruce McConachie, "New York Opera-going, 1825–1850," *American Music* 6:2 (Summer 1988), 184–6; quote in Foster, 90–91. Upon the Astor's quick demise after the fateful riot of 1849, New York's Academy of Music was built and opened in 1854, financed by 200 wealthy stockholders. It in turn was displaced by the Metropolitan Opera, built in 1883, as the place of fashion. See Ahlquist, 26–27, 33, 37–8. The Academy of Music in Philadelphia opened in 1857 and, despite earlier plans, the policies were exclusionary. See Dizikes, 163–5.

20. McConachie, 184, on dress code.

21. "The Italian Opera House and the Bowery, New York," *Spirit of the Times* (February 6, 1847), 590. The title refers to the Astor Place Opera House.

22. Teran, 29, on performers as servants; 49–55, on the Diamond Horseshoe.

Chapter 5. Matinee Ladies: Re-gendering Theater Audiences

1. Robert Wiebe, *The Opening of American Society* (New York: Knopf, 1984), ch. 16; Karen Haltunnen, *Confidence Men and Painted Women: A Study of Middle Class Culture in America, 1830–1870* (New Haven: Yale,

1982); John Kasson, *Rudeness and Civility: Manners in Nineteenth Century America* (New York: Hill & Wang, 1990).

2. On gender and public space, see Mary Ryan, *Women in Public* (Baltimore: Johns Hopkins, 1990); Dorothy O. Helly and Susan Reverby, eds., *Gendered Domains: Rethinking Public and Private in Women's History* (Ithaca, NY: Cornell University Press, 1992); Glenna Matthews, *The Rise of Public Woman: Woman's Power and Woman's Place in the U.S., 1630–1970* (New York: Oxford University Press, 1992); Sarah Deutsch, "Reconceiving the City: Women, Space and Power in Boston, 1870–1910," *Gender & History* 6:2 (August 1994), 202–23.

3. On commercial public spaces, see Ryan, *Women in Public*; Kathy Peiss, "Going Public"; Elaine Abelson, *When Ladies Go A-Thieving: Middle-Class Shoplifters in the Victorian Department Store* (New York: Oxford University Press, 1989), ch. 1.

4. Quinn, I 310–15, 445.

5. Richardson Wright, *Forgotten Ladies: Nine Portraits from the American Family Album* (Philadelphia: Lippincott, 1928), 190–216.

6. William Leach, "Transformations in a Culture of Consumption: Women and Department Stores, 1890–1925," *Journal of American History* 71 (1984), 319–42; on retail district, see M. Christine Boyer, *Manhattan Manners: Architecture and Style, 1850–1900* (New York: Rizzoli, 1985); Peiss, "Going Public."

7. Count of performances compiled from Arthur Herman Wilson, *A History of the Philadelphia Theatre, 1835 to 1855* (New York: Greenwood Press, 1968); Thomas Scharf, *History of Baltimore*, I 691; on the three Macbeths, see Richard Moody, *The Astor Place Riot* (Bloomington, IN: Indiana University Press, 1958), 104; on Spartacus, etc., see Barnard Hewitt, *Theater U.S.A., 1665–1957* (New York: McGraw Hill, 1959), 105–7, 145–7.

8. Hewitt, 92–103; quote on 98. By contrast, Junius Booth's son, Edwin, the leading male star after the Civil War, was described as "pale, thin and intellectual," Hewitt, 189. On Cooper, see John Bernard, *Retrospections of America, 1797–1811* (New York: Harper and Brothers, 1887), 166–7, and H. P. Phelps, *Players of a Century: A Record of the Albany Stage* (Albany: Joseph McDonough, 1880), 98–99.

9. Claudia Johnson, "That Guilty Third Tier: Prostitution in Nineteenth Century American Theaters," in Daniel Walker Howe, ed., *Victorian America* (Philadelphia, 1976), 111–120; Rosemarie Bank, "Hustlers in the House," Ron Engle and Tice Miller, eds., *The American Stage* (Cambridge University Press, 1993). On brothels near theaters, see Gilfoyle, *City of Eros*, 111–12. By the 1830s, prostitutes in theaters were a common practice in most cities. As we will see, this was also when a movement began to remove them.

10. Frances Trollope, *Domestic Manners of the Americans*, Donald Smalley, ed., (New York: Knopf, 1949), 74; Kemble, I 56; Tyrone Power, *Impressions of America; During the Years 1833, 1834, and 1835* (London: Richard Bentley, 1836), 72–73. There was an actual decline in women attending in

Charleston after 1815, when the audience became more heterogeneous. Pamela Adams, "The Audience in Charleston's Theaters, 1790–1860" (Ph.D., University of South Carolina, 1983), 18, 30, 34.

11. On coffee rooms, see Reese Davis James, *Cradle of Culture: 1800–1810, The Philadelphia Stage* (Philadelphia: University of Pennsylvania Press, 1957), 107; and William Dunlap, *History of the American Theatre* (New York: Burt Franklin, 1963), II 246; on Drake, see Dormon, 62; Ludlow, 477–8.

12. Ben Graf Henneke, "The Playgoer in America," 77; *New-York Mirror* quoted in Theodore Shank, "The Bowery Theater, 1826–1836" (Ph.D., Stanford University, 1956), 28. Also see Power, II 172; William K. Northall, *Before and Behind the Curtain,* 176–7; Carson, 42; George MacMinn, *The Theater of the Golden Era in California,* 279; Harold E. and Ernestine Bennett Briggs, "The Theater in Early Kansas City," *Mid-America* 32 (1950), 102.

13. Ben Graf Henneke, "The Playgoer in America," 75–86.

14. Mark Antony DeWolfe Howe, ed., *The Articulate Sisters* (Cambridge, MA: Harvard University Press, 1946), 202–18

15. Quote in Arthur Hornblow, *A History of the Theatre in America* (New York: Benjamin Blom, 1965), II 97; *Sprit of the Times* (June 15, 1850), 204, on Cushman; Power, II 172, on behavior. See also Power, II 172–3; Kemble, II 2–3. George Foster, *New York by Gas-Light,* 86–87, 88.

16. Kemble, I 59, 66, 147, 256–7, 311.

17. For an extended treatment of museum theaters and moral reform melodrama, see McConachie, *Melodramatic Formations,* ch. 6.

18. Arthur Hornblow, *A History of the Theatre in America,* I 291.

19. McConachie, 162–9; Hornblow, II 148.

20. McConachie, 168; Zachary Bloomfield, "Baptism of a Deacon's Theatre: Audience Development at the Boston Museum, 1841–1861," 180–1, 185–6, 199, 217–23.

21. McConachie, 176; Claire McGlinchee, *The First Decade of the Boston Museum* (Boston: Bruce Humphries, 1940), 37, 45; Conteur, "Our Theaters after the Civil War," *Cincinnati Enquirer* (October 15, 1922).

22. Barnard Hewitt, *Theatre U.S.A., 1665–1957,* 173–4; Charles Durang, *The Philadelphia Stage,* VI 368.

23. Karen Halttunen, *Confidence Men and Painted Women,* 93; Ann Douglas, *The Feminization of American Culture* (New York: Knopf, 1977); Kasson, *Rudeness and Civility.*

24. Peter Buckley, "To the Opera House," 114, on Ludlow; Irwin Glazer, *Philadelphia Theatres, A–Z* (Westport, CT: Greenwood Press, 1986), 12, on Arch Street Theater; "Editor's Easy Chair," *Harper's New Monthly Magazine* 40 (March 1870), 605–6.

25. Northall, 75.

26. Playbill in George C. D. Odell, *Annals of the New York Stage,* V 447. Even the working-class Pelby's National Theater in Boston in 1844 announced it would no longer sell liquor. Bloomfield, 219.

27. Bayard, "Theatres and Things Theatrical," *Wilkes' Spirit of the Times* (November 9, 1861), 160.

28. Henneke, 12–14 and 77–78. J. T. Mayne, 32, noted in 1869 that the pit and the first circle were cushioned and priced alike at 50 cents in most American theaters.

29. Richard Stott, *Workers in the Metropolis: Class, Ethnicity and Youth in Ante-bellum New York City* (Ithaca, NY: Cornell University Press, 1990), 272. Also Elliott Gorn, *The Manly Art: Bare-Knuckle Prize Fighting in America* (Ithaca, NY: Cornell University Press, 1986), 158–9, 194–206. On women's reform efforts against masculine culture, see Mary Ann Clawson, *Constructing Brotherhood: Class, Gender and Fraternalism* (Princeton: Princeton University Press, 1989), 161–4; Carroll Smith-Rosenberg, "Beauty, the Beast and the Militant Woman," in *Disorderly Conduct* (Oxford, UK: Oxford University Press, 1985), 109–28.

30. George C. D. Odell, *Annals of the New York Stage* I 443; IV 101, 103, 243, 308, 564, 571, 641; V 23, 26, 33, 39, 45, 197, 257; VI 71–3, 168, 247, 249, 309–12, 317, 459; VII 43, 332, 563.

31. Leon Beauvallet, *Rachel and the New World,* Colin Clair, trans. and ed. (New York: Abelard–Schuman, 1967; orig., 1856), 119; Lois Banner, *American Beauty,* 69.

32. On Laura Keene, Odell, VII 130, 132, and Helen Waverly Deutsch, "Laura Keene's Theatrical Management" (Ph.D., Tufts University, 1992), 155–6, 207–8; on opera matinees, Odell, VII 158 and *Spirit of the Times* (May 1, 1858), 136.

33. "Things Theatrical," *Spirit of the Times* (October 9, 1858), 420.

34. *New York Times* (October 1, 1860), 5.

35. *New York Times* (October 3, 1860), 4.

36. Peter A. Davis, "From Stock to Combination: The Panic of 1873 and its Effects on the American Theatre Industry," *Theater History Studies* 8 (1988), 1–9; and William Reardon and Eugene Bristow, "The American Theatre, 1864–1870: An Economic Portrait," *Speech Monographs* 33:4 (November 1966), 438–43, on marginal profits in the 1860s. On escorts, see *New York Times* (October 1, 1860), 5; and Shirley Madeline Harrison, "The Grand Opera House of New Orleans, Louisiana, 1871 to 1906" (Ph.D., Louisiana State University, 1965), 95. Banner, *American Beauty,* 79, claims that chaperonage in New York was enforced less before the war.

37. *New York Clipper* (April 8, 1865), 414.

38. Odell, VIII 420, 562; quote from Dio Lewis, *Our Girls* (New York: Harper and Bros., 1871), 230–1.

39. *Wilkes' Spirit of the Times* (October 27, 1866), 144.

40. Lois Banner, *American Beauty,* 40–44, 78; Karen Halttunen, *Confidence Men and Painted Women,* 161; playbill of the Walnut Street Theater, September 8, 1874, Philadelphia Free Library. Also Angus, 132, on actresses as models of fashion.

41. Banner, 122; Marilyn Moses, "Lydia Thompson and the 'British Blondes' in the United States" (Ph.D., University of Oregon, 1978).

42. McConachie, *Melodramatic Formations,* 206, 211, 221–2.

43. J. A. Mangan and James Walvin, eds., *Manliness and Morality: Middle-Class Masculinity in Britain and America, 1800–1940* (Manchester, UK: 1987), 1, 3, 10, 36, 42; Mark Carnes and Clyde Griffen, eds., *Meanings for Manhood: Constructions of Masculinity in Victorian America* (Chicago: University of Chicago Press, 1990), 191. Elliott Gorn, *The Manly Art,* 158–9, 194–206, and Richard Stott, *Workers in the Metropolis,* 272–5, discuss middle-class men's attractions to the male working-class world of saloons and prizefights.

44. *Spirit of the Times,* founded in 1831, reported on theater, sports, and agriculture. In the 1830s, two of its eight pages, including the front page, were devoted to the stage, mixed congenially with turf coverage. By the 1860s, stage coverage was reduced to a column on the back page and the magazine was devoted increasingly to turf news and secondarily to other gentlemanly sports.

45. Robert C. Allen, *Horrible Prettiness,* 96–117; Shirley Madeline Harrison, "The Grand Opera House of New Orleans, Louisiana, 1871 to 1906" (Ph.D., Louisiana State University, 1965), 116, 247, 373.

46. Henneke, "The Playgoer in America," 139; Olive Logan, *Before the Footlights and Behind the Scenes* (Philadelphia: Parmalee, 1870), 382; also Henry Irving, "The American Audience," *The Fortnightly* 43 (1885), 199.

47. J. Albert Brackett, *Theatre Law* (Boston: C. M. Clark, 1907), 209–12; Walter Swan, "The Rights of the Holder of a Theater Ticket," *Case and Comment* 18:10 (March 1912), 574–7.

48. "Americans at the Theater," *Every Saturday* (May 18, 1871), 451; "Theaters and Things Theatrical," *Spirit of the Times* (October 27, 1866), 144; also Joseph Hatton, "American Audiences and Actors," *The Theatre* (May, 1881), 257–66.

49. Henneke, 12–14, 77; "Theaters and Things Theatrical," *Wilkes Spirit of the Times* (October 26, 1861), 128. On boys in the gallery, see Chapter 9.

50. Faye Dudden, *Women in the American Theatre* (New Haven: Yale University Press, 1994), 132–8; "Editor's Easy Chair," *Harper's Monthly* (March 1870), 605; Shirley Madeline Harrison, "The Grand Opera House of New Orleans, Louisiana, 1871 to 1906" (Ph.D., Louisiana State University, 1965), 286. "Woman's plays" were offered in the eighteenth century to attract female auditors, as noted in Chapter 1, but the profits of the theater at that time did not depend upon women's patronage.

51. On ladies' night, see Odell, X 157, 331, 343, 537; on Wallack's, see "Causerie," *Spirit of the Times* (September 28, 1878), 214; "The Matinee Girl," *New-York Mirror* (February 9, 1889), 11.

52. James L. Ford "The Rentz-Santley Organization," unidentified newspaper clipping. Tony Pastor Scrapbook, New York Public Library, Billy Rose Theater Collection.

53. Walter Prichard Eaton, "Women as Theater-Goers," *Woman's Home Companion* 37 (October 1910), 13; survey in "Gallery Gods Have Made Their Way for Second Balcony Goddesses," typescript, New York Public Library, Billy Rose Theater Collection clipping file; Clayton Hamilton, "Organizing the Audience," *The Bookman* 34 (October 1911), 163–4.

54. On women and work, see Michael J. Carter and Susan Boslego Carter, "Women's Recent Progress in the Professions or, 'Women Get a Ticket to Ride After the Gravy Train Has Left the Station,'" *Feminist Studies* 7:8 (Fall, 1981), 477–504; on parallel between proletarianization of work and of leisure see Richard Butsch, "The Commodification of Leisure: The Case of the Model Airplane Hobby," *Qualitative Sociology* 7:3 (1984): 217–35.

55. Henneke, 168–75; William Northall, *Before and Behind the Curtain: or Fifty Years' Observations among the Theatres of New York* (New York: W. F. Burgess, 1851), 70, 74; Joseph Roppolo, "Áudiences in New Orleans Theatres, 1845–1861," *Tulane Studies in English* [annual] 2 (1950), 126–129.

56. Joseph Jefferson, *The Autobiography of Joseph Jefferson,* Alan Downer, ed., (Cambridge: Harvard University Press, 1964), 319.

57. Unidentified newspaper clipping, Locke scrapbook, vol. 348, p. 31, New York Public Library, Billy Rose Theater Collection.

Chapter 6. Blackface, Whiteface

1. *Putnam's Monthly* 5 (January 1855), 72. Also see Dale Cockrell, *Demons of Disorder* (Cambridge University Press, 1997). Minstrelsy began in northeastern cities and spread from there.

2. On the African Grove, see Edith Isaacs, *The Negro in the American Theatre* (New York: Theatre Arts, 1947), 19; Peter Buckley, "To the Opera House: Culture and Society in New York City, 1820–1860" (Ph.D., SUNY-Stony Brook, 1984), 166–8; George C. D. Odell, *Annals of the New York Stage* (New York: Columbia University Press, 1927), III 35–37, 70–71; playbill in Laurence Hutton, "The Negro on the Stage," *Harper's* 79 (1889), 133; Herbert Marshall and Mildred Stock, *Ira Aldridge, The Negro Tragedian* (London: Rockliff, 1958), 32–36. Carl Wittke, *Tambo and Bones: A History of the American Minstrel Stage* (New York: Greenwood Press, 1968), 9, mentioned a troupe in Boston in 1795. On black theater history, see James Hatch, "Here Comes Everybody: Scholarship and Black Theatre History," in Thomas Postlewait and Bruce McConachie, eds., *Interpreting the Theatrical Past* (Iowa City: University of Iowa Press, 1989); Edward G. Smith, "Black Theatre," in Maxine Seller, ed., *Ethnic Theatre in the United States* (Westport, CT: Greenwood Press, 1983), 37–66; Helene Keyssar, *The Curtain and the Veil: Strategies in Black Drama* (New York: Burt Franklin, 1981), ch. 1; Carl Van Vecten, *In the Garret* (New York: Knopf, 1920), ch. 3. On antebellum black entertainers, see Robert Toll, *Blacking Up: The Minstrel Show in Nineteenth-Century America* (New York: Oxford University Press, 1974), 196–202; Eric Lott, *Love and Theft: Blackface Minstrelsy and the American Working Class* (New York: Oxford University Press, 1995), 112–15, 235; Edward Dicey, *Spectator of America* (Chicago: Quadrangle, 1971) [orig., 1863], 198; Marshall and Stock, 31–32; George MacMinn, *Theatre of the Golden Era in California* (Caldwell, ID:

Caxton Printers, 1941), 425, n5; Ike Simond, *Old Slack: Reminiscences and Pocket History of the Colored Profession from 1865 to 1891* (Bowling Green, OH: Bowling Green University Press, 1974 [orig., 1891]), xviii.

3. Playbills for theaters, circuses, and variety halls regularly listed separate seating and prices for blacks. See playbills at Philadelphia Free Library Theater Collection; Harvard Theater Collection. Blacks were excluded from Charleston theaters in 1795 for fear of the Haitian Revolution. See Pamela Adams, "The Audience in Charleston Theaters, 1790–1860" (Ph.D., Univ. of South Carolina, 1983), 23. On frontier, see Briggs, "Early Theatre in the Upper Mississippi Valley," *Mid-America* 31:3 (July 1949), 132, MacMinn, 44; on blacks contesting segregation in theaters see Walter Swan, "The Right of the Holder of a Theater Ticket," *Case and Comment* 18 (March 1912), 574–7; Howard Goodson, "South of the North; North of the South" (Ph.D., Emory University, 1995), 292–302.

4. George Pierson, *Tocqueville and Beaumont in America* (New York: Oxford University Press, 1938), 513, 628; George Foster, 77; *William Johnson' Natchez: The Ante-Bellum Diary of a Free Negro,* William Ranson Hogan and Edwin Adams Davis, eds. (Baton Rouge: Louisiana State University Press, 1979), 22–23, 40–41, 114; also Francis Grund, *Aristocracy in America* (New York: Harper, 1959) [orig., 1839], 76; n.a., *Particular Account of the Dreadful Fire at Richmond, Virginia* (Baltimore: J. Kingston, 1812), 16; James Dormon, *Theatre in the Antebellum South* (Chapel Hill, NC: University of North Carolina Press, 1967), 233–4, 249; Sellers, 150, on New Orleans. Nothing has been written on nineteenth century black audiences and very little on the twentieth century. See Thomas Parley, "The Black Theatre Audience," *Players* 46 (August/September 1971), 257–61; Brooks Atkinson, "The Play," *New York Times* (March 12, 1936), 18.

5. Sol Smith, *Theatrical Management, in the West and South for Thirty Years* (New York: Harper, 1869), 209; *William Johnson's Natchez,* 40–1; Dormon, 234, on an incident of rowdiness.

6. Cockrell, 50ff, and Hans Nathan, *Dan Emmet and the Rise of Early Negro Minstrelsy* (Norman, OK: University of Oklahoma Press, 1962), chs. 1–7; "Editor's Table," *The Knickerbocker* (July 16, 1840), 84, on Rice.

7. Cockrell, 149; Nathan, ch. 11.

8. Wittke, 58, on three shows a day.

9. Wittke, 66, and Toll, 32, on long runs; Lawrence Estavan, ed., "Minstrelsy," Vol. 13, San Francisco Theatre Research Project (San Francisco: WPA, 1939), 55–6; Wittke, 72–3, 79, Harry Edwall, "The Golden Era of Minstrelsy in Memphis," *The West Tennessee Historical Society Papers* 9 (1955), 35, 43; and Elbert Bowen, "Negro Minstrelsy in Early Rural Missouri," *Missouri Historical Review* 47:2 (January 1953), 107–8; MacMinn, 432–3; Alice Ernst, *Trouping in the Oregon Country* (Portland, OR: Oregon Historical Society, 1961), 90–1, on touring; Billy Bryant, *Children of Ol' Man River* (Chicago: Lakeside Press, 1988), xxx–xxxix; Edwall 44–5, Bowen, 106–7, on river boats.

10. Allan Nevins, *The Diary of Philip Hone*, 710; Nathan, 158; Wittke, 68; Frank Davidson, "The Rise, Development and Decline of the American Minstrel Show" (Ph.D., New York University, 1952), 90.

11. William Wood, *Personal Recollections of the Stage* (Philadelphia: Henry Carey Baird, 1855), 465; Davidson, 91, on German; Odell, VII 88, on Holland; Wittke, 60, on the *Clipper*. In 1875, impressario Dan Frohman still found it easier to book theaters for Callender Minstrels than his brother Charles could for "high-class" comedies. See Toll, 204.

12. Nathan, 230; Toll, 52–7. See Odell, VII 7:90 for a bill showing each act of each part for 1857. "Bones" were originally cow ribs, two held in each hand and beat again each other.

13. *Tribune*, quoted in Lott, 270 n34; MacMinn, 434; also Saxton, 173. Maudlin ballads fit culture of sentimentalism and a growing female audience. See Lott, 187–8. On the mobile city population, see Stuart Blumin, "Mobility and Change in Ante-bellum Philadelphia," Stephan Thernstrom and Richard Sennett, eds., *Nineteenth Century Cities* (New Haven: Yale University Press, 1969).

14. Toll, *Blacking Up*, 93–7.

15. Zanger, 36–7.

16. For example, David Roediger, *Wages of Whiteness: Race and the Making of the American Working Class* (New York: Verso, 1991), 123. Saxton, 16, describes it as expressing the hegemony of the Jacksonian democrats, a political block that allied northern workers and southern planters. On concepts of oppositional, residual, and emergent cultures, see Raymond Williams, *Marxism and Literature* (London: Oxford University Press, 1977).

17. U.S. Bureau of the Census, *Historical Statistics of the U.S.,* (Washington, DC: USGPO, 1975), I 22; Lott, 112–13, on Barnum; also Toll, 38–40, Lott, 269 n26; Roediger, 117, and Lott, 20–1, on whiteface.

18. Dicey, 198; Toll, 38, on northern astonishment.

19. Toll, 88, 97.

20. Based on a sampling of *Liberator* issues from the 1850s. On mocking women and suffragists, see pictures in Robert Toll, *On with the Show* (New York: Oxford University Press), 98–9; MacMinn, 422.

21. Dale Cockrell, *Demons of Disorder: Early Blackface Minstrels and Their World* (New York: Cambridge University Press, 1997), 150–2.

22. On aesthetic criticism, see *Spirit of the Times* (July 20, 1861), 320; Philip Hone, 710; Olive Logan, "The Ancestry of Brudder Bones," *Harper's* 58 (April, 1879), 687.

23. On decline, see Wittke, 120–3 n113; Brander Matthews, 1913; "Negro Minstrelsy – Ancient and Modern," *Putnam's Monthly* 5 (January 1855), 75–6. Jon Finson, *The Voices That Are Gone: Themes in 19th-Century Popular Songs* (New York: Oxford University Press, 1994), 108–9 on Root.

24. [R. P. Nevins], "Stephen Foster and Negro Minstrelsy," *Atlantic Monthly* 20 (November 1867), 608–16, quote from 611; also Finson, 33–40.

25. Even fond reminisces of antebellum minstrelsy say little about audiences. See Brander Matthews, "The Rise and Fall of Negro Minstrelsy" *Scribner's*

(June, 1915) 754–59; Ralph Keeler, "Three Years as a Negro Minstrel," *Atlantic Monthly* (July 1869).

26. "Obituary, Not Eulogistic: Negro Minstrelsy Is Dead," *Journal of Music* 13:18 (1858), 118.

27. I reviewed each issue of *Spirit of the Times* from March 1847 to its last issue in June 1861, *Porter's Spirit of the Times* from September 1856 to its end in November 1861, and *Wilkes' Spirit of the Times* from September 1859 to 1865. On the overlap of the three papers, see Norris Yeates, *William T. Porter and the Spirit of the Times* (Baton Rouge: Louisiana State University Press, 1957), 190–7.

28. I sampled issues of the *New York Herald* for 1851 and 1855.

29. Robert Toll, "Blackface Minstrelsy in Nineteenth Century America" (Ph.D., Berkeley, 1972) 60–1, 66, and 221–2. Thanks to Robert Toll for bringing these to my attention.

30. Bowen, 107, on Twain; Michael Leavitt, *Fifty Years in Theatrical Management* (New York: Broadway Publications, 1912), 21, 23; Toll, *Blacking Up*, 33, on Cotton and several others; also see Logan, 687; Ralph Keeler, *Vagabond Adventures* (Boston: Fields Osgood, 1870), 157.

31. Keeler, 132–3, 156–8.

32. John Kasson, *Rudeness and Civility: Manners in Nineteenth-Century Urban America* (New York: Hill and Wang, 1990) ch. 4, on bodily constraint; Edwall, 37–8, on Memphis.

33. Jimmy Dalton Baines, "Samuel S. Sanford and Negro Minstrelsy" (Ph.D., Tulane University, 1967), 156–9; also Odell, VI 583, on Christy and Wood giving out kites.

34. Finson, 187–9; Harvard Theatre Collection, minstrel box on White's bill.

35. New York Public Library, Billy Rose Theater Collection, minstrels – U.S. file on playbills; Edwall, 36, on door prizes.

36. On the term "concerts," see Cockrell, 150–1; Edwall, 36ff; Finson, 190, on Foster and gentility.

37. "A New Theater," *Spirit of the Times* (October 24, 1857), 436.

38. Baines, 89; Estavan, 56; Edwall, 41, on Memphis; also *Spirit of the Times* (April 3, 1847), 72; Wittke, 74–5

39. Roediger, 115; Saxton, 169, 171; Lott, 138–9. Roediger cites Wittke (58–65) and Toll (10–13) to substantiate his claim of a working-class audience, but nowhere in these pages does either author make such a claim.

40. Nathan, 144, on Gratton; also *Spirit of the Times,* (March 2, 1850), 24. See Appendix on ticket prices and wages.

41. Toll, *Blacking Up*, 115–16, on attacks; 57, on formalized structure. Minstrelsy fits the spectator style of participation that Pierre Bourdieu, *Distinction* (Cambridge, MA: Harvard University Press, 1984), 4, described as working class.

42. Wittke, 74, on Cleveland.

43. *Spirit of the Times* (March 29, 1845), 56; (June 28, 1845), 212; (July 5, 1845), 224; (April 6, 1850), 84; (March 23, 1850), 60; (April 20, 1850), 108.

44. "Obituary, Not Eulogistic: Negro Minstrelsy Is Dead," *Journal of Music* 13:18 (1858), 118; Wittke, 120; Albert Beveridge, *Abraham Lincoln, 1809–1858*, Vol. 1 (Boston: Houghton Mifflin, 1928), 536; Finson, 185.
45. Roediger, 127, argues that racist minstrelsy united whites across class, ethnicity, and religion. However, they may not have been in the same audiences at the same shows.
46. Toll, *Blacking Up*, 34; Davidson, 114.
47. Hill, "A History of Variety – Vaudeville in Minneapolis" (Ph.D., University of Minnesota, 1979), 33.
48. James McCabe, *New York by Sunlight and Gaslight* (Philadelphia: Douglas Bros., 1882), 485–6. The "tired businessman" would be a common reference for vaudeville and legitimate theater through the 1920s.
49. Davidson, 118, 150; Toll, *Blacking Up*, 135, 163, 173, 181.
50. Toll, 146; Nathan, 228 n10, on *Clipper; Clipper* quoted by Toll, 139.
51. Toll, 138–40.
52. Toll, 149.
53. Robert C. Allen, *Horrible Prettiness: Burlesque and American Culture* (Chapel Hill, NC: University of North Carolina Press, 1991), 166, on *Clipper;* Harvard Theater Collection, minstrel box on *Eagle;* Estavan, 131, on San Francisco; Matthews, 758–9.

Chapter 7. Variety, Liquor, and Lust

1. Variety and minstrelsy were both fast-paced and always changing. Early variety also began with a troupe performing all the acts, as with minstrelsy, and even adopted minstrelsy's three-part division. See Parker Zellars, "The Cradle of Variety: The Concert Saloon," *Educational Theater Journal* 20 (December 1968), 53–60; Eugene Elliot, *History of Variety – Vaudeville from the Beginning to 1914* (Seattle: University of Washington Press, 1941), 6–7.
2. John Jennings, *Theatrical and Circus Life* (St. Louis: Sun Publishing, 1882), 393; similarly Raymond Calkins, *Substitutes for the Saloon: An Investigation for the Committee of Fifty* (Boston: Houghton Mifflin, 1901), 22.
3. Newspapers and magazines rarely gave more than the shortest reviews of this entertainment, nor did performers write memoirs, leaving as the principal historical record the controversy over morality.
4. Timothy Gilfoyle, *City of Eros: New York City, Prostitution, and the Commericalization of Sex, 1790–1920* (New York: Norton, 1992); Ann-Louise Shapiro, "Working Girls," *International Labor and Working Class History* 45 (Spring 1994), 96–107; Caroll Smith-Rosenberg, "Beauty, the Beast and the Militant Woman," *Disorderly Conduct,* (New York: Knopf, 1985). On bourgeois men's free range across these divided spheres, see Judith Walkowitz, *City of Dreadful Delights* (Chicago: University of Chicago Press, 1992), 15–24; and Richard Sennett, *The Fall of Public Man,* (New York: Knopf, 1977), 136–7.
5. George C. D. Odell, *Annals of the New York Stage* (New York: Columbia University Press, 1927), VI 589–91, VII 92, 183, 282, 352; *New York*

Times (March 28, 1874), 8; *New York Times* (January 5, 1862); Zellars, "The Cradle of Variety," 579, on small towns; Michael Leavitt, *Fifty Years in Theatrical Management* (New York: Broadway Publishing, 1912), 184–5. Also see Eugene Bristow, "Look Out for Saturday Night: A Social History of Variety Theater in Memphis Tennessee, 1859–1860" (Ph. D., University of Iowa, 1956), 47, 66; Perry Duis, *The Saloon: Public Drinking in Chicago and Boston, 1880–1920* (Urbana: University of Illinois Press, 1983), 237; Alice Henson Ernst, *Trouping in the Oregon Country* (Portland: Oregon Historical Society, 1961), 102; David Brundage, *The Making of Western Labor Radicalism* (Urbana: University of Illinois Press, 1994), 68.

6. See Appendix for admission prices; *The Night Side of New York* (New York: J. C. Haney, 1866), 11. Other descriptions of audiences in Odell VII 287; *New York Times* (March 28, 1874), 8; "Sketches of People Who Oppose our Sunday Laws," *Harper's Weekly* (October 8, 1859), 641; "The New York Concert Saloons," *New York Evening Post* (January 2, 1862); *Spirit of the Times* (1864); Matthew Hale Smith, *Sunshine and Shadow in New York* (Hartford: J. B. Burr, 1869), 215–19; and Leavitt, 184–5. The central place of sexuality in concert saloons and the sexual threat represented by black men in racist mythology of the time (e.g., see Eric Lott, *Love and Theft: Blackface Minstrelsy and the American Working Class,* Oxford University Press, 1993, on the confused mix of gender and racial ideologies) most likely meant that black men were excluded from white concert saloons. There is no mention in contemporary accounts of blacks in the audiences, and playbills rarely mentioned colored galleries or admission prices, as in theaters. Two Philadelphia halls in 1863 advertised colored galleries and admission prices, but also accommodations for ladies and children, suggesting that sex was downplayed at these particular halls. Nor are there any references to black concert saloons. No doubt there were establishments that offered urban black men the recipe of sex and liquor, but they are absent from the record, even of "Light and Shadow" books that purveyed lurid tales of such "exotic" places. There are occasional references to black prostitutes at the lowest-class "dives," but no mention of black patrons.

7. Odell, VI 592; VII 93, 187, 285–9, 359–60.

8. Gilfoyle, 224–32, offers a rather lurid and uniform interpretation of concert saloons. However, with few exceptions his sources do not refer to the Broadway saloons of controversy here.

9. "Sketches…," *Harper's Weekly* (October 8, 1859), 641.

10. "Music and the Drama," *Wilkes' Spirit of the Times,* issues from April to September 1861.

11. "Music and the Drama," *Wilkes' Spirit of the Times* (October 12, 1861), 96. The changed tone may have been an example of the sensationalism publisher George Wilkes also used in his *National Police Gazette.* On Wilkes and *The Spirit,* see Alexander Saxton, *The Rise and Fall of the White Republic: Class Politics and Mass Culture in Nineteenth Century America* (London: Verso, 1990), 212–15; Norris Yates, *William T. Porter*

and the Spirit of the Times (Louisiana State University Press, 1957), 192–6.

12. "The Concert Saloons," *New York Times* (January 5, 1862), 5.
13. "The New York Concert Saloons," *New York Evening Post* (January 2, 1862).
14. Parker Zellars, "The Cradle of Variety," 583; Odell, VII 438; "The Concert Saloon Reform," *New York Times* (April 25, 1862), 5. The *Times* typically was prudish in matters of respectability and class. See Chapter 5 on its reaction to theater matinees.
15. Advertisement, *New York Herald* (April 30, 1862), 7.
16. "Theaters and Things Theatrical," *Wilkes' Spirit of the Times* (May 21, 1864), 181. Parker Zellars, "Tony Pastor: Manager and Impresario of the American Variety Stage" (Ph.D., University of Iowa, 1964), 73–86, also discusses the crackdown. A letter to the editor of the *New York Times* (June 2, 1865) from a "mother of the old school" called for exclusion of known prostitutes from places of amusement and suggested establishment of "asylums" for their residence and reform as a humane way of eliminating the worst aspect of concert saloons.
17. Edward Winslow Martin (pseudonym of James McCabe), *The Secrets of the Great City* (Philadelphia: National Publishing Co., 1868), 312. Bowery saloons sometimes were described in dark terms. But the workingman's *New York Herald* was more tolerant; "the patrons of the Bowery amusements have little time for sentiment, but just enough time for fun and that relief from the exacting obligations of everyday life ... for they have neither the leisure nor the means to enjoy them in any other way" (October 2, 1865, quoted in Matlaw, *Tony the Trouper,* 90).
18. Music and the Drama," *Wilkes' Spirit* (July 20, 1861), 320; Odell, VII 287; Faye Dudden, *Women in the American Theatre: Actresses and Audiences, 1790–1870* (New Haven: Yale University Press, 1994), 132, on Laura Keene. See Peter Bailey, ed., *Music Hall: The Business of Pleasure* (Milton Keynes, UK: Open University Press, 1986), for similar distinctions between first-class and lesser British music halls.
19. Zellars, "Tony Pastor" 77 n97; Odell, VII 288, 289, 291, 352, 433.
20. Bills from Philadelphia Free Library Theater Collection and Zellars, "Tony Pastor" 46–8, on matinees; John Frick, "The Rialto: A Study of Union Square, the Center of New York's First Theater District" (Ph.D., New York University, 1983), 194–5 on the Palace Garden.
21. Bills from Philadelphia Free Library Theater Collection.
22. Beer halls, like concert saloons, were distinguished from neighborhood saloons. Saloons were generally male affairs, offered lunch for workers, and were more likely attended on weekdays. Beer halls were Sunday affairs for the whole family and charged an admission (e.g., 25 cents).
23. Edward Dicey, *Spectator of America* (Chicago: Quadrangle Co., 1971), 197–8; also George Foster, *New York by Gaslight* (New York: Dewitt and Davenport, 1850), 89–90; Israel Benjamin, *Three Years in America,* trans. Charles Reznikoff (New York: Arno Press, 1975), 192; David Gerber, "The Germans Take Care of Our Celebrations," in Kathryn Grover, ed., *Hard at*

Play: Leisure in America, 1840–1940 (Amherst: University of Massachusetts Press, 1992), 52–4.

24. "Teutonic Sunday Amusements," *New York Herald* (April 25, 1859), 1. *The Nightside of New York, by Members of the New York Press* (New York: Haney, 1866), 54–7, gave a very similar description.

25. Steven Ross, *Workers on the Edge* (New York: Columbia University Press, 1985), 173; Charles MacKay, *Life and Liberty in America* (New York: Harper, 1859), 137; Kathleen Conzen, *Immigrant Milwaukee* (Cambridge, MA: Harvard University Press, 1976), 158.

26. Eugene Bristow, "Look Out for Saturday Night: A Social History of Professional Variety Theater in Memphis Tennessee" (Ph. D., University of Iowa, 1956), 49–50, 73–9.

27. On frontier concert saloons, see George MacMinn, *Theater of the Golden Age in California* (Caldwell, ID: Caxton Printers, 1941), 61–6, Walter Leman, *Memories of an Old Actor* (San Francisco: A. Roman, 1886), 233–4; Eugene Elliott, *A History of Variety – Vaudeville in Seattle* (Seattle: University of Washington Press, 1944); Rex Myers, "Chicago Joe and Her Hurdy-Gurdy Girls," *Montana, the Magazine of Western History* (Spring 1977), 24–32; Robert Dykstra, *The Cattle Towns: A Social History of the Kansas Cattle Trading Centers, 1867–1885* (New York: Knopf, 1968), 100–6; Harold Briggs, "Early Variety Theater in the Trans-Mississippi West," *Mid-America* 34 (July 1952), 196–8. According to a county official in Deadwood, North Dakota in the 1870s, many of the girls working in these saloons committed suicide. See Briggs, 198.

28. Harold Briggs, "The Theater in Early Kansas City," *Mid-America* 32 (July 1950), 102–3.

29. Raymond Calkins, 165. Similarly Walter Reckless, *Vice in Chicago* (Chicago: University of Chicago Press, 1933), 99, quoting a Chicago vice report.

30. Shirley Staples, *Male-Female Comedy Teams in American Vaudeville, 1865–1932* (Ann Arbor: UMI Research Press, 1984), 29, 30; Briggs, "Kansas City," 100–1.

31. H. Hutton, "The Green Table," *Southern Magazine* 9 (September 1871), 373–81; quotes from 375–6, 376–7.

32. "Variety Shows: Their Origin and History," *New York Times* (March 28, 1874), 8; Peter Davis, "From Stock to Combination: The Panic of 1873 and its Effects on the American Theatre Industry," *Theater History Studies* 8 (1988), 6. Odell, IX 472, referred to "the great epidemic of variety" in New York in 1873–74, replacing stock company drama.

33. *New York Times* (March 28, 1874), 8.

34. "The Variety Theatres," *New York Mirror* (January 18, 1879), 4.

35. Harold and Ernestine Briggs, "Early Theater in the Upper Mississippi Valley," *Mid-America* 31 (July 1949), 151. The term "legitimate" was now attached to drama rather than the house, indicating a shift in meaning from the respectability of the house to the quality of the drama.

36. Nor were innovations exclusive to the East. Coates Opera House in Kansas City opened in 1870 with matinees for women and children. Apparently

women did attend, as the management printed a request that "ladies remove their hats during the performance." See Briggs, "Kansas City," 103.

37. Pastor's mother ran a saloon and he early began performing in minstrelsy, circus, and variety. See Frederick Snyder, "American Vaudeville – Theatre in a Package" (Ph.D., Yale University, 1970), 13.

38. Parker Zellars, "Tony Pastor," 140–56, 160–1; Robert W. Snyder, *Voice of the City: Vaudeville and Popular Culture in New York* (New York: Oxford University Press, 1989), 13–16.

39. Zellars, 180–91, 165–6, on neighborhood. *The Figaro* trade paper confirmed his house had become a "family resort." See Staples, 40.

40. Zellars, 234–6; *Clipper* quoted in Zellars, 236. On Union Square as a theater district, see John Frick, "The Rialto".

41. Turn-of-the-century music publisher Edward Marks claimed that while some theaters marketed their respectability, ironically the place where respectable "parlor" songs were marketed in the 1890s were in the less-respectable houses. The male patrons took the song out and sang it in the street, where respectable ladies would hear it and then rush to buy the song sheet to play it at home. Edward B. Marks, *They All Sang, From Tony Pastor to Rudy Vallee* (New York: Viking, 1934), 3, 8, 38, 59–62, 129–34.

42. Jennings, 395–404. Alvin Harlow, *The Serene Cincinnatians* (New York: Dutton, 1950), 264, indicated that Cincinnati's saloon entertainment was concentrated on Vine Street and that the neighboring Germans were not pleased.

43. Jennings, 401.

44. Jennings, 281–3, 291–4, 398–400, 403–4. See Gilfoyle, 173–4, for similar stories of prostitutes in "panel houses" fleecing customers.

Chapter 8. Vaudeville, Incorporated

1. Laurence Senelick, "Variety into Vaudeville, The Process Observed in Two Manuscript Gagbooks," *Theatre Survey* 19:1 (May 1978), 1–15. On turns in vaudeville, see Parker Zellars, "Tony Pastor: Manager and Impresario of the American Variety Stage" (Ph.D., University of Iowa, 1964), 184.

2. Robert W. Snyder, *Voices of the City: Vaudeville and Popular Culture in New York* (Oxford University Press, 1989); Frederick Snyder, "American Vaudeville – Theater in a package" (Ph.D., Yale University, 1970); Vera Moorhouse, "Benjamin Franklin Keith: Vaudeville Magnate" (MA thesis, Eastern Michigan University, 1975); William Marston and John Feller, *F. F. Proctor: Vaudeville Pioneer* (New York: Richard R. Smith, 1943).

3. Robert Grau, *The Businessman in the Amusement World* (New York: Broadway Publishing, 1910), 109. *Equity Magazine* counted 62 big-time and 800 small-time houses in 1923. See Gregory Waller, *Mainstreet Amusements: Movies and Commercial Entertainment in a Southern City, 1896–1930* (Washington, DC: Smithsonian Institution Press, 1995), 202.

4. Marston and Feller, 109–10; Eddie Shayne, *Down Front on the Aisle* (Denver: Parkway Publishing, 1929), 12–25. Also see Percy William, "The Headliner and the Box Office," *Variety* (December 12, 1908), 20;

Grau, *The Businessman in the Amusement World* (1910), 112; Raymond Calkins, *Substitutes for the Saloon* (Boston: Houghton Mifflin, 1901), 22–23; Robert W. Snyder, 83, 192 n4; Bill Smith, *The Vaudevillians* (New York: MacMillan, 1976), 7–8. *Variety* reporter Bill Smith defined big-time at the turn of the century as two shows a day (matinee and evening) in good theaters with a large orchestra; small time meant four or five shows a day in lodge halls, storefronts, riverboats, or wagon shows, with music by a pianist. On small-time as a mix of movies and vaudeville, see Chapter 10.

5. See Chapter 5 on matinee, and Zachary Bloomfield, "Deacon's Theater: The Boston Museum" (Ph.D., University of Missouri, 1991), 148–223, on Kimball's strategies.

6. Moorehouse, 40–44, 49, 52; quote from *Keith News* (September 19, 1904), 3. Continuous vaudeville provided flexibility of schedule for the viewer, somewhat like the VCR did for TV viewing.

7. Moorhouse, 66, 77–8; Robert Snyder, 29; Shirley Staples, *Male-Female Comedy Teams in American Vaudeville, 1865–1932* (Ann Arbor: UMI Research Press, 1984), 78, on *Dramatic Mirror*.

8. Staples, 76; "The Gallery Gods Must be Suppressed," *Philadelphia Inquirer Halftone Magazine* (October 5, 1902), 3. He squelched the gallery gods in Providence too. See Moorhouse, 73–4.

9. "The Girl Behind the Pen," *Keith News*, various columns from September 5, 1904 to November 20, 1916. Keith/Albee Collection, University of Iowa Library. Thanks to Alison Kibler for bringing these to my attention.

10. Moorhouse, 88ff, 115; Douglas Gomery, *Shared Pleasures: A History of Movie Presentation in the United States* (Madison, WI: University of Wisconsin Press, 1992).

11. Marston and Feller, 48, on judge; 75, 79, on rest. *Journal* quote from New York Public Library Theater Collection, Tony Pastor scrapbook. Keith's Union Square theater also catered to shoppers, according to Robert Grau, *The Businessman in the Amusement World*, 108. Marston, 49–51, claimed the theater was so safe some parents sent their children there all day unescorted.

12. Marston, 158–9; Moorhouse, 50.

13. Leavitt, 196.

14. Leavitt, 198; Douglas Gilbert, *American Vaudeville: Its Life and Times* (New York: Dover, 1940), 198, 218–23, 228–30; Frederick Snyder, 35–8.

15. Frederick Snyder, 45ff; also Caroline Caffin, *Vaudeville, the Book* (New York: Mitchell Kennerly, 1914), 10; Percy Williams, 20. Robert Snyder, 66, 68, suggests there was less standardization and more variation of the bill from theater to theater.

16. "Decay of Vaudeville," *American Magazine* (April 1910), 846, on shock and Jolson; *Dramatic Mirror* cited in John DeMeglio, *Vaudeville, U.S.A.* (Bowling Green, OH: Bowling Green University Press, 1973), 52; similarly Robert O. Bartholomew, "Report of Censorship of Motion Pictures and of Investigation of Motion Picture Theaters of Cleveland" (Cleveland, OH: City of Cleveland, 1913), 13–14.

17. Michael Davis, "The Exploitation of Pleasure," 32; "Decay of Vaudeville," *American Magazine* (1910), 840; Arthur Swan, "Vaudevillitis and Its Cure," *The Drama*, 2:5 (February 1912), 209–18; Louis Reeves Harrison, "Is 'Vodeveal' Necessary?" *Moving Picture World* 8:14 (April 8, 1911), 758–60. These criticisms contrast starkly with the nostalgic descriptions of the old days in reminiscences by vaudevillians in the 1930s, 1940s, and 1950s after the demise of vaudeville.
18. "Decay of Vaudeville," *American Magazine* (April 1910); Caffin, 10–12.
19. Blacks in vaudeville audiences were rare according to interviews by Robert W. Snyder, 192, and DeMeglio, 109–18; also Helen Armstead-Johnson, "Blacks in Vaudeville: Broadway and Beyond," in Myron Matlaw, ed., *American Popular Entertainment* (Westport, CT: Greenwood Press, 1977), 85, on segregation. Mary Carbine, "The Finest Outside the Loop: Motion Picture Exhibition in Chicago's Black Metropolis," *Camera Obscura* n23 (May 1990), 21–22, mentions a separate black circuit, the Theater Owner's Booking Association formed in 1909.
20. See Appendix on prices.
21. Staples, 127–8; Hartley Davis, "In Vaudeville," *Everybody's Magazine* 13 (August 1905), 235.
22. Edwin Royle, "The Vaudeville Theatre," *Scribner's Magazine* 26 (1899), 487; Caffin, 16, 18; Elbert Hubbard, *In the Spotlight* (East Aurora, NY: Roycrofters, 1917), 20. On Hubbard, see William Leach, *Land of Desire: Merchants, Power and the Rise of a New American Culture* (New York: Pantheon, 1993), 41.
23. Hubbard, 20; Alison Kibler, *Rank Ladies: Gender and Cultural Hierarchy in American Vaudeville* (Chapel Hill, NC: University of North Carolina Press, 1999), 81.
24. Kibler, 91.
25. Kibler, 93–4.
26. George M. Cohan and George Jean Nathan, "The Mechanics of Emotion" *McClure* (November, 1913) 95–96, on "mechanics"; Henry Jenkins, *What Made Pistachio Nuts: Early Sound Comedy and the Vaudeville Aesthetic* (New York: Columbia University Press, 1992), 32–7, 73.
27. Mary Cass Canfield, "The Great American Art," *New Republic* 32 (November 22, 1922), 355, on artifical intimacy; Jenkins, 77, on "plants."
28. Cyrus T. Brady, "A Vaudeville Turn," *Scribner's Magazine* 30 (1901), 351–355.
29. On knowingness in British music hall, see Peter Bailey, "Conspiracies of Meaning: Music Hall and the Knowingness of Popular Culture," *Past and Present* 144 (August 1994), 138–70.
30. Robert W. Snyder, 125; Gilbert, 218, 216.
31. Grau, *The Businessman in the Amusement World*, 242–5, claimed amateur night began in the Bowery around 1890 at Miner's, that better theaters who had introduced it stopped around 1910 when it spread to "thousands of lower-grade houses." Also DeMeglio, ch. 6.
32. Caffin, 20; DeMeglio, 65–7. Elbert Hubbard, 13, related a story of an amateur night in a Chicago theater. A Miss Cummings began to sing terribly

when "from the gallery came a foghorn voice, 'This isn't Miss Cummings; this is Miss Gings! Back to the Garden, Violet, back to the Garden!'"
33. Kibler, 92.
34. Kibler, 101–8.
35. Bartholomew, 14–15.
36. DeMeglio, 181, 186, 187. For a variation of the Groucho story, see Charles and Louise Samuels, *Once Upon a Stage: The Merry World of Vaudeville* (New York: Dodd, Mead, 1974), 143. Performers did not always take criticism well. When a Sharon, PA audience was unsympathetic to Eva Tanguay's dispute with the manager, she called them "a lot of small town saps." See Samuels, 62.
37. On the Cherry Sisters, see Anthony Slide, ed., *Selected Vaudeville Criticism* (Metuchen, NJ: Scarecrow Press, 1988), 46, and DeMeglio, 184.
38. On college students, see DeMeglio, 176–7, 182, 42–3; Samuels, 59; "Now the City is Football Mad" *New York Herald* (November 30, 1893), 5.

Chapter 9. "Legitimate" and "Illegitimate" Theater Around the Turn of the Century

1. Influential critics referred to the star, Mrs. Leslie Carter's acting as "hysterical theatrics" and "mechanical." Garff Wilson, *Three Hundred Years of American Drama and Theatre* (Englewood Cliffs, NJ: Prentice Hall, 1973), 294–5.
2. Walter Prichard Eaton, "The Insurgent Public," *American Magazine* (April 1912), 744–753; Rachel Crothers, "Four Kinds of Audiences," *Drama Magazine* 10 (May 1920), 273; Adele Heller and Lois Rudnick, eds., *1915, The Cultural Moment: The New Politics, the New Woman, the New Psychology, the New Art, and the New Theatre in America* (New Brunswick, NJ: Rutgers University Press, 1991). The movement had a social-reform as well as artistic branch, but both thought in terms of cultural hierarchy and of drama as art.
3. On usage of the term, see "The Variety Theatres," *New York Mirror* (January 18, 1879), 4; *Autobiography of Joseph Jefferson*, Alan S. Downer, ed. (Cambridge, MA: Harvard University Press, 1964), 50 n7; Lawrence Levine, *High Brow/Low Brow: The Emergence of Cultural Hierarchy in America* (Cambridge, MA: Harvard University Press, 1988), 75–6; *Oxford English Dictionary* (London: Oxford University Press, 1971), 1600. Jefferson also defined "legitimate comedian" as one who played "characters in old English and Shakespearean comedies." See *Autobiography of Joseph Jefferson*, 312.
4. Walter Prichard Eaton, "Women as Theater-Goers," *Woman's Home Companion* 37 (October 1910), 13.
5. Clayton Hamilton, "The Psychology of Theatre Audiences," *The Forum* 39 (October 1907), 236–8, 245.
6. "Up in the Theatre Gallery," New York Public Library, Billy Rose Theater Collection, clipping file: audience-theater-gallery.

7. David Carroll, *The Matinee Idols* (New York: Arbor House, 1972), 12, 15.
8. "The Matinee Girl," *Munsey's* 18 (October 1897), 38.
9. For example, plays *The Matinee Hero* (1918), *A Matinee Idol* (1910), *The Matinee Girl* (1926); "Matinee Hero Worship" (illustration) *Vanity Fair* (November 1899); E. MacCaulley, "His Matinee Girl," *Lippincott's Monthly Magazine* 71 (May 1903), 702–5.
10. Carroll, 16; Mrs. Richard Mansfield, "Metropolitan Audiences," *Cosmopolitan* 36 (April 1904), 667–9; Juliet Thompkins, "The Brutality of the Matinee Girl," *Lippincott's Monthly Magazine* 80 (November 1907), 687–8; George Jenks, "When Mabel Meets the Actors," *The Theatre* 18 (August 1913), 48, viii; "Hugged the Handsome Tenor," (illustration), theater audience file, Bettman Archive.
11. "The Theatre as it Is To-day," *Ladies' Home Journal* 16 (October 1899), 18.
12. Edward Bok, "The Young Girl at the Matinee," *Ladies' Home Journal* 20 (June 1903), 161.
13. "The Matinee Girl," *Munsey's* 18 (October 1897), 39.
14. *The Morning Telegraph* [title unclear] (February 25, 1901), 2, and editorial (February 27, 1901), 6. On "nervous prostration," see Carroll Smith-Rosenberg, "The Hysterical Woman," in *Disorderly Conduct: Visions of Gender in Victorian America* (New York: Oxford University Press, 1985), 197–216.
15. On women's magazines, see John Tebbel and Mary Ellen Zuckerman, *The Magazine in America, 1741–1990* (New York: Oxford University Press, 1991), chs. 4 and 9. On mass culture, see Andreas Huyssen, "Mass Culture as Woman: Modernism's Other," in Tania Modleski, ed., *Studies in Entertainment: Critical Approaches to Mass Culture* (Bloomington: Indiana University Press, 1986), 188–207; Tania Modleski, "Femininity as Mas(s)querade: A Feminist Approach to Mass Culture," in Colin MacCabe, ed., *High Theory/Low Culture: Analyzing Popular Television and Film* (Manchester, UK: Manchester University Press, 1986).
16. Alfred Ayers, "Players and Playgoers," *Theatre Magazine* 1:6 (August 1901), 16; "The Latter-Day Audience: Its Characteristics and Habits," *Harper's Weekly* 46 (May 17, 1902), 632; "Music Art and the Drama," *Current Literature* 34 (January 1903), 65; Winthrop Ames, "The Ills of the Theatre," *Theatre Magazine* 24 (July 1916), 2, 41; Clayton Hamilton, "The Psychology of Theatre Audiences," *Forum* 39 (October 1907), 234–48; and "Emotional Contagion in the Theatre," *The Bookman* (April 1914), 139–47.
17. "Rudeness in the Theatre," *Theater Magazine* 7 (August 1907), iii, reprinted from the *New York Times*.
18. Hamilton, "Emotional Contagion in the Theatre" 141; "The Stage," *Munsey's* (December 1910), 404; Mrs. Richard Mansfield, "Metropolitan Audiences," *Cosmopolitan* 36 (April 1904), 667–76; "The Latter-Day Audience: Its Characteristics and Habits," *Harper's Weekly* 46 (May 17, 1902), 632.
19. Rachel Crowther, "Four Kinds of Audiences," 273–5.

20. Harriet Fish cartoons in Dorothy Parker, et. al., *High Society* (New York: G. P. Putnam's Sons, 1920), 4–5, 16–17, 48–9, 54.
21. Articles from *Theater Magazine* are Harriet Kent, "After the Play is Over," 28 (November 1918), 286; Lisle Bell, "Look Around Now," 35 (March 1922), 148; F. A. Austin, "The Playgoers," 36 (July 1922), 16. For cartoons, see *Theater Magazine* 36 (August 1922), 78; 39 (January 1924), 8, 25; 40 (August 1924), 29; 42 (December, 1925), 11.
22. "William Faversham Wants to Know What Has Become of the Gallery God"; "The Gallery Gods Have Made Way for Second Balcony Goddesses," clipping file: audience-theater-gallery, New York Public Library, Billy Rose Theater Collection, both circa 1910.
23. For sex ratio, see Michael Davis, *Exploitation of Pleasure* (New York: Russell Sage Foundation, 1910), 37. For Shubert survey, see "The Gallery Gods Have Made Way for Second Balcony Goddesses."
24. "The Gallery Gods Must be Suppressed," *Philadelphia Inquirer Magazine* (October 5, 1902), 3. About the only criticism after that was by Winthrop Ames who, perhaps bitter at the failure of his Little Theater, blamed the "ills of the Theatre" on the growing presence in the audience of the "lower middle class' taxi drivers and such" who had become theater's "great, new, eager, childlike, tasteless, honest, crude, general public" (1916, 41). In 1893 the *Atlanta Journal* complained of the same gallery pranks there. See Howard Goodson, "South of the North, North of the South" (Ph.D., Emory University, 1995), 51.
25. Mrs. Richard Mansfield, "Metropolitan Audiences," 667–76. See Barnard Hewitt, *Theatre U.S.A. 1665 to 1957* (New York: McGraw-Hill, 1959), 280, on Richard Mansfield's reform efforts. Actor David Warfield, whose characterization of a Jewish immigrant made him famous, defended the old gallery. He contrasted the gallery to the boxes, sympathetically describing the galleries' sense of humanity and justifying their desire to hiss the villain. See David Warfield, "The Top Gallery vs. The Boxes," *The Independent* 54 (February 27, 1902), 503–6.
26. Arthur Pollock, "What the Gallery Wants," *Harper's Weekly* 59 (October 24, 1914), 401.
27. F. C. Russell, "Confessions of a Gallery God," *Theatre Magazine* 30 (December 1919), 378; W. Lee Dickson, "The Audience Upstairs," *Theatre Magazine* 32 (September 1920), 100.
28. "Mr. Aborn on the Gallery," *New York Times* (January 23, 1921), VI 1; "The Good Old Gallery," *New York Times* (February 20, 1921), VI 1; "The Turning Worm," (September 19, 1926), IX 2.
29. Howard Barnes, "Bringing Back the Gods to the Top Gallery," *Herald Tribune* (September 23, 1928), VII 2, 4; F. Kleber, "Gallery Maxims," *New York Dramatic Mirror* (April 15, 1916), 4, excused the boy's antics.
30. "Hissing the Villains in Hoboken," *Literary Digest* (April 6, 1929), 24–25.
31. On Progressive reformers and working-class leisure, see Dominick Cavallo, *Muscles and Morals: Organized Playgrounds and Urban Reform, 1880–1920* (Philadelphia: University of Pennsylvania Press, 1981); Paul Boyer, *Urban Masses and Moral Order in America,*

1820–1920 (Cambridge, MA: Harvard University Press, 1978); Cary Goodman, *Choosing Sides: Playgrounds and Street Life on the Lower East Side* (New York: Schocken Books, 1979); Steve Hardy, *How Boston Played: Sport, Recreation and Community, 1865–1915* (Boston: Northeastern University Press, 1982). Another discourse, stemming from the Eugenics movement of the time, was not so kind about working-class audiences. See Henry Jenkins, *What Made Pistacio Nuts: Sound Comedy and the Vaudeville Aesthetic* (New York: Columbia University Press, 1992), 28–32.

32. Elizabeth McCracken, "The Play and the Gallery," *Atlantic* 89 (April 1902), 497–507; Jane Addams, *The Spirit of Youth and the City Streets* (New York: MacMillan, 1912), 89; Mrs. Richard Mansfield, 674; also Bessie Van Vorst, *The Woman Who Toils: Being the Experiences of Two Ladies as Factory Girls* (New York: Doubleday, Page, 1903), 93–4.

33. "Rudeness in the Theatre" reprinted from the *New York Times;* Annie Marion MacLean, *Wage-Earning Women* (New York: MacMillan, 1910), 52, 83, 137; Lester Scott, "Play-Going for Working People," *New Boston* (1915), 237–41.

34. James McCabe, *Light and Shadows* (1872), 481. A recurring image in descriptions of working-class audiences is the mother and infant, representing perhaps the earthiness and the "prolific breeding" believed to typify the lower classes. It never appears in descriptions of middle or upper-class audiences. Thanks to Robert Zecker and Alison Kibler both for bringing this image to my attention.

35. Channing Pollock, *The Footlights Fore and Aft* (Boston: Gorham Press, 1911), 378–93; also see "The Bowery Theatres," *Harper's Weekly* (May 10, 1890), 370–2; see Frank Rahill, *The World of Melodrama* (Pennsylvania State University Press, 1967), 274–5, on the dispersion of cheap theaters across the city.

36. On other ethnic theaters, see Maxine Seller, *Ethnic Theater in the U.S.* (Westport, CT: Greenwood Press, 1983). Michael Davis excluded German theater from his review of ethnic theater on the grounds that their plays were of "literary significance" (35). Non-English sources constitute another potentially revealing discourse, but the limits of this study do not allow such pursuit. For use of such sources, see, e.g., Robert Zecker, "'All Our Own Kin': The Creation of a Slovak-American Community in Philadelphia, 1890–1945" (Ph.D., University of Pennsylvania, 1998).

37. Chinese audiences exhibited similarities to – and some differences from – European immigrant audiences. Chinese entertainments arrived in San Francisco in the 1850s. These included puppet shows performed on the street, acrobats, orchestras, and theater troupes. See George MacMinn, *Theater of the Golden Era in California* (Caldwell, ID: Caxton Printers, 1941), 504; Benjamin E. Lloyd, *Lights and Shades in San Francisco* (San Francisco: A. L. Bancroft, 1876), 265–6; John Jenning, *Theatrical and Cirus Life* (St. Louis: Sun Publishing, 1882), 344; Michael Davis, 35.

38. John Corbin, "How the Other Half Laughs," *Harper's Weekly* 30, 31, 36; A. Richard Sogliuzzo, "Notes for a History of the Italian American Theatre

of New York," *Theatre Survey* 14:2 (November 1973), 59–75; Emelise Aleandri and Maxine Schwartz Seller, "Italian-American Theatre," in Seller, 237–76.

39. Giuseppe Cautella, "The Bowery," *American Mercury* 9:35 (November 1926), 365–8.

40. Seller, 266; Carl Van Vechten, "A Night with Farfariello," *Theatre Magazine* 29 (January 1919), 32, 34; Deanna Paoli Gumina, *"Connazionali, Stenterello,* and *Farfariello:* Italian Variety theater in San Francisco," *California Historical Quarterly* 54 (Spring 1975), 29–36.

41. Aleandri and Seller, in Seller, 249–50; J. M. Scanlan, "An Italian Quarter Mosaic," *Overland Monthly* 47 (April 1906), 327–34.

42. Victor Rousseau, "A Puppet Play which Lasts Two Months," *Harper's Weekly* (October 3, 1908), 15–16. Behavior of immigrants was much like that of their compatriots back in Sicily. See Isabel Emerson, "The Sicilian Marionettes," *The Contemporary Review* [London] 137 (1930), 369–72.

43. *Current Literature* 27 (January 1900), 3–4 (quoted from the *Brooklyn Eagle*); Victor Rousseau, 15–16.

44. Rousseau; Lois Adler, "Sicilian Puppets," *Drama Review* 2:2 (June 1976), 25–30, and "Mulberry Dolls," *The Stage* (April 1933).

45. Diane Cypkin, "Second Avenue: The Yiddish Broadway" (Ph.D, New York University, 1986), 62–3; David Lifson, *The Yiddish Theatre in America* (New York: Thomas Yoseloff, 1965), 169; "The Theatre of the Ghetto," *Theatre Magazine* 21 (February 1915), 91; Hershel Zohn, *The Story of the Yiddish Theatre* (Las Cruces, NM: Zohn, 1979), 63; Marvin Seiger, "A History of the Yiddish Theatre in New York City to 1892," (Ph.D., Indiana University, 1960), 180–3; Irving Howe, *World of Our Fathers* (New York: Harcourt Brace Jovanovich, 1976), 460–96; quote from Hutchins Hapgood, *The Spirit of the Ghetto* (New York: Fund & Wagnall, 1902), 116.

46. Hutchins Hapgood, 118; Annie Marion MacLean, *Wage-Earning Women* (New York: MacMillan, 1910), 52, on Jewish girls' attendance; John Corbin, 39, 47, on girls' income and family expenditure on theater.

47. Hutchins Hapgood, 115; "The Spectator," *The Outlook* 79 (March 1905), 522.

48. Sandrow, 101–2, on *patriotten* and funeral of Mogulesko; "The Theatre of the Ghetto," *Theatre Magazine* 91, on Adler's fans.

49. Nahma Sandrow, *Vagabond Stars: A History of Yiddish Theater* (New York: Harper and Row, 1977), 94; Lifson, *The Yiddish Theatre,* 175; Cypkin, 36; Howe, 484, quoting complaint; Carl Van Vecten, *In the Garret* (New York: Knopf, 1920), 325.

50. Zohn, 49.

51. Corbin, 38; Hutchins Hapgood, 116; "The Theatre of the Ghetto," *Theatre Magazine* 91; "The Spectator," *The Outlook* 79 (March 1905), 522; Sandrow, 92.

52. *Outlook 79,* 522, Hapgood, 115, on organizational benefits; Corbin, 38, on curtain call; Sandrow, 102–3, on blurring line between actor and character.

53. Sandrow, 102, on Lear and Feinman incidents; "The Theatre of the Ghetto," *Theatre Magazine,* on fainting.

54. Michael Davis, 35–36. This combined with the rapid turnover of populations in neighborhoods, the many alternative "stimuli" New York offered, and licensing ordinances that disadvantaged the small theaters. Similarly, John Corbin, in 1899, thought that the Italians assimilated so quickly, speaking mostly in English even in the Italian theater, that they soon left behind this ethnic entertainment. See "How the Other Half Laughs," 30–48. See W. I. Thomas and Florian Znanzieki, *The Polish Peasant in Europe and America, 1918–1920* (Chicago: University of Chicago Press, 1918), on the second-generation immigrants' disenchantment with their ethnic identity and desire for assimilation.

55. William Slout, *Theater in a Tent: The Deveolpment of a Provincial Entertainment* (Bowling Green, OH: Bowling Green University Popular Press, 1972), ch. 1; Marian Spitzer, "Ten-Twenty-Thirty: The Passing of the Popular Circuit," *Saturday Evening Post* (August 22, 1935), 40–41, 48; Arthur Ruhl, "Ten-Twenty-Thirty," *The Outlook* 98 (August 19, 1911), 886–91.

56. Slout, 51–5; Spitzer, 40; Ray Henderson, "The Other Hundred Million," *Theater Guild* (June 1931), 9–11. On the death of touring companies, see Thomas Gale Moore, *The Economics of the American Theater* (Durham, NC: Duke University Press, 1968), 95–101; Jack Poggi, *Theater in America: The Impact of Economic Forces, 1870–1967* (Ithaca: Cornell University Press, 1968), ch. 2; and Alfred Bernheim, *The Business of the Theatre: An Economic History of the American Theatre, 1750–1932* (New York: Benjamin Blom, 1932), chs. 16 and 17.

57. *Report of the Committee of the Senate upon the Relations Between Labor and Capital*, vol. I, *Testimony* (Washington, DC: U.S. Government Printing Office, 1885), 47.

58. William Dillon, *Life Doubles in Brass* (Ithaca: The House of Nollid, 1944), 45; Lewin Goff, "The Popular Priced Melodrama in America, 1890–1910" (Ph.D., Western Reserve University, 1948), 155, on Brooklyn; Porter Emerson Browne, "The Mellowdrammer," *Everybody's Magazine* (September 1909), 354.

59. Goff, 146–53; Browne, 349–50; Roy Rosenzweig, *Eight Hours for What We Will* (London: Cambridge University Press, 1983), 200–1.

60. Dillon, 50–53.

61. Mary Shaw, "The Psychology of the Audience," *Saturday Evening Post* (February 18, 1911), 6–7, 25.

62. *Trenton Times* (April 12, 1904); Dillon, 43, 59.

63. Calkins (1901), 172–3; Michael Davis (1910). See also David Nasaw, *Going Out: The Rise and Fall of Public Amusements* (Basic Books, 1993), ch. 4, for other quotes and also for a current confirmation of the opinion that cheap theaters were a benefit to the working classes. Also see In the *New York Times*, criticizing the "legit" audience: "Why they Attend" (April 29, 1923) VII 1; "The Audience Performs" (January 9, 1921) VI 1; "The Barkless Audience" (December 3, 1921) 12; "Audience Criticized" (January 3, 1922) 16.

64. On the natural man in American culture, see Richard Slotkin, *Gunfighter Nation: The Myth of the Frontier in Twentieth Century America* (New York: Atheneum, 1992), ch. 1. With the closing of the frontier, the working class became a surrogate for the savage and the frontiersman, the new "natural man," just as the struggle between civilization and savage had been a surrogate for European class struggles.

Chapter 10. The Celluloid Stage: Nikelodeon Audiences

1. Gordon Hendricks, *The Kinetoscope* (New York: Beginnings of the American Film Press, 1966), 64–9.
2. Sherman Kingsley, "The Penny Arcade and the Cheap Theatre," *Charities and the Commons* 18 (June 8, 1907), 295–7; John Collier, "Cheap Amusements," *Survey* 20 (April 11, 1908), 75; "Penny Arcades," *Outlook* (October 26, 1912), 376–7; Benjamin Hampton, *A History of the Movies* (New York: Covici-Friede, 1931), 17.
3. Hendricks, 143; "Penny Arcades," *Outlook* (October 26 1912), 376.
4. *Complete Illustrated Catalog of Moving Picture Machines* (Chicago: Kleine Optical Co., 1905), 206–7; Charles Musser, *The Emergence of Cinema: The American Screen to 1907* (Berkeley: University of California Press, 1990), 116–18, 122–9, 183–7.
5. Robert Grau, *The Business Man in the Amusement World* (New York: Broadway Publishing, 1910), 108–10; Robert C. Allen, "Vaudeville and Film, 1895–1915" (Ph.D., University of Iowa, 1977), esp. 161–2. Musser, 276, and Garth Jowett, *Film, the Democratic Art: A Social History of American Film* (Boston: Little, Brown, 1976), 29 n33, differ with Allen.
6. "Nickel Vaudeville," *Variety* (March 17, 1906), 4; "Moving Pictures," *Billboard* 18:41 (October 13, 1906), 21; "The Nickelodeon," *The Moving Picture World and View Photographer* 1:9 (May 7, 1907), 140; Kenneth MacGowan, *Behind the Screen: The History and Technique of the Motion Picture* (New York: Dell, 1965), 129, on number of nickelodeons; Douglas Gomery, *Shared Pleasures: A History of Movie Presentation in the United States* (Madison: University of Wisconsin Press, 1992), 22–9, Gregory Waller, *Main Street Amusements: Movies and Commerical Entertainment in a Southern City, 1896–1930* (Washington, DC: Smithsonian Institution Press, 1995), and Katherine Fuller, *At the Picture Show: Small Town Audiences and the Creation of the Movie Fan* (Washington, DC: Smithsonian Institution Press, 1996), on small towns.
7. George Pratt, *Spellbound in Darkness: A History of Silent Film* (Greenwich, CT: New York Graphic Society, 1973), 44–6, on morning-to-night hours; MacGowan, 130, on film length; Robart Sklar, *Movie-Made America: A Cultural History of American Movies* (New York: Vintage, 1975), 17, on projector quality.
8. Film historians continue to dispute the makeup of the nickelodeon audience. See Robert Sklar, "*Oh Althusser:* Historiography and the Rise of Cinema Studies," in Sklar and Charles Musser, eds., *Resisting Images: Essays on Cinema and History* (Philadelphia: Temple University Press,

1990), 12–35; Ben Singer, "Mahattan Nickelodeons: New Data on Audiences and Exhibitors," *Cinema Journal* 35:3 (Spring 1995), 5–35; Robert C. Allen, "Manhattan Myopia; or Oh! Iowa!" *Cinema Journal* 6:3 (Spring 1996), 75–128; and Steven Ross, *Working-Class Hollywood: Silent Film and the Shaping of Class in America* (Princeton, NJ: Princeton University Press, 1998).

9. For debate on location, see Ben Singer, "Manhattan Nickelodeons"; Robert C. Allen, "Manhattan Myopia"; Douglas Gomery, "Movie Audiences, Urban Geography, and the History of the American Film," *The Velvet Light Trap* 19 (Spring 1982), 23–29. Michael Davis, *The Exploitation of Pleasure* (New York: Russell Sage Foundation, 1910), 30, and Charles Stelzle, "How 1000 Working Men Spend Their Spare Time," *Outlook* (April 4, 1914), 762, found movies very popular among working men.

10. Annie Marion MacLean, *Wage-Earning Women* (New York: MacMillan, 1910), 143–53, on Pennsylvania mining towns; Margaret Byington, *Homestead: The Households of a Mill Town* (New York: Charities Publication Committee, 1909), 40; see also Roy Rosenzweig, *Eight Hours for What We Will: Workers and Liesure in an Industrial City, 1870–1920* (Cambridge, UK: Cambridge University Press, 1983), 193.

11. Handbook quote in Robert Sklar, *Movie Made America*, 16.

12. On smell, see Raymond Fosdick, "Report on Motion Picture Theatres of Greater New York," (March 22, 1911); Elaine Bowser, *The Tranformation of the Cinema, 1907–1915* (Berkeley: University of California Press, 1990), 1, for quote from *Moving Picture World*.

13. Bowser, 122–3, on Audubon Theater.

14. Alan Havig, "The Commercial Amusement Audience in Early Twentieth-Century American Cities," *Journal of American Culture* 5 (Spring 1982), 1–19; Musser, 425, on shoppers.

15. Robert Merritt, "Nickelodeon Theaters 1905–1914," in Tino Balio, ed., *The American Film Industry*, rev. ed. (Madison: University of Wisconsin Press, 1985), 68, on Boston; Paul Swan, "Jules Mastbaum and the Philadelphia Picture Palaces," in Vincent Mosco and Janet Wasko, eds., *Popular Culture and Media Events* (Norwood, NJ: Ablex, 1985), 28, on Philadelphia; Douglas Gomery, "Saxe Amusement Enterprises," *Milwaukee History* 2:1 (Spring 1979), 18–28; Allen, "Vaudeville and Film" and Kathy Peiss, *Cheap Amusements: Working Woman and Leisure in Turn-of-the-Century New York* (Philadelphia: Temple University Press, 1986), on New York City; Gomery, "The Movie Palace Comes to America's Cities," in Richard Butsch, ed., *For Fun and Profit: The Transformation of Leisure into Consumption* (Philadelphia: Temple University Press, 1990), 136–51; Musser, 421–4, on Chicago; "Recreational Survey of Cincinnati" (Cincinnati: Juvenile Protective Association, 1913), 26.

16. Wagenknecht, 12–24; on Lawndale, see Peter d'A. Jones and Melvin G. Holli, *Ethnic Chicago* (Grand Rapids MI: William Eerdmans, 1981), 64–71. Thanks to Liz Cohen for identifying the class and ethnic makeup

of Lawndale. For numerous quotes of people similarly remembering their childhood moviegoing, see Gregg Paul Bachman, "The Last of the Silent Generation: Oral Histories of Silent Movie Patrons" (Ph.D., Union Institute Cincinnati, Ohio, 1995).

17. Kathryn Fuller, *At the Picture Show*.

18. Bowser, 37, on Northwest, 122, on broad clientele. The mixed classes no doubt led to different dynamics within the audience and within the theater, than at neighborhood nickelodeons in large cities with homogeneous audiences.

19. Merritt, 69, on relative profitability.

20. On stage versus movies, see Jowett, 35–8.

21. On legal history of movie house segregation, see Robert McKay, "Segregation and Public Recreation," *Virginia Law Review* 40:6 (October 1954), 697–731; Max Turner and Frank Kennedy, "Exclusion, Ejection and Segregation of Theater Patrons," *Iowa Law Review* 32:4 (May 1947), 625–58.

22. Bowser, 9–10, for estimated numbers; Mary Carbine, "'Finest Outside the Loop': Motion Picture Exhibition in Chicago's Black Metropolis, 1905–1928," *Camera Obscura*, 23 (May 1990), 9–41; Gomery, *Shared Pleasures*, ch. 8; Fuller, *At the Picture Show*, 31–4, 38–9; Waller, 167 ch. 7; Fuller, *At the Picture Show*, 31–4.

23. Peiss, 148, on trade journal; Musser, 433, for Troy photo; Sklar and Musser, 23, photo; Peiss, 148, and Robert Bartholomew, "Report of Censorship of Motion Pictures" (Cleveland: City of Cleveland, 1913), 11, on baby carriages; Peiss, 150, on Mary Heaton Vorse quote. On women, see Peiss; Elizabeth Ewen, "City Lights: Immigrant Women and the Rise of the Movies," in Catherine Stimpson, Elsa Dixler, Martha Nelson, and Kathryn Yatrakis, eds., *Women and the American City* (Chicago: University of Chicago Press, 1981); Lauren Rabinowitz, "Temptations of Pleasure: Nickelodeons, Amusement Parks and the Sights of Female Sexuality," *Camera Obscura* 23 (May 1990), 72–89. Fuller, *At the Picture Show*, 35–41, notes that women's access in small towns varied by region and religious beliefs.

24. See recurring references to babies in Chapter 9.

25. Musser, 432, on Maine; Peiss, 150, on boys unescorted.

26. William Foster, "Vaudeville and Motion Picture Shows," Reed College Record No. 16 (September 1914), 17, 18, on Portland; Musser, 433, on Pittsburgh; Rowland Haynes, "Recreation Survey, Detroit, Michigan" (Detroit Board of Commerce, 1913), 15–16; "Madison Recreational Survey" (Madison Board of Commerce, 1915), 53–54; Raymond Fosdick, "Report on Motion Picture Theatres of Greater New York" (March 22, 1911); Bartholomew, 28, on Cleveland; Lauren Rabinovitz, 73, on Chicago; also Peiss, 151–3, on unchaperoned girls.

27. Elizabeth Ewen, "City Lights," 55.

28. "Recreation Survey of Cincinnati", (1913), 26–7; "Madison Recreational Survey," 52–5; also Rowland Haynes, "Recreation Survey, Detroit, Michigan" (1913).

29. Miriam Hansen, *Babel and Babylon: Spectatorship in American Silent Film* (Cambridge, MA: Harvard University Press, 1991), says, "the recently urbanized working class, new immigrants, and, overlapping with themes of class and ethnicity, women … had not previously been considered an audience in the sense of a 'viewing public'" (1991, 91). Jowett (1974, 48) said, "the large urban working class who seldom went anywhere near live theatrical entertainment." Judith Mayne, "Immigrants and Spectators," 5:2 *Wide Angle* (Summer, 1982), 38, said, "The earliest U.S. film viewers – urban, proletarian, immigrant – never before had been referred to as an audience."

30. Gomery, *Shared Pleasures*, 33, on decentralized production; Hansen (1991), 71, on ethnic films; Daniel Leab, "'All-Colored' – But Not Much Different: Films Made for Negro Ghetto Audiences, 1913–1928" *Phylon* 36:3 (September, 1975), 321–39, on black productions. The Motion Picture Patent Company formed in January 1909 and briefly held great power and potential, controlling the source of film stock from Eastman Kodak. But it quickly fell apart beginning in February 1911. See Bowser, 21, 31, 33. Musser (434–8) notes that 15 exchanges in Chicago by 1907 controlled 80 percent of rental business in the United States, but many more soon formed in many cities across the country.

31. "Recreational Survey of Cincinnati" and Jane Addams, *The Spirit of Youth and the City Streets,* (New York: Macmillan, 1912), 95, suggest movies displaced for children other activities and even "doing nothing"; also Ellen Wartella and Sharon Mazzarella, "A Historical Comparison of Children's Use of Leisure Time," in Richard Butsch, ed., *For Fun and Profit,* 173–94.

32. Michael Davis, 25–8, on New York; estimates for New York and Chicago in "The Moving Picture and the National Character," *American Review of Reviews* (September 1910), 315; Rowland Haynes, "Recreation Survey, Milwaukee, Wisconsin," (Milwaukee: Child Welfare Commission, 1912) 38–66.

33. Alfred Bernheim, *The Business of the Theatre* (New York: Benjamin Blom, 1932), 87; also Jowett, 36–7; Robert and Helen Merrill Lynd, *Middletown: A Study in Modern American Culture* (New York: Harcourt Brace, 1929), 263–5, indicated that movies significantly increased entertainment opportunities in the small city. The Opera House of the 1890s was often closed between shows, sometimes for a week or more, especially during the summer. By contrast, the nine movie houses in 1923 were open from one to eleven, seven days a week, winter and summer.

34. Robert E. Davis, "Response to Innovation; A Study of Popular Argument About New Mass Media" (Ph.D., University of Iowa, 1965), 55, on *Independent* quote; Havig on prewar attendance.

35. Lewis Palmer, "The World in Motion," *Survey* 22 (June 5, 1909), 356; Foster, "Vaudeville and Motion Picture Shows," 27–8; also Addams, *Spirit of Youth,* 85–6; Olivia Dunbar, "The Lure of the Movies," *Harper's Weekly,* 57 (January 18, 1913), 22; Rosenzweig, 201–3; Hansen, ch. 3, on nickelodeon as an alternative public sphere.

36. Bowser, 2, on Willamantic *Journal;* Stelzle, 162; Lynd, *Middletown,* 265; also Bartholomew, 7.

37. Elizabeth Fones Wolf, "Sound Comes to the Movies," *Pennsylvania Magazine* 118:1 (January 1994), 6, and Kozarski, 54–61.
38. Fones-Wolf (1994), 4–8, 12; Margolies and Gwathmey, *Ticket to Paradise* (1991); Gregg Paul Bachman, "The Last of the Silent Generation" quotes invariably indicate *female* piano players; Tim Anderson, "Reforming 'Jackass Music': The Problematic Aesthetics of Early American Film Music," *Cinema Journal* 37:1 (Fall 1997), 3–22.
39. Bowser, 15–18; Musser, 434, 440; Michael Davis, 24.
40. Francis Couvares and Daniel Czitrom, "Real Life? Movies and Audiences in Early Twentieth Century America," *Lowell Conference on Industrial History* (October 1985), 4, 22.
41. Lynd (1929), 265; Daniel Czitrom, "The Politics of Performance: From Theater Licensing to Movie Censorship," *American Quarterly* 44:4 (December 1992), 536–7, on 1907 recession; Day Allen Willie, "The Theatre's New Rival," *Lippincott's* 84 (October 1909), 458; *World's Work* (1910 and 1911), on closings cited by Robert E. Davis, "Response to Innovation," 467–8; Grau (1910), 172; Lary May, *Screening Out the Past: The Birth of Mass Culture and the Motion Picture Industry* (New York: Oxford University Press, 1980), 35, on *Daily Forward* quote; also see Walter Pritchard Eaton, "The Menace of the Movies," *American Magazine* 76 (September 1913), 58, and "Class Consciousness and the Movies," *Atlantic* (January 1915), 48–56.
42. Jack Poggi, *Theater in America: The Impact of Economic Forces* (Ithaca: Cornell University Press, 1968), 33–43; George Bevans, "How Working Men Spend Their Spare Time" (Ph.D., Columbia University, 1913), 37–43. For description of the impact of the decline of the road on particular cities, see Lynd, 40–1; Jerry Henderson, "Nashville in the Decline of Southern Legitimate Theater During the Beginning of the Twentieth Century," *Southern Speech Journal* 29 (Fall 1963), 26–33; and G. Harrison Orians, "History of the American Music Hall [Toledo]," *Northwest Ohio Quarterly* 36:4 (1964), 182–93. Theater in New York began to decline after 1925–27. See Poggi, 47, 49–51. Sound movies accelerated the decline. See Poggi, 56.
43. Poggi, 42–3; The Drama Committee, "The Amusement Situation in the City of Boston" (Boston: Twentieth Century Club, 1910), 5, 8, 10–11, 16–17.
44. Poggi, 78–84, on impact of movies on New York drama theater; Jowett, 31, on Loew.
45. Robert C. Allen, "Vaudeville and Film", 298–303; Jowett, 30–31; "The Decay of Vaudeville," *American Magazine* 69 (April 1910), 840–8; W. A. S. Douglass, "The Passing of Vaudeville," *American Mercury* (October 1927), 188–94.
46. Linda Gordon, *Heroes of Their Own Lives* (New York: Viking Press, 1988), ch. 2; Anthony Platt, *The Child-Savers: The Invention of Delinquency* (Chicago: University of Chicago Press, 1969), ch. 2.
47. See Ellen Wartella and Sharon Mazzarella, "A Historical Comparison of Children's Use of Leisure Time," in Butsch, 174–5, on new concept of ado-

lescence in relation to media use; Czitrom, "The Politics of Performance," Hansen, 63–8, on early criticism and censorship of movies.

48. Jane Addams, *Spirit of Youth* 86, 91–92; also Louise de Koven Bowen, "Five and Ten Cent Theatres" (Chicago: Juvenile Protection Association, 1910), a friend of Addams, claimed "children stood around [outside nickelodeons] pilfering or begging in order to obtain the price of admission" (p. 2).

49. Addams, 92, and Chicago Motion Picture Committee, "Report" (1920), 121–6, claimed movies made children nervous. This concern was voiced at the turn of the century about matinee plays and later about radio shows. See Chapters 9 and 13.

50. Addams, 93; Kingsley (1907); "In the Interpreter's House," *American Magazine* (August 1913), 92–5; Bartholomew, 23; R. E. Davis, 256–61, on other examples. A few articles in the mid-1910s began to challenge this view. See Barton Currie, "The Nickel Madness," *Harper's Weekly* 51 (August 24, 1907), 1246; Robert E. Davis, 260–1.

51. Bowser, 48–52; Czitrom, "The Politics of Performance," on development of censorship; Bartholomew, 27. Henry Spurr, "The Nickelodeons: A Boon and a Menace," *Case and Comment* 18:10 (March 1912), 571–2, on local laws on motion picture theaters.

52. Louise deKoven Bowen, "Five and Ten Cent Theatres," (Chicago: Juvenile Protective Association of Chicago, 1910), 3–5; Michael Davis, 34. Nevertheless the Board came under criticism and government boards were launched or proposed. After World War I the industry again stemmed the criticism by forming the Motion Picture Producers and Distributors Association and hiring Will Hays, former Postmaster General, to direct the industry's self-regulation, stressing the responsibility to children, which stemmed criticism until the late 1920s. See Robert E. Davis, 21–5.

53. "The White Slave Films: A Review," *Outlook* (February 14, 1914), 345–50; "'Movie' Manners and Morals," *Outlook* (July 26, 1916), 695.

54. Reverend H. A. Jump, "The Social Influence of the Moving Picture" (New York: Playground and Recreation Association of America, 1911); Maurice Willows, "The Nickel Theater," *Annals of the American Academy of Political and Social Science* (July 1911), 95–9; quote of Munsterberg in Garth Jowett, "Social Science as a Weapon: The Origins of the Payne Fund Studies, 1926–1929," *Communication* 13:3 (December 1992), 213.

55. Mrs. W. I. Thomas, "The Five Cent Theatre," *Proceedings of the National Conference of Charities and Corrections* (1910), 148; Michael Davis, 23; Bartholomew, 12; "In the Interpreter's House," *American Magazine*, 93; Michael Davis, 54, and Bartholomew, 8, on lurid posters.

56. Bowen, 2, 4–5, 9. For a brief history of amateur night, see Grau (1910), 242–6. Addams, (1912) described "amateur night" where children performed "stunts," for which, if they pleased the audience, they may be paid and given the address of a booking agent, falsely raising their hopes (p. 87). Boys and girls attended in groups and frequented the same theater each night in order to better their chances of being selected to perform on "amateur night" (pp. 80–1, 91).

57. Mrs. W. I. Thomas, 148.
58. Peiss, 152, on neighborhood institution; Michael Davis 24; Bartholomew, 13–15.
59. Revered H. A. Jump, 8.
60. "Madison Recreational Survey," 52, 54, 59; "Recreation Survey of Cincinnati," 27–9.
61. Adele Woodard, "Motion Pictures for Children," *Social Service Review* (September 1917), 10–11.
62. Jane Stannard Johnson, "Children and Their Movies," *Social Service Review* (September 1917), 11–12; Mrs. F. Michael, "Better Films," *Child Welfare Magazine* 12 (November 1917), 41–42; Richard DeCordova, "Ethnography and Exhibition: The Child Audience, The Hays Office and Saturday Matinees," *Camera Obscura* 23 (May 1990), 91–106.
63. On underlying class issues in Progressive reforms, see Linda Gordon, *Heroes of Their Own Lives;* Anthony Platt, *The Child Savers;* Sonya Michel, "The Limits of Maternalism," in Seth Koven and Sonya Michel, eds., *Mothers of the New World* (Routledge, 1993).
64. R. E. Davis, 234, for 1909 quote; "'Movie' Manners and Morals" (July 26, 1916), 694.
65. Mrs. W. I. Thomas, 147; "The White Slave Films: A Review, *Outlook* (February 1914), 345; also Robert E. Davis, 55ff, 134ff, 139ff, 142ff; Bowser, 38–9; Czitrom, 539.
66. On the class nature of Progressive reforms, see e.g., Paul Boyer, *Urban Mass and Moral Order in America* (Cambridge: Harvard University Press, 1978), part four; Cary Goodman, *Choosing Sides* (New York: Schocken, 1979), part one; Stephen Hardy, *How Boston Played* (Northeastern University Press, 1982), part two. On conservatives and lower-class immigrants, see e.g., Leon Kamin, *The Science and Politics of I.Q.* (Potomac, MD: Lawrence Erlbaum, 1974), ch. 2.

Chapter 11.   Storefronts to Theaters: Seeking the Middle Class

1. Charles Musser, *The Emergence of Cinema: The American Screen to 1907,* (Berkeley: University of California Press, 1990), 432–3; Lary May, *Screening Out the Past: The Birth of Mass Culture and the Motion Picture Industry* (New York: Oxford University Press, 1980), 27–36, 148ff; Elaine Bowser, *The Transformation of Cinema: 1907–1915,* (Berkeley: University of California Press, 1990), 42–3, 122ff.
2. Gregory Waller, *Main Street Amusements: Movies and Commercial Entertainment in a Southern City, 1896–1930* (Washington, DC: Smithsonian Institution Press, 1995), 68–9, 87–8; Douglas Gomery, "Saxe Amusement Enterprises: The Movies Come to Milwaukee," *Milwaukee History* 2:1 (Spring 1979), 23.
3. Roberta Pearson, "Cultivated Folks and the Better Classes: Class Conflict and Representation in Early American Film," *Journal of Popular Film and Television* 15:3 (Fall 1987), 124, on redecorating; Robert E. Davis, "Response to Innovation: A Study of Popular Argument about New Mass

Media" (Ph.D., University of Iowa, 1965), 466–8, on nickelodeon profits; Paul O'Malley, "Neighborhood Nickelodeons: Residential Theaters in South Denver from 1907 to 1917," *Colorado Heritage* 3 (1984), 49–58.

4. Robert C. Allen, "Vaudeville and Film, 1895–1915" (Ph.D., University of Iowa, 1977), 230.

5. Robert Grau, *The Theatre of Science* (New York: Benjamin Blom, 1969) [orig., 1914], 18–19, and Bosley Crowther, *The Lion's Share* (New York: Dutton, 1957), 19–32, on growth of Lowe chain; Robert C. Allen, "Vaudeville and Film," 238, on Shubert backing Loew.

6. Allen, "Vaudeville and Film," 244–6; Robert Grau, *The Businessman in the Amusement World* (New York: Broadway Publishing, 1910), 113–18; Gregory Waller, *Main Street Amusements*, 105.

7. Grau (1910), 113–18, and Grau (1914), 28–35, on Mr. Shepard; Lewis Palmer, "The World in Motion," *Survey* 22 (June 5, 1909), 359.

8. The Drama Committee, "The Amusement Situation in the City of Boston" (Boston: Twentieth Century Club, 1910), 5, 10–11; Robert Grau (1910), 118; Grau (1914), 18-19. On smaller cities, see Waller, *Main Street Amusements*, 106, 110; Douglas Gomery, "Movie Exhibition in Milwaukee," *Milwaukee History* 2:1 (Spring 1979), 8–17.

9. Allen, "Vaudeville and Film," 233, on Dewey Theater; Douglas Gomery, "Saxe Amusement Enterprises: The Movies Come to Milwaukee," *Milwaukee History* 2:1 (Spring 1979), 21–2; photograph of Bijou Dream in Palmer (1909), 355; Douglas Gomery, "History of the American Movie Palace," *Marquee* 6:2 (Spring 1984), 5–10, lists sources on these buildings. Cartoon from the *New Yorker* (February 23, 1929), 16. Robert Snyder, "Big Time, Small Time, All Around the Town: New York Vaudeville in the Early Twentieth Century," in Richard Butsch, ed., *For Fun and Profit: The Transformation of Leisure into Consumption* (Philadelphia: Temple University Press, 1990), 123, noted how vaudeville anticipated the movie palace, although the vaudeville palaces were smaller.

10. Douglas Gomery, "The Movie Palace Comes to America's Cities," in Butsch, ed., *For Fun and Profit*, 139–40; Gomery, "Movie Audiences, Urban Geography and the History of the American Film," *Velvet Light Trap*, 19 *(1982)*, 23–29 on location in middle-class neighborhoods; see also Lary May, 149–50; Gomery in Butsch, 141–6, on strategies to attract middle class; Lynd (1929), 263–5.

11. Roy Rosenzweig, *Eight Hours for What We Will: Workers and Leisure in an Industrial City, 1870–1920* (Cambridge, UK: Cambridge University Press, 1983), 220–1. "Handling Crowds at the Roxy," *New York Times* (September 29, 1929), IX, 8, described evening audiences at one of the largest movie palaces in New York as mostly couples, on Saturdays most young couples.

12. Olivia Howard Dunbar, "The Lure of the Movies," *Harper's Weekly* 57 (January 18, 1913), 22; Robert. E. Davis, 173; *American Magazine* (August 1913), 93.

13. Marion Reedy, "Movie Crimes Against Good Taste," *Literary Digest* (September 18, 1915), 592–3.

14. Walter Prichard Eaton, "The Menace of the Movies," *American Magazine* 76 (September 1913), 55–60; Eaton, "The Theatre and the Motion Picture," *Vanity Fair* 27 (October 1926), 73, 118. In "Class Consciousness and the 'Movies,'" *Atlantic* 115 (January 1915), 48–56, Eaton was not quite ready to blame movies for the demise of theater, but argued the class distinction between movies and live drama. Responding to Eaton and others, the *New York Times* ["The Menace of the Movies," June 28, 1920, 14] claimed movies and stage drama were complementary, not opposed.

15. William Johnston, "The Structure of the Motion Picture Industry," *Annals of the Academy of Political and Social Science* 128 (November 1926), 25–7; Alice Mitchell, *Children and Movies* (Chicago: University of Chicago Press, 1929), 66–9, on Chicago. Richard Koszarski, *An Evening's Entertainment: The Age of the Silent Feature Picture, 1915–1928,* (Berkeley: University of California Press, 1990), 9–10, 13, states that even in the twenties there were few picture palaces, only 66 in 1927, but this seems a very low estimate. Gomery, "The History of the American Movie Palace," estimated about 1,000 palaces, defined broadly. Waller, *Main Street Amusements,* 194–8, argues against the palace as typical.

16. Elaine Bowser, *The Transformation of Cinema,* 127, on prefabricated façades; Lizabeth Cohen, *Making a New Deal: Industrial Workers in Chicago, 1919–1939* (New York: Cambridge University Press, 1990), 121–9, on Chicago.

17. Forrester Washington, "Recreation Facilities for the Negro," *Annals of the Academy of Political and Social Science* 140 (November 1928), 272–82. In Atlanta in 1928 blacks boycotted a new theater that established a separate entrance policy, and the owner soon allowed them to enter through the front door.

18. Bowser, 9, on Rochester. State courts, dating back to the Reconstruction era, upheld legislation prohibiting racial discrimination in places of public amusement, even while the U.S. Supreme Court judged a Congressional civil rights bill guaranteeing equal access to theaters and amusements to be unconstitutional. See Walter Swan, "The Rights of the Holder of a Theater Ticket," *Case and Comment* 18:10 (March 1912), 575. Mary Carbine, "The Finest Outside the Loop: Motion Picture Exhibition in Chicago's Black Metropolis, 1905–1928," *Camera Obscura* 23 (May 1990), 18, on ruses.

19. Mary Carbine, "Finest Outside the Loop," 9–41. Some of these houses exhibited movies by black producers with black cast and with pro-black themes, including feature film responses to *Birth of a Nation*. See Daniel Leab, "'All-Colored' – But Not Much Different: Films Made for Negro Ghetto Audiences, 1913–1928," *Phylon* 36:3 (September 1975), 321–39.

20. Gregory Waller, *Main Street Amusements,* 168–78, 240–7. Washington found movie theaters for blacks in only three of fifty-seven cities of his survey; Bowser, 9–10, on estimate on number of black nickelodeons.

21. Waller, 164–5; Mary Carbine, "Finest Outside the Loop," 23–4, 28–31.
22. Rob Wagner, "You at the Movies," *American Magazine* (December 1920), 44, 211; *New York Times*, "Movie Titles Read Aloud; Objector Is Beaten: Sues" (April 7, 1927), 8, and "Stamping at Movies" (October 20, 1929), IX 17. In a letter to a friend, playwright Booth Tarkington observed that movie audiences often laughed at low-brow films meant to be taken seriously. See Alan Downer, ed., *On Plays, Playwrights and Playgoers: Selections from the Letters of Booth Tarkington* (Princeton, NJ: Princeton University Library, 1959), 49.
23. See summary of studies of children's movie attendance in Edgar Dale, *Children's Attendance at Motion Pictures* (New York: MacMillan, 1935), 3–4, 42–3; Alice Mitchell, *Children and Movies* (Chicago: University of Chicago Press, 1929), 17, 22, 55, on children as the primary audience, quote from p. 17; photo in *The Woman Citizen* (November 13, 1920), 659; Robert and Helen Merrill Lynd, *Middletown: A Study in Modern American Culture* (New York: Harcourt Brace, 1929), 263–5.
24. The Saturday matinee, created by reformers in the 1910s, was promoted again by the censorship office of Will Hays for the motion picture producers, in 1925–26. See Richard deCordova, "Ethnography and Exhibition: The Child Audience, the Hays Office and Saturday Matinees," *Camera Obscura* 23 (May 1990), 91–107. Quotes from John Margolies and Emily Gwathmey, *Ticket to Paradise: American Movie Theaters and How We Had Fun* (Boston: Little, Brown, 1991), 44.
25. On history of the Payne Fund, see Garth Jowett, Ian Jarvie, and Kathryn Fuller, *Children and the Movies: Media Influence and the Payne Fund Controversy* (Cambridge, UK: Cambridge University Press, 1996); *An Introduction to the Frances Payne Bolton Papers* (Cleveland: Western Reserve Historical Society, 1984), 28; and the unpublished register to the Payne Fund Records at the Western Reserve Historical Society. Payne studies cited were all published by Macmillan in 1933: Ruth Peterson and Louis Thurstone, *Motion Pictures and the Social Attitudes of Children;* William Dysinger, *The Emotional Responses of Children to the Motion Picture Situation;* Herbert Blumer and Philip Hauser, *Movies, Delinquency and Crime;* William Charters, *Motion Pictures and Youth.* Edgar Dale, *Children's Attendance at Motion Pictures,* 42–3, cited other studies not by the Payne Fund, published between 1927 and 1931 on children and movies. The New Deal soon would add recreation surveys of specific cities that concentrated primarily on children's attendance and on their preferences for types of movies.
26. Lynn Bloom, "It's All For Your Own Good: Parent-Child Relationships in Popular American Child-Rearing Literature, 1820–1970," *Journal of Popular Culture* 10:1 (Summer 1976), 194; Paula Fass, *The Damned and the Beautiful: American Youth in the 1920s* (New York: Oxford University Press, 1977); quote of E A. Ross in Norman Denzin, *Symbolic Interactionism and Cultural Studies* (Cambridge MA: Basil Blackwell, 1992), 104.

27. Alice Mitchell, *Children and Movies* (Chicago: University of Chicago Press, 1929), 78–88. Boys preferred playing football or baseball over going to the movies. Even among girls, only a slight majority preferred movies over baseball. All children, boys and girls, grade and high school, Scouts and delinquents, preferred parties and automobile rides over movies.

28. Garth Jowett, Ian Jarvie, and Katherine Fuller, *Children and the Movies,* 58–64; Denzin, 104–5, on the Chicago sociologists involved in the Payne studies. Market research on movie audiences, which began in the late 1930s, also ignored behavior and focused almost exclusively on demographic composition. See Leo Handel, *Hollywood Looks at its Audience: A Report of Film Audience Research,* (Urbana, IL: University of Illinois Press, 1950), 3–4; Paul Lazarsfeld, "Audience Research in the Movie Field," *Annals of the Academy of Political and Social Science,* 254 (November 1947), 162.

29. Blumer quoted from Denzin, 106–7, 109–10. Also see Patricia Clough, "The Movies and Social Observation: Reading Blumer's *Movies and Conduct,"* *Symbolic Interaction* 11:1 (1988), 85–97.

30. Margolies and Gwathemey, *Ticket to Paradise,* 44; Lizabeth Cohen, *Making a New Deal,* 128.

31. Elizabeth Fones-Wolf, "Sound Comes to the Movies: The Philadelphia Musicians' Struggle Against Recorded Music," *Pennsylvania Magazine of History & Biography* 68 (January/April 1994), 14–16, 18–23, 27–8.

32. "Stamping at Movies," *New York Times* (October 20, 1929), IX 17; "Audiences and Sound," *New York Times* (January 4, 1931), VIII 6. In 1929 the *Times* began a separate index heading for sound movies, listing numerous articles on the technology, very few even peripherally about audiences.

33. Lary May, "Making the American Way: Modern Theatres, Audiences and the Film Industry, 1929–1945," *Prospects* 12 (1987), 92, 108, 110. On movies as second most popular, see "The Leisure Hours of 5,000 People," National Recreation Association, (1934). On movies as percent of expenditures, see Bruce Austin, *Immediate Seating, A Look At Movie Audiences* (Belmont, CA: Wadsworth, 1989), 36. A different pattern emerged from interviews with "business girls" in their twenties. Only one in six mentioned going to the movies as a leisure activity. See Janet Fowler Nelson, "Leisure Time Interest and Activities of Business Girls" (New York: The Woman's Press for YWCA National Board, 1933), 23, 35–7.

34. Lary May, "Making the American Way," 104, 111. None of these new 1930s moderne-style theaters were listed as Negro theaters. When the Lynds returned to Middletown in the mid-1930s they found seven movie theaters, only one a large movie palace. See Robert and Helen Merrell Lynd, *Middletown in Transition* (New York: Harcourt, 1937), 260–2.

35. Douglas Gomery, "The Popularity of Film-going in the U.S. 1930–1950," in Colin McCabe, ed., *High Theory/Low Culture* (New York: St. Martin's, 1986), 71–79.

36. Thomas Pryor, "The Audience at Play: Games and Premiums Rival Hollywood's Stars as Box Office Attractions," *New York Times* (April 24,

1938), X 4; Robert and Helen Lynd, *Middletown in Transition*, 260–2; See also Gomery in McCabe, on premiums and bingo.

37. Richard deCordova, "Tracing the Child Audience: The Case of Disney, 1929–1933," in *Prima dei codici 2. Alle porte di Hays* (Venezia: Fabbri Editori, 1991), 217–21. Movies were used quite early to sell other products. See Jeanne Allen, "The Film Viewer as Consumer," *Quarterly Review of Film Studies* 5:4 (Fall 1980), 481–99; and Richard de Cordova, "The Mickey in Macy's Window: Childhood, Consumerism and Disney Animation," in Eric Smoodin, ed., *Producing the Magic Kingdom* (Routledge, 1995).

38. The Lynds (1937), 260–2; on New Haven see Frank Shuttleworth and Mark May, *The Social Conduct and Attitudes of Movie Fans* (New York: MacMillan, 1933), 7, 8; Dorothy Reed, "Leisure Time of Girls in 'Little Italy'" (Ph.D., Columbia University, 1932); on Chicago, see Kenneth Lewis Heaton, "A Study of the Recreational Life of High School Students" (Ph.D., University of Chicago, 1933), 222; on Philadelphia, see Elmer Cressman, "The Out of School Activities of Junior High School" (D.Ed., Penn State College, 1937).

39. "Mayor Sees Audience's Antics and Closes Bay State Theatre," *New York Times* (February 13, 1930), 21; Margolies, *Ticket to Paradise,* 100.

40. In the *New York Times:* "A Woman on Women's Hats," (April 1, 1936), 24; on noise of candy wrappers, "Nuisance" (April 5, 1936), IV 9; "Hissing the President" (April 10, 1938), IV 9; "Bronx Cheer for Kibitzers in Movie Upheld by Court" (November 2, 1939), 27; "Curb on Hissing Suggested to Movie Theatre Managers" (August 11, 1940), IV 9; "Hissing Not Illegal" (August 15, 1940), 18; "Hissing: Silence Preferred" (August 18, 1940), IV 7; "Bars Bronx(ville) Cheer" (October 19, 1940), 11; "Plenty of Idle Time" (April 12, 1938), 22, and response, "Respite from Trouble" (April 16, 1938), 12. Hissing newsreels was not new. Robert Wagner, "You – at the Movies," 211, noted hissing of newsreels in 1920. In contrast to the complaints and the long tradition of publishing theater etiquette rules, an article in 1940 listed suggestions for audience members to make themselves more comfortable, including taking off one's shoes, wearing a loose collar, closing one's eyes for a few seconds at slow points in the movie. "Weekly Round-up of Screen Events" (June 23, 1940) IX 3.

41. Lazarsfeld [*Annals*, 1947, 162–3] claimed the young were heavier moviegoers. On annoyances, see "A Word to the Audience: Shhhhh!" *New York Times* (December 10, 1972); "Theatergoer's Got a Little List ... of Pests Who Sit around Him," *Philadelphia Bulletin* (March 24, 1974); "Quiet Please, I'd Like to Hear the Movie," *New York Times* (March 23, 1980); "Those Off Screen Commentators Are a Pain in the Ear," *Philadelphia Bulletin* (December 28, 1980), D 14; "When Movie Theaters and Audiences Are Obnoxious," *New York Times* (February 7, 1982), 19, 24; "Harassment at Movies: Complaints Rare," *New York Times* (November 17, 1982), "Go to the Movies and Shut Up!" *New York Times* (September 11, 1991), A 27. On youth, see Patricia Gallo, "Saturday Movies for Kids: A Constant in a Changing World," *Philadelphia Evening Bulletin* (March

22, 1974), 9. Perhaps most distinct among these youth audiences has been the urban working-class black teenage audience in downtown movie houses featuring "blaxploitation" movies. They have yet to be studied.

Chapter 12. Voices from the Ether: Early Radio Listening

1. Thomas Edison demonstrated the phonograph in 1877, but its use as an entertainment instrument was delayed. Sound quality improved slowly and prices remained high until the electric microphone replaced acoustical recording in 1926. A Victrola cost $150 in 1922. See Roland Gellat, *The Fabulous Phonograph: From Edison to Stereo* (New York: Appleton Century, 1954); "The 50 Year Story of RCA Victor Records" (New York: Radio Corporation of America, 1953); Charles Schicke, *Revolution in Sound: A Biography of the Recording Industry* (Boston: Little, Brown, 1974).

2. On cultural changes, see Paula Fass, *The Damned and the Beautiful* (Oxford University Press, 1977). On technological changes, see David Nye, *Electrifying America: Social Meanings of a New Technology, 1880–1940* (MIT Press, 1990); Mark Rose, *Cities of Light and Heat: Domesticating Gas and Electricity in Urban America* (State College, PA: Penn State University Press, 1995); Ruth Schwartz Cowan, *More Work for Mother: The Ironies of Household Technology from the Open Hearth to the Microwave* (Basic Books, 1983). Also see Robert and Hellen Merrill Lynd, *Middletown* (New York: Harcourt Brace, 1929) and *Middletown in Transition* (New York: Harcourt Brace, 1937).

3. George Burghard, "Eighteen Years of Amateur Radio," *Radio Broadcast* (August 1923), 29–98; Susan Douglas, *Inventing American Broadcasting, 1899–1922* (Baltimore: Johns Hopkins University Press, 1987), ch. 6. The positive characterizations of these middle-class boys as providing a valuable social service with their radios stood in contrast to the negative characterization of working-class nickelodeon patrons in the same decade.

4. Important to the new advances were vacuum tubes that first appeared in 1919 and replaced the spark. See *Radio News* (July 1923), 103. On manufacturers' influence on government favoring broadcast over the amateurs, see Susan Douglas; Robert McChesney, "The Battle for the U.S. Airwaves, 1928–1935," *Journal of Communication* 40:2 (Autumn 1990), 29–57.

5. Susan Douglas, 299–300 on KDKA; quote from J. C. Gilbert, "Rural Life Modernized," *Wireless Age* (March 1925), 25; numbers of stations from "Who Will Ultimately Do the Broadcasting," *Radio Broadcast* (April 1923), 524; also Elaine Prostak, "Up in the Air: The Debate Over Radio Use During the 1920s" (Ph.D., University of Kansas, 1983), 34–5. *Radio Broadcast* printed complete lists periodically including names of owners of all stations. Robert McChesney, "The Battle for U.S. Airwaves," 30, indicates figures significantly different from these sources.

6. On people's reactions, see Cathy Covert, "'We Hear too Much': American Sensibility and the Response to Radio, 1919–1924," in Covert and John

Stevens, eds., *Mass Media Between the Wars: Perceptions of Cultural Tension, 1918–1941* (Syracuse, NY: Syracuse University Press, 1984), 201–2; Credo Fitch Harris, *Microphone Memoirs* (New York: Bobbs Merrill, 1937), 99–103.

7. On demand for parts, see "Radio Currents," *Radio Broadcast* (May 1922), 1; "Just to Please the Wife," *Radio Broadcast* (December 1923), 139–42; also letters in *Radio News* (October 1922), 742, and *Radio Broadcast* (April 1924), 528.

8. Writers used the term "saturation" from the 1920s through the early 1950s. The 1952 "Videotown" study [see Chapter 16] and *Variety* ["Bigger than Both of Us," January 21, 1953, 29] still referred to saturation rate. In the mid-1950s a new term, "penetration," came into use, a notable change in imagery. See *Sales Management* (November 20, 1955), 30.

9. On relative growth of radio, telephone, and auto, see E. W. Burgess, "Communication," *American Journal of Sociology* 34 (1928), 127; "Statistical Survey of the Radio," *Radio Retailing* (January 1927), 30. Radio growth estimates vary. See Charles Parlin, *The Merchandising of Radio* (Philadelphia: Curtis Publishing, 1925), 4, 6; Leslie J. Page, Jr., "The Nature of the Broadcast Receiver and Its Market in the U.S. from 1922 to 1927," *Journal of Broadcasting* 4:2 (Spring 1960), 174–82.

10. On region and race, see Herman Hettinger, *A Decade of Radio Advertising* (University of Chicago Press, 1933), 43, 49; NBC map, box 278, Clark series 45, National Museum of American History (NMAH) Archive Center. On income, see CBS, *Vertical Study of Radio Ownership, 1930–1933* (New York: CBS, 1933); Affie Hammond, "Listeners' Survey of Radio," *Radio News* 14:6 (December 1932), 331–4; R. F. Elder, "Measuring Radio Advertising Sales Power," *Broadcasting* (November 1, 1931), 11, 32.

11. See price lists for 1922–23 in Warshaw Collection, Radio, box 2, NMAH Archive Center. Contrasting emphases in RCA ads for different sets reflected the limitations of the lower-price models. In 1925 its two-tube Radiola III at $35 was "less than the cost of building such a set"; its console Radiola Super-VIII in a fine cabinet for $425. "With no wires, and no connections of any kind, it picks up stations far across the country … with no interference from powerful nearby stations." See ads in Clark Collection, series 45, box 280, NMAH Archive Center.

12. *QST* quoted in *Literary Digest* (December 2, 1922), 29. The semantic distinction between amateur and "listener-in" was significant. The term "amateur" was reserved for those who were dedicated to using radio as a wireless telephone and therefore had or aspired to a license to transmit, which required passing a federal licensing test after 1911. According to Gernsback [*Radio News,* February 1923, 1450], the popular man-in-the-street definition of radio amateur was "an experimenter who tinkers with radio apparatus." The term "ham" sometimes was used in radio magazines of the 1920s to refer to amateur transmitters. See Mathews, 769.

13. Armstrong Perry, "Is the Radio Amateur Doomed?" *Radio News* (October 1922); prize essays were published in the February through July 1923 issues.

14. Orange Edward McMeans, "The Great Audience Invisible," *Scribner's Magazine* 73:4 (April 1923), 410–16; examples of metaphors in "It's Great to be a Radio Maniac," in *Colliers* (September 13, 1924) and "Confessions of an Unmade Man," *Radio Broadcast* (May 1923). See Smulyan, 19, on listeners vs. DXers.

15. "The March of Radio," *Radio Broadcast* (August 1927), 205; John Wallace, "The DX Listener Finds a Friend," *Radio Broadcast* (December 1927), 140; John Wallace, "The Listeners' Point of View: What Many Listeners Think About Broadcasting," *Radio Broadcast* (April 1927), 567. Daniel Starch, "Revised Study of Radio Broadcasting" (New York: NBC, 1930), 34.

16. On difficulties and instructions, see William Cary, "How to Go About Buying a Set," *Radio Broadcast* (April 1924), 521–3; "Radio Enters the Home," Radio Corporation of America (1922); Powell Crosley, Jr., "Souvenir Letters Commenting on the Chain-Broadcast of the WLW Organ," Gray Museum Collection Broadcast Archive, Cincinnati Historical Society; "Tuning Radio Receivers: An Explanation for Novices," *Radio News* (June 1923), 2092; "Operating the Dials Is an Exact Art," *Radio World* (April 19, 1924), 10; "Broadcast Listener," *Popular Radio* (April 1926), 379; John Wallace, "The Listeners' Point of View," *Radio Broadcast* (June 1927), 97–8.

17. On the neutrodyne introduced in 1924, see Thomas Volek, "Examining Radio Receiver Technology Through Magazine Advertising in the 1920s and 1930s" (Ph.D., University of Minnesota, 1991), 128–31; on tuning, see "Progress of Radio Receiving Equipment," *Radio Craft* (March 1938), 615.

18. On fathers and sons, e.g., see illustration, *Wireless Age* (February 1924), 33; wife's quote in "What Our Readers Write Us," *Radio Broadcast* (April 1924), 530.

19. Another suggested term was "broadcatcher." See "The Radio 'Broadcatcher' Is Revealed," *New York Times* (November 14, 1926), IV 5.

20. Covert, 205, on de-masculinizing; editorial, *Radio Broadcast* (April 1927), 558; "The Listeners' Point of View," *Radio Broadcast* (November 1927), 38.

21. A representative of the *Chicago Tribune* stated that radio fan magazines peaked in 1924, declined in 1925 and 1926, and revived slightly in 1927; and that radio dealer trade magazines declined significantly from 1922 to 1927. See "Discusses Radio Programs," *New York Times* (April 26, 1928), 14.

22. Susan Douglas, 295.

23. Grandparents also were a recurring image of the domestication of radio. The January 1925 cover of *Wireless Age* showed "grandpa" playing "air" piano to the music from the radio headphones. A Crosley radio ad [December 1924, 97] recommended buying a radio for "dear old mother,

confined to the house by the rigors of winter." The covers did not, how-ever, include blue collar and poor or black, Asian, or ethnic. The people on the covers are upper-middle-class Anglos.

24. The December 1922 issue included an article titled "The Housewife's Radio." The June 1923 cover featured a woman operating a radio for her-self in headphones. That same issue included a logo for a technical advice column titled "Broadcast Listener," which depicted a woman operating an expensive radio with a speaker for her family.

25. "Correspondence from Readers," *Radio News* (November 1922), 914. Hugo Gernsback was a science fiction magazine pioneer and advocate of the social value of technology, particularly radio. See Damon Knight, *The Futurians* (New York: John Day, 1977), 1–3.

26. For a summary, see Clyde Griffen, "Reconstructing Masculinity from the Evangelical Revival to the Waning of Progressivism: A Speculative Synthesis," in Mark Carnes and Clyde Griffen, eds., *Meanings for Manhood: Constructing Masculinity in Victorian America* (University of Chicago Press, 1990), 198–204.

27. See many examples in the two magazines in 1922 and 1923. In early 1924 the magazines cut back significantly on their reprinting of cartoons about radio. Comic stories also expressed the same themes, e.g., "Dad Answers When He's Asked," *Wireless Age* (October 1922), 30; Harry Shumway, "Just to Please the Wife," *Radio Broadcast* (December 1923), 139–42.

28. On the decline and backlash to feminism in the 1920s, see Nancy Cott, *The Grounding of Modern Feminism* (New Haven: Yale University Press, 1987), chs. 6, 8; J. Stanley Lemons, *The Woman Citizen: Social Feminism in the 1920s* (Urbana: University of Illinois Press, 1973); Rayna Rapp and Ellen Ross, "The 1920s Feminism, Consumerism, and Political Backlash in the United States," in Judith Friedlander, et al., *Women in Culture and Politics: A Century of Change* (Bloomington: Indiana University Press, 1986), 52–61; on women achieving masculine feats and entering other male spheres, see Cott, ch. 7. For a contempo-rary account of the "flapper," see Frederick Lewis Allen, *Only Yesterday: An Informal History of the 1920s* (New York: Harper & Bros., 1931), 88–90, 103–8.

29. On the "generation gap" between younger and older women, see Rayna Rapp and Ellen Ross, 54–5; on consumerism and the popular discourse on women, see Estelle Freedman, "The New Woman: Changing Views of Women in the 1920s," and Mary Ryan, "The Projection of a New Womanhood: The Movie Moderns in the 1920s," both in Lois Scharf and Joan Jensen, eds., *Decades of Discontent: The Women's Movement, 1920–1940* (Westport, CT: Greenwood Press, 1983). On magazine and newspaper articles, see Francesca Cancian, *Love in America* (Cambridge University Press, 1987), 163–4. On cosmetics, see Kathy Peiss, *Hope in a Jar: The Making of American Beauty Culture* (New York: Metropolitan Books, 1998).

30. For example, Covert, 204–5.

31. Elizabeth Bergner, "Woman's Part in Radio," *Radio Age* (July 1922), 10; Alfred Caddell, "A Woman Who Makes Receiving Sets," *Radio Broadcast* (November 1923), 29–33.

32. She was the wife of a lawyer, lived in the suburbs of New York, and had a maid.

33. "Radio and the Woman," *Radio World* (April 15, 1922); (May 20, 1922), 21; (June 10, 1922), 13; (June 17, 1922), 15; (June 3, 1922), 14; (July 1, 1922), 15; (October 28, 1922), 15.

34. Eleanor Poelher, "My Happy Radio Career," *Wireless Age* (December 1924), 30; Christine Frederick, "How I Made a Career Out of Home and Radio," *Wireless Age* (August 1924), 34; also see Golda Goldman, "The Women's Hour" (March 1925), 34; Christine Frederick, "Radio and the Girl" (August 1925), 16.

35. March 1924 cover for wash on aerial; April 1925 cover on kitchen radio; high heels on May 1925 cover; nipples on September 1925 cover.

36. Harry Irving Shumway, "Just to Please the Wife," *Radio Broadcast* (December 1923), 139–42; Alwyn Covell, "Decorating the Radio Room," *House and Garden* (August 1923). On the other hand, see the letter from one woman in "Correspondence," *Radio Broadcast* (June 1927), 100.

37. "Radio" (Philadelphia: Atwater Kent, 1925), 9, Warshaw Collection, radio box 2, NMAH Archive Center. The "even a woman can do it" strategy was also used for piloting airplanes in the late 1920s. See Joseph Corn, "Making Flying 'Thinkable': Women Pilots and the Selling of Aviation 1927–1940," *American Quarterly* 31 (Fall 1979), 559–60.

38. Ruth Schwartz Cowan, *More Work for Mother,* 172–90; Susan Smulyan, *Selling Radio: The Commercialization of American Broadcasting, 1920–1934* (Washington, DC: Smithsonian Institution Press, 1994), 86–92. Similarly in England, Germany, and Australia, see Shaun Moores, "The Box on the Dresser: Memories of Early Radio and Everyday Life," *Media, Culture & Society* 10:1 (1988), 23–40; Kate Lacey, *Feminine Frequencies: Gender, German Radio and the Public Sphere, 1923–1945* (Ann Arbor: University of Michigan Press, 1996); Lesley Johnson, "Radio and Everyday Life: The Early Years of Broadcasting in Australia," *Media, Culture & Society* 3 (1981), 167–78.

39. Announcers often asked listeners to write and offered prizes or other incentives to do so. Advertisers provided "applause cards" which listeners could fill out and send to the stations they tuned in. Letters and cards were used as the first measure of audiences. Some of these have been preserved among the papers of stations, advertisers, and performers. Newspapers and magazines, especially radio magazines, published letters from listeners. While of limited validity for a variety of reasons [Frederick Lumley, *Measurement in Radio* (Columbus: Ohio State University, 1934), ch. 3], fan mail is one of the few direct expressions by radio listeners and can offer us some insights about how they constructed their own listening practices.

40. Credo Fitch Harris, *Microphone Memoirs of the Horse and Buggy Days of Radio* (Indianapolis: Bobbs-Merrill, 1937), 54–5, 155–9, 166; See Chapter 14 on rural radio re Wendell Hall.

41. Smulyan, *Selling Radio,* 87, says radio promoters used the idea of the announcer as a guest in the listener's home to entice advertisers to use radio.
42. Robert and Helen Merrell Lynd, *Middletown,* 269–71; John Wallace, "What Many Listeners Think," *Radio Broadcast* (April 1927), 566.
43. For pictures of people listening in streets to sports broadcasts, see *Wireless Age* (August 1922), 27; *Popular Radio* (November 1923), 530; *Popular Radio* (July 1922), 230, and *Radio Retailer* (October 1927), 79. On other public listening, see photo captioned "A Johnny-on-the-Spot Receiving Station," *Popular Radio* (June 1925), 579; Reynold Wik, "Radio in the 1920s," *South Dakota History* 11 (Spring 1981); "Radio and the Woman," *Radio World* (September 30, 1922), 15; "Radio and the Woman," *Radio World* (January 13, 1923), 15.
44. "Radio and the Woman," *Radio World* (July 1, 1922), 15; "What Our Readers Write," *Radio Broadcast* (November 1924), 82; also examples in Ray Barfield, *Listening to Radio, 1920–1950* (New York: Praeger, 1996), 4, 8, 13.
45. John Wallace, "What Many Listeners Think About Broadcasting," *Radio Broadcast* (April 1927), 566; "Radio and the Woman," *Radio World* (February 17, 1923), 18; (January 13, 1923), 15; (December 15, 1923), 5; (September 30, 1922), 15.
46. "Rules of Etiquette Lacking to Guide the Radio Listener," *New York Times* (September 23, 1928), X 2; "Audience Without Group Mind," *New York Times* (June 1, 1930), III 6.
47. Lizabeth Cohen, *Making a New Deal: Industrial Workers in Chicago, 1919–1939* (Cambridge, UK: Cambridge University Press, 1990), 133, on Chicago; Frederick Lumley, *Measurement in Radio,* 271, on Virginia; also Barfield, *Listening to Radio,* 16.
48. Frank Ernest Hill and W. E. Williams, *Radio's Listening Groups* (New York: Columbia University Press, 1941), 5, 21–2, 28, 29, 46, 47, 59, 63–4. *American Town Meeting* began May 1935 and continued on television into the late 1950s; see J. Fred MacDonald, *Don't Touch That Dial: Radio Programming in American Life from 1920 to 1960* (Chicago: Nelson-Hall, 1979), 289.
49. In the early 1920s the U.S. Department of Commerce assigned the same wavelength to all commercial stations, even in the same city, who were expected to work out broadcast hours among themselves so they would not overlap. Agreements were not always achieved nor cooperation sustained. Further wavelengths were added and in January 1925 wavelengths reassigned. In January 1926 the Department of Commerce stopped issuing licenses because of congestion. At that point voluntary cooperation began to collapse. See George Douglas, ch. 7; Edward Sarno, "The National Radio Conferences" and Marvin Bensman "The Regulation of Broadcasting by the Department of Commerce, 1921–1927," in Lawrence Lichty and Malachi Topping, *American Broadcasting: A Source Book on the History of Radio and Television* (New York: Hastings House, 1975), 534–55.

50. Eric Barnouw, *A Tower in Babel*, 93, on the various cities; W. S. Hedges, "Fans to Ballot on 'Silent Night' Plan" (November 11, 1922), Radio section, 1, and "Give Views on Opera and on Silent Night" (November 18, 1922), Radio Section, 1, *Chicago Daily News*. The *Chicago Daily News*, which owned one of the major stations, reported all this in a tone of high civic-mindedness, as if it were acting out of altruism; Chester Caton, "Radio Station WMAQ: A History of its Independent Years, 1922–1931" (Ph.D., Northwestern University, 1951), 83–5.

51. *New York Times*, "Chicago Radio Fans Plan 'General Strike'" (August 7, 1925), 13; "Yield to Radio 'Strikers'" (August 28, 1925), 16; "Radio 'Strikers' Winning" (September 25, 1925), 25; "Chicago Broadcasters Silent Monday Nights" (October 4, 1925), X 18; "All Chicago Stations Silent Monday Nights" (November 29, 1925), IX 14. Two months after the boycotts reestablished unanimous participation in silent night, Chicago broadcasters "civic-mindedly" participated with stations across the United States and around the world in international experiments for distance reception in January 1926. Over a series of Monday evenings radio stations across the United States went off the air, so DXers could try to receive stations in Europe and South America, in efforts to test the limits of reception. ["England is Silent," January 25, 1926, 14, and "British Stations on Ether To-Night," January 26, 1926, 16, *Chicago Daily News*].

52. "Chicago Silent Night Put Up to Listeners," *New York Times* (March 20, 1927), 13; "Silent Night Retained," *New York Times* (March 25, 1927), 26; "Chicago Ends 'Silent Nights,'" *New York Times* (November 16, 1927), 20; "Chicago Abandons its Silent Nights," *New York Times* (December 4, 1927), XI 15; "Silent Night Is Ended," *Chicago Daily News* (November 16, 1927), 39; "Local Fans Get Distant Stations," *Chicago Daily News* (November 19, 1927), 12; "Federal Commission Acts to Give Distance Fans Chance at Big Stations," *Chicago Daily News* (November 19, 1927), 12; "DX Fan Not What He Used to Be," *Chicago Daily News* (November 21, 1927), 38.

53. "New York Studios Not Likely to Adopt Silent Night Plan," *New York Times* (June 14, 1925), IX 16.

54. "Campaign Planned to Close New York Stations on Friday," *New York Times* (October 18 1925), X 18; "League Opposes Silent Night in New York," *New York Times* (October 25 1925), IX 16; "The Broadcast Listener," *Popular Radio* (December 1925), 473; (March 1926).

55. "Listeners Complain WNYC's Wave Causes Interference," *New York Times* (July 20, 1924), VIII 15; "Topics of the Times: Far Harder to Bear than Static," *New York Times* (January 12, 1925), 14; "Letter to the Editor: Radio Interference," *New York Times* (March 18, 1925), 20; "Radio Super-Station Causes Some Protest," *New York Times* (December 12, 1925), 3; "Protest High Power Broadcasting," *New York Times* (December 19, 1925), 10; "Aims to Ban Radio Squeals," *New York Times* (February 7, 1926), 14.

56. On Cincinnati, see "Radio Listeners Organize," *Chicago Daily News* (February 5, 1926), 20; on Indianapolis, see "QRM War Declared by Radio

Listeners," *Chicago Daily News* (February 9, 1926), 16; on politicians, see "Blooper Foes Mobilize," *Chicago Daily News* (February 11, 1926), 20. The Indianapolis group continued into 1927 and opposed the 1927 Radio Act. See "Listeners Recommend New Bills Be Drafted," *New York Times* (January 9, 1927), VIII 11.

57. "'Service' Is Keynote of Listeners' League," *Cleveland Plain Dealer* (March 7, 1926), All Feature section, 8.
58. Thomas Watson, "A National Association of Radio Listeners," December 1925 typescript, New York Public Library, Billy Rose Theater Collection.
59. "The Weak Radio Listener Organization," *Radio Broadcast* (April 1927), 558; Francis St. Austell, "Direct Selling by Radio," *Radio Broadcast* (May 1928), 58–9.

Chapter 13. Radio Cabinets and Network Chains

1. Christine Frederick, "Home Comforts," *Wireless Age* (January 1925), 36–8, 83, 85–6; see Atwater Kent ad, *Ladies' Home Journal* (December 1925), 179.
2. Alwyn Covell, "Decorating the Radio Room," *House and Garden* 44 (August 1923), 50–1; "The Aristocracy of Radio Receivers," *Radio Broadcast* (January 1924), 207, 209; Thomas Volek, "Examining Radio Receiver Technology Through Magazine Advertising in the 1920s and 1930s" (Ph.D., University of Minnesota, 1990), 120, on phonographs.
3. See battery problems in "Bozo Learns about Women – and Batteries," *Radio* (November 1923), 12, 61; and Valspar ad in *Saturday Evening Post* (February 16, 1924), 77. George Douglas, *The Early Days of Radio Broadcasting* (Jefferson, NC: McFarland, 1987), 49, noted that a cheap AC tube to work with house current appeared only in 1927. Dealers claimed that the higher cost of "socket sets" retarded their acceptance. In small towns battery sets outsold "socket sets" almost 5 to 1, even though 85 percent of homes in these towns (not the surrounding countryside) had electricity. See "1927 Statistical Review," *Radio Retailing* (June 1927), 74.
4. "The Year's Trend in Set Design," *Radio Retailing* (January 1927), 55; "The 1927–28 Trends in Cabinet and Circuit Designs," *Radio Retailing* (February 1927), 36–37; "Listeners' Point of View," *Radio Broadcast* (October 1926), 532; "Sizing Up the Radio Audience," *Literary Digest* (January 1929), 54, on Starch survey. Atwater Kent and RCA advertised the ease of use of their new radio models. See 1925 A-K and RCA ads in National Museum of American History (NMAH) Warshaw Collection, Radio, box 2, and Clark series 45, box 280.
5. Cabinetry caused radio prices to rise through the 1920s, peaking in 1929 at an average of $133. But radios were available in a wide range of prices from cabinet models costing far more than a working family's week's wages, to the simple crystal set for $10. See "Selling Cabinets Requires a New Technique," *Radio Retailing* (December 1927), 60; Mean family income in 1929 was $2,335 and in 1935, $1,631. See U.S. Bureau of the Census *Historical Statistics of U.S.* (Washington, DC: USGPO 1975).

6. "Selling Cabinets," *Radio Retailing* (December 1927), 60; ad in *Saturday Evening Post* (October 22, 1927), 123. An Atwater Kent ad of 1925 announced, "Women Are Deciding Now." See *Good Housekeeping* (October 1925), 253.

7. "Selling Cabinets," *Radio Retailing* (December 1927), 60; Orrin Dunlap Jr., "Radio," *New York Times* (November 29, 1930) in NMAH, Clark Collection, series, 45, box 280.

8. Orrin Dunlap, "Looking Ahead a Few Months," *New York Times* (November 23, 1930), 16, called it a musical instrument; "You Are Selling Music, Not Radio," *Radio Retailing* (April 1927), 26–27; "Music Will Sell the Unsold Eighty Million," *Radio Retailing* (May 1927), 46–7; RCA ads in NMAH, Clark Collection, series 45, boxes 280 and 277; Herald loudspeaker ad, *Radio World* (March 1, 1924), 35. Sports was another programming attraction. Ads promoted radios to World Series fans and to college graduates who could not go to their alma mater's football games but who could listen over radio. See *Radio Retailing* (October 1927), 79 captioned, "The World Series, a Radio Opportunity"; (November 1927), 73, captioned, "Football Fans Need Radio."

9. On domestication strategies, see Susan Smulyan, *Selling Radio: The Commericalization of American Broadcasting, 1920–1934* (Washington, DC: Smithsonian Institution Press, 1994), 86–92; Shawn Moores, "The Box on the Dresser," *Media Culture and Society* 10 (1988), 23–40; Kate Lacey, "From *plauderei* to Propaganda," *Media Culture and Society* 16 (1994) 589–607; and Louis Johnson, "Radio and Everyday Life," *Media Culture and Society* 3 (1981), 167–78. Moores, 24–5, notes ensuing privatization of the English working class. Roland Marchand, *Advertising the American Dream* (Berkeley: University of California Press, 1985), 66, said in the 1920s advertisers believed they were talking primarily to women. See also Michael Schudson, *Advertising, The Uneasy Persuasion: Its Dubious Impact on American Society* (New York: Basic Books, 1984), 178–208.

10. RCA ads in NMAH Clark collection, series A, box 8, and series 45, box 277; Family listening, see *Life* (December 16, 1926), 32; *Good Housekeeping* (October 1925), 281. Grandma with headphones, see *Saturday Evening Post* (December 15, 1923), 72–3, for RCA; (February 2, 1924), for Matched Tone headsets; and *American Magazine* (December 1924), 135, for Crosley and with a speaker see *American Magazine* (October 1926), 91; *American Magazine* (January 1927), 111,

11. See several "Radio and the Woman" columns in *Radio World;* "Home Comforts," *Wireless Age* (January 1925); Stewart-Warner ad in *Saturday Evening Post* (November 13, 1926), 54; Herald ad in *Radio World* (March 1, 1924), 35. Home entertaining ads in Volek, II 29, 75, 59; *American Magazine* (August 1924), 88; *Atlantic Monthly* (August 1926), 43; *Ladies' Home Journal* (November 1925), 176–7; also Volek, 160–1.

12. Thomas Eoyang, "An Economic Study of the Radio Industry in the U.S.A." (Ph.D., Columbia University, 1936), 89. Through the mid-1930s radio prices remained relatively stable but began to fall again in 1938 even when general business improved sharply. See "Are New Radios Good

Enough," *Radio Retailing* (March 1939), 18. On income and radio, see William Gray and Ruth Munroe, *Reading Interests and Habits of Adults* (New York: MacMillan, 1929); Daniel Starch, "Revised Study of Radio Broadcasting" (New York: NBC, 1930), 18; Hadley Cantril and Gordon Allport, *The Psychology of Radio* (New York: Harper & Bros., 1935), 86–7; Frederick Lumley, *Measurement in Radio* (Columbus: Ohio State University Press, 1934), 199; Paul Lazarsfeld, *Radio and the Printed Page* (New York: Duell, Sloan and Pierce, 1940), 18, 103, 136–8. On hours of use, see Daniel Starch (1936); "Radio Takes to the Road" (New York: NBC, 1936), NMAH Clark collection, series 45, box 279; Lumley, 196; "The Joint Committee Study of Rural Radio Ownership and Use in the United States" (New York: NBC and CBS, February 1939).

13. Previously critics had questioned whether drama was appropriate to radio. See "Why Shakespeare Is Easy to Broadcast" (July 1926), 285; "The Coming of the Radio Drama" (September 1926), 480–1; "The Struggling Efforts of the 'Radio Drama'" (October 1926), 600, 602–3, all in *Popular Radio*.

14. Lumley, bibliography; Price Waterhouse & Co., "Price, Waterhouse Survey of Radio Network Popularity" (New York: CBS, 1931), Acknowledgments, on CBS survey. See also Mark James Banks, "A History of Broadcast Audience Research in the United States, 1920–1980, with an Emphasis on the Rating Services" (Ph.D., University of Tennessee, 1981); Donald Hurwitz, "Market Research and the Study of the U.S. Radio Audience," *Communication* 10:1 (December 1987), 223–41.

15. On validity of mail as a measure of audience see Lumley, ch. 3. There was much interest in measuring audiences even in the 1920s. Articles in the *New York Times* in 1924 to 1926 concerning radio audiences were exclusively about estimating its size. One of the earliest magazine reports was "How Big Is the Radio Audience," *Wireless Age* (September 1923), 23–6.

16. On Starch, see "Sizing Up the Radio Audience," *Literary Digest* (January 19, 1929), 54–5. Others doing early research included WKY in Oklahoma City, WLW in Cincinnati, WGAR and WTAM in Cleveland, WTMJ (*Milwaukee Journal*) in Milwaukee, *Columbus Dispatch* in Columbus Ohio. See the numerous studies cited by Lumley in his bibliography and discussed in his text. Lumley helped to correct the common misconception that the large stations and networks in New York and the Northeast initiated the only early research. The effort was in fact more widespread.

17. Herman Hettinger, *A Decade of Radio Advertising* (Chicago: University of Chicago Press, 1933), 54–5n. Hadley Cantril of Princeton would conduct public opinion polling but refused to do contracted market research.

18. Herman Beville, "Social Stratification of the Radio Audience," Princeton Radio Research Project (1939), 3, 8–9, on origins of Crossley and Hooper ratings; Mark James Banks, "A History of Broadcast Audience Research in the United States" (Ph.D., University of Tennessee, 1981), 34–6, 60.

19. Lumley, 194–5, 199, on day parts and audience segments; Lumley, 192, 199, and Starch (1930), 26 on families listening together. On program preferences, see Lumley, 276, and Starch (1930), 30.

20. Robert and Helen Merrell Lynd, *Middletown in Transition* (New York: Harcourt Brace, 1937), 263–4; William Kornhauser, *The Politics of Mass Society* (New York: Free Press, 1959), ch. 1; on the Lynds' observation, see Salvadore Giner, *Mass Society* (New York: Academic Press, 1976), 118; more recently Robert Putnam has argued that television has caused postwar civic disengagement. See Robert Putnam, "The Strange Disappearance of Civic America," *American Prospect* 24 (Winter 1996), 34–48. On the simultaneous processes of globalization and localization in late-twentieth-century media, see Kevin Robins, "Reimagined Communities?" *Cultural Studies* 3:2 (1989), 145–65.

21. Charles Wolfe, "The Triumph of the Hills: Country Radio, 1920–1950," in Paul Kingsbury, *Country: The Music and the Musicians* (New York: The Country Music Foundation, 1988), 63; Frances Holter, "Radio Among the Unemployed," *Journal of Applied Psychology* 23 (February 1939), 163–9. Selling the radio was also an embarrassment to teenage children, who depended upon the radio for dance music when inviting friends over.

22. Starch (1930), 26; Clifford Kirkpatrick, *Report of a Research into the Attitudes and Habits of Radio Listeners* (St. Paul, MN: Webb Book Publishing, 1933), 24. On working while listening, see Lumley, 202; Herman Hettinger, "What Do We Know About the Listening Audience?" in Levering Tyson, *Radio in Education*, vol. 3 (Chicago: University of Chicago Press, 1933), 50. Ads sometimes showed radios providing background music for conversation with guests, an addendum to the activity rather than the center of attention. See ads in Volek II 29, 59, 75, 160–1; *American Magazine* (August 1924), 88; *Atlantic Monthly* (August 1926), 43; *Ladies' Home Journal* (November 1925), 176–7.

23. The volume of letters was often commented upon, most of them responses to free offers. Richard B. O'Brien, "Filling Up the Mailbags," *New York Times* (May 17, 1931), IX 11; "Listening In," *New York Times* (February 15, 1931), VIII 16; "The Avalanche of Letters" *New York Times* (July 19, 1931), IX 13; "Letters from Home," *New York Times* (January 19, 1936), IX 15; "Behind the Scenes," *New York Times* (December 20, 1936), XI 14; Lumley, 49–52, 57, 70.

24. Lumley, 167–8.

25. Lowell Thomas, *Fan Mail* (New York: Dodge Publishing, 1935), 96–149, 106–7, 136, 148; on premier of Thomas' show, see Harrison B. Summers, ed., *A Thirty Year History of Programs Carried on National Radio Networks in the United States, 1926–1956* (New York: Arno Press, 1971), 21.

26. Letters to Baldwin Piano Company, see Wulsin Family Papers, box 277, folder 5, "Listener Responses," Cincinnati Historical Society.

27. NBC and New York City station WJZ in 1927 identified daytime as the "women's hours." Bertha Brainard, manager of WJZ, described the change: "Women discovered that during the day, while the men were out of the house, they could gain a wealth of diversion from their radio sets."

28. The apt description is from Raymond William Stedman, "A History of the Broadcasting of Daytime Serial Dramas in the United States" (Ph.D., University of Southern California, 1959), 67.
29. Irna Philips papers in State Historical Society of Wisconsin (SHSW) notes on premier date of 1929. On growth of serials, see Stedman, 115–16, 257; Frances Farmer Wilder, *Radio's Daytime Serial* (New York: CBS, 1945), 16; Rudolf Arnheim, "The World of the Daytime Serial," in Paul Lazarsfeld and Frank Stanton, *Radio Research, 1942–43* (New York: Duell, Sloan and Pearce, 1944), 36–7. Homemaker programs survived in the form of morning and luncheon talk shows. See Morleen Getz Rouse, "Daytime Radio Programming for the Homemaker, 1926–1956," *Journal of Popular Culture* 12 (Fall 1979), 315–20.
30. See Leda Summers, *Daytime Serials and Iowa Women* (Des Moines: Radio Station WHO, 1943), 3, 7; also Herta Herzog, "What Do We Really Know About Day-Time Serial Listeners?" in Lazarsfeld and Stanton, *Radio Research, 1942–43*, 32.
31. On New Rochelle, see Stedman, 143; "Women Reward 9 Radio Programs," *New York Times* (May 20, 1942), 40; text of speech and NBC's internal memo in NBC files, SHSW. See also Mero-Irion's attack on children's programs in 1935, in Chapter 15.
32. *The Beast in Me* (1948), 191, 251–8. The Buffalo doctor is mentioned also by Stedman, 174–7.
33. Tania Modleski, *Loving with a Vengeance: Mass-Produced Fantasies for Women* (Hamden, CT: Archon Books, 1982), 11–12; on Milwaukee doctor see Chapter 9, Stedman, 218, on *Sponsor* magazine; on nineteenth-century criticism of women's reading see Barbara Sicherman, "Sense and Sensibility: A Case Study of Women's Reading in Late Victorian America," in Cathy Davidson, ed., *Reading in America: Literature and Social History* (Baltimore: Johns Hopkins, 1989), 208–9, 212–13.
34. There was little examination of serial audiences before the 1940s. The first survey to mention serials, Crossley's 1932 study, simply listed them in program preferences [Lumley, 275]. Before that, preferences of housewives are listed as programs that help them with their housework. See Hettinger in Tyson, 59–60. H. M. Beville, director of research for NBC, produced the first survey on serial audiences in 1937, reporting simply that serial listening decreased with increasing income [Stedman, 148]. These surveys give no information on men who might have listened to serials, given the high levels of unemployment at the time. In recent years, men made up a sixth to a fifth of the audience for daytime television serials in 1979–1980. See Robert Lindsey, "Soap Operas: Men Are Tuning In," *New York Times* (February 21, 1979), sec. 3, 1; Mary Cassata and Thomas Skill, "Television Soap Operas: What's Been Going On Anyway – Revisited," in *Life on Daytime Television: Tuning in American Serial Drama* (Norwood, NJ: Ablex, 1983), 160–1.
35. Ruth Palter, "Radio's Attraction for Housewives," *Hollywood Quarterly* (Spring 1948), 251, 253; on daytime programming as companionship, see

Morleen Getz Rouse, "Daytime Radio Programming for the Homemaker, 1926–1956," *Journal of Popular Culture* 12 (Fall 1979), 315–20.

36. Palter, 253; Donald Horton and Richard Wohl, "Mass Communication and Para-social Interaction," *Psychiatry* 9 (1956), 215–29; Chapters 4 and 9 on green'un stories.

37. Herta Herzog, "What Do We Really Know About Day-Time Serial Listeners?" in Paul Lazarsfeld and Frank Stanton, *Radio Research, 1942–43* (New York: Duell, Sloan and Pearce, 1944), 24–5, 27–31; Leda Summers, *Daytime Serials and Iowa Women* (Des Moines: WHO, 1943); Frances Farmer Wilder, *Radio's Daytime Serial* (New York: CBS, 1945), 8–11, 18–19. Ruth Palter, Herta Herzog, and Leda Summers were all associated with the Office of Radio Research originated by Hadley Cantril and directed by Paul Lazarsfeld. See Chapter 15 on the Office.

38. Helen Papashvily, *All the Happy Endings: A Study of the Domestic Novel in America, the Women Who Wrote It, the Women Who Read It, in the Nineteenth Century* (New York: Harper and Row, 1956); Robert C. Allen, *Speaking of Soap Operas* (Chapel Hill: University of North Carolina Press, 1985), 140–7; Janice Radway, *Reading the Romance* (Chapel Hill: University of North Carolina Press, 1984); and Chapter 19 on resistance. Allen, 140–7, links the nineteenth-century domestic novel through magazines after 1880 to the radio soap.

39. The fan letters to Irna Phillips are a modest collection of about 100 fan letters from 1944 in her papers at the State Historical Society of Wisconsin. On Irna Phillips, see *Don't Touch That Dial*, 250–2 and her papers at the SHSW. Compare these to the 1920s Wendell Hall letters and the Radio Guild letters in Chapters 14 and 15. On soap fans who wrote letters, see Leda Summers, 13.

40. John Clarke, "Populism vs. Pessimism," in Butsch, *For Fun and Profit* (1990), 40, warned against presuming that alternative readings of popular culture per se constituted a progressive advance.

41. Mark Newman, *Entrepreneurs of Profit and Pride: From Black Appeal to Radio Soul* (Westport, CT: Praeger, 1988), 7, 46.

42. Newman, 6–7, 59; William Barlow, *Looking Up at Down: The Emergence of Blues Culture* (Philadelphia: Temple University Press, 1989), ch. 5. According to Barlow, these early recordings were of vaudeville musicians.

43. Newman, 56, 59, on WSBC; Theodore C. Grame, "Ethnic Broadcasting in the U.S.," American Folklife Center, Library of Congress, publ. no. 4 (1980), 61; Lizabeth Cohen, *Making a New Deal: Industrial Workers in Chicago, 1919–1939* (Cambridge University Press, 1990), 135; Nathan Godfried, "The Origins of Labor Radio: WCFL, the 'Voice of Labor,' 1925–28", *Historical Journal of Film Radio and Television* 7:2 (1987), 143–59; Jorge Schement and Ricardo Flores, "The Origins of Spanish-Language Radio: The Case of San Antonio Texas," *Journalism History* 4 (Summer 1977), 56–8, 61.

44. Grame, 63–4; Rudolf Arnheim and Martha Collins Bayne, "Foreign Language Broadcasts Over Local American Stations," in Paul Lazarsfeld

and Frank Stanton, *Radio Research, 1941* (New York: Duell, Sloan and Pearce, 1941), 3–63.

45. William I. Thomas and Florian Znaniecki, *The Polish Peasant in Europe and America, 1918–1920* (Chicago: University of Chicago Press, 1918–20); Lizabeth Cohen, *Making a New Deal*, emphasizes radio's cohesive and progressive effects.

46. An RCA sales department presentation to retail dealers predicted that 2/3 to 3/4 of fall 1931 sales would be replacement sales. See RCA sales letters, NMAH, Clark Collection series 45, box 281, 8–9.

47. "Far from Broadway," *New York Times* (August 20, 1933), IX 7. On car radio ads, see Volek, I 181–2. On saturation rates, see Table 12.1; NBC, "Radio Takes to the Road," see NMAH, Clark series 45, box 279; "Radio in 1937," CBS (1937), 10; W. Carl Dorf, "Car Dealers Don't Have Auto-Radio Sewed Up," *Radio Retailing* (February 1941), 22.

48. "The 1927–28 Trends in Cabinet and Circuit Designs," *Radio Retailing* (February 1927), 37; Atwater Kent ad in *Saturday Evening Post* (July 13, 1929), 104; also see *Collier's* (October 15, 1938), 31; Crosley, see NMAH, Clark series 45, box 280 (1930). In the earliest mention of multiple sets, Christine Frederick (*Wireless Age*, January 1925) considered it useful to have three sets: one for the servants, one on the second floor, and one on the first floor.

49. On saturation rates, see "The Joint Committee Study of Rural Radio Ownership and Use in the United States" (New York: NBC and CBS, 1939); *Electric Merchandising* (January 1940), in NMAH, Clark series 45, box 278. On portables, see *Collier's* (September 16, 1939), 53; "1940 Figures," *Radio & Television Retailing* (January 1941), 15; W. Carl Dorf, "Music to Take Out," *Radio Retailing* (April 1941), 14; "One Radio Doesn't Make a Sale," *Radio & Television Retailing* (January 1941), 16, emphasis in original; photo of bootblack in *Radio Retailing* (August 1941), 13.

50. Admiral ad, *Radio Retailing* (April 1941), 31; cover, *Radio Retailing* (May 1941).

51. I. Keith Tyler, "How Does Radio Influence Your Child?" *California Parent-Teacher* 12 (November 1935), 14–15, 27; Ruth Palter, "Radio's Attraction for Housewives," *Hollywood Quarterly* (Spring 1948), 254–5. The California study also found large numbers of students "did their reading and studying to the accompaniment of the radio."

Chapter 14.   Rural Radio: "We Are Seldom Lonely Anymore"

1. W. M. Jardine, "Radio Serves the Farmer," *Radio Retailing* (July 1927), 77; also Morse Salisbury, "Radio and the Farmer," *Annals of the Academy of Political and Social Sciences* 177 (January 1935), on low farm income and radio sales; Reynold Wik, "The USDA and the Development of Radio in Rural America," *Agricultural History* 62 (Spring 1988), 186–7 on cost of battery charge. In the early years of broadcasting the presence or absence of a nearby broadcast station also affected purchase. See S. R.

Winters, "Erratic Distribution of Radio Sets on Farms," *Radio World* (February 2, 1924), 10, reported radios were widespread in one county nearer broadcast stations, and almost absent in another.

2. F. Howard Forsyth, "The Radio and Rural Research," *Rural Sociology* 4 (March 1939), 68; Charles Wilson, "Money at the Crossroads: An Intimate Study of Radio's Influence Upon a Great Market of 60,000,000 People" (New York: NBC, 1937), 17–18, on Montana, etc.; Edmund Brunner, *Radio and the Farmer* (New York: Radio Institute of the Audible Arts, 1936), 28, on Missouri.

3. *Broadcasting Yearbook 1939*, in NMAH, Clark collection, series 45, box 278; see also "The Joint Committee Study of Rural Radio" (New York: NBC and CBS, 1939); James West, *Plainville, U.S.A.* (New York: Columbia University Press, 1945), 15–16. By 1938–39, Liston Pope noted in his study of Gaston County, North Carolina, that "Most mill [workers'] homes now have a radio and an automobile of one vintage or another." See Liston Pope, *Millhands and Preachers* (New Haven: Yale University Press, 1942), 67.

4. Reynold Wik, "The USDA and the Development of Radio in Rural America," *Agricultural History* 62 (Spring 1988), 177–88; on rural weather and market broadcasts, see John C. Baker, *Farm Broadcasting: The First Sixty Years* (Ames, IA: Iowa State University Press, 1981), 18–25.

5. John C. Baker, *Farm Broadcasting The First Sixty Years* (Ames IA: Iowa State University Press, 1981), 14–15, 137; W. M. Jardine, "Radio Serves the Farmer," *Radio Retailing* (July 1927), 77–8; "The Story of Kentucky's Famed Mountain Listening Centers," *Rural Radio* (April 1938), 11–12.

6. "What Our Readers Write Us," *Radio Broadcast* (November 1924), 82. Radio continued to play an important role for farmers into the 1940s. On the plains in 1940 it was common to hear men ask, "Have you heard the radio? What's the news? What's the market like? What's the weather gonna be?" See L. L. Longsdorf, "Is Anyone Listening In?" *Extension Service Review* 7 (November 1936), 174; West, 16.

7. Shirley Blakely, "I Follow the Crops," *Radio Retailing* (December 1927), 52–4.

8. Charles Class, "Some Social, Educational and Economic Aspects of Radio in Relation to Rural Life" (MS, Ohio State University, 1927); Brunner (1936); Wilson (1937); West (1940).

9. Class (1927), on primacy of information in the 1920s; on country music, see Charles Wolfe, "The Triumph of the Hills: Country Radio, 1920–1950," in Paul Kingsbury, ed., *Country: The Music and the Musicians* (New York: The Country Music Foundation, 1988), 59.

10. On Wisconsin, see Brunner, 23; on musicians, see William Barlow, *Lookin Up at Down: The Emergence of Blues Culture* (Philadelphia: Temple University Press, 1989), and Peter Guralnick, *The Listener's Guide to the Blues* (New York: Facts on File, 1982). Musical instruments were common in farm homes. A survey of children in West Virginia in 1928 found three of five farm homes had a phonograph, three of five had a piano or organ, one-fourth had a radio. See Ella Gardner and Caroline E. Legg, *Leisure*

Time Activities of Rural Children in Selected Areas of West Virginia (Washington, DC: U.S. Government Printing Office, 1931), 30.

11. Vera Brady Shipman, "Mr. and Mrs. Kansas Listen In," *Country Gentleman* (July 25, 1925), 16; Brunner, 21; Harry Dice, "Radio Crystal Sets," *Cedar County [Iowa] Historical Review* (July 1978), 70.

12. L. L. Longsdorf, "Is Anyone Listening In?" 174; W. Carl Dorf, "New Rural Radios," *Radio Retailing* (January 1941), 20; Charles Wilson, "Money at the Crossroads" 4.

13. Brunner, 12–13.

14. Brunner, 23–4. There were occasional mentions of farm men listening while they worked, but with no reference to loneliness. See Brunner, 27, 20; various RCA photos, NMAH, Clark collection, series A, box 8; West, 16.

15. "Attitudes of Rural People Toward Radio Service: A Nationwide Survey of Farm and Small-Town People" (Washington, DC: USDA Bureau of Agricultural Economics, 1946), 2; on Oregon, see Brunner (1936), 18.

16. Evelyn Birkby, *Neighboring on the Air: Cooking with the KMA Radio Homemakers* (Iowa City: University of Iowa Press, 1991); Robert Birkby, *KMA Radio: The First Sixty Years* (Shenandoah, IA: May Broadcasting, 1985); Jane and Michael Stern, "Neighboring," *New Yorker* (April 15, 1990), 78–93; Susan Smulyan, *Selling Radio: The Commercialization of American Broadcasting, 1920–1934* (Washington, DC: Smithsonian Institution Press, 1994) 89–90.

17. E. Birkby, 20, 31; Jane and Michael Stern, "Neighboring," *New Yorker* (April 15, 1990), 78–93; also Robert Birkby, *KMA Radio: The First Sixty Years* (Omaha: Barnhart Press, 1985).

18. John C. Baker, *Farm Broadcasting: The First Sixty Years* (Ames, IA: Iowa State University Press, 1981), 126–7; Francis St. Austell, "Direct Selling by Radio: Is It a Menace to the Retail Business Structure?" *Radio Broadcast* (May, 1928), 58, and "Letters from Readers" (July 1928), 179.

19. Wendell Hall Papers, State Historical Society of Wisconsin, Mass Communication History Center; F. G. Fritz, "Wendell Hall: Early Radio Performer," in Lawrence Lichty and Malachi Topping, eds., *American Broadcasting: A Sourcebook on the History of Radio and Television* (New York: Hastings House, 1975), 276–83.

20. The discussion is based on 167 letters and cards in the Wendell Hall papers. Writers were about evenly split between men and women.

21. Hall had at least some black listeners as well. As part of his act Hall mimicked a black singer, minstrel style. One black listener wrote, "Your numbers were enjoyed until you gave your joke on the 'Negro.' There are thousands of intelligent self-respecting Negro 'listeners in' who resent such jokes."

22. Morse Salisbury, "Radio and the Farmer," 142.

23. J. C. Gilbert, "Rural Life Modernized," *Wireless Age* (March 1925), 70–71; "How Radio Helps the Farm," *Farming – The Business Magazine* (November 1925), 220.

24. Susan Opt, "The Development of Rural Wired Radio Systems in Upstate South Carolina," *Journal of Radio Studies* 1 (1992), 71–81, documents

several such systems in rural South Carolina in the 1930s. No one as yet has investigated such systems in other locales.

25. On Missouri, O. M. Kile, "How Broadcasting Helps the Country Store," *Wireless Age* (November 1923), 37; also see cover, *Radio News* (August 1922); on banks, see Ward Seeley, "The Farm Moves Nearer the City," *Wireless Age* (January 1923), 25; *Post-Dispatch* survey in *Wireless Age* (September 1923), 24; photo in J. Farrell, "Large Scale Rural Radio," *Wireless Age* (November 1923), 29.

26. Photo of schoolhouse radio lecture in Seeley, 26; Illinois survey in "Radio on Our American Farms," *Radio World* (March 22, 1924), 17; Brunner (1936); James West, *Plainville*, 16; William Robinson, "Radio Comes to the Farmer," in Paul Lazarsfeld and Frank Stanton, *Radio Research, 1941* (New York: Duell, Sloan and Pearce, 1941), 284.

27. Charles Wolfe, "The Triumph of the Hills," 53–54.

28. Frederick Lumley, *Measurement in Radio* (Columbus, OH: Ohio State University Press, 1934), 271, on Virginia; on North Dakota and Ontario, see Wolfe, 62–3; on Wyoming, see Brunner, 20.

29. Brunner, 5, 12, 13, 21; William S. Robinson, "Radio Comes to the Farmer," 278–9, 284.

30. F. Howard Forsyth, "The Radio and Rural Research," *Rural Sociology* 4 (March 1939), 70–1; Brunner, 20, 22; John M. Gillette, "Rural Life," *American Journal of Sociology* 34 (1928), 1093; on Illinois, see Salisbury, *Annals* (1935), 141; Lynd, 264.

31. Edmund Brunner and Irving Lorge, *Rural Trends in Depression Years: A Survey of Village-Centered Agricultural Communities, 1930–1936* (New York: Columbia University Press, 1937), 251; Robinson, "Radio Comes to the Farmer," 278–85.

Chapter 15.   Fears and Dreams: Public Discourses About Radio

1. "Radiophone Fills Vacant Pulpit," *Wireless Age* (September 1921), 14; "Radio and Church Attendance," *Radio World* (November 3, 1923), 16; "Radio Substitutes for Absent Pastor," *Radio World* (April 19, 1924), 9; "Religion by Radio," *Literary Digest* (August 23, 1924), 31–2.

2. Richard Butsch, "Introduction: Leisure and Hegemony," *For Fun and Profit: The Transformation of Leisure into Consumption* (Philadelphia: Temple University Press, 1990), 13.

3. James West, *Plainville U.S.A.* (New York: Columbia University Press, 1945), 17, stated that few people in his rural Midwest village ever condemned radios as sinful or dangerous to the community; nor did preachers attack radio listening. To the contrary, radio magazines in the early 1920s often cited cases where religious services and sermons were brought to a broader audience, especially the "shut-in" and rural folk, via broadcasts. Roland Marchand, *Advertising the American Dream: Making Way for Modernity, 1920–1940* (Berkeley: University of California Press), ch. 1 and 89–94, on "apostles of modernity"; Paula Fass, *The Damned and the Beautiful: American Youth in the 1920s* (New York: Oxford

University Press 1977), esp. introduction and conclusion, on the changing bases of norms among the younger generation.

4. Marian Spitzer, "The Freedom of the Breeze," *Saturday Evening Post* (December 6, 1924), 74; for other examples of alarm, see quotes in "Audiences" in Lawrence Lichty and Malachi Topping, *American Broadcasting: A Source Book* (New York: Hastings House, 1975), 449, 462–66. The decline in drama theater attendance had preceded radio and was more affected by the introduction of movies, and especially talking movies, than by radio. See Chapter 11 on movies, and Jack Poggi, *Theater in America: The Impact of Economic Forces, 1870–1967* (Ithaca: Cornell University Press, 1968), ch. 4.

5. "Theater Flings Down the Glove," *Literary Digest* (January 24, 1925), 29; on copyright dispute, see "Clear the Air for the Theater," *Wireless Age* (June 1923), 30.

6. "Theater Flings Down the Glove"; Arthur Hornblow, "Will Radio Hurt the Theatre?" *Theatre Magazine* 41 (March 1925), 7, reprinted in Lichty, 462; Stewart-Warner radio ad in *Saturday Evening Post* (November 13, 1926), 54. "The Radio Woman" of *Radio World* (September 15, 1923), 7, said they enjoy their radio so much that she and her husband go less to the theater.

7. "The 50-Year Story of RCA Victor Records" (New York: Radio Corporation of America, 1953), 24, 26; H. S. Maraniss, "A Dog Has Nine Lives: The Story of the Phonograph," *Annals of the American Academy of Political Science* 193 (1937), 9–10; U.S. Bureau of the Census, *Historical Statistics of the United States, Colonial Times to 1970,* part 2 (Washington DC: U.S. Government Printing Office, 1975), 696; Thomas Eoyang, "An Economic Study of the Radio Industry in the U.S.A." (Ph.D., Columbia University, 1936), 71; ASCAP leaflet in Arthur Ord-Hume, *Pianola: The History of the Self-Playing Piano* (Boston: Allen & Unwin, 1984), 46.

8. On Herbert and Sousa, see Spitzer, "The Freedom of the Breeze", 23; on Gluck, see "Interesting Things Interestingly Said," *Radio Broadcast* (March 1926), 559; on ASCAP, see "Composers and Publishers Cut Programs," *Wireless Age* (June 23, 1923), 31, 42, and "'Pay if You Profit' Say Copyright Owners," *Wireless Age* (July 1923), 43–4. For a history of ASCAP see John Ryan, *The Production of Culture in the Music Industry* (Lanham, MD: University Press of America, 1985), 31–7. In contrast, country musicians received little or no royalties from recording and found radio paid better. See Charles Wolfe, "The Triumph of the Hills: Country Radio, 1920–1950," in Paul Kingsbury, ed., *Country: The Music and the Musicians* (New York: Country Music Foundation, 1988), 83–4.

9. Vern Countryman, "The Organized Musician, II," *University of Chicago Law Review* 16:2 (Winter 1949), 239–97.

10. "Will the Great Artists Continue?" *Wireless Age* (June 1923), 22–9.

11. Elaine J. Prostak, "'Up in the Air': The Debates Over Radio Use During the 1920s" (Ph.D., University of Kansas, 1983), 200–2.

12. On Minneapolis, see Clifford Kirkpatrick, *Report of a Research into the Attitudes and Habits of Radio Listeners* (St. Paul, MN: Webb Book

Publishers, 1933), 45–6; Edmund Brunner, *Radio and the Farmer* (New York: Radio Institute of the Audible Arts, 1936), 20. In the late 1940s, however, Paul Lazarsfeld found that heavy radio listeners were also heavy moviegoers and vice versa. See Paul Lazarsfeld and Patricia Kendall, *Radio Listening in America* (New York: Prentice-Hall, 1948), 6–7.

13. On AP and UPI, see Marshall Beuick, "The Limited Social Effects of Radio," *American Journal of Sociology* 32 (1926), 617; James D. Young, "Is the Radio Newspaper Next?" *Radio Broadcast* (September 1925), 576–80; for optimism, see Sarah Strier, from *Brooklyn Daily Times*, quoted in "The Newspaper and Radio," *Radio World* (December 8, 1923), 16; "The Daily Newspaper and Radio," *Radio World* (February 9, 1924), 16. M. E. Tracy, "Radio in America" *Proceedings of the Fourth Annual Convention* (Radio Manufacturers Association, 1928), 17; on ANPA, see Beuick, 617. Paul Lazarsfeld, *Radio and the Printed Page* (New York: Duall Sloan and Pearce, 1940), 258ff, found that radio enhanced use of newspapers to interpret events announced on radio, but did reduce circulation of extra editions for breaking new stories.

14. *San Francisco Examiner* cartoon reprinted in *Wireless Age* (November 1922), 45; *Chicago News* cartoon reprinted in *Wireless Age* (June 1922), 47; "Why I Became a Radio Fan: A Symposium," *Wireless Age* (February 1924), 18.

15. G. Stone, "Radio has Gripped Chicago," *Radio Broadcast* (October 1922), 501.

16. Roland Marchand, *Advertising the American Dream* 90; Magnavox and Crosley ads in *Radio World* (November 3, 1923), 21; (February 2, 1924), 21; (July 5, 1924), 2; "You Are Selling Music, not Radio," *Radio Retailing* (April 1927), 26.

17. "Chain Broadcasting an Economy," *Radio Broadcast* (February 1926), 518; "The Commission Regulates Broadcasting for the Broadcasters, not the Listener," *Radio Broadcast* (August 1927), 204, 205, and "The Listeners' Point of View," *Radio Broadcast* (April 1926), 670, and (October 1926), 532, on eliminating mediocre stations; cartoon reprinted in *Radio Retailing* (January 1927), 49.

18. "Giving Public What It Wants," *Wireless Age* (May 1923); "Radio the Musical Educator," *Wireless Age* (September 1923); John Tasker Howard, "Discrimination in Listening Homes," *Wireless Age* (October 1923), 34; C. M. Tremaine, "Radio, the Musical Educator," *Wireless Age* (September 1923), 39–40; "Rudy Wiedoeft Says," *Wireless Age* (June 1922), 33; "John C. Fruend maintains that radio will be a potent force in bringing music home to the masses" (May 1922), 36; "Marie Sundelius Says," (May 1922), 29.

19. Lee DeForest, "Opera Audience of Tomorrow," *Radio World* (August 5, 1922), 13; "Radio Audiences Superior to Theater's," *Radio World* (June 28, 1924), 29; "Radio Cultivates Taste for Better Music," *Radio World* (July 19, 1924), 24; "Radio the Culture Builder," *Radio World* (November 24, 1923), 16; "Radio Adds 5,000 Words to the Language," *Radio*

Broadcast (July 19, 1924), 30; "Music Taste Changes from Bananas to Bach," *Radio World* (February 25, 1928), 12.

20. "The Listeners' Point of View," *Radio Broadcast* (April 1926), (June 1926), (May 1927), 32. These surveys used samples biased toward the affluent and adult and those who were more likely to support classical music. Atwater-Kent radios were among the most expensive available. WJZ was a principal broadcaster of classical music, so its listeners would naturally prefer such music. And *Radio Broadcast* itself had an upscale readership. *Radio Broadcast* (November 1923), 70, "We Have the Most – Let's Have the Best," published a letter to the editor that claimed radio was "the greatest institution of learning that can be conceived" and cited the broadcast of classical concerts with explanations by announcers as examples.

21. The association of jazz with lower class was also expressed by George Jean Nathan, drama critic for *American Mercury*, in "Nightly the Front Parlors of the Proletariat Resound to the Strains of Alley Jazz [from Radio]," *Radio Broadcast* (December 1925), 177.

22. *Radio Broadcast* (January 1928), 219–23.

23. Wallace's denigration of the radio audience was perhaps acceptable to the upscale *Radio Broadcast* readership, who could consider themselves distinct from the "average listener" whom Wallace disparaged. A survey conducted by the magazine and reported in the October 1926 column, 531, revealed that almost 40 percent of those responding were engaged in the radio business as engineers, manufacturers, and dealers. Professionals, merchants, and executives each represented 12 percent of respondents, white-collar workers another 10 percent.

24. On class of listeners, see William Gray and Ruth Munroe, *Reading Interests and Habits of Adults* (New York: MacMillan, 1929), on Chicago; Kirkpatrick (1932), 25, 28, on Minneapolis.

25. Walter Damrosch, "What Does the Public Really Want?" *The Etude* (October, 1934), 579–80; on Damrosch, see Elaine J. Prostak, "'Up in the Air': The Debates Over Radio Use During the 1920's" (Ph.D., University of Kansas, 1983), 200–2; William Orton, "The Level of Thirteen-Year-Olds," *Atlantic Monthly* (January, 1931), 1–10.

26. Levering Tyson, "National Advisory Council on Radio in Education," in Mary Ely, ed., *Adult Education in Action* (New York: American Association for Adult Education, 1936), and Levering Tyson, *Radio and Education*, vols. 1–4 (Chicago: University of Chicago Press, 1931–34), for annual proceedings of the organization.

27. Sherwood Gates, "Radio in Relation to Recreation and Culture," *Annals of the American Academy of Political and Social Sciences* 213 (January 1941), 9; "Women Reward 9 Radio Programs," *New York Times* (May 20, 1942), 40.

28. Frederick Lumley, *Measurement in Radio* (Columbus: Ohio State University Press, 1934), 276–7. This strong preference for popular over classical was also indicated in a 1943 survey of Iowa households; 47 percent of adult listeners named popular music as one of their five best-liked

types of programs, ranked third after news and comedians, but only 17 percent included classical music in their top five. It ranked thirteenth among all adult preferences. See Forest Whan, "A Study of Radio Listening Habits in the State of Iowa" (Des Moines: IA: Central Broadcasting Co., 1943), 53. On struggles between middle-brow and high-brow, see Joan Rubin, *The Making of Middle Brow Culture* (Chapel Hill: University of North Carolina Press, 1992), and Michael Kammen, *The Lively Arts: Gilbert Seldes and the Transformation of Cultural Criticism in the United States* (New York: Oxford University Press, 1996).

29. "Listeners' Point of View," *Radio Broadcast* (June 1925), 580; (April 1927), 568; J. Andrew White, "Educate the Masses!" *Radio Broadcast* (December 1926), 166.

30. "The Broadcast Listener," *Popular Radio* (June 1925), 577–80; (July 1925), 88.

31. "The Broadcast Listener," *Popular Radio* (January 1926), 74; (October 1925), 371; (February 1926); see also "Musical Appreciation and the Radio," *Popular Radio* (November 1927), 370, 372.

32. Elaine Prostak, 194–6. Prostak describes the old-time movement as part of a larger reactionary resistance to modern ideas, a conflict between traditional and modern values in the 1920s.

33. Brunner, 25–6. Very few favored classical music. A county agent in Missouri commented that radio enabled farmers to "listen to the very best musical programs." President of the Ohio Farm Bureau Federation claimed that radio caused "increasing demand for high-class music rather than the jazz sort." See Brunner, 24–5.

34. Letters from NBC files at the State Historical Society of Wisconsin, Mass Communication History Center. Some letters also mentioned a Tuesday-night drama hour.

35. On class differences in viewing styles, see chapter 17

36. On the 1920s, see Paula Fass, *The Damned and the Beautiful: American Youth in the 1920s* (New York: Oxford, 1977), especially 14, where she discusses the shift of concern from controlling working-class kids to shock at their own children.

37. Azriel Eisenberg, *Children and Radio Programs* (New York: Columbia University Press, 1936), 5–6, on growth of children's programs; on Scarsdale, see "Mothers Protest 'Bogeyman' on Radio," *New York Times* (February 27, 1933), 17, and "A 'New Deal' for Youth," *New York Times* (September 10, 1933), X, 7.

38. On Council, see Eisenberg, 18–21. The Council is not the Payne Fund National Committee on Education by Radio, but an organization founded in 1930 by the American Association for Adult Education. On the Council, see its annual proceedings in Levering Tyson, *Radio and Education*, vols. 1–4 (University of Chicago Press, 1931–1934). On Mero-Irion, see "W.C.T.U. Speaker Assails the Radio," *New York Times* (September 12, 1935), 27; see chapter 13 on Mero-Irion 1942 attack on soap operas. On physical education professor, see "Radio Denounced as Peril to Young," *New York Times* (March 31, 1938), 35; also "School Aid

Urged in Traffic Safety," *New York Times* (October 4, 1939), 30. On Chicago, see John DeBoer, "The Emotional Responses of Children to Radio Drama" (Ph.D., University of Chicago, 1940), 106; also reported in "Radio's Effect on Youth," *New York Times* (November 13, 1938), IX 12. On General Federation, etc., see "Radio Reforms for Youth, Aim of Joint Drive," *New York Times* (April 30, 1939), II 4. On Rev. Long, see "Radio Thrillers Scored," *New York Times* (January 25, 1940), 42.

39. John Hutchens, "Tracy, Superman, et al. Go to War," *New York Times* (November 21, 1943), VI 14.

40. Eisenberg, 21–31.

41. Payne Fund Records register, p. 36, Western Reserve Historical Society; Garth Jowett, "Social Science as a Weapon," *Communication* 13 (December 1992), 212; Eisenberg 24–5; Lumley, v.

42. Eisenberg, 32, 138–9. Eisenberg also received support from NBC, CBS, and Bamberger Broadcasting, owner of WOR, Newark, NJ. See Eisenberg, "Acknowledgments," viii. His studies surveyed program preferences of children, research useful to broadcasters. Tyler, "How Does Radio Influence Your Child?" *California Parent-Teacher* 12 (November 1935), 14–15, also found many high school students listened while studying.

43. Everett Rogers, *A History of Communication Study* (New York: Free Press, 1994), 267–73; Lazarsfeld, *Radio and the Printed Page*, vii–ix. Stanton received his Ph.D. from Ohio State in 1935 and almost certainly knew the work of Charters' Bureau there. The Radio Research Project produced several books and numerous articles, including a special issue of the *Journal of Applied Psychology* 23 (February 1939); Lazarsfeld, *Radio and the Printed Page* (1940); Hadley Cantril, *The Invasion from Mars* (Princeton University Press, 1940); research articles collected in three volumes by Lazarsfeld and Stanton, titled *Radio Research* (Duell, Sloan and Pearce, 1942, 1944, and 1949); Lazarsfeld, Bernard Berelson, and Hazel Gaudet, *The People's Choice* (New York: Duell, Sloan and Pearce, 1944); Lazarsfeld and Patricia Kendall, *The People Look at Radio* (Chapel Hill: University of North Carolina Press, 1946); Lazarsfeld and Kendall, *Radio Listening in America* (New York: Prentice-Hall, 1948).

44. Such an approach was also maximally compatible with market research, trying to establish buyers' response to a specific product, contributing to Lazarsfeld's success in funding basic research through marketing research contracts.

45. His research was funded by NBC, CBS, the National Association of Broadcasters, and other interested companies, such as the Book of the Month Club. See Paul Lazarsfeld, *Radio and the Printed Page* viii–ix; Lazarsfeld and Patricia Kendall, *The People Look at Radio,* vii. Lazarsfeld was not averse to corporate funding, and supported much of his radio research by contracting to do market research on everything from toothpaste to *Time* magazine. See Rogers, 290, 294. Cantril and Allport's research was also supported by powerful broadcasting corporations. In

their preface, viii, they thanked the Edison Electric and Westinghouse stations in Boston, NBC, and CBS, and the NAB.

Chapter 16. The Electronic Cyclops: Fifties Television

1. "Television's Audience Problems," *Business Week* (September 13, 1947), 71; "1948 – Year of Television Progress," *Radio and Television News* (December 1948), 38; U.S. Bureau of the Census, *Statistical Abstracts* (Washington, DC: USGPO, 1995). Television broadcasting blossomed in 1948, much as radio did in 1922 and spread quickly, despite an FCC freeze on new station licenses from 1948 to 1952. By mid 1955, 96 percent of American homes were within reception distance of at least one television station, according to "TV in 10 Years Transforms America," *Sales Management* (November 20, 1955), 30.

2. On income skew, see "TV Slump: The Old One-Two," *Business Week* (May 5, 1951), 88; "Saturation in TV Sets? SRC Survey Says Yes," *Business Week* (August 6, 1955), 48; "Two Thirds of US Homes Now Boast Television Sets," *Sales Management* (November 20, 1955), 32; "When Television Comes to Town," *Electrical West* (December 1948), 104. For prices, see "Video Visions," *Business Week* (November 29, 1947), 38; "1948 – Year of Television Progress," *Radio and Television News* (December 1948), 38; "What Every Family Wants to Know About Television," *Science Illustrated* (January 1949), 24–5; "A Hard Look at TV's Future," *Business Week* (October 30, 1948), 72. See *Consumer Electronics Annual Review: 1985 Industry Facts and Figures* (Washington, D.C.: Electronics Industry Association, 1985), 7, on the decline in costs of televisions relative to the consumer price index from 1953; Alfred R. Oxenfeldt, *Marketing Practices in the TV Set Industry* (New York: Columbia University Press, 1964), 10–14. On short supply of lower-price sets, see "When Television Comes to Town," *Electrical West* (December 1948), 104.

3. See map in "What Every Family Wants to Know About Television," *Science Illustrated* (January 1949), 26–7; and tables listing stations in "1948-Year of Television Progress," 36–7. Regional saturation in 1955 was 80% in the Northeast 72% in the Northcentral, 62% in the West, and 53% in the South. See "Two Thirds of U.S. Homes Now Boast Television Sets," *Sales Management* (November 20, 1955), 32.

4. "Viewing Trends: From '50s to '80s," *Television/Radio Age* (July 22, 1985), 49.

5. "One Sunday Afternoon," *Newsweek* (November 22, 1954), 93.

6. For example, Ella April Codel, "Television Has Changed our Lives," *Parents Magazine* (December 1948), 64–5; Dorothy McFadden, "Television Comes to Our Children," *Parents Magazine* (January 1949), 26–7.

7. Calder Willingham, "Television: Giant in the Living Room," *American Mercury* (February 1952), 114–15; "The New Cyclops," *Business Week* (March 10, 1956), 76–104.

8. Leo Bogart, *The Age of Television,* 3rd ed. (New York: Frederick Ungar, 1972), 94–5.

9. Austin Lescarboura, "Television for Taverns," *Radio and Television Retailing* (August 1941), 29; "1948 – Year of Television Progress," 38; tables in *Televiser* (March 1948), 31; (October 1949), 16; (December 1950), 21. See also "Report on Los Angeles Television Survey," *Radio News* (December 1947), 196; "When Television Comes to Town," *Electrical West* (December 1948), 104.

10. "What's Happening to Leisure Time in Television Homes," (Boston: Batten, Barton, Durstine and Osborn, 1951). A salesman who had a television at home said that he was "glad that all the bars he goes to have a set." See Margaret Midas, "Without TV," *American Quarterly* 3:2 (Summer 1951), 164.

11. "Television's Audience Problem," *Business Week* (September 13, 1947), 70; on improved business, see "Barrooms with a View," *Time* (March 24, 1947), 63; also "Television in the Tavern," *Newsweek* (June 16, 1947), 64; on fight telecast, see "At the Knife and Fork," *The New Yorker* (June 29, 1946), 16–17; "Viewers Credo," *TV Guide* (August 6–13, 1949), 20. An alternative to the bar was the "$12 Portable Radio in the Bedroom," *TV Guide* (July 8–14, 1950), 20.

12. Cartoons in the *New Yorker* (December 3, 1949), 79, (December 10, 1949), 30; "Talk of the Town," *New Yorker* (October 29, 1949), 20; Philip Hamburger, "Television," *New Yorker* (October 29, 1949), 91. See also cartoons in *The $64,000,000 Answer* (New York: Berkley, 1955).

13. Anna McCarthy, "'The Front Row Is Reserved for Scotch Drinkers': Early Television's Tavern Audience," *Cinema Journal* 34:4 (Summer 1995), 34–35; "Television's Audience Problem," *Business Week* (September 13, 1947), 70; "Television in the Tavern," *Newsweek* (June 16, 1947), 64.

14. "Report on Los Angeles Television Survey," *Radio News* (December 1947), 196; Videotown study cited in Herbert Marx, "Television Takes Over," in *Television and Radio in American Life* (New York: H. W. Wilson Co., 1953), 9–10; Raymond Stewart, "The Social Impact of Television on Atlanta Households" (Atlanta: Emory University, 1952), 52; "How to Decorate for Television," *House Beautiful* (August 1949), 66–9; "Television in Your Life," *House and Garden* (April 1950), 140–1. A *New Yorker* cartoon [August 13, 1949, 18] showed a couple putting every chair in the house in front of the television for visitors.

15. "Viewers Credo," *TV Guide* (August 6–13, 1949), 20; Jack Gould, "Family Life, 1948 A.T. (After Television)," *New York Times Magazine* (August 1, 1948), 12–13.

16. Paul Ritts, *The TV Jeebies* (Philadelphia: John C. Winston, 1951), 96, 99–105.

17. Robert Rice, "Onward and Upward with the Arts: Diary of a Viewer," *New Yorker* (August 30, 1947), 44–55.

18. Jack Gould, "Family Life, 1948 A.T. (After Television)," 12–13.

19. Codel, 65; "Should You Tear 'Em Away?" *Better Homes and Garden* (September 1950), 56; Josette Frank, "Is Television Good or Bad for

Children?" *Woman's Home Companion* (November 1950), 70; Bianca Bradbury, "Is Television Mama's Friend or Foe?" *Good Housekeeping* (November 1950), 263; Howard Lane, "What Shall We Do About Television?" *Parents Magazine* (December 1950), 37, 100; *Architectural FORUM* (September 1948), 118; "Letter to the Editor," *TV Guide* (September 10, 1949), 4; Ritts, 93–6.

20. Raymond Stewart, "The Social Impact of Television on Atlanta Households," 73; May Seagoe, "Children's Television Habits and Preferences," *Quarterly of Film, Radio and Television* 6 (Winter 1951), 148; also Eleanor Maccoby, "Why Children Watch TV," *Public Opinion Quarterly* 15:3 (Fall 1951), 425.

21. Maccoby, 426; also Stewart, 73. In my own childhood, my playmates in 1955 would stop playing abruptly at five o'clock and rush each to their separate homes to watch the new Mickey Mouse Club show.

22. Ritts; Rice, *New Yorker;* Maccoby, 434.

23. Cartoon in *New Yorker* (May 13, 1950), 26–7; Maccoby, 427; also see Ritts, 93, and a cartoon in *Business Week* (March 10, 1956), 80.

24. *The First Decade of Television in Videotown, 1948–1957* (New York: Cunningham and Walsh, Inc., 1957), 19, 38; John McGeehan and Robert Maranville, "Television: Impact and Reaction in Lexington, Kentucky," Occasional Contribution, no. 50, University of Kentucky (March 1953), 9.

25. A number of surveys found what economists call substitution of television for radio during evenings, among both adults and children. See Charles Aldredge, "Television: Its Effects on Family Habits in Washington D.C." (Washington, DC: Charles Alldredge Public Relations, January 1950), 11; "Videotown," 13–16; Thomas Coffin, "Television Effects on Leisure Time Activities," *Journal of Applied Psychology* 32 (1948), 550–8; "What's Happening to Leisure Time in Television Homes? A Study of the Activities of 5,657 Persons in Urban America" (Boston: Batten, Barton, Durstine and Osborn, 1951); May Seagoe, 148. For ratings, see Lawrence Lichty and Malachi Topping, *American Broadcasting: A Source Book on the History of Radio and Television* (New York: Hastings House, 1975), 455; Erik Barnouw, *The Golden Web: A History of Broadcasting in the United States,* vol 2 (New York: Oxford University Press, 1968), II 288.

26. Data compiled from Tim Brooks and Earle Marsh, *The Complete Directory to Prime Time Network TV Shows* (New York: Ballantine, 1988), 987–90 and individual program entries. Even defunct radio programs were revived for television. A few shows appeared first on TV and transferred to radio. "Radio Doomed By TV: It Is! It Isn't..." *Editor and Publisher* (May 21, 1949), 54. Radio stations shifted to local programming of music and news and for specialized markets. See "On Radio Row: Broadcasters Go local to Meet TV Competition," *Barrons* (February 22, 1954), 13.

27. Clifton Utley, "How Illiterate Can Television Make Us?" *Commonweal* (November 19, 1948), 138; see also John Harmon, "Television and the Leisure Time Activities of Children," *Education* (October 1950), 126; "Television's Audience Problem," *Business Week* (September 13, 1947), 70.

28. Codel, "Television Has Changed Our Lives," 65–6; "Television's Audience Problem," *Business Week* (September 13, 1947), 70; Mary Hornaday, "End of Conversation?" *Christian Science Monitor Magazine* (March 19, 1949), 5; "How Illiterate Can Television Make Us?" *Commonweal*. On conversation and viewing, see Cecilia Tichi, *Electronic Hearth: Creating an American Television Culture* (New York: Oxford University Press, 1991), 28–29 on TV quiz; Utley (1948); Gould (1948); Hornaday (1949); Willingham (1952).

29. Leo Bogart, *The Age of Television*, 129–30, also Ch. 6.

30. Nielsen Television Index Reports, A. C. Nielsen papers, boxes 22–24, State Historical Society of Wisconsin; on serial ratings, see Helen Slotta, "A Study of the Ways in Which Network Radio Has Met the Impact of Television," (MA, Pennsylvania State University), 58; On locations of TVs and radios, see Slotta, 49, and Alfred Politz, "What Is Radio's Place in People's Daily Lives?" *Advertising Agency* (September 1953), 76–7, 142, 144.

31. Lynn Spigel, *Make Room for TV: Television and the Family Ideal in Postwar America* (University of Chicago Press, 1992), 76–7.

32. Federick Stuart, "The Effects of Television on the Motion Picture and Radio Industries" (Ph. D., Columbia University, 1960), reprinted, Arno (1975).

33. Charles Alldredge, 8, 12; May Seagoe, 148; "The First Decade of Television in Videotown," 12; Ralph Austrian, "Effect of Television on Motion Picture Attendance," *Journal of Society of Motion Picture Engineers* (January 1949), 12–18; Thomas Coffin, "Television Effects on Leisure Time Activities" 550–8; "What's Happening…"; Raymond Stewart, "The Social Impact of Television on Atlanta Households," 22, 34; McGeehan, 8; *The $64.000.00 Answer* (New York: Berkley Publishing, 1955).

34. "Book Publishers, Movie Moguls," *Printers Ink* (December 15, 1950), 101; Paul Raibourn, "Outlook for Television, Radio and Motion Pictures," *Commercial and Financial Chronicle* (March 15, 1951), 6; on mutual benefits, see "Top Pix into TV Homes – Zukor," *Variety* (March 4, 1953), 3; also on Paramount, see "TV – Who's Afraid," *Fortune* (July 1950), 56.

35. On recent expressions, see "Scholarly Controversy: Mass Culture," *International Labor and Working-Class History* 37 (Spring 1990), 2–40; Robert Putnam, *American Prospect*.

36. Stuart, 18–19, but see table, p. 20, on rural drop. Market researcher Daniel Starch pointed out in a 1951 study that the movie audience began to shrink long before the number of TV sets in homes was significant but the decline in movie attendance accelerated as TV spread. See "Magazine Readership Unaffected by TV," *Printers' Ink* (November 9, 1951), 40.

37. Kenneth Jackson, *Crabgrass Frontier: The Suburbanization of the United States* (New York: Oxford University Press, 1985), 233, 238, 245, 326.

38. Douglas Gomery, *Shared Pleasures: A History of Movie Presentation in the United States* (Madison: University of Wisconsin Press, 1992), 83–8.

39. On communal places, see Ray Oldenburg, *The Great Good Place* (New York: Paragon House, 1989).

40. Elaine Tyler May, *Homeward Bound* (New York: Basic Books, 1988), 14, ch. 1; Jackson, *Crabgrass Frontier*, 232, 280–2.

41. "Television," *Architectural FORUM* (September 1948), 119; Hi Sibley, "Seating Your Audience," *Popular Mechanics* (September 1950), 187; "Television in Your Life," *House and Garden* (April 1950), 140–41; "How to Decorate for Television," *House Beautiful* (August 1949), 66–9; Elaine Tyler May, *Homeward Bound*, 23. Lynn Spigel, *Make Room for TV*, 38, found television sometimes pictured as the replacement for the piano, a very different domestic image. Alldredge (1950), 3, suggested a parallel to the pot-bellied stove. Tichi, 53–6, argues that the image of the hearth recurred through American history whenever turbulence unsettled the certitudes of life.

42. John Riley, Frank Cantwell, and Katherine Ruttiger, "Some Observations on the Social Effects of Television," *Public Opinion Quarterly* 13 (Summer 1949), 232; Maccoby, 424–9; see also Raymond Stewart, "The Social Impact of Television on Atlanta Households," 59; Bradbury, 263; Battle, 57.

43. Spigel, 69.

44. Motorola ad from *Life* magazine, New York Public Library Picture Collection, television audience file.

45. "For the Ladies," *TV Guide* (July 8–14, 1950), 20; RCA ad in *Printer's Ink* (December 1, 1950), 83; "TV Slump: The Old One-Two," *Business Week* (May 5, 1951), 91; Tichi, 68, 69, on Dumont ad and portables. Still in 1955, less than 4 percent of families had more than one set. See American Research Bureau, "Television Set Distribution Figures" pamphlet, NMAH, Dumont Collection, series 4, box 32.

46. Cartoons in *New Yorker* (November 20, 1948), 48, (September 15, 1956), 38; Dumont ad in Spigel, 71; Spigel, 65–72, on conflict.

47. Coffin (1948); Alldredge, 8, 11–12; Raymond Stewart, "The Social Impact of Television on Atlanta Households," 51, 54; McGeehan and Maranville, "Television: Impact and Reaction in Lexington, Kentucky," 7, 10; "What's Happening to Leisure Time in Television Homes."

48. "Viewing Trends: From '50s to '80s," *Television/Radio Age* (July 22, 1985), 49; Haluk Sahin and John P. Robinson, "Beyond the Realm of Necessity: Television and the Colonization of Leisure," *Media, Culture and Society*, 3:1 (1980), 85–95. Leo Bogart, *The Age of Television*, 399, cited an unpublished report that there was no change in visiting and increases in other activities outside the home from 1950 to 1967; on continuing decline, see Ronald Frank and Marshall Greenberg *The Public's Use of Television: Who Watches and Why* (Beverly Hills, CA: Sage, 1980), 90. Robert Kubey and Mihaly Csikszentmihalyi, *Television and the Quality of Life: How Viewing Shapes Everyday Experience* (Hillsdale, NJ: Erlbaum, 1990), 171–4, attribute television's pull in terms of its low cost, time, skill, and effort relative to other activities.

49. Ellen Wartella and Sharon Mazzarella, "A Historical Comparison of Children's Use of Leisure Time," in *For Fun or Profit*, 183–6, 190, review the displacement versus reorganization debate. Displacement argues for a

narrow impact directly substituting TV for some other medium. Reorganization proposes a broader transformation of all activities, including nonmedia.

50. Bogart, 399; Robert Putnam, "The Strange Disappearance of Civic America," *American Prospect* 24 (Winter 1996), and responses, 25 (Spring 1996).

Chapter 17.   A TV in Every Home: Television "Effects"

1. Ira Glick and Sidney Levy, *Living with Television* (Chicago: Aldine, 1962), 26–36, on sentiments toward first sets 1957 to 1961. Leo Bogart, *The Age of Television*, 3rd ed. (New York: Frederick Ungar, 1972), 96, cited a survey in 1954 with 85 percent of sets in living rooms. In 1970 the main sets were in family rooms, others in bedrooms. See Robert Bower, *Television and the Public* (New York: Holt, Rinehart and Winston 1973), 145; also Margaret Andreason, "Evolution in the Family's Use of Television: Normative Data from Industry and Academe," in Jennings Bryant, *Television and the American Family* (Hillsdale, NJ: Erlbaum, 1990), 31.

2. On cultural capital, see Pierre Bourdieu, *Distinction: A Social Critique of the Judgement of Taste*, trans. Richard Nice (Cambridge: Harvard University Press, 1984), 48.

3. Mary Hornaday, "End of Conversation?" *Christian Science Monitor Magazine* (March 19, 1949), 5. Hornaday and others called such claims extravagant and exaggerated.

4. Jack Gould, "The Low State of TV," *New York Times* (October 19, 1952), X-13; Gilbert Seldes, *The Great Audience* (New York: Viking Press, 1950), 173, 178, 182; Norman Cousins, "The Time Trap," *Saturday Review* (December 24, 1949), 20; see also Philip Gufstafson, "Nickelodeon Days of Television," *Nation's Business* (July 1947), 37, 73; John Tebbel, "TV and Radio," *New American Mercury* (February 1951), 235–8; Calder Willingham, "Television: Giant in the Living Room," *American Mercury* (February 1952), 114–19. On Seldes, see Michael Kammen, *The Lively Arts: Gilbert Seldes and The Transformation of Cultural Criticism in the United States* (New York: Oxford University Press, 1996).

5. Philip Hamburger, "Television," *New Yorker* (October 29, 1949), 91; (November 5, 1949), 126; (December 17, 1949), 77–9; (November 26, 1949), 111–12; See Matthew Murray, "NBC Program Clearance Policies During the 1950s: Nationalizing Trends and Regional Resistance," *The Velvet Light Trap* 33 (Spring 1994), on network executives' boasts.

6. John Crosby, "Seven Deadly Sins of the Air," *Life* (November 6, 1950), 147–8+; Seldes, *Great Audience*, 181–2; John Fischer, "TV and its Critics," *Harpers* (1959), 12–16; John Tebbell, "TV and Radio," *New American Mercury* (February 1951), 235–38.

7. Matthew Murray, 38; Hornaday, "End of Conversation?" *Christian Science Monitor Magazine* (March 19, 1949), 5; William Bird, "'The Drama of Enterprise' Comes to Television," Research Seminar Paper No.

4, Hagley Museum & Library (January 1993); Brooks and Marsh, *The Complete Directory of Prime Time Network TV Shows;* on BBD&O, see Roland Marchand, *Advertising the American Dream: Making Way for Modernity, 1920–1940* (University of California Press, 1985), *Creating the Corporate Soul: The Rise of Public Relations and Corporate Imagery in American Big Business* (University of California Press, 1998), and William Leach, *Land of Desire: Merchants, Power, and the Rise of a New American Culture* (New York: Pantheon, 1993). As in the 1920s, many people resented being "uplifted" by New York executives. They complained to local affiliated stations, especially about indecency on television. See Murray, "NBC Program Clearance."

8. John Fischer, "New Hope for Television" *Harper's* (January 1960), 12, 14, 19–21; Martin Mayer, "Boris for the Millions," *Harper's* (June 1961), 22, 24–7; Martin Mayer, "How Good Is TV at Its Best?" *Harpers* (August 1960), 89, and (September 1960), 88; Schlesinger quote in Norman Jacobs, ed., *Culture for the Millions?* (Boston: Beacon Press, 1964), 148; Griffith and Suskind quoted in Wilbur Schramm, Jack Lyle, and Edwin Parker, *Television in the Lives of Our Children* (Palo Alto, CA: Stanford University Press, 1961), 3.

9. See Bernard Rosenberg and David M. White, eds., *Mass Culture: The Popular Arts in America* (New York: Free Press, 1957); "Mass Culture and Mass Media: Special Issue," *Daedalus* 89 (Spring 1960), republished as Norman Jacobs, *Culture for the Millions?* After this time, criticisms of television became the conventional wisdom, with occasional individual restatements, such as Marie Winn, *The Plug-in Drug* (New York: Viking Press, 1977), rather than a chorus of intellectual hysteria.

10. Cecilia Tichi, *Electronic Hearth: Creating an American Television Culture* (New York: Oxford University Press, 1991), 186–7 on quote, ch. 8, on reading vs. TV debate.

11. John Harmon, "Television and the Leisure Time Activities of Children," *Education* (October 1950), 127; Henrietta Battle, "Television and Your Child," *Parents Magazine* (November 1949), 58; Josette Frank, "Is Television Good or Bad for Children?" *Woman's Home Companion* (November 1950), 50–1; Bianca Bradbury, "Is Television Mama's Friend or Foe?" *Good Housekeeping* (November 1950), 58, 263; Harry Kenney, "Children Are Watching," *Christian Science Monitor Magazine* (April 9, 1949), 5; "Television Comes to Our Children," *Parents Magazine* (January 1949), 26–7, 73–5.

12. Walter Brahm, "They Proclaim Calamity," *Library Journal* 76 (August 1951), 1186–7; Joan Whitbread and Vivian Cadden, "The Real Menace of TV," *Harper's* (October 1954), 81–3.

13. Robert Goldenson, "Television and Our Children," *Parents Magazine* (December 1954), 36–7, 76, 78–81.

14. See prefaces and acknowledgments of the various reports. During the 1960s academic research produced thousands of studies, overshadowing broadcaster-sponsored output. Most major studies by this time were funded by the federal government.

15. Ad in NMAH, Warshaw Collection, box 1, folder 2.

16. "Television Makers' Ad Campaign Revised as Protests Mount Over Snob Appeal," *Printer's Ink* (November 24, 1950), 105, 107, 114, 141.

17. Margaret Midas, "Without TV," *American Quarterly* 3:2 (Summer 1951), 152–66; "Television Makers' Ad Campaign Revised," *Printer's Ink* (November 24, 1950), 106; "Ad Says Children Need TV," *Editor and Publisher* (November 25, 1950), 5.

18. "Book Publishers, Movie Moguls Launch Anti-TV Campaign," *Printer's Ink* (December 15, 1950), 83.

19. Lynn Spigel, *Make Room for TV* (University of Chicago Press, 1992) 49.

20. "The Audience," *Time* (November 8, 1968), 98.

21. Wallace Markfield, "Oh, Mass Man! Oh, Lumpen Lug! Why Do You Watch TV?" *Saturday Evening Post* (November 30, 1968), 28–9, 72

22. Bogart, 108; *Television in the Lives of Our Children*, according to Schramm, inspired hundreds of later studies as well as the Surgeon General's $2 million research program. The book was based upon a series of studies of adolescents mostly in cities of the western United States conducted between 1958 and 1960. It was funded by the National Educational Television and Radio Center, the forerunner of NET, funded by the Ford Foundation. Everett Rogers, *A History of Communication Study* (Free Press, 1994), 471, on its influence.

23. Glick and Levy, *Living with Television*, part two.

24. Glick and Levy, 63.

25. The influential work of Steven Chaffee, Jack MacLeod, and associates [e.g., "Parental Influences on Adolescent Media Use," *American Behavioral Scientist* 14:4 (1971), 323–40] contrasts two styles, concept-oriented vs. socio-oriented that clearly match class differences described by sociologists [e.g., Melvin Kohn, "Social Class and Parent-Child Relationships," *American Journal of Sociology* 68 (January 1963), 471–80]. However, they do not explicitly mention class. A less-well-known study, Robert Blood, "Social Class and Family Control of Television Viewing," *Merrill-Palmer Quarterly* 7 (July 1961), 205–22, is explicit in favoring middle-class over working-class styles.

26. Leo Bogart, *The Age of Television*, 267, 270.

27. Gary Steiner, *The People Look at Television* (New York: Knopf, 1963), 87–9

28. Schramm, et. al., *Television in the Lives of Our Children*, 181–3.

29. Robert Bower, *Television and the Public* (New York: Holt, Rinehart, and Winston, 1973), 173.

30. Elliott Medrich, "Constant Television: A Background to Daily Life," *Journal of Communication* 29:3 (Summer 1979), 171–6.

31. "Television Violence," *AMA Proceedings* (1976), 80; "TV Violence," *AMA Proceedings* (1982), 278; American Academy of Pediatrics Committee on Communications, "Children, Adolescents and Television," *Pediatrics* 96 (1995), 786–7; "Media Education" *Pediatrics* 104 (August 1999), 341–43; *Physician Guide to Media Violence* (Chicago: AMA, 1996).

32. This presumed pathogenic nature of television has been extended in recent years to other television-related activities of video games and computers. Researchers have sometimes contradicted the conventional belief, arguing that the problem inheres in the child (and their parents) rather than in television. See, e.g., Schramm, Lyle and Parker, 181.

33. On passivity and the drug metaphor see Spigel, 62; Tichi, 105–10; Robin Smith, "Television Addiction," in Jennings Bryant and Dolf Zillmann, eds., *Persepctives on Media Effects* (Hillsdale, NJ: Erlbaum, 1986), 109–28; Douglas Davis, *The Five Myths of Television Power* (New York: Simon and Schuster, 1993), ch. 4. Katz claimed the history of communications research oscillates between emphases on passive or active audiences. See Elihu Katz, "On Conceptualizing Media Effects," *Studies in Communication* 1(1980), 119–41.

34. Joseph Klapper claimed the concern about passivity was a popular one, expressed by media critics and child rearing professionals such as Bruno Bettelheim, not by communications researchers, and that the concern was much more pronounced with the arrival of television. See Joseph Klapper, *The Effects of Mass Communication* (New York: Free Press, 1960), 235, 239, 241, 246, 248; Bruno Bettleheim, *The Informed Heart: Autonomy in a Mass Age* (New York: Free Press, 1960), 49–50. Other researchers, who substituted their own "what do people do with television" for the effects question "what does television do to people," criticized the effect approach for inherently assuming a passive audience. See, e.g., Elihu Katz, Jay Blumler, and Michael Gurevitch, "Utilization of Mass Communication by the Individual," in *Uses of Mass Communication* (1974), 21.

35. Examples are the roundly condemned TV talk shows. In a rare exception, Sonia Livingstone and Peter Hunt reconsidered whether the talk show may in fact have some beneficial functions for its viewers, creating a new public space for political debate. See *Talk on Television: Audience Participation and Public Debate* (London: Routledge, 1994).

36. "Housewives Skip Picture on TV Sets," *Editor and Publisher* (May 28, 1955), 14; Robert Bechtel, Clark Achelpohl, and Roger Akers, "Correlates Between Observed Behavior and Questionnaire Responses on Television Viewing," *Television and Social Behavior, Vol. IV: Television in Day-to-Day Life* (Washington, DC: U.S. GPO, 1972), 294, 297; also Robert Kubey and Mihaly Csikszentmihalyi, *Television and the Quality of Life: How Viewing Shapes Everyday Experience* (Hillsdale, NJ: Erlbaum, 1990).

37. Gans noted sharp differences between men and women in viewing preferences. The women preferred programs that Berger characterized as "middle class," suggesting that working-class women were not "resistant." Since these researchers gave little attention to gender – Gans's one observation being the exception – it is difficult to say how women responded. Recent studies of working-class women viewers of soaps indicate distinctly female forms of resistant viewing. See Conclusion.

38. Bennett Berger, *Working Class Suburb: A Study of Auto Workers in Suburbia* (University of California Press, 1960), 74–5.

39. *The Urban Villagers: Group and Class in the Life of Italian-Americans* (New York: Free Press, 1962), 187–96; *The Levittowners: Ways of Life and Politics in a New Suburban Community,* (New York: Pantheon, 1967), 190–3. On portrayals of class and gender, see Richard Butsch, "Class and Gender in Four Decades of Television Situation Comedies," *Critical Studies in Mass Communication* 9 (December 1992), 387–99. On the "emasculated man" and television during the 1950s, see Spigel, 60–5; "What Happened to Men," *TV Guide* and letter to editor.

40. "Lower-class Negro Television Spectators: Pseudo-Jovial Skepticism," in Arthur Shostak and Adeline Gomberg, eds., *Blue Collar World: Studies of the American Worker* (Englewood Cliffs, NJ: Prentice Hall, 1964), 431.

41. Robert Bechtel, Clark Achelpohl, and Roger Akers, "Correlates Between Observed Behavior and Questionnaire Responses on Television Viewing," *Television and Social Behavior,* vol. IV (Washington, DC: U.S. Dept. of HEW, 1972), 297. This talking back is an oppositional form of parasocial interaction, whereas Horton and Wohl conceived it as a conforming response, accepting the authority of the television figure. Donald Horton and Richard Wohl (1954).

42. Vidmar and Rokeach (1974); Brigham and Giesbrecht; Surlin and Tate.

Chapter 18.   Homevideo: Viewer Autonomy?

1. On the growth of independent stations, see John Dempsey, "Unwired Webs Big Biz for Indies," *Variety* (November 16, 1988), 1, 44; Bill Carter, "From Baltimore, Dave Smith Stares Down the Networks," *New York Times* (October 4, 1998), BU1, 14–15.

2. On the rise of VCR and the failure of videodisc, see Richard Butsch, "Home Video and Corporate Plans," in *For Fun and Profit: The Transformation of Leisure into Consumption* (Philadelphia: Temple University Press, 1990), 215–35.

3. On the "prehistory" of VCRs, see Don Agostino and Associates, "Home Video: A Report on the Status, Projected Development and Consumer Use of Videocassette Recorders and Videodisc Players in the U.S.," prepared for the FCC Network Inquiry Special Staff (Washington, DC: Federal Communications Commission, November 1979), 7–17.

4. See "X-Rated Sales as High as 70% of Total Prerecorded Market in '79," *Merchandising* (January 1980), 72. By the fall of 1980 X-rated accounted for only about 20–25 percent of the market. See "Incompatible Units Confuse Market," *Variety* (October 1, 1980), 1.

5. "The Coming VCR Glut," *Fortune* (August 19, 1985), 77; "VCRs: Ogre or Opportunity?" *Marketing and Media Decisions* (September 1984), 49; "VCRs Bring Big Changes in Use of Leisure," *New York Times* (March 3, 1985), 1; "VCRs," *Broadcasting* (August 20, 1984), 43.

6. On the demise of Sony's Beta format, see "Matsushita Takes the Lead in Video Recorders," *Fortune* (July 16, 1979), 110; "To the Beta End," *Forbes* (December 16, 1985), 178; "Beta's in Trouble Say Video Distribs; Some Hanging On," *Variety* (January 15, 1986), 41.

7. "Simultaneous Release of New Films, Prerecorded Tapes Due by Spring," *Merchandising* (February 1980), 58; "MGM Film Forms Venture with CBS for Video Cassettes," *Wall Street Journal* (June 5, 1980), 17; "Fox's Magnetic Video Licenses 250 United Artists Feature Pix," *Variety* (July 23, 1980), 1; "ITA Scouts Video Revolution; Film Majors Merit Biz Boom," *Variety* (March 18, 1981), 277, 296, reported an estimated 12,000 titles available.

8. "Videalers Prefer Rent to Sale, Two New Indie Surveys Show," *Variety* (September 1, 1982), 57; "Home Truths for Hollywood," *The Economist* (July 30, 1983), 72–3. In 1985 the average inventory of video stores was only 2300 tapes. See "VSDA Survey Says Sales Volume 15%," *Variety* (June 26, 1985), 84.

9. "Tenth Annual Consumer Survey," *Merchandising* (May 1982), 22; "Firms Renting Videocassettes Worry Studios," *Wall Street Journal* (March 27, 1981), 31; "Rental Route as Copyright Hold," *Variety* (November 11, 1981), 1; "ITA Scouts Video Revolution; Film Majors Merit Biz Boom," *Variety* (March 18, 1981), 277, 296; "Videalers Prefer Rent to Sale, Two New Indie Surveys Show," *Variety* (September 1, 1982), 57; "3M Report Studies HV Rental Patterns," *Variety* (September 19, 1984), 113.

10. "Disney's Rental-Only Cassettes Could Presage Industry Trend," *Variety* (July 15, 1981), 42; "Rental Route as Copyright Hold," *Variety* (November 11, 1981), 1; "MGM/CBS Video Introduces 'First Run' Rental Plan," *Merchandising* (January 1982), 46; "Warner Gets Mixed Reaction in Texas on Rental Program," *Merchandising* (December 1981), 44, 63.

11. The Video Software Dealers Association formed in December 1981; another retail organization formed as well but folded in 1982. See *VideoNews* (December 11, 1981), 7. On repeal, see "Vestron and Karl Home Video Execs Claim First Sale Repeal Would Hinder, Not Aid Vid Biz," *Variety* (June 13, 1984), 37; "Valenti, Wayman Trade Slams Over First Sale In Warmup for Fall Legislative Battles," *Variety* (August 31, 1983), 34.

12. "VideoDiscs: A Three-Way Race for a Billion-Dollar Jackpot," *Business Week* (July 7, 1980) 74; "The Fortune 500 Directory," *Fortune* (May 5, 1980), 274–301.

13. *Broadcasting* (March 21, 1966), 160; "Videodisc: The Expensive Race to be First," *Business Week* (September 15, 1975), 58, 64; "Report RCA Makes Breakthrough in Videodisc Development Work," *Merchandising Week* (July 31, 1972), 9; "Philips Unveils Video Disk Unit," *Electronic News* (September 11, 1972), 16; "MCA Enters Disk in Marketing Race for TV Playbacks," *Broadcasting* (December 18, 1972), 49; "Zenith in Big R&D Outlay on Video Discs," *Merchandising Week* (April 30, 1973), 3.

14. "Special Report: Videodisk," *Broadcasting* (February 2, 1981), 36; "Videodisc: A Three Way Race," *Business Week* (July 7, 1980) 72–4; "RCA's Biggest Gamble Ever," *Business Week* (March 9, 1981), 79; "Vidisk Hour of Truth Approaching," *Variety* (February 17, 1982), 43–4; "Third Vidisk System (JVC) Placed on 'Indefinite' U.S. & U.K. Hold," *Variety*

(November 24, 1982), 31; "With Zenith's Exit, RCA Faces Lonely Haul in Vidisk Hardware," *Variety* (January 26, 1983), 39; "After RCA: Others to Exit U.S. Video Disk Player Mkt.," *Electronic News* (April 16, 1984), 20; "RCA's Vidisk Losses," *Variety* (March 10, 1982), 35; "Philips Opens Books on LV; Messerschmitt Cites $400 Mil Marketing Development Tab," *Variety* (March 10, 1982), 35.

15. Industry personnel and researchers have coined numerous new terms to describe uses of VCRs and RCD, with unclear and overlapping definitions. Susan Eastman and Gregory Newton, "Delineating Grazing: Observations of Remote Control Use," *Journal of Broadcasting* 45:1 (Winter 1995), 77–82, discuss the confusion of terminology.

16. "The Impact of Cable Television on Subscriber and Nonsubscriber Behavior," *Journal of Advertising Research* 23:4 (August/September 1983), 15–23.

17. "Consumer Vid Spending in '85 Exceeds U.S. Theatrical B.O.; H'wood Studios Reap $1.8 Bil," *Variety* (January 15, 1986), 41. The drop in the late 1980s and early 1990s was within the range of normal annual fluctuations. Several reasons have been offered why people continued to go to the movie theater, including simply that going out is an event. See "At the Movies," *New York Times* (April 27, 1997), Sec. 4, p. 2. On industry worries of the time, see "Col Survey Shows Vid Rentals Far Outdistance Admissions," *Variety* (May 21, 1986), 3, 44; "Teens Leaving Theaters for Homevid," *Variety* (February 26, 1986), 3; "VCRs Bring Big Changes in Use of Leisure," *New York Times* (March 3, 1985), 1; "Say VCR Effect on Tix Sales Peaking," *Variety* (January 15, 1986), 36; "'Staggering' VCR Growth Cited," *Variety* (May 21, 1986), 3.

18. "Of Popcorn, Loneliness and VCRs," *New York Times* (August 27, 1985); Bradley Greenberg and Carrie Heeter, "VCRs and Young People," *American Behavioral Scientists* 30:5 (May/June 1987), 518.

19. On group viewing, see "Home VCR Study: Kids Lead Adults by Almost Double," *Variety* (June 22, 1988), 1; Stuart Miller, "MTV Wants its Collegiate Crowd," *Variety* (May 20, 1991), 27; a participant observation study conducted in spring 1993 under my supervision, observed group viewers in dorms and student apartments of an Eastern private college.

20. Nielsen claimed that households specialized in their uses of VCRs and identified three types: those that use the VCR with video cameras, those that used the VCR primarily for time-shifting, and those that used it primarily for pre-recorded cassettes. See "Soaps Top Pix in VCR Taping, Per Nielsen Poll," *Variety* (May 2, 1984), 44.

21. "First Look at Cassette Audience," *Media Decisions* (March 1979), 147; "Home Tapers Tapping Cable Programming," *Advertising Age* (May 31, 1984), 40; Opinion Research Center, "Recent Media Trends," 2; "Nets Audience May Be Widened by VCR Use," *Advertising Age* (June 10, 1985), 60.

22. "First Look at Cassette Audience," *Media Decisions* (March 1979), 149; "Soaps Top Pix in VCR Taping," *Variety* (May 2, 1984), 44; Mark Levy, "Program Playback Preferences in VCR Households," *Journal of*

Broadcasting 24 (Summer 1980), 332, 334; "VCRs: The Saga Continues," *Marketing & Media Decisions* (September 1985), 156.

23. "VCRs," *Broadcasting* (August 20, 1984), 48; "Neilsen Attacks VCR Zap Factor," *Advertising Age* (November 19, 1984), 92; Opinion Research Corp., "Recent Media Trends," *Public Opinion Index* 18: 6 (June 1985), 2; "As VCRs Advance, Agencies Fear TV Viewers Will Zap More Ads," *Wall Street Journal* (January 4, 1991), B3.

24. Carrie Heeter and Bradley Greenberg, "A Theoretical Overview of the Program Choice Process," in *Cableviewing* (Norwood, NJ: Ablex, 1988); B. Klopfenstein, "From Gadget to Necessity: The Diffusion of Remote Control Technology," in James Walker and Robert Bellamy, *The Remote Control in the New Age of Television* (Westport, CT: Praeger, 1993), 23–39; Robert Bellamy and James Walker, *Television and the Remote Control* (New York: Guilford, 1996), 18–21.

25. Bellamy and Walker, 35, 45–6, 100, 101, 137–9.

26. Bellamy and Walker 112.

27. "Intro Course Focus: How to Stop Surfing," *Variety* (January 5, 1997), 1–2; Susan Eastman, Jeffrey Neal-Lunsford, and Karen Riggs, "Coping with Grazing: Prime-Time Strategies for Accelerated Program Transitions," *Journal of Broadcasting and Electronic Media* 39 (1995), 92–108; Bellamy and Walker 49–94.

28. On bypassing networks, see "By-passing Networks Could Mean Big Profits," *Variety* (August 25, 1984), 1; "Is it Time for a Fourth Network?" *New York Times* (August 28, 1983), 1H; "M-E Joint Deal to Counter Webs," *Variety* (January 19, 1983), 77; "Program Suppliers Eye Satellites to Counter Nets," *Variety* (September 30, 1981), 60; "Fox Hatches Indie Web," *Variety* (May 14, 1986), 50.

29. Independent broadcast stations' share of the audience grew from 10 percent of total television viewing in 1975 to 21 percent in 1985, but then declined to 12 percent in 1996 as the new movie studio networks began. Data supplied by Nielsen Media Research; also "Viewing Trends from '50's to '80's," *Television/Radio Age* (July 22, 1985), 49; "Indie TV: It's Come a Long Way Baby," *Variety* (January 1, 1986), 29.

30. Numerous articles in the trade press note the panic of networks over their share losses and describe many new programming strategies to halt the losses, to no avail. See, e.g., Stuart Miller, "Web Losing Fight Against Erosion," *Variety* (December 23, 1996), 34; Joe Flint, "Intro Course Focus: How to Stop Surfing," *Variety* (December 23, 1996), 31; Bill Carter, "Where Did the Reliable Old TV Season Go?" *New York Times* (April 20, 1997), H1, 30; Susan Tyler Eastman, Jeffrey Neal-Lunsford, and Karen Riggs, "Coping with Grazing: Prime-Time Strategies for Accelerated Program Transitions," *Journal of Broadcasting & Electronic Media* 39 (1995), 92–108; D. M. Davis and J. R. Walker, "Countering the New Media: The Resurgence of Share Maintenance in Primetime Network Television," *Journal of Broadcasting & Electronic Media* 34 (1990), 487–93.

31. *New York Times* (1986); (1987); *Variety.* On reversal, see "A Racial Divide Widens on Network TV," *New York Times* (December 29, 1998), 1, A12.

32. "New Nielsen Study Boosts Numbers," *Variety* (November 19, 1990), 38; Richard Huff, "Nielsen, Nets Launch Viewership Study," *Variety* (April 6, 1992), 34

33. Elizabeth Kolbert, "Networks Press Nielsen to Count the Barfly Too," *New York Times* (March 15, 1993), D1.

34. From a study conducted in spring 1993 at an Eastern private college; also Dafna Lemish, "The Rules of Viewing Television in Public Places," *Journal of Broadcasting* 26:4 (Fall 1982), 757–81.

35. Stuart Miller, "TV Viewing's No Dating Game," *Variety* (August 24, 1992), 15–16.

36. "Home VCR Study: Kids Lead Adults by Almost Double," *Variety* (June 22, 1988), 1, 77; Marie-Louise Mares, "Children's Use of VCRs," *Annals of the American Academy of the Political and Social Sciences* 557 (May 1998), 121.

37. See Bill Carter, "Does More Time On Line Mean Reduced TV Time?" *New York Times* (January 31, 1997), D5; Bill Carter, "Networks Battle Nielsen as Young Viewers Turn Up Missing," *New York Times* (December 21, 1998), B1; Richard Katz, "Young Auds Seek Web, Not Webs," *Variety* (January 4, 1999), 65.

38. Jon Katz, "Old Media, New Media and a Middle Way," *New York Times* (January 19, 1997), H43; Amy Jordan and Kathleen Hall Jamieson, eds., "Children and Television," special issue, *Annals of the American Academy of Political and Social Science* 557 (May 1998).

39. Laurie Hays, "PCs May Be Teaching Kids the Wrong Lessons," *Wall Street Journal* (April 24, 1995), B1; on addiction, see Thomas DeLoughry, "Snared by the Internet," *Chronicle of Higher Education* (March 1, 1996), A25, 27.

Chapter 19.   Conclusion: From Effects to Resistance and Beyond

1. See, e.g., Philip Palmgreen, Lawrence Wenner, Karl Erik Rosengren, "Uses and Gratifications Research: The Past Ten Years," in Rosengren, Wenner, and Palmgreen, *Media Gratifications Research: Current Perspectives* (Beverly Hills: Sage 1985), 11–37; Sonia Livingstone, *Making Sense of Television: The Psychology of Audience Interpretation* (New York: Pergamon, 1990), 7–17; Everett Dennis and Ellen Wartella, *American Communication Research – The Remembered History* (Mahwah, NJ: L Erlbaum, 1996); Everett Rogers, *A History of Communication Study: A Biographical Approach* (New York: Free Press, 1994); Jesse Delia, "Communication Research: A History," in Charles Berger and Steven Chaffee, *Handbook of Communication Science* (Beverly Hills: Sage, 1987), 20–99; The future of the field II issue, *Journal of Communication* 43:4 (Autumn 1993); Elihu Katz, "Communications Research since Lazarsfeld," *Public Opinion Quarterly* 51:4 (1987), S25–S45.

2. See, e.g., Joseph Klapper, *The Effects of Mass Communication* (Glencoe, IL: Free Press, 1960), 234–8. Sociologist Herbert Gans claimed that in the absence of research into effects of media, the "public" turns to "essayists"

who simply asserted the power of media and the helplessness of audiences. See "Reopening the Black Box," *Journal of Communication* 43 (Autumn 1993), 29.

3. The tradition that political scientist Harold Lasswell invented the "hypodermic theory" in the 1920s is apparently false. See Dennis and Wartella, *American Communication Research* (1996), 172.

4. Everett Dennis stated that "For at least two generations, not only were media scholars cautious [about claiming powerful media and passive audiences] but they lent support to a generalized attitude in American universities that suggested a minimal impact of media in a variety of arenas." See Everette Dennis, "Preface," Everette Dennis and Ellen Wartella, eds., *American Communication Research: The Remembered History* (Mahwah, NJ: Erlbaum, 1996). Katz described the early Lazarsfeld studies as beginning "to perceive the mass audience as somehow more active, more involved, and more political." Eliha Katz, "Diffusion Research at Columbia," in Dennis and Wartella, 63.

5. Jesse Delia, "Communication Research: A History," in Charles Berger and Steven Chaffee, eds., *Handbook of Communication Research* (Beverly Hills: Sage 1987), 59–60, 63–9, on the shift from Lazarsfeld's applied research tradition to experimental social psychology paradigm. Wartella argues that each new medium attracted a new generation of researchers who began with a passive hypothesis from public debate. Ellen Wartella, "The History Reconsidered," in Dennis and Wartella, 177–8.

6. George Gerbner and his colleagues argue that both the Lazarsfeld and social psychological traditions of research have failed to find strong effects because of their focus on the *short-term* impact of single stimuli. They instead argued for study of long-term effects of repeated pervasive messages. This "cultivation analysis" approach concentrated on documenting a pervasive environment of ideas. See Shearon Lowry and Melvin DeFleur, *Milestones in Mass Communications Research* (White Plains, NY: Longman, 1983), 304, 381–3; Nancy Signorielli and Michael Morgan, "Cultivation Analysis: Conceptualization and Methodology," in *Cultivation Analysis: New Directions in Media Effects Research* (Beverly Hills: Sage, 1990), 17–19.

7. Elihu Katz, Jay Blumler, and Michael Gurevitch, "Uses and Gratifications Research," *Public Opinion Quarterly* 37 (Winter 1973–74), 509; the slogan first appeared in Elihu Katz, "Mass Communication Research and the Study of Culture," *Studies in Public Communication* 2 (1959), 1–6.

8. For an early critique of the approach, see Philip Elliot, "Uses and Gratifications: A Critique and a Sociological Alternative," in Jay Blumler and Elihu Katz, *Use of Mass Communication* (Beverly Hills: Sage, 1974).

9. See James Lull's autobiographical account in *Inside Family Viewing* (New York Routledge, 1990), 11–12; special ethnographic issue of *Journal of Broadcasting* 26:4 (Fall 1982); Thomas Lindlof and Timothy Meyer, "Mediated Communication as Ways of Seeing, Acting and Constructing Culture: The Tools and Foundations of Qualitative Research," in Lindlof, ed., *Natural Audiences: Qualitative Research and Media Uses and*

Effects (Norwood, NJ: Ablex, 1987), 1–30. Herbert Gans, in Withey and Ron Abeles (1980), 69, advocated an ethnographic approach such as he used for *Urban Villagers*. Also see Wilbur Schramm, *Television in the Lives of Our Children* (1961), 35.

10. Quote from Lindlof and Meyer, 4 Ira Glick and Sidney Levy, 49, already in the late 1950s saw television as part of the daily routine. But separation of mass communication and interpersonal communication within the discipline tended to retard pursuit of this reasonable observation. See James Lull, *Inside Television Viewing*, 12. The focus on embeddedness was stimulated by research on how VCRs changed family viewing patterns.

11. For critiques of the cultural studies ethnographic approach, see Janice Radway, "Reception Study: Ethnography and the Problems of Dispersed Audiences and Nomadic Subjects," *Cultural Studies* 2:3 (1988), 359–76; Virginia Nightingale, "What's 'Ethnographic' About Ethnographic Audience Research?" *Australian Journal of Communication* 16 (December 1989), 50–63.

12. Raymond Williams, *Marxism and Literature* (London: Oxford University Press, 1977), 113, 122–6. Stuart Hall applied Williams' term "oppositional" to what came to be called "reading against the grain" in his 1973 paper, "Encoding and Decoding in the Television Discourse," reprinted in Simon During, ed., *The Cultural Studies Reader* (London: Routledge, 1993), 103.

13. Stuart Hall, "Encoding and Decoding in the Television Discourse"; "Reflections on the Encoding/Decoding Model: An Interview with Stuart Hall," in Jon Cruz and Justin Lewis, *Viewing, Reading, Listening* (Boulder, Co.: Westview, 1994), 253–74. For early cultural studies of television audiences, see Stuart Hall "Introduction to Media Studies at the Centre," in *Culture, Media and Language* (London: Unwin Hyman, 1980), 117–21; Graeme Turner, *British Cultural Studies: An Introduction* (London: Routledge, 1990), ch. 4.

14. Stuart Hall and Tony Jefferson, eds., *Resistance Through Ritual: Youth Subcultures in Post-War Britain* (London: Hutchinson, 1976); John Clarke, Chas Critcher, Richard Johnson, eds., *Working Class Culture: Studies in History and Theory* (London: Hutchinson, 1979); Dick Hebdige, *Subculture: The Meaning of Style* (London: Methuen, 1979).

15. David Scholle, "Resistance: Pinning Down a Wandering Concept in Cultural Studies Discourse," *Journal of Urban and Cultural Studies* 1:1 (1990), 87–105; Sonia Livingstone, "The Rise and Fall of Audience Research," *Journal of Communication* 43:4 (Autumn 1993), 9; Ronald Lembo and Kenneth Tucker, "Culture, Television, and Opposition: Rethinking Cultural Studies," and William Evans, "The Interpretive Turn in Media Research: Innovation, Iteration, or Illusion," *Critical Studies in Mass Communication* 7:2 (June 1990), 100–3, 258–61.

16. Meagan Morris, "Banality of Cultural Studies," in Patricia Mellencamp, *Logics of Television: Essays in Cultural Criticism* (Bloomington: Indiana University Press, 1990), 14–43; Celeste Michelle Condit, "The Rhetorical Limits of Polysemy," in Robert Avery and David Eason, eds., *Critical*

Perspectives on Media and Society (New York: Guilford Press, 1991), 365–86; Tamar Liebes and Elihu Katz, "On the Critical Abilities of Television Viewers," in Ellen Seiter, Hans Borchers, Gabriele Kreutzner, and Eva-Maria Warth, eds., *Remote Control: Television, Audiences, and Cultural Power* (London: Routledge, 1989), 219; William Seaman, "Active Audience Theory: Pointless Populism," *Media Culture and Society* 14 (1992), 301–11; Justin Lewis and Sut Jhally, "The Politics of Cultural Studies: Racism, Hegemony and Resistance," and response by Herman Gray, *American Quarterly* 46:1 (March 1994), 114–20; Tania Modleski, "Introduction," *Studies in Entertainment* (Bloomington: Indiana University Press, 1986). Some writers within cultural studies have argued for integrating these opposite views. See John Clarke, "Pessimism vs. Populism," in Richard Butsch, ed. *For Fun and Profit: The Transformation of Leisure into Consumption* (Philadelphia: Temple University Press, 1990), 28–44; Lawrence Grossberg, "Cultural Studies vs. Politcal Economy: Is Anybody Else Bored with This Debate?" *Critical Studies in Mass Communication* 12:1 (March 1995), 72–81; Jim McGuigan, *Cultural Populism* (London: Routledge, 1992). For an interesting reflection on their own previous work, see David Morley, *Television, Audiences and Cultural Studies* (London: Routledge, 1992) and Dick Hebdige, *Hiding in the Light* (London: Comedia, 1988). Re: broader attacks on cultural studies, see Michael Denning, "The Academic Left and the Rise of Cultural Studies," *Radical History Review* (Fall 1992), 21–47.

17. Graeme Turner, *British Cultural Studies* (London: Routledge, 1992), 122; see also Judith Williamson, "The Problem of Being Popular," *New Socialist* (September 1986), 14–15.

18. Meaghan Morris, 25, 30, 29, 31.

19. Raymond Williams, "Base and Superstructure," in *Problems in Materialism and Culture: Selected Essays* (London: Verso, 1980), 38. This essay was originally published in *New Left Review* 82 (November–December 1973) and later expanded into *Marxism and Literature.*

20. Stuart Hall, "Notes on Deconstructing the Popular," in Raphael Samuel, ed., *People's History and Socialist Theory* (London: Routledge & Kegan Paul, 1981), 239.

21. Ien Ang, *Living Room Wars: Rethinking Media Audiences for a Postmodern World* (London: Routledge, 1996), 8–10, 43.

22. Williams, *Marxism and Literature,* ch. 8, 121–8, and Hebdige, *Subculture,* 92–9, on incorporation.

23. Robin Kelley emphasizes the collective nature of daily acts of black working-class resistance. Even seemingly individualistic acts may have larger significance when they are part of a subculture. See Robin Kelley, "'We Are Not What We Seem': Rethinking Black Working-Class Opposition in the Jim Crow South," *Journal of American History* 80:1 (June 1993), 75–112.

24. For example, Gaye Tuchman, Arlene Kaplan Daniels, and James Benet, *Hearth and Home: Images of Women in the Mass Media* (New York:

Oxford University Press, 1978); Mary Cassata and Thomas Skill, *Life on Daytime Television: Tuning-in American Serial Drama* (Norwood, NJ: Ablex, 1983); Laura Mulvey, "Visual Pleasure and Narrative Cinema," *Screen* 16:3 (1975) 6–18; Tania Modleski, *Loving with a Vengeance: Mass-Produced Fantasies for Women* (Hamden, CT: Archon Books, 1982).

25. For reviews of this literature, see Ien Ang, *Living Room Wars,* 110–15, and Jackie Stacey, "From Male Gaze to Female Spectator," in *Star Gazing: Hollywood Cinema and Female Spectatorship* (London: Routledge, 1994), 19–48; Jim McGuigan, *Cultural Populism* (London: Routledge, 1992), 140–51.

26. Modleski particularly was criticized for presuming that all viewers would adopt the "ideal mother image" she attributed to soap opera text. See Ang, *Living Room Wars,* 112.

27. Charlotte Brunsdon, "Crossroads: Notes on Soap Opera," *Screen* 22:4 (1981); Dorothy Hobson, *Crossroads: The Drama of a Soap Opera* (London: Methuen, 1982); Ien Ang, *Watching Dallas: Soap Opera and the Melodramatic Imagination,* Della Couling, trans., (London: Methuen, 1985); Ellen Seiter, Hans Borchers, Gabriele Kreutzner, and Eva-Maria Warth, "'Don't Treat Us Like We're So Stupid and Naïve': Toward an Ethnography of Soap Opera Viewers," in *Remote Control: Television, Audiences and Cultural Power* (New York: Routledge, 1989); Andrea Press, *Women Watching Television: Gender, Class and Generation in the American Television Experience* (Philadelphia: University of Pennsylvania Press, 1991). On the two research traditions in film studies and television studies, see Annette Kuhn, "Women's Genres," *Screen* 25:1 (January/February 1984), 18–28; and Stacey, *Star Gazing* (1994).

28. Ellen Seiter, et al., "Don't Treat Us Like We're So Stupid and Naïve," 240–2. Andrea Press, *Women Watching Television,* too found women reading soap operas resistively. By the mid-1990s this approach was being refined by Ien Ang, *Living Room Wars* (1996); Stacey, *Star Gazing* (1994). Again reflecting a general shift in women's studies, Ang (117–19, 120, 126) argued for the need to examine the "articulation" of gender with media consumption. "Articulation" is a term borrowed by Stuart Hall from Laclau, used in cultural studies from early on. See David Morley, "Text, Readers, Subject," in Stuart Hall, Dorothy Hobson, A. Lowe, and Paul Willis, *Culture, Media, Language* (London: Hutchinson, 1980), 165.

29. Tania Modleski, "The Rhythms of Reception: Daytime Television and Women's Work," in E. Ann Kaplan, ed., *Regarding Television: Critical Approaches – An Anthology* (Frederick, MD: University Publications of America, 1983), 71–3; Modleski, *Loving with a Vengeance* (1982), 100–2. Sandy Flitterman, "The Real Soap Operas: TV Commercials," in Kaplan, *Regarding Television,* 84–5, also notes the "staccato, ruptured attention." Similar interrupted styles were found in early radio listening. See Chapter 13.

30. Stuart Hall, "Encode/Decode," noted people's familiarity with forms and conventions.

31. John Hartley, "Invisible Fictions: Television Audiences, Paedocracy, Pleasure," *Textual Practice* 1:2 (1988), 121–38; Ien Ang, *Desperately Seeking the Audience* (London: Routledge 1991); Martin Allor, "Relocating the Site of the Audience," *Critical Studies in Mass Communication* 5:3 (1988), 217–33; Graeme Turner, *British Cultural Studies: An Introduction* (London: Routledge, 1990), 149, 161–6.

32. Elizabeth Long, on the other hand, did study preexisting groups and explored their relation to collective action. See "Textual Interpretation as Collective Action," in Jon Cruz and Justin Lewis, eds., *Viewing, Reading, Listening: Audiences and Cultural Reception* (Boulden, CO: Westview, 1994), 181–212.

33. On interpretive communities, see Stanley Fish, *Is There a Text in This Class?: The Authority of Interpretive Communities* (Cambridge: Harvard University Press, 1980).

34. See Virginia Nightingale, "What's 'Ethnographic' About Ethnographic Audience Research?" *Australian Journal of Communication* 16 (December 1989), 59–60, on difference between subculture and TV reception. A few ethnographic studies over the decades have found people use their own experience and communities as context to judge and interpret media. See Hortense Powdermaker, "Mississippi," *Strangers and Friends; The Way of an Anthropologist* (New York; Norton, 1966); Rosalind Brunt, "Engaging with the Popular: Audiences for Mass Culture and What to Say About Them," in Lawrence Grossberg, Cary Nelson, Paula Treichler, eds., *Cultural Studies* (London: Routledge, 1992), 72; and Chapter 17 on working-class viewers.

35. On images of fans, see Joli Jensen, "Fandom as Pathology: The Consequences of Characterization," and John Fiske, "The Cultural Economy of Fandom," in Lisa Lewis, *The Adoring Audience* (London: Routledge, 1992), 9–29, 30–49. Camille Bacon-Smith, *Enterprising Women: Television Fandom and the Creation of Popular Myth* (Philadelphia: University of Pennsylvania Press, 1992), 17–18, found a high proportion of fans are women, although this varied by particular show and fan activity.

36. Henry Jenkins, *Textual Poachers: Television Fans and Participatory Culture* (New York: Routledge, 1992), 277–82, 283–7; John Fiske, *Understanding Popular Culture* (Unwin Hyman, 1989), 146–50; Bacon-Smith, *Enterprising Women,* 319–22 distinguishes casual fans from core fans who "draw their social lives from the structures of fandom." Jenkins describes core fans who constitute and sustain the fan subcultures.

37. Fiske in Lewis, 37, on semiotic production. Seiter, "Don't Talk to Us Like We're So Stupid and Naïve"; Andrea Press, *Women Watching Television,* on group viewing. Again, E. Long is an exception.

38. Kari Whittenberger-Keith, "Understanding Fandom Rhetorically: The Case of Beauty and the Beast," in Andrew King, ed., *Postmodern Political Communication: The Fringe Challenges the Center* (Westport, CT: Praeger, 1992), 131–51. Whittenberger-Keith noted most rhetoric in letters from fanzines sustained the community. Fans are more like hobbyists

than counterculturalists. On hobbyists, see Dale Dannefer, "Rationality and Passion in Private Experience: Modern Consciousness and the Social World of Old-Car Collectors," *Social Problems* 27:4 (April 1980), 392–412; Richard Butsch, "The Commodification of Leisure: The Case of the Model Airplane Hobby and Industry," *Qualitative Sociology* 7:3 (Fall 1984), 217–35; Bert Moorhouse, "Organizing Hot Rods: Sport and Specialist Magazines," *British Journal of Sports History* 3:1 (May 1986), 81–98.

39. See Steve Duncombe, "Notes from the Underground: Zines and the Politics of Underground Culture," (Ph.D., CUNY, 1996).

40. John Tulloch and Henry Jenkins, *Science Fiction Audiences: Watching Dr. Who and Star Trek* (London: Routledge, 1995), 196–7.

41. Stuart Hall and Tony Jefferson, *Resistance Through Ritual;* Dick Hebdige, *Subculture: The Meaning of Style* (London: Methuen, 1979); also see Theodore Roszak, *The Making of a Counter Culture* (Garden City, NY: Doubleday, 1969).

Appendix: Availability, Affordability, Admission Price

1. William Reardon and Eugene Bristow, "The American Theatre, 1860–1870: An Economic Portrait," *Speech Monographs* 33:4 (November 1966), 438–43; Peter Davis, "From Stock to Combination: The Panic of 1873 and Its Effects on American Theater," *Theater History Studies* 8 (1988), 1–9.

Selected Bibliography

This bibliography lists only a few of the numerous, primary sources from periodicals used in this research. A complete list would take up dozens of pages and would repeat information found in the notes. Many can be found under various headings, such as "audience," "theater," "gallery," "radio," and so forth, in *Poole's Index, Reader's Guide, The New York Times Index,* the *New York Post* general news index 1873–1921, and Frederick Faxon, Mary Bates, and Anne Sutherland, eds., *Cumulative Dramatic Index 1909–1949* (Boston: G. K. Hall, 1965). Claudia Johnson and E. Vernon, *Nineteenth Century Theatrical Memoirs* (Westport CT: Greenwood Press, 1982), indexes references to audiences in memoirs. Frederick Litto, *American Dissertations on the Drama and the Theatre: A Bibliography* (Kent, OH: Kent State University, 1969) helped to locate relevant secondary sources; and Marsha Appel, *Illustration Index* (Metuchen, NJ: Scarecrow, 1980) helped to locate pictures of audiences. George C. D. Odell, *Annals of the New York Stage,* was unique among theater histories in indexing the subject of audiences. In addition, I found information illuminating audiences in the archives and newspapers and magazines listed below.

Archives

Bettmann Archive: audience files.

Cincinnati Historical Society: Fan mail from Powell Crosley and Wulsin Family papers.

Columbia University Rare Book and Manuscript Library: George C. D. O'Dell, Paul Lazarsfeld, Erik Barnouw papers; Fanny Kemble and Brander Matthews letters; Augustin Daly's theater collection.

Free Library of Philadelphia Theatre Collection: Playbills and clipping files on audiences, vaudeville, minstrelsy.

Harvard University Pusey Library Theater Collection: Playbills and clipping files on audiences, minstrelsy and vaudeville/variety.

Historical Society of Pennsylvania: Playbills and theater scrapbooks (13 vols.); scrapbook of Charles Durang, "The Philadelphia Stage from the Year 1749 to the Year 1855," 1868, arranged and illustrated by Thomas Westcott from Philadelphia *Sunday Dispatch,* from May 7, 1854 on.

University of Iowa Libraries Special Collections: Keith/Albee Collection.

Library of Congress Manuscript Division: Austin Brown papers 1830–1901, Laura Keene papers.

Museum of the City of New York: Yiddish theater collection; Byron Company photographs of theatrical scene in New York City, 1896–1918.

National Museum of American History (NMAH) Archive Center: Ayer, Clark, Dumont, and Warshaw collections.

National Archives: WPA Recreation Programs Records 1935–1939; Bureau of Labor Statistics Cost of Living Survey, 1918–19, completed questionnaires.

New York Historical Society: Henry Southworth theater diary, 1850–51.

New York Public Library, Billy Rose Theater Collection: Epes Sargent, Tony Pastor scrapbooks; Robinson Locke scrapbook collection; and clippings files.

New York Public Library Picture Collection.

University of Pennsylvania Van Pelt Library Special Collections: Edwin Forrest papers.

Princeton University Mudd Manuscript Library: Playbills and Office of Radio Research papers, 1937–39.

State Historical Society of Wisconsin (SHSW), Mass Communication Collection: NBC Records; papers of researchers Edgar P. James, Daniel Starch, C. E. Hooper, Inc., A C. Nielsen, Inc.; fan mail of John Daly, Wendall Hall, Hal Kanter, NBC, Irna Philips, Rod Serling, Clifton Utley; papers of Women's National Radio Committee, 1942.

Trenton Public Library, Trentoniana Collection: William Green theatre record and scrapbook, 1900–02; John J. Cleary scrapbook of Trenton history.

Western Reserve Historical Society: The Payne Fund Records.

Newspapers and Magazines

Chicago *Daily News,* radio section, 1922–27; New York *Clipper,* 1866–85; New York *Dramatic Mirror,* 1879–1922; New York *Herald,* minstrelsy column, 1850–60; *Keith News;* New York *Times,* 1860s–1970s; *Popular Radio,* 1922–29; *Radio* 1921–23; *Radio Age,* 1922–27; *Radio Broadcast,* 1922–30; *Radio Digest,* 1923–30; *Radio-Music Merchant,* 1930; *Radio News,* 1920–23, 1932; *Radio Retailing,* various, 1925–41; *Radio World,* 1922–28; *Rural Radio,* 1939; *The Spirit of the Times,* 1830s–60s; *Televiser,* 1944–51; *Theatre Magazine,* 1901–27; *Variety,* 1975–95; *Wireless Age,* 1919–25.

General: Eighteenth- and Nineteenth-Century Sources

Gustave De Beaumont, *Marie, or Slavery in the United States* (Palo Alto, CA: Stanford University Press, 1958), trans. Barbara Chapman. [orig., 1835].

Edward Dicey, *Spectator of America* (Chicago: Quadrangle, 1971) [orig., 1863].

Henry Bradshaw Fearon, *Sketches of America* (New York: Augustus Kelley, 1970; London: Longman, Hurst, Rees, Orme and Brown, 1818).

David Edelstein, *Joel Munsell: Printer and Antiquarian* (New York: Columbia University Press, 1950).

George Foster, *New York by Gaslight* (New York: Dewitt & Davenport, 1850).

Benjamin French, *Witness to the Young Republic: A Yankee's Journal* (Hanover, NH: University Press of New England, 1989).

Francis J. Grund, *Aristocracy in America: From the Sketch-book of a German Nobleman* (New York: Harper, 1959) [orig., London: Richard Bentley, 1839].

Thomas Butler Gunn, *The Physiology of New York Boarding-Houses* (New York: Mason Brothers, 1857).

John Hewitt, *Shadows on the Wall* (New York: AMS Press, 1971) [orig., Baltimore, 1877].

William Ranson Hogan and Edwin Adams Davis, eds., *William Johnson's Natchez: The Ante-Bellum Diary of a Free Negro* (Baton Rouge: Louisiana State University Press, 1979).

Philip Hone, *The Diary of Philip Hone, 1828–1851*, Allan Nevins, ed. (New York: Dodd, Mead, 1927).

Mark Antony DeWolfe Howe, ed., *The Articulate Sisters* (Cambridge, MA: Harvard University Press, 1946).

Dio Lewis, *Our Girls* (New York: Harper and Bros., 1871).

Benjamin E. Lloyd, *Lights and Shades in San Francisco* (San Francisco: A.L. Bancroft, 1876).

Ferdinand Longchamp, *Asmodeus in New York* (New York: Longchamps, 1866).

J. T. Mayne, *Short Notes of Tours in America and India* (Madras: Gantz Bros., 1869).

Edward Martin [James McCabe], *The Secrets of the Great City* (Philadelphia: National, 1868).

James McCabe, *Light and Shadows of New York Life* (Philadelphia: National, 1872).

James McCabe, *New York by Sunlight and Gaslight* (Philadelphia: Douglas Bros., 1882).

John Melish, *Travels through the US of A in the Years 1806 & 1807 and 1809, 1810 & 1811* (Philadelphia: John Melish, 1815).

George W. Pierson, *Tocqueville and Beaumont in America* (New York: Oxford University Press 1938).

William Priest, *Travels in the U S of A Commencing in the year 1793 and ending in 1797* (London: Printed for J. Johnson, 1802).

Charles H. Sherrill, *French Memories of Eighteenth-Century America* (New York: Charles Scribner's Sons, 1915).

Matthew Smith, *Sunshine and Shadow in New York* (Hartford, CT: J. B. Ban, 1869).

Frances Trollope, *Domestic Manners of the Americans,* Donald Smalley ed. (New York: Knopf, 1949) [orig., London, 1832].

Isaac Weld, Jr. *Travels Through North America: 1795–97,* vol. I, 4th ed. (New York: Augustus Kelley, 1969) [orig., London: Lane, Newman, 1807].

General: Twentieth-Century Sources

"The Leisure Hours of 5,000 People," National Recreation Association (1934).

"Madison Recreational Survey" (Madison, WIS: Madison Board of Commerce, 1915).

"Recreational Survey of Cincinnati" (Cincinnati: Juvenile Protection Association, 1913).

Elaine Abelson, *When Ladies Go A-Thieving: Middle-Class Shoplifters in Victorian Department Stores* (New York: Oxford University Press, 1989)

D. R. Adams, "Wage Rates in the Early National Period, Philadelphia, 1785–1830," *Journal of Economic History* (1968), 404–27.

Jane Addams, *The Spirit of Youth and the City Streets* (New York: MacMillan, 1912).

Stanley Benn and Gerald Gaus, eds., *Public and Private in Social Life* (London: Croom Helm, 1983).

Bennett Berger, *Working Class Suburb: A Study of Auto Workers in Suburbia* (Berkeley University of California Press, 1960).

George Bevans, "How Working Men Spend Their Spare Time" (Ph.D., Columbia University, 1913).

Lynn Bloom, "It's All for Your Own Good: Parent-Child Relationships in Popular American Child-Rearing Literature, 1820–1970," *Journal of Popular Culture* 10:1 (Summer 1976), 194–204.

Stuart Blumin, "Mobility and Change in Ante-bellum Philadelphia," in Stephan Thernstrom and Richard Sennett, eds., *Nineteenth Century Cities* (New Haven: Yale University Press, 1969).

John Bohstedt, "The Moral Economy and the Discipline of Historical Context," *Journal of Social History* 26 (Winter 1992), 265–84.

Pierre Bourdieu, *Distinction: A Social Critique of the Judgement of Taste,* trans. Richard Nice (Cambridge: Harvard University Press, 1984).

M. Christine Boyer, *Manhattan Manners: Architecture and Style, 1850–1900* (New York: Rizzoli, 1985).

Paul Boyer, *Urban Masses and Moral Order in America, 1820–1920* (Cambridge: Harvard University Press, 1978).

Adam Brown, *Fanatics: Power, Identity and Fandom in Football* (London: Routledge, 1998).

Peter Burke, *Popular Culture in Early Modern Europe* (London: Temple Smith, 1978).

Richard Butsch, ed., *For Fun and Profit: The Transformation of Leisure into Consumption* (Philadelphia: Temple University Press, 1990).

Craig Calhoun, *Habermas and the Public Sphere* (Cambridge, MA: MIT Press, 1992).

Mark Carnes and Clyde Griffen, eds., *Meanings for Manhood: Constructions of Masculinity in Victorian America* (Chicago: University of Chicago Press, 1990).

Dominick Cavallo, *Muscles and Morals: Organized Playgrounds and Urban Reform, 1880–1920* (Philadelphia: University of Pennsylvania Press, 1981).

John Clarke, "Pessimism vs. Populism," in Richard Butsch, ed. *For Fun and Profit: The Transformation of Leisure into Consumption* (Philadelphia: Temple University Press, 1990) 28–44.

John Clarke, Chas Critcher, Richard Johnson, eds., *Working Class Culture: Studies in History and Theory* (London: Hutchinson, 1979).

Lizabeth Cohen, *Making a New Deal: Industrial Workers in Chicago, 1919–1939* (New York: Cambridge University Press, 1990).

Patricia Cline Cohen, "Unregulated Youth: Masculinity and Murder in the 1830s City," *Radical History Review* 52 (Winter 1992), 33–52.

Kathleen Conzen, *Immigrant Milwaukee* (Cambridge: Harvard University Press, 1976).

David Courtwright, *Violent Land: Single Men and Social Disorder* (Cambridge: Harvard University Press, 1996).

Ruth Schwartz Cowan, *More Work for Mother: The Ironies of Household Technology from the Open Hearth to the Microwave* (New York: Basic Books, 1983).

Elmer Cressman, "The Out of School Activities of Junior High School" (D.Ed., Penn State College, 1937).

Cathy Davidson, ed., *Reading in America: Literature and Social History* (Baltimore: Johns Hopkins, 1989).

Michael Davis, *Exploitation of Pleasure* (New York: Russell Sage Foundation, 1910)

Michael Denning, *Mechanic Accents: Dime Novels and Working-Class Culture in America* (New York: Verso, 1987).

Michael Denning, "The End of Mass Culture" and responses *International Labor and Working Class History* 37–39 (Spring 1990 to Spring 1991).

Michael Denning, "The Academic Left and the Rise of Cultural Studies," *Radical History Review* (Fall 1992), 21–47.

Norman Denzin, *Symbolic Interactionism and Cultural Studies* (Cambridge, MA: Basil Blackwell, 1992).

Sarah Deutsch, "Reconceiving the City: Women, Space and Power in Boston, 1870–1910," *Gender & History* 6:2 (August 1994), 202–23.

Ann Douglas, *The Feminization of American Culture* (New York: Knopf, 1977).

Steve Duncombe, "Notes from the Underground: Zines and the Politics of Underground Culture" (Ph.D., CUNY, 1996.)

Robert Dykstra, *The Cattle Towns: A Social History of the Kansas Cattle Trading Centers, 1867–1885* (New York: Knopf, 1968).

Ron Eyerman and Andrew Jamison, "Social Movements and Cultural Transformation: Popular Music in the 1960s," *Media, Culture and Society* 17 (1995), 449–68.

Paula Fass, *The Damned and the Beautiful: American Youth in the 1920s* (New York: Oxford University Press, 1977).

Michael Feldberg, "The Crowd in Philadelphia History," *Labor History* 15:3 (Summer 1974), 323–36.

Stanley Fish, *Is There a Text in This Class?: The Authority of Interpretive Communities* (Cambridge: Harvard University Press, 1980).

John Fiske, *Understanding Popular Culture* (Boston: Unwin Hyman, 1989).

William Gamson, *Talking Politics* (New York: Cambridge University Press, 1992).

Herbert Gans, *The Urban Villagers: Group and Class in the Life of Italian-Americans* (New York: Free Press, 1962).

Herbert Gans, *The Levittowners* (New York: Pantheon, 1967).

Ella Gardner and Caroline Legg, *Leisure Time Activities of Rural Children in Selected Areas of West Virginia* (Washington: U.S. GPO, 1931).

Timothy Gilfoyle, *City of Eros: New York City, Prostitution, and the Commercialization of Sex, 1790–1920* (New York: Norton, 1992).

Paul Gilje, *The Road to Mobocracy: Popular Disorder in New York City, 1763–1834* (Chapel Hill: University of North Carolina Press, 1987).

Paul Gilje, *Rioting in America* (Bloomington: Indiana University Press, 1996).

Salvador Giner, *Mass Society* (New York: Academic Press, 1976).

David Grimsted, "The Purple Rose of Popular Culture Theory," *American Quarterly* 43:4 (December 1991), 541–78.

Lawrence Grossberg, "Cultural Studies vs. Political Economy: Is Anybody Else Bored with This Debate?" *Critical Studies in Mass Communication* 12:1 (March 1995), 72–81.

Lawrence Grossberg, Cary Nelson, Paula Treichler, eds., *Cultural Studies* (New York: Routledge, 1992).

Stuart Hall and Tony Jefferson, eds., *Resistance through Ritual: Youth Subcultures in Post-War Britain* (London: Hutchinson, 1976).

Stuart Hall, "Notes on Deconstructing the Popular," in Raphael Samuel, ed., *People's History and Socialist Theory* (London: Routledge & Kegan Paul, 1981), 227–40.

Karen Halttunen, *Confidence Men and Painted Women: A Study of Middle-Class Culture in America, 1830–1870* (New Haven: Yale University Press, 1982).

Hutchins Hapgood, *The Spirit of the Ghetto* (New York: Funk & Wagnalls, 1902).

Steve Hardy, *How Boston Played: Sport, Recreation and Community, 1865–1915* (Boston: Northeastern University Press, 1982).

Alan Havig, "The Commercial Amusement Audience in Early Twentieth-Century American Cities," *Journal of American Culture* 5 (Spring 1982), 1–19.

Rowland Haynes, "Recreation Survey, Milwaukee" (Milwaukee: Child Welfare Commission, 1912).

Rowland Haynes, "Recreation Survey, Detroit, Michigan" (Detroit: Detroit Board of Commerce, 1913).

Rowland Haynes and F. F. McClure, "Recreation Survey of Kansas City, Missouri" (New York: Playground and Recreation Association of America, 1912).

Kenneth Lewis Heaton, "A Study of the Recreational Life of High School Students" (Ph.D., University of Chicago, 1933).

Dick Hebdige, *Subculture: The Meaning of Style* (London: Methuen, 1979).

Dick Hebdige, *Hiding in the Light: On Images and Things* (Routledge, 1988).

Adele Heller and Lois Rudnick, eds., *1915, The Cultural Moment: The New Politics, the New Woman, the New Psychology, the New Art, and the New Theatre in America* (New Brunswick, NJ: Rutgers University Press, 1991).

Dorothy O. Helly and Susan Reverby, eds., *Gendered Domains: Rethinking Public and Private in Women's History* (Ithaca, NY: Cornell University Press, 1992).

Irving Howe, *World of Our Fathers* (New York: Harcourt Brace Jovanovich, 1976).

Andreas Huyssen, "Mass Culture as Woman: Modernism's Other," in Tania Modleski, ed., *Studies in Entertainment: Critical Approaches to Mass Culture* (Bloomington: Indiana University Press, 1986), 188–207.

Kenneth Jackson, *Crabgrass Frontier: The Suburbanization of the United States* (New York: Oxford University Press 1985).

Norman Jacobs, ed., *Culture for the Millions?* (Boston: Beacon Press, 1964).

Peter d'A. Jones and Melvin G. Holli, *Ethnic Chicago* (Grand Rapids MI: William Eerdmans, 1981).

Patrick Joyce, *Visions of the People: Industrial England and the Question of Class, 1840–1914* (London: Cambridge University Press, 1991).

Michael Kammen, *The Lively Arts: Gilbert Seldes and the Transformation of Cultural Criticism in the Unites States* (New York: Oxford University Press, 1996).

John Kasson, *Rudeness and Civility: Manners in Nineteenth-Century Urban America* (New York: Hill and Wang, 1990).

Robin Kelley, "'We Are Not What We Seem': Rethinking Black Working-Class Opposition in the Jim Crow South," *Journal of American History* 80:1 (June 1993), 75–112.

Linda Kerber, *Women of the Republic* (Chapel Hill: University of North Carolina Press, 1980).

Melvin Kohn, "Social Class and Parent-Child Relationships," *American Journal of Sociology* 68 (January 1963), 471–80.

William Kornhauser, *The Politics of Mass Society* (New York: Free Press, 1959).

Bruce Laurie, *Working People of Philadelphia, 1800–1850* (Philadelphia: Temple University Press, 1980).

William Leach, "Transformations in a Culture of Consumption: Women and Department Stores, 1890–1925," *Journal of American History* 71 (1984), 319–342.

William Leach, *Land of Desire: Merchants, Power and the Rise of a New American Culture* (New York: Pantheon, 1993).

J. P. Lichtenberge, ed., Country life issue, *American Academy of Political and Social Science* 40 n129 (1912).

Elizabeth Long, "Women, Reading and Cultural Authority: Some Implications of the Audience Perspective in Cultural Studies," *American Quarterly* 38 (Fall 1986), 591–612.

Elizabeth Long, "Textual Interpretation as Collective Action" in Jon Cruz and Justin Lewis, eds., *Viewing, Reading, Listening: Audiences and Cultural Reception* (Boulder, CO: Westview, 1994), 181–211.

Robert and Helen Merrill Lynd, *Middletown A Study in Modern American Culture* (New York: Harcourt, Brace, 1929)

Robert and Helen Merrill Lynd, *Middletown in Transition* (New York: Harcourt, 1937).

Annie Marion MacLean, *Wage-Earning Women* (New York: MacMillan, 1910).

Roland Marchand, *Advertising the American Dream* (Berkeley: University of California Press, 1985).

Roland Marchand, *Creating the Corporate Soul: The Rise of Public Relations and Corporate Imagery in American Big Business* (Berkeley: University of California Press, 1998).

Glenna Matthews, *The Rise of Public Woman: Woman's Power and Woman's Place in the U.S., 1630–1970* (New York, Oxford University Press 1992).

Elaine Tyler May, *Homeward Bound* (New York: Basic Books, 1988).

Jim McGuigan, *Cultural Populism* (London: Routledge, 1992).

Robert McKay, "Segregation and Public Recreation," *Virginia Law Review* 40:6 (October 1954), 697–731.

Edward Montgomery, "The Urbanization of Rural Recreation" (Ph.D., University of Chicago, 1934).

David Nasaw, *Children of the City: At Work and at Play* (Garden City: Doubleday, 1985).

David Nasaw, *Going Out* (New York Basic Books, 1995).

Janet Fowler Nelson, "Leisure Time Interest and Activities of Business Girls" (New York: The Woman's Press for YWCA National Board, 1933).

Roger Nichols, ed., *American Frontier and Western Issues: An Historiographical Review* (Westport, CT: Greenwood Press, 1986).

Francis North, "A Recreational Survey of the City of Providence, Rhode Island" (Providence, RI: Providence Playground Association, 1912).

Francis North, "A Recreational Survey of the City of Waltham, Massachusetts" (Waltham, MA: Barry, 1913).

David Nye, *Electrifying America: Social Meanings of a New Technology, 1880–1940* (Cambridge, MA: MIT Press, 1990).

Ray Oldenburg, *The Great Good Place* (New York: Paragon House, 1989)

Helen Papashvily, *All the Happy Endings: A Study of the Domestic Novel in America, The Women Who Wrote It, The Women Who Read It, in the Nineteenth Century* (New York: Harper and Row, 1956).

Kathy Peiss, *Cheap Amusements: Working Women and Leisure in Turn-of-the-Century New York* (Philadelphia: Temple University Press, 1986),

Kathy Peiss, *Hope in a Jar: The Making of America's Beauty Culture* (New York: Metropolitan Books, 1998)

Anthony Platt, *The Child-Savers: the Invention of Delinquency* (Chicago: University of Chicago Press, 1969).

Robert Putnam, "The Strange Disappearance of Civic America," *American Prospect* 24 (Winter 1996), 34–48, and responses in 25 (March–April, 1996), 17–28, and 26 (May–June, 1996), 16–21, 94.

Lauren Rabinowitz, *For the Love of Pleasure* (New Brunswick, NJ: Rutgers University Press, 1998).

Janice Radway, *Reading the Romance* (Chapel Hill University of North Carolina Press, 1984).

Clarence Rainwater, "The Play Movement in the U.S.: A Study of Community Recreation" (Ph.D., University of Chicago, 1921).

Charles Raitt, "A Survey of Recreational Facilities in Rochester, NY" (Rochester, NY: J.M. Egloff, 1929).

Rayna Rapp and Ellen Ross, "The 1920s Feminism, Consumerism, and Political Backlash in the United States," in Judith Friedlander, et al., *Women in Culture and Politics: A Century of Change* (Bloomington: Indiana University Press, 1986), 52–61.

Walter Reckless, *Vice in Chicago* (Chicago: University of Chicago Press, 1933).

Dorothy Reed, "Leisure Time of Girls in 'Little Italy'" (Ph.D., Columbia University, 1932).

David Roediger, *Wages of Whiteness: Race and the Making of the American Working Class* (New York: Verso, 1991).

Malcolm Rohrbough, *Days of Gold: The California Gold Rush and the American Nation* (Berkeley: University of California Press, 1997).

Bernard Rosenberg and David M. White, eds., *Mass Culture: The Popular Arts in America* (New York: Free Press, 1957).

Roy Rosenzweig, *Eight Hours for What We Will* (London: Cambridge University Press, 1983).

Steven Ross, *Workers on the Edge: Urban Leisure and Politics in Industrializing Cincinnati, 1788–1890* (New York: Columbia University Press, 1985).

Theodore Roszak, *The Making of A Counter Culture* (Garden City, NY: Doubleday, 1969).

Joan Rubin, *The Making of Middle Brow Culture* (Chapel. Hill: University of North Carolina Press, 1992)

George Rude, *Ideology and Popular Protest* (New York: Pantheon, 1980).

Mary Ryan, *Women in Public: Between Banners and Ballots, 1825–1880* (Baltimore: Johns Hopkins University Press, 1990).

Alexander Saxton, *The Rise and Fall of the White Republic: Class Politics and Mass Culture in Nineteenth Century America* (London: Verso, 1990).

Lois Scharf and Joan Jensen, eds., *Decades of Discontent: The Women's Movement 1920–1940* (Westport, CT: Greenwood Press, 1983).

David Scobey, "Anatomy of the Promenade: The Politics of Bourgeois Sociability in Nineteenth Century New York," *Social History* 17 (May 1992), 203–28.

James Scott, *Domination and the Arts of Resistance* (New Haven, CT: Yale University Press, 1990).

Joan Scott, *Gender and the Politics of History* (New York; Columbia University Press, 1988).

Gilbert Seldes, *The Great Audience* (New York: Viking Press, 1950).

Richard Sennett, *The Fall of Public Man* (New York: Knopf, 1977).

David Scholle, "Resistance: Pinning Down a Wandering Concept in Cultural Studies Discourse," *Journal of Urban and Cultural Studies* 1:1 (1990), 87–105.

James Sharp, *American Politics in the Early Republic: The New Nation in Crisis* (New Haven, CT: Yale University Press, 1993).

Beverly Skeggs, *Formations of Class and Gender: Becoming Respectable* (London: Routledge, 1997).

Richard Slotkin, *The Fatal Environment: The Myth of the Frontier in the Age of Industrialization, 1800–1890* (New York: Atheneum, 1985).

Carroll Smith-Rosenberg, *Disorderly Conduct* (New York: Knopf, 1985).

Peter Stallybrass and Allon White, *The Politics and Peotics of Transgression* (Ithaca, NY: Cornell University Press, 1986).

Christine Stansell, *City of Women: Sex and Class in New York 1789–1860* (New York: Knopf, 1982).

Catherine Stimpson, Elsa Dixler, Martha Nelson, and Kathryn Yatrakis, eds., *Women and the American City* (Chicago: University of Chicago Press, 1981).

Richard Stott, *Workers in the Metropolis: Class, Ethnicity and Youth in Antebellum New York City* (Ithaca, NY: Cornell University Press, 1990).

Thomas Strychacz, "American Sports Writers and 'Unruly Rooters': The Significance of Orderly Spectating," *Journal of American Studies* 28:1 (April 1994), 84–9.

Alan Swingewood, *The Myth of Mass Culture* (Atlantic Highlands, NJ: Humanities Press, 1977).

Rogan Taylor, *Football and Its Fans: Supporters and Their Relations with the Game, 1885–1985* (Leicester, UK: Leicester University Press, 1992).

John Tebbel and Mary Ellen Zuckerman, *The Magazine in America, 1741–1990* (New York: Oxford University Press, 1991).

William I. Thomas and Florian Znaniecki, *The Polish Peasant in Europe and America, 1918–1920* (Chicago: University of Chicago Press, 1918–20).

Edwin P. Thompson, "The Moral Economy of the English Crowd in the Eighteenth Century," *Past and Present* 50 (February 1971), 76–136.

Charles Tilly, *From Mobilization to Revolution* (Reading, MA: Addison-Wesley, 1978).

Arthur Todd, ed., *Chicago Recreation Survey*, IV (Washington, DC: WPA, 1939).

Graeme Turner, *British Cultural Studies* (London Routledge, 1992).

U.S. Bureau of the Census, *Historical Statistics of the United States, Colonial Times to 1970*, part 2 (Washington DC: U.S. Government Printing Office, 1975).

Bessie Van Vorst, *The Woman Who Toils: Being the Experiences of Two Ladies as Factory Girls* (New York: Doubleday, Page, 1903).

Richard Wade, *The Urban Frontier: The Rise of Western Cities, 1790–1830* (Cambridge, MA: Harvard University Press, 1959).

Judith Walkowitz, *City of Dreadful Delights* (Chicago: University of Chicago Press, 1992).

Forrester Washington, "Recreation Facilities for the Negro," *Annals of the Academy of Politcal and Social Science* 140 (November 1928), 272–82.

Steven Watts, *The Republic Reborn* (Baltimore: Johns Hopkins University Press, 1987).

Jeffrey Weintraub and Krishan Kumar, eds., *Public and Private in Thought and Practice: Perspectives on a Grand Dichotomy* (Chicago: University of Chicago Press, 1997).

Elliott West, *The Saloon on the Rocky Mountain Mining Frontier* (Lincoln: University of Nebraska Press, 1979).

James West, *Plainville, U.S.A.* (New York: Columbia University Press, 1945).

Robert Wiebe, *The Opening of American Society* (New York: Knopf, 1984).

Sean Wilentz, *Chants Democratic: New York City and the Rise of the American Working Class, 1788–1850* (New York: Oxford University Press, 1984).

Raymond Williams, *Marxism and Literature* (London: Oxford University Press, 1977).

Raymond Williams, *Sociology of Culture* (New York: Schocken, 1982).

Gordon S. Wood, *The Radicalism of the American Revolution* (New York: Knopf, 1992).

Richardson Wright, *Forgotten Ladies: Nine Portraits from the American Family Album* (Philadelphia: Lippincott, 1928).

Norris Yeates, *William T. Porter and the Spirit of the Times* (Baton Rouge: Louisiana State University Press, 1957).

Stage: Eighteenth- and Nineteenth-Century Sources

"For the Centinel, Mr. Russell [editor]," *Columbian Centinel* (September 15, 1793), 3.

"The Italian Opera House and the Bowery, New York," *Spirit of the Times* 16:50 (February 6, 1847), 590.

Letter to the editor of the *New York Times* [June 2, 1865] from a "mother of the old school."

"The Matinee Girl," *New York Mirror* (February 9, 1889), 11.

"The New York Concert Saloons," *New York Evening Post* (January 2, 1862).

The Nightside of New York, by Members of the New York Press (New York: J. C. Haney, 1866).

"Obituary, Not Eulogistic: Negro Minstrelsy Is Dead," *Journal of Music* 13:18 (1858), 118.

"Scene," *Boston Gazette* (March 12, 1801), 1.

"Sketches of People Who Oppose Our Sunday Laws," *Harper's Weekly* (October 8, 1859), 641.

"Teutonic Sunday Amusements," *New York Herald* (April 25, 1859), 1.

"Theater and Its Friends," *Harpers Weekly"* (January 31, 1857).

"The Variety Theatres," *New York Mirror* (January 18, 1879), 4.

"Variety Shows: Their Origin and History," *New York Times* (March 28, 1874), 8.

William Alger, *Life of Edwin Forrest* (Philadelphia: Lippincott, 1877).

Benjamin Baker, *A Glance at New York* (New York: Samuel French, 1857).

Leon Beauvallet, *Rachel and the New World,* Colin Clair, trans. and ed. (New York: Abelard-Schuman, 1967), [orig., New York: Dix Edwards, 1856].

Israel Benjamin, *Three Years in America,* Charles Reznikoff, trans. (New York: Arno Press, 1975).

John Bernard, *Retrospections of America, 1797–1811* (New York: Harper's, 1887).

William Clapp, *A Record of the Boston Stage* (Boston: James Munroe, 1853).

John Corbin, "How the Other Half Laughs," *Harper's Weekly* 98 (1899), 30–48.

Joseph Cowell, *Thirty Years Passed Among the Players in England and America* (New York: Harper, 1844).

Charles P. Daly, *First Theater in America* (New York: Burt Franklin, 1896).

Charles Day, *Fun in Black; or, Sketches of Minstrel Life* (New York: R. M. DeWitt, 1874).

William Dunlap, *History of the American Theatre* (New York: Burt Franklin, 1963). [orig., London: Richard Bentley, 1833].

John Gardiner, *Speech of John Gardiner, Esquire on Repealing the Law Against Theatrical Exhibition* (Boston, 1792).

Joseph Hatton, "American Audiences and Actors," *The Theatre* (May 1881), 257–66.

H. Hutton, "The Green Table," *Southern Magazine* 9 (September 1871), 373–81.

Henry Irving, "The American Audience," *The Fortnightly* 43 (1885), 197–201.

Washington Irving, *The Letters of Jonathan Oldstyle,* Bruce Granger and Martha Hertzog, eds. (Boston: Twayne Publishing, 1977).

Joseph Jefferson, *The Autobiography of Joseph Jefferson,* Alan Downer, ed. (Cambridge: Harvard University Press, 1964).

John Jennings, *Theatrical and Circus Life* (St. Louis: Sun Publishing, 1882).

Ralph Keeler, *Vagabond Adventures* (Boston: Fields Osgood, 1870).

Fanny Kemble, *The Journal of Frances Anne Butler* (New York: Benjamin Blom, 1970) [orig., London: John Murray, 1835].

Walter Leman, *Memories of an Old Actor* (San Francisco: A. Roman, 1886).

Olive Logan, *Before the Footlights and Behind the Scenes* (Philadelphia: Parmalee, 1870).

Noah Ludlow, *Dramatic Life as I Found It* (St Louis: G. I. Jones, 1880).

[R. P. Nevins] "Stephen Foster and Negro Minstrelsy," *Atlantic Monthly* 20 (November 1867), 608–16.

William Northall, *Before and Behind the Curtains* (New York: W. F. Burgess, 1851).

H. P. Phelps, *Players of a Century: A Record of the Albany Stage* (Albany: Jos. McDonough, 1880).

Tyrone Power, *Impressions of America* (London: Richard Bentley, 1836).

Orville Roorbach, *Minstrel Gags and Endmen's Handbook* (New York: Happy Hours, 1875).

Ike Simond, *Old Slack: Reminiscences and Pocket History of the Colored Profession from 1865 to 1891* (Bowling Green University Press, 1943) [orig., 1891].

Maud and Otis Skinner, *One Man in His Time: The Adventures of H. Watkins, Strolling Player, 1845–1863, From His Journal* (Philadelphia: University of Pennsylvania Press, 1938).

Sol Smith, *Theatrical Management in the West and South for Thirty Years* (New York: Harper & Bros., 1869).

Joseph Thompson, *Theatrial Amusements: A Discourse on the Character and Influence of the Theater* (New York: Baker & Scribner, 1847).

[J. C. Trux] "Negro Minstrelsy – Ancient and Modern," *Putnam's Monthly* 5 (January 1855), 75–6.

Walt Whitman, "The Bowery," in Justin Kaplan, *Walt Whitman: Prose and Poetry* (New York: Library of America, 1982), 1186–9.

Walt Whitman, "Miserable State of the Stage," in Montrose Moses and John Brown, eds., *The American Theater as Seen by Its Critics* (New York: Cooper Square, 1967), 71–2.

W. H. Whittaker, "The Law of the Theater," *Central Law Journal* 12 (January–June, 1881), 390–3.

George Willard, *History of the Providence Stage* (Rhode Island News Co., 1891).

John Witherspoon, *A Serious Inquiry into the Nature and Effects of the Stage* (New York: Whiting and Watson, 1812).

William Wood, *Personal Recollections of the Stage* (Philadelphia: Henry Carey Baird, 1855).

Stage: Twentieth-Century Sources

"The Gallery Gods Have Made Way for Second Balcony Goddesses," clipping file: Audience-theater-gallery, NYPL, Billy Rose Theater Collection, circa 1910.

"The Gallery Gods Must Be Suppressed," *Philadelphia Inquirer Halftone Magazine* (October 5, 1902), 3.

"The Girl Behind the Pen," *Keith News,* various columns from September 5, 1904 To November 20, 1916. Keith/Albee Collection, University of Iowa Library.

"The Good Old Gallery," *New York Times* (February 20, 1921), VI: 1.

"Hissing the Villains in Hoboken," *Literary Digest* (April 6, 1929), 24–5.

"The Latter-Day Audience: Its Characteristics and Habits," *Harper's Weekly* 46 (May 17, 1902), 632.

"Mulberry Dolls," *The Stage* (April 1933).

"The Matinee Girl," *Munsey's* 18 (October 1897), 38.

"Rudeness in the Theatre," *Theater Magazine* 7 (August 1907), iii.

"Up in the Theatre Gallery," New York Public Library, Billy Rose Theater Collection, clipping file: Audience-theater-gallery.

"The Variety Stage: Something of its Early History," *Harper's Weekly* (March 22, 1902), 380.

Pamela Adams, "The Audience in Charleston's Theaters, 1790–1860" (Ph.D., University of South Carolina, 1983).

Lois Adler, "Sicilian Puppets," *Drama Review* 2:2 (June 1976), 25–30.

Karen Alhquist, "Opera, Theater and Audience in Antebellum New York" (Ph.D., University of Michigan, 1991).

Robert C. Allen, *Horrible Prettiness: Burlesque and American Culture* (Chapel Hill; University of North Carolina Press, 1991).

Brooks Atkinson, "The Play," *New York Times* (March 12, 1936), 18.

F. A. Austin, "The Playgoers" *Theatre Magazine* 36 (July 1922), 16.

Alfred Ayers, "Players and Playgoers," *Theatre Magazine* 1:6 (August 1901), 16.

Marc Baer, *Theatre and Disorder in Late Georgian London* (London: Oxford University Press, 1992).

Peter Bailey, ed., *Music Hall: The Business of Pleasure* (Milton Keynes, UK: Open University Press, 1986).

Peter Bailey, "Conspiracies of Meaning: Music-Hall and the Knowingness of Popular Culture," *Past and Present* 144 (August 1994), 138–170.

Jimmy Dalton Baines, "Samuel S. Sanford and Negro Minstrelsy" (Ph.D., Tulane University Press, 1967).

Rosemarie Bank, "Hustlers in the House," Ron Engle and Tice Miller, eds., *The American Stage* (Cambridge, UK: Cambridge University Press, 1993).

Howard Barnes, "Bringing Back the Gods to the Top Gallery," *New York Herald Tribune* (September, 23, 1928), VII: 2, 4.

Robert O. Bartholomew, "Report of Censorship of Motion Pictures and of Investigation of Motion Picture Theaters of Cleveland" (1913).

Alfred Bernheim, *The Business of the Theatre: An Economic History of the American Theatre, 1750–1932* (New York: Benjamin Blom, 1932).

Herbert Blau, *The Audience* (Baltimore: Johns Hopkins University Press, 1990).

Zachary Bloomfield, "Baptism of a Deacon's Theatre: Audience Development at the Boston Museum, 1841–1861" (Ph.D., University of Missouri, 1991).

Edward Bok, "The Young Girl at the Matinee," *Ladies' Home Journal* 20 (June 1903), 161.

Elbert Bowen, "Negro Minstrelsy in Early Rural Missouri," *Missouri Historical Review* 47:2 (January 1953), 107–8.

J. Albert Brackett, *Theatre Law* (Boston: C. M. Clark, 1907).

Cyrus T. Brady, "A Vaudeville Turn," *Scribner's Magazine* 30 (1901), 351–5.

Harold and Ernestine Briggs, "The Early Theatre in the Upper Mississippi," *Mid-America* 31:3 [ns20] (July 1949), 131–62.

Harold and Ernestine Briggs, "The Theater in Early Kansas City," *Mid-America* 32 (July 1950), 89–103.

Harold Briggs, "Early Variety Theater in the Trans.-Mississippi West," *Mid-America* 34 (July 1952), 188–202.

David Brigham, *Public Culture in the Early Republic: Peale's Museum and its Audience* (Washington, DC: Smithsonian Institution Press, 1995).

Eugene Bristow, "Look Out for Saturday Night: A Social History of Variety Theater in Memphis Tennessee, 1859–1860" (Ph.D., University of Iowa, 1956).

Jared Brown "A Note on British Military Theatre in New York at the End of the American Revolution," *New York History* 62 (April 1981), 177–87.

Porter Emerson Browne, "The Mellowdrammer," *Everybody's Magazine* (September 1909), 347–54.

Robert Brustein, *The Theater in Revolt* (New York: Ivan R. Dee, 1991).

Billy Bryant, *Children of Ol' Man River: The Life and Times of a Showboat Trouper* (Chicago: Lakeside Press, 1988).

Peter Buckley, "To the Opera House: Culture and Society in New York City, 1820–1860" (Ph.D., SUNY Stony Brook, 1984).

Ann Burk, "The Mining Camp Saloon as Social Center," *Red River Valley Historical Review* 2 (Fall 1975), 381–392.

Anne Butler, *Daughters of Joys, Sisters of Mercy: Prostitutes in the American West, 1865–1890* (Urbana: University of Illinois Press, 1987).

Richard Butsch, "American Theater Riots and Class Relations, 1754–1849," *Theatre Annual* 48 (1995), 41–59.

David Carroll, *The Matinee Idols* (New York: Arbor House, 1972).

Caroline Caffin, *Vaudeville, the Book* (New York: Mitchell Kennerly, 1914).

Raymond Calkins, *Substitutes for the Saloon: An Investigation for the Committee of Fifty* (Boston: Houghton Mifflin, 1901).

William Carson, *The Theater on the Frontier* (New York: Benjamin Blom 1965).

Giuseppe Cautella, "The Bowery," *The American Mercury* 9:35 (November 1926), 365–368.

Patricia Click, *Spirit of the Times: Amusements in Nineteenth Century Baltimore, Norfolk and Richmond* (Charlottesville, VA: University of Virginia Press, 1989).

Dale Cockrell, *Demons of Disorder: Early Blackface Minstrels and Their World* (New York: Cambridge University Press, 1997).

George M. Cohan and George Jean Nathan, "The Mechanics of Emotion" *McClure's* (November 1913), 95.96.

Conteur, "Our Theaters After the Civil War," *Cincinnati Enquirer* (October 15, 1922).

Ann Cook, *The Privileged Playgoers of Shakespeare's London, 1576–1642* (Princeton, NJ: Princeton University Press, 1981).

Rachel Crowther, "Four Kinds of Audiences," *Drama Magazine* 10 (May 1920), 273–5.

Diane Cypkin, "Second Avenue: The Yiddish Broadway" (Ph.D., New York University, 1986).

Frank Davidson, "The Rise, Development and Decline of the American Minstrel Show" (Ph.D., New York University, 1952).

Peter A. Davis, "From Stock to Combination: The Panic of 1873 and its Effects on the American Theatre Industry," *Theater History Studies* 8 (1988), 1–9.

Peter A. Davis, "Puritan Mercantilism and the Politics of Anti-Theatrical Legislation in Colonial America," in Ron Engle and Tice Miller, eds., *The American Stage: Social and Economic Issues from the Colonial Period to the Present* (Cambridge, UK: Cambridge University Press, 1993), 18–29.

Michael Davis, *The Exploitation of Pleasure: A Study of Commercial Recreation in New York City* (New York: Russell Sage Foundation, 1910).

John DeMeglio, *Vaudeville, U.S.A.* (Bowling Green, OH: Bowling Green University Press, 1973).

Helen Waverly Deutsch, "Laura Keene's Theatrical Management: Profile of a Profession in Transition" (Ph.D., Tufts University, 1992).

W. Lee Dickson, "The Audience Upstairs," *Theatre Magazine* 32 (September 1920) 100.

William Dillon, *Life Doubles in Brass* (Ithaca, NY: The House of Nollid, 1944).

John Dizikes, *Opera in America: A Cultural History* (New Haven, CT: Yale University Press, 1993).

James Dormon, *Theater in the Antebellum South, 1815–1861* (Chapel Hill: University of North Carolina Press, 1967).

Richard Dorson, "Mose, the Far Famed and World Renowned," *American Literature* 15 (1943), 288–300.

W. A. S. Douglass, "The Passing of Vaudeville," *American Mercury* (October 1927), 188–94.

The Drama Committee, "The Amusement Situation in the City of Boston" (Boston: Twentieth Century Club, 1910).

Faye Dudden, *Women in the American Theatre* (New Haven: Yale University Press, 1994).

James Dunlap, "Sophisticates and Dupes: Cincinnati Audiences, 1851," *Bulletin of the Historical and Philosophical Society of Ohio* 13:2 (April 1955), 87–97.

William Dye, "Pennsylvania vs. Theatre," *Pennsylvania Magazine* 55 (1931), 333–72.

Walter Prichard Eaton, "Women as Theater-Goers," *Woman's Home Companion* 37 (October 1910), 13.

Walter Prichard Eaton, "The Insurgent Public," *American Magazine* (April 1912), 744–753.

Harry Edwall, "The Golden Era of Minstrelsy in Memphis," *The West Tennessee Historical Society Papers* 9 (1955), 29–47.

Eugene Elliot, *History of Variety-Vaudeville from the Beginning to 1914* (Seattle: University of Washington Press, 1941).

Alice Ernst, *Trouping in the Oregon Country* (Portland: Oregon Historical Society, 1961).

Lawrence Estavan, ed., "Minstrelsy," 13, *San Francisco Theatre Research Project* (San Francisco: WPA of Northern California, 1939).

Jon Finson, *The Voices That Are Gone: Themes in 19th Century Song* (New York: Oxford University Press, 1994)

Duane K. Ford, "Factors Influencing Audience Response to Popular Price Melodrama, circa 1890–1910" (M.A.: University of Florida, 1970).

John Frick, "The Rialto: A Study of Union Square, the Center of New York's First Theater District" (Ph.D., New York University, 1983).

William Gates, "The Theatre in Natchez," *Journal of Mississippi History* 3:2 (April 1941), 71–129.

David George and Christopher Gossip, eds., *Studies in the Commedia dell'Arte* (Cardiff: University of Wales Press, 1993).

David Gerber, "The Germans Take Care of Our Celebrations," in Kathryn Grover, ed., *Hard at Play: Leisure in America, 1840–1940* (Amherst: University of Massachusetts Press, 1992), 39–60.

Douglas Gilbert, *American Vaudeville: Its Life and Times* (New York: Dover, 1940),

Irwin Glazer, *Philadelphia Theatres, A-Z* (Westport, CT: Greenwood Press, 1986),

Lewin Goff, "The Popular Priced Melodrama in America, 1890–1910" (Ph.D., Western Reserve University, 1948).

Howard Goodson, "South of the North, North of the South: Public Entertainment in Atlanta, 1880–1930" (Ph.D., Emory University 1995).

Philip Graham, *Showboats* (Austin: University of Texas Press, 1951).

David Grimsted, *Melodrama Unveiled* (University of Chicago, 1968).

Deanna Paoli Gumina, "*Connazionali, Stenterello,* and *Farfariello:* Italian Variety Theater in San Francisco," *California Historical Quarterly* 54 (Spring 1975), 27–36.

Andrew Gurr, *Play-going in Shakespeare's London* (Cambridge, UK: Cambridge University Press, 1987);

Clayton Hamilton, "The Psychology of Theatre Audiences," *The Forum* 39 (October 1907), 234–48.

Clayton Hamilton, "Organizing the Audience," *The Bookman* 34 (October 1911), 163–4.

Clayton Hamilton, "Emotional Contagion in the Theatre," *The Bookman* (April 1914), 139–47.

Frank Burton Harrison, "London Theater Audiences of the Nineteenth Century" (Ph.D., Yale University, 1953).

Louis Reeves Harrison, "Is 'Vodeveal' Necessary?" *Moving Picture World* 8:14 (April 8, 1911), 758–60.

Shirley Madeline Harrison, "The Grand Opera House of New Orleans, Louisiana, 1871 to 1906" (Ph.D., Louisiana State University, 1965).

Jerry Henderson, "Nashville in the Decline of Southern Legitimate Theater During the Beginning of the Twentieth Century," *Southern Speech Journal* 29 (Fall 1963), 26–33.

Ray Henderson, "The Other Hundred Million," *Theater Guild Magazine* (June 1931), 9–11.

Ben Graf Henneke, "The Playgoer in America" (Ph.D., University of Illinois, 1956).

Barnard Hewitt, *Theater U.S.A., 1665–1957* (New York: McGraw Hill, 1959).

Lawrence Hill, "A History of Variety-Vaudeville in Minneapolis" (Ph.D., University of Minnesota, 1979).

Francis Hodge, *Yankee Theatre: The Image of America on the Stage, 1825–1850* (Austin: University of Texas Press, 1964).

Arthur Hornblow, *A History of the Theatre in America* (New York: Benjamin Blom, 1965) [orig., Lippincott, 1919], two vols.

Arthur Hornblow, "A Disgraceful Exhibition," *Theatre Magazine* 41 (January 1925), 7.

Elbert Hubbard, *In the Spotlight: Personal Experiences of Elbert Hubbard on the American Stage* (East Aurora, NY: Roycrofters, 1917).

Edith Isaacs, *The Negro in the American Theatre* (New York: Theatre Arts, 1947).

Reese James, *Cradle of Culture, 1800–1810: The Philadelphia Stage* (Philadelphia: University of Pennsylvania Press, 1957).

Henry Jenkins, *What Made Pistachio Nuts: Early Sound Comedy and the Vaudeville Aesthetic* (New York: Columbia University Press, 1992).

George Jenks, "When Mabel Meets the Actors," *The Theatre* 18 (August 1913), 48, viii.

Claudia Johnson, "That Guilty Third Tier: Prostitution in Nineteenth Century American Theaters," in Daniel Walker Howe, ed., *Victorian America* (Philadelphia: University of Pennsylvania Press, 1976), 111–20.

James Johnston, *Listening in Paris: A Cultural History* (University of California Press, 1995).

John Kendall, *The Golden Age of the New Orleans Theater* (Baton Rouge: Louisiana State University Press, 1952).

Alison Kibler, *Rank Ladies: Gender and Cultural Hierarchy in American Vaudeville* (Chapel Hill: University of North Carolina Press, 1999).

F. Kleber, "Gallery Maxims," *New York Dramatic Mirror* (April 15, 1916), 4.

Michael Leavitt, *Fifty Years in Theatrical Management* (New York: Broadway Publications, 1912).

Lawrence Levine, *High Brow/Low Brow: The Emergence of Cultural Hierarchy in America* (Cambridge, MA: Harvard University Press, 1988).

David Lifson, *The Yiddish Theatre in America* (New York: Thomas Yoseloff, 1965).

Eric Lott, *Love and Theft: Blackface Minstrelsy and the American Working Class* (New York: Oxford University Press, 1995).

John Lough, *Paris Theatre Audiences in the Seventeenth and Eighteenth Centuries* (London: Oxford University Press, 1957).

James Lynch, *Box, Pit and Gallery: Stage and Society in Johnson's London* (New York: Russell & Russell, 1953).

E. MacCaulley, "His Matinee Girl," *Lippincott's Monthly Magazine* 71 (May 1903), 702–5.

George MacMinn, *Theater of the Golden Era in California* (Caldwell, ID: Caxton Printers, 1941).

Mrs. Richard Mansfield, "Metropolitan Audiences," *Cosmopolitan* 36 (April 1904), 667–76.

Edward B. Marks, *They All Sang, From Tony Pastor to Rudy Vallee* (New York: Viking, 1934).

Selected Bibliography

Herbert Marshall and Mildred Stock, *Ira Aldredge: The Negro Tragedian* (London: Rockliff, 1958).

William Marston and John Feller, *F.F. Proctor: Vaudeville Pioneer* (New York: Richard R. Smith, 1943).

Julian Mates, *The American Musical Stage Before 1800* (New Brauswich, NJ: Rutgers University Press, 1962).

Myron Matlaw, "Tony the Trouper: Pastor's Early Years," *Theatre Annual* 34 (1968), 70–90.

Bruce McConachie, "New York Opera-going, 1825–1850," *American Music* 6:2 (Summer 1988), 181–92.

Bruce McConachie, *Melodramatic Formations* (University of Iowa Press, 1992).

Bruce McConachie and Daniel Friedman, *Theatre for Working Class Audiences in the U.S. 1830–1980* (Westport CT: Greenwood Press, 1985).

Elizabeth McCracken, "The Play and the Gallery," *Atlantic* 89 (April 1902), 497–507.

Claire McGlinchee, *The First Decade of the Boston Museum* (Boston: Bruce Humphries, 1940).

Ruth Harsha McKensie, "Organization, Production and Management at the Chestnut Street Theatre, Philadelphia, 1791–1820" (Ph.D., Stanford University, 1952).

Brooks McNamara, *The American Playhouse in the Eighteenth Century* (Cambridge MA: Harvard University Press, 1969).

Paul McPharlin, *The Puppet Theatre in America: A History* (New York: Harper & Bros., 1949).

Richard Moody, *The Astor Place Riot* (Bloomington, IN: Indiana University Press, 1958).

Thomas Gale Moore, *The Economics of the American Theater* (Durham: Duke University Press, 1968).

Vera Moorhouse, "Benjamin Franklin Keith: Vaudeville Magnate" (M.A.: Eastern Michigan University, 1975).

Edmund S. Morgan, "Puritan Hostility to the Theatre," *Proceedings of the American Philosophical Society* 110 (1966), 340–7.

Montrose Moses and John M. Brown, eds., *The American Theatre as Seen by its Critics, 1752–1934* (New York: Norton, 1934).

Marilyn Moses, "Lydia Thompson and the 'British Blondes' in the United States" (Ph.D., University of Oregon, 1978).

Steven Mullaney, *The Place of the Stage* (Chicago: University of Chicago Press, 1988).

Rex Myers, "Chicago Joe and Her Hurdy-Gurdy Girls," *Montana, the Magazine of Western History* (Spring 1977), 24–33

George Jean Nathan, *The Popular Theatre* (New York: Knopf, 1918).

Hans Nathan, *Dan Emmet and the Rise of Early Negro Minstrelsy* (Norman: University of Oklahoma Press, 1962).

George C. D. Odell, *Annals of the New York Stage* (New York: Columbia University Press, 1927–1949).

Thomas Parley, "The Black Theatre Audience," *Players* 46 (August/September 1971).

Harry W. Pedicord, *The Theatrical Public in the Time of Garrick* (New York: Columbia University Press, 1954).

Jack Poggi, *Theater in America: The Impact of Economic Forces, 1870–1967* (Ithaca, New York: Cornell University Press, 1968).

Arthur Pollock, "What the Gallery Wants," *Harper's Weekly* 59 (October 24, 1914), 401.

Channing Pollock, *The Footlights Fore and Aft* (Boston: Gorham Press, 1911).

Thomas Pollock, *The Philadelphia Theatre in the Eighteenth Century* (Philadelphia: University of Pennsylvania Press, 1933).

Thomas Postlewait and Bruce McConachie, eds., *Interpreting the Theatrical Past* (Iowa City: University of Iowa Press, 1989).

Judith Pratt, "The Vaudeville Criticism of Epes Winthrop Sargent, 1890–1910" (Ph.D., University of Nebraska, 1984).

Arthur Hobson Quinn, *A History of the American Drama*, 2nd ed. (Appleton-Century-Crofts, 1943), two volumes.

Frank Rahill, *The World of Melodrama* (State College: Pennsylvania State University Press, 1967).

Hugh Rankin, *The Theater in Colonial America* (Chapel Hill: University of North Carolina Press, 1960).

William Reardon and Eugene Bristow, "The American Theatre, 1864–1870: An Economic Portrait," *Speech Monographs* 33:4 (November 1966), 438–43.

Ettore Rella, "A History of Burlesque," Vol. 14 *San Francisco Theater Research Series* (San Francisco: W.P.A. of Northern California, 1940).

David Rinear, *The Temple of Momus: Mitchell's Olympic Theatre, 1839–1848* (Metuchen, NJ: Scarecrow Press, 1987).

David Roberts, *The Ladies: Female Patronage of Restoration Drama, 1660–1700* (Oxford University Press, 1989).

Joseph Roppolo, "Audiences in New Orleans Theaters, 1845–1861," *Tulane Studies in English* 2 (1950), 121–35.

John Rosselli, *The Opera Industry in Italy from Cimarosa to Verdi* (Cambridge University Press, 1984).

Victor Rousseau, "A Puppet Play Which Lasts Two Months," *Harper's Weekly* (October 3, 1908), 15–16.

Arthur Ruhl, "Ten-Twenty-Thirty," *Outlook* 98 (August 19, 1911), 886–91.

F. C. Russell, "Confessions of a Gallery God," *Theatre Magazine* 30 (December 1919), 378.

Charles and Louise Samuels, *Once Upon a Stage: The Merry World of Vaudeville* (New York: Dodd, Mead, 1974).

Nahma Sandrow, *Vagabond Stars: A History of Yiddish Theater* (New York: Harper and Row, 1977).

A. Saxon, "A Brief History of the Claque," *Theatre Survey* 5:1 (May 1964), 10–26.

J. M. Scanlan, "An Italian Quarter Mosaic," *Overland Monthly* 47 (April 1906), 327–334.

Lester Scott, "Play-Going for Working People," *New Boston* (1915), 237–41.

Marvin Seiger, "A History of the Yiddish Theatre in New York City to 1892" (Ph.D., Indiana University, 1960).

Maxine Seller, *Ethnic Theater in the U.S.* (Westport, CT: Greenwood Press, 1983).

Laurence Senelick, "Variety into Vaudeville, The Process Observed in Two Manuscript Gagbooks," *Theatre Survey* 19:1 (May 1978), 1–15.

Theodore Shank, "The Bowery Theater, 1826–1836" (Ph.D., Stanford University, 1956).

Mary Shaw, "The Psychology of the Audience," *Saturday Evening Post* (February 18, 1911), 6–7, 25.

Eddie Shayne, *Down Front on the Aisle* (Denver: Parkway Publishing 1929).

Anthony Slide, *Selected Vaudeville Criticism* (Metuchen, NJ: Scarecrow Press, 1988).

William Slout, *Theater in a Tent: The Development of a Provincial Entertainment* (Bowling Green, OH: Bowling Green University Popular Press, 1972).

Bill Smith, *The Vaudevillians* (New York: MacMillan, 1976).

Frederick Snyder, "American Vaudeville – Theatre in a Package" (Ph.D., Yale University, 1970).

Robert W. Snyder, *Voice of the City: Vaudeville and Popular Culture in New York* (New York: Oxford University Press, 1989).

A. Richard Sogliuzzo, "Notes for a History of the Italian American Theatre of New York," *Theatre Survey* 14:2 (November 1973), 59–75.

Marian Spitzer, "Ten-Twenty-Thirty: The Passing of the Popular Circuit," *Saturday Evening Post* (August 22, 1935), 40–41, 48.

Shirley Staples, *Male-Female Comedy Teams in American Vaudeville, 1865–1932* (Ann Arbor: UMI Research Press, 1984).

Charles Stein, *American Vaudeville as Seen by its Contemporaries* (New York: Knopf, 1984).

Walter Swan, "The Rights of the Holder of a Theater Ticket," *Case and Comment* 18:10 (March 1912), 574–7.

Stephen Tait, "English Theatre Riots," *Theatre Arts* 24 (1940), 97–104.

Jay Teran, "The New York Opera Audience: 1825–1974" (Ph.D., New York University, 1974).

Carl Thomas, "The Restoration Theatre Audience" (Ph.D., University of Southern California, 1952).

Juliet Thompkins, "The Brutality of the Matinee Girl," *Lippincott's Monthly Magazine* 80 (November 1907), 687–8.

Robert Toll, *Blacking Up: The Minstrel Show in Nineteenth-Century America* (New York: Oxford University Press, 1974).

Robert Toll, *On with the Show* (New York: Oxford University Press, 1976).

Carl Van Vecten, *In the Garret* (New York: Knopf, 1920).

Gregory Waller, *Mainstreet Amusements: Movies and Commercial Entertainment in a Southern City, 1896–1930* (Washington, DC: Smithsonian Institution Press, 1995).

David Warfield, "The Top Gallery vs. The Boxes," *The Independent* 54 (February 27, 1902), 503–6.

Nina Warnke, "Immigrant Popular Culture as Contested Space," *Theatre Journal* 48 (1996), 321–35.

Margaret Watson, *Silver Theatre: Amusements of Nevada's Mining Frontier* (Glendale CA: Arthur H. Clark, 1964).

Mark West, "A Spectrum of Spectators: Circus Audiences in Nineteenth Century America," *Journal of Social History* 15:2 (Winter 1981), 265–70.

Eola Willis, *The Charleston Stage in the Eighteenth Century* (Columbia, SC: State Company, 1924).

Claire Willson, "From Variety Theater to Coffee Shoppe," *Arizona Historical Review* 6 (April 1935), 3–13.

Arthur Herman Wilson, *A History of the Philadelphia Theatre, 1835 to 1855* (New York: Greenwood Press, 1968).

Carl Wittke, *Tambo and Bones: A History of the American Minstrel Stage* (New York: Greenwood Press, 1968).

Jules Zanger, "The Minstrel Show as Theater of Misrule," *Quarterly Journal of Speech* 60:1 (February 1974), 33–6.

Parker Zellars, "Tony Pastor: Manager and Impresario of the American Variety Stage" (Ph.D., University of Iowa, 1964).

Parker Zellars, "The Cradle of Variety: The Concert Saloon," *Educational Theater Journal* 20 (December 1968), 53–60.

Sheldon Zitner, "The English Theatre Audience: 1660–1700" (Ph.D., Duke University 1955).

Hershel Zohn, *The Story of the Yiddish Theatre* (Las Cruces, NM: Zohn, 1979).

Mass Media

"Attitudes of Rural People Toward Radio Service: A Nationwide Survey of Farm and Small-town People" (Washington, DC: USDA Bureau of Agricultural Economics, 1946).

The First Decade of Television in Videotown, 1948–1957 (New York: Cunningham and Walsh, 1957)

"Go to the Movies and Shut Up!" *New York Times* (September 11, 1991), A27.

"Handling Crowds at the Roxy," *New York Times* (September 29, 1929), IX, 8.

"Hissing Not Illegal," *New York Times* (August 15, 1940), 18.

"How Radio Helps the Farm," *Farming – The Business Magazine* (November 1925), 220.

"The Joint Committee Study of Rural Radio Ownership and Use in the United States" (NBC and CBS, February 1939).

"Local Drawing Power of Pictures Vary According to Occupations of Patrons," *Moving Picture World* (October 30, 1920), 1207–14.

"Movie Manners and Morals," *Outlook* (July 26, 1916), 694–5.

"The New Cyclops," *Business Week* (March 10, 1956), 76–104.

"Penny Arcades," *Outlook* (October 26, 1912), 376–7.

Physician Guide to Media Violence (American Medical Association, 1996).

"Stamping at Movies," *New York Times* (October 20, 1929), IX 17.

"Television in the Tavern," *Newsweek* (June 16, 1947), 64.

"Those Off Screen Commentators Are a Pain in the Ear," *Philadelphia Bulletin* (December 28, 1980), D14.

"$12 Portable Radio in the Bedroom," *TV Guide* (July 8–14, 1950), 20.

"VCRs Bring Big Changes in Use of Leisure," *New York Times* (March 3, 1985), 1.

"Viewing Trends from '50s to '80s," *Television/Radio Age* (July 22, 1985), 49.

"The White Slave Films: A Review," *Outlook* (February 14, 1914), 345–50.

"A Word to the Audience: Shhhhh!," *New York Times* (December 10, 1972).

"When Movie Theaters and Audiences Are Obnoxious," *New York Times* (February 7, 1982), 19, 24.

Nicholas Abercrombie and Brian Longhurst, *Audiences: A Sociological Theory of Performance and Imagination* (London: Sage Publications, 1998).

Paul Adams, "Television as a Gathering Place," *Annals of the Association of American Geographers* 82:1 (March 1992), 117–35.

Charles Aldredge, "Television: Its Effects on Family Habits in Washington D.C.," Charles Alldredge Public Relations (January 1950).

Jeanne Allen, "The Film Viewer as Consumer," *Quarterly Review of Film Studies* 5:4 (Fall 1980), 481–99.

Robert C. Allen, "Vaudeville and Film, 1895–1915" (Ph.D., University of Iowa, 1977),

Robert C. Allen, *Speaking of Soap Operas* (University of North Carolina Press, 1985).

Robert C. Allen, "From Exhibition to Reception: Reflections on the Film Audience in Film History," *Screen* 31:4 (Winter 1990), 347–56.

Robert C. Allen, "Manhattan Myopia; or Oh! Iowa!" *Cinema Journal* 6:3 (Spring 1996), 75–128.

Martin Allor, "Relocating the Site of the Audience," *Critical Studies in Mass Communication* 5:3 (1988), 217–33.

American Academy of Pediatrics Committee on Communications, "Children, Adolescents and Television," *Pediatrics* 96 (1995), 786–7.

Tim Anderson, "Reforming 'Jackass Music': The Problematic Aesthetics of Early American Film Music," *Cinema Journal* 37:1 (Fall 1997), 3–22.

Margaret Andreason, "Evolution in the Family's Use of Television: Normative Data from Industry and Academe," in Jennings Bryant, ed., *Television and the American Family* (Hillsdale, NJ: Erlbaum, 1990), 3–55.

Ien Ang, *Desperately Seeking the Audience* (London: Routledge, 1991).

Ien Ang, *Living Room Wars: Rethinking Media Audiences for a Postmodern World* (London: Routledge, 1996).

Robert Armour, "Effects of Censorship on the New York Nickelodeon Market, 1907–1909," *Film History* 4:2 (1990).

Ralph Austrian, "Effect of Television on Motion Picture Attendance," *Journal of Society of Motion Picture Engineers* (January 1949), 12–18.

Camille Bacon-Smith, *Enterprising Women: Television Fandom and the Creation of Popular Myth* (Philadelphia: University of Pennsylvania Press, 1992).

Gregg Paul Bachman, "The Last of the Silent Generation: Oral Histories of Silent Movie Patrons" (Ph.D., Union Institute, Cincinnati, Ohio, 1995).

Kenneth Baker, "Radio Listening and Socio-economic Status," *Psychological Record* 1(1937), 99–144.

Mark James Banks, "A History of Broadcast Audience Research in the United States, 1920–1980, with an Emphasis on the Rating Services" (Ph.D., University of Tennessee, 1981).

Francis Barcus, "Parental Influence on Children's Television Viewing," *Television Quarterly* 7:3 (1969), 63–74.

Ray Barfield, *Listening to Radio, 1920–1950* (Westport, CT.: Praeger, 1996).

Eric Barnouw, *A History of Broadcasting in the United States,* 3 volumes (New York: Oxford University Press, 1966–70).

Robert Bartholomew, "Report of Censorship of Motion Pictures and of Investigation of Motion Picture Theaters of Cleveland," (Cleveland, OH: City of Cleveland, 1913).

Batten, Barton, Durstine, and Osborn, Inc., "What's Happening to Leisure Time in Television Homes? A Study of the Activities of 5,657 Persons in Urban America" (Boston: Batten, Barton, Durstine and Osborn, 1951).

Robert Bechtel, Clark Achelpohl, and Roger Akers, "Correlates Between Observed Behavior and Questionnaire Responses on Television Viewing," *Television and Social Behavior, Vol. IV: Television in Day-to-Day Life* (Washington, DC: U.S. GPO, 1972), 274–344.

Robert Bellamy and James Walker, *Television and the Remote Control: Grazing on a Vast Wasteland* (New York: Guilford, 1996).

Marshall Beuick, "The Limited Social Effects of Radio," *American Journal of Sociology* 32 (1926), 617.

Herman Beville, "Social Stratification of the Radio Audience" (Princeton: Office of Radio Research, Princeton University, 1939).

Robert Blood, "Social Class and Family Control of Television Viewing," *Merrill-Palmer Quarterly* 7:3 (July 1961), 205–22.

Samuel Bloom, "A Social Psychological Study of Motion Picture Audience Behavior: A Case Study of the Negro Image in Mass Communication" (Ph.D., University of Wisconsin, 1956).

Alan Blum, "Lower Class Negro Television Spectators: Pseudo-Jovial Skepticism," in Arthur Shostak and Adeline Gomberg, eds., *Blue Collar World: Studies of the American Worker* (Englewood Cliffs, NJ: Prentice Hall, 1964), 429–35.

Herbert Blumer, *Movies and Conduct* (New York: MacMillan, 1933).

Herbert Blumer and Philip Hauser, *Movies, Delinquency and Crime* (New York: MacMillan 1933).

Leo Bogart, *The Age of Television,* 3rd ed. (New York: Frederick Ungar, 1972).

Louise deKoven Bowen, "Five and Ten Cent Theatres" (Chicago: Chicago Juvenile Protection Association, 1910).

Robert Bower, *Television and the Public* (New York: Holt, Rinehart and Winston, 1973).

Elaine Bowser, *The Transformation of the Cinema, 1907–1915* (Berkeley: University of California Press, 1990).

Steuart H. Britt, "A Study of Drive-in Theater Audiences" (Chicago: Screen Advertising Bureau, April 1960).

Mary Ellen Brown, *Soap Opera and Women's Talk: The Pleasure of Resistance* (Beverly Hills, CA: Sage, 1994).

Edmund Brunner, *Radio and the Farmer* (New York: Radio Institute of the Audible Arts, 1936).

Charlotte Brunsdon, *Screen Tastes: From Soap Opera to Satellite Dish* (London: Routledge, 1997).

Jennings Bryant, ed., *Television and the American Family* (Hillsdale, NJ: Erlbaum, 1990).

E. W. Burgess, "Communication," *American Journal of Sociology* 34 (1928), 127.

Richard Butsch, "Home Video and Corporate Plans," in *For Fun and Profit: The Transformation of Leisure into Consumption* (Philadelphia: Temple University Press, 1990), 215–35.

CBS, *Vertical Study of Radio Ownership, 1930–1933* (New York: CBS, 1933).

CBS, *Radio in 1937* (New York: Columbia Broadcasting System, 1937).

Hadley Cantril and Gordon Allport, *The Psychology of Radio* (New York: Harper & Bros., 1935).

Hadley Cantril, *The Invasion from Mars: A Study in the Psychology of Panic* (Princeton, NJ: Princeton University Press, 1940).

Mary Carbine, "'Finest Outside the Loop': Motion Picture Exhibition in Chicago's Black Metropolis, 1905–1928," *Camera Obscura,* 23 (May 1990), 9–41.

Louis Carlat, "'A Cleanser for the Mind': Marketing Radio Receivers for the American Home, 1922–1932," in Roger Horowitz and Arwen Mohun, eds., *His and Hers: Gender, Consumption and Technology* (Charlottesville: University Press of Virginia, 1998).

Diane Carouthers, *Radio Broadcasting from 1920 to 1990, An Annotated Bibliography* (New York: Garland Press, 1991).

Chester Caton, "Radio Station WMAQ: A History of its Independent Years, 1922–1931" (Ph.D. Northwestern University, 1951).

Steven Chaffee and Jack MacLeod, "Parental Influences on Adolescent Media Use," *American Behavioral Scientist* 14:4 (1971), 323–40.

William Charters, *Motion Pictures and Youth* (New York: MacMillan, 1933).

Chicago Motion Picture Committee, "Report" (1920).

Chicago Tribune Research Division, "A View from the Balcony: A Study of Moviegoers' Habits and Attitudes," *Chicago Tribune* (June 1969).

Patricia Clough, "The Movies and Social Observation: Reading Blumer's *Movies and Conduct" Symbolic Interaction* 11:1 (1988), 85–97.

Paul Cobley, "Throwing Out the Baby: Populism and Active Audience Theory," *Media Culture and Society* 16 (1994), 677–87.

Thomas Coffin, "Television Effects on Leisure Time Activities," *Journal of Applied Psychology* 32 (1948), 550–8.

John Collier, "Cheap Amusements," *Survey* 20 (April 11, 1908), 73–76.

Celeste Michelle Condit, "The Rhetorical Limits of Polysemy," in Robert Avery and David Eason, eds., *Critical Perspectives on Media and Society* (New York: Guilford Press, 1991), 365–86.

Norman Cousins, "The Time Trap," *Saturday Review* (December 24, 1949), 20.

Cathy Covert and John Stevens, eds., *Mass Media Between the Wars: Perceptions of Cultural Tension, 1918–1941* (Syracuse, NY: Syracuse University Press, 1984).

Bosley Crowther, *The Lion's Share* (New York: E. P. Dutton, 1957).

Jon Cruz and Justin Lewis, *Viewing, Reading, Listening: Audiences and Cultural Reception* (Boulder, CO: Westview, 1994).

Barton Currie, "The Nickel Madness," *Harper's Weekly* 51 (August 24, 1907), 1246–7.

Daniel Czitrom, "The Politics of Performance: From Theater Licensing to Movie Censorship," *American Quarterly* 44:4 (December 1992), 525–53.

Edgar Dale, *Children's Attendance at Motion Pictures* (New York: Macmillan, 1935).

Peter Dahlgren, *Television and the Public Sphere: Citizenship, Democracy and the Media* (Sage, 1995).

Walter Damrosch, "What Does the Public Really Want?" *Etude* (October 1934), 579–80.

Robert E. Davis, "Response to Innovation: A Study of Popular Argument about New Mass Media" (Ph.D., University of Iowa, 1965).

John DeBoer, "The Emotional Responses of Children to Radio Drama" (Ph.D., University of Chicago, 1940).

Richard deCordova, "Ethnography and Exhibition: The Child Audience, the Hays Office and Saturday Matinees," *Camera Obscura* 23 (May 1990), 91–107.

Richard deCordova, "Tracing the Child Audience: The Case of Disney, 1929–1933," in *Prima dei codici 2. Alle porte di Hays* (Venezia: Fabbri Editori, 1991), 217–21.

Richard deCordova, "The Mickey in Macy's Window: Childhood, Consumerism and Disney Animation," in Eric Smoodin ed., *Producing the Magic Kingdom* (New York: Routledge, 1995).

Lloyd DeGrane, *Tuned In: Television in American Life* (Urbana: University of Illinois Press, 1991).

Jesse Delia, "Communication Research: A History," in Charles Berger and Steven Chaffee, *Handbook of Communication Science* (Beverly Hills, CA: Sage, 1987), 20–99

Chad Dell, "Researching Historical Broadcast Audiences: Female Fandom of Professional Wrestling, 1945–1960" (Ph.D., University of Wisconsin-Madison, 1997).

Thomas DeLoughry, "Snared by the Internet," *Chronicle of Higher Education* (March 1, 1996), A25, 27.

Everett Dennis and Ellen Wartella, *American Communication Research – The Remembered History* (Mahwah, NJ: Erlbaum, 1996).

E. Deidre, *Female Spectators: Looking at Film and Television* (New York: Verso, 1988).

David Denby, "Buried Alive," *New Yorker* (July 15, 1996), 48–58.

Julie Dobrow, ed., *Social and Cultural Aspects of VCR Use* (Hillsdale, NJ: Erlbaum, 1991).

George Douglas, *The Early Days of Radio Broadcasting* (Jefferson, NC: McFarland, 1987).

Susan Douglas, *Inventing American Broadcasting, 1899–1922* (Baltimore: Johns Hopkins University Press, 1987).

Susan Douglas, "Notes Toward a History of Media Audiences," *Radical History Review* 54 (Fall 1992), 127–38.

The Drama Committee for the Twentieth Century Club, "The Amusement Situation in the City of Boston" (Boston: Twentieth Century Club, 1910).

Olivia Howard Dunbar, "The Lure of the Movies," *Harper's Weekly* 57 (January 18, 1913), 20, 22.

William Dysinger, *The Emotional Responses of Children to the Motion Picture Situation* (New York: MacMillan, 1933).

Susan Eastman and Gregory Newton, "Delineating Grazing: Observations of Remote Control Use," *Journal of Broadcasting* 40:1 (Winter 1995), 77–95.

Walter Pritchard Eaton, "The Menace of the Movies," *American Magazine* 76 (September 1913), 55–60.

Walter Prichard Eaton, "Class Consciousness and the Movies," *Atlantic* (January 1915), 48–56.

Walter Prichard Eaton, "The Theatre and the Motion Picture," *Vanity Fair* 27 (October 1926), 73, 118.

Harold Edwards, "Menace of the Movies," *Theatre Magazine* 22 (October 1915), 176–8.

Azriel Eisenberg, *Children and Radio Programs* (New York: Columbia University Press, 1936).

Ethnographic audience research issue, *Journal of Broadcasting* 26:4 (Fall 1982).

Thomas Eoyang, "An Economic Study of the Radio Industry in the U.S.A." (Ph.D., Columbia University, 1936).

James Ettema and D. Charles Whitney, *Audience-making: How the Media Create the Audience* (Beverly Hills: Sage, 1994).

William Evans, "The Interpretive Turn in Media Research: Innovation, Iteration, or Illusion," *Critical Studies in Mass Communication* 7:2 (June 1990), 258–61.

Elizabeth Ewen, "City Lights: Immigrant Women and the Rise of Movies," in Catherine Stimson, ed., *Women and the American City* (University of Chicago Press, 1981), 42–62.

Marjorie Ferguson, ed., *Public Communications, the New Imperatives: Future Directions in Media Research* (Beverly Hills: Sage, 1990).

John Fiske, "The Cultural Economy of Fandom," in Lisa Lewis, ed., *The Adoring Audience: Fan Culture and Popular Media* (London: Routledge, 1992), 30–49.

Elizabeth Fones-Wolf, "Sound Comes to the Movies: The Philadelphia Musicians' Struggle Against Recorded Music," *Pennsylvania Magazine of History & Biography* 68 (January/April 1994).

Raymond Fosdick, "Report on Motion Picture Theatres of Greater New York" (New York: City of New York, March 22, 1911).

William Foster, "Vaudeville and Motion Picture Shows," *Reed College Record* 16 (September 1914).

Katherine Fuller, *At the Picture Show: Small-Town Audiences and the Creation of the Movie Fan* (Smithsonian Institution Press, 1996).

Patricia Gallo, "Saturday Movies for Kids: A Constant in a Changing World," *Philadelphia Evening Bulletin* (March 22, 1974), 9.

Lorraine Gammon and Margaret Marshment, eds., *The Female Gaze: Women as Viewers of Popular Culture* (London: Women's Press, 1988).

Ella Gardner and Caroline E. Legg, *Leisure Time Activities of Rural Children in Selected Areas of West Virginia* (Washington, DC: U.S. Government Printing Office, 1931), 30.

Sherwood Gates, "Radio in Relation to Recreation and Culture," *Annals of the American Academy of Political and Social Sciences* 213 (January 1941), 9–14.

Joseph Geiger, "The Effects of the Motion Picture on the Mind and Morals of the Young," *International Journal of Ethics* 34 (October 1923), 69–83.

Roland Gellat, *The Fabulous Phonograph: From Edison to Stereo* (New York: Appleton Century, 1954).

Ira Glick and Sidney Levy, *Living with Television* (Chicago: Aldine, 1962).

Douglas Gomery, "Movie Audiences, Urban Geography, and the History of the American Film," *The Velvet Light Trap* 19 (Spring 1982), 23–29.

Douglas Gomery, "The Popularity of Film Going in the U.S. 1930–1950," in Colin McCabe, ed., *High Theory/Low Culture* (New York: St. Martin's, 1986), 71–79.

Douglas Gomery, *Shared Pleasures: A History of Movie Presentation in the United States* (Madison: University of Wisconsin Press, 1992).

Theodore C. Grame, "Ethnic Broadcasting in the U.S.," American Folklife Center, Library of Congress, publication no. 4 (1980).

Bradley Greenberg and Carrie Heeter, "VCRs and Young People," *American Behavioral Scientists* 30:5 (May/June 1987), 509–21.

Robert Grau, *Forty Years' Observation of Music and the Drama* (New York: Broadway Publishing, 1909).

Robert Grau, *The Business Man in the Amusement World* (New York: Broadway Publishing, 1910).

Robert Grau, *The Theatre of Science* (New York: Benjamin Blom, 1969) [orig., 1914].

William Gray and Ruth Munroe, *Reading Interests and Habits of Adults* (New York: Macmillan, 1929).

Stuart Hall, Dorothy Hobson, Andrew Lowe, and Paul Willis, *Culture, Media, Language* (London: Hutchinson, 1980).

Stuart Hall, "Encoding and Decoding in the Television Discourse," reprinted in Simon During, ed. *The Cultural Studies Reader* (London Routledge, 1993), 90–103.

Stuart Hall, "Reflections on the Encoding/Decoding Model: An Interview with Stuart Hall," in Jon Cruz and Justin Lewis, *Viewing, Reading, Listening* (Boulder, CO: Westview, 1994), 253–74.

Leo Handel, *Hollywood Looks at its Audience: A Report of Film Audince Research* (Urbana: University of Illinois Press, 1950).

Miriam Hansen, *Babel and Babylon: Spectatorship in American Silent Film* (Combridge, MA: Harvard University Press, 1991).

Credo Fitch Harris, *Microphone Memoirs* (New York: Bobbs Merrill, 1937).

Cheryl Harris and Alison Alexander, eds., *Theorizing Fandom: Fans, Subcultures and Identity* (Cresskill, NJ: Hampton Press, 1995).

C. Lee Harrington and Denise Bielby, *Soap Fans: Pursuing Pleasure and Making Sense in Everyday Life* (Routledge, 1995).

John Hartley, "Invisible Fictions: Television Audiences, Paedocracy, Pleasure," *Textual Practice* 1:2 (1988), 121–38.

John Hartley, *The Politics of Pictures: The Creation of the Public in the Age of Popular Media* (London: Routledge, 1992).

Alan Havig, "The Commercial Amusement Audience in Early Twentieth Century American Cities," *Journal of American Culture* 5 (Spring 1982), 1–19.

James Hay, Larry Grossberg, and Ellen Wartella, *The Audience and Its Landscape* (Boulder CO: Westview Press, 1996).

Greg Hearn, "Active and Passive Conceptions of the Television Audience: Effects of a Change in Viewing Routine," *Human Relations* 42 (October 1989), 857–75.

Gordon Hendricks, *The Kinetoscope* (New York: Beginnings of the American Film Press, 1966).

Herta Herzog, "What Do We Really Know about Day-Time Serial Listeners?" Paul Lazarsfeld and Frank Stanton, *Radio Research, 1942–43* (New York: Duell Sloan, Pearce, 1944), 3–33.

Frank Ernest Hill and W. E. Williams, *Radio's Listening Groups* (New York: Columbia University Press, 1941).

Dorothy Hobson, *Crossroads: The Drama of a Soap Opera* (London: Methuen, 1982).

Robert Hodge and David Tripp, *Children and Television* (Cambridge, UK: Polity Press, 1986).

Frances Holter, "Radio among the Unemployed," *Journal of Applied Psychology* 23 (February 1939), 163–9.

Donald Horton and Richard Wohl, "Mass Communication and Para-social Interaction," *Psychiatry* 9 (1956), 215–29.

Henry Jenkins, *Textual Poachers: Television Fans and Participatory Culture* (London: Routledge, 1992).

Joli Jensen, "Fandom as Pathology," in Lisa Lewis, ed., *The Adoring Audience: Fan Culture and Popular Media* (London: Routledge, 1992), 9–29.

Jane Stannard Johnson, "Children and their Movies," *Social Service Review* (September 1917), 11–12.

Lesley Johnson, "Radio and Everyday Life: The Early Years of Broadcasting in Australia," *Media, Culture & Society* 3 (1981), 167–78.

Amy Jordan and Kathleen Hall Jamieson, eds., "Children and Television," special issue, *Annals of the American Academy of Political and Social Science* 557 (May 1998).

Garth Jowett, *Film, the Democratic Art: A Social History of American Film* (Boston: Little, Brown, 1976).

Garth Jowett, "Social Science as a Weapon: The Origins of the Payne Fund Studies, 1926–1929," *Communication* 13:3 (December 1992), 211–25.

Garth Jowett, Ian Jarvie, and Kathryn Fuller, *Children and the Movies: Media Influence and the Payne Fund Controversy* (Cambridge, UK: Cambridge University Press, 1996).

Reverend H. A. Jump, "The Social Influence of the Moving Picture," (New York: Playground and Recreation Association of America, 1911).

Elihu Katz, Jay Blumler, and Michael Gurevitch, "Uses and Gratifications Research," *Public Opinion Quarterly* 37 (Winter 1973–74), 509–23.

Elihu Katz, "Communications Research Since Lazarsfeld," *Public Opinion Quarterly* 51:4 (1987), S25–45.

Sherman Kingsley, "The Penny Arcade and the Cheap Theatre," *Charities and the Commons* 18 (June 8, 1907), 295–97.

Clifford Kirkpatrick, *Report of a Research into the Attitudes and Habits of Radio Listeners* (St. Paul, MN: Webb Book Publishing, 1933).

Joseph Klapper, *The Effects of Mass Communication* (New York: Free Press, 1960).

Daniel Klenow and Jeffrey Crane, "Selected Characteristics of the X-Rated Movie Audience: Toward a National Profile of the Recidivist," *Sociological Symposium* 20 (Fall 1977), 73–83.

Richard Koszarski, *An Evening's Entertainment: The Age of the Silent Feature Picture, 1915–1928*, (Berkeley: University of California Press, 1990).

Robert Kubey and Mihaly Csikszentmihalyi, *Television and the Quality of Life: How Viewing Shapes Everyday Experience* (Hillsdale, NJ: Erlbaum, 1990).

Kate Lacey, *Feminine Frequencies: Gender, German Radio and the Public Sphere, 1923–1945* (Ann Arbor: University of Michigan Press, 1996).

Paul Lazarsfeld, ed., Radio issue of the *Journal of Applied Psychology* 23 (February 1939).

Paul Lazarsfeld, *Radio and the Printed Page* (New York: Duell, Sloan and Pearce, 1940).

Paul Lazarsfeld, "Audience Research in the Movie Field," *Annals of the Academy of Political and Social Science* 254 (November 1947), 160–8.

Paul Lazarsfeld and Patricia Kendall, *Radio Listening in America* (New York: Prentice-Hall, 1948).

Paul Lazarsfeld and Frank Stanton, *Radio Research, 1941* (New York: Duell, Sloan and Pearce, 1941).

Paul Lazarsfeld and Frank Stanton, *Radio Research, 1942–43* (New York: Duell, Sloan and Pearce, 1944).

Paul Lazarsfeld, Bernard Berelson, and Hazel Gaudet, *The People's Choice* (New York: Duell, Sloan and Pearce, 1944).

Paul Lazarsfeld and Patricia Kendall, *The People Look at Radio* (Chapel Hill: University of North Carolina Press, 1946).

Daniel Leab, "'All-Colored' – But Not Much Different: Films Made for Negro Ghetto Audiences, 1913–1928," *Phylon* 36:3 (September 1975), 321–39.

Ronald Lembo and Kenneth Tucker, "Culture, Television, and Opposition: Rethinking Cultural Studies," *Critical Studies in Mass Communication* 7:2 (June 1990), 97–116.

Dafna Lemish, "The Rules of Viewing Television in Public Places," *Journal of Broadcasting* 26:4 (Fall 1982), 757–81.

Justin Lewis, *The Ideological Octopus: An Exploration of Television and its Audience* (New York: Routlege, 1991).

Justin Lewis and Sut Jhally, "The Politics of Cultural Studies: Racism, Hegemony and Resistance," and response by Herman Gray, *American Quarterly* 46:1 (March 1994), 114–20.

Lisa Lewis, *The Adoring Audience: Fan Culture and Popular Media* (Routledge, 1992).

Lawrence Lichty and Malachi Topping, *American Broadcasting: A Source Book on the History of Radio and Television* (New York: Hastings House, 1975).

Thomas Lindlof, ed., *Natural Audiences: Qualitative Research and Media Uses and Effects* (Norwood, NJ: Ablex, 1987).

Sonia Livingstone, *Making Sense of Television: The Psychology of Audience Interpretation* (New York: Pergamon, 1990).

Sonia Livingstone, "The Rise and Fall of Audience Research," *Journal of Communication* 43:4 (Autumn 1993), 5–12.

Sonia Livingstone and Peter Lunt, *Talk on Television: Audience Participation and Public Debate* (London: Routledge, 1994).

Authur Loesser, *Men, Women and Pianos: A Social History* (New York: Simon and Schuster, 1954).

Shearon Lowry and Melvin DeFleur, *Milestones in Mass Communications Research* (New York: Longman, 1983).

James Lull, *Inside Family Viewing: Ethnographic Research on Television's Audiences* (London: Routledge, 1990).

Frederick Lumley, *Measurement in Radio* (Columbus: Ohio State University, 1934).

Eleanor Maccoby, "Why Children Watch TV," *Public Opinion Quarterly* 15:3 (Fall 1951), 421–44.

J. Fred MacDonald, *Don't Touch That Dial: Radio Programming in American Life from 1920 to 1960* (Chicago: Nelson-Hall, 1979).

John Margolies and Emily Gwathmey, *Ticket to Paradise: American Movie Theaters and How We Had Fun* (Boston: Little, Brown, 1991).

Herbert Marx, ed., *Television and Radio in American Life* (New York: H. W. Wilson, 1953).

Mary Mauder, "The Public Debate About Broadcasting in the Twenties: An Interpretive History," *Journal of Broadcasting* 28:2 (Spring 1984), 167–85.

Lary May, *Screening out the Past: The Birth of Mass Culture and the Motion Picture Industry* (New York: Oxford University Press, 1980).

Lary May, "Making the American Way: Modern Theatres, Audiences and the Film Industry, 1929–1945," *Prospects* 12 (1987) 89–124.

Judith Mayne, "Immigrants and Spectators", *Wide Angle* 5:2 (Summer, 1982) 32–40

Anna McCarthy, "'The Front Row is Reserved for Scotch Drinkers': Early Television's Tavern Audience," *Cinema Journal* 34:4 (Summer 1995), 31–49.

Robert McChesney, "The Battle for the U.S. Airwaves, 1928–1935," *Journal of Communication* 40:2 (Autumn 1990), 29–57.

John McGeehan and Robert Maranville, "Television: Impact and Reaction in Lexington, Kentucky," Occasional Contribution, no. 50, University of Kentucky (March 1953).

Samuel McKelvie, "What the Movies Mean to the Farmer," *Annals of the Academy of Political and Social Science* 128 (November 1926), 131–2.

Orange Edward McMeans, "The Great Audience Invisible," *Scribner's* 73:4 (April 1923), 410–16.

Elliott Medrich, "Constant Television: A Background to Daily Life," *Journal of Communication* 29:3 (Summer 1979), 171–6.

Patricia Mellencamp, *Logics of Television: Essays in Cultural Criticism* (Bloomington: Indiana University Press, 1990).

Russell Merritt, "Nickelodeon Theaters 1905–1914," in Tino Balio, ed., *The American Film Industry*, rev. ed. (Madison: University of Wisconsin Press, 1985), 83–102.

Margaret Midas, "Without TV," *American Quarterly* 3:2 (Summer 1951), 152–66.

Alice Mitchell, *Children and Movies* (Chicago: University of Chicago Press, 1929).

Irene Mix and John Wallace, "The Listener's Point of View," *Radio Broadcast* column (1925–28).

Tania Modleski, *Loving with a Vengeance: Mass-Produced Fantasies for Women* (Hamden, CT: Archon Books, 1982).

Tania Modleski, "The Rhythms of Reception: Daytime Television and Women's Work," in E. Ann Kaplan, ed., *Regarding Television: Critical Approaches – An Anthology* (Frederick, MD: University Publications of America, 1983), 71–3.

Tania Modleski, *Studies in Entertainment* (Bloomington: Indiana University Press, 1986).

Shaun Moores, "The Box on the Dresser: Memories of Early Radio and Everyday Life," *Media, Culture & Society* 10:1 (1988), 23–40.

Shaun Moores, *Interpreting Audiences: The Ethnography of Media Consumption* (Beverly Hills, CA: Sage, 1994).

David Morley, *Television, Audiences, and Cultural Studies* (London: Routledge, 1992).

David Morrison, "The Transference of Experience and the Impact of Ideas: Paul Lazarsfeld and Mass Communication Research," *Communication* 10 (1988), 185–209.

Laura Mulvey, "Visual Pleasure and Narrative Cinema," *Screen* 16:3 (1975), 6–18.

Matthew Murray, "NBC Program Clearance Policies During the 1950s: Nationalizing Trends and Regional Resistance," *The Velvet Light Trap* 33 (Spring 1994).

Charles Musser, *The Emergence of Cinema: The American Screen to 1907* (Berkeley: University of California Press, 1990).

Charles Musser, "Reading Local Histories of Early Film Exhibition," *Historical Journal of Film, Radio and Television* 15:4 (1995), 581–5.

NBC, "Radio Takes to the Road" (New York: NBC, 1936).

W. Russell Neuman, *The Future of the Mass Audience* (Cambridge, UK: Cambridge University Press, 1991).

Mark Newman, *Entrepreneurs of Profit and Pride: From Black Appeal to Radio Soul* (Westport, CT: Praeger, 1988).

Virginia Nightingale, "What's 'Ethnographic' about Ethnographic Audience Research?" *Australian Journal of Communication* 16 (December 1989), 50–63.

Susan Ohmer, "Gallup Looks at the Movies: George Gallup and Audience Research in Hollywood" (Ph.D., New York University, 1990).

Paul O'Malley, "Neighborhood Nickelodeons: Residential Theaters in South Denver from 1907 to 1917," *Colorado Heritage* 3 (1984), 49–58.

Opinion Research Corp., "Recent Media Trends," *Public Opinion Index* 18 (June 1985),

Susan Opt, "The Development of Rural Wired Radio Systems in Upstate South Carolina," *Journal of Radio Studies* 1 (1992), 71–81.

Arthur Ord-Hume, *Pianola: The History of the Self-Playing Piano* (Boston: Allen & Unwin, 1984).

Lewis Palmer, "The World in Motion," *Survey* 22 (June 5, 1909), 355–65.

Ruth Palter, "Radio's Attraction for Housewives," *Hollywood Quarterly* 3 (Spring 1948), 248–57.

Joseph Patterson, "The Nickelodeon," *Saturday Evening Post* (November 23, 1907), 10–11, 38.

Roberta Pearson, "Cultivated Folks and the Better Classes: Class Conflict and Representation in Early American Film," *Journal of Popular Film and Television* 15:3 (Fall 1987), 120–8.

Ruth Peterson and Louis Thurstone, *Motion Pictures and the Social Attitudes of Children* (New York: MacMillan, 1933).

Andrea Press, *Women Watching Television: Gender, Class and Generation in the American Television Experience* (Philadelphia: University of Pennsylvania Press, 1991).

Charles Preston, ed., *The $64,000,000 Answer* (New York: Berkley Publishing, 1955).

Price Waterhouse & Co., "Price, Waterhouse Survey of Radio Network Popularity" (New York: CBS, 1931).

Elaine Prostak, "Up in the Air: The Debate Over Radio Use During the 1920s" (Ph.D., University of Kansas, 1983).

Thomas Pryor, "The Audience at Play: Games and Premiums Rival Hollywood's Stars as Box Office Attractions," *New York Times* (April 24, 1938), X, 4.

Janice Radway, "Reception Study: Ethnography and the Problems of Dispersed Audiences and Nomadic Subjects," *Cultural Studies* 2:3 (1988), 359–76.

Marion Reedy, "Movie Crimes Against Good Taste," *Literary Digest* (September 18, 1915), 592–3.

Louis Reid, "The Psychology of Fan Mail," *Broadcasting* (September 15, 1932), 10.

Robert Rice, "Onward and Upward with the Arts: Diary of a Viewer," *New Yorker* (August 30, 1947), 44–55.

John Riley, Frank Cantwell, and Katherine Ruttiger, "Some Observations on the Social Effects of Television," *Public Opinion Quarterly* 13 (Summer 1949), 223–34.

Paul Ritts, *The TV Jeebies* (Philadelphia: John C. Winston, 1951).

Robert Roberts, "Those Who Do Not Watch Television," *Sociology and Social Research* 71 (January 1987), 105–7.

Norbert Rodeman, "The Development of Academic Research in Radio and Television for the First Half of the Twentieth Century" (Ph.D., Northwestern, 1951).

Everett Rogers, *A History of Communication Study* (New York: Free Press, 1994).

Bernard Rosenberg and David White, *Mass Culture: The Popular Arts in America* (New York: Free Press 1957).

Karl Erik Rosengren, Lawrence Wenner, and Philip Palmgreen, *Media Gratifications Research: Current Perspectives* (Beverly Hills: Sage, 1985).

Steven Ross, *Working-Class Hollywood: Silent Film and the Shaping of Class in America* (Princeton, NJ: Princeton University Press, 1998).

Morleen Getz Rouse, "Daytime Radio Programming for the Homemaker, 1926–1956," *Journal of Popular Culture* 12 (Fall 1979), 315–20.

Haluk Sahin and John P. Robinson, "Beyond the Realm of Necessity: Television and the Colonization of Leisure," *Media, Culture and Society* 3:1 (1980), 85–95.

Morse Salisbury, "Radio and the Farmer," *Annals of the Academy of Political and Social Sciences* 177 (January 1935), 141–6.

Jorge Schement and Ricardo Flores, "The Origins of Spanish-Language Radio: The Case of San Antonio Texas," *Journalism History* 4 (Summer 1977), 56–58, 61.

Wilbur Schramm, Jack Lyle, and Edwin Parker, *Television in the Lives of Our Children* (Palo Alto, CA: Stanford University Press, 1961).

May Seagoe, "Children's Television Habits and Preferences," *Quarterly of Film, Radio and Television* 6 (Winter 1951), 143–53.

William Seaman, "Active Audience Theory: Pointless Populism," *Media Culture and Society* 14 (1992), 301–11.

Ellen Seiter, Hans Borchers, Gabriele Kreutzner, and Eva-Maria Warth, *Remote Control: Television, Audiences and Cultural Power* (New York: Routledge, 1989).

Frank Shuttleworth and Mark May, *The Social Conduct and Attitudes of Movie Fans* (New York: Macmillan, 1933).

Nancy Signorielli and Michael Morgan, eds., *Cultivation Analysis: New Directions in Media Effects Research* (Beverly Hills, CA: Sage, 1990).

Sime [Silverman], "Nickel Vaudeville," *Variety* (March 17, 1906), 4.

Ben Singer, "Manhattan Nickelodeons: New Data on Audiences and Exhibitors," *Cinema Journal* 35:3 (Spring 1995), 5–35.

Jerome and Dorothy Singer, *Television, Imagination and Aggression: A Study of Pre-Schoolers* (Hillsdale, NJ: Erlbaum, 1981).

Robert Sklar, *Movie Made America: A Cultural History of American Movies* (New York: Random House, 1975).

Robert Sklar, "*Oh Althusser:* Historiography and the Rise of Cinema Studies," in Robert Sklar and Charles Musser, eds., *Resisting Images: Essays on Cinema and History* (Philadelphia: Temple University Press, 1990).

Robin Smith, "Television Addiction," in Jennings Bryant and Dolf Zillmann, eds., *Perspectives on Media Effects* (Hillsdale, NJ: Erlbaum, 1986), 109–28.

Susan Smulyan, "Radio Advertising to Women in 1920s America," *Historical Journal of Film, Radio and Television* 13:3 (1993), 299–314.

Susan Smulyan, *Selling Radio: The Commercialization of American Broadcasting, 1920–1934* (Washington, DC: Smithsonian Institution Press, 1994).

Dallas Smythe, Parker Lusk, and Charles Lewis, "Portrait of an Art Theater Audience," *Quarterly of Film Radio and Television* 8:1 (Fall 1953), 28–50.

Lynn Spigel, *Make Room for TV: Television and the Family Ideal in Postwar America* (University of Chicago Press, 1992).

Henry Spurr, "The Nickelodeons: A Boon and a Menace," *Case and Comment* 18:10 (March 1912), 565–73.

Jackie Stacey, *Star Gazing: Hollywood Cinema and Female Spectatorship* (London: Routledge, 1994).

Charles Stamps, "The Concept of Mass Audience in American Broadcasting: An Historical Descriptive Study" (Ph.D., Northwestern University, 1956).

Daniel Starch, *Revised Study of Radio Broadcasting* (New York: NBC, 1930).

Raymond William Stedman, "A History of the Broadcasting of Daytime Serial Dramas in the United States" (Ph.D., University of Southern California, 1959).

Janet Steiger, "The Handmaiden of Villainy: Methods and Problems in Studying Historical Reception of Film," *Wide Angle* 8:1 (1986) 19–28.

Gary Steiner, *The People Look at Television* (New York: Knopf, 1963).

Alice Sterner, "Radio, Motion Picture and Reading Interests" (New York: Columbia University Teachers College, 1947).

Irwin Stewart, Radio issue, *Annals of the American Academy of Political and Social Science* 142 (March 1929), Supplement.

Raymond Stewart, "The Social Impact of Television on Atlanta Households" (Ph.D., Emory University, 1952).

Frederic Stuart, "The Effects of Television on the Motion Picture Industry, 1948–1960," in Gorham Kindem, ed., *The American Movie Industry* (Carbondale IL: Southern Illinois University Press, 1982), 257–307.

Leda Summers, *Daytime Serials and Iowa Women* (Des Moines: Radio Station WHO, 1943).

Harrison B. Summers, ed., *A Thirty Year History of Programs Carried on National Radio Networks in the United States, 1926–1956* (New York: Arno Press, 1971).

"Crystal D. Tector," "Radio and the Woman," *Radio World* column (1922–24).

Cecilia Tichi, *Electronic Hearth: Creating an American Television Culture* (New York: Oxford University Press, 1991).

Lowell Thomas, *Fan Mail* (New York: Dodge Publishing, 1935).

Mrs. W. I. Thomas, "The Five Cent Theatre," *Proceedings of the National Conference of Charities and Corrections* (1910), 145–49.

James Thurber, *The Beast in Me* (London: Hamilton, 1949).

Gaye Tuchman, Arlene Kaplan Daniels, and James Benet, *Hearth and Home: Images of Women in the Mass Media* (New York: Oxford University Press, 1978).

John Tulloch and Henry Jenkins, *Science Fiction Audiences: Watching Dr. Who and Star Trek* (London: Routledge, 1995).

Max Turner and Frank Kennedy, "Exclusion, Ejection and Segregation of Theater Patrons," *Iowa Law Review* 32:4 (May 1947), 625–58.

I. Keith Tyler, "How Does Radio Influence Your Child?" *California Parent-Teacher* 12 (November 1935), 14–15, 27.

Levering Tyson, *Radio and Education*, Vols. 1–4 (Chicago: University of Chicago Press, 1931–34).

Thomas Volek, "Examining Radio Receiver Technology Through Magazine Advertising in the 1920s and 1930s" (Ph.D., University of Minnesota, 1991).

Rob Wagner, "You at the Movies," *American Magazine* (December 1920), 42–44, 210–11.

James Walker and Robert Bellamy, *The Remote Control in the New Age of Television* (Westport, CT: Praeger, 1993).

Gregory Waller, *Main Street Amusements: Movies and Commerical Entertainment in a Southern City, 1896–1930* (Washington, DC: Smithsonian Institution Press, 1995).

William Lloyd Warner, "The Radio Daytime Serial," *Genetic Psychology Monograph* 37:1 (February 1948), 3–71.

Ellen Wartella and Sharon Mazzarella, "A Historical Comparison of Children's Use of Leisure Time," in Richard Butsch, ed., *For Fun and Profit*, (Philadelphia: Temple University Press, 1990) 173–194.

Ellen Wartella and Byron Reeves, "Historical Trends in Research on Children and the Media, 1900–1960," *Journal of Communication* 35:2 (Spring 1985), 118–33.

James Webster and Patricia Phalan, *The Mass Audience: Rediscovering the Dominant Model* (Hillsdale, NJ: Erlbaum, 1996).

Forest Whan, "A Study of Radio Listening Habits in the State of Iowa" (Des Moines, Iowa: Central Broadcasting Co., 1943).

Kari Whittenberger-Keith, "Understanding Fandom Rhetorically: The Case of *Beauty and the Beast*," in Andrew King, ed., *Postmodern Political Communication: The Fringe Challenges the Center* (Westport, CT: Praeger, 1992), 131–51.

Reynold Wik, "Radio in the 1920s," *South Dakota History* 11:2 (Spring 1981), 93–109.

Reynold Wik, "The USDA and the Development of Radio in Rural America," *Agricultural History* 62 (Spring 1988), 177–88.

Frances Farmer Wilder, *Radio's Daytime Serial* (New York: CBS, September 1945),

Tannis Williams and Gordon Handford, *The Impact of Television* (New York: Academic Press, 1986).

Day Allen Willie, "The Theatre's New Rival," *Lippincott's* 84 (October 1909), 454–8.

Maurice Willows, "The Nickel Theater," *Annals of the American Academy of Political and Social Science* (July 1911), 95–9.

Charles Wilson, "Money at the Crossroads: An Intimate Study of Radio's Influence upon a Great Market of 60,000,000 People" (New York: NBC, 1937).

Marie Winn, *The Plug-In Drug* (New York: Viking Press, 1977).

Charles Wolfe, "The Triumph of the Hills: Country Radio, 1920–1950," in Paul Kingsbury, *Country: The Music and the Musicians* (New York: Country Music Foundation, 1988), 53–87.

Adele Woodard, "Motion Pictures for Children," *Social Service Review* (September 1917), 10–11.

Francis Yates, "The Broadcast Listener," *Popular Radio* column (1925–28).

Index